KNOWLEDGE AND REALITY

Classic and Contemporary Readings

Edited by

STEVEN M. CAHN
MAUREEN ECKERT
ROBERT BUCKLEY

The City University of New York

Upper Saddle River, New Jersey 07458

Library of Congress Cataloging-in-Publication Data

Knowledge and reality : classic and contemporary readings / edited by Steven M. Cahn, Maureen Eckert, Robert Buckley.

p. cm.
ISBN 0-13-042401-3 (paper)
1. Knowledge, Theory of. 2. Metaphysics. I. Cahn, Steven M. II. Eckert, Maureen (date) III. Buckley, Robert (date)

BD161 .K585 2004
110—dc21

2002034388

VP/Editorial Director: Charlyce Jones Owen
Senior Acquisitions Editor: Ross Miller
Assistant Editor: Wendy Yurash
Editorial Assistant: Carla Worner
Editorial/production supervision and interior design: Mary Araneo
Marketing Manager: Chris Ruel
Prepress and Manufacturing Buyer: Brian Mackey
Cover Art Director: Jayne Conte
Cover Designer: Bruce Kenselaar
Cover photos: NASA and Library of Congress

This book was set in 10/11 Times by Interactive Composition Corporation and was printed and bound by Courier Companies. The cover was printed by Phoenix Color Corp.

PEARSON
Prentice Hall

Printed in the United States of America

10 9 8 7 6 5 4 3 2 1

ISBN 0-13-042401-3

Pearson Education LTD., London
Pearson Education Australia PTY, Limited, Sydney
Pearson Education Singapore, Pte. Ltd
Pearson Education North Asia Ltd, Hong Kong
Pearson Education Canada, Ltd., Toronto
Pearson Educación de Mexico, S.A. de C.V.
Pearson Education—Japan, Tokyo
Pearson Education Malaysia, Pte. Ltd
Pearson Education, Upper Saddle River, New Jersey

To my parents, John and Agnes Eckert, for their love and support.

—M. E.

To Anne and Felicia Maviglia, for their boundless love and encouragement.

—R. B.

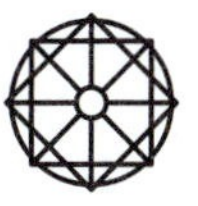

CONTENTS

PREFACE

This volume includes forty-seven selections from over thirty philosophers past and present. Philosophical questions have a perennial appeal and we have chosen selections that represent the most important, interesting, and instructive examples of inquiries into the central questions of epistemology and metaphysics. Issues that receive in-depth treatment include the problem of *a priori* knowledge, skepticism, foundationalism versus coherentism, the problems of universals, identity and change, causation, and the relationship between perception and the external world. We have made a concerted effort to represent less frequently covered topics such as reliabilism, virtue epistemology, and trope theory, thereby showcasing to readers both time honored positions on the enduring questions of epistemology and metaphysics as well as burgeoning philosophical trends.

Our book is both distinctive and unusual in its range and flexibility. Historical figures such as Plato, Aristotle, Zeno, and Heraclitus appear alongside contemporary thinkers like W. V. O. Quine, Nelson Goodman, Ernest Sosa, Donald Davidson, David Lewis, and others. The reader can thus see how significant problems concerning knowledge and reality were given early expression and how they have evolved over time.

The editors of *Knowledge and Reality: Classic and Contemporary Readings* are pleased to present this collection of some of the most fascinating works in epistemology and metaphysics.

KNOWLEDGE

CHAPTER ONE

WHAT IS KNOWLEDGE?

Plato gives us what is often considered the classic view of knowledge, that knowledge consists of beliefs that are true and also guaranteed in some significant way, that is, justified. In the *Meno,* he contrasts a man who happens to have the right opinion about the way to the town of Larissa, with a man who not only has this right opinion, but has also gone there himself. Both men may give you directions that get you to your destination, yet, intuitively, we understand that the right opinion of the man who has been there is not a matter of good luck. A definition of knowledge will be incomplete if it does not include a condition that captures the difference between true beliefs and those that also have further warrant or justification. For Plato this amounts to a world of difference: one who has knowledge of anything must have knowledge of the form of the thing in question, not just empirical familiarity with it. Unlike Plato, modern epistemologists have disentangled their views of knowledge from metaphysics and focus on the issues like what counts as justification and avoiding skepticism. Defenses of Foundationalism and Coherentism aim to answer just such questions.

Yet, the definition of knowledge as true, justified, belief, underwent an important assault by the philosopher Edmund Gettier in his paper, "Is True Justified Belief Knowledge?" In this paper, Gettier gives his famous cases that have been taken to show that even true, justified beliefs fail to yield knowledge. If Gettier is right, then the definition of knowledge requires a stronger condition, or, perhaps, needs to be rethought altogether. Other papers, from contemporary philosophers, in other chapters are inspired by the Gettier cases. David Lewis's paper, "Elusive Knowledge," found in Chapter 2, attempts to solve the Gettier cases through epistemic contextualism. Reliabilism, represented by Alvin

Goldman, and virtue epistemology, represented by Ernest Sosa in Chapter 3, attempt to keep the classical view of knowledge alive in light of the Gettier cases through substantial revisions of the condition of justification. A massive literature exists that attempts to solve the Gettier cases directly, but for the purpose of this volume, we have included papers that represent entire trends in the field of epistemology influenced by Gettier.

 1 

Meno

PLATO

. . .

SOC. I am afraid, Meno, that you and I are not good for much, and that Gorgias has been as poor an educator of you as Prodicus has been of me. Certainly we shall have to look to ourselves, and try to find someone who will help in some way or other to improve us. This I say, because I observe that, absurdly enough, in the previous discussion none of us remarked that right and good action is possible to man under other guidance than that of knowledge (ἐπιστήμη). Perhaps that is the reason why we have failed to discover how good men are produced.

MEN. How do you mean, Socrates?

SOC. You will see. Good men are necessarily useful; were we not right in admitting this? It must be so.

MEN. Yes.

SOC. And in supposing that they will be useful if they are true guides to us of action—there we were also right?

MEN. Yes.

SOC. But when we said that a man cannot be a good guide unless he have knowledge (φρόνησις), in this we seem to have made a wrong admission.

MEN. What do you mean by 'a good guide'?

SOC. I will explain. If a man knew the way to Larisa, or anywhere else, and went to the place and led others thither, would he not be a right and good guide?

MEN. Certainly.

SOC. And a person who had a right opinion about the way, but had never been and did not know, would be a good guide also, would he not?

MEN. Certainly.

SOC. And while he has true opinion about that which the other knows, he will be just as good a guide if he only thinks the truth, as he who knows the truth?

Source: Plato, *Meno,* from *The Dialogues of Plato,* translated by Benjamin Jowett, 2nd edition, Oxford: Clarendon Press, 1875.

MEN. Exactly.

SOC. Then true opinion is as good a guide to correct action as knowledge; and that was the point which we omitted in our speculation about the nature of virtue, when we said that knowledge only is the guide of right action; whereas there is also true opinion.

MEN. So it seems.

SOC. Then right opinion is not less useful than knowledge?

MEN. There is a difference, Socrates; he who has knowledge will always be right, but he who has right opinion will sometimes be right, and sometimes not.

SOC. What do you mean? Can he be wrong who has right opinion, so long as he has right opinion?

MEN. I admit the cogency of your argument, and therefore, Socrates, I wonder that knowledge should ever be prized far above right opinion—or why they should ever differ.

SOC. And shall I explain this wonder to you?

MEN. Do tell me.

SOC. You would not wonder if you had ever observed the images of Daedalus; but perhaps you have not got them in your country?

MEN. What have they to do with the question?

SOC. Because they require to be fastened in order to keep them, and if they are not fastened they will run away like fugitive slaves.

MEN. Well, what of that?

SOC. I mean to say that, like runaway slaves, they are not very valuable possessions if they are at liberty, for they will walk off; but when fastened they are of great value, for they are really beautiful works of art. Now this is an illustration of the nature of true opinions: while they abide with us they are beautiful and fruitful of nothing but good, but they run away out of the human soul, and do not care to remain long, and therefore they are not of much value until they are fastened by a reasoned understanding of causes; and this fastening of them, friend Meno, is recollection, as you and I have agreed to call it. But when they are bound, in the first place, they attain to be knowledge; and, in the second place, they are abiding. And this is why knowledge is more honourable and excellent than right opinion, because fastened by a chain.

MEN. Indeed, Socrates, something of the kind seems probable.

SOC. I too speak rather in ignorance; I only conjecture. And yet that knowledge differs from right opinion is no matter of conjecture with me. There are not many things which I profess to know, but this is most certainly one of them. . . .

2

Is Justified True Belief Knowledge?

EDMUND L. GETTIER

Various attempts have been made in recent years to state necessary and sufficient conditions for someone's knowing a given proposition. The attempts have often been such that they can be stated in a form similar to the following:[1]

(a) S knows that P *IFF* (i) P is true,
(ii) S believes that P, and
(iii) S is justified in believing that P.

For example, Chisholm has held that the following gives the necessary and sufficient conditions for knowledge:[2]

(b) S knows that P *IFF* (i) S accepts P,
(ii) S has adequate evidence for P, and
(iii) P is true.

Source: Edmund Gettier, "Is Justified True Belief Knowledge?" Analysis, 23 (1963), pp. 121–123. Reprinted by permission of the author.

Ayer has stated the necessary and sufficient conditions for knowledge as follows:[3]

(c) S knows that P *IFF* (i) P is true,
(ii) S is sure that P is true, and
(iii) S has the right to be sure that P is true.

I shall argue that (a) is false in that the conditions stated therein do not constitute a *sufficient* condition for the truth of the proposition that S knows that P. The same argument will show that (b) and (c) fail if 'has adequate evidence for' or 'has the right to be sure that' is substituted for 'is justified in believing that' throughout.

I shall begin by noting two points. First, in that sense of 'justified' in which S's being justified in believing P is a necessary condition of S's knowing that P, it is possible for a person to be justified in believing a proposition that is in fact false. Secondly, for any proposition P, if S is justified in believing P, and P entails Q, and

S deduces Q from P and accepts Q as a result of this deduction, then S is justified in believing Q. Keeping these two points in mind, I shall now present two cases in which the conditions stated in (a) are true for some proposition, though it is at the same time false that the person in question knows that proposition.

Case I:
Suppose that Smith and Jones have applied for a certain job. And suppose that Smith has strong evidence for the following conjunctive proposition:

(d) Jones is the man who will get the job, and Jones has ten coins in his pocket.

Smith's evidence for (d) might be that the president of the company assured him that Jones would in the end be selected, and that he, Smith, had counted the coins in Jones's pocket ten minutes ago. Proposition (d) entails:

(e) The man who will get the job has ten coins in his pocket.

Let us suppose that Smith sees the entailment from (d) to (e), and accepts (e) on the grounds of (d), for which he has strong evidence. In this case, Smith is clearly justified in believing that (e) is true.

But imagine, further, that unknown to Smith, he himself, not Jones, will get the job. And, also, unknown to Smith, he himself has ten coins in his pocket. Proposition (e) is then true, though proposition (d), from which Smith inferred (e), is false. In our example, then, all of the following are true: (*i*) (e) is true, (*ii*) Smith believes that (e) is true, and (*iii*) Smith is justified in believing that (e) is true. But it is equally clear that Smith does not *know* that (e) is true; for (e) is true in virtue of the number of coins in Smith's pocket, while Smith does not know how many coins are in Smith's pocket, and bases his belief in (e) on a count of the coins in Jones's pocket, whom he falsely believes to be the man who will get the job.

Case II:
Let us suppose that Smith has strong evidence for the following proposition:

(f) Jones owns a Ford.

Smith's evidence might be that Jones has at all times in the past within Smith's memory owned a car, and always a Ford, and that Jones has just offered Smith a ride while driving a Ford. Let us imagine, now, that Smith has another friend, Brown, of whose whereabouts he is totally ignorant. Smith selects three place-names quite at random, and constructs the following three propositions:

(g) Either Jones owns a Ford, or Brown is in Boston;

(h) Either Jones owns a Ford, or Brown is in Barcelona;

(i) Either Jones owns a Ford, or Brown is in Brest-Litovsk.

Each of these propositions is entailed by (f). Imagine that Smith realizes the entailment of each of these propositions he has constructed by (f), and proceeds to accept (g), (h), and (i) on the basis of (f). Smith has correctly inferred (g), (h), and (i) from a proposition for which he has strong evidence. Smith is therefore completely justified in believing each of these three propositions. Smith, of course, has no idea where Brown is.

But imagine now that two further conditions hold. First, Jones does *not* own a Ford, but is at present driving a rented car. And secondly, by the sheerest coincidence, and entirely unknown to Smith, the place mentioned in proposition (h) happens really to be the place where Brown is.

If these two conditions hold then Smith does *not* know that (h) is true, even though (*i*) (h) *is* true, (*ii*) Smith does believe that (h) is true, and (*iii*) Smith is justified in believing that (h) is true.

These two examples show that definition (a) does not state a *sufficient* condition for someone's knowing a given proposition. The same cases, with appropriate changes, will suffice to show that neither definition (b) nor definition (c) do so either.

NOTES

1. Plato seems to be considering some such definition at *Tbeaetetus* 201, and perhaps accepting one at *Meno* 98.
2. Roderick M. Chisholm, *Perceiving: a Philosophical Study*, Cornell University Press (Ithaca, New York, 1957), p. 16.
3. A. J. Ayer, *The Problem of Knowledge*, Macmillan (London, 1956), p. 34.

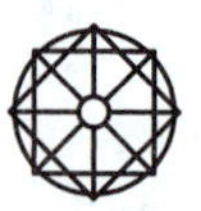

CHAPTER TWO
SKEPTICISM

The skeptic doubts that knowledge in general (globally) or within a specific field of inquiry (locally) is possible. Philosophical skepticism comes in different forms and the goal of this section is to introduce the reader to a few of them.

We present a portion of Sextus Empiricus's *Outlines of Pyrrhonism* as one of the forms of Ancient Skepticism. This selection provides insight into the systematic and holistic viewpoint of Pyrrhonic skepticism. According to Empiricus, appearances (phantasies)—our passively received sensory appearances—cannot be doubted. But the Pyrrhonic skeptic refrains entirely from drawing any conclusions about these appearances. No beliefs based on appearances can ever be ascertained as true beyond all reasonable doubt. The skeptic withholds assent to any beliefs and is thus agnostic (does not know one way or the other). Do our perceptions conform to reality? We do not know. Is there an external reality? We do not know. *The Outlines of Pyrrhonism* provides the methods (tropoi), which the skeptic can employ to counterbalance any positive beliefs he or she has with opposing accounts. The balancing of argument with counterargument results in Epoche, the suspension of judgement, which is a state of the intellect on account of which we neither affirm nor deny anything. One cannot know if anything beyond one's immediate sense perceptions is real, so one will not commit oneself to any beliefs about them. Through suspending all our beliefs and doubting the ultimate reality of everything, we find inner peace and tranquility, ataraxia, and become imperturbable. Importantly, in the closing excerpt, a famous skeptical problem "The Problem of the Criterion," is presented. Empiricus presents this problem in which, when we are asked to give an account of something that we know, we must also know the criteria for knowing it, yet to give an account of these criteria we must already *have* criteria for this.

The next selection is from David Hume, a British empiricist and a skeptic. He is perhaps most famous for criticizing the teleological proof for God's existence and raising the problem of justifying inductive inferences. In the excerpt from *A Treatise on Human Nature,* Hume turns to the question of why we believe in material objects whose identity persist over time. According to his empiricist theory of meaning, any meaningful idea must be rooted in sense experience (some "impression"). However, when it comes to external objects, our impressions are always fragmented. We never have an uninterrupted or constant impression of anything. We invariably blink, lose focus, or turn away completely from the objects we experience. Hence our belief in persistent material objects cannot be justified as rational since we do not have the requisite sense impressions with which to ground such a belief. Hume argues that such a belief must be explained psychologically, if it cannot be justified epistemically. He then offers a psychological account of why we attribute identity to external objects on the basis of the barrage of fragmented sense impressions offered to us by experience.

The twentieth-century British philosopher G. E. Moore defends our commonsense notions of the external world against skepticism. In "A Defence of Common Sense" he claims that we can be sure of our commonsense knowledge of the truth of ordinary propositions about ourselves, bodies, and other people, and it is the analysis of these propositions that creates disagreement among philosophers. It is simply too implausible to deny our commonsense knowledge about the world.

In the selection, "Elusive Knowledge," contemporary philosopher David Lewis defends the view of epistemic contextualism. In advocating this view, Lewis attempts both to maintain certainty in our commonsense knowledge, as G. E. Moore suggests, and to explain the variable epistemic standards that arise in particular contexts in which we are asked to defend our claims to knowledge. Philosophy itself is a context in which the standards of certainty are so high that skepticism enters the picture.

Peter Unger, another contemporary philosopher, argues in "A Defense of Skepticism" that, contrary to the Moorean position on our commonsense knowledge, we hardly ever know anything with any certainty. This is because, like other basic terms in our language, which he calls "absolute," our use of the term "know" does entail skepticism even about ordinary commonsense beliefs. Unger's linguistic analysis challenges the idea that skepticism is an implausible thesis.

1

Outlines of Pyrrhonism, excerpts

SEXTUS EMPIRICUS

CHAPTER IV
The Meaning of Scepticism

Scepticism is an ability to place in antithesis, in any manner whatever, appearances and judgements, and thus—because of the equality of force in the objects and arguments opposed—to come first of all to a suspension of judgement and then to mental tranquillity. Now, we call it an "ability" not in any peculiar sense of the word,[1] but simply as it denotes a "being able." "Appearances" we take as meaning the objects of sense-perception;[2] hence we set over against them the objects of thought. The phrase "in any manner whatever" may attach itself to "ability," so that we may understand that word (as we have said) in its simple sense, or it may be understood as modifying the phrase "to place in antithesis appearances and judgements." For since the antitheses we make take various forms, appearances opposed to appearances, judgements to judgements, or appearances to judgements, we say "in any manner whatever" in order to include all the antitheses. Or, we may understand it as "any manner of appearances and judgements whatever," in order to relieve ourselves of the inquiry into how appearances appear or how judgements are formed, and thus take them at their face value.[3] When we speak of arguments which are "opposed," we do not at all mean denial and affirmation, but use this word in the sense of "conflicting."[4] By "equality of force" we mean equality in respect of credibility and incredibility, since we do not admit that any of the conflicting arguments can take precedence over another on grounds of its being more credible.[5] "Suspension of judgement" is a cessation of the thought processes in

---

Source: Sextus Empiricus, *Scepticism, Man and God,* ed. P. Hallie, trans. S. Etheridge. Middletown, CT: Wesleyan University Press, 1964, pp. 32–34, 35, 37–38, 42–44, 59, 62. Reprinted by permission of the publisher.

consequence of which we neither deny nor affirm anything. "Mental tranquillity" is an undisturbed and calm state of soul. . . .

CHAPTER VI
THE PRINCIPLES OF SCEPTICISM

Scepticism has its inception and cause, we say, in the hope of attaining mental tranquillity.[6] Men of noble nature had been disturbed at the irregularity in things, and puzzled as to where they should place their belief. Thus they were led on to investigate both truth and falsehood in things, in order that, when truth and falsehood were determined, they might attain tranquillity of mind. Now, the principle fundamental to the existence of Scepticism is the proposition, "To every argument an equal argument is opposed," for we believe that it is in consequence of this principle that we are brought to a point where we cease to dogmatize. . . .

CHAPTER VIII
DOES THE SCEPTIC HAVE A SYSTEM?

Our attitude is the same when we are asked whether the Sceptic has a system. For if one defines "system" as "an adherence to a set of numerous dogmas which are consistent both with one another and with appearances," and if "dogma" is defined as "assent to a non-evident thing," then we shall say that we have no system. But if one means by "system" a "discipline which, in accordance with appearance, follows a certain line of reasoning, that line of reasoning indicating how it is possible to seem to live rightly ('rightly' understood not only with reference to virtue, but more simply),[7] and extending also to the ability to suspend judgement," then we say that we do have a system. For we follow a certain line of reasoning which indicates to us, in a manner consistent with appearances, how to live in accordance with the customs, the laws, and the institutions of our country, and with our own natural feelings. . . .

CHAPTER X
DO THE SCEPTICS DENY APPEARANCES?

Those who say that the Sceptics deny appearances seem to me to be ignorant of what we say. As we said above, we do not deny those things which, in accordance with the passivity of our sense-impressions,[8] lead us involuntarily to give our assent to them; and these are the appearances. And when we inquire whether an object is such as it appears, we grant the fact of its appearance. Our inquiry is thus not directed at the appearance itself. Rather, it is a question of what is predicated of it, and this is a different thing from investigating the fact of the appearance itself. For example, honey appears to us to have a sweetening quality. This much we concede, because it affects us with a sensation of sweetness. The question, however, is whether it is sweet in an absolute[9] sense. Hence not the appearance is questioned, but that which is predicated of the appearance. Whenever we do expound arguments directly against appearances, we do so not with the intention of denying them, but in order to point out the hasty judgement of the dogmatists. For if reason is such a rogue as to all but snatch even the appearances from under our very eyes, should we not by all means be wary of it, at least not be hasty to follow it, in the case of things non-evident?[10] . . .

CHAPTER XIII
GENERAL INTRODUCTION TO THE MODES OF SUSPENSION OF JUDGEMENT

We were saying that mental tranquillity follows on suspension of judgement in regard to all things. Next, it would be proper for us to state how we attain suspension of judgement. As a general rule, this suspension of judgement is effected by our setting things in opposition. We oppose appearances to appearances, or thoughts to thoughts, or appearances to thoughts. For example, when we say, "The same tower appears round from a distance, but square from close by," we are opposing appearances to appearances. When a person is trying to prove the existence of providence from the order of the celestial bodies, and we counter him with the observation that the good often fare ill while the evil prosper and then conclude from this that there is no providence, we are opposing thoughts to thoughts. And then appearances may be opposed to thoughts. Anaxagoras,[11] for instance, could oppose to the fact that snow is white his reasoning that "Snow is frozen water, and water is black, snow therefore is black also." And sometimes, from the point of view of a different concept, we oppose present things to present things, as in the foregoing, and sometimes present things to past or future things. An example of this is the following. Whenever someone propounds an argument that we are not able to dispose of, we make this reply: "Before the birth of the founder of the school to which you belong, this argument of your school was not yet seen to be a sound argument. From the point of view of nature, however, it existed all the while as such. In like manner it is possible, as far as nature is concerned, that an argument antithetical to the one now set forth by you is in existence, though as yet unknown to us. This being so, the fact that an argument seems valid to us now is not yet a sufficient reason why we must assent to it."

But for a better understanding of these antitheses, I shall now present also the modes by which suspension of judgement is induced. I cannot, however, vouch for their number or validity, since it is possible that they are unsound, and that there are more of them than the ones to be discussed.

CHAPTER XIV
THE TEN MODES

With the older Sceptics the usual teaching is that the modes by which suspension of judgement seems to be brought about are ten in number, which they also term synonymously "arguments" and "forms." These are as follows. First is that in which suspension is caused by the variation in animals. In the second it is caused by the differences in human beings. Third, by the differences in the construction of the organs of sense. Fourth, by the circumstances. Fifth, by the positions, distances, and places involved. Sixth, by the admixtures present. Seventh, by the quantities and compoundings of the underlying objects. Eighth, by the relativity of things. Ninth, by the frequency or rarity of occurrence. Tenth, by the institutions, customs, laws, mythical beliefs, and dogmatic notions. This order, however, is merely arbitrary. . . .

THE FOURTH MODE

But we can also reach suspension by basing our argument on each sense separately, or even by disregarding the senses. To this end we employ the fourth mode of suspension, which we call the mode based on the circumstances. We understand by "circumstances" the states in which we are. This mode, we say, is seen in cases of natural or unnatural states, in states of waking or sleeping, in cases where age, motion or rest, hating or loving are involved; or where the determining factor is a state of want or satiety, drunkenness or soberness; in cases of predispositions, or when it is a question of confidence or fear, or grief or joy. For example, things appear dissimilar according to whether we are in a natural or unnatural state; delirious people, and those who are possessed by a god, think that they hear divine voices, while we do not. Often they claim that they perceive, among a number of other things, the odour of storax or frankincense, or something of that sort, where we perceive nothing. And the same water that seems hot to a person when poured on inflamed parts seems lukewarm to us. The coat which appears yellowish-orange to men with bloodshot eyes does not appear so to me, yet it is the same coat. And the same honey that appears sweet to me appears bitter to those suffering from jaundice. . . .

The discrepancy between such impressions is irresolvable on other grounds also, for if a person prefers one sense-impression to another, and one circumstance to another, he does so either without judging and without proof or by judging and offering proof. But he cannot do so without judgement and proof, for then he will be discredited. Nor can he do so even with judgement and proof, for if he judges the impressions, he must at all events use a criterion in judging them. And this criterion he will declare to be either true or false. If false, he will not be worthy of belief; but if he claims it is true, then his statement that the criterion is true will be offered either without proof or with proof. If without proof, again he will not be worthy of belief; but if he offers proof for his statement, the proof must in any case be a true one, otherwise he will not be worthy of belief. Now, if he says that the proof employed for the confirmation of his criterion is true, will he say this after having passed judgement on the proof, or without having judged it? If he has not judged it, he will not be worthy of belief, but if he has, obviously he will say he has used a criterion in his judgement. We shall ask for a proof for this criterion, and for this proof another criterion. For the proof always needs a criterion to confirm it, and the criterion needs a proof to show that it is true. A proof cannot be sound without the pre-existence of a true criterion, and a criterion cannot be true either without prior confirmation of the proof. And so both the criterion and the proof fall into circular argument, in which both are found to be untrustworthy. The fact that each expects confirmation from the other makes both of them equally untrustworthy. It is impossible, then, for a person to give the preference to one sense-impression over another. This being so, such differences in sense-impressions as arise from a disparity of states will be irresolvable. As a result, this mode also serves to introduce suspension of judgement with regard to the nature of external objects. . . .

NOTES

Notes have been renumbered consecutively throughout these excerpts to avoid confusion.

1. Not in the full, complicated sense in which Aristotle used the term "potency," or *dynamis,* because potency in his system was a metaphysical notion involving powers not directly experienced by us, the way the smooth redness of an apple is experienced. Sextus is trying to stay close to what we might now call a "phenomenological" description of the mind, a plain description of what we experience.
2. Sextus is concerned not with the objects that help cause sense-perception, the hidden potencies of things, but with objects, like the yellow smoothness of the apple that we experience facing us, which are the "objects of sense-perception." These are the "objects" with which we are directly "acquainted" in sense-experience, and which do not require a metaphysical system for their description. Of course, there are differences amongst all these terms, but the similarities are important enough to warrant our putting them all in the same group: directly experienced objects.
3. Another key phrase of Scepticism, related to the notion of sense-objects discussed in the preceding footnote. The Sceptic is not undertaking psychology (the depth study of the soul or mind), nor is he expounding the metaphysics of mind; he is not studying the hidden or inferred causes or structures of judgements or appearances. All he wants is to study the experienced relations, observable in experience, that hold amongst judgements and appearances.

4. To deny something is to assert its falsity, just as to affirm it is to assert its truth; the Sceptic is not making such assertions, is not letting himself assert the falsity or the truth of a metaphysical claim. He is *suspending* judgement on such claims *via* pointing out the conflicts or oppositions between them. To involve himself in denial or affirmation would be to make the Sceptic a rival metaphysician with all the others. And so he withholds assent or denial, and observes how that rogue reason can make any metaphysical claim as plausible (or implausible) as it likes. The device of the Sceptic is the balance-scale: he suspends arguments against each other, and does not come down hard for or against any of them. Doubt then is the withholding of assent *and* of denial, the mere recognition of the conflicts or oppositions between equally plausible (or equally implausible) claims. Many who talk about Scepticism do not see this all-important point. . . .
5. This equality of force is not determined by the Sceptics by means of some measuring or weighing machine which tells us exactly how much truth and how much falsity there is in a given argument. The device of the balance-scale is therefore a misleading one as far as the Sceptics' position is concerned: they have no way of determining the precise amount of truth or falsity in a claim in any precise way. If they did, they would be dogmatists, stopping their investigations when they come to the weightiest claim. As it is, they are observers of the complex set of mutually conflicting claims that make up the history of metaphysical philosophy, observers who notice that with ingenuity and luck as strong a defence can be made for any one claim as for any other. And this notion of "strength" is broad and qualitative, not as precise and quantitative as the balance-scale would suggest. This "equality" simply means that reason is a rogue, that having no decisive grounds for proving matters beyond everyday experience and custom it can make anything as plausible (or implausible) as anything else.
6. Scepticism is a *practical-wisdom philosophy,* one that seeks (as did post-Christian Stoicism and Epicureanism) *eudaimonia,* "happiness," by way of peace of mind, or *ataraxia.* The truth is not its ultimate goal. Moreover, the proof of the *falsity* of particular dogmatic claims is not its motivation or goal either. The *arche* of Scepticism is peaceful happiness by way of a suspension of judgement.
7. Notice the emphasis upon "simple," or everyday, obvious uses of words like "rightly." What the Sceptic is doing in general is to try to get back to plain talk.
8. There are at least two important meanings to this notion of "passivity," or "involuntariness" of our sense-experience: (1) When a knife cuts through one's skin, one is not free to eliminate the pain; the pain follows the knife-cut regardless of our volition or voluntary activity—we are passive to the affective consequences of our sense-experience; (2) When we see an apple as red, we believe it to be red, without any act of choosing or volition having to come between the perception and the belief. Seeing *is* believing. But the dogmatist believes in a hidden reality with special traits, while the Sceptic, and the ordinary man, simply believes what he sees as he sees it.
9. As we shall presently be seeing by way of the modes, we can speak of appearances only in a sense that keeps us mindful of the relativity of our perceptions to ourselves and to our conditions.
10. Again, the Sceptics want to keep "reason" (in the form of a dogmatic analysis of the causes "behind" experience) from turning our attention away from plain experience and towards matters that produce endless squabbling and groundless zeal. Appearances themselves are not subject to question as appearances.
11. Anaxagoras of Clazomenae lived around 450 B.C. and was a friend of Euripides and Pericles. He taught that a supreme intelligence (*nus*) ruled all things by composing and decomposing numberless "seeds of all things," or basic, elemental, indivisible building blocks of the universe.

2

A Treatise of Human Nature, excerpts

DAVID HUME

SECTION II
OF SCEPTICISM WITH REGARD TO THE SENSES

Thus the sceptic still continues to reason and believe, even tho' he asserts, that he cannot defend his reason by reason; and by the same rule he must assent to the principle concerning the existence of body, tho' he cannot pretend by any arguments of philosophy to maintain its veracity. Nature has not left this to his choice, and has doubtless esteem'd it an affair of too great importance to be trusted to our uncertain reasonings and speculations. We may well ask, *What causes induce us to believe in the existence of body?* but 'tis in vain to ask, *Whether there be body or not?* That is a point, which we must take for granted in all our reasonings.

The subject, then, of our present enquiry is concerning the *causes* which induce us to believe in the existence of body: And my reasonings on this head I shall begin with a distinction, which at first sight may seem superfluous, but which will contribute very much to the perfect understanding of what follows. We ought to examine apart those two questions, which are commonly confounded together, *viz.* Why we attribute a CONTINU'D existence to objects, even when they are not present to the senses; and why we suppose them to have an existence DISTINCT from the mind and perception. Under this last head I comprehend their situation as well as relations, their *external* position as well as the *independence* of their existence and operation. These two questions concerning the continu'd and distinct existence of body are intimately connected together. For if the objects of our senses continue to exist, even when they are not perceiv'd, their existence is of course independent of and distinct from the perception; and *vice versa,* if their existence be independent of the perception and distinct from it, they must continue to exist, even tho' they be not perceiv'd. But tho' the

Source: David Hume, *A Treatise of Human Nature,* originally published 1739–1740.

decision of the one question decides the other; yet that we may the more easily discover the principles of human nature, from whence the decision arises, we shall carry along with us this distinction, and shall consider, whether it be the *senses, reason,* or the *imagination,* that produces the opinion of a *continu'd* or of a *distinct* existence. These are the only questions, that are intelligible on the present subject. For as to the notion of external existence, when taken for something specifically different from our perceptions,[1] we have already shewn its absurdity.

To begin with the SENSES, 'tis evident these faculties are incapable of giving rise to the notion of the *continu'd* existence of their objects, after they no longer appear to the senses. For that is a contradiction in terms, and supposes that the senses continue to operate, even after they have ceas'd all manner of operation. These faculties, therefore, if they have any influence in the present case, must produce the opinion of a distinct, not of a continu'd existence; and in order to that, must present their impressions either as images and representations, or as these very distinct and external existences.

That our senses offer not their impressions as the images of something *distinct,* or *independent,* and *external,* is evident; because they convey to us nothing but a single perception, and never give us the least intimation of any thing beyond. A single perception can never produce the idea of a double existence, but by some inference either of the reason or imagination. When the mind looks farther than what immediately appears to it, its conclusions can never be put to the account of the senses; and it certainly looks farther, when from a single perception it infers a double existence, and supposes the relations of resemblance and causation betwixt them.

If our senses, therefore, suggest any idea of distinct existences, they must convey the impressions as those very existences, by a kind of fallacy and illusion. Upon this head we may observe, that all sensations are felt by the mind, such as they really are, and that when we doubt, whether they present themselves as distinct objects, or as mere impressions, the difficulty is not concerning their nature, but concerning their relations and situation. Now if the senses presented our impressions as external to, and independent of ourselves, both the objects and ourselves must be obvious to our senses, otherwise they cou'd not be compar'd by these faculties. The difficulty, then, is how far we are *ourselves* the objects of our senses.

'Tis certain there is no question in philosophy more abstruse than that concerning identity, and the nature of the uniting principle, which constitutes a person. So far from being able by our senses merely to determine this question, we must have recourse to the most profound metaphysics to give a satisfactory answer to it; and in common life 'tis evident these ideas of self and person are never very fix'd nor determinate. 'Tis absurd, therefore, to imagine the senses can ever distinguish betwixt ourselves and external objects. . . .

But not to lose time in examining, whether 'tis possible for our senses to deceive us, and represent our perceptions as distinct from ourselves, that is as *external* to and *independent* of us; let us consider whether they really do so, and whether this error proceeds from an immediate sensation, or from some other causes.

To begin with the question concerning *external* existence, it may perhaps be said, that setting aside the metaphysical question of the identity of a thinking substance, our own body evidently belongs to us; and as several impressions appear exterior to the body, we suppose them also exterior to ourselves. The paper, on which I write at present, is beyond my hand. The table is beyond the paper. The walls of the chamber beyond the table. And in casting my eye towards the window, I perceive a great extent of fields and buildings beyond my chamber. From all this it may be infer'd, that no other faculty is requir'd, beside the senses, to convince us of the external existence of body. But to prevent this inference, we need only weigh the three following considerations. *First,* That, properly speaking, 'tis not our body we perceive, when we regard our limbs and members, but certain impressions, which enter by the senses; so that the ascribing a real and corporeal existence to these impressions, or to their objects, is an act of the mind as difficult to explain, as that which we examine at present. *Secondly,* Sounds, and tastes, and smells, tho' commonly regarded by the mind as continu'd independent qualities, appear not to have any existence in extension, and consequently cannot appear to the senses as situated externally to the body. The reason, why we ascribe a place to them, shall be consider'd[2] afterwards. *Thirdly,* Even our sight informs us not of distance or outness (so to speak) immediately and without a certain reasoning and experience, as is acknowledg'd by the most rational philosophers.

As to the *independency* of our perceptions on ourselves, this can never be an object of the senses; but any opinion we form concerning it, must be deriv'd from experience and observation: And we shall see afterwards, that our conclusions from experience are far from being favourable to the doctrine of the independency of our perceptions. Mean while we may observe that when we talk of real distinct existences, we have commonly more in our eye their independency than external situation in place, and think an object has a sufficient reality, when its Being is uninterrupted, and independent of the incessant revolutions, which we are conscious of in ourselves.

Thus to resume what I have said concerning the senses; they give us no notion of continu'd existence, because they cannot operate beyond the extent, in which they really operate. They as little produce the opinion of a distinct existence, because they neither can offer it to the mind as represented, nor as original. To offer it as represented, they must present both an object and an image. To make it appear as original, they must convey a falshood; and this falshood must lie in the relations and situation: In order to which they must be able to compare the object with ourselves; and even in that case they do not, nor is it possible they shou'd, deceive us. We may, therefore, conclude with certainty, that the opinion of a continu'd and of a distinct existence never arises from the senses.

To confirm this we may observe, that there are three different kinds of impressions convey'd by the senses. The first are those of the figure, bulk, motion and solidity of bodies. The second those of colours, tastes, smells, sounds, heat and cold. The third are the pains and pleasures, that arise from the application of objects to our bodies, as by the cutting of our flesh with steel, and such like. Both philosophers and the vulgar suppose the first of these to have a distinct continu'd existence. The vulgar only regard the second as on the same footing. Both philosophers and the vulgar, again, esteem the third to be merely perceptions; and consequently interrupted and dependent beings.

Now 'tis evident, that, whatever may be our philosophical opinion, colours, sounds, heat and cold, as far as appears to the senses, exist after the same manner with motion and solidity, and that the difference we make betwixt them in this respect, arises not from the mere perception. So strong is the prejudice for the distinct continu'd existence of the former qualities, that when the contrary opinion is advanc'd by modern philosophers, people imagine they can almost refute it from their feeling and experience, and that their very senses contradict this philosophy. 'Tis also evident, that colours, sounds, *&c.* are originally on the same footing with the pain that arises from steel, and pleasure that proceeds from a fire; and that the difference betwixt them is founded neither on perception nor reason, but on the imagination. For as they are confest to be, both of them, nothing but perceptions arising from the particular configurations and motions of the parts of body, wherein possibly can their difference consist? Upon the whole, then, we may conclude, that as far as the senses are judges, all perceptions are the same in the manner of their existence. . . .

Since all impressions are internal and perishing existences, and appear as such, the notion of their distinct and continu'd existence must arise from a concurrence of some of their qualities with the qualities of the imagination; and since this notion does not extend to all of them, it must arise from certain qualities peculiar to some impressions. 'Twill therefore be easy for us to discover these qualities by a comparison of the impressions, to which we attribute a distinct and continu'd existence, with those, which we regard as internal and perishing.

We may observe, then, that 'tis neither upon account of the involuntariness of certain impressions, as is commonly suppos'd, nor of their superior force and violence, that we attribute to them a reality, and continu'd existence, which we refuse to others, that are voluntary or feeble. For 'tis evident our pains and pleasures, our passions and affections, which we never suppose to have any existence beyond our perception, operate with greater violence, and are equally involuntary, as the impressions of figure and extension, colour and sound, which we suppose to be permanent beings. The heat of a fire, when moderate, is suppos'd to exist in the fire; but the pain, which it causes upon a near approach, is not taken to have any being except in the perception. . . .

After a little examination, we shall find, that all those objects, to which we attribute a continu'd existence, have a peculiar *constancy,* which distinguishes them from the impressions, whose existence depends upon our perception. These mountains, and houses, and trees, which lie at present under my eye, have always appear'd to me in the same order; and when I lose sight of them by shutting my eyes or turning my head, I soon after find them return upon me without the least alteration. My bed and table, my books and papers, present themselves in the same uniform manner, and change not upon account of any interruption in my seeing or perceiving them. This is the case with all the impressions, whose objects are suppos'd to have an external existence; and is the case with no other impressions, whether gentle or violent, voluntary or involuntary.

This constancy, however, is not so perfect as not to admit of very considerable exceptions. Bodies often change their position and qualities, and after a little absence or interruption may become hardly knowable. But here 'tis observable, that even in these changes they preserve a *coherence,* and have a regular dependence on each other; which is the foundation of a kind of reasoning from causation, and produces the opinion of their continu'd existence. When I return to my chamber after an hour's absence, I find not my fire in the same situation, in which I left it: But then I am accustom'd in other instances to see a like alteration produc'd in a like time, whether I am present or absent, near or remote. This coherence, therefore, in their changes is one of the characteristics of external objects, as well as their constancy.

Having found that the opinion of the continu'd existence of body depends on the COHERENCE and CONSTANCY of certain impressions, I now proceed to examine after what manner these qualities give rise to so extraordinary an opinion. To begin with the coherence; we may observe, that tho' those internal impressions, which we regard as fleeting and perishing, have also a certain coherence or regularity in their appearances, yet 'tis of somewhat a different nature, from that which we discover in bodies. Our passions are found by experience to have a mutual connexion with and dependance on each other; but on no occasion is it necessary to suppose, that they have existed and operated, when they were not perceiv'd, in order to preserve the same dependance and connexion, of which we have had experience. The case is not the same with relation to external objects. Those require a continu'd existence, or otherwise lose, in a great measure, the regularity of their operation. I am here seated in my chamber with my face to the fire; and all the objects, that strike my senses, are contain'd in a few yards around me. My memory, indeed, informs me of the existence of many objects; but then this information extends not beyond their past existence, nor do either my senses or memory give any testimony to the continuance of their being. When therefore I am thus seated, and revolve over these thoughts, I hear on a sudden a noise as of a door turning upon its hinges; and a little after see a porter, who advances towards me. This gives occasion to many new reflexions and reasonings. First, I never have observ'd, that this noise cou'd proceed from any thing but the motion of a door; and therefore conclude, that the present phænomenon is a contradiction to all past experience, unless the door, which I remember on t'other side the chamber, be still in being. Again, I have always found, that a human body was possest of a quality, which I call gravity, and which hinders it from mounting in the air, as this porter must have done to arrive at my chamber, unless the stairs I remember be not annihilated by my absence. But this is not all. I receive a letter, which upon opening it I perceive by the hand-writing and subscription to have come from a friend, who says he is two hundred leagues distant. 'Tis evident I can never account for this phænomenon, conformable to my experience in other instances, without spreading out in my mind the whole sea and continent between us, and supposing the effects and continu'd existence of posts and ferries, according to my memory and observation. To consider these phænomena of the porter and letter in a certain light, they are contradictions to common experience, and may be regarded as objections to those maxims, which we form concerning the connexions of causes and effects. I am accustom'd to hear such a sound, and see such an object in motion at the same time. I have not receiv'd in this particular instance both these perceptions. These observations are contrary, unless I suppose that the door still remains, and that it was open'd without my perceiving it: And this supposition, which was at first entirely arbitrary and hypothetical, acquires a force and evidence by its being the only one, upon which I can reconcile these contradictions. There is scarce a moment of my life, wherein there is not a similar instance presented to me, and I have not occasion to suppose the continu'd existence of objects, in order to connect their past and present appearances, and give them such an union with each other, as I have found by experience to be suitable to their particular natures and circumstances. Here then I am naturally led to regard the world, as something real and durable, and as preserving its existence, even when it is no longer present to my perception.

But tho' this conclusion from the coherence of appearances may seem to be of the same nature with our reasonings concerning causes and effects; as being deriv'd from custom, and regulated by past experience; we shall find upon examination, that they are at the bottom considerably different from each other, and that this inference arises from the understanding, and from custom in an indirect and oblique manner. For 'twill readily be allow'd, that since nothing is ever really present to the mind, besides its own perceptions, 'tis not only impossible, that any habit shou'd ever be acquir'd otherwise than by the regular succession of these perceptions, but also that any habit shou'd ever exceed that degree of regularity. Any degree, therefore, of regularity in our perceptions, can never be a foundation for us to infer a greater degree of regularity in some objects, which are not perceiv'd; since this supposes a contradiction, *viz.* a habit acquir'd by what was never present to the mind. But 'tis evident, that whenever we infer the continu'd existence of the objects of sense from their coherence, and the frequency of their union, 'tis in order to bestow on the objects a greater regularity than what is observ'd in our mere perceptions. We remark a connexion betwixt two kinds of objects in their past appearance to the senses, but are not able to observe this connexion to be perfectly constant, since the turning about of our head, or the shutting of our eyes is able to break it. What then do we suppose in this case, but that these objects still continue their usual connexion, notwithstanding their apparent interruption, and that the irregular appearances are join'd by something, of which we are insensible? But as all reasoning concerning matters of fact arises only from custom, and custom can only be the effect of repeated perceptions, the extending of custom and reasoning beyond the perceptions can never be the direct and natural effect of the constant repetition and connexion, but must arise from the co-operation of some other principles.

I have already[3] observ'd, in examining the foundation of mathematics, that the imagination, when set into any train of thinking, is apt to continue, even when its object fails it, and like a galley put in motion by the oars, carries on its course without any new impulse. This I have assign'd for the reason, why, after considering several loose standards of equality, and correcting them by each other, we proceed to imagine so correct and exact a standard of that relation, as is not liable to the least error or variation. The same principle makes us easily entertain this opinion of the continu'd existence of body. Objects have a certain coherence even as they appear to our senses; but this coherence is much greater and more uniform, if we suppose the objects to have a continu'd existence; and as the mind is once in the train of observing an uniformity among objects, it naturally continues, till it renders the uniformity as compleat as possible. The simple supposition of their continu'd existence suffices for this purpose, and gives us a notion of a much greater regularity among objects, than what they have when we look no farther than our senses.

But whatever force we may ascribe to this principle, I am afraid 'tis too weak to support alone so vast an edifice, as is that of the continu'd existence of all external bodies; and that we must join the *constancy* of their appearance to the *coherence,* in order to give a satisfactory account of that opinion. As the explication of this will lead me into a considerable compass of very profound reasoning; I think it proper, in order to avoid confusion, to give a short sketch or abridgment of my system, and afterwards draw out all its parts in their full compass. This inference from the constancy of our perceptions, like the precedent from their coherence, gives rise to the opinion of the *continu'd* existence of body, which is prior to that of its *distinct* existence, and produces that latter principle.

When we have been accustom'd to observe a constancy in certain impressions, and have found, that the perception of the sun or ocean, for instance, returns upon us after an absence or annihilation with like parts and in a like order, as at its first appearance, we are not apt to regard these interrupted perceptions as different, (which they really are) but on the contrary consider them as individually the same, upon account of their resemblance. But as this interruption of their existence is contrary to their perfect identity, and makes us regard the first impression as annihilated, and the second as newly created, we find ourselves somewhat at a loss, and are involv'd in a kind of contradiction. In order to free ourselves from this difficulty, we disguise, as much as possible, the interruption, or rather remove it entirely, by supposing that these interrupted perceptions are connected by a real existence, of which we are insensible. This supposition, or idea of continu'd existence, acquires a force and vivacity from the memory of these broken impressions, and from that propensity, which they give us, to suppose them the same; and according to the precedent reasoning, the very essence of belief consists in the force and vivacity of the conception. . . .

But as we here not only *feign* but *believe* this continu'd existence, the question is, *from whence arises such a belief;* and this question leads us to the *fourth* member of this system. It has been prov'd already, that belief in general consists in nothing, but the vivacity of an idea; and that an idea may acquire this vivacity by its relation to some present impression.

Impressions are naturally the most vivid perceptions of the mind; and this quality is in part convey'd by the relation to every connected idea. The relation causes a smooth passage from the impression to the idea, and even gives a propensity to that passage. The mind falls so easily from the one perception to the other, that it scarce perceives the change, but retains in the second a considerable share of the vivacity of the first. It is excited by the lively impression; and this vivacity is convey'd to the related idea without any great diminution in the passage, by reason of the smooth transition and the propensity of the imagination.

But suppose, that this propensity arises from some other principle, besides that of relation; 'tis evident it must still have the same effect, and convey the vivacity from the impression to the idea. Now this is exactly the present case. Our memory presents us with a vast number of instances of perceptions perfectly resembling each other, that return at different distances of time, and after considerable interruptions. This resemblance gives us a propension to consider these interrupted perceptions as the same; and also a propension to connect them by a continu'd existence, in order to justify this identity, and avoid the contradiction, in which the interrupted appearance of these perceptions seems necessarily to involve us. Here then we have a propensity to feign the continu'd existence of all sensible objects; and as this propensity arises from some lively impressions of the memory, it bestows a vivacity on that fiction; or in other words, makes us believe the continu'd existence of body. If sometimes we ascribe a continu'd existence to objects, which are perfectly new to us, and of whose constancy and coherence we have no experience, 'tis because the manner, in which they present themselves to our senses, resembles that of constant and coherent objects; and this resemblance is a source of reasoning and analogy, and leads us to attribute the same qualities to the similar objects.

I believe an intelligent reader will find less difficulty to assent to this system, than to comprehend it fully and distinctly, and will allow, after a little reflection, that every part carries its own proof along with it. 'Tis indeed evident, that as the vulgar *suppose* their perceptions to be their only objects, and at the same time *believe* the continu'd existence of matter, we must account for the origin of the belief upon that supposition. Now upon that supposition, 'tis a false opinion that any of our objects, or perceptions, are identically the same after an interruption; and consequently the opinion of their identity can never arise from reason, but must arise from the imagination. The imagination is seduc'd into such an opinion only by means of the resemblance of certain perceptions; since we find they are only our resembling perceptions, which we have a propension to suppose the same. This propension to bestow an identity on our resembling perceptions, produces the fiction of a continu'd existence; since that fiction, as well as the identity, is really false, as is acknowledg'd by all philosophers, and has no other effect than to remedy the interruption of our perceptions, which is the only circumstance that is contrary to their identity. In the last place this propension causes belief by means of the present impressions of the memory; since without the remembrance of former sensations, 'tis plain we never shou'd have any belief of the continu'd existence of body. Thus in examining all these parts, we find that each of them is supported by the strongest proofs; and that all of them together form a consistent system, which is perfectly convincing. A strong propensity or inclination alone, without any present impression, will sometimes cause a belief or opinion. How much more when aided by that circumstance?

But tho' we are led after this manner, by the natural propensity of the imagination, to ascribe a continu'd existence to those sensible objects or perceptions, which we find to resemble each other in their interrupted appearance; yet a very little reflection and philosophy is sufficient to make us perceive the fallacy of that opinion. I have already observ'd, that there is an intimate connexion betwixt those two principles, of a *continu'd* and of a *distinct* or *independent* existence, and that we no sooner establish the one than the other follows, as a necessary consequence. 'Tis the opinion of a continu'd existence, which first takes place, and without much study or reflection draws the other along with it, wherever the mind follows its first and most natural tendency. But when we compare experiments, and reason a little upon them, we quickly perceive, that the doctrine of the independent existence of our sensible perceptions is contrary to the plainest experience. This leads us backward upon our footsteps to perceive our error in attributing a continu'd existence to our perceptions, and is the origin of many very curious opinions, which we shall here endeavour to account for.

'Twill first be proper to observe a few of those experiments, which convince us, that our perceptions are not possest of any independent existence. When we press one eye with a finger, we immediately perceive all the objects to become double, and one half of them to be remov'd from their common and natural position. But as we do not attribute a continu'd existence to both these perceptions, and as they are both of the same nature, we clearly perceive, that all our perceptions are dependent on our organs, and the disposition of our nerves and animal spirits. This opinion is confirm'd by the seeming encrease and diminution of objects, according to their distance; by the apparent alterations in their figure; by the changes in their colour and other qualities from our sickness and distempers; and by an infinite number of other experiments of the same kind; from all which we learn, that our sensible perceptions are not possest of any distinct or independent existence.

The natural consequence of this reasoning shou'd be, that our perceptions have no more a continu'd than an independent existence; and indeed philosophers have so far run into this opinion, that they change their system, and distinguish, (as we shall do for the future) betwixt perceptions and objects, of which the former are suppos'd to be interrupted, and perishing, and different at every different return; the latter to be uninterrupted, and to preserve a continu'd existence and identity. But however philosophical this new system may be esteem'd, I assert that 'tis only a palliative remedy, and that it contains all the difficulties of the vulgar system, with some others, that are peculiar to itself. There are no principles either of the understanding or fancy, which lead us directly to embrace this opinion of the double existence of perceptions and objects, nor can we arrive at it but by passing thro' the common hypothesis of the identity and continuance of our interrupted perceptions. Were we not first perswaded, that our perceptions are our only objects, and continue to exist even when they no longer make their appearance to the senses, we shou'd never be led to think, that our perceptions and objects are different, and that our objects alone preserve a continu'd existence. 'The latter hypothesis has no primary recommendation either to reason or the imagination, but acquires all its influence on the imagination from the former.' This proposition contains two parts, which we shall endeavour to prove as distinctly and clearly, as such abstruse subjects will permit.

As to the first part of the proposition, *that this philosophical hypothesis has no primary recommendation, either to reason or the imagination,* we may soon satisfy ourselves with regard to *reason* by the following reflections. The only existences, of which we are certain, are perceptions, which being immediately present to us by consciousness, command our strongest assent, and are the first foundation of all our conclusions. The only conclusion we can draw from the existence of one thing to that of another, is by means of the relation of cause and effect, which shews, that there is a connexion betwixt them, and that the existence of one is dependent on that of the other. The idea of this relation is deriv'd from past experience, by which we find, that two beings are constantly conjoin'd together, and are always present at once to the mind. But as no beings are ever present to the mind but perceptions; it follows that we may observe a conjunction or a relation of cause and effect between different perceptions, but can never observe it between perceptions and objects. 'Tis impossible, therefore, that from the existence or any of the qualities of the former, we can ever form any conclusion concerning the existence of the latter, or ever satisfy our reason in this particular.

'Tis no less certain, that this philosophical system has no primary recommendation to the *imagination,* and that that faculty wou'd never, of itself, and by its original tendency, have fallen upon such a principle. I confess it will be somewhat difficult to prove this to the full satisfaction of the reader; because it implies a negative, which in many cases will not admit of any positive proof. If any one wou'd take the pains to examine this question, and wou'd invent a system, to account for the direct origin of this opinion from the imagination, we shou'd be able, by the examination of that system, to pronounce a certain judgement in the present subject. Let it be taken for granted, that our perceptions are broken, and interrupted, and however like, are still different from each other; and let any one upon this supposition shew why the fancy, directly and immediately, proceeds to the belief of another existence, resembling these perceptions in their nature, but yet continu'd, and uninterrupted, and identical; and after he has done this to my satisfaction, I promise to renounce my present opinion. Mean while I cannot forbear concluding, from the very abstractedness and difficulty of the first supposition, that 'tis an improper subject for the fancy to work upon. Whoever wou'd explain the origin of the *common* opinion concerning the continu'd and distinct existence of body, must take the mind in its *common* situation, and must proceed upon the supposition, that our perceptions are our only objects, and continue to exist even when they are not perceiv'd. Tho' this opinion be false, 'tis the most natural of any, and has alone any primary recommendation to the fancy.

As to the second part of the proposition, *that the philosophical system acquires all its influence on the imagination from the vulgar one;* we may observe, that this is a natural and unavoidable consequence of the foregoing conclusion, *that it has no primary recommendation to reason or the imagination.* For as the philosophical system is found by experience to take hold of many minds, and in particular of all those, who reflect ever so little on this subject, it must derive all its authority from the vulgar system; since it has no original authority of its own. The manner, in which these two systems, tho' directly contrary, are connected together, may be explain'd, as follows.

The imagination naturally runs on in this train of thinking. Our perceptions are our only objects: Resembling perceptions are the same, however broken or uninterrupted in their appearance: This appearing interruption is contrary to the identity: The interruption consequently extends not beyond the appearance, and the perception or object really continues to exist, even when absent from us: Our sensible perceptions have, therefore, a continu'd and uninterrupted existence. But as a little reflection destroys this conclusion, that our perceptions have a continu'd existence, by shewing that they have a dependent one, 'twou'd naturally be expected, that we must altogether reject the opinion, that there is such a thing in nature as a continu'd existence, which is preserv'd even when it no longer appears to the senses. The case, however, is otherwise. Philosophers are so far from rejecting the opinion of a continu'd existence upon rejecting that of the independence and continuance of our sensible perceptions, that tho' all sects agree in the latter sentiment, the former, which is, in a manner, its necessary consequence, has been peculiar to a few extravagant sceptics; who after all maintain'd that opinion in words only, and were never able to bring themselves sincerely to believe it.

There is a great difference betwixt such opinions as we form after a calm and profound reflection, and such as we embrace by a kind of instinct or natural impulse, on account of their suitableness and conformity to the mind. If these opinions become contrary, 'tis not difficult to foresee which of them will have the advantage. As long as our attention is bent upon the subject, the philosophical and study'd principle may prevail; but the moment we relax our thoughts, nature will display herself, and draw us back to our former opinion. Nay she has sometimes such an influence, that she can stop our progress, even in the midst of our most profound reflections, and keep us from running on with all the consequences of any philosophical opinion. Thus tho' we clearly perceive the dependence and interruption of our perceptions, we stop short in our carreer, and never upon that account reject that notion of an independent and continu'd existence. That opinion has taken such deep root in the imagination, that 'tis impossible ever to eradicate it, nor will any strain'd metaphysical conviction of the dependence of our perceptions be sufficient for that purpose.

But tho' our natural and obvious principles here prevail above our study'd reflections, 'tis certain there must be some struggle and opposition in the case; at least so long as these reflections retain any force or vivacity. In order to set ourselves at ease in this particular, we contrive a new hypothesis, which seems to comprehend both these principles of reason and imagination. This hypothesis is the philosophical one of the double existence of perceptions and objects; which pleases our reason, in allowing, that our dependent perceptions are interrupted and different; and at the same time is agreeable to the imagination, in attributing a continu'd existence to something else, which we call *objects*. This philosophical system, therefore, is the monstrous offspring of two principles, which are contrary to each other, which are both at once embrac'd by the mind, and which are unable mutually to destroy each other. The imagination tells us, that our resembling perceptions have a continu'd and uninterrupted existence, and are not annihilated by their absence. Reflection tells us, that even our resembling perceptions are interrupted in their existence, and different from each other. The contradiction betwixt these opinions we elude by a new fiction, which is conformable to the hypotheses both of reflection and fancy, by ascribing these contrary qualities to different existences; the *interruption* to perceptions, and the *continuance* to objects. Nature is obstinate, and will not quit the field, however strongly attack'd by reason; and at the same time reason is so clear in the point, that there is no possibility of disguising her. Not being able to reconcile these two enemies, we endeavour to set ourselves at ease as much as possible, by successively granting to each whatever it demands, and by feigning a double existence, where each may find something, that has all the conditions it desires. Were we fully convinc'd, that our resembling perceptions are continu'd, and identical, and independent, we shou'd never run into this opinion of a double existence; since we shou'd find satisfaction in our first supposition, and wou'd not look beyond. Again, were we fully convinc'd, that our perceptions are dependent, and interrupted, and different, we shou'd be as little inclin'd to embrace the opinion of a double existence; since in that case we shou'd clearly perceive the error of our first supposition of a continu'd existence, and wou'd never regard it any farther. 'Tis therefore from the intermediate situation of the mind, that this opinion arises, and from such an adherence to these two contrary principles, as makes us seek some pretext to justify our receiving both; which happily at last is found in the system of a double existence.

NOTES

1. Part II. sect. 6.
2. Sect. 5.
3. Part II. sect. 4.

3

A Defence of Common Sense

G. E. MOORE

In what follows I have merely tried to state, one by one, some of the most important points in which my philosophical position differs from positions which have been taken up by *some* other philosophers. It may be that the points which I have had room to mention are not really the most important, and possibly some of them may be points as to which no philosopher has ever really differed from me. But, to the best of my belief, each is a point as to which many have really differed; although (in most cases, at all events) each is also a point as to which many have agreed with me.

I. The first point is a point which embraces a great many other points. And it is one which I cannot state as clearly as I wish to state it, except at some length. The method I am going to use for stating it is this. I am going to begin by enunciating, under the heading (1), a whole long list of propositions, which may seem, at first sight, such obvious truisms as not to be worth stating: they are, in fact, a set of propositions, every one of which (in my own opinion) I *know,* with certainty, to be true. I shall, next, under the heading (2), state a single proposition which makes an assertion about a whole set of *classes* of propositions—each class being defined, as the class consisting of all propositions which resemble *one* of the propositions in (1) in a certain respect. (2), therefore, is a proposition which could not be stated, until the list of propositions in (1), or some similar list, had already been given. (2) is itself a proposition which may seem such an obvious truism as not to be worth stating: and it is also a proposition which (in my own opinion) I *know,* with certainty, to be true. But, nevertheless, it is, to the best of my belief, a proposition with regard to which many philosophers have, for different reasons, differed from me; even if they have not

Source: G. E. Moore, *Philosophical Papers*. London: George Allen and Unwin, 1959. Used with permission of the Estate of G. E. Moore.

directly denied (2) itself, they have held views incompatible with it. My first point, then, may be said to be that (2), together with all its implications, some of which I shall expressly mention, is true.

(1) I begin, then, with my list of truisms, every one of which (in my own opinion) I *know*, with certainty, to be true. The propositions to be included in this list are the following:

There exists at present a living human body, which is *my* body. This body was born at a certain time in the past, and has existed continuously ever since, though not without undergoing changes; it was, for instance, much smaller when it was born, and for some time afterwards, than it is now. Ever since it was born, it has been either in contact with or not far from the surface of the earth; and, at every moment since it was born, there have also existed many other things, having shape and size in three dimensions (in the same familiar sense in which it has), from which it has been *at various distances* (in the familiar sense in which it is now at a distance both from that mantelpiece and from that bookcase, and at a greater distance from the bookcase than it is from the mantelpiece); also there have (very often, at all events) existed some other things of this kind with which it was *in contact* (in the familiar sense in which it is now in contact with the pen I am holding in my right hand and with some of the clothes I am wearing). Among the things which have, in this sense, formed part of its environment (i.e. have been either in contact with it, or at *some* distance from it, however *great*) there have, at every moment since its birth, been large numbers of other living human bodies, each of which has, like it, (*a*) at some time been born, (*b*) continued to exist from some time after birth, (*c*) been, at every moment of its life after birth, either in contact with or not far from the surface of the earth; and many of these bodies have already died and ceased to exist. But the earth had existed also for many years before my body was born; and for many of these years, also, large numbers of human bodies had, at every moment, been alive upon it; and many of these bodies had died and ceased to exist before it was born. Finally (to come to a different class of propositions), I am a human being, and I have, at different times since my body was born, had many different experiences, of each of many different kinds: e.g. I have often perceived both my own body and other things which formed part of its environment, including other human bodies; I have not only perceived things of this kind, but have also observed facts about them, such as, for instance, the fact which I am now observing, that that mantelpiece is at present nearer to my body than that bookcase; I have been aware of other facts, which I was not at the time observing, such as, for instance, the fact, of which I am now aware, that my body existed yesterday and was then also for some time nearer to that mantelpiece than to that bookcase; I have had expectations with regard to the future, and many beliefs of other kinds, both true and false; I have thought of imaginary things and persons and incidents, in the reality of which I did not believe; I have had dreams; and I have had feelings of many different kinds. And, just as my body has been the body of a human being, namely myself, who has, during his lifetime, had many experiences of each of these (and other) different kinds; so, in the case of very many of the other human bodies which have lived upon the earth, each has been the body of a different human being, who has, during the lifetime of that body, had many different experiences of each of these (and other) different kinds.

(2) I now come to the single truism which, as will be seen, could not be stated except by reference to the whole list of truisms, just given in (1). This truism also (in my own opinion) I *know*, with certainty, to be true; and it is as follows:

In the case of *very many* (I do not say *all*) of the human beings belonging to the class (which includes myself) defined in the following way, i.e. as human beings who have had human bodies, that were born and lived for some time upon the earth, and who have, during the lifetime of those bodies, had many different experiences of each of the kinds mentioned in (1), it is true that each has frequently, during the life of his body, known, with regard to *himself* or *his* body, and with regard to some time earlier than any of the times at which I wrote down the propositions in (1), a proposition *corresponding* to each of the propositions in (1), in the sense that it asserts with regard to *himself* or *his* body and the earlier time in question (namely, in each case, the time at which he knew it), just what the corresponding proposition in (1) asserts with regard to *me* or *my* body and the time at which I wrote that proposition down.

In other words what (2) asserts is only (what seems an obvious enough truism) that each of *us* (meaning by 'us', very many human beings of the class defined) has frequently *known,* with regard to *himself* or *his* body and the time at which he knew it, everything which, in writing down my list of propositions in (1), I was claiming to know about *my*self or *my* body and the time at which I wrote that proposition down, i.e. just as *I* knew (when I wrote it down) 'There exists at present a living human body which is my body', so each of us has frequently known with regard to himself and some other time the different but corresponding proposition, which *he* could *then* have properly expressed by, 'There exists *at present* a human body which is *my* body'; just as *I* know 'Many human bodies other than mine have before now lived on the earth', so each of us has frequently known the different but corresponding proposition 'Many human bodies other than *mine* have before *now* lived on the earth'; just as *I* know 'Many human beings other than myself have before now perceived, and dreamed, and felt', so each of *us* has frequently known the different but corresponding proposition 'Many human beings other than *myself* have before *now* perceived, and dreamed, and felt'; and so on, in the case of *each* of the propositions enumerated in (1).

I hope there is no difficulty in understanding, so far, what this proposition (2) asserts. I have tried to make clear by examples what I mean by 'propositions *corresponding* to each of the propositions in (1)'. And what (2) asserts is merely that each of us has frequently known to be true a proposition *corresponding* (in that sense) to each of the propositions in (1)—a *different* corresponding proposition, of course, at each of the times at which he knew such a proposition to be true.

But there remain two points, which, in view of the way in which some philosophers have used the English language, ought, I think, to be expressly mentioned, if I am to make quite clear exactly how much I am asserting in asserting (2).

The first point is this. Some philosophers seem to have thought it legitimate to use the word 'true' in such a sense that a proposition which is partially false may nevertheless also be true; and some of these, therefore, would perhaps *say* that propositions like those enumerated in (1) are, in their view, true, when all the time they believe that every such proposition is partially false. I wish, therefore, to make it quite plain that I am not using 'true' in any such sense. I am using it in such a sense (and I think this is the ordinary usage) that if a proposition is partially false, it follows that it is *not* true, though, of course, it may be *partially* true. I am maintaining, in short, that all the propositions in (1), and also many propositions corresponding to each of these, are *wholly* true; I am asserting this in asserting (2). And hence any philosopher, who does in fact believe, with regard to any or all of these classes of propositions, that every proposition of the class in question is partially false, is, in fact, disagreeing with me and holding a view incompatible with (2), even though he may think himself justified in *saying* that he believes some propositions belonging to all of these classes to be 'true'.

And the second point is this. Some philosophers seem to have thought it legitimate to use such expressions as, e.g. 'The earth has existed for many years past', as if they expressed something which they really believed, when in fact they believe that every proposition, which such an expression would *ordinarily* be understood to express, is, at least partially, false; and all they really believe is that there is some *other* set of propositions, related in a certain way to those which such expressions do actually express, which, unlike these, really are true. That is to say, they use the expression 'The earth has existed for many years past' to express, not what it would ordinarily be understood to express, but the proposition that some proposition, related to this in a certain way, is true; when all the time they believe that the proposition, which this expression would ordinarily be understood to express, is, at least partially, false. I wish, therefore, to make it quite plain that I was not using the expressions I used in (1) in any such subtle sense. I meant by each of them precisely what every reader, in reading them, will have understood me to mean. And any philosopher, therefore, who holds that any of these expressions, if understood in this popular manner, expresses a proposition which embodies some popular error, is disagreeing with me and holding a view incompatible with (2), even though he may hold that there is some *other,* true, proposition which the expression in question might be legitimately used to express.

In what I have just said, I have assumed that there is some meaning which is *the* ordinary or popular meaning of such expressions as 'The earth has existed for many years past'. And this, I am afraid, is an assumption which some philosophers are capable of disputing. They seem to think that the question 'Do you believe that the earth has existed for many years past?' is not a plain question, such as should be met either by a plain 'Yes' or 'No', or by a plain 'I can't make up my mind', but is the sort of question which can be properly met by: 'It all depends on what you mean by "the earth" and "exists" and "years": if you mean so and so, and so and so, and so and so, then I do; but if you mean so and so, and so and so, and so and so, or so and so, and so and so, and so and so, or so and so, and so and so, and so and so, then I don't, or at least I think it is extremely doubtful.' It seems to me that such a view is as profoundly mistaken as any view can be. Such an expression as 'The earth has existed for many years past' is the very type of an unambiguous expression, the meaning of which we all understand. Anyone who takes a contrary view must, I suppose, be confusing the question whether we understand its meaning (which we all certainly do) with the entirely different question whether we *know what it means,* in the sense that we are able to *give a correct analysis* of its meaning. The question what is the correct analysis of *the* proposition meant *on any occasion* (for, of course, as I insisted in defining (2), a different proposition is meant at every different time at which the expression is used) by 'The earth has existed for many years past' is, it seems to me, a profoundly difficult question, and one to which, as I shall presently urge, no one knows the answer. But to hold that we do not know what, in certain respects, is the analysis of what we understand by such an expression, is an entirely different thing from holding that we do not understand the expression. It is obvious that we cannot even raise the question how what we do understand by it is to be analysed, unless we do understand it. So soon, therefore, as we know that a person who uses such an expression is using it in its ordinary sense, we understand his meaning. So that in explaining that I was using the expressions used in (1) in their ordinary sense (those of them which have an ordinary sense, which is not the case with quite all of them), I have done all that is required to make my meaning clear.

But now, assuming that the expressions which I have used to express (2) are understood, I think, as I have said, that many philosophers have really held views incompatible with (2). And the philosophers who have done so may, I think, be divided into two main groups. A. What (2) asserts is, with regard to a whole set of *classes* of propositions, that we have, each of us, frequently *known* to be true propositions belonging to *each* of these classes. And one way of holding a view incompatible with this proposition is, of course, to hold, with regard to one or more of the classes in question, that *no* propositions of that class *are* true—that all of them are, at least partially, false; since if, in the case of any one of these classes, *no* propositions of that class *are* true, it is obvious that nobody can have *known* any propositions of that class to be true, and therefore that *we* cannot have known to be true propositions belonging to *each* of these classes. And my first group of philosophers consists of philosophers who have held views incompatible with (2) for this reason. They have held, with regard to one or more of the classes in question, simply that no propositions of that class *are* true. Some of them have held this with regard to *all* the classes in question; some only with regard to *some* of them. But, of course, whichever of these two views they have held, they have been holding a view inconsistent with (2). B. Some philosophers, on the other hand, have not ventured to assert, with regard to *any* of the classes in (2), that no propositions of that class *are* true, but what they have asserted is that, in the case of some of these classes, no human being has ever *known,* with certainty, that any propositions of the class in question are true. That is to say, they differ profoundly from philosophers of group A, in that they hold that propositions of *all* these classes *may* be true; but nevertheless they hold a view incompatible with (2) since they hold, with regard to some of these classes, that none of us has ever *known* a proposition of the class in question to be true.

A. I said that some philosophers, belonging to this group, have held that no propositions belonging to *any* of the classes in (2) are wholly true, while others have only held this with regard to *some* of the classes in (2). And I think the chief division of this kind has been the following. Some of the propositions in (1) (and, therefore, of course, all propositions belonging to the corresponding classes in (2)) are propositions which cannot be true, unless some *material things* have existed and have stood *in spatial relations* to one another: that is to say, they are propositions which, *in a certain sense,* imply *the reality of material things,* and *the reality of Space*. E.g. the proposition that my body has existed for many years past, and has, at every moment during that time been either in contact with or not far from the earth, is a proposition which implies both the *reality of material things* (provided you use 'material things' in such a sense that to deny the reality of material things implies that no proposition which asserts that human bodies have existed, or that the earth has existed, is wholly true) and also the *reality of Space* (provided, again, that you use 'Space' in such a sense that to deny the reality of Space implies that no proposition which asserts that anything has ever been in contact with or at a distance from another, in the familiar senses pointed out in (1), is wholly true). But others among the propositions in (1) (and, therefore, propositions belonging to the corresponding classes in (2)), do not (at least obviously) imply either the reality of material things or the reality of Space: e.g. the propositions that I have often had dreams, and have had many different feelings at different times. It is true that propositions of this second class do imply one thing which is also implied by all propositions of the first, namely that (*in a certain sense*) *Time is real,* and imply also one thing not implied by propositions of the first class, namely that (*in a certain sense*) *at least one Self is real.* But I think there are some philosophers, who, while denying that (in the senses in question) either material things or Space are real, have been willing to admit that Selves and Time are real, in the sense required. Other philosophers, on the other hand, have used the expression 'Time is not real', to express some view that they held; and some, at least, of these have, I think, meant by this expression something which is incompatible with the truth of *any* of the propositions in (1)—they have meant, namely, that *every* proposition of the sort that is expressed by the use of 'now' or 'at present', e.g. 'I am now both seeing and hearing' or 'There exists at present a living human body', or by the use of a *past* tense, e.g. 'I *have* had many experiences in the past', or 'The earth *has* existed for many years', are, at least partially, false.

All the four expressions I have just introduced, namely, 'Material things are not real', 'Space is not real', 'Time is not real', 'The Self is not real', are, I think, unlike the expressions I used in (1), really ambiguous. And it may be that, in the case of each of them, some philosopher has used the expression in question to express some view he held which was not incompatible with (2). With such philosophers, if there are any, I am not, of course, at present concerned. But it seems to me that the most natural and proper usage of each of these expressions is a usage in which it *does* express a view incompatible with (2); and, in the case of each of them, some philosophers have, I think, really used the expression in question to express such a view. All such philosophers have, therefore, been holding a view incompatible with (2).

All such views, whether incompatible with *all* of the propositions in (1), or only with *some* of them, seem to me to be quite certainly false; and I think the following points are specially deserving of notice with regard to them:

(*a*) If *any* of the classes of propositions in (2) is such that no proposition of that class is true, then no philosopher has ever existed, and therefore none can ever have held with regard to any such class, that no proposition belonging to it is true. In other words, the proposition that some propositions belonging to each of these classes are true is a proposition which has the peculiarity, that, if any philosopher has ever denied it, it follows from the fact that he has denied it, that he must have been wrong in denying it. For when I speak of 'philosophers' I mean, of course (as we all do), exclusively philosophers who have been human beings, with human bodies that have lived upon the earth, and who have at different times had many different experiences. If, therefore, there have been any philosophers, there have been human beings of this class; and if there have been human beings of this class, all the rest of what is asserted in (1) is certainly true too. Any view, therefore, incompatible with the propositions that many propositions corresponding to each of the propositions in (1) are true, can only be true, on the hypothesis that no philosopher has ever held any such view. It follows, therefore, that, in considering whether this proposition is true, I cannot consistently regard the fact that many philosophers, whom I respect, have, to the best of my belief, held views incompatible with it, as having any weight at all against it. Since, if I know that they have held such views, I am, *ipso facto,* knowing that they were mistaken; and, if I have no reason to believe that the proposition in question is true, I have still less reason to believe that they have held views incompatible with it; since I am more certain that they have existed and held *some* views, i.e. that the proposition in question is true, than that they have held any views incompatible with it.

(*b*) It is, of course, the case that all philosophers who have held such views have repeatedly, even in their philosophical works, expressed other views inconsistent with them: i.e. no philosopher has ever been able to hold such views consistently. One way in which they have betrayed this inconsistency, is by alluding to the existence of other philosophers. Another way is by alluding to the existence of the human race, and in particular by using 'we' in the sense in which I have already constantly used it, in which any philosopher who asserts that 'we' do so and so, e.g. that '*we* sometimes believe propositions that are not true', is asserting not only that he himself has done the thing in question, but that *very many other human beings, who have had bodies and lived upon the earth,* have done the same. The fact is, of course, that all philosophers have belonged to the class of human beings which exists only if (2) be true: that is to say, to the class of human beings who have frequently *known* propositions corresponding to each of the propositions in (1). In holding views incompatible with the proposition that propositions of all these classes are true, they have, therefore, been holding views inconsistent with propositions which they themselves *knew* to be true; and it was, therefore, only to be expected that they should sometimes betray their knowledge of such propositions. The strange thing is that philosophers should have been able to hold sincerely, as part of their philosophical creed, propositions inconsistent with what they themselves *knew* to be true; and yet, so far as I can make out, this has really frequently happened. My position, therefore, on this first point differs from that of philosophers belonging to this group A, not in that I hold anything which they don't hold, but only in that I don't hold, as part of my philosophical creed, things which they do hold as part of theirs—that is to say, propositions inconsistent with some which they and I both hold in common. But this difference seems to me to be an important one.

(*c*) Some of these philosophers have brought forward, in favour of their position, arguments designed to show, in the case of some or all of the propositions in (1), that no propositions of that type can possibly be wholly true, because every such proposition entails both of two incompatible propositions. And I admit, of course, that if any of the propositions in (1) did entail both of two incompatible propositions it could not be true. But it seems to me I have an absolutely conclusive argument to show that none of them does entail both of two incompatible propositions. Namely this: All of the propositions in (1) are true; no true proposition entails both of two incompatible propositions; therefore, none of the propositions in (1) entails both of two incompatible propositions.

(*d*) Although, as I have urged, no philosopher who has held with regard to any of these types of proposition that no propositions of that type are true, has failed to hold also other views inconsistent with his view in this respect, yet I do not think that the view, with regard to any or all of these types, that no proposition belonging to them is true, is *in itself* a self-contradictory view, i.e. entails both of two incompatible propositions. On the contrary, it seems to me quite clear that it *might* have been the case that Time was not real, material things not real, Space not real, selves not real. And in favour of my view that none of these things, which might have been the case, *is* in fact the case, I have, I think, no better argument than simply this—namely, that all the propositions in (1) are, in fact, true.

B. This view, which is usually considered a much more modest view than A, has, I think, the defect that, unlike A, it really is self-contradictory, i.e. entails both of two mutually incompatible propositions.

Most philosophers who have held this view, have held, I think, that though each of us knows propositions corresponding to *some* of the propositions in (1), namely to those which merely assert that *I* myself have had in the past experiences of certain kinds at many different times, yet none of us knows *for certain* any propositions either of the type (*a*) which assert the existence of *material things* or of the type (*b*) which assert the existence of *other* selves, beside myself, and that *they* also have had experiences. They admit that we do in fact *believe* propositions of both these types, and that they *may* be true: some would even say that we know them to be highly probable; but they deny that we ever know them, *for certain,* to be true. Some of them have spoken of such beliefs as 'beliefs of Common Sense', expressing thereby their conviction that beliefs of this kind are very commonly entertained by mankind: but they are convinced that these things are, in all cases, only *believed,* not known for certain; and some have expressed this by saying that they are matters of Faith, not of Knowledge.

Now the remarkable thing which those who take this view have not, I think, in general duly appreciated, is that, in each case, the philosopher who takes it is making an assertion about 'us'—that is to say, not merely about himself, but about *many other human beings as well.* When he says 'No human being has ever *known* of the existence of other human beings', he is saying: 'There have been many other human beings beside myself, and none of them (including myself) has ever known of the existence of other human beings.' If he says: 'These beliefs are beliefs of Common Sense, but they are not matters of *knowledge'*, he is saying: 'There have been many other human beings, beside myself, who have shared these beliefs, but neither I nor any of the rest has ever known them to be true.' In other words, he asserts with confidence that these beliefs *are* beliefs of Common Sense, and seems often to fail to notice that, *if* they are, they must be true; since the proposition that they are beliefs of Common Sense is one which logically entails propositions both of type (*a*) and of type (*b*); it logically entails the proposition that many human beings, beside the philosopher himself, have had human bodies, which lived upon the earth, and have had various experiences, including beliefs of this kind. This is why this position, as contrasted with positions of group A, seems to me to be self-contradictory. Its difference from A consists in the fact that it is making a proposition about *human knowledge* in general, and therefore is actually asserting the existence of many human beings, whereas philosophers of group A in stating their position are not doing this: they are only contradicting *other* things which they hold. It is true that a philosopher who says 'There have existed many human beings beside myself, and none of us has ever known of the existence of any human beings beside himself', is only contradicting himself if what he holds is 'There have *certainly* existed many human beings beside myself' or, in other words, '*I* know that there have existed other human beings beside myself'. But this, it seems to me, is what such philosophers have in fact been generally doing. They seem to me constantly to betray the fact that they regard the proposition that those beliefs *are* beliefs of Common Sense, or the proposition that they themselves are not the only members of the human race, as not merely true, but *certainly* true; and *certainly* true it cannot be, unless one member, at least, of the human race, namely themselves, has *known* the very things which that member is declaring that no human being has ever known.

Nevertheless, my position that I *know,* with certainty, to be true all of the propositions in (1), is certainly not a position, the denial of which entails both of two incompatible propositions. If I do *know* all these propositions to be true, then, I think, it is quite certain that other human beings also have known corresponding propositions: that is to say (2) also *is* true, and *I* know it to be true. But do I really *know* all the propositions in (1) to be true? Isn't it possible that I merely believe them? Or know them to be highly probable? In answer to this question, I think I have nothing better to say than that it seems to me that I *do* know them, with certainty. It is, indeed, obvious that, in the case of most of them, I do not know them *directly:* that is to say, I only know them because, in the past, I have known to be true *other* propositions which were evidence for them. If, for instance, I do know that the earth had existed for many years before I was born, I certainly only know this because I have known other things in the past which were evidence for it. And I certainly do not know exactly what the evidence was. Yet all this seems to me to be no good reason for doubting that I do know it. We are all, I think, in this strange position that we do *know* many things, with regard to which we *know* further that we must have had evidence for them, and yet we do not know *how* we know them, i.e. we do not know what the evidence was. If there is any 'we', and if we know that there is, this must be so: for that there is a 'we' is one of the things in question. And that I do know that there is a 'we', that is to say, that many other human beings, with human bodies, have lived upon the earth, it seems to me that I do know, for certain.

If this first point in my philosophical position, namely my belief in (2), is to be given any name, which has actually been used by philosophers in classifying the positions of other philosophers, it would have, I think, to be expressed by saying that I am one of those philosophers who have held that the 'Common Sense view of the world' is, in certain fundamental features, *wholly* true. But it must be remembered that, according to me, *all* philosophers, without exception, have agreed with me in holding this: and that the real difference, which is commonly expressed in this way, is only a difference between those philosophers, who have *also* held views inconsistent with these features in 'the Common Sense view of the world', and those who have not.

The features in question (namely, propositions of any of the classes defined in defining (2)) are all of them features, which have this peculiar property—namely, that *if we know that they are features in the 'Common Sense view of the world', it follows that they are true*: it is self-contradictory to maintain that *we* know them to be features in the Common Sense view, and that yet they are not true; since to say that *we* know this, is to say that they are true. And many of them also have the further peculiar property that, *if they are features in the Common Sense view of the world (whether 'we' know this or not), it follows that they are true,* since to say that there is a 'Common Sense view of the world', is to say that they are true. The phrases 'Common Sense view of the world' or 'Common Sense beliefs' (as used by philosophers) are, of course, extraordinarily vague; and, for all I know, there may be many propositions which may be properly called features in 'the Common Sense view of the world' or 'Common Sense beliefs', which are not true, and which deserve to be mentioned with the contempt with which some philosophers speak of 'Common Sense beliefs'. But to speak with contempt of those 'Common Sense beliefs' which I have mentioned is quite certainly the height of absurdity. And there are, of course, enormous numbers of other features in 'the Common Sense view of the world' which, if these are true, are quite certainly true too: e.g. that there have lived upon the surface of the earth not only human beings, but also many different species of plants and animals, etc. etc.

II. What seems to me the next in importance of the points in which my philosophical position differs from positions held by *some* other philosophers, is one which I will express in the following way. I hold, namely, that there is no good reason to suppose either (A) that *every* physical fact is *logically* dependent upon some mental fact or (B) that *every* physical fact is *causally* dependent upon some mental fact. In saying this, I am not, of course, saying that there *are* any physical facts which are wholly independent (i.e. both logically and causally) of mental facts: I do, in fact, believe that there are; but that is not what I am asserting. I am only asserting that there is *no good reason* to suppose the contrary; by which I mean, of course, that none of the human beings, who have had human bodies that lived upon the earth, have, during the lifetime of their bodies, had any good reason to suppose the contrary. Many philosophers have, I think, not only believed either that *every* physical fact is *logically* dependent upon some mental fact ('physical fact' and 'mental fact' being understood in the sense in which I am using these terms) or that *every* physical fact is *causally* dependent upon some mental fact, or both, but also that they themselves had good reason for these beliefs. In this respect, therefore, I differ from them.

In the case of the term 'physical fact', I can only explain how I am using it by giving examples. I mean by 'physical facts', facts *like* the following: 'That mantelpiece is at present nearer to this body than that bookcase is', 'The earth has existed for many years past', 'The moon has at every moment for many years past been nearer to the earth than to the sun', 'That mantelpiece is of a light colour'. But, when I say 'facts *like* these', I mean, of course, facts like them *in a certain respect;* and what this respect is I cannot define. The term 'physical fact' is, however, in common use; and I think that I am using it in its ordinary sense. Moreover, there is no need for a definition to make my point clear; since among the examples I have given there are some with regard to which I hold that there is no reason to suppose *them* (i.e. these particular physical facts) either logically or causally dependent upon any mental fact.

'Mental fact', on the other hand, is a much more unusual expression, and I am using it in a specially limited sense, which, though I think it is a natural one, does need to be explained. There may be many other senses in which the term can be properly used, but I am only concerned with this one; and hence it is essential that I should explain what it is.

There may, possibly, I hold, be 'mental facts' of three different kinds. It is only with regard to the first kind that I am sure that there are facts of that kind; but if there were any facts of either of the other two kinds, they would be 'mental facts' in my limited sense, and therefore I must explain what is meant by the hypothesis that there are facts of those two kinds.

(*a*) My first kind is this. I am conscious now; and also I am seeing something now. These two facts are both of them mental facts of my first kind; and my first kind consists exclusively of facts which resemble one or other of the two *in a certain respect.*

(α) The fact that I am conscious now is obviously, in a certain sense, a fact, with regard to a particular individual and a particular time, to the effect that that individual is conscious at that time. And every fact which resembles this one in that respect is to be included in my first kind of mental fact. Thus the fact that I was also conscious at many different times yesterday is not itself a fact of this kind: but it entails that there *are* (or, as we should commonly say, because the times in question are past times, 'were') many other facts of this kind, namely each of the facts, which, at each of the times in question, I could have properly expressed by 'I am conscious *now*'. *Any* fact which is, in this sense, a fact with regard to an individual and a time (whether the individual be myself or another, and whether the time be past or present), to the effect that that individual *is* conscious at that time, is to be included in my first kind of mental fact: and I call such facts, facts of class (α).

(β) The second example I gave, namely the fact that I am seeing something now, is obviously related to the fact that I am conscious now in a peculiar manner. It not only *entails* the fact that I am conscious now (for from the fact that I am seeing something it *follows* that I am conscious: I *could* not have been seeing anything, unless I had been conscious, though I might quite well have been conscious without seeing anything) but it also is a fact, with regard to a *specific way* (or mode) of being conscious, to the effect that I am conscious in that way: in the same sense in which the proposition (with regard to any particular thing) 'This is red' both entails the proposition (with regard to the same thing) 'This is coloured', and is also a proposition, with regard to a *specific way* of being coloured, to the effect that that thing is coloured in that way. And any fact which is related in this peculiar manner to any fact of class (α), is also to be included in my first kind of mental fact, and is to be called a fact of class (β). Thus the fact that I am hearing now is, like the fact that I am seeing now, a fact of class (β); and so is any fact, with regard to myself and a past time, which could at that time have been properly expressed by 'I am dreaming now', 'I am imagining now', 'I am at present aware of the fact that . . .', etc. etc. In short, any fact, which is a fact with regard to a particular individual (myself or another), a particular time (past or present), and *any particular kind of experience,* to the effect that that individual is having at that time an experience of that particular kind, is a fact of class (β): and only such facts are facts of class (β).

My first kind of mental facts consists exclusively of facts of classes (α) and (β), and consists of *all* facts of either of these kinds.

(*b*) That there are many facts of classes (α) and (β) seems to me perfectly certain. But many philosophers seem to me to have held a certain view with regard to the *analysis* of facts of class (α), which is such that, if it were true, there would be facts of another kind, which I should wish also to call 'mental facts'. I don't feel at all sure that this analysis is true; but it seems to me that it *may* be true; and since we can understand what is meant by the supposition that it is true, we can also understand what is meant by the supposition that there are 'mental facts' of this second kind.

Many philosophers have, I think, held the following view as to the analysis of what each of us knows, when he knows (at any time) 'I am conscious now'. They have held, namely, that there is a certain intrinsic property (with which we are all of us familiar and which might be called that of 'being an experience') which is such that, at any time at which any man knows 'I am conscious now', he is knowing, with regard to that property and himself and the time in question, 'There is occurring now an event which has this property (i.e. "is an experience") and which is an experience of *mine',* and such that this fact is what he expresses by 'I am conscious now'. And if this view is true, there must be many facts of each of three kinds, each of which I should wish to call 'mental facts'; viz. (1) facts with regard to some event, which has this supposed intrinsic property, and to some time, to the effect that that event is occurring at that time, (2) facts with regard to this supposed intrinsic property and some time, to the effect that *some* event which has that property is occurring at that time, and (3) facts with regard to some property, which is a *specific way* of having the supposed intrinsic property (in the sense above explained in which 'being red' is a specific way of 'being coloured') and some time, to the effect that some event which has that specific property is occurring at that time. Of course, there not only are not, but *cannot* be, facts of any of these kinds, unless there is an intrinsic property related to what each of us (on any occasion) expresses by 'I am conscious now', in the manner defined above; and I feel very doubtful whether there is any such property; in other words, although I know for certain both that I have had many experiences, and that I have had experiences of many different kinds, I feel very doubtful whether to say the first is the same thing as to say that there have been many events, each of which was an experience and an experience of mine, and whether to say the second is the same thing as to say that there have been many events, each of which was an experience of mine, and each of which also had a different property, which was a specific way of being an experience. The proposition that I have had experiences does not necessarily entail the proposition that there have been any events which were experiences; and I cannot satisfy myself that I am acquainted with any events of the supposed kind. But yet it seems to me possible that the proposed analysis of 'I am conscious now' is correct: that I am really acquainted with events of the supposed kind, though I cannot see that I am. And *if* I am, then I should wish to call the three kinds of facts defined above 'mental facts'. Of course, if there are 'experiences' in the sense defined, it would be possible (as many have held) that there *can* be no experiences which are not *some individual's* experiences; and in that case any fact of any of these three kinds would be logically dependent on, though not necessarily identical with, some fact of class (α) or class (β). But it seems to me also a possibility that, if there are 'experiences', there might be experiences which did not belong to any individual; and, in that case, there would be 'mental facts' which were neither identical with nor logically dependent on any fact of class (α) or class (β).

(*c*) Finally some philosophers have, so far as I can make out, held that there are or may be facts which are facts with regard to some individual, to the effect that he is conscious, or is conscious in some specific way, but which differ from facts of classes (α) and (β), in the important respect that they are not facts *with regard to any time:* they have conceived the possibility that there may be one or more individuals, who are *timelessly* conscious, and timelessly conscious in specific modes. And others, again, have, I think, conceived the hypothesis that the intrinsic property defined in (*b*) may be one which does not belong only to *events,* but may also belong to one or more wholes, which do *not* occur at any time: in other words, that there may be one or more *timeless* experiences, which might or might not be the experiences of some individual. It seems to me very doubtful whether any of these hypotheses are even possibly true; but I cannot see for certain that they are not possible: and, if they are possible, then I should wish to give the name 'mental fact' to any fact (if there were any) of any of the five following kinds, viz. (1) to any fact which is the fact, with regard to any individual, that he is *timelessly* conscious, (2) to any fact which is the fact, with regard to any individual, that he is *timelessly* conscious in any specific way, (3) to any fact which is the fact with regard to a *timeless* experience that it exists, (4) to any fact which is the fact with regard to the supposed intrinsic property 'being an experience', that something timelessly exists which has that property, and (5) to any fact which is the fact, with regard to any property, which is a specific mode of this supposed intrinsic property, that something timelessly exists which has that property.

I have, then, defined three different kinds of facts, each of which is such that, if there *were* any facts of that kind (as there certainly *are,* in the case of the first kind), the facts in question *would be* 'mental facts' in my sense; and to complete the definition of the limited sense in which I am using 'mental facts', I have only to add that I wish also to apply the name to one *fourth* class of facts: namely to any fact, which is the fact, with regard to any of these three kinds of facts, or any kinds included in them, *that there are facts of the kind in question;* i.e. not only will each individual fact of class (α) be, in my sense, a 'mental fact', but also the general fact 'that there are facts of class (α)', will itself be a 'mental fact'; and similarly in all other cases: e.g. not only will the fact that I am now perceiving (which is a fact of class (β)) be a 'mental fact', but also the general fact that *there are* facts, with regard to individuals and times, to the effect that the individual in question is perceiving at the time in question, will be a 'mental fact'.

A. Understanding 'physical fact' and 'mental fact' in the senses just explained, I hold, then, that there is no good reason to suppose that *every* physical fact is *logically* dependent upon some mental fact. And I use the phrase, with regard to two facts, F_1 and F_2, 'F_1 is *logically dependent* on F_2', wherever and only where F_1 *entails* F_2, either in the sense in which the proposition 'I am seeing now' *entails* the proposition 'I am conscious now', or the proposition (with regard to any particular thing) 'This is red' entails the proposition (with regard to the same thing) 'This is coloured', or else in the more strictly logical sense in which (for instance) the conjunctive proposition 'All men are mortal, and Mr Baldwin is a man' entails the proposition 'Mr Baldwin is mortal'. To say, then, of two facts, F_1 and F_2, that F_1 is *not* logically dependent upon F_2, is only to say that F_1 *might* have been a fact, even if there had been no such fact as F_2; or that the conjunctive proposition 'F_1 is a fact, but there is no such fact as F_2' is a proposition which is not self-contradictory, i.e. does not entail both of two mutually incompatible propositions.

I hold, then, that, in the case of *some* physical facts, there is no good reason to suppose that there is some mental fact, such that the physical fact in question could not have been a fact unless the mental fact in question had also been one. And my position is perfectly definite, since I hold that this is the case with all the four physical facts, which I have given as examples of physical facts. For example, there is no good reason to suppose that there is any mental fact whatever, such that the fact that that mantelpiece is at present nearer to my body than that bookcase could not have been a fact, unless the mental fact in question had also been a fact; and, similarly, in all the other three cases.

In holding this I am certainly differing from some philosophers. I am, for instance, differing from Berkeley, who held that that mantelpiece, that bookcase, and my body are, all of them, either 'ideas' or 'constituted by ideas', and that no 'idea' can possibly exist without being perceived. He held, that is, that this physical fact is logically dependent upon a mental fact of my fourth class: namely a fact which is the fact that there is at least one fact, which is a fact with regard to an individual and the present time, to the effect that that individual is now perceiving something. He does not say that this physical fact is logically dependent upon any fact which is a fact of any of my first three classes, e.g. on any fact which is the fact, with regard to a particular individual and the present time, that *that* individual is now perceiving something: what he does say is that the physical fact couldn't have been a fact, unless it had been a fact that there was *some* mental fact of this sort. And it seems to me that many philosophers, who would perhaps disagree either with Berkeley's assumption that my body is an 'idea' or 'constituted by ideas', or with his assumption that 'ideas' cannot exist without being perceived, or with both, nevertheless would agree with him in thinking that this physical fact is logically dependent upon *some* 'mental fact': e.g. they might say that it could not have been a fact, unless there had been, at some time or other, or, were timelessly, *some* 'experience'. Many, indeed, so far as I can make out, have held that *every* fact is logically dependent on every other fact. And, of course, they have held in the case of their opinions, as Berkeley did in the case of his, that they had good reasons for them.

B. I also hold that there is no good reason to suppose that *every* physical fact is *causally* dependent upon some mental fact. By saying that F_1 is *causally* dependent on F_2, I mean only that F_1 *wouldn't* have been a fact unless F_2 had been; *not* (which is what 'logically dependent' asserts) that F_1 *couldn't conceivably* have been a fact, unless F_2 had been. And I can illustrate my meaning by reference to the example which I have just given. The fact that that mantelpiece is at present nearer to my body than that bookcase, is (as I have just explained) so far as I can see, not *logically* dependent upon any mental fact; it *might* have been a fact, even if there had been no mental facts. But it certainly is *causally* dependent on many mental facts: my body *would* not have been here unless I had been conscious in various ways in the past; and the mantelpiece and the bookcase certainly *would* not have existed, unless other men had been conscious too.

But with regard to two of the facts, which I gave as instances of physical facts, namely the fact that the earth has existed for many years past, and the fact that the moon has for many years past been nearer to the earth than to the sun, I hold that there is no good reason to suppose that these are *causally* dependent upon any mental fact. So far as I can see, there is no reason to suppose that there is any mental fact of which it could be truly said: unless this fact had been a fact, the earth would not have existed for many years past. And in holding this, again, I think I differ from some philosophers. I differ, for instance, from those who have held that all material things were created by God, and that they had good reasons for supposing this.

III. I have just explained that I differ from those philosophers who have held that there is good reason to suppose that all material things were created by God. And it is, I think, an important point in my position, which should be mentioned, that I differ also from all philosophers who have held that there is good reason to suppose that there is a God at all, whether or not they have held it likely that he created all material things.

And similarly, whereas some philosophers have held that there is good reason to suppose that we, human beings, shall continue to exist and to be conscious after the death of our bodies, I hold that there is no good reason to suppose this.

IV. I now come to a point of a very different order.

As I have explained under I., I am not at all sceptical as to the *truth* of such propositions as 'The earth has existed for many years past', 'Many human bodies have each lived for many years upon it', i.e. propositions which assert the existence of material things: on the contrary, I hold that we all know, with certainty, many such propositions to be true. But I am very sceptical as to what, in certain respects, the correct *analysis* of such propositions is. And this is a matter as to which I think I differ from many philosophers. Many seem to hold that there is no doubt at all as to their *analysis,* nor, therefore, as to the analysis of the proposition 'Material things have existed', in certain respects in which I hold that the analysis of the propositions in question is extremely doubtful; and some of them, as we have seen, while holding that there is no doubt as to their *analysis,* seem to have doubted whether any such propositions are *true*. I, on the other hand, while holding that there is no doubt whatever that many such propositions are wholly true, hold also that no philosopher, hitherto, has succeeded in suggesting an analysis of them, as regards certain important points, which comes anywhere near to being certainly true.

It seems to me quite evident that the question how propositions of the type I have just given are to be analysed, depends on the question how propositions of another and simpler type are to be analysed. I know, at present, that I am perceiving a human hand, a pen, a sheet of paper, etc.; and it seems to me that I cannot know how the proposition 'Material things exist' is to be analysed, until I know how, in certain respects, these simpler propositions are to be analysed. But even these are not simple enough. It seems to me quite evident that my knowledge that I am now perceiving a human hand is a deduction from a pair of propositions simpler still—propositions which I can only express in the form 'I am perceiving *this*' and '*This* is a human hand'. It is the analysis of propositions of the latter kind which seems to me to present such great difficulties, while nevertheless the whole question as to the *nature* of material things obviously depends upon their analysis. It seems to me a surprising thing that so few philosophers, while saying a great deal as to what material things *are* and as to what it is to perceive them, have attempted to give a clear account as to what precisely they suppose themselves to *know* (or to *judge,* in case they have held that we don't *know* any such propositions to be true, or even that no such propositions *are* true) when they know or judge such things as 'This is a hand,' 'That is the sun', 'This is a dog', etc. etc. etc.

Two things only seem to me to be quite certain about the analysis of such propositions (and even with regard to these I am afraid some philosophers would differ from me) namely that whenever I know, or judge, such a proposition to be true, (1) there is always some *sense-datum* about which the proposition in question is a proposition—some sense-datum which is *a* subject (and, in a certain sense, the principal or ultimate subject) of the proposition in question, and (2) that, nevertheless, *what* I am knowing or judging to be true about this sense-datum is not (in general) that it is *itself* a hand, or a dog, or the sun, etc. etc., as the case may be.

Some philosophers have I think doubted whether there are any such things as other philosophers have meant by 'sense-data' or 'sensa'. And I think it is quite possible that some philosophers (including myself, in the past) have used these terms in senses such that it is really doubtful whether there are any such things. But there is no doubt at all that there are sense-data, in the sense in which I am now using that term. I am at present seeing a great number of them, and feeling others. And in order to point out to the reader what sort of things I mean by sense-data, I need only ask him to look at his own right hand. If he does this he will be able to pick out something (and, unless he is seeing double, *only* one thing) with regard to which he will see that it is, at first sight, a natural view to take that that thing is identical, not, indeed, with his whole right hand, but with that part of its surface which he is actually seeing, but will also (on a little reflection) be able to see that it is doubtful whether it can be identical with the part of the surface of his hand in question. Things *of the sort* (in a certain respect) of which this thing is, which he sees in looking at his hand, and with regard to which he can understand how some philosophers should have supposed it to *be* the part of the surface of his hand which he is seeing, while others have supposed that it can't be, are what I mean by 'sense-data'. I therefore define the term in such a way that it is an open question whether the sense-datum which I now see in looking at my hand and which is a sense-datum of my hand is or is not identical with that part of its surface which I am now actually seeing.

That what I know, with regard to this sense-datum, when I know 'This is a human hand', is not that it is *itself* a human hand, seems to me certain because I know that my hand has many parts (e.g. its other side, and the bones inside it), which are quite certainly *not* parts of this sense-datum.

I think it certain, therefore, that the analysis of the proposition 'This is a human hand' is, roughly at least, of the form 'There is a thing, and only one thing, of which it is true both that it is a human hand and that *this surface* is a part of its surface'. In other words, to put my view in terms of the phrase 'theory of representative perception', I hold it to be quite certain that I do not *directly* perceive *my hand;* and that when I am said (as I may be correctly said) to 'perceive' it, that I 'perceive' it means that I perceive (in a different and more fundamental sense) something which is (in a suitable sense) *representative* of it, namely, a certain part of its surface.

This is all that I hold to be *certain* about the analysis of the proposition 'This is a human hand'. We have seen that it includes in its analysis a proposition of the form 'This is part of the surface of a human hand' (where 'This', of course, has a different meaning from that which it has in the original proposition which has now been analysed). But this proposition also is undoubtedly a proposition about the sense-datum, which I am seeing, which is a sense-datum *of* my hand. And hence the further question arises: *What,* when I know '*This is part of the surface of* a human hand', am I knowing about the sense-datum in question? Am I, in this case, really knowing about the sense-datum in question that it *itself* is part of the surface of a human hand? Or, just as we found in the case of 'This is a human hand', that what I was knowing about the sense-datum was certainly not that it *itself* was a human hand, so, is it perhaps the case, with this new proposition, that even here I am not knowing, with regard to the sense-datum, that it is *itself* part of the surface of a hand? And, if so, what is it that I am knowing about the sense-datum itself?

This is the question to which, as it seems to me, no philosopher has hitherto suggested an answer which comes anywhere near to being *certainly* true.

There seem to me to be three, and only three, alternative types of answer possible; and to any answer yet suggested, of any of these types, there seem to me to be very grave objections.

(1) Of the first type, there is but one answer: namely, that in this case what I am knowing really is that the sense-datum *itself* is part of the surface of a human hand. In other words that, though I don't perceive *my hand* directly, I do *directly* perceive part of its surface; that the sense-datum itself *is* this part of its surface and not merely something which (in a sense yet to be determined) 'represents' this part of its surface; and that hence the sense in which I 'perceive' this part of the surface of my hand, is not in its turn a sense which needs to be defined by reference to yet a third more ultimate sense of 'perceive', which is the only one in which perception is direct, namely that in which I perceive the sense-datum.

If this view is true (as I think it may just possibly be), it seems to me certain that we must abandon a view which has been held to be certainly true by most philosophers, namely the view that our sense-data always really have the qualities which they sensibly appear to us to have. For I know that if another man were looking through a microscope at the same surface which I am seeing with the naked eye, the sense-datum which he saw would sensibly appear to him to have qualities very different from and incompatible with those which my sense-datum sensibly appears to me to have: and yet, if my sense-datum is identical with the surface we are both of us seeing, his must be identical with it also. My sense-datum can, therefore, be identical with this surface only on condition that it is identical with his sense-datum; and, since his sense-datum sensibly appears to him to have qualities incompatible with those which mine sensibly appears to me to have, his sense-datum can be identical with mine only on condition that the sense-datum in question either has not got the qualities which it sensibly appears to me to have, or has not got those which it sensibly appears to him to have.

I do not, however, think that this is a fatal objection to this first type of view. A far more serious objection seems to me to be that, when we see a thing double (have what is called 'a double image' of it), we certainly have *two* sense-data each of which is *of* the surface seen, and which cannot therefore both be identical with it; and that yet it seems as if, if any sense-datum is ever identical with the surface *of* which it is a sense-datum, each of these so-called 'images' must be so. It looks, therefore, as if every sense-datum is, after all, only 'representative' of the surface, *of* which it is a sense-datum.

(2) But, if so, what relation has it to the surface in question?

This second type of view is one which holds that when I know 'This is part of the surface of a human hand', what I am knowing with regard to the sense-datum which is *of* that surface, is, *not* that it is *itself* part of the surface of a human hand, but something of the following kind. There is, it says, *some* relation, R, such that what I am knowing with regard to the sense-datum is either 'There is one thing and only one thing, of which it is true both that it is a part of the surface of a human hand, and that it has R to this sense-datum', or else 'There are a set of things, of which it is true both that that set, taken collectively, *are* part of the surface of a human hand, and also that each member of the set has R to this sense-datum, and that nothing which is not a member of the set has R to it'.

Obviously, in the case of this second type, many different views are possible, differing according to the view they take as to what the relation R is. But there is only one of them, which seems to me to have any plausibility; namely that which holds that R is an ultimate and unanalysable relation, which might be expressed by saying that 'xRy' means the same as 'y is an appearance or manifestation of x'. I.e. the analysis which this answer would give of 'This is part of the surface of a human hand' would be 'There is one and only one thing of which it is true both that it is part of the surface of a human hand, and that this sense-datum is an appearance or manifestation of it'.

To this view also there seem to me to be very grave objections, chiefly drawn from a consideration of the questions how we can possibly *know* with regard to any of our sense-data that there is one thing and one thing only which has to them such a supposed ultimate relation; and how, if we do, we can possibly *know* anything further about such things, e.g. of what size or shape they are.

(3) The third type of answer, which seems to me to be the only possible alternative if (1) and (2) are rejected, is the type of answer which J. S. Mill seems to have been implying to be the true one when he said that material things are 'permanent possibilities of sensation'. He seems to have thought that when I know such a fact as 'This is part of the surface of a human hand', what I am knowing with regard to the sense-datum which is the principal subject of that fact, is not that it is itself part of the surface of a human hand, nor yet, with regard to any relation, that *the* thing which has to it that relation is part of the surface of a human hand, but a whole set of hypothetical facts each of which is a fact of the form 'If *these* conditions had been fulfilled, I should have been perceiving a sense-datum intrinsically related to *this* sense-datum in *this* way', 'If *these* (other) conditions had been fulfilled, I should have been perceiving a sense-datum intrinsically related to *this* sense-datum in *this* (other) way', etc. etc.

With regard to this third type of view as to the analysis of propositions of the kind we are considering, it seems to me, again, just *possible* that it is a true one; but to hold (as Mill himself and others seem to have held) that it is *certainly,* or nearly certainly, true, seems to me as great a mistake, as to hold with regard either to (1) or to (2), that they are *certainly,* or nearly certainly, true. There seem to me to be very grave objections to it; in particular the three, (*a*) that though, in general, when I know such a fact as 'This is a hand', I certainly do know some hypothetical facts of the form 'If *these* conditions had been fulfilled, I should have been perceiving a sense-datum of *this* kind, which would have been a sense-datum of the same surface of which *this* is a sense-datum', it seems doubtful whether any conditions with regard to which I know this are not themselves conditions of the form 'If this and that *material thing* had been in those positions and conditions . . . ', (*b*) that it seems again very doubtful whether there is any intrinsic relation, such that my knowledge that (under *these* conditions) I should have been perceiving a sense-datum of *this* kind, which would have been a sense-datum of the same surface of which *this* is a sense-datum, is equivalent to a knowledge, with regard to that relation, that I should, under those conditions, have been perceiving a sense-datum related by it to *this* sense-datum, and (*c*) that, if it were true, the sense in which a material surface is 'round' or 'square', would necessarily be utterly different from that in which our sense-data sensibly appear to us to be 'round' or 'square'.

V. Just as I hold that the proposition 'There are and have been material things' is quite certainly true, but that the question how this proposition is to be analysed is one to which no answer that has been hitherto given is anywhere near certainly true; so I hold that the proposition 'There are and have been many Selves' is quite certainly true, but that here again all the analyses of this proposition that have been suggested by philosophers are highly doubtful.

That I am now perceiving many different sense-data, and that I have at many times in the past perceived many different sense-data, I know for certain—that is to say, I know that there are mental facts of class (β), connected in a way which it is proper to express by saying that they are all of them facts about *me;* but how this kind of connection is to be analysed, I do not know for certain, nor do I think that any other philosopher knows with any approach to certainty. Just as in the case of the proposition 'This is part of the surface of a human hand', there are several extremely different views as to its analysis, each of which seems to me *possible,* but none nearly certain, so also in the case of the proposition 'This, that and that sense-datum are all at present being perceived by *me',* and still more so in the case of the proposition '*I* am now perceiving this sense-datum, and *I* have in the past perceived sense-data of these other kinds'. Of the *truth* of these propositions there seems to me to be no doubt, but as to what is the correct analysis of them there seems to me to be the gravest doubt—the true analysis may, for instance, *possibly* be quite as paradoxical as is the third view given above under IV as to the analysis of 'This is part of the surface of a human hand'; but whether it *is* as paradoxical as this seems to me to be quite as doubtful as in that case. Many philosophers, on the other hand, seem to me to have assumed that there is little or no doubt as to the correct analysis of such propositions; and many of these, just reversing my position, have also held that the propositions themselves are not true.

 4 

Elusive Knowledge

DAVID LEWIS

We know a lot. I know what food penguins eat. I know that phones used to ring, but nowadays squeal, when someone calls up. I know that Essendon won the 1993 Grand Final. I know that here is a hand, and here is another.

We have all sorts of everyday knowledge, and we have it in abundance. To doubt that would be absurd. At any rate, to doubt it in any serious and lasting way would be absurd; and even philosophical and temporary doubt, under the influence of argument, is more than a little peculiar. It is a Moorean fact that we know a lot. It is one of those things that we know better than we know the premises of any philosophical argument to the contrary.

Besides knowing a lot that is everyday and trite, I myself think that we know a lot that is interesting and esoteric and controversial. We know a lot about things unseen: tiny particles and pervasive fields, not to mention one another's underwear. Sometimes we even know what an author meant by his writings. But on these questions, let us agree to disagree peacefully with the champions of 'post-knowledgeism'. The most trite and ordinary parts of our knowledge will be problem enough.

For no sooner do we engage in epistemology—the systematic philosophical examination of knowledge—than we meet a compelling argument that we know next to nothing. The sceptical argument is nothing new or fancy. It is just this: it seems as if knowledge must be by definition infallible. If you claim that *S* knows that *P*, and yet you grant that *S* cannot eliminate a certain possibility in which not-*P*, it certainly seems as if you have granted that *S* does not after all know that *P*. To speak of fallible knowledge, of knowledge despite uneliminated possibilities of error, just *sounds* contradictory.

Source: David Lewis, "Elusive Knowledge," *Australasian Journal of Philosophy,* vol. 74, No. 4 (1996), pp. 549–560. Reprinted by permission of the publisher and permission of David Lewis's estate.

Blind Freddy can see where this will lead. Let your paranoid fantasies rip—CIA plots, hallucinogens in the tap water, conspiracies to deceive, old Nick himself—and soon you find that uneliminated possibilities of error are everywhere. Those possibilities of error are far-fetched, of course, but possibilities all the same. They bite into even our most everyday knowledge. We never have infallible knowledge.

Never—well, hardly ever. Some say we have infallible knowledge of a few simple, axiomatic necessary truths; and of our own present experience. They say that I simply cannot be wrong that a part of a part of something is itself a part of that thing; or that it seems to me now (as I sit here at the keyboard) exactly as if I am hearing clicking noises on top of a steady whirring. Some say so. Others deny it. No matter; let it be granted, at least for the sake of the argument. It is not nearly enough. If we have only that much infallible knowledge, yet knowledge is by definition infallible, then we have very little knowledge indeed—not the abundant everyday knowledge we thought we had. That is still absurd.

So we know a lot; knowledge must be infallible; yet we have fallible knowledge or none (or next to none). We are caught between the rock of fallibilism and the whirlpool of scepticism. Both are mad!

Yet fallibilism is the less intrusive madness. It demands less frequent corrections of what we want to say. So, if forced to choose, I choose fallibilism. (And so say all of us.) We can get used to it, and some of us have done. No joy there—we know that people can get used to the most crazy philosophical sayings imaginable. If you are a contented fallibilist, I implore you to be honest, be naive, hear it afresh. 'He knows, yet he has not eliminated all possibilities of error.' Even if you've numbed your ears, doesn't this overt, explicit fallibilism *still* sound wrong?

Better fallibilism than scepticism; but it would be better still to dodge the choice. I think we can. We will be alarmingly close to the rock, and also alarmingly close to the whirlpool, but if we steer with care, we can—just barely—escape them both.

Maybe epistemology is the culprit. Maybe this extraordinary pastime robs us of our knowledge. Maybe we do know a lot in daily life; but maybe when we look hard at our knowledge, it goes away. But only when we look at it harder than the sane ever do in daily life; only when we let our paranoid fantasies rip. That is when we are forced to admit that there always are uneliminated possibilities of error, so that we have fallible knowledge or none.

Much that we say is context-dependent, in simple ways or subtle ways. Simple: 'it's evening' is truly said when, and only when, it is said in the evening. Subtle: it could well be true, and not just by luck, that Essendon played rottenly, the Easybeats played brilliantly, yet Essendon won. Different contexts evoke different standards of evaluation. Talking about the Easybeats we apply lax standards, else we could scarcely distinguish their better days from their worse ones. In talking about Essendon, no such laxity is required. Essendon won because play that is rotten by demanding standards suffices to beat play that is brilliant by lax standards.

Maybe ascriptions of knowledge are subtly context-dependent, and maybe epistemology is a context that makes them go false. Then epistemology would be an investigation that destroys its own subject matter. If so, the sceptical argument might be flawless, when we engage in epistemology—and only then![1]

If you start from the ancient idea that justification is the mark that distinguishes knowledge from mere opinion (even true opinion), then you well might conclude that ascriptions of knowledge are context-dependent because standards for adequate justification are context-dependent. As follows: opinion, even if true, deserves the name of knowledge only if it is adequately supported by reasons; to deserve that name in the especially demanding context of epistemology, the arguments from supporting reasons must be especially watertight; but the special standards of justification that this special context demands never can be met (well, hardly ever). In the strict context of epistemology we know nothing, yet in laxer contexts we know a lot.

But I myself cannot subscribe to this account of the context-dependence of knowledge, because I question its starting point. I don't agree that the mark of knowledge is justification.[2] First, because justification is not sufficient: your true opinion that you will lose the lottery isn't knowledge, whatever the odds. Suppose you know that it is a fair lottery with one winning ticket and many losing tickets, and you know how many losing tickets there are. The greater the number of losing tickets, the better is your justification for believing you will lose. Yet there is no number great enough to transform your fallible opinion into knowledge—after all, you just might win. No justification is good enough—or none short of a watertight deductive argument, and all but the sceptics will agree that this is too much to demand.[3]

Second, because justification is not always necessary. What (non-circular) argument supports our reliance on perception, on memory, and on testimony?[4] And yet we do gain knowledge by these means. And sometimes, far from having supporting arguments, we don't even know how we know. We once had evidence, drew conclusions, and thereby gained knowledge; now we have forgotten our reasons, yet still we retain our knowledge. Or we know the name that goes with the face, or the sex of the chicken, by relying on subtle visual cues, without knowing what those cues may be.

The link between knowledge and justification must be broken. But if we break that link, then it is not—or not entirely, or not exactly—by raising the standards of justification that epistemology destroys knowledge. I need some different story.

To that end, I propose to take the infallibility of knowledge as my starting point.[5] Must infallibilist epistemology end in scepticism? Not quite. Wait and see. Anyway, here is the definition. Subject *S* *knows* proposition *P* iff *P* holds in every possibility left uneliminated by *S*'s evidence; equivalently, iff *S*'s evidence eliminates every possibility in which not-*P*.

The definition is short, the commentary upon it is longer. In the first place, there is the proposition, *P*. What I choose to call 'propositions' are individuated coarsely, by necessary equivalence. For instance, there is only one necessary proposition. It holds in every possibility; hence in every possibility left uneliminated by *S*'s evidence, no matter who *S* may be and no matter what his evidence may be. So the necessary proposition is known always and everywhere. Yet this known proposition may go unrecognised when presented in impenetrable linguistic disguise, say as the proposition that every even number is the sum of two primes. . . .

Next, there are the possibilities. We needn't enter here into the question whether these are concreta, abstract constructions, or abstract simples. Further, we needn't decide whether they must always be maximally specific possibilities, or whether they need only be specific enough for the purpose at hand. A possibility will be specific enough if it cannot be split into subcases in such a way that anything we have said about possibilities, or anything we are going to say before we are done, applies to some subcases and not to others. For instance, it should never happen that proposition *P* holds in some but not all subcases; or that some but not all subcases are eliminated by *S*'s evidence.

But we do need to stipulate that they are not just possibilities as to how the whole world is; they also include possibilities as to which part of the world is oneself, and as to when it now is. We need these possibilities *de se et nunc* because the propositions that may be known include propositions *de se et nunc*.[6] Not only do I know that there are hands in this world somewhere and somewhen. I know that *I* have hands, or anyway I have them *now*. Such propositions aren't just made true or made false by the whole world once and for all. They are true for some of us and not for others, or true at some times and not others, or both. . . .

So, next, we need to say what it means for a possibility to be eliminated or not. Here I say that the uneliminated possibilities are those in which the subject's entire perceptual experience and memory are just as they actually are. There is one possibility that actually obtains (for the subject and at the time in question); call it *actuality*. Then a possibility *W* is *uneliminated* iff the subject's perceptual experience and memory in *W* exactly match his perceptual experience and memory in actuality. (If you want to include other alleged forms of basic evidence, such as the evidence of our extrasensory faculties, or an innate disposition to believe in God, be my guest. If they exist, they should be included. If not, no harm done if we have included them conditionally.) . . .

Finally, we must attend to the word 'every'. What does it mean to say that every possibility in which not-*P* is eliminated? An idiom of quantification, like 'every', is normally restricted to some limited domain. If I say that every glass is empty, so it's time for another round, doubtless I and my audience are ignoring most of all the glasses there are in the whole wide world throughout all of time. They are outside the domain. They are irrelevant to the truth of what was said.

Likewise, if I say that every uneliminated possibility is one in which *P*, or words to that effect, I am doubtless ignoring some of all the uneliminated alternative possibilities that there are. They are outside the domain, they are irrelevant to the truth of what was said.

But, of course, I am not entitled to ignore just any possibility I please. Else true ascriptions of knowledge, whether to myself or to others, would be cheap indeed. I may properly ignore some uneliminated possibilities; I may not properly ignore others. Our definition of knowledge requires a *sotto voce* proviso. *S* *knows* that *P* iff *S*'s evidence eliminates every possibility in which not-*P*—Psst!—except for those possibilities that we are properly ignoring.

Unger suggests an instructive parallel.[7] Just as *P* is known iff there are no uneliminated possibilities of error, so likewise a surface is flat iff there are no bumps on it. We must add the proviso: Psst!—except for those bumps that we are properly ignoring. Else we will conclude, absurdly, that nothing is flat. (Simplify by ignoring departures from flatness that consist of gentle curvature.)

We can restate the definition. Say that we *presuppose* proposition *Q* iff we ignore all possibilities in which not-*Q*. To close the circle: we *ignore* just those possibilities that falsify our presuppositions. *Proper* presupposition corresponds, of course, to proper ignoring. Then *S* knows that *P* iff *S*'s evidence eliminates every possibility in which not-*P*—Psst!—except for those possibilities that conflict with our proper presuppositions.[8]

The rest of (modal) epistemology examines the *sotto voce* proviso. It asks: what may we properly presuppose in our ascriptions of knowledge? Which of all the uneliminated alternative possibilities may not properly be ignored? Which ones are the 'relevant alternatives'?—relevant, that is, to what the subject does and doesn't know?[9] In reply, we can list several rules.[10] We begin with three prohibitions: rules to tell us what possibilities we may not properly ignore.

First, there is the *Rule of Actuality*. The possibility that actually obtains is never properly ignored; actuality is always a relevant alternative; nothing false may properly be presupposed. It follows that only what is true is known, wherefore we did not have to include truth in our definition of knowledge. The rule is 'externalist'—the subject himself may not be able to tell what is properly ignored. In judging which of his ignorings are proper, hence what he knows, we judge his success in knowing—not how well he tried.

When the Rule of Actuality tells us that actuality may never be properly ignored, we can ask: *whose* actuality? Ours, when we ascribe knowledge or ignorance to others? Or the subject's? In simple cases, the question is silly. (In fact, it sounds like the sort of pernicious nonsense we would expect from someone who mixes up what is true with what is believed.) There is just one actual world, we the ascribers live in that world, the subject lives there too, so the subject's actuality is the same as ours.

But there are other cases, less simple, in which the question makes perfect sense and needs an answer. Someone may or may not know who he is; someone may or may not know what time it is. Therefore I insisted that the propositions that may be known must include propositions *de se et nunc;* and likewise that the possibilities that may be eliminated or ignored must include possibilities *de se et nunc.* Now we have a good sense in which the subject's actuality may be different from ours. I ask today what Fred knew yesterday. In particular, did he then know who he was? Did he know what day it was? Fred's actuality is the possibility *de se et nunc* of being Fred on September 19th at such-and-such possible world; whereas my actuality is the possibility *de se et nunc* of being David on September 20th at such-and-such world. So far as the world goes, there is no difference: Fred and I are worldmates, his actual world is the same as mine. But when we build subject and time into the possibilities *de se et nunc,* then his actuality yesterday does indeed differ from mine today. . . .

Or suppose we ask modal questions about the subject: what must he have known, what might he have known? Again we are considering the subject as he is not here, but off at other possible worlds. Likewise if we ask questions about knowledge of knowledge: what does he (or what do we) know that he knows?

So the question 'whose actuality?' is not a silly question after all. And when the question matters, as it does in the cases just considered, the right answer is that it is the subject's actuality, not the ascriber's, that never can be properly ignored.

Next, there is the *Rule of Belief.* A possibility that the subject believes to obtain is not properly ignored, whether or not he is right to so believe. Neither is one that he ought to believe to obtain—one that evidence and arguments justify him in believing—whether or not he does so believe.

That is rough. Since belief admits of degree, and since some possibilities are more specific than others, we ought to reformulate the rule in terms of degree of belief, compared to a standard set by the unspecificity of the possibility in question. A possibility may not be properly ignored if the subject gives it, or ought to give it, a degree of belief that is sufficiently high, and high not just because the possibility in question is unspecific.

How high is 'sufficiently high'? That may depend on how much is at stake. When error would be especially disastrous, few possibilities may be properly ignored. Then even quite a low degree of belief may be 'sufficiently high' to bring the Rule of Belief into play. The jurors know that the accused is guilty only if his guilt has been proved beyond reasonable doubt.[11]. . .

Next, there is the *Rule of Resemblance.* Suppose one possibility saliently resembles another. Then if one of them may not be properly ignored, neither may the other. (Or rather, we should say that if one of them may not properly be ignored *in virtue of rules other than this rule,* then neither may the other. Else nothing could be properly ignored; because enough little steps of resemblance can take us from anywhere to anywhere.) Or suppose one possibility saliently resembles two or more others, one in one respect and another in another, and suppose that each of these may not properly be ignored (in virtue of rules other than this rule). Then these resemblances may have an additive effect, doing more together than any one of them would separately. . . .

It is the Rule of Resemblance that explains why you do not know that you will lose the lottery; no matter what the odds are against you and no matter how sure you should therefore be that you will lose. For every ticket, there is the possibility that it will win. These possibilities are saliently similar to one another: so either every one of them may be properly ignored, or else none may. But one of them may not properly be ignored: the one that actually obtains.

The Rule of Resemblance also is the rule that solves the Gettier problems: other cases of justified true belief that are not knowledge.[12]

(1) I think that Nogot owns a Ford, because I have seen him driving one; but unbeknownst to me he does not own the Ford he drives, or any other Ford. Unbeknownst to me, Havit does own a Ford, though I have no reason to think so because he never drives it, and in fact I have often seen him taking the tram. My justified true belief is that one of the two owns a Ford. But I do not know it; I am right by accident. Diagnosis: I do not know, because I have not eliminated the possibility that Nogot drives a Ford he does not own whereas Havit neither drives nor owns a car. This possibility may not properly be ignored. Because, first, actuality may not properly be ignored; and, second, this possibility saliently resembles actuality. It resembles actuality perfectly so far as Nogot is concerned; and it resembles actuality well so far as Havit is concerned, since it matches actuality both with respect to Havit's carless habits and with respect to the general correlation between carless habits and carlessness. In addition, this possibility saliently resembles a third possibility: one in which Nogot drives a Ford he owns while Havit neither drives nor owns a car. This third possibility may not properly be ignored, because of the degree to which it is believed. This time, the resemblance is perfect so far as Havit is concerned, rather good so far as Nogot is concerned.

(2) The stopped clock is right twice a day. It says 4:39, as it has done for weeks. I look at it at 4:39; by luck I pick up a true belief. I have ignored the uneliminated possibility that I looked at it at 4:22 while it was stopped saying 4:39. That possibility was not properly ignored. It resembles actuality perfectly so far as the stopped clock goes.

(3) Unbeknownst to me, I am travelling in the land of the bogus barns; but my eye falls on one of the few real ones. I don't know that I am seeing a barn, because I may not properly ignore the possibility that I am seeing yet another of the abundant bogus barns. This possibility saliently resembles actuality in respect of the abundance of bogus barns, and the scarcity of real ones, hereabouts.

(4) Donald is in San Francisco, just as I have every reason to think he is. But, bent on deception, he is writing me letters and having them posted to me by his accomplice in Italy. If I had seen the phoney letters, with their Italian stamps and postmarks, I would have concluded that Donald was in Italy. Luckily, I have not yet seen any of them. I ignore the uneliminated possibility that Donald has gone to Italy and is sending me letters from there. But this possibility is not properly ignored, because it resembles actuality both with respect to the fact that the letters are coming to me from Italy and with respect to the fact that those letters come, ultimately, from Donald. So I don't know that Donald is in San Francisco.

Next, there is the *Rule of Reliability*. This time, we have a presumptive rule about what *may* be properly ignored; and it is by means of this rule that we capture what is right about causal or reliabilist theories of knowing. Consider processes whereby information is transmitted to us: perception, memory, and testimony. These processes are fairly reliable.[13] Within limits, we are entitled to take them for granted. We may properly presuppose that they work without a glitch in the case under consideration.

Defeasibly—*very* defeasibly!—a possibility in which they fail may properly be ignored.

My visual experience, for instance, depends causally on the scene before my eyes, and what I believe about the scene before my eyes depends in turn on my visual experience. Each dependence covers a wide and varied range of alternatives.[14] Of course, it is possible to hallucinate—even to hallucinate in such a way that all my perceptual experience and memory would be just as they actually are. That possibility never can be eliminated. But it can be ignored. And if it is properly ignored—as it mostly is—then vision gives me knowledge. Sometimes, though, the possibility of hallucination is not properly ignored; for sometimes we really do hallucinate. The Rule of Reliability may be defeated by the Rule of Actuality. Or it may be defeated by the Rules of Actuality and of Resemblance working together, in a Gettier problem: if I am not hallucinating, but unbeknownst to me I live in a world where people mostly do hallucinate and I myself have only narrowly escaped, then the uneliminated possibility of hallucination is too close to actuality to be properly ignored.

We do not, of course, presuppose that nowhere ever is there a failure of, say, vision. The general presupposition that vision is reliable consists, rather, of a standing disposition to presuppose, concerning whatever particular case may be under consideration, that we have no failure in that case.

In similar fashion, we have two permissive *Rules of Method*. We are entitled to presuppose—again, very defeasibly—that a sample is representative; and that the best explanation of our evidence is the true explanation. That is, we are entitled properly to ignore possible failures in these two standard methods of nondeductive inference. Again, the general rule consists of a standing disposition to presuppose reliability in whatever particular case may come before us.

Yet another permissive rule is the *Rule of Conservatism*. Suppose that those around us normally do ignore certain possibilities, and it is common knowledge that they do. (They do, they expect each other to, they expect each other to expect each other to, . . .) Then—again, very defeasibly!—these generally ignored possibilities may properly be ignored. We are permitted, defeasibly, to adopt the usual and mutually expected presuppositions of those around us. . . .

Our final rule is the *Rule of Attention*. But it is more a triviality than a rule. When we say that a possibility *is* properly ignored, we mean exactly that; we do not mean that it *could have been* properly ignored. Accordingly, a possibility not ignored at all is *ipso facto* not properly ignored. What is and what is not being ignored is a feature of the particular conversational context. No matter how far-fetched a certain possibility may be, no matter how properly we might have ignored it in some other context, if in *this* context we are not in fact ignoring it but attending to it, then for us now it is a relevant alternative. It is in the contextually determined domain. If it is an uneliminated possibility in which not-*P*, then it will do as a counter-example to the claim that *P* holds in every possibility left uneliminated by *S*'s evidence. That is, it will do as a counter-example to the claim that *S* knows that *P*.

Do some epistemology. Let your fantasies rip. Find uneliminated possibilities of error everywhere. Now that you are attending to them, just as I told you to, you are no longer ignoring them, properly or otherwise. So you have landed in a context with an enormously rich domain of potential counter-examples to ascriptions of knowledge. In such an extraordinary context, with such a rich domain, it never can happen (well, hardly ever) that an ascription of knowledge is true. Not an ascription of knowledge to yourself (either to your present self or to your earlier self, untainted by epistemology); and not an ascription of knowledge to others. That is how epistemology destroys knowledge. But it does so only temporarily. The pastime of epistemology does not plunge us forevermore into its special context. We can still do a lot of proper ignoring, a lot of knowing, and a lot of true ascribing of knowledge to ourselves and others, the rest of the time.

What is epistemology all about? The epistemology we've just been doing, at any rate, soon became an investigation of the ignoring of possibilities. But to investigate the ignoring of them was *ipso facto* not to ignore them. Unless this investigation of ours was an altogether atypical sample of epistemology, it will be inevitable that epistemology must destroy knowledge. That is how knowledge is elusive. Examine it, and straightway it vanishes. . . .

NOTES

Notes have been renumbered consecutively to avoid confusion.

1. The suggestion that ascriptions of knowledge go false in the context of epistemology is to be found in Barry Stroud, 'Understanding Human Knowledge in General' in Marjorie Clay and Keith Lehrer (eds.), *Knowledge and Skepticism* (Boulder: Westview Press, 1989); and in Stephen Hetherington, 'Lacking Knowledge and Justification by Theorising About Them' (lecture at the University of New South Wales, August 1992). Neither of them tells the story just as I do, however it may be that their versions do not conflict with mine.
2. Unless, like some, we simply define 'justification' as 'whatever it takes to turn true opinion into knowledge' regardless of whether what it takes turns out to involve argument from supporting reasons.
3. The problem of the lottery was introduced in Henry Kyburg, *Probability and the Logic of Rational Belief* (Middletown, CT: Wesleyan University Press, 1961), and in Carl Hempel, 'Deductive-Nomological vs. Statistical Explanation' in Herbert Feigl and Grover Maxwell (eds.), *Minnesota Studies in the Philosophy of Science,* Vol. II (Minneapolis: University of Minnesota Press, 1962). It has been much discussed since, as a problem both about knowledge and about our everyday, non-quantitative concept of belief.
4. The case of testimony is less discussed than the others; but see C. A. J. Coady, *Testimony: A Philosophical Study* (Oxford: Clarendon Press, 1992) pp. 79–129.
5. I follow Peter Unger, *Ignorance: A Case for Skepticism* (New York: Oxford University Press, 1975). But I shall not let him lead me into scepticism.
6. See my 'Attitudes *De Dicto* and *De Se*', *The Philosophical Review* 88 (1979) pp. 513–543; and R. M. Chisholm, 'The Indirect Reflexive' in C. Diamond and J. Teichman (eds.), *Intention and Intentionality: Essays in Honour of G.E.M. Anscombe* (Brighton: Harvester, 1979).
7. Peter Unger, *Ignorance,* chapter II. I discuss the case, and briefly foreshadow the present paper, in my 'Scorekeeping in a Language Game', *Journal of Philosophical Logic* 8 (1979) pp. 339–359, esp. pp. 353–355.
8. See Robert Stalnaker, 'Presuppositions', *Journal of Philosophical Logic* 2 (1973) pp. 447–457; and 'Pragmatic Presuppositions' in Milton Munitz and Peter Unger (eds.), *Semantics and Philosophy* (New York: New York University Press, 1974). See also my 'Scorekeeping in a Language Game'.

   The definition restated in terms of presupposition resembles the treatment of knowledge in Kenneth S. Ferguson, *Philosophical Scepticism* (Cornell University doctoral dissertation, 1980).
9. See Fred Dretske, 'Epistemic Operators', *The Journal of Philosophy* 67 (1970) pp. 1007–1022, and 'The Pragmatic Dimension of Knowledge', *Philosophical Studies* 40 (1981) pp. 363–378; Alvin Goldman, 'Discrimination and Perceptual Knowledge', *The Journal of Philosophy* 73 (1976) pp. 771–791; G. C. Stine, 'Skepticism, Relevant Alternatives, and Deductive Closure', *Philosophical*

Studies 29 (1976) pp. 249–261; and Stewart Cohen, 'How to be A Fallibilist', *Philosophical Perspectives* 2 (1988) pp. 91–123.

10. Some of them, but only some, taken from the authors just cited.
11. Instead of complicating the Rule of Belief as I have just done, I might equivalently have introduced a separate Rule of High Stakes saying that when error would be especially disastrous, few possibilities are properly ignored.
12. See Edmund Gettier, 'Is Justified True Belief Knowledge?', *Analysis* 23 (1963) pp. 121–123. Diagnoses have varied widely. The four examples below come from: (1) Keith Lehrer and Thomas Paxson Jr., 'Knowledge: Undefeated True Belief', *The Journal of Philosophy* 66 (1969) pp. 225–237; (2) Bertrand Russell, *Human Knowledge: Its Scope and Limits* (London: Allen and Unwin, 1948) p. 154; (3) Alvin Goldman, 'Discrimination and Perceptual Knowledge', op. cit.; (4) Gilbert Harman, *Thought* (Princeton, NJ: Princeton University Press, 1973) p. 143.

    Though the lottery problem is another case of justified true belief without knowledge, it is not normally counted among the Gettier problems. It is interesting to find that it yields to the same remedy.
13. See Alvin Goldman, 'A Causal Theory of Knowing', *The Journal of Philosophy* 64 (1967) pp. 357–372; D.M. Armstrong, *Belief, Truth and Knowledge* (Cambridge: Cambridge University Press, 1973).
14. See my 'Veridical Hallucination and Prosthetic Vision', *Australasian Journal of Philosophy* 58 (1980) pp. 239–249. John Bigelow has proposed to model knowledge-delivering processes generally on those found in vision.

5

A Defense of Skepticism

PETER UNGER

The skepticism that I will defend is a negative thesis concerning what we know. I happily accept the fact that there is much that many of us correctly and reasonably believe, but much more than that is needed for us to know even a fair amount. Here I will not argue that nobody knows anything about anything, though that would be quite consistent with the skeptical thesis for which I will argue. The somewhat less radical thesis which I will defend is this one: every human being knows, at best, hardly anything to be so. More specifically, I will argue that hardly anyone knows that 45 and 56 are equal to 101, if anyone at all. On this skeptical thesis, no one will know the thesis to be true. But this is all right. For I only want to argue that it may be reasonable for us to suppose the thesis to be true, not that we should ever know it to be true.

Source: From *Philosophical Review* 80 (1971).

Few philosophers now take skepticism seriously. With philosophers, even the most powerful of traditional skeptical argument has little force to tempt them nowadays. Indeed, nowadays, philosophers tend to think skepticism interesting only as a formal challenge to which positive accounts of our common-sense knowledge are the gratifying responses. Consequently, I find it at least somewhat natural to offer a defense of skepticism.[1]

My defense of skepticism will be quite unlike traditional arguments for this thesis. This is largely because I write at a time when there is a common faith that, so far as expressing truths is concerned, all is well with the language that we speak. Against this common, optimistic assumption, I shall illustrate how our language habits might serve us well in practical ways, even while they involve us in saying what is false rather than true. And this often does occur, I will maintain, when our positive assertions contain terms with special features of a certain kind, which I call *absolute* terms. Among these terms, "flat" and "certain" are *basic* ones. Due to these terms' characteristic features, and because the world is not so simple as it might be, we do not speak truly, at least as a rule, when we say of a real object, "That has a top which is flat" or when we say of a real person, "He is certain that it is raining." And just as basic absolute terms generally fail to apply to the world, so other absolute terms, which are at least partially defined by the basic ones, will fail to apply as well. Thus, we also speak falsely when we say of a real object or person, "That is a cube" or "He knows that it is raining." For an object is a cube only if it has surfaces which are flat, and, as I shall argue, a person knows something to be so only if he is certain of it.

I. SOPHISTICATED WORRIES ABOUT WHAT SKEPTICISM REQUIRES

The reason contemporary sophisticated philosophers do not take skepticism seriously can be stated broadly and simply. They think that skepticism implies certain things which are, upon a bit of reflection, quite impossible to accept. These unacceptable implications concern the functioning of our language.

Concerning our language and how it functions, the most obvious requirement of skepticism is that some common terms of our language will involve us in error systematically. These will be such terms as "know" and "knowledge," which may be called the "terms of knowledge." If skepticism is right, then while we go around saying "I know," "He knows," and so on, and while we believe what we say to be true, all the while what we say and believe will actually be false. If our beliefs to the effect that we know something or other are so consistently false, then the terms of knowledge lead us into error systematically. But if these beliefs really are false, should we not have experiences which force the realization of their falsity upon us, and indeed abandon these beliefs? Consequently, shouldn't our experiences get us to stop thinking in these terms which thus systematically involve us in error? So, as we continue to think in the terms of knowledge and to believe ourselves to know all sorts of things, this would seem to show that the beliefs are not false ones and the terms are responsible for no error. Isn't it only reasonable, then, to reject a view which requires that such helpful common terms as "knows" and "knowledge" lead us into error systematically?

So go some worrisome thoughts which might lead us to dismiss skepticism out of hand. But it seems to me that there is no real need for our false beliefs to clash with our experiences in any easily noticeable way. Suppose, for instance, that you falsely believe that a certain region of space is a vacuum. Suppose that, contrary to your belief, the region does contain some gaseous stuff, though only the slightest trace. Now, for practical purposes, we may suppose that, so far as gaseous contents go, it is not important whether that region really is a vacuum or whether it contains whatever gaseous stuff it does contain. Once this is supposed, then it is reasonable to suppose as well that, for practical purposes, it makes no important difference whether you falsely believe that the region is a vacuum or truly believe this last thing—namely, that, for practical purposes, it is not important whether the region is a vacuum or whether it contains that much gaseous stuff.

We may notice that this supposed truth is entailed by what you believe but does not entail it. In other words, a region's being a vacuum entails that, for practical purposes, there is no important difference between whether the region is a vacuum or whether it contains whatever gaseous stuff it does contain. For, if the region *is* a vacuum, whatever gas it contains is nil, and so there is no difference at all, for any sort of purpose, between the region's being a vacuum and its having that much gaseous stuff. But the entailment does not go the other way, and this is where we may take a special interest. For while a region may not be a vacuum, it may contain so little gaseous stuff that, so far as gaseous contents go, for practical purposes there is no important difference between the region's being a vacuum and its containing whatever gaseous stuff it does contain. So if this entailed truth lies behind the believed falsehood, your false belief, though false, may not be harmful. Indeed, generally, it may even be helpful for you to have this false belief rather than having none and rather than having almost any other belief about the matter that you might have. On this pattern, we may have many false beliefs about regions being vacuums even while these beliefs will suffer no important clash with the experiences of life.

More to our central topic, suppose that, as skepticism might have it, you falsely believe that you *know* that there are elephants. As before, there is a true thing which is entailed by what you falsely believe and which we should notice. The thing here, which presumably you do not actually believe, is this: that, with respect to the matter of whether there are elephants, for practical purposes there is no important difference between whether you know that there are elephants or whether you are in that position with respect to the matter that you actually are in. This latter, true thing is entailed by the false thing you believe—namely, that you know that there are elephants. For if you do know, then, with respect to the matter of the elephants, there is no difference at all, for any purpose of any sort, between your knowing and your being in the position you actually are in. On the other hand, the entailment does not go the other way and, again, this is where our pattern allows a false belief to be helpful. For even if you do not really know, still, it may be that for practical purposes you are in a position with respect to the matter (of the elephants) which is not importantly different from knowing. If this is so, then it may be better, practically speaking, for you to believe falsely that you know than to have no belief at all here. Thus, not only with beliefs to the effect that specified regions are vacuums, but also with beliefs to the effect that we know certain things, it may be that there are very many of them which, though false, it is helpful for us to have. In both cases, the beliefs will not noticeably clash with the experiences of life. Without some further reason for doing so, then, noting the smooth functioning of our "terms of knowledge" gives us no powerful reason for dismissing the thesis of skepticism.

There is, however, a second worry which will tend to keep sophisticates far from embracing skepticism, and this worry is, I think, rather more profound than the first. Consequently, I shall devote most of the remainder to treating this second worry. The worry to which I shall be so devoted is this: that, if skepticism is right, then the terms of knowledge, unlike other terms of our language, will never or hardly ever be used to make simple, positive assertions that are true. In other words, skepticism will require the terms of knowledge to be isolated freaks of our language. But even with familiar, persuasive arguments for skepticism, it is implausible to think that our language is plagued by an isolated little group of troublesome freaks. So, by being so hard on knowledge alone, skepticism seems implausible once one reflects on the exclusiveness of its persecution.

II. ABSOLUTE TERMS AND RELATIVE TERMS

Against the worry that skepticism will require the terms of knowledge to be isolated freaks, I shall argue that, on the contrary, a variety of other terms is similarly troublesome. As skepticism becomes more plausible with an examination of the terms of knowledge, so other originally surprising theses become more plausible once their key terms are critically examined. When all of the key terms are understood to have essential features in common, the truth of any of these theses need not be felt as such a surprise.

The terms of knowledge, along with many other troublesome terms, belong to a class of terms that is quite pervasive in our language. I call these terms *absolute terms*. The term "flat," in its central, literal meaning, is an absolute term. (With other meanings, as in "His voice is flat" and "The beer is flat," I have no direct interest.) To say that something is flat is no different from saying that it is absolutely, or perfectly, flat. To say that a surface is flat is to say that some things or properties *which are matters of degree* are *not* instanced in the surface *to any degree at all*. Thus, something which is flat is not at all bumpy, and not at all curved. Bumpiness and curvature are matters of degree. When we say of a surface that it is bumpy, or that it is curved, we use the *relative terms* "bumpy" and "curved" to talk about the surface. Thus, absolute terms and relative terms go together, in at least one important way, while other terms, like "unmarried," have only the most distant connections with terms of either of these two sorts.

There seems to be a syntactic feature which is common to relative terms and to certain absolute terms, while it is found with no other terms. This feature is that each of these terms may be modified by a variety of terms that serve to indicate (matters of) degree. Thus, we find "The table is *very* bumpy" and "The table is *very* flat" but not "The lawyer is *very* unmarried." Among those absolute terms which admit such qualification are all those absolute terms which are *basic* ones. A basic absolute term is an absolute term which is not (naturally) defined in terms of some other absolute term, not even partially so. I suspect that "straight" is such a term, and perhaps "flat" is as well. But in its central (geometrical) meaning, "cube" quite clearly is not a basic absolute term even though it is an absolute term. For "cube" means, among other things, "having edges that are *straight* and surfaces which are *flat*": and "straight" and "flat" are absolute terms. While "cube" does not admit of qualification of degree, "flat" and "straight" do admit of such qualification. Thus, all relative terms and all basic absolute terms admit of constructions of degree. While this is another way in which these two sorts of terms go together, we must now ask: how may we distinguish terms of the one sort from those of the other?

But is there now anything to distinguish here? For if absolute terms admit of degree construction, why think that any of these terms is not a relative term, why think that they do not purport to predicate things or properties which are, as they now look to be, matters of degree? If we may say that a table is very flat, then why not think flatness a matter of degree? Isn't this essentially the same as our saying of a table that it is very bumpy, with bumpiness being a matter of degree? So perhaps "flat," like "bumpy" and like all terms that take degree constructions, is, fittingly, a relative term. But basic absolute terms may be distinguished from relatives even where degree constructions conspire to make things look otherwise.

To advance the wanted distinction, we may look to a procedure for paraphrase. Now, we have granted that it is common for us to say of a surface that it is pretty, or very, or extremely, flat. And it is also common for us to say that, in saying such things of surfaces, we are saying *how* flat the surfaces are. What we say here seems of a piece with our saying of a surface that it is pretty, or very, or extremely, bumpy, and our then saying that, in doing this, we are saying *how* bumpy the surface is. But, even intuitively, we may notice a difference here. For only with our talk about "flat," we have the idea that these locutions are only convenient means for saying how closely a surface approximates, or *how close it comes to being,* a surface which is (absolutely) flat. Thus, it is intuitively plausible, and far from being a nonsensical interpretation, to paraphrase things so our result with our "flat" locutions is this: what we have said of a surface is that it is pretty *nearly* flat, or very *nearly* flat, or extremely *close to being* flat and, in doing that, we have said, not simply how flat the surface is, but rather *how close* the surface is *to being* flat. This form of paraphrase gives a plausible interpretation of our talk of flatness while allowing the term "flat" to lose its appearance of being a relative term. How will this form of paraphrase work with "bumpy," where, presumably, a genuine relative term occurs in our locutions?

What do we say when we say of a surface that it is pretty bumpy, or very bumpy, or extremely so? Of course, it at least appears that we say *how* bumpy the surface is. The paraphrase has it that what we are saying is that the surface is pretty *nearly* bumpy, or very *nearly* bumpy, or extremely *close to being* bumpy. In other words, according to the paraphrase, we are saying *how close* the surface is *to being* bumpy. But anything of this sort is, quite obviously, a terribly poor interpretation of what we are saying about the surface. Unfortunately for the paraphrase, if we say that a surface is very bumpy it is entailed by what we say that the surface is bumpy, while if we say that the surface is very close to being bumpy it is entailed that the surface is *not* bumpy. Thus, unlike the case with "flat," our paraphrase cannot apply with "bumpy." Consequently, by means of our paraphrase we may distinguish between absolute terms and relative ones.

Another way of noticing how our paraphrase lends support to the distinction between absolute and relative terms is this: the initial data are that such terms as "very," which standardly serve to indicate that there is a great deal of something, serve with opposite effect when they modify terms like "flat"—terms which I have called basic absolute terms. That is, when we say, for example, that something is (really) very flat, then, so far as flatness is concerned, we seem to say less of the thing than when we say, simply, that it is (really) flat. The augmenting function of "very" is turned on its head so that the term serves to diminish. What can resolve this conflict? It seems that our paraphrase can. For on the paraphrase, what we are saying of the thing is that it is very *nearly* flat, and so, by implication, that it is *not* flat (but only very nearly so). Once the paraphrase is exploited, the term "very" may be understood to have its standard augmenting function. At the same time, "very" functions without conflict with "bumpy." Happily, the term "very" is far from being unique here; we get the same results with other augmenting modifiers: "extremely," "especially," and so on.

For our paraphrastic procedure to be comprehensive, it must work with contexts containing explicitly comparative locutions. Indeed, with these contexts, we have a common form of talk where the appearance of relativeness is most striking of all. What shall we think of our saying, for example, that one surface is not *as* flat as another, where things strikingly look to be a matter of degree? It seems that we must allow that in such a suggested comparison, the surface which is said to be the *flatter* of the two may be, so far as logic goes, (absolutely) flat. Thus, we should *not* paraphrase this comparative context as "the one surface is not as *nearly* flat as the other." For this form of paraphrase would imply that the second surface is not flat, and so it gives us a poor interpretation of the original, which has no such implication. But then, a paraphrase with no bad implications is not far removed. Instead of simply inserting our "nearly" or our "close to being," we may allow for the possibility of (absolute) flatness by putting things in a way which is only somewhat more complex. For we may paraphrase our original by saying: the first surface is *either not flat though the second is, or else it is* not as *nearly* flat as the second. Similarly, where we say that one surface is flatter than another, we may paraphrase things like this: the first surface is *either flat though the second is not or else it is closer to being flat* than the second. But in contrast to all this, with comparisons of bumpiness, no paraphrase is available. To say that one surface is not as bumpy as another is not to say either that the first surface is not bumpy though the second is, or else that it is not as nearly bumpy as the second one.

Our noting the availability of degree constructions allow us to class together relative terms and basic absolute terms, as against any other terms. And our noting that only with the absolute terms do our constructions admit of our paraphrase allows us to distinguish between the relative terms and the basic absolute terms. Now that these terms may be quite clearly distinguished, we may restate without pain of vacuity those ideas on which we relied to introduce our terminology. Thus, to draw the *connection* between terms of the two sorts we may now say this: every basic absolute term, and so every absolute term whatever, may be defined, at least partially, by means of certain relative terms. The defining conditions presented by means of the relative terms are negative ones; they say that what the relative term purports to denote is *not* present *at all,* or *in the least,* where the absolute term correctly applies. Thus, these negative conditions are logically necessary ones for basic absolute terms, and so for absolute terms which are defined by means of the basic ones. Thus, something is flat, in the central, literal sense of "flat," only if it is not at all, or not in the least, curved or bumpy. And similarly, something is a cube, in the central, literal sense of "cube," only if it has surfaces which are not at all, or not in the least, bumpy or curved. In noting these demanding *negative relative requirements,* we may begin to appreciate, I think, that a variety of absolute terms, if not all of them, might well be quite troublesome to apply, perhaps even failing consistently in application to real things.

In a final general remark about these terms, I should like to motivate my choice of terminology for them. A reason I call terms of the one sort "absolute" is that, at least in the case of the basic ones, the term may always be modified, grammatically, with the term "absolutely." And indeed, this modification fits so well that it is, I think, always redundant. Thus, something is flat if and only if it is absolutely flat. In contrast, the term "absolutely" never gives a standard, grammatical modification for any of our relative terms: nothing which is bumpy is absolutely bumpy. On the other hand, each of the relative terms takes "relatively" quite smoothly as a grammatical modifier. (And, though it is far from being clear, it is at least arguable, I think, that this modifier is redundant for these terms. Thus, it is at least arguable that something is bumpy if and only if it is relatively bumpy.) In any event, with absolute terms, while "relatively" is grammatically quite all right as a modifier, the construction thus obtained must be understood in terms of our paraphrase. Thus, as before, something is relatively flat if and only if it is relatively close to being (absolutely) flat, and so only if it is not flat.

In this terminology, and in line with our linguistic tests, I think that the first term of each of the following pairs is a relative term while the second is an absolute one: "wet" and "dry," "crooked" and "straight," "important" and "crucial," "incomplete" and "complete," "useful" and "useless," and so on. I think that both "empty" and "full" are absolute terms, while "good" and "bad," "rich" and "poor," and "happy" and "unhappy" are all relative terms. Finally, I think that, in the sense defined by our tests, each of the following is neither an absolute term nor a relative one: "married" and "unmarried," "true" and "false," and "right" and "wrong." In other plausible senses, though, some or all of this last group might be called "absolute."

III. ON CERTAINTY AND CERTAIN RELATED THINGS

Certain terms of our language are standardly followed by propositional clauses, and, indeed, it is plausible to think that wherever they occur they *must* be followed by such clauses on pain of otherwise occurring in a sentence which is elliptical or incomplete. We may call terms which take these clauses *propositional terms* and we may then ask: are some propositional terms absolute ones, while others are relative terms? By means of our tests, I will argue that "certain" is an absolute term, while "confident," "doubtful," and "uncertain" are all relative terms.

With regard to being certain, there are two ideas which are important: first, the idea of something's being certain, where that which is certain is *not* certain *of* anything, and, second, the idea of a being's being certain, where that which is certain *is* certain *of* something. A paradigm context for the first idea is the context "It is certain that it is raining" where the term "it" has no apparent reference. I will call such contexts *impersonal* contexts, and the idea of certainty which they serve to express, thus, the impersonal idea of certainty. In contrast, a paradigm context for the second idea is this one: "He is certain that it is raining"—where, of course, the term "he" purports to refer as clearly as one might like. In the latter context, which we may call the *personal* context, we express the personal idea of certainty. This last may be allowed, I think, even though in ordinary conversations we may speak of dogs as being certain; presumably, we treat dogs there the way we typically treat persons.

Though there are these two important sorts of context, I think that "certain" must mean the same in both. In both cases, we must be struck by the thought that the presence of certainty amounts to the complete absence of doubt, or doubtfulness. This thought leads me to say that "It is certain that *p*" means, within the bounds of nuance, "It is not at all doubtful that *p*." The idea of personal certainty may then be defined accordingly; we relate what is said in the impersonal form to the mind of the person, or subject, who is said to be certain of something. Thus, "He is certain that *p*" means, within the bounds of nuance, "*In his mind,* it is not at all doubtful that *p*." Where a man is certain of something, then, concerning that thing, all doubt is absent in that man's mind. With these definitions available, we may now say this: connected negative definitions of certainty suggest that, in its central, literal meaning, "certain" is an absolute term.

But we should like firmer evidence for thinking that "certain" is an absolute term. To be consistent, we turn to our procedure for paraphrase. I will exhibit the evidence for personal contexts and then say a word about impersonal ones. In any event, we want contrasting results for "certain" as against some related relative terms. One term which now suggests itself for contrast is, of course, "doubtful." Another is, of course, "uncertain." And we will get the desired results with these terms. But it is, I think, more interesting to consider the term "confident."

In quick discussions of these matters, one might speak indifferently of a man's being confident of something and of his being certain of it. But on reflection there is a difference between confidence and certainty. Indeed, when I say that I am certain of something, I tell you that I am not confident of it but that I am *more than* that. And if I say that I am confident that so-and-so, I tell you that I am *not so much as* certain of the thing. Thus, there is an important difference between the two. At least part of this difference is, I suggest, reflected by our procedure for paraphrase.

We may begin to apply our procedure by resolving the problem of augmenting modifiers. Paradoxically, when I say that I am (really) very certain of something, I say *less* of myself, so far as certainty is concerned, than I do when I say, simply, that I am (really) certain of the thing. How may we resolve this paradox? Our paraphrase explains things as before. In the first case, what I am really saying is that I am very *nearly* certain, and so, in effect, that I am not really certain. But in the second case, I say that I really am. Further, we may notice that, in contrast, in the case of "confident" and "uncertain," and "doubtful" as well, no problem with augmenting arises in the first place. For when I say that I am very confident of something, I say more of myself, so far as confidence is concerned, than I do when I simply say that I am confident of the thing. And again our paraphrastic procedure yields us the lack of any problems here. For the augmented statement cannot be sensibly interpreted as saying that I am very nearly confident of the thing. Indeed, with any modifier weaker than "absolutely," our paraphrase works well with "certain" but produces only a nonsensical interpretation with "confident" and other contrasting terms. For example, what might it mean to say of someone that he was rather confident of something? Would this be to say that he was rather close to being confident of the thing? Surely not.

Turning to comparative constructions, our paraphrase separates things just as we should expect. For example, from "He is more certain that *p* than he is that *q*" we get "He is either certain that *p* while not certain that *q*, or else he is more nearly certain that *p* than he is that *q*." But from "He is more confident that *p* than he is that *q*" we do *not* get "He is either confident that *p* while not confident that *q*, or else he is more nearly confident that *p* than he is that *q*." For he may well already be confident of both things. Further comparative constructions are similarly distinguished when subjected to our paraphrase. And no matter what locutions we try, the separation is as convincing with impersonal contexts as it is with personal ones, so long as there are contexts which are comparable. Of course, "confident" has no impersonal contexts; we cannot say "It is confident that *p*," where the "it" has no purported reference. But where comparable contexts do exist, as with "doubtful" and "uncertain," further evidence is available. Thus, we may reasonably assert that "certain" is an absolute term while "confident," "doubtful," and "uncertain" are relative terms.

IV. THE DOUBTFUL APPLICABILITY OF SOME ABSOLUTE TERMS

If my account of absolute terms is essentially correct, then, at least in the case of some of these terms, fairly reasonable suppositions about the world make it somewhat doubtful that the terms properly apply. (In certain contexts, generally where what we are talking about divides into discrete units, the presence of an absolute term need cause no doubts. Thus, considering the absolute term "complete," the truth of "His set of steins is now complete" may be allowed without hesitation, but the truth of "His explanation is now complete" may well be doubted. It is with the latter, more interesting contexts, I think, that we shall be concerned in what follows.) For example, while we say of many surfaces of physical things that they are flat, a rather reasonable interpretation of what we do observe makes it at least somewhat doubtful that these surfaces actually *are* flat. When we look at a rather smooth block of stone through a powerful microscope, the observed surface appears to us to be rife with irregularities. And this irregular appearance seems best explained, not by being taken as an illusory optical phenomenon, but by taking it to be a finer, more revealing look of a surface which is, in fact, rife with smallish bumps and crevices. Further, we account for bumps and crevices by supposing that the stone is composed of much smaller things, molecules and so on, which are in such a combination that, while a large and sturdy stone is the upshot, no stone with a flat surface is found to obtain.

Indeed, what follows from my account of "flat" is this: that, as a matter of logical necessity, if a surface is flat, then there never is any surface which is flatter than it is. For on our paraphrase, if the second surface is flatter than the first, then either the second surface is flat while the first is not, or else the second is more nearly flat than the first, neither surface being flat. So if there is such a second, flatter surface, then the first surface is not flat after all, contrary to our supposition. Thus there cannot be any second, flatter surface. Or in other words, if it is logically possible that there be a surface which is flatter than a given one, then that given surface is not really a flat one. Now, in the case of the observed surface of the stone, owing to the stone's irregular composition, the surface is *not* one such that it is logically impossible that there be a flatter one. (For example, we might veridically observe a surface through a microscope of the same power which did not appear to have any bumps or crevices.) Thus it is only reasonable to suppose that the surface of this stone is not really flat.

Our understanding of the stone's composition, that it is composed of molecules and so on, makes it reasonable for us to suppose as well that any similarly sized or larger surfaces will fail to be flat just as the observed surface fails to be flat. At the same time, it would be perhaps a bit rash to suppose that much smaller surfaces would fail to be flat as well. Beneath the level of our observation perhaps there are small areas of the stone's surface which are flat. If so, then perhaps there are small objects that have surfaces which are flat, like this area of the stone's surface: for instance, chipping off a small part of the stone might yield such a small object. So perhaps there are physical objects with surfaces which are flat, and perhaps it is not now reasonable for us to assume that there are no such objects. But even if this strong assumption is not now reasonable, one thing which does seem quite reasonable for us now to assume is this: we should at least suspend judgement on the matter of whether there are any physical objects with flat surfaces. That there are such objects is something it is not now reasonable for us to believe.

It is at least somewhat doubtful, then, that "flat" ever applies to actual physical objects or to their surfaces. And the thought must strike us that if "flat" has no such application, this must be due in part to the fact that "flat" is an absolute term. We may then do well to be a bit doubtful about the applicability of any other given absolute term and, in particular, about the applicability of the term "certain." As in the case of "flat," our paraphrase highlights the absolute character of "certain." As a matter of logical necessity, if someone is certain of something, then there never is anything of which he is more certain. For on our paraphrase, if the person is more certain of any other thing, then either he is certain of the other thing while not being certain of the first, or else he is more nearly certain of the other thing than he is of the first; that is, he is certain of neither. Thus, if it is logically possible that there be something of which a person might be more certain than he now is of a given thing, then he is not really certain of that given thing.

Thus it is reasonable to suppose, I think, that hardly anyone, if anyone at all, is certain that 45 and 56 are 101. For it is reasonable to suppose that hardly anyone, if anyone at all, is so certain of that particular calculation that it is impossible for there to be anything of which he might be yet more certain. But this is not surprising; for hardly anyone *feels* certain that those two numbers have that sum. What, then, about something of which people commonly do feel absolutely certain—say, of the existence of automobiles?

Is it reasonable for us now actually to believe that many people are certain that there are automobiles? If it is, then it is reasonable for us to believe as well that for each of them it is not possible for there to be anything of which he might be more certain than he now is of there being automobiles. In particular, we must then believe of these people that it is impossible for any of them ever to be more certain of his own existence than all of them now are of the existence of automobiles. While these people *might* all actually be as certain of the automobiles as this, just as each of them *feels* himself to be, I think it somewhat rash for us actually to believe that they *are* all so certain. Certainty being an absolute and our understanding of people being rather rudimentary and incomplete, I think it more reasonable for us now to suspend judgement on the matter. And, since there is nothing importantly peculiar about the matter of the automobiles, the same cautious position recommends itself quite generally: so far as actual human beings go, the most reasonable course for us now is to suspend judgement as to whether any of them is certain of more than hardly anything, if anything at all.[2]

V. DOES KNOWING REQUIRE BEING CERTAIN?

One tradition in philosophy holds that knowing requires being certain. As a matter of logical necessity, a man knows something only if he is certain of the thing. In this tradition, certainty is not taken lightly; rather, it is equated with absolute certainty. Even that most famous contemporary defender of common sense, G. E. Moore, is willing to equate knowing something with knowing the thing with absolute certainty.[3] I am rather inclined to hold with this traditional view, and it is now my purpose to argue that this view is at least a fairly reasonable one.

To a philosopher like Moore, I would have nothing left to say in my defense of skepticism. But recently some philosophers have contended that not certainty, but only belief, is required for knowing.[4] According to these thinkers, if a man's belief meets certain conditions not connected with his being certain, that mere belief may properly be counted as an instance or a bit of knowledge. And even more recently some philosophers have held that not even so much as belief is required for a man to know that something is so.[5] Thus, I must argue for the traditional view of knowing. But then what has led philosophers to move further and further away from the traditional strong assertion that knowing something requires being certain of the thing?

My diagnosis of the situation is this. In everyday affairs we often speak loosely, charitably, and casually; we tend to let what we say pass as being true. I want to suggest that it is by being wrongly serious about this casual talk that philosophers (myself included) have come to think it rather easy to know things to be so. In particular, they have come to think that certainty is not needed. Thus typical in the contemporary literature is this sort of exchange. An examiner asks a student when a certain battle was fought. The student fumbles about and, eventually, unconfidently says what is true: "The Battle of Hastings was fought in 1066." It is supposed, quite properly, that this correct answer is a result of the student's reading. The examiner, being an ordinary mortal, allows that the student knows the answer; he judges that the student knows that the Battle of Hastings was fought in 1066. Surely, it is suggested, the examiner is correct in his judgement even though this student clearly is not certain of the thing; therefore, knowing does not require being certain. But is the examiner really correct in asserting that the student knows the date of this battle? That is, do such exchanges give us good reason to think that knowing does not require certainty?

My recommendation is this. Let us try focusing on just those words most directly employed in expressing the concept whose conditions are our object of inquiry. This principle is quite generally applicable and, I think, quite easily applied. We may apply it by suitably juxtaposing certain terms, like "really" and "actually," with the terms most in question (here, the term "knows"). More strikingly, we may *emphasize* the terms in question. Thus, instead of looking at something as innocent as "He knows that they are alive," let us consider the more relevant "He (really) *knows* that they are alive."

Let us build some confidence that this principle is quite generally applicable, and that it will give us trustworthy results. Toward this end, we may focus on some thoughts about definite descriptions—that is, about expressions of the form "the so-and-so." About these expressions, it is a tradition to hold that they require uniqueness, or unique satisfaction, for their proper application. Thus, just as it is traditional to hold that a man knows something only if he is certain of it, so it is also traditional to hold that there is something which is the chair with seventeen legs only if there is exactly one chair with just that many legs. But, again, by being wrongly serious about our casual everyday talk, philosophers may come to deny the traditional view. They may do this by being wrongly serious, I think, about the following sort of ordinary exchange. Suppose an examiner asks a student, "Who is the father of Nelson Rockefeller, the present Governor of New York State?" The student replies, "Nelson Rockefeller is the son of John D. Rockefeller, Jr." No doubt, the examiner will allow that, by implication, the student got the right answer; he will judge that what the student said is true even though the examiner is correctly confident that the elder Rockefeller sired other sons. Just so, one might well argue that definite descriptions, like "the son of *X*," do not require uniqueness. But against this argument from the everyday flow of talk, let us insist that we focus on the relevant conception by employing our standard means for emphasizing the most directly relevant term. Thus, while we might feel nothing contradictory at first in saying, "Nelson Rockefeller is the son of John D. Rockefeller, Jr., and so is Winthrop Rockefeller," we must confess that even initially we would have quite different feelings about our saying "Nelson Rockefeller is actually *the* son of John D. Rockefeller, Jr., and so is Winthrop Rockefeller." With the latter, where emphasis is brought to bear, we cannot help but feel that what is asserted is inconsistent. And, with this, we feel differently about the original remark, feeling it to be essentially the same assertion and so inconsistent as well. Thus, it seems that when we focus on things properly, we may assume that definite descriptions do require uniqueness.

Let us now apply our principle to the question of knowing. Here, while we might feel nothing contradictory at first in saying "He knows that it is raining, but he isn't certain of it," we would feel differently about our saying "He really *knows* that it is raining, but he isn't certain of it." And, if anything, this feeling of contradiction is only enhanced when we further emphasize, "He really *knows* that it is raining, but he isn't actually *certain* of it." Thus it is plausible to suppose that what we said at first is actually inconsistent, and so that knowing does require being certain.

For my defense of skepticism, it now remains only to combine the result we have just reached with that at which we arrived in the previous section. Now, I have argued that each of two propositions deserves, if not our acceptance, at least the suspension of our judgement:

That, in the case of every human being, there is hardly anything, if anything at all, of which he is certain.

That (as a matter of necessity), in the case of every human being, the person knows something to be so only if he is certain of it.

But I think I have done more than just that. For the strength of the arguments given for this position on each of these two propositions is, I think, sufficient for warranting a similar position on propositions which are quite obvious consequences of the two of them together. One such consequential proposition is this:

That, in the case of every human being, there is hardly anything, if anything at all, which the person knows to be so.

And so this third proposition, which is just the thesis of skepticism, also deserves, if not our acceptance, at least the suspension of our judgement. If this thesis is not reasonable to accept, then neither is its negation, the thesis of "common sense."

VI. A PROSPECTUS AND A RETROSPECTIVE

I have argued that we know hardly anything, if anything, because we are certain of hardly anything, if anything. My offering this argument will strike many philosophers as peculiar, even many who have some sympathy with skepticism. For it is natural to think that, except for the requirement of the truth of what is known, the requirement of "attitude," in this case of personal certainty, is the *least* problematic requirement of knowing. Much more difficult to fulfill, one would think, would be requirements about one's justification, about one's grounds, and so on. And, quite candidly, I am inclined to agree with these thoughts. Why, then, have I chosen to defend skepticism by picking on what is just about the easiest requirement of knowledge? My thinking has been this: the requirement of being certain will, most likely, not be independent of more difficult requirements; indeed, any more difficult requirement will entail this simpler one. Thus one more difficult requirement might be that the knower be completely *justified* in being certain, which entails the requirement that the man be certain. And, in any case, for purposes of establishing some clarity, I wanted this defense to avoid the more difficult requirements because they rely on normative terms—for example, the term "justified." The application of normative terms presents problems which, while worked over by many philosophers, are still too difficult to handle at all adequately. By staying away from more difficult requirements, and so from normative terms, I hoped to raise doubts in a simpler, clearer context. When the time comes for a more powerful defense of skepticism, the more difficult requirements will be pressed. Then normative conditions will be examined and, for this examination, declared inapplicable. But these normative conditions will, most likely, concern one's being certain; no justification of mere belief or confidence will be the issue in the more powerful defenses. By offering my defense, I hoped to lay part of the groundwork for more powerful defenses of skepticism.

I would end with this explanation but for the fact that my present views contradict claims I made previously, and others have discussed critically these earlier claims about knowledge.[6] Before, I strove to show that knowledge was rather easy to come by, that the conditions of knowledge could be met rather easily. To connect my arguments, I offered a unified analysis:

> For any sentential value of *p*, (at a time *t*) a man knows that *p* if and only if (at *t*) it is not at all accidental that the man is right about its being the case that *p*.

And, in arguing for the analysis, I tried to understand its defining condition just so liberally that it would allow men to know things rather easily. Because I did this, I used the analysis to argue against skepticism—that is, against the thesis which I have just defended.

Given my present views, while I must find the criticisms of my earlier claims more interesting than convincing, I must find my analysis to be more accurate than I was in my too liberal application of it. For, however bad the analysis might be in various respects, it does assert that knowledge is an absolute. In terms of my currently favored distinctions, "accidental" is quite clearly a relative term, as are other terms which I might have selected in its stead: "coincidental," "matter of luck," "lucky," and so on. Operating on these terms with expressions such as "not at all" and "not in the least degree" will yield us absolute expressions, the equivalent of absolute terms. Thus, the condition that I offered is not at all likely to be one that is easily met. My main error, then, was not that of giving too vague or liberal a defining condition, but rather that of too liberally interpreting a condition which is in fact strict.

But I am quite uncertain that my analysis is correct in any case, and even that one can analyze knowledge. Still, so far as analyzing knowledge goes, the main plea of this paper must be this: whatever analysis of knowledge is adequate, if any such there be, it must allow that the thesis of skepticism be at least fairly plausible. For this plea only follows from my broader one: that philosophers take skepticism seriously and not casually suppose, as I have often done, that this unpopular thesis simply must be false.[7]

NOTES

1. Among G. E. Moore's most influential papers against skepticism are "A Defense of Common Sense," "Four Forms of Scepticism," and "Certainty." These papers are now available in Moore's *Philosophical Papers* (New York, 1962). More recent representatives of the same anti-skeptical persuasion include A. J. Ayer's *The Problem of Knowledge* (Baltimore, 1956) and two books by Roderick M. Chisholm: *Perceiving* (Ithaca, 1957) and *Theory of Knowledge* (Englewood Cliffs, N.J., 1966). Among the many recent journal articles against skepticism are three papers of my own: "Experience and Factual Knowledge," *Journal of Philosophy,* vol. 64, no. 5 (1967), "An Analysis of Factual Knowledge," *Journal of Philosophy,* vol. 65, no. 6 (1968), and "Our Knowledge of the Material World," *Studies in the Theory of Knowledge, American Philosophical Quarterly Monograph* No. 4 (1970). At the same time, a survey of the recent journal literature reveals very few papers where skepticism is defended or favored. With recent papers which do favor skepticism, however, I can mention at least two. A fledgling skepticism is persuasively advanced by Brian Skyrms in his "The Explication of '*X* Knows that *p*,'" *Journal of Philosophy,* vol. 64, no. 12 (1967). And in William W. Rozeboom's "Why I Know So Much More Than You Do," *American Philosophical Quarterly,* vol. 4, no. 4 (1967), we have a refreshingly strong statement of skepticism in the context of recent discussion.
2. For an interesting discussion of impersonal certainty, which in some ways is rather in line with my own discussion while in other ways against it, one might see Michael Anthony Slote's "Empirical Certainty and the Theory of Important Criteria," *Inquiry,* vol. 10 (1967). Also, Slote makes helpful references to other writers in the philosophy of certainty.
3. See Moore's cited papers, especially "Certainty," p. 232.
4. An influential statement of this view is Roderick M. Chisholm's, to be found in the first chapter of each of his cited books. In "Experience and Factual Knowledge," I suggest a very similar view.
5. This view is advanced influentially by Colin Radford in "Knowledge by Examples," *Analysis,* 27 (October, 1966). In "An Analysis of Factual Knowledge," and especially in "Our Knowledge of The Material World," I suggest this view.
6. See my cited papers and these interesting discussions of them: Gilbert H. Harman, "Unger on Knowledge," *Journal of Philosophy,* 64 (1967), 353–359; Ruth Anna Putnam, "On Empirical Knowledge," *Boston Studies in the Philosophy of Science,* IV, 392–410; Arthur C. Danto, *Analytical Philosophy of Knowledge* (Cambridge, 1968), pp. 130 ff. and 144 ff.; Keith Lehrer and Thomas Paxson, Jr., "Knowledge: Undefeated Justified True Belief," *Journal of Philosophy,* 66 (1969), 225–237; J. L. Mackie, "The Possibility of Innate Knowledge," *Proceedings of the Aristotelian Society* (1970), pp. 245–257.
7. Ancestors of the present paper were discussed in philosophy colloquia at the following schools: Brooklyn College of The City University of New York, The University of California at Berkeley, Columbia University, The University of Illinois at Chicago Circle, The Rockefeller University, Stanford University, and The University of Wisconsin at Madison. I am thankful to those who participated in the discussion. I would also like to thank each of these many people for help in getting to the present defense: Peter M. Brown, Richard Cartwright, Fred I. Dretske, Hartry Field, Bruce Freed, H. P. Grice, Robert Hambourger, Saul A. Kripke, Stephen Schiffer, Michael A. Slote, Sydney S. Shoemaker, Dennis W. Stampe, Julius Weinberg, and Margaret Wilson, *all* of whom remain at least somewhat skeptical. Finally, I would like to thank the Graduate School of The University of Wisconsin at Madison for financial assistance during the preparation of this defense.

CHAPTER THREE

FOUNDATIONALISM, COHERENTISM, RELIABILISM, AND VIRTUE EPISTEMOLOGY

This section presents four views concerning the justification of knowledge. Some of the central questions include the following. Must our knowledge be ultimately founded on an indubitable, self-evident ground? Or can our true beliefs be justified through their connection with other true beliefs? Must we ourselves be aware of the means by which we acquire our beliefs?

We begin this section with Ernest Sosa's paper, "The Raft and the Pyramid," which clearly explicates the positions of foundationalism and coherentism in epistemology through the metaphors of the pyramid and the raft. Foundationalism, with its pyramid structure, holds that knowledge must ultimately be justified by inference or derivation from a terminal, basic, and indubitable proposition. Coherentism about knowledge, modeled on the raft or Neurath's ship at sea, holds that beliefs are justified through their coherence within a comprehensive system of beliefs. In addition to examining the structures of these positions, Sosa examines arguments against foundationalism, showing that these arguments pose problems for both coherentism and foundationalism alike. Substantial foundationalism and coherentism are more similar than they appear initially, and Sosa suggests that that although foundationalism is the stronger view, a third view—reliabilism—may provide a better account of justification than either of these positions.

We have chosen Roderick Chisholm's "A Version of Foundationalism" as a relatively contemporary representative of this view. (Selections from Descartes found in "Reality," Chapter 3 of this anthology, also represent the foundationalist view.) Chisholm argues for a version of foundationalism that bases knowledge ultimately in self-presenting properties of an individual's intentional states, i.e., those properties which one must have necessarily if one has them at all (i.e., a sensation of pain). These self-evident properties of mental states provide the needed evidence base for a foundation of one's knowledge.

Donald Davidson represents the Coherentist view, which holds that knowledge is justified through its connections with other beliefs. Davidson presents his own version of this view, in which the coherence theory of truth and the coherence theory of knowledge are tied together. Davidson holds that we have reason to think that our beliefs are, in fact, coherent and that most of the beliefs found in a coherent total set of beliefs are true. All consistent beliefs of a rational believer constitute knowledge. In contrast to the coherentism found in Idealism, Davidson further argues that the coherence theory of truth and knowledge is consistent with realism.

Alvin Goldman develops the externalist notion of justification in his essay, "What is Justified Belief?" Here, he presents the view known as Reliabilism, which holds that knowledge is justified if it is caused by a reliable mechanism. This view contrasts with the internalist view of justification held by foundationalists such as Descartes and Chisholm. Internalism requires that the knower be cognizant of the source or means by which her beliefs are justified. Under externalism, the knower need not herself be aware of the reliable source of her knowledge, but insofar as her beliefs are true and produced by a normally reliable mechanism, she has justified true beliefs. Carl Ginet, in "Contra Reliabilism" argues that reliabilism leaves us with cases in which what justifies our beliefs is not the same as what causes them. Reliabilism is thus an insufficient account of justification.

Finally, in "Knowledge and Intellectual Virtue" Ernest Sosa discusses the notion of "intellectual virtues," qualities which maximize truth over error. Rational deduction, memory, intuition, and perceptual faculties are all involved in generating and transmitting knowledge. The virtue of maximizing truth over error becomes significant if we are invoking reliable causal mechanisms in justifying knowledge because we need to understand what is involved in ensuring this reliability. Intellectual virtue, the ability to infallibly or reliably distinguish truth from error, strengthens the condition of epistemic justification, which, according to Sosa, cannot be done away with as a condition for knowledge.

The Raft and the Pyramid

Coherence versus Foundations in the Theory of Knowledge

ERNEST SOSA

Contemporary epistemology must choose between the solid security of the ancient foundationalist pyramid and the risky adventure of the new coherentist raft. Our main objective will be to understand, as deeply as we can, the nature of the controversy and the reasons for and against each of the two options. But first of all we take note of two underlying assumptions.

1. *Two assumptions*

(A1) Not everything believed is known, but nothing can be known without being at least believed (or accepted, presumed, taken for granted, or the like) in some broad sense. What additional requirements must a belief fill in order to be knowledge? There are surely at least the following two: (a) it must be true, and (b) it must be justified (or warranted, reasonable, correct, or the like).

(A2) Let us assume, moreover, with respect to the second condition A1(b): first, that it involves a normative or evaluative property; and, second, that the relevant sort of justification is that which pertains to knowledge: epistemic (or theoretical) justification. Someone seriously ill may have two sorts of justification for believing he will recover: the practical justification that derives from the contribution such belief will make to his recovery and the theoretical justification provided by the lab results, the doctor's diagnosis and prognosis, and so on. Only the latter is relevant to the question whether he knows.

Source: Sosa, Ernest, "The Raft and the Pyramid: Coherence Versus Foundations in the Theory of Knowledge," in Peter French, Howard Wettstein, and Theodore Uehling, eds., *Midwest Studies in Philosophy V: Studies in Epistemology* (University of Minnesota Press, 1980), pp. 3–25. Reprinted with permission of the publisher.

2. *Knowledge and criteria (or canons, methods, or the like)*

   a. There are two key questions of the theory of knowledge:

      (i) What do we know?
      (ii) How do we know?

      The answer to the first would be a list of bits of knowledge or at least of types of knowledge: of the self, of the external world, of other minds, and so on. An answer to the second would give us criteria (or canons, methods, principles, or the like) that would explain how we know whatever it is that we do know.

   b. In developing a theory of knowledge, we can begin either with a(i) or with a(ii). Particularism would have us begin with an answer to a(i) and only then take up a(ii) on the basis of that answer. Quite to the contrary, methodism would reverse that order. The particularist thus tends to be antiskeptical on principle. But the methodist is as such equally receptive to skepticism and to the contrary. Hume, for example, was no less a methodist than Descartes. Each accepted, in effect, that only the obvious and what is proved deductively on its basis can possibly be known.

   c. What, then, is the obvious? For Descartes it is what we know by intuition, what is clear and distinct, what is indubitable and credible with no fear of error. Thus for Descartes basic knowledge is always an infallible belief in an indubitable truth. All other knowledge must stand on that basis through deductive proof. Starting from such criteria (canons, methods, etc.), Descartes concluded that knowledge extended about as far as his contemporaries believed.[1] Starting from similar criteria, however, Hume concluded that both science and common sense made claims far beyond their rightful limits.

   d. Philosophical posterity has rejected Descartes's theory for one main reason: that it admits too easily as obvious what is nothing of the sort. Descartes's reasoning is beautifully simple: God exists; no omnipotent perfectly good being would descend to deceit; but if our common sense beliefs were radically false, that would represent deceit on His part. Therefore, our common sense beliefs must be true or at least cannot be radically false. But in order to buttress this line of reasoning and fill in details, Descartes appeals to various principles that appear something less than indubitable.

   e. For his part, Hume rejects all but a minuscule portion of our supposed common sense knowledge. He establishes first that there is no way to prove such supposed knowledge on the basis of what is obvious at any given moment through reason or experience. And he concludes, in keeping with this methodism, that in point of fact there really is no such knowledge.

3. *Two metaphors: the raft and the pyramid*

   Both metaphors concern the body or system of knowledge in a given mind. But the mind is of course a more complex marvel than is sometimes supposed. Here I do not allude to the depths plumbed by Freud, nor even to Chomsky's. Nor need we recall the labyrinths inhabited by statesmen and diplomats, nor the rich patterns of some novels or theories. We need look no further than the most common, everyday beliefs. Take, for instance, the belief that driving tonight will be dangerous. Brief reflection should reveal that any of us with that belief will join to it several other closely related beliefs on which the given belief depends for its existence or (at least) its justification. Among such beliefs we could presumably find some or all of the following: that the road will be icy or snowy; that driving on ice or snow is dangerous; that it will rain or snow tonight; that the temperature will be below freezing; appropriate beliefs about the forecast and its reliability; and so on.

How must such beliefs be interrelated in order to help justify my belief about the danger of driving tonight? Here foundationalism and coherentism disagree, each offering its own metaphor. Let us have a closer look at this dispute, starting with foundationalism.

Both Descartes and Hume attribute to human knowledge an architectonic structure. There is a nonsymmetric relation of physical support such that any two floors of a building are tied by that relation: one of the two supports (or at least helps support) the other. And there is, moreover, a part with a special status: the foundation, which is supported by none of the floors while supporting them all.

With respect to a body of knowledge K (in someone's possession), foundationalism implies that K can be divided into parts K_1, K_2, . . . , such that there is some nonsymmetric relation R (analogous to the relation of physical support) which orders those parts in such a way that there is one—call it F—that bears R to every other part while none of them bears R in turn of F.

According to foundationalism, each piece of knowledge lies on a pyramid such as the following:

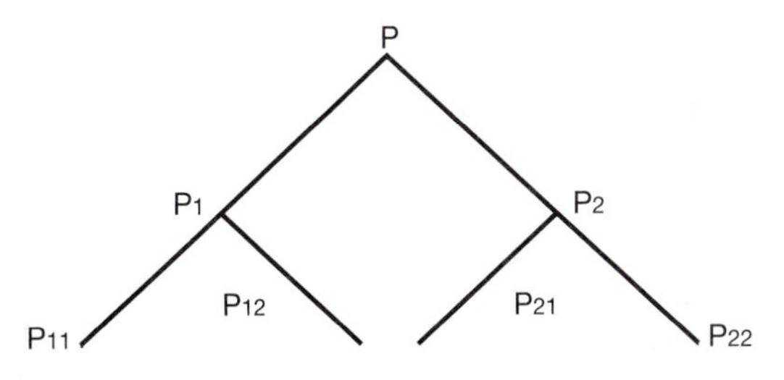

The nodes of such a pyramid (for a proposition P relative to a subject S and a time t) must obey the following requirements:

a. The set of all nodes that succeed (directly) any given node must serve jointly as a base that properly supports that node (for S at t).
b. Each node must be a proposition that S is justified in believing at t.
c. If a node is not self-evident (for S at t), it must have successors (that serve jointly as a base that properly supports that node).
d. Each branch of an epistemic pyramid must terminate.

For the foundationalist Descartes, for instance, each terminating node must be an indubitable proposition that S believes at t with no possibility of error. As for the nonterminal nodes, each of them represents inferential knowledge, derived by deduction from more basic beliefs.

Such radical foundationalism suffers from a fatal weakness that is twofold:

a. there are not so many perfectly obvious truths as Descartes thought; and
b. once we restrict ourselves to what is truly obvious in any given context, very little of one's supposed common sense knowledge can be proved on that basis.

If we adhere to such radical foundationalism, therefore, we are just wrong in thinking we know so much.

Note that in citing such a "fatal weakness" of radical foundationalism, we favor particularism as against the methodism of Descartes and Hume. For we reject the methods or criteria of Descartes and Hume when we realize that they plunge us in a deep skepticism. If such criteria are incompatible with our enjoyment of the rich body of knowledge that we commonly take for granted, then as good particularists we hold on to the knowledge and reject the criteria.

If we reject radical foundationalism, however, what are we to put in its place? Here epistemology faces a dilemma that different epistemologists resolve differently. Some reject radical foundationalism but retain some more moderate form of foundationalism. Others react more vigorously, however, by rejecting all forms of foundationalism in favor of a radically different coherentism. Coherentism is associated with idealism—of both the German and the British variety—and has recently acquired new vigor and interest.

The coherentists reject the metaphor of the pyramid in favor of one that they owe to the positivist Neurath, according to whom our body of knowledge is a raft that floats free of any anchor or tie. Repairs must be made afloat, and though no part is untouchable, we must stand on some in order to replace or repair others. Not every part can go at once.

According to the new metaphor, what justifies a belief is not that it be an infallible belief with an indubitable object, nor that it have been proved deductively on such a basis, but that it cohere with a comprehensive system of beliefs.

4. *A coherentist critique of foundationalism*

What reasons do coherentists offer for their total rejection of foundationalism? The argument that follows below summarizes much of what is alleged against foundationalism. But first we must distinguish between subjective states that incorporate a propositional attitude and those that do not. A propositional attitude is a mental state of someone with a proposition for its object: beliefs, hopes, and fears provide examples. By way of contrast, a headache does not incorporate any such attitude. One can of course be conscious of a headache, but the headache itself does not constitute or incorporate any attitude with a proposition for its object. With this distinction in the background, here is the antifoundationalist argument, which has two lemmas—a(iv) and b(iii)—and a principal conclusion.

a. (i) If a mental state incorporates a propositional attitude, then it does not give us direct contact with reality, e.g., with pure experience, unfiltered by concepts or beliefs.
(ii) If a mental state does not give us direct contact with reality, then it provides no guarantee against error.
(iii) If a mental state provides no guarantee against error, then it cannot serve as a foundation for knowledge.
(iv) Therefore, if a mental state incorporates a propositional attitude, then it cannot serve as a foundation for knowledge.

b. (i) If a mental state does not incorporate a propositional attitude, then it is an enigma how such a state can provide support for any hypothesis, raising its credibility selectively by contrast with its alternatives. (If the mental state has no conceptual or propositional content, then what logical relation can it possibly bear to any hypothesis? Belief in a hypothesis would be a propositional attitude with the hypothesis itself as object. How can one depend logically for such a belief on an experience with no propositional content?)
(ii) If a mental state has no propositional content and cannot provide logical support for any hypothesis, then it cannot serve as a foundation for knowledge.
(iii) Therefore, if a mental state does not incorporate a propositional attitude, then it cannot serve as a foundation for knowledge.

c. Every mental state either does or does not incorporate a propositional attitude.

d. Therefore, no mental state can serve as a foundation for knowledge. (From a(iv), b(iii), and c.)

According to the coherentist critic, foundationalism is run through by this dilemma. Let us take a closer look.[2]

In the first place, what reason is there to think, in accordance with premise b(i), that only propositional attitudes can give support to their own kind? Consider practices—e.g., broad policies or customs. Could not some person or group be justified in a practice because of its consequences: that is, could not the consequences of a practice make it a good practice? But among the consequences of a practice may surely be found, for example, a more just distribution of goods and less suffering than there would be under its alternatives. And neither the more just distribution nor the lower degree of suffering is a propositional attitude. This provides an example in which propositional attitudes (the intentions that sustain the practice) are justified by consequences that are not propositional attitudes. That being so, is it not conceivable that the justification of belief that matters for knowledge be analogous to the objective justification by consequences that we find in ethics?

Is it not possible, for instance, that a belief that there is something red before one be justified in part because it has its origin in one's visual experience of red when one looks at an apple in daylight? If we accept such examples, they show us a source of justification that serves as such without incorporating a propositional attitude.

As for premise a(iii), it is already under suspicion from our earlier exploration of premise b(i). A mental state M can be nonpropositional and hence not a candidate for so much as truth, much less infallibility, while it serves, in spite of that, as a foundation of knowledge. Leaving that aside, let us suppose that the relevant mental state is indeed propositional. Must it then be infallible in order to serve as a foundation of justification and knowledge? That is so far from being obvious that it seems more likely false when compared with an analogue in ethics. With respect to beliefs, we may distinguish between their being true and their being justified. Analogously, with respect to actions, we may distinguish between their being optimal (best of all alternatives, all things considered) and their being (subjectively) justified. In practical deliberation on alternatives for action, is it inconceivable that the most *eligible* alternative *not* be objectively the best, all things considered? Can there not be another alternative—perhaps a most repugnant one worth little if any consideration—that in point of fact would have a much better total set of consequences and would thus be better, all things considered? Take the physician attending to Frau Hitler at the birth of little Adolf. Is it not possible that if he had acted less morally, that would have proved better in the fullness of time? And if that is so in ethics, may not its likeness hold good in epistemology? Might there not be justified (reasonable, warranted) beliefs that are not even true, much less infallible? That seems to me not just a conceivable possibility, but indeed a familiar fact of everyday life, where observational beliefs too often prove illusory but no less reasonable for being false.

If the foregoing is on the right track, then the antifoundationalist is far astray. What has led him there?

As a diagnosis of the antifoundationalist argument before us, and more particularly of its second lemma, I would suggest that it rests on an Intellectualist Model of Justification.

According to such a model, the justification of belief (and psychological states generally) is parasitical on certain logical relations among propositions. For example, my belief (i) that the streets are wet, is justified by my pair of beliefs (ii) that it is raining, and (iii) that if it is raining, the streets are wet. Thus we have a structure such as this:

B(Q) is justified by the fact that B(Q) is grounded on (B(P), B(P⊃Q)).

And according to an Intellectualist Model, this is parasitical on the fact that

P and (P⊃Q) together logically imply Q.

Concerning this attack on foundationalism I will argue (a) that it is useless to the coherentist, since if the antifoundationalist dilemma impales the foundationalist, a form of it can be turned against the coherentist to the same effect; (b) that the dilemma would be lethal not only to foundationalism and coherentism but also to the very possibility of substantive epistemology; and (c) that a form of it would have the same effect on normative ethics.

a. According to coherentism, what justifies a belief is its membership in a coherent and comprehensive set of beliefs. But whereas being grounded on B(P) and (B(P⊃Q) is a property of a belief B(Q) that yields immediately the logical implication of Q and P and (P⊃Q) as the logical source of that property's justificatory power, the property of being a member of a coherent set is not one that immediately yields any such implication.

   It may be argued, nevertheless, (i) that the property of being a member of a coherent set would supervene in any actual instance on the property of being a member of a particular set *a* that is in fact coherent, and (ii) that this would enable us to preserve our Intellectualist Model, since (iii) the justification of the member belief B(Q) by its membership in *a* would then be parasitical on the logical relations among the beliefs in *a* which constitute the coherence of that set of beliefs, and (iv) the justification of B(Q) by the fact that it is part of a coherent set would then be *indirectly* parasitical on logical relations among propositions after all.

   But if such an indirect form of parasitism is allowed, then the experience of pain may perhaps be said to justify belief in its existence parasitically on the fact that P logically implies P! The Intellectualist Model seems either so trivial as to be dull, or else sharp enough to cut equally against both foundationalism and coherentism.

b. If (i) only propositional attitudes can justify such propositional attitudes as belief, and if (ii) to do so they must in turn be justified by yet other propositional attitudes, it seems clear that (iii) there is no hope of constructing a complete epistemology, one which would give us, in theory, an account of what the justification of any justified belief would supervene on. For (i) and (ii) would rule out the possibility of a finite regress of justification.

c. If only propositional attitudes can justify propositional attitudes, and if to do so they must in turn be justified by yet other propositional attitudes, it seems clear that there is no hope of constructing a complete normative ethics, one which would give us, in theory, an account of what the justification of any possible justified action would supervene upon. For the justification of an action presumably depends on the intentions it embeds and the justification of these, and here we are already within the net of propositional attitudes from which, for the intellectualist, there is no escape.

It seems fair to conclude that our coherentist takes his antifoundationalist zeal too far. His antifoundationalist argument helps expose some valuable insights but falls short of its malicious intent. The foundationalist emerges showing no serious damage. Indeed, he now demands equal time for a positive brief in defense of his position.

5. *The regress argument*

a. The regress argument in epistemology concludes that we must countenance beliefs that are justified in the absence of justification by other beliefs. But it reaches that conclusion only by rejecting the possibility in principle of an infinite regress of justification. It thus opts for foundational beliefs justified in some non-inferential way by ruling out a chain or pyramid of justification that has justifiers, and justifiers of justifiers, and so on *without end.* One may well find this too short a route to foundationalism, however, and demand more compelling reasons for thus rejecting an infinite regress as vicious. We shall find indeed that it is not easy to meet this demand.

b. We have seen how even the most ordinary of everyday beliefs is the tip of an iceberg. A closer look below the surface reveals a complex structure that ramifies with no end in sight. Take again my belief that driving will be dangerous tonight, at the tip of an iceberg, (I), that looks like this:

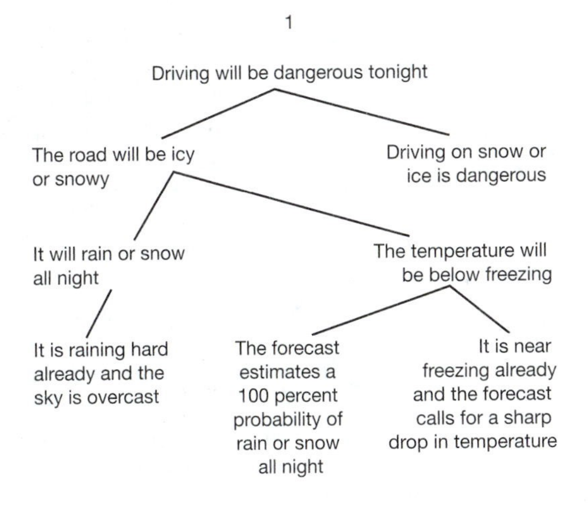

The immediate cause of my belief that driving will be hazardous tonight is the sound of raindrops on the windowpane. All but one or two members of the underlying iceberg are as far as they can be from my thoughts at the time. In what sense, then, do they form an iceberg whose tip breaks the calm surface of my consciousness?

Here I will assume that the members of (I) are beliefs of the subject, even if unconscious or subconscious, that causally buttress and thus justify his prediction about the driving conditions.

Can the iceberg extend without end? It may appear obvious that it cannot do so, and one may jump to the conclusion that any piece of knowledge must be ultimately founded on beliefs that are *not* (inferentially) justified or warranted by other beliefs. This is a doctrine of *epistemic foundationalism.*

Let us focus not so much on the *giving* of justification as on the *having* of it. *Can* there be a belief that is justified in part by other beliefs, some of which are in turn justified by yet other beliefs, and so on without end? Can there be an endless regress of justification?

c. There are several familiar objections to such a regress:

(i) *Objection:* "It is incompatible with human limitations. No human subject could harbor the required infinity of beliefs." *Reply:* It is mere presumption to fathom with such assurance the depths of the mind, and especially its unconscious and dispositional depths. Besides, our object here is the nature of epistemic justification in itself and not only that of such justification as is accessible to humans. Our question is not whether humans could harbor an infinite iceberg of justification. Our question is rather whether *any* mind, no matter how deep, could do so. Or is it ruled out *in principle* by the very nature of justification?

(ii) *Objection:* "An infinite regress is indeed ruled out in principle, for if justification were thus infinite how could it possible end? *Reply:* (i) If the end mentioned is *temporal,* then why must there be such an end? In the first place, the subject may be eternal. Even if he is not eternal, moreover, why must belief acquisition and justification occur seriatim? What precludes an infinite body of beliefs acquired at a single stroke? Human limitations may rule this out for humans, but we have yet to be shown that it is precluded in principle, by the very nature of justification. (ii) If the end mentioned is justificatory, on the other hand, then to ask how justification could possibly end is just to beg the question.

(iii) *Objection:* "Let us make two assumptions: first, that S's belief of q justifies his belief of p only if it works together with a justified belief on his part that q provides good evidence for p; and, second, that if S is to be justified in believing p on the basis of his belief of q and is to be justified in believing q on the basis of his belief of r, then S must be justified in believing that r provides good evidence for p via q. These assumptions imply that an actual regress of justification requires belief in an infinite proposition. Since no one (or at least no human) can believe an infinite proposition, no one (no human) can be a subject of such an actual regress."[3]

Reply: Neither of the two assumptions is beyond question, but even granting them both, it may still be doubted that the conclusion follows. It is true that each finitely complex belief of the form "r provides good evidence for p via $q_1, \ldots, q_n$" will *omit* how some members of the full infinite regress are epistemically tied to belief of p. But that seems irrelevant given the fact that for each member r of the regress, such that r is tied epistemically to belief of p, there *is* a finite belief of the required sort ("r provides good evidence for p via $q_1, \ldots, q_n$") that ties the two together. Consequently, there is no apparent reason to suppose—even granted the two assumptions—that an infinite regress will require a single belief in an infinite proposition, and not just an infinity of beliefs in increasingly complex finite propositions.

(iv) *Objection:* "But if it is allowed that justification extend infinitely, then it is too easy to justify any belief at all or too many beliefs altogether. Take, for instance, the belief that there are perfect numbers greater than 100. And suppose a mind powerful enough to believe every member of the following sequence:

(σ1) There is at least one perfect number > 100
There are at least two perfect numbers > 100
There are at least three perfect numbers > 100

If such a believer has no other belief about perfect numbers save the belief that a perfect number is a whole number equal to the sum of its whole factors, then surely he is *not* justified in believing that there are perfect numbers greater than 100. He is quite unjustified in believing any of the members of sequence (σ1), in spite of the fact that a challenge to any can be met easily by appeal to its successor. Thus it cannot be allowed after all that justification extend infinitely, and an infinite regress is ruled out."

Reply: We must distinguish between regresses of justification that are actual and those that are merely potential. The difference is *not* simply that an actual regress is composed of actual beliefs. For even if all members of the regress are actual beliefs, the regress may still be *merely potential* in the following sense: while it is true that *if* any member *were* justified then its predecessors *would* be, still none is in fact justified. Anyone with our series of beliefs about perfect numbers in the absence of any further relevant information on such numbers would presumably be the subject of such a merely potential justificatory regress.

(v) *Objection:* "But defenders of infinite justificatory regresses cannot distinguish thus between actual regresses and those that are merely potential. There is no real distinction to be drawn between the two. For if any regress ever justifies the belief at its head, then every regress must always do so. But obviously not every regress does so (as we have seen by examples), and hence no regress can do so."[4]

Reply: One can in fact distinguish between actual justificatory regresses and merely potential ones, and one can do so both abstractly and by examples.

What an actual regress has that a merely potential regress lacks is the property of containing only justified beliefs as members. What they both share is the property of containing no member without successors that would jointly justify it.

Recall our regress about perfect numbers greater than 100: i.e., there is at least one; there are at least two; there are at least three; and so on. Each member has a successor that would justify it, but no member is justified (in the absence of further information external to the regress). That is therefore a merely potential infinite regress. As for an actual regress, I see no compelling reason why someone (if not a human, then some more powerful mind) could not hold an infinite series of actually justified beliefs as follows:

(σ2) There is at least one even number
There are at least two even numbers
" three "

It may be that no one could be the subject of such a series of justified beliefs unless he had a proof that there is a denumerable infinity of even numbers. But even if that should be so, it would not take away the fact of the infinite regress of potential justifiers, each of which is actually justified, and hence it would not take away the fact of the actual endless regress of justification.

The objection under discussion is confused, moreover, on the nature of the issue before us. Our question is *not* whether there can be an infinite potential regress, each member of which would be justified by its successors, such that the belief at its head is justified in virtue of its position there, at the head of such a regress. The existence and even the possibility of a single such regress with a belief at its head that was *not* justified in virtue of its position there would of course settle that question in the negative. Our question is, rather, whether there can be an actual infinite regress of justification, and the fact that a belief at the head of a potential regress might still fail to be justified despite its position does *not* settle this question. For even if there can be a merely potential regress with an unjustified belief at its head, that leaves open the possibility of an infinite regress, each member of which is justified by its immediate successors working jointly, where every member of the regress is in addition actually justified.

6. *The relation of justification and foundationalist strategy*

The foregoing discussion is predicated on a simple conception of justification such that a set of beliefs β conditionally justifies (*would* justify) a belief X iff, necessarily, if all members of β are justified then X is also justified (if it exists). The fact that on such a conception of justification actual endless regresses—such as (σ2)—seem quite possible blocks a straightforward regress argument in favor of foundations. For it shows that an actual infinite regress cannot be dismissed out of hand.

Perhaps the foundationalist could introduce some relation of justification—presumably more complex and yet to be explicated—with respect to which it could be argued more plausibly that an actual endless regress is out of the question.

There is, however, a more straightforward strategy open to the foundationalist. For he *need not* object to the possibility of an endless regress of justification. His essential creed is the more positive belief that every justified belief must be at the head of a terminating regress. Fortunately, to affirm the universal necessity of a terminating regress is *not* to deny the bare possibility of a nonterminating regress. For a single belief can trail at once regresses of both sorts: one terminating and one not. Thus the proof of the denumerably infinite cardinality of the set of evens may provide for a powerful enough intellect a *terminating* regress for each member of the *endless* series of justified beliefs:

(σ2) There is at least one even number
There are at least two even numbers
" three "

At the same time, it is obvious that each member of (σ2) lies at the head of an actual endless regress of justification, on the assumption that each member is conditionally justified by its successor, which is in turn actually justified.

"Thank you so much," the foundationalist may sneer, "but I really do not need that kind of help. Nor do I need to be reminded of my essential creed, which I know as well as anyone. Indeed my rejection of endless regresses of justification is only a means of supporting my view that every justified belief must rest ultimately on foundations, on a terminating regress. You reject that strategy much too casually, in my view, but I will not object here. So we put that strategy aside. And now, my helpful friend, just what do we put in its place."

Fair enough. How then could one show the need for foundations if an endless regress is not ruled out?

7. *Two levels of foundationalism*

a. We need to distinguish, first, between two forms of foundationalism: one *formal,* the other *substantive*. A type of *formal foundationalism* with respect to a normative or evaluative property ϕ is the view that the conditions (actual and possible) within which ϕ would apply can be specified in general, perhaps recursively. *Substantive foundationalism* is only a particular way of doing so, and coherentism is another.

Simpleminded hedonism is the view that:

(i) every instance of pleasure is good,
(ii) everything that causes something good is itself good, and
(iii) everything that is good is so in virtue of (i) or (ii) above.

Simpleminded hedonism is a type of formal foundationalism with respect to the good.

Classical foundationalism in epistemology is the view that:

(i) every infallible, indubitable belief is justified,
(ii) every belief deductively inferred from justified beliefs is itself justified, and
(iii) every belief that is justified is so in virtue of (i) or (ii) above.

Classical foundationalism is a type of formal foundationalism with respect to epistemic justification.

Both of the foregoing theories—simpleminded hedonism in ethics, and classical foundationalism in epistemology—are of course flawed. But they both remain examples of formal foundationalist theories.

b. One way of arguing in favor of formal foundationalism in epistemology is to formulate a convincing formal foundationalist theory of justification. But classical foundationalism in epistemology no longer has for many the attraction that it had for Descartes, nor has any other form of epistemic foundationalism won general acceptance. Indeed epistemic foundationalism has been generally abandoned and its advocates have been put on the defensive by the writings of Wittgenstein, Quine, Sellars, Rescher, Aune, Harman, Lehrer, and others. It is lamentable that in our headlong rush away from foundationalism we have lost sight of the different types of foundationalism (formal vs. substantive) and of the different grades of each type. Too many of us now see it as a blur to be decried and avoided. Thus our present attempt to bring it all into better focus.

c. If we cannot argue from a generally accepted foundationalist theory, what reason is there to accept formal foundationalism? There is no reason to think that the conditions (actual and possible) within which an object is spherical are generally specifiable in nongeometric terms. Why should we think that the conditions (actual and possible) within which a belief is epistemically justified are generally specifiable in nonepistemic terms?

   So far as I can see, the main reason for accepting formal foundationalism in the absence of an actual, convincing formal foundationalist theory is the very plausible idea that epistemic justification is subject to the supervenience that characterizes normative and evaluative properties generally. Thus, if a car is a good car, then any physical replica of that car must be just as good. If it is a good car in virtue of such properties as being economical, little prone to break down, etc., then surely any exact replica would share all such properties and would thus be equally good. Similarly, if a belief is epistemically justified, it is presumably so in virtue of its character and its basis in perception, memory, or inference (if any). Thus any belief exactly like it in its character and its basis must be equally well justified. Epistemic justification is supervenient. The justification of a belief supervenes on such properties of it as its content and its basis (if any) in perception, memory, or inference. Such a doctrine of supervenience may itself be considered, with considerable justice, a grade of foundationalism. For it entails that every instance of justified belief is founded on a number of its nonepistemic properties, such as its having a certain basis in perception, memory, and inference, or the like.

   But there are higher grades of foundationalism as well. There is, for instance, the doctrine that the conditions (actual and possible) within which a belief would be epistemically justified *can be specified* in general, perhaps recursively (and by reference to such notions as perception, memory, and inference).

   A higher grade yet of formal foundationalism requires not only that the conditions for justified belief be specifiable, in general, but that they be specifiable by a simple, comprehensive theory.

d. Simpleminded hedonism is a formal foundationalist theory of the highest grade. If it is true, then in every possible world goodness supervenes on pleasure and causation in a way that is recursively specifiable by means of a very simple theory.

   Classical foundationalism in epistemology is also a formal foundationalist theory of the highest grade. If it is true, then in every possible world epistemic justification supervenes on infallibility cum indubitability and deductive inference in a way that is recursively specifiable by means of a very simple theory.

   Surprisingly enough, coherentism may also turn out to be formal foundationalism of the highest grade, provided only that the concept of coherence is itself both simple enough and free of any normative or evaluative admixture. Given these provisos coherentism explains how epistemic justification supervenes on the nonepistemic in a theory of remarkable simplicity: a belief is justified iff it has a place within a system of beliefs that is coherent and comprehensive.

   It is a goal of ethics to explain how the ethical rightness of an action supervenes on what is not ethically evaluative or normative. Similarly, it is a goal of epistemology to explain how the epistemic justification of a belief supervenes on what is not epistemically evaluative or normative. If coherentism aims at this goal, that imposes restrictions on the notion of coherence, which must now be conceived innocent of epistemically evaluative or normative admixture. Its substance must therefore consist of such concepts as explanation, probability, and logical implication—with these conceived, in turn, innocent of normative or evaluative content.

e. We have found a surprising kinship between coherentism and substantive foundationalism, both of which turn out to be varieties of a deeper foundationalism. This deeper foundationalism is applicable to any normative or evaluative property ϕ, and it comes in three grades. The *first* or lowest is simply the supervenience of ϕ: the idea that whenever something has ϕ its having it is founded on certain others of its properties which fall into certain restricted sorts. The *second* is the explicable supervenience of ϕ: the idea that there are formulable principles that explain in quite general terms the conditions (actual and possible) within which ϕ applies. The *third* and highest is the easily explicable supervenience of ϕ: the idea that there is a *simple* theory that explains the conditions within which ϕ applies. We have found the coherentist and the substantive foundationalist sharing a primary goal: the development of a formal foundationalist theory of the highest grade. For they both want a simple theory that explains precisely how epistemic justification supervenes, in general, on the nonepistemic. This insight gives us an unusual viewpoint on some recent attacks against foundationalism. Let us now consider as an example a certain simple form of argument distilled from the recent antifoundationalist literature.[5]

8. *Doxastic ascent arguments*

Several attacks on foundationalism turn on a sort of "doxastic ascent" argument that calls for closer scrutiny.[6] Here are two examples:

A. A belief B is foundationally justified for S in virtue of having property F only if S is justified in believing (1) that most at least of his beliefs with property F are true, and (2) that B has property F. But this means that belief B is not foundational after all, and indeed that the very notion of (empirical) foundational belief is incoherent.

It is sometimes held, for example, that perceptual or observational beliefs are often justified through their origin in the exercise of one or more of our five senses in standard conditions of perception. The advocate of doxastic ascent would raise a vigorous protest, however, for in his view the mere fact of such sensory prompting is importent to justify the belief prompted. Such prompting must be coupled with the further belief that one's senses work well in the circumstances, or the like. For we are dealing here with *knowledge,* which requires not blind faith but *reasoned* trust. But now surely the further belief about the reliability of one's senses itself cannot rest on blind faith but requires its own backing of reasons, and we are off on the regress.

B. A belief B of proposition P is foundationally justified for S only if S is justified in believing that there are no factors present that would cause him to make mistakes on the matter of the proposition P. But, again, this means that belief B is not foundational after all and indeed that the notion of (empirical) foundational belief is incoherent.

From the vantage point of formal foundationalism, neither of these arguments seems persuasive. In the first place, as we have seen, what makes a belief foundational (formally) is its having a property that is nonepistemic (not evaluative in the epistemic or cognitive mode), and does not involve inference from other beliefs, but guarantees, via a necessary principle, that the belief in question is justified. A belief B is made foundational by having some such nonepistemic property that yields its justification. Take my belief that I am in pain in a context where it is caused by my being in pain. The property that my belief then has, of being a self-attribution of pain caused by one's own pain is, let us suppose, a nonepistemic property that yields the justification of any belief that has it. So my belief that I am in pain is in that context foundationally justified. Along with my belief that I am in pain, however, there come other beliefs that are equally well justified, such as my belief that someone is in pain. Thus I am foundationally justified in believing that I am in pain only if I am justified in believing that someone is in pain. Those who object to foundationalism as in A or B above are hence mistaken in thinking that their premises would refute foundationalism. The fact is that they would not touch it. For a belief is no less foundationally justified for having its justification yoked to that of another closely related belief.

The advocate of arguments like A and B must apparently strengthen his premises. He must apparently claim that the beliefs whose justification is entailed by the foundationally justified status of belief B must in some sense function as a *necessary source* of the justification of B. And this would of course preclude giving B foundationally justified status. For if the *being justified* of those beliefs is an *essential* part of the source of the justification of B, then it is ruled out that there be a wholly *nonepistemic* source of B's justification.

That brings us to a second point about A and B, for it should now be clear that these cannot be selectively aimed at foundationalism. In particular, they seem neither more nor less valid objections to coherentism than to foundationalism, or so I will now argue about each of them in turn.

A′. A belief X is justified for S in virtue of membership in a coherent set only if S is justified in believing (1) that most at least of his beliefs with the property of thus cohering are true, and (2) that X has that property.

Any coherentist who accepts A seems bound to accept A′. For what could be possibly appeal to as a relevant difference? But A′ is a quicksand of endless depth. (How is he justified in believing A′(1)? Partly through justified belief that *it* coheres? And what would justify *this?* And so on . . .).

B′. A belief X is justified for S only if S is justified in believing that there are no factors present that would cause him to make mistakes on the subject matter of that belief.

Again, any coherentist who accepts B seems bound to accept B′. But this is just another road to the quicksand. (For S is justified in believing that there are no such factors only if . . . and so on.)

Why are such regresses vicious? The key is again, to my mind, the doctrine of supervenience. Such regresses are vicious because they would be logically incompatible with the supervenience of epistemic justification on such nonepistemic facts as the totality of a subject's beliefs, his cognitive and experiential history, and as many other nonepistemic facts as may seem at all relevant. The idea is that there is a set of such nonepistemic facts surrounding a justified belief such that no belief could possibly have been surrounded by those very facts without being justified. Advocates of A or B run afoul of such supervenience, since they are surely committed to the more general views derivable from either of A or B by deleting 'foundationally' from its first sentence. In each case the more general view would then preclude the possibility of supervenience, since it would entail that the source of justification *always* includes an *epistemic* component.

9. *Coherentism and substantive foundationalism*

   a. The notions of coherentism and substantive foundationalism remain unexplicated. We have relied so far on our intuitive grasp of them. In this section we shall consider reasons for the view that substantive foundationalism is superior to coherentism. To assess these reasons, we need some more explicit account of the difference between the two.

      By coherentism we shall mean any view according to which the ultimate sources of justification for any belief lie in relations among that belief and other beliefs of the subject: explanatory relations, perhaps, or relations of probability or logic.

      According to substantive foundationalism, as it is to be understood here, there are ultimate sources of justification other than relations among beliefs. Traditionally these additional sources have pertained to the special content of the belief or its special relations to the subjective experience of the believer.

   b. The view that justification is a matter of relations among beliefs is open to an objection from alternative coherent systems or detachment from reality, depending on one's perspective. From the latter perspective the body of beliefs is held constant and the surrounding world is allowed to vary, whereas from the former perspective it is the surrounding world that is held constant while the body of beliefs is allowed to vary. In either case, according to the coherentist, there could be no effect on the justification for any belief.

      Let us sharpen the question before us as follows. Is there reason to think that there is a least one system B′, alternative to our actual system of beliefs B, such that B′ contains a belief X with the following properties:

      (i) in our present nonbelief circumstances we would not be justified in having belief X even if we accepted along with that belief (as our total system of beliefs) the entire belief system B′ in which it is embedded (no matter how acceptance of B′ were brought about); and
      (ii) that is so despite the fact that belief X coheres with in B′ at least as fully as does some actual justified belief of ours within our actual belief system B (where the justification of that actual justified belief is alleged by the coherentist to derive solely from its coherence within our actual body of beliefs B).

      The coherentist is vulnerable to counterexamples of this sort right at the surface of his body of beliefs, where we find beliefs with minimal coherence, whose detachment and replacement with contrary beliefs would have little effect on the coherence of the body. Thus take my belief that I have a headache when I do have a splitting headache, and let us suppose that this *does* cohere within my present body of beliefs. (Thus I have no reason to doubt my present introspective beliefs, and so on. And if my belief does *not* cohere, so much the worse for coherentism, since my belief is surely justified.) Here then we have a perfectly justified or warranted belief. And yet such a belief may well have relevant relations of explanation, logic, or probability with at most a small set of other beliefs of mine at the time: say, that I am not free of headache, that I am in pain, that someone is in pain, and the like. If so, then an equally coherent alternative is not far to seek. Let everything remain constant, *including* the splitting headache, except for the following: replace the belief that I have a headache with the belief that I do *not* have a headache, the belief that I am in pain with the belief that I am *not* in pain, the belief that someone is in pain with the belief that someone is *not* in pain, and so on. I contend that my resulting hypothetical system of beliefs would cohere as fully as does my actual system of beliefs, and yet my hypothetical belief that I do *not* have a headache would not therefore be justified. What makes this difference concerning justification between my actual belief that I have a headache and the hypothetical belief that I am free of headache, each as coherent as the other within its own system, if not the actual splitting headache? But the headache is *not* itself a belief nor a relation among beliefs and is thus in no way constitutive of the internal coherence of my body of beliefs.

Some might be tempted to respond by alleging that one's belief about whether or not one has a headache is always *infallible.* But since we could devise similar examples for the various sensory modalities and propositional attitudes, the response given for the case of headache would have to be generalized. In effect, it would have to cover "peripheral" beliefs generally—beliefs at the periphery of one's body of beliefs, minimally coherent with the rest. These peripheral beliefs would all be said to be infallible. That is, again, a possible response, but it leads to a capitulation by the coherentist to the radical foundationalist on a crucial issue that has traditionally divided them: the infallibility of beliefs about one's own subjective states.

What is more, not all peripheral beliefs are about one's own subjective states. The direct realist is probably right that some beliefs about our surroundings are uninferred and yet justified. Consider my present belief that the table before me is oblong. This presumably coheres with such other beliefs of mine as that the table has the same shape as the piece of paper before me, which is oblong, and a different shape than the window frame here, which is square, and so on. So far as I can see, however, there is no insurmountable obstacle to replacing that whole set of coherent beliefs with an equally coherent set as follows: that the table before me is square, that the table has the same shape as the square window frame, and a different shape than the piece of paper, which is oblong, and so on. The important points are (a) that this replacement may be made without changing the rest of one's body of beliefs or any aspect of the world beyond, including one's present visual experience of something oblong, not square, as one looks at the table before one; and (b) that is so, in part, because of the fact (c) that the subject need not have any beliefs about his present sensory experience.

Some might be tempted to respond by alleging that one's present experience is *self-intimating,* i.e., always necessarily taken note of and reflected in one's beliefs. Thus if anyone has visual experience of something oblong, then he believes that he has such experience. But this would involve a further important concession by the coherentist to the radical foundationalist, who would have been granted two of his most cherished doctrines: the infallibility of introspective belief and the self-intimation of experience.

10. *The foundationalist's dilemma*

The antifoundationalist zeal of recent years has left several forms of foundationalism standing. These all share the conviction that a belief can be justified not only by its coherence within a comprehensive system but also by an appropriate combination of observational content and origin in the use of the senses in standard conditions. What follows presents a dilemma for any foundationalism based on any such idea.

a. We may surely suppose that beings with observational mechanisms radically unlike ours might also have knowledge of their environment. (That seems possible even if the radical difference in observational mechanisms precludes overlap in substantive concepts and beliefs.)

b. Let us suppose that there is such a being, for whom experience of type ϕ (of which we have no notion) has a role with respect to his beliefs of type ϕ analogous to the role that our visual experience has with respect to our visual beliefs. Thus we might have a schema such as the following:

Human	*Extraterrestial being*
Visual experience	ϕ experience
Experience of something red	Experience of something F
Belief that there is something red before one	Belief that there is something F before one

c. It is often recognized that our visual experience intervenes in two ways with respect to our visual beliefs: as cause and as justification. But these are not wholly independent. Presumably, the justification of the belief that something here is red derives at least in part from the fact that it originates in a visual experience of something red that takes place in normal circumstances.

d. Analogously, the extraterrestial belief that something here has the property of being F might be justified partly by the fact that it originates in a ϕ experience of something F that takes place in normal circumstances.

e. A simple question presents the foundationalist's dilemma: regarding the epistemic principle that underlies our justification for believing that something here is red on the basis of our visual experience of something red, is it proposed as a fundamental principle or as a derived generalization? Let us compare the famous Principle of Utility of value theory, according to which it is best for that to happen which, of all the possible alternatives in the circumstances, would bring with it into the world the greatest balance of pleasure over pain, joy over sorrow, happiness over unhappiness, content over discontent, or the like. Upon this fundamental principle one may then base various generalizations, rules of thumb, and maxims of public health, nutrition, legislation, etiquette, hygiene, and so on. But these are all then derived generalizations which rest for their validity on the fundamental principle. Similarly, one may also ask, with respect to the generalizations advanced by our foundationalist, whether these are proposed as fundamental principles or as derived maxims or the like. This sets him face to face with a dilemma, each of whose alternatives is problematic. If his proposals are meant to have the status of secondary or derived maxims, for instance, then it would be quite unphilosophical to stop there. Let us turn, therefore, to the other alternative.

f. On reflection it seems rather unlikely that epistemic principles for the justification of observational beliefs by their origin in sensory experience could have a status more fundamental than that of derived generalizations. For by granting such principles fundamental status we would open the door to a multitude of equally basic principles with no unifying factor.

There would be some for vision, some for hearing, etc., without even mentioning the corresponding extraterrestial principles.

g. It may appear that there is after all an idea, however, that unifies our multitude of principles. For they all involve sensory experience and sensible characteristics. But what is a sensible characteristic? Aristotle's answer appeals to examples: colors, shapes, sounds, and so on. Such a notion might enable us to unify perceptual epistemic principles under some more fundamental principle such as the following:

   If σ is a sensible characteristic, then the belief that there is something with σ before one is (prima facie) justified if it is based on a visual experience of something with σ in conditions that are normal with respect to σ.

h. There are at least two difficulties with such a suggestion, however, and neither one can be brushed aside easily. First, it is not clear that we can have a viable notion of sensible characteristic on the basis of examples so diverse as colors, shapes, tones, odors, and so on. Second, the authority of such a principle apparently derives from contingent circumstances concerning the reliability of beliefs prompted by sensory experiences of certain sorts. According to the foundationalist, our visual beliefs are justified by their origin in our visual experience or the like. Would such beliefs be equally well justified in a world where beliefs with such an origin were nearly always false?

i. In addition, finally, even if we had a viable notion of such characteristics, it is not obvious that fundamental knowledge of reality would have to derive causally or otherwise from sensory experience of such characteristics. How could one impose reasonable limits on extraterrestial mechanisms for noninferential acquisition of beliefs? Is it not possible that such mechanisms need not always function through sensory experience of any sort? Would such beings necessarily be denied any knowledge of their surroundings and indeed of any contingent spatio-temporal fact? Let us suppose them to possess a complex system of true beliefs concerning their surroundings, the structures below the surface of things, exact details of history and geography, all constituted by concepts none of which corresponds to any of our sensible characteristics. What then? Is it not possible that their basic beliefs should all concern fields of force, waves, mathematical structures, and numerical assignments to variables in several dimensions? This is no doubt an exotic notion, but even so it still seems conceivable. And if it is in fact possible, what then shall we say of the noninferential beliefs of such beings? Would we have to concede the existence of special epistemic principles that can validate their noninferential beliefs? Would it not be preferable to formulate more abstract principles that can cover both human and extraterrestial foundations? If such more abstract principles are in fact accessible, then the less general principles that define the human foundations and those that define the extraterrestial foundations are both derived principles whose validity depends on that of the more abstract principles. In this the human and extraterrestial epistemic principles would resemble rules of good nutrition for an infant and an adult. The infant's rules would of course be quite unlike those valid for the adult. But both would still be based on a more fundamental principle that postulates the ends of well-being and good health. What more fundamental principles might support both human and extraterrestial knowledge in the way that those concerning good health and well-being support rules of nutrition for both the infant and the adult?

11. *Reliabilism: an ethics of moral virtues and an epistemology of intellectual virtues*

In what sense is the doctor attending Frau Hitler justified in performing an action that brings with it far less value than one of its accessible alternatives? According to one promising idea, the key is to be found in the rules that he embodies through stable dispositions. His action is the result of certain stable virtues, and there are no equally virtuous alternate *dispositions* that, given his cognitive limitations, he might have embodied with equal or better total consequences, and that would have led him to infanticide in the circumstances. The important move for our purpose is the stratification of justification. Primary justification attaches to virtues and other dispositions, to stable dispositions to act, through their greater contribution of value when compared with alternatives. Secondary justification attaches to particular acts in virtue of their source in virtues or other such justified dispositions.

The same strategy may also prove fruitful in epistemology. Here primary justification would apply to *intellectual* virtues, to stable dispositions for belief acquisition, through their greater contribution toward getting us to the truth. Secondary justification would then attach to particular beliefs in virtue of their source in intellectual virtues or other such justified dispositions.[7]

That raises parallel questions for ethics and epistemology. We need to consider more carefully the concept of a virtue and the distinction between moral and intellectual virtues. In epistemology, there is reason to think that the most useful and illuminating notion of intellectual virtue will prove broader than our tradition would suggest and must give due weight not only to the subject and his intrinsic nature but also to his environment and to his epistemic community. This is a large topic, however, to which I hope some of us will turn with more space, and insight, than I can now command.[8]

NOTES

1. But Descartes's methodism was at most partial. James Van Cleve has supplied the materials for a convincing argument that the way out of the Cartesian circle is through a particularism of basic knowledge. (See James Van Cleve, "Foundationalism, Epistemic Principles, and the Cartesian Circle," *The Philosophical Review* 88 (1979): 55–91.) But this is, of course, compatible with methodism on inferred knowledge. Whether Descartes subscribed to such methodism is hard (perhaps impossible) to determine, since in the end he makes room for all the kinds of knowledge required by particularism. But his language when he introduces the method of hyperbolic doubt, and the order in which he proceeds, suggest that he did subscribe to such methodism.
2. Cf. Laurence Bonjour "The Coherence Theory of Truth," *Philosophical Studies* 30 (1976): 281–312; and, especially, Michael Williams, *Groundless Belief* (New Haven, 1977); and L. Bonjour, "Can Empirical Knowledge Have a Foundation?" *American Philosophical Quarterly* 15 (1978): 1–15.
3. Cf. Richard Foley, "Inferential Justification and the Infinite Regress," *American Philosophical Quarterly* 15 (1978): 311–16.
4. Cf. John Post, "Infinite Regress Arguments," *Philosophical Studies* 34 (1980).
5. The argument of this whole section is developed in greater detail in my paper "The Foundations of Foundationalism" *Nous* (1980).
6. For some examples of the influence of doxastic ascent arguments, see Wilfrid Sellars's writing in epistemology: e.g., "Empiricism and the Philosophy of Mind" in *Science, Perception, and Reality,* especially section VIII, and particularly p. 168. Also I. T. Oakley, "An Argument

for Skepticism Concerning Justified Beliefs," *American Philosophical Quarterly* 13 (1976): 221–28; and Bonjour, "Can Empirical Knowledge Have a Foundation?"

7. This puts in a more traditional perspective the contemporary effort to develop a "causal theory of knowing." From our viewpoint, this effort is better understood not as an attempt to *define* propositional knowledge but as an attempt to formulate fundamental principles of justification.

   Cf. the work of D. Armstrong, *Belief, Truth and Knowledge* (London, 1973); and that of F. Dretske, A. Goldman, and M. Swain, whose relevant already published work is included in *Essays on Knowledge and Justification,* ed. G. Pappas and M. Swain (Ithaca and London, 1978). But the theory is still under development by Goldman and by Swain, who have reached general conclusions about it similar to those suggested here, though not necessarily—so far as I know—for the same reasons or in the same overall context.

8. I am indebted above all to Roderick Chisholm: for his writings and for innumerable discussions. The main ideas in the present paper were first presented in a seminar of 1976–77 at the University of Texas. I am grateful to Anthony Anderson, David and Jean Blumenfeld, Laurence Bonjour, and Martin Perlmutter, who made that seminar a valuable stimulus. Subsequent criticism by my colleague James Van Cleve has also been valuable and stimulating.

2

A Version of Foundationalism

RODERICK M. CHISHOLM

I shall here set forth a version of "foundationalism" in the theory of knowledge. I believe that if we have such a theory before us, rather than a mere program for a theory, then the philosophical issues that foundationalism involves can be more adequately understood. It is my hope that non-foundationalists may thus be encouraged to formulate actual versions of the alternatives to foundationalism.

As a result of criticisms by several philosophers, I have been able to correct and otherwise improve upon my earlier attempts to state such a theory.[1]

I shall accommodate my formulation to a general theory about what is expressed by first-person sentences: these sentences do not express first-person propositions (for there are no first-person propositions); they express, rather, the direct attribution of properties to oneself.

I begin, then, by summarizing my general conception of the primary *object* of intentional attitudes—attitudes like knowing, believing, and desiring.

THE PRIMARY OBJECT OF INTENTIONAL ATTITUDES

It is only within the last decade that philosophers have come to appreciate the difficulties involved in what might be called "the 'he, himself' locution"—the locution 'There exists an x such that x believes *himself* to be wise', as contrasted with "There exists an x such that x believes x to be wise." The difficulties are due to the fact that the first locution implies the second and not conversely, thus leaving us with the question "What does the first tell us that the second does not?"

Source: Roderick Chisholm, "A Version of Foundationalism" in Peter French, Howard Wettstein, and Theodore Uehling, eds., *Midwest Studies in Philosophy V: Studies in Epistemology* (University of Minnesota Press, 1980), pp. 543–564. Reprinted with permission of the publisher.

The second locution could be true and the first false in the following situation. I look in the mirror, or look at my hand, and believe with respect to the person that I see that he is wise: I am then an x such that x believes x to be wise. But it may yet be at the same time that I do not believe *myself* to be wise, for I may have a very poor opinion of myself and not realize that *I* am the person I am looking at.

To understand the difference between the two locutions, we have to rethink the nature of believing and of other so-called propositional attitudes. Instead of thinking of these attitudes as involving, in the first instance, a relation between a person and a *proposition,* we think of them as involving a relation between a person and a *property*—a property that the person attributes to himself. If I believe myself to be wise, then I directly attribute the property of wisdom to myself. If I believe *you* to be wise, then there is a certain *other* property which is such that, in directly attributing *that* property to myself, I *indirectly* attribute to you the property of being wise. Suppose, for example, that you are the only person I am talking with. And suppose I (directly) attribute to myself the following property—that of talking with exactly one person and with a person who is a philosopher. Then I indirectly attribute to you the property of being a philosopher. The property I attribute to myself singles you out as the thing to which I bear a certain relation; by directly attributing the one property to me, I indirectly attribute the other property to you.

Thus we begin with the undefined locution 'x directly attributes to y the property of being F'. And we assume that direct attribution is necessarily such that, for every x and y, if x directly attributes a certain property to y, then x is identical with y. Given this undefined locution, we may now define the locution 'x *indirectly attributes* to y the property of being F' as follows: "There is a property H and a relation R of the following sort: (i) x directly attributes H to x; (ii) x bears R to y and only to y; (iii) H is necessarily such that whatever has it bears R to just one thing and to a thing that is F; and (iv) if R logically implies the property of being F, then R is necessarily such that whoever conceives it conceives the property of being F."

So-called *de dicto* believing—the acceptance of propositions—may be viewed as one type of indirect attribution. If I accept a certain proposition, then I indirectly attribute to it the property of being true. (In so doing, I will single it out as the sole thing I am conceiving in a certain way. The proposition, say, that all men are mortal may be the sole thing pertaining to mortality that I am now conceiving.) But we shall assume that whenever I do attribute a property to myself, then I *also* accept a certain proposition. Thus if I attribute wisdom to myself, I will also accept the proposition that someone is wise.[2]

The version of epistemology that follows, then, presupposes this general theory of believing. But everything that I shall say is readily adaptable to the view that the basic form of believing is propositional. Indeed, if that view were true, the following could be considerably simplified.

PRESUPPOSITIONS OF THE THEORY OF EVIDENCE

The problems of the theory of evidence, like all other genuinely philosophical problems, arise when we consider the consequences of certain presuppositions. Each of the presuppositions seems to be inescapable, and yet, when we combine them, they give rise to philosophical perplexity. The perplexity is philosophical in that, it would seem, we cannot resolve it by appeal to the particular sciences. We must rely instead upon our own deliberation and reflection.

What, then, are the presuppositions of "the theory of evidence"? I shall list six such suppositions. In formulating them, I shall use the first person, but I am quite confident, however, that I am speaking for all of us.

(1) There are certain things I know and certain things I do not know. I can give examples of each. Like Moore, I know that this is a hand and that the earth has existed for hundreds of years past. But I do not know whether it will rain here a year from today and I do not know how many people there are now in East Jaffrey. This first presupposition can be put more generally: there are certain things I am justified in believing and certain other things I am not justified in believing.

(2) The distinction between the things I am justified in believing and the things I am not justified in believing need not coincide with the distinction between those of my beliefs that are true and those of my beliefs that are false. In other words, it is quite possible that some of the things I am justified in believing are false and that some of the things I am *not* justified in believing are true. Possibly my senses are deceiving me, but even if they are, I am now justified in believing they are not. And obviously, many of the things I am not justified in believing are true. I cannot *now* say, of course, which of my justified beliefs are false. Perhaps there was a time when people were justified in believing the false proposition that all swans are white. This means that they were not justified in believing the true proposition that some swans are not white.

We may say, of the relation between epistemic justification and truth, what John Maynard Keynes said about the relation between probability and truth: ". . . there is no direct relation between the truth of a proposition and its probability. Probability begins and ends with probability. That a scientific investigation pursued on account of its probability will generally lead to truth, rather than falsehood, is at best only probable."[3]

(3) Yet there *is* a positive relation between the epistemically justified and the true. For one thing, I am justified in believing a given proposition if and only if I am justified in believing that that proposition is *true*. There is still another point about the relation between epistemic justification and truth, but this point is somewhat more difficult to formulate. For the present, we may put it by saying that, if I want to believe what is true and not to believe what is false, then the most reasonable thing for me to do is to believe what is justified and not to believe what is not justified.

(4) Epistemic justification, unlike truth, is capable of degrees. Of the things that we are justified in believing, some are more justified than others. We may say, more generally, that certain attitudes are *more reasonable* on certain occasions than are other attitudes on those occasions. (As we shall see, the concepts of the theory of evidence may be explicated in terms of the undefined epistemic locution. '______ is more reasonable for S at t than ______'.)

(5) Some of the things I know, or am justified in believing, are justified by certain *other* things that I know, or am justified in believing. For example, I know—and am therefore justified in believing—that there were people in this building earlier today. What justifies me in believing this may include the fact that certain people have told me so and that I am justified in believing what they said. And presumably my justification also includes certain general information I have about buildings like this and the communities in which they exist.

(6) Some of the things I am justified in believing are such that by reflection I can *know* that I am justified in believing them; and I can find out just *what,* if anything, justifies me in believing them. Thus Russell once observed: "The degree of credibility attaching to a proposition is itself sometimes a datum. I think we should also hold that the degree of credibility to be attached to a *datum* is sometimes a datum."[4] This will hold for so-called empirical or *a posteriori* beliefs as well as for beliefs that are *a priori*. Hence, the present concept of the justified differs from the concept of the true in another respect. For in the case of what is empirical or

a posteriori, deliberation or reflection is *not* sufficient to enable us to find out whether it is true. It is important to distinguish this final point from the first. According to the first, there are some things I am justified in believing and some things I am not justified in believing. And according to the present point, some of the things I am justified in believing are such that I can find out by reflection that they *are* things I am justified in believing; and similarly for some of the things I am not justified in believing.[5]

It may be noted that these presuppositions of the theory of evidence are analogous, in fundamental respects, to the presuppositions of ethics.

SOME EPISTEMIC CONCEPTS

Traditionally, knowledge may be identified with justified true belief. If, as we have assumed, the basic sense of believing is direct attribution, then there is a kind of knowledge that may be associated with justified true direct attribution. We now consider this knowledge.

The simplest way of setting forth the vocabulary of the theory of evidence, or epistemology, is to take as undefined the locution, '______ is more reasonable than ______ for S at t' (or, alternatively, '______ is epistemically preferable to ______ for S at t'). Epistemically reasonability could be understood in terms of the general requirement to try to have the largest possible set of logically independent beliefs which is such that the true beliefs outnumber the false beliefs. The principles of epistemic preferability are the principles one should follow if one is to fulfill this requirement. (It should be noted that the requirement is so formulated that the requirement to have true beliefs receives greater emphasis than the requirement not to have false beliefs.)

The epistemic locution we have taken as undefined is obviously applicable to propositional acceptance, or *de dicto* belief, where we can say that accepting one proposition is more or less reasonable than accepting another. But its application can readily be extended to direct attribution.

In order to characterize the relevant epistemic concepts in their application to such attribution, we shall introduce the concept of *withholding* the attribution of a property. Consider a person and a property such that (a) the person does *not* directly attribute that property to himself and (b) he does not directly attribute the *negation* of that property to himself: such a person may be said to *withhold* the direct attribution of that property.

Among the general principles of epistemic preferability is the fact that such preferability is transitive and asymmetric. If one attribution, or withholding, is more reasonable for a given subject at a given time than a second, and if the second is more reasonable than a third, then the first is more reasonable than the third. And if one is more reasonable than another, then the other is not more reasonable than the one.

We may also affirm the following principle: If, for a certain subject at a certain time, withholding the direct attribution of a given property is *not* more reasonable than the direct attribution of that property, then the direct attribution of that property *is* more reasonable than the direct attribution of the negation of that property. This principle has its analogue in the following *de dicto* epistemic principle: if withholding a proposition is *not* more reasonable than accepting it, then accepting it is more reasonable than accepting its negation. "If agnosticism is not more reasonable than theism, then theism is more reasonable than atheism."[6]

Given these principles and others, we may formulate definitions of a variety of fundamental epistemic concepts. We could say, for example, that the direct attribution of a given property is epistemically *unacceptable* for a given subject at a given time, provided only that withholding that property is more reasonable for that subject at that time than directly attributing it. In saying that the attitude is "unacceptable," I do not mean that the believer *finds* it unacceptable. I mean something more objective—something that could also be put by saying that the attitude ought not to be taken, or that it is an attitude that it would be unreasonable to take. We could say that an attribution is *counterbalanced* if and only if the direct attribution of that property is no more nor less reasonable than is the direct attribution of the negation of that property.

We may also distinguish several different epistemic levels that the direct attribution of a property may occupy for a given subject at a given time. Thus we have:

having some presumption in its favor;
acceptability;
being beyond reasonable doubt;
being evident;
being certain.

Each of these concepts may be said to provide a sense for the expression 'epistemically justified'—"certainty" constituting the highest degree of epistemic justification and "having some presumption in its favor" the lowest.

A direct attribution of a property could be said to *have some presumption in its favor* provided only that the direct attribution of that property is more reasonable than the direct attribution of its negation. A direct attribution of a property is *acceptable* if it is not unacceptable. A direct attribution of a property could be said to be *beyond reasonable doubt* provided only that the direct attribution of that property is more reasonable than withholding that property.

Ascending to still higher epistemic levels, we may now consider *the evident*—where the evident is thought of as that which distinguishes knowledge from true belief that is not knowledge. We may say that the direct attribution of a property is *evident* if the attribution is beyond reasonable doubt and if it is even *more* reasonable than withholding what is counterbalanced. (We have said that the attribution of a property is counterbalanced provided that the attribution of that property is no more nor less reasonable than is the attribution of its negation.) A counterbalanced attribution would provide a paradigm case of that which it is reasonable to withhold. But we are saying that an evident attribution is even *more* reasonable than is any such withholding. (In thus countenancing the category of the evident, we give sense to the remark that the principles of epistemic preferability give "believing the true" a greater emphasis than "not believing the false." Indeed, one of the principles of epistemic preferability could be put by saying this: It is possible that there are properties P and Q such that P is counterbalanced and attributing Q is more reasonable than withholding the attribution of P.)

Finally there is the concept of objective certainty. The direct attribution of a property may be said to be objectively *certain* for a person provided these conditions hold: the direct attribution of that property is beyond reasonable doubt for that person; and it is at least as reasonable for him as is the direct attribution of any other property. If the attribution of the property of being F is thus certain for a subject, then he may be said to be certain that *he* is F.[7]

These epistemic expressions may be read in another way. For example, if we may say, of the property of being F, that the direct attribution of that property is beyond reasonable doubt for a certain subject x, then we may also say: "It is beyond reasonable doubt for x that *he* is F." And analogously for the other epistemic concepts just defined.

We must take care not to be misled by syntax at this point. The propositional locution 'It is beyond reasonable doubt for x that *he* is F' may tempt one to suppose that there is a certain proposition corresponding to the expression 'he is F' and that this proposition is one which is beyond reasonable doubt for the subject x. But 'It is beyond reasonable for x that he is F' does not imply that there is a proposition corresponding to the expression 'he is F'. In this respect it may be compared with the locution 'He believes himself to be F'. The latter tells us only that he has directly attributed the property of being F to himself; and the former tells us only that, for him, directly attributing that property is more reasonable than withholding it.

The epistemic concepts which thus apply to direct attributions have their analogues which may be applied to propositions.

THE SELF-PRESENTING

Let us introduce the concept of a *self-presenting property*. There are certain properties—many, if not all, of them psychological or "Cartesian"—that may be said to "present themselves" to the subject who has them. One example is feeling sad: another is thinking about a golden mountain; another is believing oneself to be wise; and still another may be suggested by the awkward locution 'is appeared redly to'.

In saying that such properties are "self-presenting," I mean this: (i) they are necessarily such that if a person has them and if he considers the question whether he has them (i.e., if he considers his having them), then *ipso facto* he will directly attribute them to himself; and (ii) they are properties such that we *can* consider our having them *while* we have them. (Without the second clause, we would have to say that such properties as being unconscious are self-presenting.)[8] Feeling sad, for example, is necessarily such that if you do feel sad and if you consider the question *whether* you feel sad, then you will believe yourself to feel sad. Similarly for believing and for other intentional attitudes.

These attitudes include the property of *considering* I have just mentioned. Thus considering the question whether one is sad—considering one's being sad—is itself a property that is self-presenting.

And there are *ways of being appeared to* such that being appeared to in those ways is self-presenting. Thus there is a way of being appeared redly to which is such that if you are appeared redly to in that way, and if you consider your being appeared redly to in that way, then you will attribute to yourself the property of being appeared redly to in that way. We shall return to such ways of being appeared to below.

We may leave open the question whether certain logically necessary properties—for example, being either red or nonred—are self-presenting. If they are *not* self-presenting, then we may say that *all* self-presenting properties are psychological or "Cartesian."

We have said that the direct attribution of a property is objectively *certain* for a person provided these conditions hold: the direct attribution of that property is beyond reasonable doubt for that person; and it is at least as reasonable for him as is the direct attribution of any other property. Let us now consider the relation of such certainty to that which is self-presenting.

It will be noted that I have not *defined* self-presenting properties by reference to certainty. But if we think of certainty as constituting the highest degree of epistemic justification, then we may say that a person's self-presenting properties *are* objects of certainty for that person.

Indeed we may affirm the following "material epistemic principle" pertaining to such certainty:

P1 If the property of being F is self-presenting, then for every x, if (i) x has the property of being F, and if (ii) x considers his being F, then it is certain for x that he then has the property of being F.

If, as I have said, being sad is a self-presenting property, then if you are sad and if you consider the question whether you are sad, it will be certain for you that you are sad. And if considering is also self-presenting and if you consider your considering whether you are sad, then it will be evident to you that you are considering whether you are sad.

Every self-presenting property provides us with an instance of P1. Thus we could say:

For every x, if (i) x has the property of being sad, and if (ii) x considers his being sad, then it is certain for x that he then has the property of being sad.

Our principle illustrates what Alston and Sosa have called the "supervenient" character of epistemic justification; for it tells us how positive epistemic status "is supervenient on a set of non-epistemic facts."[9] Other material epistemic principles that I shall formulate also illustrate such supervenience. (We could say that a normative property G "supervenes upon" a nonnormative property H provided only: H is necessarily such that whatever has it has G, but not necessarily such that whoever attributes it attributes G. A "normative" property—for present purposes—could be said to be any property definable in terms of preferability.) Thus the instance of P1 cited above tells us that being certain that one is sad supervenes upon the property of being both sad and such that one considers one's being sad.

Principle P1 pertains to what we might call "nonpropositional certainty." But we may affirm as a corollary the following principle about propositional certainty: For every x, if it is certain for x that he has the property of being F, then the *proposition* that something is F is one that is empirically certain for x.

To understand principle P1, we should distinguish two closely related concepts—the concept of the *directly evident* and the concept of an *evidence-base.*

The empirical certainty that may thus be yielded by those of our properties that are self-presenting could be said to constitute that which is *directly evident.* When we have such properties, then our direct attributions of them are directly evident. So, too, for the attribution of those properties which are *entailed* by the self-presenting. (One property may be said to "entail" another if it is necessarily such that whoever attributes it attributes the other.) And the propositions that may be said to be entailed by such attributions may also be said to be directly evident.

It will also be convenient to introduce the technical concept of an *evidence-base:* a person's evidence-base at any time will be the set of those properties which are self-presenting to that person at that time or which are entailed by what is thus self-presenting.

Hence a property may be in one's evidence-base without it being directly evident to one that one has that property. For one may *have* that property and yet not *consider* one's having that property.

If, as I believe, there are no first-person propositions, then one's evidence-base cannot be identified with a set of propositions (even though, as I have said, there *are* directly evident propositions). Yet it will be convenient to speak as we would if one's evidence-base *were* a set of propositions. Thus we shall speak of the logical consequences of one's evidence-base: we shall speak of what is consistent with it, of what follows from it, and of the probability relations that it may be bear to hypotheses that refer beyond it. But this way of talking does not commit us to the hypothesis that one's evidence-base is, after all, a set of first-person propositions, for we can avoid it by using obvious circumlocutions.

Thus we may make statements like "My evidence-base *entails* that I have the property of being so-and-so." This means that the set of properties constituting my evidence-base is necessarily such that (i) whoever has them has the property of being so-and-so and (ii) whoever attributes them to himself also attributes to himself the property of being so-and-so. And if my evidence-base thus "entails that I have the property of being so-and-so," then it may also be said to "*contradict* my *not* having the property of being so-and-so."

THE UNITY OF CONSCIOUSNESS AND CERTAINTY

Kant held that the subject is "in a position" to "unite all his representations into a single consciousness."[10] What does it mean to say that the subject is "*in a position* so to unite them"? Perhaps the answer is this: "In order to see that the representations are united, the subject has only to ask himself *whether* they are united." And what is it for the representations to *be* thus united?

I suggest we may formulate the *principle of the unity of consciousness* as another material epistemic principle:

P2 For every x, if (i) it is certain for x that he is F and certain for x that he is G, and if (ii) x considers his being both F and G, then it is certain for x that he is both F and G.

Given what we have said about propositional certainty, we may add that if it is certain for a subject that he is both F and G, then the *proposition* that there is something that is both F and G is one that is certain for him.

The unity of consciousness gives us a means by which we can identify without recourse to a middle term and without appeal to a set of common properties. If there is a property G that is self-presenting to me and if there is a property H that is also self-presenting to me, then, *ipso facto,* I can be certain that I have both G and H. And if I can be certain that I have both G and H, then I can also be certain of the proposition there *is* something having both G and H.

The person's self-presenting properties, then, are such that he can be absolutely certain that they are all had by one and the same thing—namely, himself.

THE UNCONTRADICTED

In the formulation of our first epistemic principle above, we appealed to a certain "justification-making" property—that of being self-presenting—and we defined that property without making use of epistemic terms. Then we were able to say what epistemic status is supervenient upon that property (more exactly, upon that property and the fact that one considers one's *having* that property). I shall now attempt to formulate another such principle.

Let us first try to single out certain things that may be said to have *some presumption in their favor* for our subject at any given time. We have said that the direct attribution of a property has some presumption in its favor for a given subject at a given time provided that the direct attribution of that property is then more reasonable for him than is the direct attribution of its negation.

I suggest now an extremely latitudinarian principle. This is the principle that *anything* we find ourselves believing may be said to have *some* presumption in its favor—*provided* it is not explicitly contradicted by the set of other things that we believe. Hence we may say, more exactly:

P3 For every x, if (i) x directly attributes to himself the property of being F, and if (ii) x being F is not explicitly contradicted by the set of properties that x directly attributes to x, then his being F has some presumption in its favor for x.

The principle may be extended to propositional belief: for every x, if x accepts a proposition that is not explicitly contradicted by any set of propositions accepted by x, then that proposition has some presumption in its favor for x.

One proposition *explicitly* contradicts another provided only that it *entails* the negation of the other. That is to say, the one proposition is necessarily such that (a) if it is true then the negation of the other is true and (b) whoever accepts it accepts the negation of the other. Analogously, two properties may be so related that the one explicitly contradicts the other. Here, too, one may say that the one property entails the negation of the other: the one property is necessarily such that (a) if it is exemplified then the negation of the other is exemplified and (b) whoever attributes it to a thing attributes the negation of the other property to that thing.

I would take the principle just formulated to constitute one of the fundamental principles of the theory of knowledge. Here we follow Carneades who assigned a positive epistemic status to "the uncontradicted."[11] Such a principle may seem overpermissive, epistemically. But any such over-permissiveness can be corrected by reference to a certain subset of these "uncontradicted" attributions; this subset constitutes our next category.

THE EPISTEMICALLY UNSUSPECT

From among those propositions that thus have some presumption in their favor for our subject, we may single out those that are "epistemically unsuspect" or "epistemically in the clear." An attribution may be said to be *epistemically unsuspect,* or *epistemically in the clear,* for any subject, provided only that it is *not disconfirmed* by any set of properties that have some presumption in their favor for him.[12]

We must say something, then, about the relevant concept of confirmation. Confirmation is normally thought of as being a relation between propositions; but it may also be construed as a relation between properties. One property may be such that it *confirms the attribution* of another property; or, to put the matter somewhat differently, one property may be such that it *confirms that whatever has it* has the other property. The relevant relation between properties is analogous to that which holds when one proposition confirms another. Thus the property of being F could be said to *confirm* the property of being G (alternatively, to confirm that whatever has it has the property G), provided only that these conditions hold: For every x, if it is evident for x that he is F, and if everything that is evident for x is entailed by his being F, then it is epistemically acceptable for x that he is G. And analogously for disconfirmation.

For example, my belief that I am in a building with other people is epistemically in the clear for me. This means that those things having some presumption in their favor for me do *not* confirm the attribution of the property of not being in a building with other people.

According to our second material epistemic principle: anything we believe has some presumption in its favor provided it is not contradicted by anything we believe. We may now add a third material principle:

P4 For every x, whatever is epistemically in the clear for x is also epistemically acceptable for x.

Additional epistemic principles may be formulated by reference to these categories.

THE EVIDENTIAL STATUS OF BEING APPEARED TO

There are ways of being appeared to which are such that being appeared to in those ways tends to make evident the nature of what it is that appears to one in those ways. In other words, there are certain ways of appearing and certain properties which are so related that being appeared to in one of those ways tends to make it evident that one is appeared to by something having one of those properties.

The requisite sense of 'appear' is both causal and psychological: the object of perception, as a stimulus object acting upon a person's sense organs, causes the person to have certain sensations—or, as I prefer to put it, the object of perception causes the person to sense, or *to be appeared to,* in a certain way. One should note the distinction between the two locutions 'x *appears to* y in a certain way' and 'y is *appeared to* in a certain way'. The first implies the second but not conversely. The first, unlike the second, implies something about an external stimulus object and what it causes. In cases of phantasy and hallucination the second could be true and the first false.

Here we will cite a further principle:

P5 For every x, being appeared to in a way that is self-presenting tends to make it evident for x that there is something that is appearing in that way to him.

We have put our principle briefly by making use of the concept expressed by 'tends to make evident'. We may say that the property being F *tends to make evident* the attribution of the property being G provided that these conditions hold: being F is necessarily such that, for every x, if x is F and if his being G is epistemically in the clear for x, then it is evident for x that he is G. If being F does thus tend to make evident the attribution of being G and if in fact his being G *is* epistemically in the clear for x, then we may say, more simply, that being F *makes evident* for x that he is G.

An instance of our principle would be:

> Being appeared redly to tends to make it evident that something is appearing red.

The expression 'being appeared redly to', in our example, has what I have called its *non-comparative* sense in this use.[13] 'Being appeared redly to', in this use, refers to a property that is self-presenting in the sense that we have defined.

Let us now consider an important point about principle P5; this pertains to our distinction above between that which may be said to be in one's *evidence-base* and that which may be said to be *directly evident* to one. We noted that a property could be in a person's evidence-base without it being directly evident to that person that he has that property; this might be the case if the person did not *consider* his having that property. Principle P5 pertains *not* to the directly evident but to what is in one's evidence-base. Hence P1 could be fulfilled even if the subject does not consider the ways he is being appeared to. Thus Thomas Reid said that the appearance is likely to "hide itself" behind the shadow of the object perceived and to "pass through the mind unobserved."[14]

PERCEPTUAL EVIDENCE

What I would call the primary sense of perception may be expressed by saying "The property of being F is such that x *perceives* y to have it." This sense of perception may be defined as follows: "y is F; y appears to x in a manner that tends to make it evident that one is appeared to in that way by something that is F; and x directly attributes to himself the property of being appeared to in that way by something that is F." When 'perceive' is taken in this way, the expressions that may replace the letter "F" are restricted to expressions for certain sensible characteristics.

If I perceive a thing to be red, then the way the thing appears to me makes evident to me that the thing that appears to me in that way is a thing that is red. In other words, the way of appearing is necessarily such that if a thing appears to a person in that way, and if his being appeared to by something that is red is epistemically in the clear for him, then such attribution is also evident for him.

Perception, however, is not normally restricted to the attribution of such sensible characteristics. Hence we may introduce a secondary sense of perception, which could be expressed by saying "The property of being F is such that x *perceptually takes* there to be something that has it." This concept may be defined by saying: "x is appeared to in a way such that he directly attributes to himself the property of perceiving the thing that is appearing to him in that way to have the property of being F."[15]

We may now form further principles of evidence by referring to this concept of perceptual taking.

A simple form of such a principle would be illustrated by the following: If a person perceptually takes there to be a sheep in the field before him, then it is *evident* to him that there is a sheep in the field before him. Thus Meinong held, in effect, that the fact that we *think* we perceive confers "presumptive evidence (*Vermutungsevidenz*)" upon the proposition or state of affairs that is the object of our ostensible perception.[16] And H. H. Price has said that the fact that we "perceptually accept" a certain proposition is sufficient to confer some positive epistemic status on that proposition. Price put this point as follows: "We want to be able to say: the fact that a material thing is perceptually presented to the mind is *prima facie evidence* of the thing's existence and of its really having that sort of surface which it ostensibly has: or, again, that there is *some presumption in favor of* this, not merely in the sense that we do as a matter of fact presume it (which of course we do) but in the sense that we are entitled to do so."[17] But such principles, as they stand, are somewhat over-permissive, epistemically.

Using the concept of the "epistemically unsuspect," or of that which is "epistemically in the clear," we might say that certain perceptual propositions are evident—*provided* they are epistemically unsuspect. In this way we could formulate a principle that is less permissive. Thus we might say:

P6 For every subject x, if (i) x perceptually takes there to be something that is F, and if (ii) his perceiving something that is F is epistemically in the clear for x, then it is evident for x that he perceives something that is F.

Let us note that the first part of the antecedent ('x perceptually takes there to be something that is F'.) pertains to what is self-presenting and that the second part of the antecedent ('his perceiving something that is F is epistemically in the clear') pertains to the epistemically unsuspect. And it should be noted further that the final clause reads: 'it is evident for x that he *perceives something that is F*'. (One can perceive something that is F without thereby perceiving the thing *to be* F—without thereby perceiving *that* the thing is F. Thus if the person that I see is a thief, then I perceive something that is a thief. But even if I know that he is a thief, it is not likely that I *perceive* him to be a thief.)

The emphasis that we have placed in principle P6 upon that which is epistemically unsuspect, or in the clear, has applications for the so-called KK principle—the principle according to which, if one knows, then one knows that one knows. For our ordinary perceptual beliefs will not be instances of *knowing* unless they are epistemically unsuspect. But normally, whether or not such beliefs *are* epistemically unsuspect, they will not be known to be such.

It should be noted that our principle P6 states certain conditions under which we may say of a person that it is evident to him that he perceives something that is F. It does not enable us to say, *de re,* of that person and a certain external object y, that it is evident to the person that he perceives that particular thing y to be F. It may be self-presenting for x that he is *being appeared to* in a certain way (that he *senses* in a certain way). But it cannot be self-presenting to him that there is something that *is appearing* to him in that way (i.e., it cannot be self-presenting to him that an external stimulus object *causes* him to sense in that way). By means of what principle, then, can the person pass from a way of appearing to a particular physical thing that "transcends" that way of appearing? We want, then, a principle that says of two different things, x and y, that it is evident to x that y is F.

The following is a possibility:

P7 For every x and y, if (i) perceives y to be F, and if (ii) it is evident for x that he perceives something that is F, then y is such that it is evident to x that it is F.

This perceptual principle introduces the *de re* epistemic locution: "y is such that it is evident to x that it is F." Therefore, the principle is, in a certain respect, less pure than the preceding principle, P6. For, in theory at least, one can ascertain merely by reflection whether or not the antecedent condition of P6 obtains. But the present principle, P7, is not applicable unless there is an external physical thing that is causing the subject to sense in the way that he does. And this fact cannot be ascertained merely by reflection. It cannot be self-presenting to the subject that there *is* a certain thing that he perceives to be F; it can be self-presenting only that perceptually takes there to be something that is F. Hence we might call P7 a "quasi-epistemic principle."

OTHER EPISTEMIC PRINCIPLES

The perceptual principles I have tried to formulate have their analogues for memory and also, I believe, for "the problem of other minds," but I shall not attempt to formulate these additional principles here. I shall cite only one additional principle. This is a *coherence* principle, or *concurrence* principle, telling us how the members of a concurrent set of beliefs can lend each other support.

Let us say that a *concurrent* set of properties is a set of properties of the following sort: it is a set of two or more properties each of which is such that the conjunction of all the others tends to confirm it and is logically independent of it.

Our coherence principle is this:

P8 Any concurrent set of properties, each of which is acceptable for S, is such that each of its members is beyond reasonable doubt for S.

This principle has its obvious analogue for propositions.

IS THIS FOUNDATIONALISM?

In order to see the sense in which the present view may be said to be a version of "foundationalism," let us now list the eight epistemic principles we have formulated:

P1 If the property of being F is self-presenting, then for every x, if (i) x has the property of being F, and if (ii) x considers his being F, then it is certain for x that he has the property of being F.

P2 For every x, if (i) it is certain for x that he is F and certain for x that he is G, and if (ii) x considers his being both F and G, then it is certain for x that he is both F and G.

P3 For every x, if (i) x directly attributes to himself the property of being F, and if (ii) x being F is not explicitly contradicted by the set of properties that x directly attributes to x, then his being F has some presumption in its favor for x.

P4 For every x, whatever is epistemically in the clear for x is also acceptable for x.

P5 For every x, being appeared to in a way that is self-presenting tends to make it evident for x that there is something that is appearing in that way to him.

P6 For every x, if (i) x perceptually takes there to be something that is F, and if (ii) his perceiving something that is F is epistemically in the clear for x, then it is evident for x that he perceives something that is F.

P7 For every x and y, if (i) x perceives y to be F, and if (ii) it is evident for x that he perceives something that is F, then y is such that it is evident to x that it is F.

P8 Any concurrent set of properties, each of which is acceptable for S, is such that each of its members is beyond reasonable doubt for S.

We may now consider certain philosophical questions.

(1) Are there *self-justifiers*—attributions or propositions that may be said to constitute their own justification?

The self-presenting would seem to be the closest we can come to that which constitutes its own justification. The fact that one has a self-presenting property does not itself make it evident that one has that property. But the fact that one has it and also *considers* one's having it does make it evident that one has it. Self-presenting properties, moreover, are distinctive in the following respect: it can be evident to one that one has the property even though one has no non-deductive—no merely inductive—grounds for attributing that property to oneself. In other words, a self-presenting property is a property such that it can be *evident* that one has it even though the only things that *make* it evident that one has it are things that entail it.

If we look now to our principles, we will see that in our formulations of P1, P3, P5, and P6, antecedent (i) pertains to what is self-presenting. (But this is not true of P2 or P7.) And in our formulations of P1 and P2, antecedent (ii) pertains to what is self-presenting.

(2) Is there a sense in which the self-presenting may be said to justify that which is not directly evident? Principles P5 and P6 state conditions under which the self-presenting may make evident certain attributions that are not directly evident. For in the case of each of these principles, antecedent (i) refers to what is self-presenting and the consequent refers to something that is not directly evident. But application of the principles does not require that it be *evident* to the subject that he has the self-presenting properties in question—for they do not require that he *consider* his having them. It is the self-presenting, then, and not the directly evident, that may be said to justify that which is not directly evident.

(3) Is everything that is epistemically justified justified *by* that which is self-presenting? Or is there a sense in which something other than that which is self-presenting can be said to serve as a ground or foundation of our knowledge?

Examination of our principles makes it clear that, according to them, our knowledge is not a function *merely* of what is self-presenting. Principle P3 refers to what I have called "the uncontradicted"; this involves the logical relations that one attribution may bear to others. If these relations obtain, the fact that they obtain will not be self-presenting. But, I would say, one can always ascertain by reflection whether or not they obtain. Similar observations hold of "the epistemically unsuspect" (that which is "epistemically in the clear"), referred to in principles P4, P5, and P6, and of the type of "concurrence" referred to in P8.

But the *de re* principle, P7, is an exception. For antecedent (i)—'if x perceives y to be F'—is not something that can be ascertained merely by reflection. The requisite sense of 'perceives', as we have defined it, involves a causal relation between the object of perception and the perceiver.

And one cannot determine by reflection whether or not such a relation obtains. Hence I suggested that P7 might be called a "quasi-epistemic principle."

I wrote in the second edition of *Theory of Knowledge:*

> What, then, of our justification for those propositions that are indirectly evident? We might say that they are justified in three different ways. (1) They may be justified by certain relations that they bear to what is *directly* evident. (2) They may be justified by certain relations that they bear to *each other*. And (3) they may be justified *by their own nature,* so to speak, and quite independently of the relations that they bear to anything else.[18]

I would now replace 'the directly evident' above by 'the self-presenting'; otherwise, I would say, the passage describes the present version of foundationalism.

(4) Can we say that, according to our principles, the self-presenting constitutes the *foundation* or *grounds* we have for the other things we know?

We must decide, of course, how the technical term 'foundation', or 'grounds', is to be understood. We could say that a self-presenting property constitutes the *basis* for an attribution provided that the subject has that property and provided that, if he has it and if the attribution is epistemically in the clear, then the attribution is evident. But this concept of a basis is a very broad one. If a self-presenting property is thus a basis for an attribution, then any wider self-presenting property which entailed that property would also be a basis for that attribution. For example, anything that is a basis for attributing the property expressed by "being standing and such that the President is in Washington" would be, in this sense, a basis for attributing the property of standing. But it would not constitute the *ground* or *foundation* for that attribution. A ground, then, would be a special type of basis.

Let us define "The property of being G constitutes S's *grounds* for the attribution of being H" by saying: The property of being G is a basis of the attribution of being H for x, and it is entailed by everything that is a basis of the attribution of being H for x. If we take 'grounds' in this way, then we may say that, according to our principles, the self-presenting does constitute the subject's grounds for what he knows. And, moreover, the principles do not specify any type of grounds other than that which is self-presenting.

These considerations also apply to *a priori* knowledge. Thus we might define an *axiom* as a proposition that is necessarily such that (i) it is true and (ii) whoever conceives it accepts it. Then we could affirm a principle analogous to P1: "If the proposition that p is an axiom, then, for every x, if x conceives the proposition that p, it is certain for x that p." (Here 'p' is schematic, replaceable by any English sentence.) Then we could say that that self-presenting state, which is the subject conceiving the proposition that p, is the ground for his knowledge that p.

"You are saying that logic and mathematics are grounded in certain *subjective* states. That is psychologism of the worst sort!" We are saying only that even our knowledge of logic and mathematics begins with experience. We are not saying that logic and mathematics are about that which is subjective. The objection confuses the *ratio essendi* with the *ratio cognoscendi*. "But how could a proposition be an axiom if it is grounded on some other proposition?" Saying that a proposition is an axiom for a given person does not imply that that person does not ground the proposition on something else; it implies only that he does not ground it upon any other *necessary* proposition.[19]

(5) Are there any *unjustified justifiers*—justifiers that are not themselves justified?

To the extent that the self-presenting serves as a foundation or ground for other knowledge, it could be said to *justify* what is thus known.

But these self-presenting properties may serve as justifiers even when one does not *consider* one's having these properties. Hence they may serve as justifiers even when it is not evident to one that one has them. And so in this sense, the self-presenting may be a justifier that is not itself justified.[20]

OTHER SENSES OF JUSTIFICATION

The issues in theory of knowledge between "foundationalists" and "non-foundationalists," so far as I have been able to ascertain, are mostly the result of misunderstanding. Foundationalism, I believe it is agreed, is a theory about the justification of belief, but apparently those who accept it take 'justify' in one way and those who reject it take 'justify' in another way.[21]

The foundationalists take 'justify' in the *epistemic* sense. This interpretation of justification is illustrated, at least, by the concepts of epistemic perferability I have tried to explicate. And the non-foundationalists take 'justify' in one or another of several non-epistemic senses—some of which seem to presuppose some *further* sense of 'justify' and some of which do not. From the fact that foundationalism is false, if 'justify' is taken in one of its non-epistemic senses, it does not follow, of course, that it is false if 'justify' is taken in its epistemic sense.

If you present one account of justification and I present another, is the difference between us merely verbal? Not if our respective accounts are intended to be adequate to the same pre-analytic data. And there is a set of data to which most versions of foundationalism and non-foundationalism are intended to be adequate. Such data are involved in the fact that there is a valid distinction between knowledge and true belief that is not knowledge.

The term 'justification', in its pre-analytic sense, may be thought of as being the name for that which distinguishes knowledge from true belief that is not knowledge. The terms 'warrant' and 'grounds' are other possibilities, as are variants of 'evidence' and 'evident'. Other possibilities are certain broader concepts in terms of which our ordinary evidential concepts can be defined, such as "credible" or "reasonable." Thus I would prefer to make use of terms that can be defined by reference to the comparative concept, "more reasonable than." But for the present let us use 'justification'. (In considering these questions, we will do well to keep in mind that such words as 'perceive' and 'remember' are generally used in a way that implies knowing and therefore that there may be the danger of circularity if we attempt to explicate knowing in terms of perceiving and remembering.)

We presuppose, then, that there *is* a valid distinction between knowledge and true belief that is not knowledge. In other words, we presuppose that it is possible to have true belief with respect to a certain topic without having knowledge with respect to that topic. Let us cite certain examples of this distinction. For then we will be able to ask whether various proposed analyses of the distinction are adequate to the examples. I shall describe three different cases.

(a) We contrast the astronomer who believes that there are at least nine planets with the man who arrived at that belief solely on the basis of an examination of what he took the tea leaves to say.

(b) Consider a case of the sort discussed by Brentano. I happen to have a headache and you believe, solely on the basis of an exaggerated pessimism, that someone in the room has a headache; then you have mere true belief with respect to a topic concerning which I have knowledge.

(c) The possible cases need not be restricted to empirical knowledge. Suppose I believe, solely on hearsay, that a certain mathematical or logical theorem is true. And suppose the theorem is one that certain mathematicians or logicians have *proved* to be true. Then I will have true belief with respect to the theorem and they will have knowledge.

Let us, then, consider other possible theories about the *nature* of the justification in question, about the nature of that which is essential to the distinction between knowledge and true belief that is not knowledge.

Let us consider, then, some of those *other* concepts that are thought to be adequate to our pre-analytic data about justification.

(1) Sometimes it is said: "A belief is justified if and only if it is arrived at by a *reliable* method." The word 'reliable' may then be characterized either by reference to truth alone or by reference to some other sense of justification. If we take it the first way, then we could form a simple version of the "reliable method" theory by saying: "A belief is justified if and only if the method by means of which it was arrived at is, more often than not, a method that leads to beliefs that are true and not to beliefs that are false."

Given such a simple interpretation of 'reliable method', it is very difficult to distinguish this sense of 'justify' from that which might be put by saying that a belief is justified if and only if it is true. (Such a theory, of course, would not be adequate to our three examples.) If I *have* arrived at a true belief, however accidentally, then I have followed a method which, on this occasion, *has* led to a true belief. Consider, once again, our three examples above of true belief that is not knowledge. It does not take much ingenuity to formulate, for each case, a general procedure that has been followed in that case and which is such that, whenever it is followed, it leads to true belief. We need mention only our first case: the man who decided that there were nine planets as a result of reading the tea leaves in a certain way. If this reading took place, say, on a Friday afternoon at 2:17 and if, previously and subsequently, the man never consulted the tea leaves about the number of planets at that hour on a Friday afternoon, then he followed a procedure that always leads to truth—one he could describe by saying, "Whenever I want to find out anything about the number of planets, I should consult the tea leaves at 2:17 on a Friday afternoon."

The simple version of the "reliability theory," then, does not enable us to distinguish knowledge from true belief that is not knowledge. Hence one must place certain restrictions upon the simple formula I have proposed. It remains to be seen whether this can be done without importing some other sense of justification.[22]

(2) 'Justify' might be taken to refer to the procedures of decision theory, or game theory. In applying such procedures one may reach conclusions of the following sort: "A course of action is justified (or reasonable) for a particular individual at a particular time if and only if, in relation to the goals of that individual at that time and in relation to the evidence he has, it is more reasonable for him to pursue that course of action than not to pursue it." How would we apply such procedures to the acquisition of belief? One might say: "A belief is justified for a particular individual at a certain time if and only if, in relation to the goals of that individual at that time and to the *evidence* he then has, it is more reasonable for him to have that belief than not to have it." Here, once again, we have a sense of 'justify' that presupposes the epistemic sense, for it refers to the *evidence* that the individual has.

"But might not this evidence in turn be characterized by reference to the procedures of decision theory?" The answer is that the kind of regress that would then be involved will not begin in the right place. ("If there are recordings of musical performances, then there must have been at least one actual performance at some time or other." "No; for all our recordings were made from *other* recordings of musical performances.")

"It is not necessary that we characterize decision procedure epistemically. We can say that the subject should base his beliefs not on the *evidence* that he has but merely on the *other beliefs* that he has." We can, of course, formulate decision theory in such a way. But how would reference to such procedures help us to analyze our three examples?[23]

(3) Sometimes justification is characterized by reference to "science" as in: "A belief is justified if and only if it has as its object one of the statements of science." This says both too much and too little, for it is inadequate both to our first example as well as to our second example. Consider first the case involving the planets. The man who followed the tea leaves *did* accept one of the statements of science—namely, that there are nine planets. Consider next the second example who knew that he had a headache and therefore that there is someone in the room who has a headache. In what sense was the object of his belief one of the "statements of science"?

If, now, we say, "A belief is justified for a given person if and only if he arrives at it by means of a scientific procedure," then we are faced once again with the difficulties we encountered with "the reliable method" theory.

(4) Sometimes, it would seem, justification is characterized in terms of *coherence:* a belief or a statement is said to be justified in this sense provided it coheres in a certain way with certain other beliefs or statements. One may ask "In what ways?" and, more important, "With *what* other beliefs or statements?" The answer, once again, would seem to presuppose some further sense of justification. Thus I have formulated a coherence principle in P8 above, but that principle presupposes applications of our basic epistemic concept. What would be an alternative to such a principle? Here, too, programs have been formulated, but not with such detail that we can apply any of them to our present problem.[24]

(5) In recent years, it has also been contended that a belief or a statement is justified provided only it has a certain *explanatory* power.[25] But it would seem to be impossible to characterize the requisite sense of *explanation* without presupposing some other sense of justification. Normally, a hypothesis is not said to be an explanation for a particular formula unless the hypothesis has *some* positive epistemic status—unless, say, it has some presumption in its favor: ". . . the acceptability of an explanation must be assessed on the basis of the degree to which the explanans as a whole is supported by factual evidence."[26] Moreover, if the suggestion is to be applied to our three examples, then, presumably, we will need an explication, not merely of the logical locution 'E explains O', but of the relativized locution 'E explains O for S'.[27] How, then, are we to characterize the relativized locution? We will be back where we started if we say merely "S has an explanation for O." Suppose E explains O, in the logical sense of 'explains'. And suppose S has true belief, but not knowledge, about E and O. Will he then "have an explanation" for O? In *one* sense of 'have an explanation', the tea leaf man who believes that there are nine planets "has an explanation" for many astronomical phenomena. But this sense of 'have an explanation' has no relevance to the distinction between knowledge and true belief that is not knowledge.

It would seem, once again, that we are considering a theory that needs to be worked out.

(6) 'Justify' may be taken in a strictly ethical sense, as when one says "I have a right to believe whatever I want, provided no one else is affected by my beliefs." This ethical sense of 'justify' does not seem to be relevant to the issues that separate foundationalists and nonfoundationalists.[28] Certainly this concept does not help us in any obvious way with our three examples of the distinction between knowledge and true belief that is not knowledge. But I shall leave open the possibility that the epistemic sense of justification can be explicated in purely ethical terms.

NOTES

1. These critics include William P. Alston, Bruce Aune, Fred Dretske, Herbert Heidelberger, Ernest Sosa, and Timm Triplet.
2. I assume, however, that there are no "first-person propositions"—e.g., that although the first-person sentence "I am wise" expresses my direct attribution of wisdom to myself,

it does not express a proposition. My reasons for holding this are set forth in detail in: "The Self and the World," *Proceedings of the Second International Wittgenstein Symposium* (Vienna, 1978), pp. 407–10; "Objects and Persons," *Grazer philosophische Studien* 5 (1979); "The Indirect Reflexive," in *Intention and Intentionality,* ed. C. Diamond and J. Teichman (Sussex, 1979), pp. 39–53; and "The Logic of Believing," *Pacific Philosophical Quarterly* 1 (1980).

3. John Maynard Keynes, *A Treatise on Probability* (London, 1952), p. 322.
4. Bertrand Russell, *Human Knowledge: Its Scope and Limits* (New York, 1948), pp. 381–82.
5. Compare C. I. Lewis, *The Ground and Nature of the Right* (New York, 1955), chap. 2; and James Van Cleve, "Foundationalism, Epistemic Principles, and the Cartesian Circle," *The Philosophical Review* 88 (1979): 55–91, especially pp. 84–91.
6. Other principles are set forth in the second edition of my book *Theory of Knowledge* (Englewood Cliffs, N.J., 1976), pp. 138–39. The principles are there restricted to *de dicto* form; but their analogues for direct attribution are obvious.
7. To do justice to the Gettier problem, we should introduce the concept of the "non-defectively evident"—a category falling between the evident and the certain. The expression "It is non-defectively evident for x that he is F" may be spelled out as: "Either (a) it is certain for x that he is F, or (b) the property of being F is entailed by a conjunction of properties each having for x a basis that is not a basis of any false attribution for x." The relevant concept of "a basis" is defined below.
8. Shall we also say that these properties are necessarily such that a person attributes them to himself only if he has them?
9. Compare William P. Alston, "Two Types of Foundationalism," *Journal of Philosophy* 73 (1976): 165–85, especially p. 170; and Ernest Sosa, "The Foundations of Foundationalism," forthcoming in *Nous.*
10. See the *Critique of Pure Reason,* A98–130, A345–49, B131–38.
11. Compare *Sextus Empiricus,* vol. II, Loeb Classical Library (London, 1933), p. 95; "Against the Logicians," vol. I, pp. 176–77.
12. Compare the following definition proposed by John Pollock: "'p is prima facie justified for S' means: 'It is necessarily true that if S believes (or were to believe) that P, and S has no reason for thinking that it is false that P, then S is (or would be) justified in believing that P.'" John Pollock, *Knowledge and Justification* (Princeton, N.J., 1972), p. 30.
13. See the chapter "Three Uses of Appear Words," in my book *Perceiving: A Philosophical Study* (Ithaca, N.Y., 1957), pp. 43–53; the distinction is further defended in "Comments and Replies," *Philosophia* 7 (1978): 599–602.
14. Thomas Reid, *An Inquiry into the Human Mind,* chap. V, sections 2 and 8.
15. Suppose a person thus assumes he is being appeared to by something that is a philosopher; and suppose further the assumption is correct. Then he believes himself to be perceiving something to be a philosopher—where 'perceive' must now be understood in its primary sense. Since the primary sense of "perceive" is restricted to the apprehension of sensible characteristics, shall we say that, strictly speaking, the person's "perceptual taking" is false? I think that we should.
16. See A. Meinong, *Gesamtausgabe,* vol. V (Graz, 1973), pp. 398–404.
17. H. H. Price, *Perception* (New York, 1935), p. 185.
18. Chisholm, *Theory of Knowledge,* 2nd ed., p. 63.
19. Compare Franz Brentano, *Die Lehre vom richtigen Urteil* (Hamburg, 1979), p. 168.
20. Hence the classification of types of foundationalism proposed by Pastin ("modest," "radical") should be expanded. See Mark Pastin. "Modest Foundationalism and Self-Warrant," in *Essays on Knowledge and Justification,* ed. G. Pappas and M. Swain (Ithaca, N.Y., 1978), pp. 279–88.
21. This point is recognized by Frederick L. Will in *Induction and Justification* (Ithaca, N.Y., 1974), part II; compare Michael Williams in *Groundless Belief* (Oxford, 1977), p. 115.

22. See Alvin Goldman, "Discrimination and Perceptual Knowledge," in *Essays on Knowledge and Justification,* pp. 120–45. Goldman attempts to develop the "reliability" theory for perceptual knowledge; hence what he says is not strictly applicable to our three examples above. And I think he would concede, moreover, that he has set forth a program rather than a finished theory, for he makes use of the undefined expression 'S's propensity to form an F-belief as a result of percept P has an *appropriate* genesis' (p. 142, my italics). Compare Fred Dretske, *Seeing and Knowing* (London, 1969), chap. 2, and "Conclusive Reasons," in *Australasian Journal of Philosophy* 48 (1971):1–22. Compare James van Cleve's criticism of "naturalistic" theories of epistemic justification in "Foundationalism, Epistemic Principles, and the Cartesian Circle," section X.
23. One could, of course, make use of a principle such as our P3 and then compensate for its over-permissiveness by making certain further *epistemic* stipulations. Compare Keith Lehrer, *Knowledge* (Oxford, 1974), chap. 6. I believe that Lehrer does not intend his theory to be adequate to the type of example I have cited; but if this is so, then the theory should not be thought of as an alternative to the present theory.
24. Compare Lehrer, *Knowledge,* chap. 8, and Nicholas Rescher, *The Coherence Theory of Truth* (Oxford, 1973), chap. 13. The theories proposed by these authors are not readily applicable to our three cases.
25. Compare James Cornman, "Foundational versus Nonfoundational Theories of Empirical Justification," in *Essays on Knowledge and Justification,* pp. 229–52.
26. The quotation is from Jaegwon Kim's article "Explanation in Science," in *Encyclopedia of Philosophy,* ed. Paul Edwards (New York, 1967), vol. III, pp. 159–63; the quotation is from p. 161. Kim also cites additional "epistemic conditions" which must be fulfilled if a theory or hypothesis is to serve as an explanation; one of these is "the requirement of total evidence" (p. 161). Compare Lehrer, *Knowledge,* chap. 5.
27. Thus Cornman, in the article referred to in note 25, makes use of the undefined expression 'x explains y', but he does not introduce 'x explains y for S'.
28. For a definitive study of the relations between the epistemic and ethical senses of "justify," or "warrant," see Roderick Firth, "Are Epistemic Concepts Reducible to Ethical Concepts?" in *Values and Morals,* ed. A. Goldman and J. Kim (Dordrecht, 1978), pp. 215–29.

A Coherence Theory of Truth and Knowledge

DONALD DAVIDSON

In this paper I defend what may as well be called a coherence theory of truth and knowledge. The theory I defend is not in competition with a correspondence theory, but depends for its defense on an argument that purports to show that coherence yields correspondence.

The importance of the theme is obvious. If coherence is a test of truth, there is a direct connection with epistemology, for we have reason to believe many of our beliefs cohere with many others, and in that case we have reason to believe many of our beliefs are true. When the beliefs are true, then the primary conditions for knowledge would seem to be satisfied.

Someone might try to defend a coherence theory of truth without defending a coherence theory of knowledge, perhaps on the ground that the holder of a coherent set of beliefs might lack a reason to believe his beliefs coherent. This is not likely, but it may be that someone, though he has true beliefs, and good reasons for holding them, does not appreciate the relevance of reason to belief. Such a one may best be viewed as having knowledge he does not know he has: he thinks he is a skeptic. In a word, he is a philosopher.

Setting aside aberrant cases, what brings truth and knowledge together is meaning. If meanings are given by objective truth conditions there is a question how we can know that the conditions are satisfied, for this would appear to require a confrontation between what we believe and reality; and the idea of such a confrontation is absurd. But if coherence is a test of truth, then coherence is a test for judging that objective truth conditions are satisfied, and we no longer need to explain meaning on the basis of possible confrontation. My slogan is: correspondence without confrontation. Given a correct epistemology, we can be realists in all

Source: Donald Davidson, "A Coherence Theory of Truth and Knowledge" in *Truth and Interpretation: Perspectives on the Philosophy of Donald Davidson,* ed. E. Lepore, Oxford: Basil Blackwell, 1986, pp. 307–319. Reprinted with permission of the author.

departments. We can accept objective truth conditions as the key to meaning, a realist view of truth, and we can insist that knowledge is of an objective world independent of our thought or language.

Since there is not, as far as I know, a theory that deserves to be called 'the' coherence theory, let me characterize the sort of view I want to defend. It is obvious that not every consistent set of interpreted sentences contains only true sentences, since one such set might contain just the consistent sentence *S* and another just the negation of *S*. And adding more sentences, while maintaining consistency, will not help. We can imagine endless state-descriptions—maximal consistent descriptions—which do not describe our world.

My coherence theory concerns beliefs, or sentences held true by someone who understands them. I do not want to say, at this point, that every possible coherent set of beliefs is true (or contains mostly true beliefs). I shy away from this because it is so unclear what is possible. At one extreme, it might be held that the range of possible maximal sets of beliefs is as wide as the range of possible maximal sets of sentences, and then there would be no point to insisting that a defensible coherence theory concerns beliefs and not propositions or sentences. But there are other ways of conceiving what it is possible to believe which would justify saying not only that all actual coherent belief systems are largely correct but that all possible ones are also. The difference between the two notions of what it is possible to believe depends on what we suppose about the nature of belief, its interpretation, its causes, its holders, and its patterns. Beliefs for me are states of people with intentions, desires, sense organs; they are states that are caused by, and cause, events inside and outside the bodies of their entertainers. But even given all these constraints, there are many things people do believe, and many more that they could. For all such cases, the coherence theory applies.

Of course some beliefs are false. Much of the point of the concept of belief is the potential gap it introduces between what is held to be true and what is true. So mere coherence, no matter how strongly coherence is plausibly defined, cannot guarantee that what is believed is so. All that a coherence theory can maintain is that most of the beliefs in a coherent total set of beliefs are true.

This way of stating the position can at best be taken as a hint, since there is probably no useful way to count beliefs, and so no clear meaning to the idea that most of a person's beliefs are true. A somewhat better way to put the point is to say there is a presumption in favor of the truth of a belief that coheres with a significant mass of belief. Every belief in a coherent total set of beliefs is justified in the light of this presumption, much as every intentional action taken by a rational agent (one whose choices, beliefs and desires cohere in the sense of Bayesian decision theory) is justified. So to repeat, if knowledge is justified true belief, then it would seem that all the true beliefs of a consistent believer constitute knowledge. This conclusion, though too vague and hasty to be right, contains an important core of truth, as I shall argue. Meanwhile I merely note the many problems asking for treatment: what exactly does coherence demand? How much of inductive practice should be included, how much of the true theory (if there is one) of evidential support must be in there? Since no person has a completely consistent body of convictions, coherence with *which* beliefs creates a presumption of truth? Some of these problems will be put in better perspective as I go along.

It should be clear that I do not hope to define truth in terms of coherence and belief. Truth is beautifully transparent compared to belief and coherence, and I take it as primitive. Truth, as applied to utterances of sentences, shows the disquotational feature enshrined in Tarski's Convention T, and that is enough to fix its domain of application. Relative to a language or a speaker, of course, so there is more to truth then Convention T; there is whatever carries over from language to language or speaker to speaker. What Convention T, and the trite sentences it declares true, like "'Grass is green' spoken by an English speaker, is true if and only if grass is green," reveal is that the truth of an utterance depends on just two things: what the words as spoken mean, and how the world is arranged. There is no further relativism to a conceptual scheme, a way of viewing things, a perspective. Two interpreters, as unlike in culture, language and point of view as you please, can disagree over whether an utterance is true, but only if they differ on how things are in the world they share, or what the utterance means.

I think we can draw two conclusions from these simple reflections. First, truth is correspondence with the way things are. (There is no straightforward and non-misleading way to state this; to get things right, a detour is necessary through the concept of satisfaction in terms of which truth is characterized.[1] So if a coherence theory of truth is acceptable, it must be consistent with a correspondence theory. Second, a theory of knowledge that allows that we can know the truth must be a non-relativized, non-internal form of realism. So if a coherence theory of knowledge is acceptable, it must be consistent with such a form of realism. My form of realism seems to be neither Hilary Putnam's internal realism nor his metaphysical realism.[2] It is not internal realism because internal realism makes truth relative to a scheme, and this is an idea I do not think is intelligible.[3] A major reason, in fact, for accepting a coherence theory is the unintelligibility of the dualism of a conceptual scheme and a 'world' waiting to be coped with. But my realism is certainly not Putnam's metaphysical realism, for *it* is characterized by being 'radically non-epistemic', which implies that all our best researched and established thoughts and theories may be false. I think the independence of belief and truth requires only that *each* of our beliefs may be false. But of course a coherence theory cannot allow that all of them can be wrong.

But why not? Perhaps it is obvious that the coherence of a belief with a substantial body of belief enhances its chance of being true, provided there is reason to suppose the body of belief is true, or largely so. But how can coherence alone supply grounds for belief? Mayhap the best we can do to justify one belief is to appeal to other beliefs. But then the outcome would seem to be that we must accept philosophical skepticism, no matter how unshaken in practice our beliefs remain.

This is skepticism in one of its traditional garbs. It asks: Why couldn't all my beliefs hang together and yet be comprehensively false about the actual world? Mere recognition of the fact that it is absurd or worse to try to *confront* our beliefs, one by one, or as a whole, with what they are about does not answer the question nor show the question unintelligible. In short, even a mild coherence theory like mine must provide a skeptic with a reason for supposing coherent beliefs are true. The partisan of a coherence theory can't allow assurance to come from outside the system of belief, while nothing inside can produce support except as it can be shown to rest, finally or at once, on something independently trustworthy.

It is natural to distinguish coherence theories from others by reference to the question whether or not justification can or must come to an end. But this does not define the positions, it merely suggests a form the argument may take. For there are coherence theorists who hold that some beliefs can serve as the basis for the rest, while it would be possible to maintain that coherence is not enough, although giving reasons never comes to an end. What distinguishes a coherence theory is simply the claim that nothing can count as a reason for holding a belief except another belief. Its partisan rejects as unintelligible the request for a ground or source of justification of another ilk. As Rorty has put it, 'nothing counts as justification unless by reference to what we already accept, and there is no way to get outside our beliefs and our language so as to find some test other than coherence.'[4] About this I am, as you see, in agreement with Rorty. Where we differ, if we do, is on whether there remains a question how, given that we cannot 'get outside our beliefs and our language so as to find some test other than coherence', we nevertheless can have knowledge of, and talk about, an objective public world which is not of our own making. I think this question does remain, while I suspect that Rorty doesn't think so. If this is his view, then he must think I am making a mistake in trying to answer the question. Nevertheless, here goes.

It will promote matters at this point to review very hastily some of the reasons for abandoning the search for a basis for knowledge outside the scope of our beliefs. By 'basis' here I mean specifically an epistemological basis, a source of justification.

The attempts worth taking seriously attempt to ground belief in one way or another on the testimony of the senses: sensation, perception, the given, experience, sense data, the passing show. All such theories must explain at least these two things: what, exactly, is the relation between sensation and belief that allows the first to justify the second? and, why should we believe our sensations are reliable, that is, why should we trust our senses?

The simplest idea is to identify certain beliefs with sensations. Thus Hume seems not to have distinguished between perceiving a green spot and perceiving that a spot is green. (An ambiguity in the word 'idea' was a great help here.) Other philosophers noted Hume's confusion, but tried to attain the same results by reducing the gap between perception and judgement to zero by attempting to formulate judgements that do not go beyond stating that the perception or sensation or presentation exists (whatever that may mean). Such theories do not justify beliefs on the basis of sensations, but try to justify certain beliefs by claiming that they have exactly the same epistemic content as a sensation. There are two difficulties with such a view: first, if the basic beliefs do not exceed in content the corresponding sensation they cannot support any inference to an objective world; and second, there are no such beliefs.

A more plausible line is to claim that we cannot be wrong about how things appear to us to be. If we believe we have a sensation, we do; this is held to be an analytic truth, or a fact about how language is used.

It is difficult to explain this supposed connection between sensations and some beliefs in a way that does not invite skepticism about other minds, and in the absence of an adequate explanation, there should be a doubt about the implications of the connection for justification. But in any case, it is unclear how, on this line, sensations justify the belief in those sensations. The point is rather that such beliefs require no justification, for the existence of the belief entails the existence of the sensation, and so the existence of the belief entails its own truth. Unless something further is added, we are back to another form of coherence theory.

Emphasis on sensation or perception in matters epistemological springs from the obvious thought: sensations are what connect the world and our beliefs, and they are candidates for justifiers because we often are aware of them. The trouble we have been running into is that the justification seems to depend on the awareness, which is just another belief.

Let us try a bolder tack. Suppose we say that sensations themselves, verbalized or not, justify certain beliefs that go beyond what is given in sensation. So, under certain conditions, having the sensation of seeing a green light flashing may justify the belief that a green light is flashing. The problem is to see how the sensation justifies the belief. Of course if someone has the sensation of seeing a green light flashing, it is likely, under certain circumstances, that a green light is flashing. *We* can say this, since we know of his sensation, but *he* can't say it, since we are supposing he is justified without having to depend on believing he has the sensation. Suppose he believed he didn't have the sensation. Would the sensation still justify him in the belief in an objective flashing green light?

The relation between a sensation and a belief cannot be logical, since sensations are not beliefs or other propositional attitudes. What then is the relation? The answer is, I think, obvious: the relation is causal. Sensations cause some beliefs and in *this* sense are the basis or ground of those beliefs. But a causal explanation of a belief does not show how or why the belief is justified.

The difficulty of transmuting a cause into a reason plagues the anti-coherentist again if he tries to answer our second question: What justifies the belief that our senses do not systematically deceive us? For even if sensations justify belief in sensation, we do not yet see how they justify belief in external events and objects.

Quine tells us that science tells us that 'our only source of information about the external world is through the impact of light rays and molecules upon our sensory surfaces.'[5] What worries me is how to read the words 'source' and 'information'. Certainly it is true that events and objects in the external world cause us to believe things about the external world, and much, if not all, of the causality takes a route through the sense organs. The notion of information, however, applies in a non-metaphorical way only to the engendered beliefs. So 'source' has to be read simply as 'cause' and 'information' as 'true belief' or 'knowledge'. Justification of beliefs caused by our senses is not yet in sight.[6]

The approach to the problem of justification we have been tracing must be wrong. We have been trying to see it this way: a person has all his beliefs about the world—that is, all his beliefs. How can he tell if they are true, or apt to be true? Only, we have been assuming, by connecting his beliefs to the world, confronting certain of his beliefs with the deliverances of the senses one by one, or perhaps confronting the totality of his beliefs with the tribunal of experience. No such confrontation makes sense, for of course we can't get outside our skins to find out what is causing the internal happenings of which we are aware. Introducing intermediate steps or entities into the causal chain, like sensations or observations, serves only to make the epistemological problem more obvious. For if the intermediaries are merely causes, they don't justify the beliefs they cause, while if they deliver information, they may be lying. The moral is obvious. Since we can't swear intermediaries to truthfulness, we should allow no intermediaries between our beliefs and their objects in the world. Of course there are causal intermediaries. What we must guard against are epistemic intermediaries.

There are common views of language that encourage bad epistemology. This is no accident, of course, since theories of meaning are connected with epistemology through attempts to answer the question how one determines that a sentence is true. If knowing the meaning of a sentence (knowing how to give a correct interpretation of it) involves, or is, knowing how it could be recognized to be true, then the theory of meaning raises the same question we have been struggling with, for giving the meaning of a sentence will demand that we specify what would justify asserting it. Here the coherentist will hold that there is no use looking for a source of justification outside of other sentences held true, while the foundationalist will seek to anchor at least some words or sentences to nonverbal rocks. This view is held, I think, both by Quine and by Michael Dummett.

Dummett and Quine differ, to be sure. In particular, they disagree about holism, the claim that the truth of our sentences must be tested together rather than one by one. And they disagree also, and consequently, about whether there is a useful distinction between analytic and synthetic sentences, and about whether a satisfactory theory of meaning can allow the sort of indeterminacy Quine argues for. (On all these points, I am Quine's faithful student.)

But what concerns me here is that Quine and Dummett agree on a basic principle, which is that whatever there is to meaning must be traced back somehow to experience, the given, or patterns of sensory stimulation, something intermediate between belief and the usual objects our beliefs are about. Once we take this step, we open the door to skepticism, for we must then allow that a very great many—perhaps most—of the sentences we hold to be true may in fact be false. It is ironical. Trying to make meaning accessible has made truth inaccessible. When meaning goes epistemological in this way, truth and meaning are necessarily divorced. One can, of course, arrange a shotgun wedding by redefining truth as what we are justified in asserting. But this does not marry the original mates.

Take Quine's proposal that whatever there is to the meaning (information value) of an observation sentence is determined by the patterns of sensory stimulation that would cause a speaker to assent to or dissent from the sentence. This is a marvellously ingenious way of capturing what is appealing about verificationist theories without having to talk of meanings, sense-data, or sensations; for the first time it made plausible the idea that one could, and should, do what I call the theory of meaning without need of what Quine calls meanings. But Quine's proposal, like other forms of verificationism, makes for skepticism. For clearly a person's sensory stimulations could be just as they are and yet the world outside very different. (Remember the brain in the vat.)

Quine's way of doing without meanings is subtle and complicated. He ties the meanings of some sentences directly to patterns of stimulation (which also constitute the evidence, Quine thinks, for assenting to the sentence), but the meanings of further sentences are determined by how they are conditioned to the original, or observation sentences. The facts of such conditioning do not permit a sharp division between sentences held true by virtue of meaning and sentences held true on the basis of observation. Quine made this point by showing that if one way of interpreting a speaker's utterances was satisfactory, so were many others. This doctrine of the indeterminacy of translation, as Quine called it, should be viewed as neither mysterious nor threatening. It is no more mysterious than the fact that temperature can be measured in Centigrade or Fahrenheit (or any linear transformation of those numbers). And it is not threatening because the very procedure that demonstrates the degree of indeterminacy at the same time demonstrates that what is determinate is all we need.

In my view, erasing the line between the analytic and synthetic saved philosophy of language as a serious subject by showing how it could be pursued without what there cannot be: determinate meanings. I now suggest also giving up the distinction between observation sentences and the rest. For the distinction between sentences belief in whose truth is justified by sensations and sentences belief in whose truth is justified only by appeal to other sentences held true is as anathema to the conherentist as the distinction between beliefs justified by sensations and beliefs justified only by appeal to further beliefs. Accordingly, I suggest we give up the idea that meaning or knowledge is grounded on something that counts as an ultimate source of evidence. No doubt meaning and knowledge depend on experience, and experience ultimately on sensation. But this is the 'depend' of causality, not of evidence or justification.

I have now stated my problem as well as I can. The search for an empirical foundation for meaning or knowledge leads to skepticism, while a coherence theory seems at a loss to provide any reason for a believer to believe that his beliefs, if coherent, are true. We are caught between a false answer to the skeptic, and no answer.

The dilemma is not a true one. What is needed to answer the skeptic is to show that someone with a (more or less) coherent set of beliefs has a reason to suppose his beliefs are not mistaken in the main. What we have shown is that it is absurd to look for a justifying ground for the totality of beliefs, something outside this totality which we can use to test or compare with our beliefs. The answer to our problem must then be to find a *reason* for supposing most of our beliefs are true that is not a form of *evidence*.

My argument has two parts. First I urge that a correct understanding of the speech, beliefs, desires, intentions and other propositional attitudes of a person leads to the conclusion that most of a person's beliefs must be true, and so there is a legitimate presumption that any one of them, if it coheres with most of the rest, is true. Then I go on to claim that anyone with thoughts, and so in particular anyone who wonders whether he has any reason to suppose he is generally right about the nature of his environment, must know what a belief is, and how in general beliefs are to be detected and interpreted. These being perfectly general facts we cannot fail to use when we communicate with others, or when we try to communicate with others, or even when we merely think we are communicating with others, there is a pretty strong sense in which we can be said to know that there is a presumption in favor of the overall truthfulness of anyone's beliefs, including our own. So it is bootless for someone to ask for some *further* reassurance; that can only add to his stock of beliefs. All that is needed is that he recognize that belief is in its nature veridical.

Belief can be seen to be veridical by considering what determines the existence and contents of a belief. Belief, like the other so-called propositional attitudes, is supervenient on facts of various sorts, behavioral, neurophysiological, biological and physical. The reason for pointing this out is not to encourage definitional or nomological reduction of psychological phenomena to something more basic, and certainly not to suggest epistemological priorities. The point is rather understanding. We gain one kind of insight into the nature of the propositional attitudes when we relate them systematically to one another and to phenomena on other levels. Since the propositional attitudes are deeply interlocked, we cannot learn the nature of one by first winning understanding of another. As interpreters, we work our way into the whole system, depending much on the pattern of interrelationships.

Take for example the interdependence of belief and meaning. What a sentence means depends partly on the external circumstances that cause it to win some degree of conviction; and partly on the relations, grammatical, logical or less, that the sentence has to other sentences held true with varying degrees of conviction. Since these relations are themselves translated directly into beliefs, it is easy to see how meaning depends on belief. Belief, however, depends equally on meaning, for the only access to the fine structure and individuation of beliefs is through the sentences speakers and interpreters of speakers use to express and describe beliefs. If we want to illuminate the nature of meaning and belief, therefore, we need to start with something that assumes neither. Quine's suggestion, which I shall essentially follow, is to take *prompted assent* as basic, the causal relation between assenting to a sentence and the cause of such assent. This is a fair place to start the project of identifying beliefs and meanings, since a speaker's assent to a sentence depends both on what he means by the sentence and on what he believes about the world. Yet it is possible to know that a speaker assents to a sentence without knowing either what the sentence, as spoken by him, means, or what belief is expressed by it. Equally obvious is the fact that once an interpretation has been given for a sentence assented to, a belief has been attributed. If correct theories of interpretation are not unique (do not lead to uniquely correct interpretations), the same will go for attributions of belief, of course, as tied to acquiescence in particular sentences.

A speaker who wishes his words to be understood cannot systematically deceive his would-be interpreters about when he assents to sentences—that is, holds them true. As a matter of principle, then, meaning, and by its connection with meaning, belief also, are open to public determination. I shall take advantage of this fact in what follows and adopt the stance of a radical interpreter when asking about the nature of belief. What a fully informed interpreter could learn about what a speaker means is all there is to learn: the same goes for what the speaker believes.[7]

The interpreter's problem is that what he is assumed to know—the causes of assents to sentences of a speaker—is, as we have seen, the product of two things he is assumed not to know, meaning and belief. If he knew the meanings he would know the beliefs, and if he knew the beliefs expressed by sentences assented to, he would know the meanings. But how can he learn both at once, since each depends on the other?

The general lines of the solution, like the problem itself, are owed to Quine. I will, however, introduce some changes into Quine's solution, as I have into the statement of the problem. The changes are directly relevant to the issue of epistemological skepticism.

I see the aim of radical interpretation (which is much, but not entirely, like Quine's radical translation) as being to produce a Tarski-style characterization of truth for the speaker's language, and a theory of his beliefs. (The second follows from the first plus the presupposed knowledge of sentences held true.) This adds little to Quine's program of translation, since translation of the speaker's language into one's own plus a theory of truth for one's own language add up to a theory of truth for the speaker. But the shift to the semantic notion of truth from the syntactic notion of translation puts the formal restrictions of a theory of truth in the foreground, and emphasizes one aspect of the close relation between truth and meaning.

The principle of charity plays a crucial role in Quine's method, and an even more crucial role in my variant. In either case, the principle directs the interpreter to translate or interpret so as to read some of his own standards of truth into the pattern of sentences held true by the speaker. The point of the principle is to make the speaker intelligible, since too great deviations from consistency and correctness leave no common ground on which to judge either conformity or difference. From a formal point of view, the principle of charity helps solve the problem of the interaction of meaning and belief by restraining the degrees of freedom allowed belief while determining how to interpret words.

We have no choice, Quine has urged, but to read our own logic into the thoughts of a speaker; Quine says this for the sentential calculus, and I would add the same for first-order quantification theory. This leads directly to the identification of the logical constants, as well as to assigning a logical form to all sentences.

Something like charity operates in the interpretation of those sentences whose causes of assent come and go with time and place: when the interpreter finds a sentence of the speaker the speaker assents to regularly under conditions he recognizes, he takes those conditions to be the truth conditions of the speaker's sentence. This is only roughly right, as we shall see in a moment. Sentences and predicates less directly geared to easily detected goings-on can, in Quine's cannon, be interpreted at will, given only the constraints of interconnections with sentences conditioned directly to the world. Here I would extend the principle of charity to favor interpretations that as far as possible preserve truth: I think it makes for mutual understanding, and hence for better interpretation, to interpret what the speaker accepts as true when we can. In this matter, I have less choice than Quine, because I do not see how to draw the line between observation sentences and theoretical sentences at the start. There are several reasons for this, but the one most relevant to the present topic is that this distinction is ultimately based on an epistemological consideration of a sort I have renounced: observation sentences are directly based on something like sensation—patterns of sensory stimulation—and this is an idea I have been urging leads to skepticism. Without the direct tie to sensation or stimulation, the distinction between observation sentences and others can't be drawn on epistemologically significant grounds. The distinction between sentences whose causes to assent come and go with observable circumstances and those a speaker clings to through change remains however, and offers the possibility of interpreting the words and sentences beyond the logical.

The details are not here to the point. What should be clear is that if the account I have given of how belief and meaning are related and understood by an interpreter, then most of the sentences a speaker holds to be true—especially the ones he holds to most stubbornly, the ones most central to the system of his beliefs—most of these sentences *are* true, at least in the opinion of the interpreter. For the only, and therefore unimpeachable, method available to the interpreter automatically puts the speaker's beliefs in accord with the standards of logic of the interpreter, and hence credits the speaker with plain truths of logic. Needless to say there are degrees of logical and other consistency, and perfect consistency is not to be expected. What needs emphasis is only the methodological necessity for finding consistency enough.

Nor, from the interpreter's point of view, is there any way he can discover the speaker to be largely wrong about the world. For he interprets sentences held true (which is not to be distinguished from attributing beliefs) according to the events and objects in the outside world that cause the sentence to be held true.

What I take to be the important aspect of this approach is apt to be missed because the approach reverses our natural way of thinking of communication derived from situations in which understanding has already been secured. Once understanding has been secured we are able, often, to learn what a person believes quite independently of what caused him to believe it. This may lead us to the crucial, indeed fatal, conclusion that we can in general fix what someone means independently of what he believes and independently of what caused the belief. But if I am right, we can't in general first identify beliefs and meanings and then ask what caused them. The causality plays an indispensable role in determining the content of what we say and believe. This is a fact we can be led to recognize by taking up, as we have, the interpreter's point of view.

It is an artifact of the interpreter's correct interpretation of a person's speech and attitudes that there is a large degree of truth and consistency in the thought and speech of an agent. But this is truth and consistency by the interpreter's standards. Why couldn't it happen that speaker and interpreter understand one another on the basis of shared but erroneous beliefs? This can, and no doubt often does, happen. But it cannot be the rule. For imagine for a moment an interpreter who is omniscient about the world, and about what does and would cause a speaker to assent to any sentence in his (potentially unlimited) repertoire. The omniscient interpreter, using the same method as the fallible interpreter, finds the fallible speaker largely consistent and correct. By his own standards, of course, but since these are objectively correct, the fallible speaker is seen to be largely correct and consistent by objective standards. We may also, if we want, let the omniscient interpreter turn his attention to the fallible interpreter of the fallible speaker. It turns out that the fallible interpreter can be wrong about some things, but not in general; and so he cannot share universal error with the agent he is interpreting. Once we agree to the general method of interpretation I have sketched, it becomes impossible correctly to hold that anyone could be mostly wrong about how things are.

There is, as I noted above, a key difference between the method of radical interpretation I am now recommending, and Quine's method of radical translation. The difference lies in the nature of the choice of causes that govern interpretation. Quine makes interpretation depend on patterns of sensory stimulation, while I make it depend on the external events and objects the sentence is interpreted as being about. Thus Quine's notion of meaning is tied to sensory criteria, something he thinks that can be treated also as evidence. This leads Quine to give epistemic significance to the distinction between observation sentences and others, since observation sentences are supposed, by their direct conditioning to the senses, to have a kind of extra-linguistic justification. This is the view against which I argued in the first part of my paper, urging that sensory stimulations are indeed part of the causal chain that leads to belief, but cannot, without confusion, be considered to be evidence, or a source of justification, for the stimulated beliefs.

What stands in the way of global skepticism of the senses is, in my view, the fact that we must, in the plainest and methodologically most basic cases, take the objects of a belief to be the causes of that belief. And what we, as interpreters, must take them to be is what they in fact are. Communication begins where causes converge: your utterance means what mine does if belief in its truth is systematically caused by the same events and objects.[8]

The difficulties in the way of this view are obvious, but I think they can be overcome. The method applies directly, at best, only to occasion sentences—the sentences' assent to which is caused systematically by common changes in the world. Further sentences are interpreted by their conditioning to occasion sentences, and the appearance in them of words that appear also in occasion sentences. Among occasion sentences, some will vary in the credence they command not only in the face of environmental change, but also in the face of change of credence awarded related sentences. Criteria can be developed on this basis to distinguish degrees of observationality on internal grounds, without appeal to the concept of a basis for belief outside the circle of beliefs.

Related to these problems, and easier still to grasp, is the problem of error. For even in the simplest cases it is clear that the same cause (a rabbit scampers by) may engender different beliefs in speaker and observer, and so encourage assent to sentences which cannot bear the same interpretation. It is no doubt this fact that made Quine turn from rabbits to patterns of stimulation as the key to interpretation. Just as a matter of statistics, I'm not sure how much better one approach is than the other. Is the relative frequency with which identical patterns of stimulation will touch off assent to 'Gavagai' and 'Rabbit' greater than the relative frequency with which a rabbit touches off the same two responses in speaker and interpreter? Not an easy question to test in a convincing way. But let the imagined results speak for Quine's method. Then I must say, what I must say in any case, the problem of error cannot be met sentence by sentence, even at the simplest level. The best we can do is cope with error holistically, that is, we interpret so as to make an agent as intelligible as possible, given his actions, his utterances and his place in the world. About some things we will find him wrong, as the necessary cost of finding him elsewhere right. As a rough approximation, finding him right means identifying the causes with the objects of his beliefs, giving special weight to the simplest cases, and countenancing error where it can be best explained.

Suppose I am right that an interpreter must so interpret as to make a speaker or agent largely correct about the world. How does this help the person himself who wonders what reason he has to think his beliefs are mostly true? How can he learn about the causal relations between the real world and his beliefs that lead the interpreter to interpret him as being on the right track?

The answer is contained in the question. In order to doubt or wonder about the provenance of his beliefs an agent must know what belief is. This brings with it the concept of objective truth, for the notion of a belief is the notion of a state that may or may not jibe with reality. But beliefs are also identified, directly and indirectly, by their causes. What an omniscient interpreter knows a fallible interpreter gets right enough if he understands a speaker, and this is just the complicated causal truth that makes us the believers we are, and fixes the contents of our beliefs. The agent has only to reflect on what a belief is to appreciate that most of his basic beliefs are true, and among his beliefs, those most securely held and that cohere with the main body of his beliefs are the most apt to be true. The question, how do I know my beliefs are generally true? thus answers itself, simply because beliefs are by nature generally true. Rephrased or expanded, the question becomes, how can I tell whether my beliefs, which are by their nature generally true, are generally true?

All beliefs are justified in this sense: they are supported by numerous other beliefs (otherwise they wouldn't be the beliefs they are), and have a presumption in favor of their truth. The presumption increases the larger and more significant the body of beliefs with which a belief coheres, and there being no such thing as an isolated belief, there is no belief without a presumption in its favor. In this respect, interpreter and interpreted differ. From the interpreter's point of view, methodology enforces a general presumption of truth for the body of beliefs as a whole, but the interpreter does not need to presume each particular belief of someone else is true. The general presumption applied to others does not make them globally right, as I have emphasized, but provides the background against which to accuse them of error. But from each person's own vantage point, there must be a graded presumption in favor of each of his own beliefs.

We cannot, alas, draw the picturesque and pleasant conclusion that all true beliefs constitute knowledge. For though all of a believer's beliefs are to some extent justified to him, some may not be justified enough, or in the right way, to constitute knowledge. The general presumption in favor of the truth of belief serves to rescue us from a standard form of skepticism by showing why it is impossible for all our beliefs to be false together. This leaves almost untouched the task of specifying the conditions of knowledge. I have not been concerned with the canons of evidential support (if such there be), but to show that all that counts as evidence or justification for a belief must come from the same totality of belief to which it belongs.

NOTES

1. See my 'True to the Facts', *The Journal of Philosophy* (1960), pp. 216–34.
2. Hilary Putnam, *Meaning and the Moral Sciences* (Routledge and Kegan Paul, London, 1978), p. 125.
3. See my 'On the Very Idea of a Conceptual Scheme', in *Proceedings and Addresses of the American Philosophical Association* (1974), pp. 5–20.
4. Richard Rorty, *Philosophy and the Mirror of Nature* (Princeton University Press, Princeton, 1979), p. 178.
5. W. V. Quine, 'The Nature of Natural Knowledge', in *Mind and Language,* ed. S. Guttenplan, (Clarendon Press, Oxford, 1975), p. 68.
6. Many other passages in Quine suggest that Quine hopes to assimilate sensory causes to evidence. In *Word and Object* (MIT Press, Massachusetts, 1960), p. 22 he writes that 'surface irritations . . . exhaust our clues to an external world.' In *Ontological Relativity* (Columbia University Press, New York, 1969), p. 75, we find that 'The stimulation of his

sensory receptors is all the evidence anybody has had to go on, ultimately, in arriving at his picture of the world.' On the same page: 'Two cardinal tenets of empiricism remain unassailable. . . . One is that whatever evidence there *is* for science *is* sensory evidence. The other . . . is that all inculcation of meanings of words, must rest ultimately on sensory evidence.' In *The Roots of Reference* (Open Court Publishing Company, Illinois, 1974), pp. 37–8, Quine says 'observations' are basic 'both in the support of theory and in the learning of language', and then goes on, 'What are observations? They are visual, auditory, tactual, olfactory. They are sensory, evidently, and thus subjective. . . . Should we say then that the observation is not the sensation. . . . ? No . . . ' Quine goes on to abandon talk of observations for talk of observation sentences. But of course observation sentences, unlike observations, cannot play the role of evidence unless we have reason to believe they are true.

7. I now think it is essential, in doing radical interpretation, to include the desires of the speaker from the start, so that the springs of action and intention, namely both belief and desire, are related to meaning. But in the present talk it is not necessary to introduce this further factor.
8. It is clear that the causal theory of meaning has little in common with the causal theories of reference of Kripke and Putnam. Those theories look to causal relations between names and objects of which speakers may well be ignorant. The chance of systematic error is thus increased. My causal theory does the reverse by connecting the cause of a belief with its object.

Afterthoughts, 1987

(to "A Coherence Theory of Truth and Knowledge")

The paper printed here was written for a colloquium organized by Richard Rorty for a Hegel Congress at Stuttgart in 1981. W. V. Quine and Hilary Putnam were the other participants in the colloquium. Our contributions were published in *Kant oder Hegel?,* (ed. Dieter Henrich, Klett-Cotta, 1983). After Stuttgart the four of us had a more leisurely exchange on the same topics at the University of Heidelberg. When the Pacific Division of the American Philosophical Association met in March of 1983, Rorty read a paper titled "Pragmatism, Davidson, and Truth." It was in part a comment on "A Coherence Theory of Truth and Knowledge." I replied. Rorty subsequently published his paper with revisions in *Truth and Interpretation: Perspectives on the Philosophy of Donald Davidson* (ed. Ernest LePore, Blackwell, 1986). This note continues the conversation.

A few aging philosophes, which category may include Quine, Putnam, and Dummett, and certainly includes me, are still puzzling over the nature of truth and its connections or lack of connections with meaning and epistemology. Rorty thinks we should stop worrying; he believes philosophy has seen through or outgrown the puzzles and should turn to less heavy and more interesting matters. He is particularly impatient with me for not conceding that the old game is up because he finds in my work useful support for his enlightened stance; underneath my "out-dated rhetoric" he detects the outlines of a largely correct attitude.

In his paper, both early and late, Rorty urges two things: that my view of truth amounts to a rejection of both coherence and correspondence theories and should properly be classed as belonging to the pragmatist tradition, and that I should not pretend that I am answering the skeptic when I am really telling him to get lost. I pretty much concur with him on both points.

[In *Reading Rorty,* ed. Alan Malichowski, Blackwell, 1990.]

In our 1983 discussion I agreed to stop calling my position either a coherence or a correspondence theory if he would give up the pragmatist theory of truth. He has done his part; he now explicitly rejects both James and Peirce on truth. I am glad to hold to my side of the bargain. If it had not already been published, I would now change the title of "A Coherence Theory," and I would not describe the project as showing how "coherence yields correspondence." On internal evidence alone, as Rorty points out, my view cannot be called a correspondence theory. As long ago as 1969 ("True to the Facts," reprinted in *Inquiries into Truth and Interpretation,* Oxford, 1984) I argued that nothing can usefully and intelligibly be said to correspond to a sentence; and I repeated this in "A Coherence Theory." I thought then that the fact that in characterizing truth for a language it is necessary to put words into relation with objects was enough to give some grip for the idea of correspondence; but this now seems to me a mistake. The mistake is in a way only a misnomer, but terminological infelicities have a way of breeding conceptual confusion, and so it is here. Correspondence theories have always been conceived as providing an explanation or analysis of truth, and this a Tarski-style theory of truth certainly does not do. I would also now reject the point generally made against correspondence theories that there is no way we could ever tell whether our sentences or beliefs correspond to reality. This criticism is at best misleading, since no one has ever explained in what such a correspondence could consist; and, worse, it is predicated on the false assumption that truth is transparently epistemic.

I also regret having called my view a "coherence theory." My emphasis on coherence was properly just a way of making a negative point, that "all that counts as evidence or justification for a belief must come from the same totality of belief to which it belongs." Of course this negative claim has typically led those philosophers who held it to conclude that reality and truth are constructs of thought; but it does not lead me to this conclusion, and for this reason if no other I ought not to have called my view a coherence theory. There is also a less weighty reason for not stressing coherence. Coherence is nothing but consistency. It is certainly in favor of a set of beliefs that they be consistent, but there is no chance that a person's beliefs will not tend to be self-consistent, since beliefs are individuated in part by their logical properties; what is not largely consistent with many other beliefs cannot be identified as a belief. The main thrust of "A Coherence Theory" has little to do with consistency; the important thesis for which I argue is that belief is intrinsically veridical. This is the ground on which I maintain that while truth is not an epistemic concept, neither is it wholly severed from belief (as it is in different ways by both correspondence and coherence theories).

My emphasis on coherence was misplaced; calling my view a "theory" was a plain blunder. In his paper Rorty stressed a minimalist attitude toward truth that he correctly thought we shared. It could be put this way: truth is as clear and basic a concept as we have. Tarski has given us an idea of how to apply the general concept (or try to apply it) to particular languages on the assumption that we already understand it; but of course he didn't show how to define it in general (he proved, rather, that this couldn't be done). Any further attempt to explain, define, analyze or explicate the concept will be empty or wrong: correspondence theories, coherence theories, pragmatist theories, theories that identify truth with warranted assertability (perhaps under "ideal" or "optimum" conditions), theories that ask truth to explain the success of science, or serve as the ultimate outcome of science or the conversations of some eite, all such theories either add nothing to our understanding of truth or have obvious counterexamples. Why on earth should we expect to be able to reduce truth to something clearer or more fundamental? After all, the only concept Plato succeeded in defining was mud (dirt and water). Putnam's comparison of various attempts to characterize truth with the attempts to define "good" in naturalistic terms seems to me, as it does to Rorty, apt. It also seems to apply to Putnam's identification of truth with idealized warranted assertability (*Realism and Reason,* Cambridge, 1983, p. xviii).

A theory of truth for a speaker, or group of speakers, while not a definition of the general concept of truth, does give a firm sense of what the concept is good for; it allows us to say, in a compact and clear way, what someone who understands that speaker, or those speakers, knows. Such a theory also invites the question how an interpreter could confirm its truth—a question which without the theory could not be articulated. The answer will, as I try to show in "A Coherence Theory," bring out essential relations among the concepts of meaning, truth, and belief. If I am right, each of these concepts requires the others, but none is subordinate to, much less definable in terms of, the others. Truth emerges not as wholly detached from belief (as a correspondence theory would make it) nor as dependent on human methods and powers of discovery (as epistemic theories of truth would make it). What saves truth from being "radically non-epistemic" (in Putnam's words) is not that truth is epistemic but that belief, through its ties with meaning, is intrinsically veridical.

Finally, how about Rorty's admonition to stop trying to answer the skeptic, and tell him to get lost? A short response would be that the skeptic has been told this again and again over the millennia and never seems to listen; like the philosopher he is, he wants an argument. To spell this out a bit: there is perhaps the suggestion in Rorty's "Pragmatism, Davidson, and Truth" that a "naturalistic" approach to the problems of meaning and the propositional attitudes will automatically leave the skeptic no room for maneuver. This thought, whether or not it is Rorty's, is wrong. Quine's naturalized epistemology, because it is based on the empiricist premise that what we mean and what we think is conceptually (and not merely causally) founded on the testimony of the senses, is open to standard skeptical attack. I was much concerned in "A Coherence Theory" to argue for an alternative approach to meaning and knowledge, and to show that if this alternative were right, skepticism could not get off the ground. I agree with Rorty to this extent; I did not set out to "refute" the skeptic, but to give a sketch of what I think to be a correct account of the foundations of linguistic communication and its implications for truth, belief, and knowledge. If one grants the correctness of this account, one can tell the skeptic to get lost.

Where Rorty and I differ, if we do, is in the importance we attach to the arguments that lead to the skeptic's undoing, and in the interest we find in the consequences for knowledge, belief, truth, and meaning. Rorty wants to dwell on where the arguments have led: to a position which allows us to dismiss the skeptic's doubts, and so to abandon the attempt to provide a general justification for knowledge claims—a justification that is neither possible nor needed. Rorty sees the history of Western philosophy as a confused and victorless battle between unintelligible skepticism and lame attempts to answer it. Epistemology from Descartes to Quine seems to me just one complex, and by no means unilluminating, chapter in the philosophical enterprise. If that chapter is coming to a close, it will be through recourse to modes of analysis and adherence to standards of clarity that have always distinguished the best philosophy, and will, with luck and enterprise, continue to do so.

What is Justified Belief?

ALVIN I. GOLDMAN

The aim of this paper is to sketch a theory of justified belief. What I have in mind is an explanatory theory, one that explains in a general way why certain beliefs are counted as justified and others as unjustified. Unlike some traditional approaches, I do not try to prescribe standards for justification that differ from, or improve upon, our ordinary standards. I merely try to explicate the ordinary standards, which are, I believe, quite different from those of many classical, e.g., 'Cartesian', accounts.

Many epistemologists have been interested in justification because of its presumed close relationship to knowledge. This relationship is intended to be preserved in the conception of justified belief presented here. In previous papers on knowledge,[1] I have denied that justification is necessary for knowing, but there I had in mind 'Cartesian' accounts of justification. On the account of justified belief suggested here, it *is* necessary for knowing, and closely related to it.

The term 'justified', I presume, is an evaluative term, a term of appraisal. Any correct definition or synonym of it would also feature evaluative terms. I assume that such definitions or synonyms might be given, but I am not interested in them. I want a set of *substantive* conditions that specify when a belief is justified. Compare the moral term 'right'. This might be defined in other ethical terms or phrases, a task appropriate to meta-ethics. The task of normative ethics, by contrast, is to state substantive conditions for the rightness of actions. Normative ethics tries to specify non-ethical conditions that determine when an action is right. A familiar example is act-utilitarianism, which says an action is right if and only if it produces, or would produce, at least as much net happiness as any alternative open to the agent. These

Source: Alvin Goldman, "What Is Justified Belief?" from Pappas, G. S., ed., *Justification and Knowledge*. Dordrecht: D. Reidel Publishing Co., 1973, pp. 1–23 with kind permission from Kluwer Academic Publishers.

necessary and sufficient conditions clearly involve no ethical notions. Analogously, I want a theory of justified belief to specify in non-epistemic terms when a belief is justified. This is not the only kind of theory of justifiedness one might seek, but it is one important kind of theory and the kind sought here.

In order to avoid epistemic terms in our theory, we must know which terms are epistemic. Obviously, an exhaustive list cannot be given, but here are some examples: 'justified', 'warranted', 'has (good) grounds', 'has reason (to believe)', 'knows that', 'sees that', 'apprehends that', 'is probable' (in an epistemic or inductive sense), 'shows that', 'establishes that', and 'ascertains that'. By contrast, here are some sample non-epistemic expressions: 'believes that', 'is true', 'causes', 'it is necessary that', 'implies', 'is deducible from', and 'is probable' (either in the frequency sense or the propensity sense). In general, (purely) doxastic, metaphysical, modal, semantic, or syntactic expressions are not epistemic.

There is another constraint I wish to place on a theory of justified belief, in addition to the constraint that it be couched in non-epistemic language. Since I seek an explanatory theory, i.e., one that clarifies the underlying source of justificational status, it is not enough for a theory to state 'correct' necessary and sufficient conditions. Its conditions must also be appropriately deep or revelatory. Suppose, for example, that the following sufficient condition of justified belief is offered: 'If *S* senses redly at *t* and *S* believes at *t* that he is sensing redly, then *S*'s belief at *t* that he is sensing redly is justified.' This is not the kind of principle I seek; for, even if it is correct, it leaves unexplained *why* a person who senses redly and believes that he does, believes this justifiably. Not every state is such that if one is in it and believes one is in it, this belief is justified. What is distinctive about the state of sensing redly, or 'phenomenal' states in general? A theory of justified belief of the kind I seek must answer this question, and hence it must be couched at a suitably deep, general, or abstract level.

A few introductory words about my *explicandum* are appropriate at this juncture. It is often assumed that whenever a person has a justified belief, he knows that it is justified and knows what the justification is. It is further assumed that the person can state or explain what his justification is. On this view, a justification is an argument, defense, or set of reasons that can be given in support of a belief. Thus, one studies the nature of justified belief by considering what a person might *say* if asked to defend, or justify, his belief. I make none of these sorts of assumptions here. I leave it an open question whether, when a belief *is* justified, the believer *knows* it is justified. I also leave it an open question whether, when a belief is justified, the believer can *state* or *give* a justification for it. I do not even assume that when a belief is justified there is something 'possessed' by the believer which can be called a 'justification'. I do assume that a justified belief gets its status of being justified from some processes or properties that make it justified. In short, there must be some justification-conferring processes or properties. But this does not imply that there must be an argument, or reason, or anything else, 'possessed' at the time of belief by the believer.

I

A theory of justified belief will be a set of principles that specify truth-conditions for the schema ⌜*S*'s belief in *p* at time *t* is justified⌝, i.e., conditions for the satisfaction of this schema in all possible cases. It will be convenient to formulate candidate theories in a recursive or inductive format, which would include (A) one or more base clauses, (B) a set of recursive clauses (possibly null), and (C) a closure clause. In such a format, it is permissible for the predicate 'is a justified belief' to appear in recursive clauses. But neither this predicate, nor any other epistemic predicate, may appear in (the antecedent of) any base clause.[2]

Before turning to my own theory, I want to survey some other possible approaches to justified belief. Identification of problems associated with other attempts will provide some motivation for the theory I shall offer. Obviously, I cannot examine all, or even very many, alternative attempts. But a few sample attempts will be instructive.

Let us concentrate on the attempt to formulate one or more adequate base-clause principles.[3] Here is a classical candidate:

(1) If *S* believes *p* at *t*, and *p* is indubitable for *S* (at *t*), then *S*'s belief in *p* at *t* is justified.

To evaluate this principle, we need to know what 'indubitable' means. It can be understood in at least two ways. First, '*p* is indubitable for *S*' might mean: '*S* has no *grounds* for doubting *p*'. Since 'ground' is an epistemic term, however, principle (1) would be inadmissible on this reading, for epistemic terms may not legitimately appear in the antecedent of a base-clause. A second interpretation would avoid this difficulty. One might interpret '*p* is indubitable for *S*' psychologically, i.e., as meaning '*S* is psychologically incapable of doubting *p*'. This would make principle (1) admissible, but would it be correct? Surely not. A religious fanatic may be psychologically incapable of doubting the tenets of his faith, but that doesn't make his belief in them justified. Similarly, during the Watergate affair, someone may have been so blinded by the aura of the Presidency that even after the most damaging evidence against Nixon had emerged he was still incapable of doubting Nixon's veracity. It doesn't follow that his belief in Nixon's veracity was justified.

A second candidate base-clause principle is this:

(2) If *S* believes *p* at *t*, and *p* is self-evident, then *S*'s belief in *p* at *t* is justified.

To evaluate this principle, we again need an interpretation of its crucial term, in this case 'self-evident'. On one standard reading, 'evident' is a synonym for 'justified', '*Self*-evident' would therefore mean something like 'directly justified', 'intuitively justified', or 'non-derivatively justified'. On this reading 'self-evident' is an epistemic phrase, and principle (2) would be disqualified as a base-clause principle.

However, there are other possible readings of '*p* is self-evident' on which it isn't an epistemic phrase. One such reading is: 'It is impossible to understand *p* without believing it'.[4] According to this interpretation, trivial analytic and logical truths might turn out to be self-evident. Hence, any belief in such a truth would be a justified belief, according to (2).

What does 'it is *impossible* to understand *p* without believing it' mean? Does it mean '*humanly* impossible'? That reading would probably make (2) an unacceptable principle. There may well be propositions which humans have an innate and irrepressible disposition to believe, e.g., 'Some events have causes'. But it seems unlikely that people's inability to refrain from believing such a proposition makes every belief in it justified.

Should we then understand 'impossible' to mean 'impossible in principle', or 'logically impossible'? If that is the reading given, I suspect that (2) is a vacuous principle. I doubt that even trivial logical or analytic truths will satisfy this definition of 'self-evident'. Any proposition, we may assume, has two or more components that are somehow organized or juxtaposed. To understand the proposition one must 'grasp' the components and their juxtaposition. Now in the case of *complex* logical truths, there are (human) psychological operations that suffice to grasp the components and their juxtaposition but do not suffice to produce a belief that the proposition is true. But can't we at least *conceive* of an analogous set of psychological operations even for simple logical truths, operations which perhaps are not in the repertoire of human cognizers but which might be in the repertoire of some conceivable beings? That is, can't we conceive of psychological operations that would suffice to grasp the components and componential-juxtaposition of these simple propositions but do not suffice to produce *belief* in the propositions? I think we can conceive of such operations. Hence, for any proposition you choose, it will be possible for it to be understood without being believed.

Finally, even if we set these two objections aside, we must note that self-evidence can at best confer justificational status on relatively few beliefs, and the only plausible group are beliefs in necessary truths. Thus, other base-clause principles will be needed to explain the justificational status of beliefs in contingent propositions.

The notion of a base-clause principle is naturally associated with the idea of 'direct' justifiedness, and in the realm of contingent propositions first-person-current-mental-state propositions have often been assigned this role. In Chisholm's terminology, this conception is expressed by the notion of a '*self-presenting*' state or proposition. The sentence 'I am thinking', for example, expresses a self-presenting proposition. (At least I shall *call* this sort of content a 'proposition', though it only has a truth value given some assignment of a subject who utters or entertains the content and a time of entertaining.) When such a proposition is true for person *S* at time *t*, *S* is justified in believing it at *t*: in Chisholm's terminology, the proposition is 'evident' for *S* at *t*. This suggests the following base-clause principle.

(3) If *p* is a self-presenting proposition, and *p* is true for *S* at *t*, and *S* believes *p* at *t*, then *S*'s belief in *p* at *t* is justified.

What, exactly, does 'self-presenting' mean? In the second edition of *Theory of Knowledge*, Chisholm offers this definition: "*h* is self-presenting for *S* at *t* = df. *h* is true at *t*; and necessarily, if *h* is true at *t*, then *h* is evident for *S* at *t*."[5] Unfortunately, since 'evident' is an epistemic term, 'self-presenting' also becomes an epistemic term on this definition, thereby disqualifying (3) as a legitimate base-clause. Some other definition of self-presentingness must be offered if (3) is to be a suitable base-clause principle.

Another definition of self-presentation readily comes to mind. 'Self-presentation' is an approximate synonym of 'self-intimation', and a proposition may be said to be self-intimating if and only if whenever it is true of a person that person believes it. More precisely, we may give the following definition.

(SP) Proposition *p* is self-presenting if and only if: necessarily, for any *S* and any *t*, if *p* is true for *S* at *t*, then *S* believes *p* at *t*.

On this definition, 'self-presenting' is clearly not an epistemic predicate, so (3) would be an admissible principle. Moreover, there is initial plausibility in the suggestion that it is *this* feature of first-person-current-mental-state propositions—viz., their truth guarantees their being believed—that makes beliefs in them justified.

Employing this definition of self-presentation, is principle (3) correct? This cannot be decided until we define self-presentation more precisely. Since the operator 'necessarily' can be read in different ways, there are different forms of self-presentation and correspondingly different versions of principle (3). Let us focus on two of these readings: a '*nomological*' reading and a '*logical*' reading. Consider first the nomological reading. On this definition a proposition is self-presenting just in case it is nomologically necessary that if *p* is true for *S* at *t*, then *S* believes *p* at *t*.[6]

Is the nomological version of principle (3)—call it '(3_N)'—correct? Not at all. We can imagine cases in which the antecedent of (3_N) is satisfied but we would not say that the belief is justified. Suppose, for example, that *p* is the proposition expressed by the sentence 'I am in brain-state *B*', where '*B*' is shorthand for a certain highly specific neural state description. Further suppose it is a nomological truth that anyone in brain-state *B* will ipso facto *believe* he is in brain-state *B*. In other words, imagine that an occurrent belief with the content 'I am in brain-state *B*' is realized whenever one is in brain-state *B*.[7] According to (3_N), any such belief is justified. But that is clearly false. We can readily imagine circumstances in which a person goes into brain-state *B* and therefore has the belief in question, though this belief is by no means justified. For example, we can imagine that a brain-surgeon operating on *S* artificially induces brain-state *B*. This results, phenomenologically, in *S*'s suddenly believing—out of the blue—that he is in brain-state *B*, without any relevant antecedent beliefs. We would hardly say, in such a case, that *S*'s belief that he is in brain-state *B* is justified.

Let us turn next to the logical version of (3)—call it '(3_L)' – in which a proposition is defined as self-presenting just in case it is logically necessary that if *p* is true for *S* at *t*, then *S* believes *p* at *t*. This stronger version of principle (3) might seem more promising. In fact, however, it is no more successful than (3_N). Let *p* be the proposition 'I am awake' and assume that it is logically necessary that if this proposition is true for some person *S* and time *t*, then *S* believes *p* at *t*. This assumption is consistent with the further assumption that *S* frequently believes *p* when it is false, e.g., when he is dreaming. Under these circumstances, we would hardly accept the contention that *S*'s belief in this proposition is always justified. But nor should we accept the contention that the belief is justified when it is *true*. The truth of the proposition logically guarantees that the belief is *held*, but why should it guarantee that the belief is *justified?*

The foregoing criticism suggests that we have things backwards. The idea of self-presentation is that truth guarantees belief. This fails to confer justification because it is compatible with there being belief without truth. So what seems necessary—or at least sufficient—for justification is that belief should guarantee truth. Such a notion has usually gone under the label of '*infallibility*', or '*incorrigibility*'. It may be defined as follows.

(INC) Proposition *p* is incorrigible if and only if: necessarily, for any *S* and any *t*, if *S* believes *p* at *t*, then *p* is true for *S* at *t*.

Using the notion of incorrigibility, we may propose principle (4).

(4) If *p* is an incorrigible proposition, and *S* believes *p* at *t*, then *S*'s belief in *p* at *t* is justified.

As was true of self-presentation, there are different varieties of incorrigibility, corresponding to different interpretations of 'necessarily'. Accordingly, we have different versions of principle (4). Once again, let us concentrate on a nomological and a logical version, (4_N) and (4_L) respectively.

We can easily construct a counterexample to (4_N) along the lines of the belief-state/brain-state counterexample that refuted (3_N). Suppose it is nomologically necessary that if anyone believes he is in brain-state *B* then it is true that he is in brain-state *B*, for the only way this belief-state is realized is through brain-state *B* itself. It follows that 'I am in brain-state *B*' is a nomologically incorrigible proposition. Therefore, according to (4_N), whenever anyone believes this proposition at any time, that belief is justified. But we may again construct a brain-surgeon example in which someone comes to have such a belief but the belief isn't justified.

Apart from this counterexample, the general point is this. Why should the fact that *S*'s believing *p* guarantees the truth of *p* imply that *S*'s belief is justified? The nature of the guarantee might be wholly fortuitous, as the belief-state/brain-state example is intended to illustrate. To appreciate the point, consider the following related possibility. A person's mental structure might be such that whenever he believes that *p* will be true (of him) a split second later, then *p* is true (of him) a split second later. This is because, we may suppose, his believing it brings it about. But surely we would not be compelled in such a circumstance to say that a belief of this sort is justified. So why should the fact that *S*'s believing *p* guarantees the truth of *p precisely at the time of belief* imply that the belief is justified? There is no intuitive plausibility in this supposition.

The notion of *logical* incorrigibility has a more honored place in the history of conceptions of justification. But even principle (4_L), I believe, suffers from defects similar to those of (4_N). The mere fact that belief in *p* logically guarantees its truth does not confer justificational status on such a belief.

The first difficulty with (4_L) arises from logical or mathematical truths. Any true proposition of logic or mathematics is logically necessary. Hence, any such proposition *p* is logically incorrigible, since it is logically necessary that, for any *S* and any *t*, if *S* believes *p* at *t* then *p* is true (for *S* at *t*). Now assume that Nelson believes a certain very complex mathematical truth at time *t*. Since such a proposition is logically incorrigible, (4_L) implies that Nelson's belief in this truth at *t* is justified. But we may easily suppose that this belief of Nelson is not at all the result of proper mathematical reasoning, or even the result of appeal to trustworthy authority. Perhaps Nelson believes this complex truth because of utterly confused reasoning, or because of hasty and ill-founded conjecture. Then his belief is not justified, contrary to what (4_L) implies.

The case of logical or mathematical truths is admittedly peculiar, since the truth of these propositions is assured independently of any beliefs. It might seem, therefore, that we can better capture the idea of 'belief logically guaranteeing truth' in cases where the propositions in question are *contingent*. With this in mind, we might restrict (4_L) to *contingent* incorrigible propositions. Even this amendment cannot save (4_L), however, since there are counterexamples to it involving purely contingent propositions.

Suppose that Humperdink has been studying logic—or, rather, pseudo-logic—from Elmer Fraud, whom Humperdink has no reason to trust as a logician. Fraud has enunciated the principle that any disjunctive proposition consisting of at least 40 distinct disjuncts is very probably true. Humperdink now encounters the proposition *p*, a contingent proposition with 40 disjuncts, the 7th disjunct being 'I exist'. Although Humperdink grasps the proposition fully, he doesn't notice that it is entailed by 'I exist'. Rather, he is struck by the fact that it falls under the disjunction rule Fraud has enunciated (a rule I assume Humperdink is not *justified* in believing). Bearing this rule in mind, Humperdink forms a belief in *p*. Now notice that *p* is logically incorrigible. It is logically necessary that if anyone believes *p*, then *p* is true (of him at that time). This simply follows from the fact that, first, a person's believing anything entails that he exists, and second, 'I exist' entails *p*. Since *p* is logically incorrigible, principle (4_L) implies that Humperdink's belief in *p* is justified. But surely, given our example, that conclusion is false. Humperdink's belief in *p* is not at all justified.

One thing that goes wrong in this example is that while Humperdink's belief in *p* logically implies its truth, Humperdink doesn't *recognize* that his believing it implies its truth. This might move a theorist to revise (4_L) by adding the requirement that *S* 'recognize' that *p* is logically incorrigible. But this, of course, won't do. The term 'recognize' is obviously an epistemic term, so the suggested revision of (4_L) would result in an inadmissible base-clause.

II

Let us try to diagnose what has gone wrong with these attempts to produce an acceptable base-clause principle. Notice that each of the foregoing attempts confers the status of 'justified' on a belief without restriction on *why* the belief is held, i.e., on what *causally initiates* the belief or *causally sustains* it. The logical versions of principles (3) and (4), for example, clearly place no restriction on causes of belief. The same is true of the nomological versions of (3) and (4), since nomological requirements can be satisfied by simultaneity or cross-sectional laws, as illustrated by our brain-state/belief-state examples. I suggest that the absence of causal requirements accounts for the failure of the foregoing principles. Many of our counter-examples are ones in which the belief is caused in some strange or unacceptable way, e.g., by the accidental movement of a brain-surgeon's hand, by reliance on an illicit, pseudo-logical principle, or by the blinding aura of the Presidency. In general, a strategy for defeating a non-causal principle of justifiedness is to find a case in which the principle's antecedent is satisfied but the belief is caused by some faulty belief-forming process. The faultiness of the belief-forming process will incline us, intuitively, to regard the belief as unjustified. Thus, correct principles of justified belief must be principles that make causal requirements, where 'cause' is construed broadly to include sustainers as well as initiators of belief (i.e., processes that determine, or help to overdetermine, a belief's continuing to be held.)[8]

The need for causal requirements is not restricted to base-clause principles. Recursive principles will also need a causal component. One might initially suppose that the following is a good recursive principle: 'If S justifiably believes q at t, and q entails p, and S believes p at t, then S's belief in p at t is justified'. But this principle is unacceptable. S's belief in p doesn't receive justificational status simply from the fact that p is entailed by q and S justifiably believes q. If what causes S to believe p at t is entirely different, S's belief in p may well not be justified. Nor can the situation be remedied by adding to the antecedent the condition that S justifiably believes that q entails p. Even if he believes this, and believes q as well, he might not put these beliefs together. He might believe p as a result of some other wholly extraneous, considerations. So once again, conditions that fail to require appropriate causes of a belief don't guarantee justifiedness.

Granted that principles of justified belief must make reference to causes of belief, what kinds of causes confer justifiedness? We can gain insight into this problem by reviewing some faulty processes of belief-formation, i.e., processes whose belief-outputs would be classed as unjustified. Here are some examples: confused reasoning, wishful thinking, reliance on emotional attachment, mere hunch or guesswork, and hasty generalization. What do these faulty processes have in common? They share the feature of *unreliability:* they tend to produce *error* a large proportion of the time. By contrast, which species of belief-forming (or belief-sustaining) processes are intuitively justification-conferring? They include standard perceptual processes, remembering, good reasoning, and introspection. What these processes seem to have in common is *reliability:* the beliefs they produce are generally true. My positive proposal, then, is this. The justificational status of a belief is a function of the reliability of the process or processes that cause it, where (as a first approximation) reliability consists in the tendency of a process to produce beliefs that are true rather than false.

To test this thesis further, notice that justifiedness is not a purely categorical concept, although I treat it here as categorical in the interest of simplicity. We can and do regard certain beliefs as more justified than others. Furthermore, our intuitions of comparative justifiedness go along with our beliefs about the comparative reliability of the belief-causing processes.

Consider perceptual beliefs. Suppose Jones believes he has just seen a mountain-goat. Our assessment of the belief's justifiedness is determined by whether he caught a brief glimpse of the creature at a great distance, or whether he had a good look at the thing only 30 yards away. His belief in the latter sort of case is (*ceteris paribus*) more justified than in the former sort of case. And, if his belief is true, we are more prepared to say he *knows* in the latter case than in the former. The difference between the two cases seems to be this. Visual beliefs formed from brief and hasty scanning, or where the perceptual object is a long distance off, tend to be wrong more often than visual beliefs formed from detailed and leisurely scanning, or where the object is in reasonable proximity. In short, the visual processes in the former category are less reliable than those in the latter category. A similar point holds for memory beliefs. A belief that results from a hazy and indistinct memory impression is counted as less justified than a belief that arises from a distinct memory impression, and our inclination to classify those beliefs as '*knowledge*' varies in the same way. Again, the reason is associated with the comparative reliability of the processes. Hazy and indistinct memory impressions are generally less reliable indicators of what actually happened; so beliefs formed from such impressions are less likely to be true than beliefs formed from distinct impressions. Further, consider beliefs based on inference from observed samples. A belief about a population that is based on random sampling, or on instances that exhibit great variety, is intuitively more justified than a belief based on biased sampling, or on instances from a narrow sector of the population. Again, the degree of justifiedness seems to be a function of reliability. Inferences based on random or varied samples will tend to produce less error or inaccuracy than inferences based on non-random or non-varied samples.

Returning to a categorical concept of justifiedness, we might ask just *how* reliable a belief-forming process must be in order that its resultant beliefs be justified. A precise answer to this question should not be expected. Our conception of justification is *vague* in this respect. It does seem clear, however, that *perfect* reliability isn't required. Belief-forming processes that *sometimes* produce error still confer justification. It follows that there can be justified beliefs that are false.

I have characterized justification-conferring processes as ones that have a 'tendency' to produce beliefs that are true rather than false. The term 'tendency' could refer either to *actual* long-run frequency, or to a 'propensity', i.e., outcomes that would occur in merely *possible* realizations of the process. Which of these is intended? Unfortunately, I think our ordinary conception of justifiedness is vague on this dimension too. For the most part, we simply assume that the 'observed' frequency of truth versus error would be approximately replicated in the actual long-run, and also in relevant counterfactual situations, i.e., ones that are highly 'realistic', or conform closely to the circumstances of the actual world. Since we ordinarily assume these frequencies to be roughly the same, we make no concerted effort to distinguish them. Since the purpose of my present theorizing is to capture our ordinary conception of justifiedness, and since our ordinary conception is vague on this matter, it is appropriate to leave the theory vague in the same respect.

We need to say more about the notion of a belief-forming '*process*'. Let us mean by a 'process' a *functional operation* or procedure, i.e., something that generates a *mapping* from certain states—'inputs'—into other states—'outputs'. The outputs in the present case are states of believing this or that proposition at a given moment. On this interpretation, a process is a *type* as opposed to a *token*. This is fully appropriate, since it is only types that have statistical properties such as producing truth 80%

of the time; and it is precisely such statistical properties that determine the reliability of a process. Of course, we also want to speak of a process as *causing* a belief, and it looks as if types are incapable of being causes. But when we say that a belief is caused by a given process, understood as a functional procedure, we may interpret this to mean that it is caused by the particular *inputs* to the process (and by the intervening events 'through which' the functional procedure carries the inputs into the output) on the occasion in question.

What are some examples of belief-forming 'processes' construed as functional operations? One example is reasoning processes, where the inputs include antecedent beliefs and entertained hypotheses. Another example is functional procedures whose inputs include desires, hopes, or emotional states of various sorts (together with antecedent beliefs). A third example is a memory process, which takes as input beliefs or experiences at an earlier time and generates as output beliefs at a later time. For example, a memory process might take as input a belief *at* t_1 that Lincoln was born in 1809 and generate as output a belief *at* t_n that Lincoln was born in 1809. A fourth example is perceptual processes. Here it isn't clear whether inputs should include states of the environment, such as the distance of the stimulus from the cognizer, or only events within or on the surface of the organism, e.g., receptor stimulations. I shall return to this point in a moment.

A critical problem concerning our analysis is the degree of generality of the process-types in question. Input-output relations can be specified very broadly or very narrowly, and the degree of generality will partly determine the degree of reliability. A process-type might be selected so narrowly that only one instance of it ever occurs, and hence the type is either completely reliable or completely unreliable. (This assumes that reliability is a function of *actual* frequency only.) If such narrow process-types were selected, beliefs that are intuitively unjustified might be said to result from perfectly reliable processes; and beliefs that are intuitively justified might be said result from perfectly unreliable processes.

It is clear that our ordinary thought about process-types slices them broadly, but I cannot at present give a precise explication of our intuitive principles. One plausible suggestion, though, is that the relevant processes are *content-neutral*. It might be argued, for example, that the process of *inferring p whenever the Pope asserts p* could pose problems for our theory. If the Pope is infallible, this process will be perfectly reliable; yet we would not regard the belief-outputs of this process as justified. The content-neutral restriction would avert this difficulty. If relevant processes are required to admit as input beliefs (or other states) with *any* content, the aforementioned process will not count, for its input beliefs have a restricted propositional content, viz., '*the Pope asserts p*'.

In addition to the problem of 'generality' or 'abstractness' there is the previously mentioned problem of the '*extent*' of belief-forming processes. Clearly, the causal ancestry of beliefs often includes events outside the organism. Are such events to be included among the 'inputs' of belief-forming processes? Or should we restrict the extent of belief-forming processes to '*cognitive*' events, i.e., events within the organism's nervous system? I shall choose the latter course, though with some hesitation. My general grounds for this decision are roughly as follows. Justifiedness seems to be a function of how a cognizer deals with his environmental input, i.e., with the goodness or badness of the operations that register and transform the stimulation that reaches him. ('Deal with', of course, does not mean *purposeful* action; nor is it restricted to *conscious* activity.) A justified belief is, roughly speaking, one that results from cognitive operations that are, generally speaking, good or successful. But '*cognitive*' operations are most plausibly construed as operations of the cognitive faculties, i.e., 'information-processing' equipment *internal* to the organism.

With these points in mind, we may now advance the following base-clause principle for justified belief.

(5) If *S*'s believing *p* at *t* results from a reliable cognitive belief-forming process (or set of processes), then *S*'s belief in *p* at *t* is justified.

Since 'reliable belief-forming process' has been defined in terms of such notions as belief, truth, statistical frequency, and the like, it is not an epistemic term. Hence, (5) is an admissible base-clause.

It might seem as if (5) promises to be not only a successful base clause, but the only principle needed whatever, apart from a closure clause. In other words, it might seem as if it is a necessary as well as a sufficient condition of justifiedness that a belief be produced by reliable cognitive belief-forming processes. But this is not quite correct, given our provisional definition of 'reliability'.

Our provisional definition implies that a reasoning process is reliable only if it generally produces beliefs that are true, and similarly, that a memory process is reliable only if it generally yields beliefs that are true. But these requirements are too strong. A reasoning procedure cannot be expected to produce true belief if it is applied to false premisses. And memory cannot be expected to yield a true belief if the original belief it attempts to retain is false. What we need for reasoning and memory, then, is a notion of '*conditional reliability*'. A process is conditionally reliable when a sufficient proportion of its output-beliefs are true *given that its input-beliefs are true*.

With this point in mind, let us distinguish *belief-dependent* and *belief-independent* cognitive processes. The former are processes *some* of whose inputs are belief-states.[9] The latter are processes *none* of whose inputs are belief-states. We may then replace principle (5) with the following two principles, the first a base-clause principle and the second a recursive-clause principle.

(6_A) If *S*'s belief in *p* at *t* results ('immediately') from a belief-independent process that is (unconditionally) reliable, then *S*'s belief in *p at t* is justified.

(6_B) If *S*'s belief in *p* at *t* results ("immediately") from a belief-dependent process that is (at least) conditionally reliable, and if the beliefs (if any) on which this process operates in producing *S*'s belief in *p* at *t* are themselves justified, then *S*'s belief in *p* at *t* is justified.[10]

If we add to (6_A) and (6_B) the standard closure clause, we have a complete theory of justified belief. The theory says, in effect, that a belief is justified if and only it is '*well-formed*', i.e., it has an ancestry of reliable and/or conditionally reliable cognitive operations. (Since a dated belief may be over-determined, it may have a number of distinct ancestral trees. These need not all be full of reliable or conditionally reliable processes. But at least one ancestral tree must have reliable or conditionally reliable processes throughout.)

The theory of justified belief proposed here, then, is an *Historical* or *Genetic* theory. It contrasts with the dominant approach to justified belief, an approach that generates what we may call (borrowing a phrase from Robert Nozick) '*Current Time-Slice*' theories. A Current Time-Slice theory makes the justificational status of a belief wholly a function of what is true of the cognizer *at the time* of belief. An Historical theory makes the justificational status of a belief depend on its prior history. Since my Historical theory emphasizes the reliability of the belief-generating processes, it may be called '*Historical Reliabilism*'.

The most obvious examples of Current Time-Slice theories are 'Cartesian' Foundationalist theories, which trace all justificational status (at least of contingent propositions) to current mental states. The usual varieties of Coherence theories, however, are equally Current Time-Slice views, since they too make the justificational status of a belief wholly a function of *current* states of affairs. For Coherence theories, however, these current states include all other beliefs of the cognizer, which would not be considered relevant by Cartesian Foundationalism. Have there been other Historical theories of justified belief? Among contemporary writers, Quine and Popper have Historical epistemologies, though the notion of 'justification' is not their avowed *explicandum*. Among historical writers, it might seem that Locke and Hume had Genetic theories of sorts. But I think that their Genetic theories were only theories of ideas, not of knowledge or justification. Plato's theory of recollection, however, is a good example of a Genetic theory of knowing.[11] And it might be argued that Hegel and Dewey had Genetic epistemologies (if Hegel can be said to have had a clear epistemology at all).

The theory articulated by (6_A) and (6_B) might be viewed as a kind of 'Foundationalism,' because of its recursive structure. I have no objection to this label, as long as one keeps in mind how different this 'diachronic' form of Foundationalism is from Cartesian, or other 'synchronic' varieties of, Foundationalism.

Current Time-Slice theories characteristically assume that the justificational status of a belief is something which the cognizer is able to know or determine at the time of belief. This is made explicit, for example, by Chisholm.[12] The Historical theory I endorse makes no such assumption. There are many facts about a cognizer to which he lacks 'privileged access', and I regard the justificational status of his beliefs as one of those things. This is not to say that a cognizer is necessarily ignorant, at any given moment, of the justificational status of his current beliefs. It is only to deny that he necessarily has, or can get, knowledge or true belief about this status. Just as a person can know without knowing that he knows, so he can have justified belief without knowing that it is justified (or believing justifiably that it is justified.)

A characteristic case in which a belief is justified though the cognizer doesn't know that it's justified is where the original evidence for the belief has long since been forgotten. If the original evidence was compelling, the cognizer's original belief may have been justified; and this justificational status may have been preserved through memory. But since the cognizer no longer remembers how or why he came to believe, he may not know that the belief is justified. If asked now to justify his belief, he may be at a loss. Still, the belief *is* justified, though the cognizer can't demonstrate or establish this.

The Historical theory of justified belief I advocate is connected in spirit with the causal theory of knowing I have presented elsewhere.[13] I had this in mind when I remarked near the outset of the paper that my theory of justified belief makes justifiedness come out closely related to knowledge. Justified beliefs, like pieces of knowledge, have appropriate histories; but they may fail to be knowledge either because they are false or because they founder on some other requirement for knowing of the kind discussed in the post-Gettier knowledge-trade.

There is a variant of the Historical conception of justified belief that is worth mentioning in this context. It may be introduced as follows. Suppose *S* has a set *B* of beliefs at time t_0, and some of these beliefs are *un*justified. Between t_0 and t_1 he reasons from the entire set *B* to the conclusion *p*, which he then accepts at t_1. The reasoning procedure he uses is a very sound one, i.e., one that is conditionally reliable. There is a sense or respect in which we are tempted to say that *S*'s belief in *p* at t_1 is 'justified'. At any rate, it is tempting to say that the *person* is justified in believing *p* at *t*. Relative to his antecedent cognitive state, he did as well as could be expected: the *transition* from his cognitive state at t_0 to his cognitive state at t_1 was entirely sound. Although we may acknowledge this brand of justifiedness—it might be called '*Terminal-Phase Reliabilism*'—it is not a kind of justifiedness so closely related to knowing. For a person to know proposition p, it is not enough that the *final phase* of the process that leads to his belief in p be sound. It is also necessary that some entire history of the process be sound (i.e., reliable or conditionally reliable).

Let us return now to the Historical theory. In the next section of the paper, I shall adduce reasons for strengthening it a bit. Before looking at these reasons, however, I wish to review two quite different objections to the theory.

First, a critic might argue that *some* justified beliefs do not derive their justificational status from their causal ancestry. In particular, it might be argued that beliefs about one's current phenomenal states and intuitive beliefs about elementary logical or conceptual relationships do not derive their justificational status in this way. I am not persuaded by either of these examples. Introspection, I believe, should be regarded as a form of retrospection. Thus, a justified belief that I am 'now' in pain gets its justificational status from a relevant, though brief, causal history.[14] The apprehension of logical or conceptual relationships is also a cognitive process that occupies time. The psychological process of 'seeing' or 'intuiting' a simple logical truth is very fast, and we cannot introspectively dissect it into constituent parts. Nonetheless, there are mental operations going on, just as there are mental operations that occur in *idiots savants,* who are unable to report the computational processes they in fact employ.

A second objection to Historical Reliabilism focuses on the reliability element rather than the causal or historical element. Since the theory is intended to cover all possible cases, it seems to imply that for any cognitive process C, if C is reliable in possible world W, then any belief in W that results from C is justified. But doesn't this permit easy counterexamples? Surely we can imagine a possible world in which wishful thinking is reliable. We can imagine a possible world where a benevolent demon so arranges things that beliefs formed by wishful thinking usually come true. This would make wishful thinking a reliable process in that possible world, but surely we don't want to regard beliefs that result from wishful thinking as justified.

There are several possible ways to respond to this case and I am unsure which response is best, partly because my own intuitions (and those of other people I have consulted) are not entirely clear. One possibility is to say that in the possible world imagined, beliefs that result from wishful thinking *are* justified. In other words we reject the claim that wishful thinking could never, intuitively, confer justifiedness.[15]

However, for those who feel that wishful thinking couldn't confer justifiedness, even in the world imagined, there are two ways out. First, it may be suggested that the proper criterion of justifiedness is the propensity of a process to generate beliefs that are true *in a non-manipulated environment,* i.e., an environment in which there is no purposeful arrangement of the world either to accord or conflict with the beliefs that are formed. In other words, the suitability of a belief-forming process is only a function of its success in '*natural*' situations, not situations of the sort involving benevolent or malevolent demons, or any other such manipulative creatures. If we reformulate the theory to include this qualification, the counterexample in question will be averted.

Alternatively, we may reformulate our theory, or reinterpret it, as follows. Instead of construing the theory as saying that a belief in possible world W is justified if and only if it results from a cognitive process that is reliable in W, we may construe it as saying that a belief in possible world W is justified if and only if it results from a cognitive process that is reliable *in our world.* In short, our conception of justifiedness is derived as follows. We note certain cognitive processes in the actual world, and form beliefs about which of these are reliable. The ones we believe to be reliable are then regarded as justification-conferring processes. In reflecting on hypothetical beliefs, we deem them justified if and only if they result from processes already picked out as justification-conferring, or processes very similar to those. Since wishful thinking is not among these processes, a belief formed in a possible world *W* by wishful thinking would not be deemed justified, even if wishful thinking is reliable *in W*. I am not sure that this is a correct reconstruction of our intuitive conceptual scheme, but it would accommodate the benevolent demon case, at least if the proper thing to say in that case is that the wishful-thinking-caused beliefs are unjustified.

Even if we adopt this strategy, however, a problem still remains. Suppose that wishful thinking turns out to be reliable *in the actual world!*[16] This might be because, unbeknownst to us at present, there is a benevolent demon who, lazy until now, will shortly start arranging things so that our wishes come true. The long-run performance of wishful thinking will be very good, and hence even the new construal of the theory will imply that beliefs resulting from wishful thinking (in *our* world) are justified. Yet this surely contravenes our intuitive judgement on the matter.

Perhaps the moral of the case is that the standard format of a 'conceptual analysis' has its shortcomings. Let me depart from that format and try to give a better rendering of our aim and the theory that tries to achieve that aim. What we really want is an *explanation* of why we count, or would count, certain beliefs as justified and others as unjustified. Such an explanation must refer to our *beliefs* about reliability, not to the actual *facts*. The reason we *count* beliefs as justified is that they are formed by what we *believe* to be reliable belief-forming processes. Our beliefs about which belief-forming processes are reliable may be erroneous, but that does not affect the adequacy of the explanation. Since we *believe* that wishful thinking is an unreliable belief-forming process, we regard beliefs formed by wishful thinking as unjustified. What matters, then, is what we *believe* about wishful thinking, not what is *true* (in the long run) about wishful thinking. I am not sure how to express this point in the standard format of conceptual analysis, but it identifies an important point in understanding our theory.

III

Let us return, however, to the standard format of conceptual analysis, and let us consider a new objection that will require some revisions in the theory advanced until now. According to our theory, a belief is justified in case it is caused by a process that is in fact reliable, or by one we generally believe to be reliable. But suppose that although one of *S*'s beliefs satisfies this condition, *S* has no reason to believe that it does. Worse yet, suppose *S* has reason to believe that his belief is caused by an *un*reliable process (although *in fact* its causal ancestry is fully reliable). Wouldn't we deny in such circumstances that *S*'s belief is justified? This seems to show that our analysis, as presently formulated, is mistaken.

Suppose that Jones is told on fully reliable authority that a certain class of his memory beliefs are almost all mistaken. His parents fabricate a wholly false story that Jones suffered from amnesia when he was seven but later developed *pseudo*-memories of that period. Though Jones listens to what his parents say and has excellent reason to trust them, he persists in believing the ostensible memories from his seven-year-old past. Are these memory beliefs justified? Intuitively, they are not justified. But since these beliefs result from genuine memory and original perceptions, which are adequately reliable processes, our theory says that these beliefs are justified.

Can the theory be revised to meet this difficulty? One natural suggestion is that the actual reliability of a belief's ancestry is not enough for justifiedness; in addition, the cognizer must be *justified in believing* that the ancestry of his belief is reliable. Thus one might think of replacing (6_A), for example, with (7). (For simplicity, I neglect some of the details of the earlier analysis.)

(7) If *S*'s belief in *p* at *t* is caused by a reliable cognitive process, and *S* justifiably believes at *t* that his *p*-belief is so caused, then *S*'s belief in *p* at *t* is justified.

It is evident, however, that (7) will not do as a base clause, for it contains the epistemic term 'justifiably' in its antecedent.

A slightly weaker revision, without this problematic feature, might next be suggested, viz.,

(8) If *S*'s belief in *p* at *t* is caused by a reliable cognitive process, and *S* believes at *t* that his *p*-belief is so caused, then *S*'s belief in *p* at *t* is justified.

But this won't do the job. Suppose that Jones believes that his memory beliefs are reliably caused despite all the (trustworthy) contrary testimony of his parents. Principle (8) would be satisfied, yet we wouldn't say that these beliefs are justified.

Next, we might try (9), which is stronger than (8) and, unlike (7), formally admissible as a base clause.

(9) If *S*'s belief in *p* at *t* is caused by a reliable cognitive process, and *S* believes at *t* that his *p*-belief is so caused, and this meta-belief is caused by a reliable cognitive process, than *S*'s belief in *p* at *t* is justified.

A first objection to (9) is that it wrongly precludes unreflective creatures—creatures like animals or young children, who have no beliefs about the genesis of their beliefs—from having justified beliefs. If one shares my view that justified belief is, at least roughly, *well-formed* belief, surely animals and young children can have justified beliefs.

A second problem with (9) concerns its underlying rationale. Since (9) is proposed as a substitute for (6_A), it is implied that the reliability of a belief's own cognitive ancestry does not make it justified. But, the suggestion seems to be, the reliability of a *meta-belief*'s ancestry confers justifiedness on the first-order belief. Why should that be so? Perhaps one is attracted by the idea of a 'trickle-down' effect: if an n+1-level belief is justified, its justification trickles down to an n-level belief. But even if the trickle-down theory is correct, it doesn't help here. There is no assurance from the satisfaction of (9)'s antecedent that the meta-belief itself is *justified.*

To obtain a better revision of our theory, let us re-examine the Jones case. Jones has strong evidence against certain propositions concerning his past. He doesn't *use* this evidence, but if he *were* to use it properly, he would stop believing these propositions. Now the proper use of evidence would be an instance of a (conditionally) reliable process. So what we can say about Jones is that he *fails* to use a certain (conditionally) reliable process that he could and should have used. Admittedly, had he used this process, he would have 'worsened' his doxastic states: he would have replaced some true beliefs with suspension of judgement. Still, he couldn't have known this in the case in question. So, he failed to do something which, epistemically, he should have done. This diagnosis suggests a fundamental change in our theory. The justificational status of a belief is not only a function of the cognitive processes *actually* employed in producing it; it is also a function of processes that could and should be employed.

With these points in mind, we may tentatively propose the following revision of our theory, where we again focus on a base-clause principle but omit certain details in the interest of clarity.

(10) If *S*'s belief in *p* at *t* results from a reliable cognitive process, and there is no reliable or conditionally reliable process available to *S* which, had it been used by *S* in addition to the process actually used, would have resulted in *S*'s not believing *p* at *t*, the *S*'s belief in *p* at *t* is justified.

There are several problems with this proposal. First, there is a technical problem. One cannot use an additional belief-forming (or doxastic-state-forming) process *as well as* the original process if the additional one would result in a different doxastic state. One wouldn't be using the original process at all. So we need a slightly different formulation of the relevant counterfactual. Since the basic idea is reasonably clear, however, I won't try to improve on the formulation here. A second problem concerns the notion of '*available*' belief-forming (or doxastic-state-forming) processes. What is it for a process to be 'available' or a cognizer? Were scientific procedures 'available' to people who lived in pre-scientific ages? Furthermore, it seems implausible to say that all 'available' processes ought to be used, at least if we include such processes as gathering *new* evidence. Surely a belief can sometimes be justified even if additional evidence-gathering would yield a different doxastic attitude. What I think we should have in mind here are such additional processes as calling previously acquired evidence to mind, assessing the implications of that evidence, etc. This is admittedly somewhat vague, but here again our ordinary notion of justifiedness is vague, so it is appropriate for our analysans to display the same sort of vagueness.

This completes the sketch of my account of justified belief. Before concluding, however, it is essential to point out that there is an important use of 'justified' which is not captured by this account but can be captured by a closely related one.

There is a use of 'justified' in which it is not implied or presupposed that there is a *belief* that is justified. For example, if *S* is trying to decide whether to believe *p* and asks our advice, we may tell him that he is 'justified' in believing it. We do not thereby imply that he *has* a justified *belief,* since we know he is still suspending judgement. What we mean, roughly, is that he *would* or *could* be justified if he were to believe *p*. The justificational status we ascribe here cannot be a function of the causes of *S*'s believing *p*, for there is no belief by *S* in *p*. Thus, the account of justifiedness we have given thus far cannot explicate *this* use of 'justified'. (It doesn't follow that this use of 'justified' has no connection with causal ancestries. Its proper use may depend on the causal ancestry of the cognizer's cognitive state, though not on the causal ancestry of his believing *p*.)

Let us distinguish two uses of 'justified': an *ex post* use and an *ex ante* use. The *ex post* use occurs when there exists a belief, and we say *of that belief* that it is (or isn't) justified. The *ex ante* use occurs when no such belief exists, or when we wish to ignore the question of whether such a belief exists. Here we say of the *person,* independent of his doxastic state vis-à-vis *p*, that *p* is (or isn't) suitable for him to believe.[17]

Since we have given an account of *ex post* justifiedness, it will suffice if we can analyze *ex ante* justifiedness in terms of it. Such an analysis, I believe, is ready at hand. *S* is *ex ante* justified in believing *p* at *t* just in case his total cognitive state at *t* is such that from that state he could come to believe *p* in such a way that this belief would be *ex post* justified. More precisely, he is *ex ante* justified in believing *p* at *t* just in case a reliable belief-forming operation is available to him such that the application of that operation to his total cognitive state at *t* would result, more or less immediately, in his believing *p* and this belief would be *ex post* justified.

Stated formally, we have the following:

(11) Person *S* is *ex ante* justified in believing *p* at *t* if and only if there is a reliable belief-forming operation available to *S* which is such that if *S* applied that operation to his total cognitive state at *t*, *S* would believe *p* at *t*-plus-delta (for a suitably small delta) and that belief would be *ex post* justified.

For the analysans of (11) to be satisfied, the total cognitive state at *t* must have a suitable causal ancestry. Hence, (11) is implicitly an Historical account of *ex ante* justifiedness.

As indicated, the bulk of this paper was addressed to *ex post* justifiedness. This is the appropriate analysandum if one is interested in the connection between justifiedness and knowledge, since what is crucial to whether a person *knows* a proposition is whether he has an actual *belief* in the proposition that is justified. However, since many epistemologists are interested in *ex ante* justifiedness, it is proper for a general theory of justification to try to provide an account of that concept as well. Our theory does this quite naturally, for the account of *ex ante* justifiedness falls out directly from our account of *ex post* justifiedness.[18]

NOTES

1. 'A Causal Theory of Knowing,' *The Journal of Philosophy* 64, 12 (June 22, 1967): 357–372; 'Innate Knowledge,' in S. P. Stich, ed., *Innate Ideas* (Berkeley: University of California Press, 1975); and 'Discrimination and Perceptual Knowledge,' *The Journal of Philosophy* 73, 20 (November 18, 1976), 771–791.
2. Notice that the choice of a recursive format does not prejudice the case for or against any particular theory. A recursive format is perfectly general. Specifically, an explicit set of necessary and sufficient conditions is just a special case of a recursive format, i.e., one in which there is no recursive clause.
3. Many of the attempts I shall consider are suggested by material in William P. Alston, 'Varieties of Privileged Access,' *American Philosophical Quarterly* 8 (1971), 223–241.
4. Such a definition (though without the modal term) is given, for example, by W. V. Quine and J. S. Ullian in *The Web of Belief* (New York: Random House, 1970), p. 21. Statements are said to be self-evident just in case "to understand them is to believe them".
5. Englewood Cliffs, N.J.: Prentice-Hall, Inc., 1977, p. 22.
6. I assume, of course, that 'nomologically necessary' is *de re* with respect to '*S*' and '*t*' in this construction. I shall not focus on problems that may arise in this regard, since my primary concerns are with different issues.
7. This assumption violates the thesis that Davidson calls 'The Anomalism of the Mental'. Cf. 'Mental Events,' in L. Foster and J. W. Swanson, eds., *Experience and Theory* (Amherst: University of Massachusetts Press, 1970). But it is unclear that this thesis is a necessary truth. Thus, it seems fair to assume its falsity in order to produce a counterexample. The example neither entails nor precludes the mental-physical identity theory.
8. Keith Lehrer's example of the gypsy lawyer is intended to show the inappropriateness of a causal requirement. (See *Knowledge,* Oxford: University Press, 1974, pp. 124–125.) But I find this example unconvincing. To the extent that I clearly imagine that the lawyer fixes his belief solely as a result of the cards, it seems intuitively wrong to say that he *knows*—or has a *justified belief*—that his client is innocent.
9. This definition is not exactly what we need for the purposes at hand. As Ernest Sosa points out, introspection will turn out to be a belief-dependent process since sometimes the input into the process will be a belief (when the introspected content is a belief). Intuitively, however, introspection is not the sort of process which may be merely conditionally reliable. I do not know how to refine the

definition so as to avoid this difficulty, but it is a small and isolated point.

10. It may be objected that principles (6_A) and (6_B) are jointly open to analogues of the lottery paradox. A series of processes composed of reliable but less-than-perfectly-reliable processes may be extremely unreliable. Yet applications of (6_A) and (6_B) would confer justifiedness on a belief that is caused by such a series. In reply to this objection, we might simply indicate that the theory is intended to capture our ordinary notion of justifiedness, and this ordinary notion has been formed without recognition of this kind of problem. The theory is not wrong *as* a theory of the ordinary (naive) conception of justifiedness. On the other hand, if we want a theory to do more than capture the ordinary conception of justifiedness, it might be possible to strengthen the principles to avoid lottery-paradox analogues.
11. I am indebted to Mark Pastin for this point.
12. Cf. *Theory of Knowledge,* Second Edition, pp. 17, 114–116.
13. Cf. 'A Causal Theory of Knowing,' *op. cit.* The reliability aspect of my theory also has its precursors in earlier papers of mine on knowing: 'Innate Knowledge,' *op. cit.* and 'Discrimination and Perceptual Knowledge,' *op. cit.*
14. The view that introspection is retrospection was taken by Ryle, and before him (as Charles Hartshorne points out to me) by Hobbes, Whitehead, and possibly Husserl.
15. Of course, if people in world *W* learn *inductively* that wishful thinking is reliable, and regularly base their beliefs on this inductive inference, it is quite unproblematic and straightforward that their beliefs are justified. The only interesting case is where their beliefs are formed *purely* by wishful thinking, without using inductive inference. The suggestion contemplated in this paragraph of the text is that, in the world imagined, even pure wishful thinking would confer justifiedness.
16. I am indebted here to Mark Kaplan.
17. The distinction between *ex post* and *ex ante* justifiedness is similar to Roderick Firth's distinction between *doxastic* and *propositional* warrant. See his 'Are Epistemic Concepts Reducible to Ethical Concepts?', in Alvin I. Goldman and Jaegwon Kim, eds., *Values and Morals, Essays in Honor of William Frankena, Charles Stevenson, and Richard Brandt* (Dordrecht: D. Reidel, 1978).
18. Research on this paper was begun while the author was a fellow of the John Simon Guggenheim Memorial Foundation and of the Center for Advanced Study in the Behavioral Sciences. I am grateful for their support. I have received helpful comments and criticism from Holly S. Goldman, Mark Kaplan, Fred Schmitt, Stephen P. Stich, and many others at several universities where earlier drafts of the paper were read.

Contra Reliabilism

CARL GINET

The reliability of a belief-producing process is a matter of how likely it is that the process will produce beliefs that are true. The term *reliabilism* may be used to refer to any position that makes this idea of reliability central to the explication of some important epistemic concept. I know of three such positions that appeal to some epistemologists: (1) a reliabilist account of what makes a belief justified, (2) a reliabilist account of what makes a true belief knowledge, and (3) a reliabilist answer to the question of the fourth condition, the question of what must be added to justified true belief to make knowledge. Obviously these are alternative positions rather than parts of a single coherent whole. I think of the first as reliabilism's boldest stand, the second as the position to which it may retreat when the first is found untenable, and the third as its last refuge. I will criticize only the first two positions.[1]

Source: Carl Ginet, "Contra Reliabilism," *THE MONIST,* vol. 68, no. 2 (April, 1985), pp. 175–187.

1. *Reliabilism as an account of justification.*

Let us elaborate a little on what is meant by the reliability of a belief-producing process. A belief-producing process is a certain *kind* of process that produces beliefs having a certain kind of content. The kind of process is reliable just in case the beliefs of that kind that it produces are true a sufficiently high proportion of the time, or *would* be true a sufficiently high proportion of the time if the process were to occur frequently: it has a sufficiently strong propensity to produce true rather than false beliefs.

The boldest claim a reliabilist can make about the justification of belief is this: for a belief to be justified is for it to be produced by a reliable process. This simple statement needs some serious refining. For any particular belief, there will be *some* kind to which the producing process belongs and *some* kind to which the content belongs such that it will be of no significance at all that most (or all) or few (or none) of the beliefs of that kind that are (or would be) produced by processes of that kind are true. The kinds can, for example, be specified so narrowly that the production of the particular belief in question will be the only case in point that ever would occur. So the reliabilist must revise the claim to read: for a belief to be justified is for there to be a *relevant* kind to which the belief content belongs and a *relevant* kind of process by which it was produced such that that kind of process reliably produces true beliefs of that kind. It will not be trivial to specify criteria of relevance that are both plausible and informative, but let us assume that it can be done.

However this refinement is worked out, it will be unable to avoid certain clear counterexamples to this boldest of the reliabilist claims, cases where it is clear that what justifies the belief is *not* what causes it (and also, though this is not essential to the counterexample, where it is unlikely that the belief is produced by any relevant kind of reliable process). Suppose, for example, that it is a mild day in Ithaca but the weather forecast I hear on the radio says that a mass of cold air will move into the region tomorrow. As soon as I hear that, I have, we may suppose, good reason to believe that it will be colder in Ithaca tomorrow; and if I were caused to believe it by having that reason then my belief would be produced by a (relevant) reliable process. But let us suppose that I irrationally refuse to believe it until my Aunt Hattie tells me that she feels in her joints that it will be colder tomorrow. She often makes that sort of prediction and I always believe her, even if I have no other supporting evidence. She is right about as often as she is wrong. So the (relevant) process by which my belief is actually caused is not reliable. Nevertheless my belief is justified. I do have justification for it, namely, my justified belief as to what the Weather Bureau said. Thus I am protected from reproach for holding the belief, though I may deserve reproach for something else, namely, *being moved* to hold it *by* Aunt Hattie's prediction and not by the Weather Bureau's. I could rebut any reproach for my holding the belief by pointing out that I do have justification for it. My recognizing the evidential value of the Weather Bureau's forecast is quite compatible with my (irrationally) refusing to be moved to belief by that evidence.

It may help to see the matter right here to consider an analogous situation with respect to the justification of action. Suppose you and I are eating at a restaurant where the chocolate mousse is beyond compare. We both order it. After eating my portion I finish off the major part of your portion while you are away from the table. This is something I decided to do as soon as you announced your temporary departure. But as you stood up you said to me, "Please finish my mousse: I can't possibly eat any more." So I am perfectly justified in finishing your mousse. You have given me permission and I am aware of this fact and its moral relevance to my action. Still it is not because of this justification I have for it that I perform the action. I would have done it anyway. So there is something here for which I may be censured, namely, what I found to be sufficient reason to act: my gluttonous craving would have led me to eat your mousse even without your permision. But something I should *not* be blamed for is: eating your mousse. Given that I am aware of your permission and its justifying force, that action is above reproach and it would be unjust to inflict on me any of the penalities that should attach to eating someone else's chocolate mousse without their permission.

So the justification of an action or of a belief is not necessarily a matter of how it was actually caused. But the reliabilist can admit this and retreat to the claim that the justification of a belief is a matter either of how it is actually caused or of how it could have been caused in the circumstances actually present. The reliabilist can say that a belief is justified just in case either it is actually caused by a (relevant) reliable process or there are conditions present such that if they had caused the belief then it would have been caused by a reliable process. This is still too crude a formulation of the position but it is refined enough for my purposes.[2] The criticisms I have to make are directed at the basic idea.

Let us note, first, that there are cases that show that the reliabilist condition fails to be *sufficient* for justified belief. A leading reliabilist has himself described such a case. Alvin Goldman, in his paper, "What Is Justified Belief?",[3] says (p. 6):

> Suppose that *p* is the proposition expressed by the sentence 'I am in brain-state B', where 'B' is shorthand for a certain highly specific neural state-description. Further suppose it is a nomological truth that anyone in brain-state B will ipso facto *believe* he is in brain-state B.

The reliabilist position would appear to dictate that any such belief is justified, for the process producing it could not be more reliable: it is a causal law about the kind of brain-state that it always produces in its subject a belief that he or she is in a brain-state of that kind. But as Goldman himself goes on to say (p. 6), the claim that any such belief is justified

> is clearly false. We can readily imagine circumstances in which a person goes into brain-state B and therefore has the belief in question, though this belief is by no means justified. For example, we can imagine that a brain-surgeon operating on S artificially induces brain-state B. This results . . . in S's suddenly believing . . . that he is in brain-state B, *without any relevant antecedent beliefs* [my emphasis]. We would hardly say, in such a case, that S's belief that he is in brain-state B is justified.

Consider another example. Suppose some film-makers have made a film that has a happy ending although things look very bad for the protagonists most of the way through. These same film-makers had earlier put out a tragic film that had greatly upset many viewers. They want viewers of the new film not to suffer undue anxiety and so they introduce into the film the subliminal message, "Don't worry! Everything turns out all right." That is, this message appears on the screen at frequent intervals but for such a short period each time that it can be perceived only subliminally: the viewers see it but do not know they are seeing it. Their seeing it causes them to have the belief that things will turn out all right, without their knowing how they are caused to have it. It is clear that, in these circumstances, this belief is not justified. Yet the process that produced it may be extremely reliable.

Surprisingly, none of Goldman's refinements on his reliabilist condition for justified belief (in "What Is Justified Belief?") rules out these counter-examples to its sufficiency. The reliabilist might hope that a plausible account of what makes a kind of process relevant, if and when such an account is achieved, will rule that the reliable processes in these examples are not of relevant kinds. But it is hard to see how any non-ad-hoc account could do this without also ruling out kinds that should be ruled in. It would not do, for example, to say that the reliable belief-producing process must be some sort of inference from other beliefs, since there are justified beliefs that are not arrived at by inference. There is, then, reason to suspect that the reliabilist condition cannot be made both plausible and sufficient for justified belief.

As far as being *necessary* is concerned, the reliabilist condition fails no matter how relevance of the kind of process is defined. Consider, for instance, the possibility of a world run by a Cartesian demon who causes its other inhabitants to have sets of perceptual and personal-memory impressions that, though as rich and coherent as yours and mine, are all illusory. The perceptual beliefs and personal-memory beliefs that these hapless subjects are led to have are as justified as any of our current perceptual or memory beliefs. Yet the sort of process by which they are caused has no tendency to cause true beliefs. (It is the case even in this demon-world, however, that the processes producing perceptual and personal-memory beliefs *seem* reliable to the inhabitants of that world, as gauged by the purported beliefs and justified inferences therefrom. The principles of belief-justification should be such that in any possible world the beliefs they justify support the thesis that following the principles generally leads to true beliefs—even in possible worlds where that thesis is false.)

Goldman does not appear to consider just this sort of counter-example but in another connection he makes a move that may seem to help here. He says that the reliability of a kind of belief producing process is to be gauged in the actual world: if the perceptual and memory processes that cause beliefs in the demon-world are reliable in *our* world then the beliefs they produce in the demon-world are justified even though those same processes are not reliable in that world. Well, let us allow reliabilism to make this ruling in its account of justification: *we* should assess reliability, and hence justifiedness, by actual-world standards even when considering non-actual worlds. But now, what about the inhabitants of non-actual worlds? How should *they* assess justifiedness of beliefs? By the same lights, their standards cannot be those of any world but their own. If ours must be actual-world standards then theirs must be their-world standards. Yet it seems quite clear that the inhabitants of the demon-world should regard their perceptual and memory beliefs as justified—just as much so as we should—even though they are not produced by processes that are reliable in their world. If *our* world is run by a Cartesian demon, we are still justified in our present perceptual and memory beliefs (or the coherent majority of them, at any rate).

2. *Reliabilism as a non-justificationist account of knowledge.*

Here the suggestion is that for a true belief to be knowledge it is not required that the subject have justification for the belief. It is necessary only that the belief be produced by a sufficiently reliable process. I shall not argue directly for my contrary view, that no *un*justified belief can be knowledge however reliable the process by which it was produced. Rather I will rebut the various arguments I know of for the reliabilist position and against the requirement of justification.

It is difficult to find cases in the real world in which a person lacks justification for a belief that has been produced by a reliable process (Why is this?), but it is not hard to imagine them. We described two such cases in the preceding section (pp. 176–77) and here is another. Suppose that S, residing in Finland, is frequently caused to have accurate beliefs as to the current temperature in degrees Celsius in Sydney, Australia. But S herself does not know how this happens: she just suddenly finds herself with the conviction, for example, that it is now plus five degrees Celsius in Sydney. She knows nothing of the process by which these beliefs are produced and can offer no reasons for holding them, no evidence in favor of them. But, we may suppose, the process actually producing these beliefs is quite reliable. (It is unimportant exactly what this process is, but we might imagine some sort of electronic link between a thermometer in Sydney and S's brain.) My intuition is that, when S is caused in this way to have a true belief that the temperature in Sydney is +5°C, S does *not know* this if she herself has no good reason for believing it. The reliabilist position says to the contrary that, since S's belief is produced by a process that can be counted on always to produce true beliefs, S does know what the temperature is in Sydney.

The reliabilist might be tempted to try to get us to see S's belief as a case of knowledge by suggesting that the case is analogous to ordinary perceptual knowledge of the proximate environment. If we allow that I know that there is a light before me when I am caused via my organs of sight to believe that there is a light before me then, the reliabilist might say, why not allow that S knows in an analogous way that the temperature in Sydney is +5°C when S is caused, via the Sydney-temperature-detecting-apparatus attached to her brain, to have that belief? Why not see her as having a special sort of perceptual or quasi-perceptual knowledge?

Well, in perceptual knowledge—properly so called—there are facts directly accessible to the knower that *justify* the perceptual belief (without entailing its truth or that it was produced by a reliable process): facts about S's sense experience and how the perceptual belief it prompts coheres with those prompted by the rest of S's current and remembered sense experience. (The justification need not be by *inference* from these facts.) S's belief about the temperature in Sydney would need to be made similar in this respect in order to be a candidate for quasi-perceptual knowledge. But then, even if it could thereby be made a successful candidate, it would no longer support the reliabilist position now under consideration. For then S's true belief is a candidate for knowledge, not merely because of its being reliably produced, but also because of the directly accessible facts constituting S's quasi-perceptual justification for the belief.[4]

An argument that does try to support the position that S's reliably produced beliefs are knowledge even if they lack justification (whether quasi-perceptual or other) is the following. Even if S does not know that her beliefs have been reliably produced, someone else who does know this can rely on S's beliefs as a guide to the facts about the current temperature in Sydney: she can use S's beliefs as detectors of those facts. S's beliefs convey information to her and that is enough to make those beliefs knowledge. If a person's beliefs reliably convey information, in the way that a properly functioning thermometer conveys information, if they are capable of giving us knowledge, then they should be counted as knowledge.

I cannot see this. I cannot see how the fact that a person's beliefs enable others to have knowledge, through being reliable indicators of something, can make those beliefs themselves knowledge. All sort of things other than true beliefs can be reliable indicators and therefore bases or enablers of knowledge; and being a basis or enabler of knowledge must be distinguished from being knowledge, in true beliefs as in all other things. A certain category of a person's sheer *guesses,* or a certain category of her *false* beliefs, might be reliable indicators of a certain category of facts, but those guesses, or false beliefs, would not *thereby* be knowledge. I do not see why true beliefs should be any different in this respect.

Another argument I have encountered[5] points to the beliefs of animals and very young children, many of which count as knowledge even though none of them is either justified or unjustified (because animals and very young children lack the very notion of justification). If justification is irrelevant to distinguishing *their* true beliefs that are knowledge from those that are not, then, so the argument goes, it is generally irrelevant (and something else is needed, viz., being produced by a reliable process). But this does not follow. It must be admitted that animals and children do counter the claim that *no* belief is knowledge unless it is *justified.* But they do not counter the claim I subscribed to above, that no *un*justified belief can be knowledge, nor the claim that the concept of knowledge does require justification in its primary application, namely to those of us who do have the notion of a belief's being justified or not. In the natural extension of the concept to others who have beliefs this requirement must of course be dropped.

William Alston gives an example that he claims shows the possibility of knowledge without justification.[6] S has "friends" who

> convince him that for about half the time his sense experience is a radically unreliable guide to his current situation, and that he cannot tell when this is the case. They produce very impressive

> evidence. The totality of the evidence available to S strongly supports their story. S . . . justifiably believes that his senses are not to be trusted.

But there comes an occasion when S

> is about to cross a street and seems to see a truck coming down the street. In fact his perceptual belief-forming apparatus is working normally and a truck *is* coming down the street. Forgetting his skepticism for a moment he waits for the truck to pass before venturing into the street. He acquired a momentary perceptual belief that a truck was coming down the street. . . . it seems clear that he did acquire knowledge. . . . given the fact that his senses were functioning in a perfectly reliable and normal fashion, and given the fact that he thereby felt certain that a truck was coming down the street . . . , is it not clear that S *learned* (*ascertained, found out*) that a truck was coming, that he was *cognizant* of the truck, that he received *information* about the state of affairs in the street?

Perhaps there is a sense in which S received the information that a truck was coming down the street (roughly the same sense in which a video-recorder might receive that information), but it seems clear to me that S did *not* learn, ascertain, find out, or come to *know* that truth. And this is because S did lack adequate justification for believing it. Suppose we make the example clearer in this respect. Suppose that the story S's "friends" tell him is true and that S even has memories of many similar sense-experiences that his later experience gave him reason to think were illusory (or at least to mistrust). Now it is quite clear that S's total evidence does not make it likely that his visual experience of the truck is veridical, and it is quite clear to me that S therefore does not *know* that it is veridical or that he sees a truck bearing down on him.

Of course, if S *could not help* believing it then he cannot be reproached for doing so and is, in a sense, justified in doing so, though not *rationally* justified. And, whether or not S could help believing it, he was rationally justified in not taking any chances, in *acting* as if there were a truck bearing down on him. It may be easy here to fail to distinguish the truth that S is justified in the belief because he could not help it or is rationally justified in acting as if it were true from the falsehood that S *knows* what he believes. Consider an example in which such distracting truths are not present. Suppose that what S saw was something whose existence had no relevance for S's action (as far as S had any reason to believe)—say, a large blinking blue light way down the street—and suppose the sight of this neither justified nor compelled S's belief in its existence (supposing S had the same reasons as before for not trusting the general reliability of his senses) but S carelessly believed in it anyway. Does S *know* that he sees the blinking light?

3. *How voluntary is belief?*

The final argument I will discuss also tries to bolster the reliabilist position we are considering by undermining that of the justificationist. It seeks to discredit the very notion of justification of belief. The argument fastens on the fact that the notion of a belief's being justified or not requires a *voluntaristic* conception of belief and it contends that this conception is inappropriate.[7]

Being justified in believing something is possible only if it is also possible for one to be *un*justified in believing something. To be unjustified in believing something means that one *ought* not to believe it. And this can be true only if one *can* refrain from believing it, only if one has a choice between believing and not believing and makes the wrong choice. But, this argument claims, we never do have any such direct voluntary control over whether or not we believe something. It is conceptually impossible. Believing is just not the sort of thing that involves the will in the direct way that action does. One cannot just decide to believe or not to believe something and forthwith do so, in the way that one can just decide to act or not to act and forthwith do so. Thus, the argument concludes, the notion of a belief's being justified or unjustified is confused and illegitimate, implying that belief is more voluntary than it could conceivably be. Justification should be replaced in the analysis of knowledge with a reliability condition.

It seems to me that, on the contrary, belief is as voluntary as the notion of its being justified or unjustified requires. All that is needed is that direct voluntary control of one's belief should be possible, at least sometimes. If that is so, then we can interpret an ascription of unjustifiedness to a belief that the subject cannot help having as saying that, if the subject were able to help it, she ought not to hold the belief. And we do seem to think that cases of direct voluntary control of belief do actually occur. For we do sometimes reproach people for believing as they do and act as if we think that they should, and could, just stop doing so, and we swallow the voluntaristic implications with equanimity.

Of course we must recognize that many beliefs we have we could not just stop having forthwith and many we do not have we could not just adopt forthwith. I could not, for instance, just for the fun of it simply give up forthwith my belief that the earth has existed for many years past, or that I am married and a father, or that there is a chair in the room where I now sit. I could not simply adopt forthwith a belief in the contrdictory of one of these propositions, or a belief that it is at this moment raining (not raining) in Sydney, or that there are (are not) at least thirty-five planets in our galaxy that have life on them. I cannot seriously raise the question of whether or not to do one of these things.

But just the same is true concerning many *intentions* for future action I have and many others I lack. I could not simply give up forthwith my intention to eat tomorrow or to teach my courses next semester or to have clothes on whenever I appear in public. I could not simply adopt forthwith an intention with content contradictory to one of these, or the intention to jump off a tall building tomorrow or to scream loudly the next time I am in a department meeting. And no one (I hope) is going to claim that *intending* future action is not a voluntary matter evaluatable as justified or unjustified.

And no one should have trouble in recognizing that sometimes one does have a choice as to whether or not forthwith to adopt (or give up) a certain intention about one's future action. No one will see any absurdity in supposing that each of the following three alternatives is now in my power to embrace forthwith: decide to take the car to the office this afternoon, decide to walk to the office this afternoon, make no decision either way for the time being. But equally there is no absurdity in supposing that each of the following alternatives is now in my power to embrace forthwith: believe what Sally's confident memory says is the population of Syracuse, believe that her memory must be mistaken (for I seem to remember a much higher figure), believe nothing either way on the matter for the time being. In fact I frequently confront situations where conflicting evidence, or my own uncertain memory, make both my believing something and my not believing it quite *live* options for me and where which I do certainly *seems* to me to be a matter of my simply *deciding* (perhaps after some deliberation) which to do.

I have heard it argued that belief is necessarily not a voluntary matter on the ground that it is impossible to believe something for the sake of an extrinsic reward. If someone were to convince you that he would give you a million dollars if only you start believing within the next ten minutes, and without any investigation, that exactly eight females were born in Tompkins County Hospital in the last 100 hours, you could not do it. But, the argument goes, it should be possible for you to do this if belief could be a voluntary sort of thing.

There are two serious problems with this argument. In the first place, it is far from clear that it is *always* impossible to believe something for the sake of an extrinsic reward. Suppose that, as I am deliberating whether to trust Sally's memory or mine or neither regarding the population of Syracuse, she offers to bring me breakfast in bed if I decide to trust her memory. (She offers this out of an unselfish desire that I not miss out on a opportunity to believe a truth.) Might that not help me to decide to believe the figure she remembers? To be sure, if I did not already have a fairly strong evidential reason to believe it—her sincere testimony as to what she clearly remembers—if she had admittedly just guessed at the figure, then this sort of incentive (even one much greater) could not lead me to believe it. I do not think I could ever believe any such thing without some non-negligible evidential reason for doing so, and perhaps this is true of most people. But this may, for all I know, be only a contingent fact about us. I have yet to see a convincing argument that it is conceptually impossible that someone should manage to believe such a thing without having any evidence for it for the sake of an extrinsic reward. I think I can imagine observations that would be good evidence that such a thing had happened, at least as far as observations of another person can ever furnish good evidence as to what they believe. It would be amazingly irrational, but, as we all know, people do some amazingly irrational things.[8]

But even if it is a conceptual necessity that we can believe something only when we have evidential reason to do so, this is quite compatible with my deciding to believe for the sake of an extrinsic reward. It means only that a situation in which my decision to believe is motivated in that way must be prepared by my already having some evidential reason which has not yet led me to believe.

Moreover, even if it were true that an extrinsic reward could never be even part of one's motive for believing something, it would not follow that one can never be in a position where one can simply choose which of two or more incompatible alternative options to adopt in one's belief. Compare the following two bits of inner monologue:

> Should I give up my intention to refuse all invitations for the rest of the week, in light of how much I have accomplished in the last two days?
>
> Should I give up my belief that Rex was lying, in light of Lois's corroboration of his testimony?

In both cases I am deliberating a *decision* as to what my attitude will be towards a certain proposition and I expect my decision to determine my attitude equally directly in both cases.

It does seem clear that no option—whether it is for acting or intending or believing—can be *live* for me unless I have some reason to choose it. And certain sorts of things that can be reasons for adopting the attitude of believing cannot be reasons for adopting the attitude of intending, and vice versa. Possessing evidence that p is reason to believe that p but not reason to intend that p. Possessing evidence that if I act in such-and-such a way then certain results I desire will come about is reason to intend that I so act but not reason to believe that I will so act—except insofar as it is reason for intending it and intending it implies believing it: it is not reason for believing it independently of being reason for intending it. But this difference should not obscure from us the fundamental similarity in their relation to the will that there is between believing and intending: that an unchosen option is live for me only if I have some reason to choose it goes for intending as well as for believing; that conflicting options can all be live for me if I have reason to choose each of them and that when this happens (barring rather special circumstances) I can simply choose which option to adopt and forthwith do so: this goes for believing as well as for intending.

I conclude that belief is as voluntary as it needs to be for the concept of justification to apply (if intention is) and that there is no basis in the consideration of voluntariness for the suggestion that in the analysis of knowledge the notion of a belief's being justified should give way to the notion of its being produced by a reliable process.[9]

NOTES

1. The third position is probably a successful refuge. A reliability account of the fourth condition seems to me as likely to work as any, although I think that an account in terms of a certain notion of undefeated justification is equally adequate. But that is a topic for another paper.
2. In the new second disjunct, something should be said about what it is for the conditions to be present and capable of causing the belief (without actually doing so). Alvin Goldman, in his paper, "The Internalist Conception of Justification," in French, Uehling, and Wettstein, eds., *Studies in Epistemology, Midwest Studies in Philosophy V* (Minneapolis, MN: University of Minnesota Press, 1980), pp. 27–51 (which is the best-developed reliabilist account of justification I know of), allows that the conditions by which a person is justified in changing his or her beliefs should be immediately accessible to the person, a point that seems clearly right to me. He suggests further, however, (and here is the reliabilism) that what makes a complete set of justification principles (which dictate what sorts of immediately accessible facts justify what sorts of beliefs) a *correct* complete set is just the fact that if one always followed those principles in forming one's beliefs then (given the way the world is) one's beliefs would be mostly correct. He argues that there is no other way that the principles of justification can be validated. For an argument in a contrary vein, that some complete set of principles of justification must be such that one needs only to understand them in order to be justified in accepting them (that is, they must be evident a priori), see my "The Justification of Belief: A Primer", in Ginet and Shoemaker eds., *Knowledge and Mind* (Oxford University Press, 1983), p. 36.
3. In Pappas ed., *Justification and Knowledge* (Dordrecht: D. Reidel, 1979), pp. 1–24.
4. I doubt that anything we should count as a perceptual or quasi-perceptual justification could be built into the example, given the content of S's belief, which refers to a location specified by proper name rather than in terms of S's point of view and to the Centigrade measure of temperature. A better example of a possible but non-actual kind of perceptual or quasi-perceptual justification would be the following: S is caused by varying intensities of magnetic field around her to have varying intensities of a special sort of sensation and is prompted by that sensation to believe that she feels varying intensities of some sort of force impinging on her. If the content of her sensation-prompted beliefs were, however, that there were variously intense fields of *magnetic* force occurring somewhere in the basement of Goldwin Smith Hall, then her justification for them could not be purely perceptual, any more than my justification for believing that the white grains I see before me are salt obtained from beneath Cayuga Lake can be purely perceptual.
5. In, for example, William Alston's "What's Wrong with Immediate Knowledge?", *Synthese* 55 (April 1983), pp. 73–96.
6. In "Justification and Knowledge," presented at a Special Session on Knowledge and Justification at the World Congress of Philosophy, Montreal, August, 1983.
7. This argument too is suggested in Alston's paper mentioned in n5, above.
8. I would not deny that the very idea of someone's even *offering* a reward for just believing something is strikingly odd, in a way that offering a reward for *acting as if* one believed it would not be so odd. But consider the idea of someone's offering a reward for just *intending* a certain future action (not caring whether or not one carries out the intention when the time comes). That too would be very odd. The oddity in either case can be explained, I think, by two considerations. In the first place, it would

be unusual that, and hard to see why, someone would desire one to intend or believe in a particular way without this desire deriving from a desire as to how one should act (a desire whose object at least includes that one should act in the way that the belief and intention would normally lead to). And if it is one's action that is really wanted (or part of what is really wanted), then it would be more sensible to attach the reward to the action (or the whole of which it is part), for then the chances of getting what is really wanted could not be lessened and would most likely be increased. In the second place, there is the difficulty of confirming that one has met the condition for the reward by really believing or intending as required, rather than merely pretending to do so. The fact that one's motive is the reward makes confirming one's true propositional attitude more difficult than it would ordinarily be, because one might reasonably think that one could gain the reward by acting as if one believed or intended in the required way without actually troubling to believe or intend.

9. An earlier version of this paper was read at a session of the World Congress of Philosophy in Montreal in August, 1983. The revision has benefitted from comments made in the discussion on that occasion.

6

Knowledge and Intellectual Virtue

ERNEST SOSA

I

An intellectual virtue is a quality bound to help maximize one's surplus of truth over error; or so let us assume for now, though a more just conception may include as desiderata also generality, coherence, and explanatory power, unless the value of these is itself explained as derivative from the character of their contribution precisely to one's surplus of truth over error. This last is an issue I mention in order to lay it aside. Here we assume only a teleological conception of intellectual virtue, the relevant end being a proper relation to the truth, exact requirements of such propriety not here fully specified.

Whatever exactly the end may be, the virtue of a virtue derives not simply from leading us to it, perhaps accidentally, but from leading us to it reliably: e.g., "in a way *bound* to maximize one's surplus of truth over error." Rationalist intuition and deduction are thus prime candidates, since they would always lead us aright. But it is not so clearly virtuous to admit no other faculties, seeing the narrow limits beyond which intuition and deduction will never lead us. What other faculties might one admit?

II

There are faculties of two broad sorts: those that lead to beliefs from beliefs already formed, and those that lead to beliefs but not from beliefs. The first of these we call "transmission" faculties, the second "generation" faculties. Rationalist deduction is hence a transmission faculty and rationalist intuition a "generation" faculty. Supposing reason a single faculty with subfaculties of intuitive reason and inferential reason, reason itself is then both a transmission faculty and a generation faculty. The other most general

Source: Ernest Sosa, "Knowledge and Intellectual Virtue" *THE MONIST,* vol. 68, no. 2 (April, 1985), pp. 226–245.

faculties traditionally recognized are, of course, perception, introspection, and memory. Shall we simply admit these, so as to break the narrow limits of reason in our search for truth?

Memory would seem a transmission faculty.[1] If I remember that the square of the hypothenuse is equal to the sum of the squares of the legs then my present belief to that effect derives in a certain way from my earlier belief to that same effect. If we think of memory thus it is then as little fallible as deductive reason. Given the truth of its input beliefs, there is no chance whatever for a false output, just as in deduction, Indeed memory then seems if anything more secure than deduction, since the object of the input belief is the very same as that of the output belief. We go from belief at time t in the Pythagorean Theorem to belief at a later time t′ in that very same proposition. There should hence be no rationalist compunction about such transmission memory as a further faculty beside intuitive and deductive reason.

Possession of an excellent transmissive memory is yet compatible with frequent error in one's ostensible memories. Someone might have an excellent ability to retain beliefs once acquired, and yet suffer from a terrible propensity to believe new things out of the blue which come as apparent memories, as beliefs from the past.

Turn next to intuitive reason, a faculty of grasping relatively simple necessary truths, an ability or power by which one cannot consider without accepting any necessary truth that is simple enough. Someone might then be gifted with such a faculty, while all the same suffering from a terrible propensity to believe things out of the blue as apparent truths of intuitive reason, as apparently truths that he grasps just because of their simple and obvious necessity, while in fact (a) other operative causes suffice on their own to bring about the beliefs in question, and (b) the intrinsic character of the propositions believed—their simple necessity—would *not* alone call forth his assent upon consideration.

If the possibility of a propensity to error in one's ostensible intuitions does not rule out intuitive reason, then the similar potential for error in one's ostensible memories cannot alone rule out transmissive memory, even for strict rationalism.

Whereas memory is like deductive reason in being a transmission faculty, perception is rather like intuitive reason in being a generation faculty. Both the external perception of the senses and the internal perception of introspection generate beliefs out of states that are not beliefs. [More strictly: "out of states that are not beliefs at the same or at higher levels in the hierarchy of beliefs B(P), B(B(P)), B(B(B(P))),—etc." This in order to allow for the introspection of B(P) by B(B(P)).]

The perceptual faculty of sight, for example, generates beliefs about the colors and shapes of surfaces seen fully, within a certain range, and in adequate light. Such beliefs issue from visual impressions derived in turn from the seen objects. Here again we have the familiar possibility in a new form: now it is someone with excellent sight subject besides to frequent hallucinations. His ostensible visual perceptions are thus highly error-prone but that should not cancel the virtue of his faculty of sight so long as both erring intuition and erring memory retain their status. And similar reasoning applies to introspection as well.

If on the other hand perception as a faculty can ever conceivably lead us astray, then perhaps what makes a belief perceptual is its basis in experience as if P, leaving it open whether or not the belief derives from a perceptual process originating in a fact corresponding to the object of belief: namely, P. Such perception *can* of course lead us astray. It does so whenever a perceptual belief turns out to be in error. Such perception would then be *essentially* an experience-belief (input-output) device and it would seem a dubious virtue for any epistemic community so circumstanced that it nearly always would lead them astray.

That is a promising tack for external perception but dubious for other general faculties. Take for instance memory. Even if on occasion we accept P because of what seems phenomenologically a memory feeling or inclination to accept P, surely not every case of memory can be conceived thus. Here we run against the fact that nothing in the operation of memory need play experience's role as input for perception. One may simply find oneself believing that the square of the hypothenuse equals the sum of the squares of the legs with no separate memory feeling of any sort. Yet that might still be a perfectly acceptable case of remembering. And something similar holds good for reason, both intuitive and deductive.

III

What makes a faculty intellectually virtuous? *Its* performance or powers, surely? If so what is required in a faculty is that *it* not lead us astray in our quest for truth: that *it* outperform feasible competitors in its truth/error delivery differential. This even if one is often wrong, or nearly always wrong, in one's beliefs as to the outputs of that faculty. Someone may be gifted with comprehensive and accurate recall well above the average for his epistemic kind. What if in addition he is nearly always wrong when he both believes something and takes himself to believe it on the basis of memory—wrong both on the source of his belief, which in fact is not memory, and also wrong in the belief itself, which in fact is false? Would this invalidate the claim to knowledge of any deliverance of his excellent memory, even one about whose source he forms no further belief?

How to determine the truth/error delivery differential of a faculty will depend on whether it is generative or transmissive. For a generative faculty the relevant differential covers all deliverances of that faculty. But it can't be right to charge against a transmissive faculty errors that enter with its inputs, for which it bears no responsibility. The relevant differential for a transmissive faculty is accordingly the truth/error differential over outputs yielded by *true* inputs. Intuitive reason, deductive reason, and propositional memory all hence deliver a truth/error differential apparently undiminished by falsehood. But neither introspection nor perception may seem so favored.

Introspection may seem not so favored in general, if defined as acquisition or sustainment of belief about one's own mental state on the basis of one's own mental state. For one can look within and attribute n sides to a visual image that in fact has n + 1 sides. Dependent as it is on the favor of external conditions, outer perception is all the more prone to lead us astray. And it seems unavailing to plead that misleading perception is no true perception. Despite perfection *in the subject himself* outer perception can still go astray through unfavorable *external* conditions, a difference from inner perception whose consequences we need to explore.

Pure introspection, it may be argued, is not guessing or miscounting or any such error-prone process that may *build* on introspection but is not exhaustively introspection. Of course not just *any* belief about one's own mental state counts as pure introspection. Pure introspection requires a certain causal aetiology: it requires that one's belief about a mental state of one's own have its source in that very mental state. But not just in any way whatever may the mental state serve as source of one's belief: not when one miscounts the sides of one's image, for instance. Here it is not just *introspection* that plays a role, but also *counting* (a process with external application liable perhaps to lead us astray).

Pure introspection is a cognitive process that in normal conditions reflects the actual character of one's mental states and as such cannot normally cause error. Through greater attentiveness and circumspection one can normally improve the quality of one's introspection and thus enhance its accuracy. But except for rare special phenomena—excruciating pain, for example—it does seem plausible that abnormal conditions could always frustrate one's best attempts at accurate introspection. Such abnormality could derive from a variety of causes including hypnosis, brainwashing, and neural engineering.

Yet why call the source of a belief "introspection" when it derives wholly from the suggestion of a hypnotist? And if a belief is not after all a deliverance of introspection when a mere hypnotic suggestion, why call it pure introspection if it derives *even partly* from hypnosis and partly from a somewhat misdescribed internal phenomenon? If we follow this line, then pure introspection seems again no less infallible than rational intuition. In each case we have a faculty in the subject leading causally from given facts to the belief in them. The process can of course go wrong in various ways—haste, perhaps, or inattentiveness, or hypnosis—but when it goes wrong we are denied a *pure* exemplar of introspection or intuition, as the case may be.

If we do yield to such purism on reason both intuitive and deductive, on memory, and on introspection, with what right can we deny the same treatment to outer perception? When some abnormality dupes us through illusion or hallucination, we could absolve the faculty of perception by alleging that any such error cannot be charged to *pure* perception: "Pure perception requires normal conditions, internal *and* external, and hence precludes the presence of abnormalities responsible for such illusion or hallucination."

But it is hard to credit someone with good perception if he is frequently enough duped by illusion or hallucination: we need to reconsider purism in general.

IV

We are thus back to our question: If someone's ostensible intuitions, deductions, memories, introspections, and perceptions are mostly wrong, how can we credit him with intellectually virtuous faculties of reason, memory, and perception, when the virtue of such virtues would have to derive from their maximizing our differential of truth over error? There is, perhaps, a plausible response: "What makes something an *ostensible* x is that it *seems* an x, but a belief can *seem* a deliverance of reason, or of memory, or of perception, without really being such. Thus the fact that *ostensible* deliverances of X are nearly always wrong is quite compatible with *true* deliverances of X being nearly always right, and hence quite compatible with X's being an intellectually virtuous faculty." Yet it still seems absurd to credit someone with good perception if he is frequently duped by hallucination or illusion, even when such anomalies issue from a variety of sporadic causes. Most especially does that seem absurd if the responsible causes are intrinsic to the subject himself.

Someone prone to frequent illusions or hallucinations of mainly internal origin cannot be credited with good visual perception in an epistemically most relevant sense. This even if in normal external conditions he *does* reflect with unsurpassed accuracy the colors and shapes in his environment, by virtue of his excellent eyesight. Perhaps then such receptiveness is necessary for virtue but *not* sufficient. Perhaps one needs to mirror such properties not just in the sense of showing their impact when they are appropriately placed and mediated in one's environment, but in the fuller sense that includes *also* a further requirement: that one show the characteristic trace of such impact *only* under the action of the correlated sensible properties, in normal conditions.

The key element of a specific perceptual faculty would then be some quality enabling the subject to reflect accurately the presence *or absence* of some correlated range of properties and relations. The presence of such properties would project characteristic images or traces in the subject, whose presence or absence could then guide his perceptual beliefs. Under this fuller conception of a virtuous perceptual faculty, then, to the extent one is prone to illusion or hallucination in certain conditions, to that extent is diminished whatever relevant faculty one might still retain: to that extent is it diminished in its ability to justify in such conditions.

Unfortunately, that analysis does not carry over easily to other traditional faculties. There is nothing that plays for them the role played by sensory images or "traces" for outer perception. Ostensible memories, it may be recalled, will not serve, since they amount not to pre-belief images (except for the very special cases in which personal memory does function via imagistic traces), but to the beliefs themselves believed retained in memory. And something similar holds good in each of the other cases: introspection, intuition, and deduction.

For faculties other than outer perception we are hence left with a question: is there nothing in them analogous to the hallucinations or illusions that make a subject's perception less virtuous than it might be? Must we say that such faculties are always error free, since there is no way of understanding how their true operation could possibly lead to error? Our understanding of how belief can be *perceptual* though false depends on understanding perception as essentially an experience-belief mechanism fallible through the occasional failure of an experience to reflect what experience of that sort normally reflects. What can play the role of experience for any of the other faculties?

Is there any sort of belief-guiding pre-belief appearance in the operation of introspection, of memory, of intuition, or of deduction? In the absence of any such appearance, moreover, how can any belief be in error while yet an introspective, memory, intuitive or deductive belief?

Take memory. Shall we say that any belief about the past will count as a memory belief? Surely not: one can *infer* to new beliefs about the past, which do not then issue from memory. Shall we say that any belief is due to memory which is just there at a time with no inferential or experiential lineage? Surely not: a belief due to present subliminal suggestion is not a memory belief, nor is one implanted by advanced neural technology. How then can we conceive of a *memory* belief without involving its aetiology? There seems no way. But once we do involve such aetiology, how then do we understand the lineage required for legitimacy as memory while still allowing the possibility of error due to the misoperation of *memory* (and not to flaws in the original inputs)?

Suppose $B_t(P)$ can derive by memory from $B_{t'}(Q)$ where $t > t'$ and $P = Q$ (failing which it is hard to see how error could possibly arise from the operation of memory). This entails a hard question: How may P and Q be related for it to be possible that B(P) derive by memory from B(Q)? Can they differ to any width?

Everyone is of course familiar with the decay of information in memory. Thus one may ostensively remember a friend's phone number as 245–6088 when really it is 245–9088. But here we must ask: Is the presence of the '6' due to the operation of *memory*? Or is it due to nothing more than guessing in the absence of true memory, or perhaps to an unfortunate disposition to switch the '6' and the '9'? "Well, it *feels* no diferent than any of the other six digits!" True, but can that be a good guide to when we do and when we do not have memory, if a hypnotist might have created that same feeling for all seven digits, *none* in that case being a deliverance of memory? The relevant feeling, so far as I can tell, might be just the feeling of confidence in the absence of reasons, and *that* hypnosis can provide. Therefore it cannot be such a feeling that *makes* a belief a memory belief, however well or ill it might serve as symptom or criterion. And we are thus left with our main questions: (a) What then *can* constitute the character of a belief of being a memory belief if not the causal aetiology of that belief? (b) If it *is* its causal aetiology that makes a belief of P a pure memory belief, what short of an earlier belief of P can serve as relevant cause? "Nothing" seems in each case a defensible answer. And until we are shown some flaw in this answer it will seem defensible to suppose memory infallible when pure.

Since the relevant considerations seem applicable not just to memory but equally to introspection, intuition, and deduction, each of these raises the same question of how it may be understood so as to allow error. The difficulties already encountered suggest a shift in the burden of proof: Why *not* conceive of such faculties as infallible?

V

There is one other subfaculty of reason beside intuitive reason and deductive reason, and that is of course ampliative reason, whether inductive or explanatory. This is just reason in its role as seeker of coherence and comprehensiveness, however, and granted the *possibility* that our most coherent and comprehensive account of a certain matter fail to accord with the brute facts, such ampliative reason must take a place next to external perception among fallible faculties. Just as with external perception, our most justified ampliative procedure may yet lead us into error. But there is nothing here to require revision of the view that intuition, deduction, introspection, and memory are all infallible.

Yet there is one remaining scruple. We made an exception by admitting the fallibility of perception for one main reason: because there can be perceptually justified yet false beliefs. And this fits with our notion that a belief's justification derives from the endowments and conduct that lie behind it. For the falsehood of a perceptually justified belief may go unreflected in the subject's perception because of external abnormalities that he could not possibly have grasped. In such circumstances his perceptual false belief shows no defect or misconduct in the subject, and may be perceptually justified. That is why we had to allow perception to be exceptional in being fallible. But is there not a similar reason to allow fallibility in each of the other faculties?

Take a student gifted with excellent memory who attributes *An Essay Concerning Human Understanding* to David Hume. Given his excellent memory proven right on countless occasions, is he not justified in accepting what he ostensibly remembers? And don't we then have as much reason to admit the fallibility of memory as that of perception?

Take again a logician gifted with excellent deductive powers who goes through a relatively simple proof and somehow fails for once to detect an invalidating flaw. Might he not be justified still in believing the (false) conclusion on the basis of his inference from the (true) premisses? And are we not thereby forced to admit the (transmissive) fallibility of deduction?

Or take, finally, someone of normal sophistication and acumen who believes in the existence of a class of all classes that are not self-members. Given his normal ability to understand simple necessary truths and to grasp their truth, might he not be justified through intuition in accepting that untruth about classes at least until shown an opposing demonstration? And are we not thereby forced to admit the fallibility of intuition?

To the contrary, in none of these cases is there really no plausible alternative to admitting the fallibility of the relevant faculty: memory, deduction, or intuition. For in each of them it is at least equally plausible to insist that the false belief derives *not* from the operation of true memory, or true deduction, or true intuition, but from various other interfering causes. Thus, to take just one example, at the point where the logician makes his mistake he is *not* following any relevant rule of deduction. How then can that part of his procedure be true deduction as opposed to, say, blundering through inattention?

But if in no such case does the belief really have its source in the corresponding faculty, whence can it derive its justification? In each case the justification can plausibly be attributed to coherence-seeking ampliative reason, as follows. In each case, the subject (a) is aware of his gift, of his relevant faculty F and its reliability, (b) finds himself with a belief B which he justifiably attributes to his faculty F, and (c) on the basis of (a) and (b) justifiably sustains his belief B. And that is all compatible with the falsity of B. Hence the way in which ostensible memory, deduction, and intuition can lead one into error is roundabout, and compatible after all with the infallibility of the corresponding faculties. In each case, the source of the false belief is not the corresponding faculty F (memory itself, or deduction, or intuition) but rather ampliative, coherence-seeking reason. It is such reason which when provided with the assumptions: (a) that the subject's faculty F is normally reliable (as proved time and time again already), and (b) that present belief B derives from F, a reasonable assumption in the circumstances; reaches on that twofold basis the conclusion (c) that belief B must be true, which sustains the subject in upholding B. In each case, however, B turns out to be false, and—we may now reasonably add—turns out *not* to be a deliverance of F after all.

Thus may we after all explain the apparent fallibility of introspection, intuition, deduction, and memory as illusory reflections of the true fallibility of ampliative, explanatory reason, which may take a belief B for a deliverance of a faculty F when B is neither true *nor* a deliverance of F. (And the objection that no subject S is so reflective as is required by our explanation would receive a twofold response: (a) emphasis on the implicit character of the assumptions attributed to S; and (b) appeal to the distinction between animal knowledge and reflective knowledge in section IX below.)

VI

The question does remain whether intuitive reason (for example) would be of any use to epistemology if ostensible intuitions could always fail to be real and the true ones were indistinguishable from the false ones. But what is it here to distinguish a true one if not to know that it is a true one? And if that's all it is, then why can't the rationalist respond that we *can* tell a true intuition after all, since we can intuit-cum-introspect that an intuition of ours is such, *even if not all ostensible intuition-cum-introspection is real.*

But surely that response would not be plausible if ostensible intuitions almost never turned out to be real. Exactly why not, however, if in any case where ostensible intuition turned out to be real the output belief *would* come out of an infallible process (not simply a reliable process, note, but an infallibly reliable process)? Why should it make a difference how many other cases seem cases of such a process without really being so or what ratio there is of real to false ostensible cases?

Besides, why should one's fallibility with regard to the source S of one's belief B and its justification impugn such justification if the justification derives from source S itself and not from one's knowledge of it. Requiring that one always know the source of one's justification, would seem to land us in a vicious regress.

Despite such doubts from the other side, however, it still seems absurd to allow that someone can know that p because his belief that p does derive from intuition even though his ostensible intuitions almost never turn out to be real.

VII

There is anyhow an alternative to explore before yielding to anything so implausible as human infallibility. According to our alternative, we first define a *faculty* of retentive memory, and only then define a retentive memory belief as a belief deriving causally from the exercise of that faculty. This provides an alternative answer to our question: "If it is its causal aetiology that makes a belief of P a pure memory belief, what short of an earlier belief of P can serve as relevant cause?" And this alternative answer leaves it open that retentive memory be fallible. Whether it is or is not fallible now depends on how we conceive of the faculty itself, on how we define it.

Consider first the notion of a faculty in general. The primary meaning attributed to 'faculty' by my dictionary is: "ability, power." Faculties are therefore presumably in the general family of dispositions. Here are some simple examples of dispositional properties:

a. Being an incline-roller: being a thing x such that were x placed at the top of an inclined plane in certain conditions (absence of obstacles, etc.), then x would roll down.
b. Being a level-roller: being a thing x such that were x placed on a level plane surface and pushed in certain conditions, then x would roll.
c. Being a round-snug-fitter: being a thing x such that were x placed with a certain orientation on a hole of a certain diameter, x would fit snugly.

Both a basketball and a bicycle tire would have dispositions or powers a, b, and c. And in each case of an ordinary object and an ordinary disposition something intrinsic to the object would ground its having the disposition in question: some intrinsic property or some set of intrinsic properties. Thus it's the roundness of a basketball that grounds its having each of the three dispositions or powers: a, b, and c. But it's rather the cylindrical intrinsic character of the tire that grounds its possession of each of a, b, and c. How now shall we think of faculties: as dispositions or as grounding intrinsic characters of dispositions? Faculties seem abilities to do certain sorts of things in certain sorts of circumstances rather than what *underlies* the possession of such abilities. Otherwise, since many different intrinsic characters or natures can underlie possession of the same ability (as happens with a ball and a tire vis-à-vis dispositions a, b, and c) we would have to speak of different faculties in the tire and the ball, which seems wrong. (It is of course somewhat forced to speak of faculties at all in something that is not an agent, but then similar examples could surely be contrived in which a human and an extraterrestrial would take the place of the basketball and the tire respectively.)

If indeed cognitive faculties are viewed as abilities or powers, how more specifically is it done? Here is one possibility: To each faculty there corresponds a set of accomplishments of a distinctive sort. Indeed the faculty is *defined* as the ability to attain such accomplishments. Now of course an accomplishment attainable in given circumstances may be unattainable in other circumstances. Therefore, abilities correlate with accomplishments only relative to circumstances. There is for example our ability to tell (directly) the color and shape of a surface, so long as it is facing, "middle-sized," not too far, unscreened, and in enough light, and so long as one looks at it while sober, and so on. And similarly for other perceptual faculties. Compare also our ability to tell simple enough necessary truths, at least once having attained an age of reason and discernment; and our ability to retain simple enough beliefs in which we have sufficient interest. In each case our remarkably extensive species-wide accomplishments of a certain sort are explained by appeal to a corresponding ability, to a cognitive faculty; or at least we are thus provided the beginning of an explanation, an explanation sketch. But in none of these cases is there really any pretense to infallibility. All we're in a position to require is a good success ratio. Common sense is simply in no position to specify substantive circumstances in which the exercise of sight is bound to be infallible. (By substantive circumstances here is meant circumstances that are not vacuous or trivial in the way of "being such as to be right about the facing surface.") Of course that is not to say that there aren't underlying abilities which are in fact infallible: it's just to say that if there are such abilities common sense is at this point unable to formulate them. (Compare the fact that corresponding to commonsense generalizations about falling bodies and the like science did discover underlying principles with a good claim to being substantive and exceptionless.)

Any actuality involving an individual as essential constituent displays abilities or powers of that individual. The dance of a puppet displays not only abilities of the puppeteer but also powers of the puppet. The powers in the puppet that serve as partial source of its behavior are not however of the sort sufficient to make it an agent, much less a responsible agent. Similarly, someone hypnotized into believing something to his mind groundless would seem too much a puppet of external fate to count as knowing what he believes. His belief does of course display certain powers seated in him as well as certain abilities of the hypnotist. But the powers constituting susceptibility to hypnosis are hardly of the sort to give knowledge or epistemically justified belief. (At least that seems so if one is hypnotized unawares *in our world as it stands.* But it also seems plausible both (a) that we can embellish the example so that hypnosis does provide knowledge, at least in the way the reading of an encyclopedia may do so, and (b) that we can conceive of a world where even being hypnotized unawares does regularly enable people to know things by being hypnotized into believing them.)

What powers or abilities do then enable a subject to know or at least to acquire epistemic justification? They are presumably powers or abilities to distinguish the true from the false in a certain subject field, to attain truth and avoid error in that field. One's power or ability must presumably make one such that, normally at least, in one's ordinary habitat, or at least in one's ordinary circumstances when making such judgements, one *would* believe what is true and *not* believe what is false, concerning matters in that field.

Just how fields are to be defined is determined by the lay of interesting, illuminating generalizations about human cognition, which psychology and cognitive science are supposed in time to uncover. In any case, fields must not be narrowed arbitrarily so as to secure artificially a sort of pseudo-reliability. Human intellectual virtues are abilities to attain cognitive accomplishments in "natural" fields, which would stand out by their place in useful, illuminating generalizations about human cognition.

Faculty F is a *more refined subfaculty* of faculty F′ iff the field f(F) of F includes but is not included by the field f(F′) of F′. Thus the visual faculties of an expert bird-watcher would presumably include many more refined subfaculties of the faculties of color and shape perception that he shares with ordinary people. Moreover, the visual faculties of a bird-watcher with 20–20 vision would presumably include many more refined subfaculties of the faculties that he shares with those who fall well short of his visual acuity.

Faculty F is *more reliable* than faculty F′ iff the likelihood with which F would enable one to discriminate truth from falsehood in f(F) is higher than the likelihood with which F′ would enable one to make such discrimination in f(F′).

Thus may we explain why in certain conditions one is better justified in taking a surface (S) to be polygonal (P) than in taking it to be heptagonal (H): there may then be faculties F and F′ such that (a) F′ yields the belief that S is P; (b) F yields the belief that S is H; (c) F is a more refined sub-faculty of F′, and (d) F′ is more reliable than F.

VIII

Infallible faculties are required by rationalism. But pure rationalism with its *perfectly* reliable certainty is a failed epistemology. A more realistic successor claims our attention today:

> *Reliabilism* is the view that a belief is epistemically justified if and only if it is produced or sustained by a cognitive process that reliably yields truth and avoids error.

There are two main sorts of objection to such reliabilism and they pull in opposite directions. One questions the sufficiency of such reliability for justification. The other questions its necessity.

Consider first someone gifted with a sort of clairvoyance or special sense who considers the deliverances of his gift to be inexplicable superstition, and has excellent reason for his dim view. How plausible would it be to suppose him justified in his clairvoyant beliefs?[2]

From the opposite direction, consider the victim of a Cartesian Evil Demon. If his experience and reasoning are indistinguishable from those of the best justified among us, can we in fairness deny him the justification that we still claim for ourselves? Yet if we do grant him such justification, the *un*reliable processes do yield him much belief that is in fact justified (given our hypothesis).

A response to the first sort of objection modifies radical reliabilism by requiring for justification not only that the belief in question be caused by a reliable process, but also that there be no equally reliable process in the subject's repertoire whose use by him in combination with the process that he actually does use would not have yielded that same belief. Such alternative methods would of course include the recall and use through reasoning of relevant evidence previously unused though stored in memory, including evidence about the reliability of one's pertinent faculties.[3]

That revision will not deal with the problem from the other direction, however, the problem of the justified victim of the Evil Demon. And there is besides a further problem. For if a process is reliable but fallible, it can on occasion fail to operate properly. But that opens the possibility that a process yield a belief B through *improper* operation where by lucky accident B turns out to be true anyhow. Take for example memory, and suppose it fallible. Suppose, in particular, that memory could take a belief that a friend's phone number is 245–9088 as input and yield as output later belief that it is 245–6088. Might not one's memory be such that on a given occasion it *would* in fact have that unfortunate result but for the effect of extremely rare and random inversion-preventing radiation? Would the (correct) output belief properly earn it status as epistemically justified? If so, since no reasoning via falsehood seems involved, would the belief also amount to knowledge? If these are good questions, parallel questions can obviously be raised about our various perceptual faculties.

What in brief is the problem? Apparently, though a belief is caused by a reliable but fallible cognitive process, that process may actually operate improperly and cause the true belief only through the intervention of some highly unusual factor whose presence is merely a lucky accident. Would the belief then fall short of sound epistemic justification, and not be a true instance of knowledge? What might be missing? Perhaps some closer connection between the belief and its truth? Perhaps these cannot be so independent as when they come together only by lucky accident, the way they do in our example of fallible memory.

Compare the Gettier case in which S acquires the belief that p in a highly reliable way and deduces from it that-($p \vee q$), where this last belief turns out to be true but only because it's true that q, since in fact it is false that p. If S has no reason to think it true that q, and no reason to think that-($p \vee q$) except his having inferred it deductively from his belief that p, then it seems clear his belief that-($p \vee q$) turns out to be true only by luck (in some appropriate sense) and is not a case of knowledge.[4]

Finally, compare also the case where we are out driving and spot a barn by its barnlike look from our perspective on the highway; where unknown to us it is the one true barn left standing in that vicinity, in the midst of barn facades all presenting equally realistic barnlike looks, and many such facsimiles may be found for miles in either direction. If visual perception remains a reliable process, then by reliabilism our belief would seem justified, yet though true it seems clearly no knowledge.[5]

These three examples pose a problem not so much for reliabilism as a theory of justification, as for the combination of such a theory of justification with a conception of knowledge as justified true belief.

IX

Here is a short story. Superstitious S believes whatever he reads in the horoscope simply because one day in August it predicted no snow. Tricky T intends to offer S a lemon of a used car and plants the following in the horoscope under S's sign: "You will be offered a business proposition by T. The time is ripe for accepting business propositions." Does S know that T will offer him a deal? T planted the message and would have done so if he had been going to offer S a deal, and would not have done so if he had not been going to offer S a deal. So it is not *just* a lucky guess nor is it *just* a happy accident that S is right in thinking that a deal is forthcoming, given his daily use of the horoscope. In fact here S not only believes the truth that p; but also he would believe that p if it were true that p (in nearby possible worlds where it is true that p), and he would not believe that p if it were false that p (in nearby possible worlds where it is false that p). One thing seems clear: S does not know in such a case. What S lacks, I suggest, is *justification.* His reason for trusting the horoscope is not adequate—to put it kindly. What is such justification?[6]

A being of epistemic kind K is *prima facie* justified in believing P if and only if his belief of P manifests what, relative to K beings, is an intellectual virtue, a faculty that enhances their differential of truth over error. But such prima facie justification may of course be overridden in special cases: e.g., through his learning that the conditions are not normal for the use of that faculty.[7]

It is of prudential importance to the subject himself to know how reliable and trustworthy his own judgements are in various categories. That is also moreover of prudential importance to his fellows and of social importance collectively to his epistemic kind. Testimony is of paramount importance to the *epistemic* weal and progress of any social, language using species.

That is why we take an interest not only in the truth of beliefs but also in their justification. What interests us in justification is essentially the trustworthiness and reliability of the subject with regard to the field of his judgement, in situations normal for judgements in that field. That explains also why what does matter for justification is how the subject performs with regard to factors internal to him, and why it does not matter for justification if external factors are abnormal and unfavorable so that despite his impeccable performance S does not know. What we care about in justification are the epistemic endowments and conduct of the subject, his intellectual virtues.

From this standpoint we may distinguish between two general varieties of knowledge as follows.

> One has *animal knowledge* about one's environment, one's past, and one's own experience if one's judgements and beliefs about these are direct responses to their impact—e.g., through perception or memory—with little or no benefit of reflection or understanding.
>
> One has *reflective knowledge* if one's judgement or belief manifests not only such direct response to the fact known but also understanding of its place in a wider whole that includes one's belief and knowledge of it and how these come about.[8]

Since a direct response supplemented by such understanding would in general have a better chance of being right, reflective knowledge is better justified than corresponding animal knowledge.

Note that no human blessed with reason has merely animal knowledge of the sort attainable by beasts. For even when perceptual belief derives as directly as it ever does from sensory stimuli, it is still relevant that one has *not* perceived the signs of contrary testimony. A reason-endowed being automatically monitors his background information and his sensory input for contrary evidence and automatically opts for the most coherent hypothesis even when he responds most directly to sensory stimuli. For even when response to stimuli is most direct, *if* one were also to hear or see the signs of credible contrary testimony that would change one's response. The beliefs of a *rational* animal hence would seem never to issue from *unaided* introspection, memory, or perception. For reason is always at least a silent partner on the watch for other relevant data, a silent partner whose very *silence* is a contributing cause of the belief outcome.

Both animal and reflective knowledge require a true belief whose justification by its source in intellectual virtue is prima facie but not overridden. Possible overriders of such justification would have to be wider intrinsic states of the subject diminishing significantly the probability that the belief in question be true. The probability that it be true since yielded by the intellectual virtue is then significantly greater than the probability that it be true given the wider intrinsic state.

Overriders come in two varieties: the opposing and the disabling. An overrider of prima facie justification for believing P is opposing iff it would provide *prima facie* justification for believing the opposite: not-P. Otherwise it is a disabling overrider.[9]

If one has visual experience as if there is a pink surface before one, the reception of good testimony that there is no pink surface in the room would provide an opposing overrider. But if the good testimony says only that there is a red light shining on the surface before one, that provides a disabling overrider. What is it in either of these cases that defeats one's *prima facie* justification when one accepts such testimony?

In our eyes anyone who still believes in a pink surface before him after accepting either testimony above would lack justification—this because we consider rational coherence the best overall guide. Even if the testimony is in each case false, given only adequate reason to accept it, one still loses one's justification to believe in the pink surface. Ironically that is so even for someone who does respond directly to the experience of pink with the corresponding belief and whose belief turns out true while the testimony is false. Here it would *seem* that the subject is at least as well off epistemically as his neighbor who also responds to pink experience while ignorant of the (misleading) testimony, and at least as well off as the nearby young child who could not have understood the testimony even had he heard it. But that is an illusion. Once having attained years of reason and discretion, and once in possession of the credible testimony, one errs not to give it due weight, which may betray a flawed epistemic character. This is important news to fellow members of one's epistemic kind, and even to one's own higher self, as is revealed in one's loss of "justification" for belief in the pink surface.

But not just *any* sort of incoherence would betray such a flaw. The author who sincerely takes responsibility in his preface for the "errors that surely remain" is not guilty of epistemic misconduct for continuing to accept individually the contents of his carefully wrought treatise, nor would he sin by accepting their conjunction could he somehow manage to conjoin them. The convinced skeptic with the reasoned conclusion that perceptual beliefs about one's environment are never justified does not lose all justification for his many such beliefs in the course of a normal day. Yet both the author and the skeptic are of course guilty of a sort of incoherence. But how can this be so? How can such incoherence differ relevantly from that of the victim of credible-hence-accepted but misleading testimony who arbitrarily retains what the testimony discredits?

According to our leading idea, the relevant difference must reside in a difference for one's prospects towards getting in the best relation to the truth. This is borne out by reflecting that anyone who lets skeptical arguments mislead him to the cynical extent of a massive withdrawal of doxastic commitment would save his coherence at enormous cost in truth. And the same goes for the honest and sincere author at work on his preface.

X

To sum up.

An intellectual virtue is a subject-grounded ability to tell truth from error infallibly or at least reliably in a correlated field. To be epistemically justified in believing is to believe out of intellectual virtue. To know you need at least epistemic justification. But there are two prominently different sorts of knowledge: the animal and the reflective. Animal knowledge is yielded by reaction to the relevant field unaided by reflection on the place of one's belief and its object within one's wider view. Even for such knowledge it is not just the reliability of the cognitive process yielding the relevant belief that provides its justification. Nor is it enough to require further the absence of any equally reliable process in the subject's repertoire whose use by him combined with the process actually used would not have yielded that belief. For even that will not preclude a subject with excellent eyesight subject however to internal hallucinogenic interference 99% of the time, one deprived of any way to distinguish his cases of true vision from the hallucinations. Such a subject can hardly be granted even animal knowledge in his rare cases of true vision, surely, nor even warranted or justified belief. Though he has a reliable cognitive process of true vision, he yet does not have a relevant faculty in an epistemically most relevant sense: he does not have a faculty F correlated with a "natural" field f(F) such that F is constituted by the ability to discern truth from error with high reliability over f(F). Despite his occasionally operative true vision, our victim of frequent, stable, and long-standing hallucinogenic irregularities does not have the sort of ability constitutive of an epistemically relevant faculty.

Since justified belief seems anyhow insufficient for knowledge (see the objections early in section VIII above), it is tempting to bypass justification and try some wholly fresh approach.[10] Yet justification proves stubbornly required for knowledge. Section IX concludes the paper with some general reflections on the nature of justification and on two of its main varieties.[11]

NOTES

1. Actually this is true only of one sort of memory, "retention." For a notion of generative memory see Carl Ginet's *Knowledge, Perception, and Memory* (Dordrecht: D. Reidel, 1975), esp. ch. 7, sec. 2, pp. 148–53.
2. Cf. Laurence Bonjour, "Externalist Theories of Empirical Knowledge," *Midwest Studies in Philosophy* V (1980): 53–75. Cf. also William Alston, "What's Wrong with Immediate Knowledge?" *Synthese* 55 (1983): 73–97.
3. Cf. Alvin Goldman, "What Is Justified Belief?" in George S. Pappas, ed., *Justification and Knowledge* (Dordrecht: D. Reidel, 1979).
4. Cf. Edmund Gettier, "Is Justified True Belief Knowledge?" *Analysis* 23 (1963): 121–23.
5. Cf. Alvin Goldman, "Discrimination and Perceptual Knowledge," *The Journal of Philosophy* 73 (1976): 771–91.

6. For alternative reactions to our recent difficulties, see Robert Nozick, *Philosophical Explanations* (Cambridge, MA: Harvard University Press, 1981), ch. 3 esp. part I; and Peter Klein, "Real Knowledge," *Synthese* 55 (1983): 143–65.
7. That epistemic justification is prima facie and defeasible is argued already in Roderick M. Chisholm's *Theory of Knowledge,* 1st edition (Englewood Cliffs, NJ: Prentice-Hall, Inc., 1966), p. 46.
8. That "wider whole" essentially involved in good reasoning is wider than might appear is argued by Gilbert Harman in "Reasoning and Evidence One Does Not Possess," *Midwest Studies in Philosophy* 5 (1980) 163–82.
9. Cf. John Pollock, *Knowledge and Justification* (Princeton, NJ: Princeton University Press, 1974).
10. For example, Robert Nozick's in his *Philosophical Explanations, op. cit.* Compare Fred Dretske's *Knowledge and the Flow of Information* (Cambridge, MA: MIT Press/Bradford Books, 1981). For Dretske's *precis* of his book, discussion by several commentators, and replies by the author, see *The Behavioral and Brain Sciences* 6 (1983): 55–90.
11. An earlier version of this paper was part of the Special Session on Knowledge and Justification at the Twelfth World Congress of Philosophy (Montreal, August, 1983).

CHAPTER FOUR
THE *A PRIORI*

In the section that follows we turn to the question of whether human knowledge is rooted in sense experience. Empiricists like John Locke, George Berkeley, David Hume, and the twentieth-century philosopher W. V. O. Quine, among others, have argued that all knowledge is dependent on sense experience. According to these philosophers, everything we know, and the various justifications we can offer for that knowledge, must come from experience. Indeed, for W. V. O. Quine, even basic arithmetical truths like $2 + 2 = 4$ can, in principle, be revised in light of experience. Rationalists, like Plato, Descartes, Leibniz, and others have traditionally argued that at least some significant knowledge is independent of sense experience.

We present this debate with historical selections from the seventeenth century, beginning with the Empiricist, John Locke, moving to the Rationalist Leibniz, and culminating in the Transcendental Idealism of Immanuel Kant. Locke rejected the notion that we have any innate ideas, believing that the human mind is a *tabula rasa* or "empty cabinet." Knowledge, for Locke, was the perception of the agreement and disagreement of our ideas (mental representations)—ideas that have their source in sense experience. Leibniz, however, held that the distinction between necessary and contingent propositions can be found in the kind of analysis we could perform on propositions. In a "finite analysis" in which the predicate concept can be determined to be included in the subject concept we find necessary propositions, while if it merely "converges" on a component of the subject concept it is contingent. David Hume, an Empiricist, held that *a priori* or certain knowledge could only be derived from relations of ideas as opposed to matters of fact. His skepticism regarding knowledge in domains such as metaphysics, as well as his restriction of mathematical knowledge to analytic propositions, awoke Kant from his "dogmatic slumber."

Kant sought to expand the distinction between propositions known on the basis of experience and those whose truth could be grasped by merely considering the meanings of the terms employed. Mathematical propositions like "7 + 5 = 12," according to Kant, are true independent of experience, but their truth consists in more than a semantic analysis of the terms involved. We learn something that is not contained in the terms "7" "5" and "+" when we arrive at the sum of 12. Mathematical knowledge thus provides us with significant knowledge that is necessarily true for Kant.

Quine, Kripke, Kitcher and Boghossian represent the contemporary debate on the *a priori*. Explicit in this debate is the problem of whether or not scientific truths are necessary truths, and, ultimately, whether or not science supersedes philosophical analysis altogether. If the philosopher's job is to discern necessary truths through conceptual analysis, it would seem to follow that if conceptual analysis is insufficient to yield any certain knowledge, the philosopher's job is quite limited. Quine's radical Empiricism, which includes the rejection of all *a priori* knowledge and necessary truth, is a landmark in contemporary philosophy. His position is that of semantic holism, the view that our knowledge of the world must be understood as a holistic web of beliefs, which is always revisable in principle, in light of experience. Changes made at the "periphery" of the web effect others in this web. Core beliefs at the center of the web, such as the laws of logic, may resist change, but in principle all of our knowledge is contingent and *a posteriori*.

Saul Kripke's *Naming and Necessity* is a significant reply to Quine's work, for in it he makes the distinction between necessary *a posteriori* truths and those that are necessary *a priori*. In other words, unlike Quine, Kripke holds that the empirical sciences can give us necessary truths. In order to follow Kripke, we need to hold a different notion of how necessity can be established by way of reference-fixing through possible world analysis; yet he provides an appealing option to the stark, philosophical "desert landscape" to which Quine has been accused of restricting philosophy. Philip Kitcher attempts to construct a way to maintain Quinean Empiricism and also hold that there can be *a priori* knowledge without the metaphysical and semantic commitments required by Kripke's position. Paul Boghossian replies directly to Quine's "Two Dogmas of Empiricism," attempting to prove that analyticity has not been undermined by Quine's arguments and that a workable notion of analyticity can be constructed.

An Essay Concerning Human Understanding

JOHN LOCKE

NO INNATE PRINCIPLES IN THE MIND

1. *The way shown how we come by any Knowledge, sufficient to prove it not innate.* It is an established opinion amongst some men that there are in the understanding certain *innate principles,* some primary notions, κοιναὶ ἔννοιαι, characters, as it were stamped upon the mind of man, which the soul receives in its very first being, and brings into the world with it. It would be sufficient to convince unprejudiced readers of the falseness of this supposition, if I should only show (as I hope I shall in the following parts of this Discourse) how men, barely by the use of their natural faculties, may attain to all the knowledge they have, without the help of any innate impressions, and may arrive at certainty, without any such original notions or principles.

2. *General Assent the great Argument.* There is nothing more commonly taken for granted than that there are certain *principles,* both *speculative* and *practical* (for they speak of both), universally agreed upon by all mankind: which therefore, they argue, must needs be constant impressions which the souls of men receive in their first beings, and which they bring into the world with them, as necessarily and really as they do any of their inherent faculties.

3. *Universal Consent proves nothing innate.* This argument, drawn from universal consent, has this misfortune in it, that, if it were true in matter of fact that there were certain truths wherein all mankind agreed, it would not prove them innate, if there can be any other way shown how men may come to that universal agreement in the things they do consent in, which I presume may be done.

4. *"What is, is," and "It is impossible for the same Thing to be and not to be" not universally assented to.* But, which is worse, this argument of universal consent, which is made use of to prove innate principles, seems to me a demonstration that there are none such, because there

---

Source: John Locke, *An Essay Concerning Human Nature,* first published in 1690.

are none to which all mankind give an universal assent. I shall begin with the speculative, and instance in those magnified principles of demonstration, "Whatsoever is, is," and "It is impossible for the same thing to be and not to be," which, of all others, I think have the most allowed title to innate. These have so settled a reputation of maxims universally received that it will no doubt be thought strange if anyone should seem to question it. But yet I take liberty to say that these propositions are so far from having an universal assent, that there are a great part of mankind to whom they are not so much as known.

5. *Not on the Mind naturally imprinted, because not known to Children, Idiots, &c.* For, first, it is evident, that all children and idiots have not the least apprehension or thought of them. And the want of that is enough to destroy that universal assent which must needs be the necessary concomitant of all innate truths; it seeming to me near a contradiction to say, that there are truths imprinted on the soul, which it perceives or understands not: imprinting, if it signify anything, being nothing else but the making certain truths to be perceived. For to imprint anything on the mind without the mind's perceiving it seems to me hardly intelligible. If therefore children and idiots have souls, have minds, with those impressions upon them, they must unavoidably perceive them, and necessarily know and assent to these truths; which since they do not, it is evident that there are no such impressions. For if they are not notions naturally imprinted, how can they be innate? And if they are notions imprinted, how can they be unknown? To say a notion is imprinted on the mind, and yet at the same time to say that the mind is ignorant of it and never yet took notice of it, is to make this impression nothing. No proposition can be said to be in the mind which it never yet knew, which it was never yet conscious of. For if any one may, then, by the same reason, all propositions that are true, and the mind is capable ever of assenting to, may be said to be in the mind, and to be imprinted; since, if any one can be said to be in the mind, which it never yet knew, it must be only because it is capable of knowing it; and so the mind is of all truths it ever shall know. Nay, thus truths may be imprinted on the mind which it never did, nor ever shall know; for a man may live long, and die at last in ignorance of many truths which his mind was capable of knowing, and that with certainty. So that if the capacity of knowing be the natural impression contended for, all the truths a man ever comes to know will, by this account, be every one of them innate; and this great point will amount to no more, but only to a very improper way of speaking; which, whilst it pretends to assert the contrary, says nothing different from those who deny innate principles. For nobody, I think, ever denied that the mind was capable of knowing several truths. The capacity, they say, is innate, the knowledge acquired. But then to what end such contest for certain innate maxims? If truths can be imprinted on the understanding without being perceived, I can see no difference there can be between any truths the mind is capable of knowing in respect of their original: they must all be innate or all adventitious; in vain shall a man go about to distinguish them.

6. *That men know them when they come to the Use of Reason answered.* To avoid this, it is usually answered that all men know and assent to them, *when they come to the use of reason;* and this is enough to prove them innate.

7. This answer must signify one of these two things: either that as soon as men come to the use of reason these supposed native inscriptions come to be known and observed by them; or else, that the use and exercise of men's reasons assists them in the discovery of these principles, and certainly makes them known to them.

8. *If Reason discovered them, that would not prove them innate.* If they mean that by the use of reason men may discover these principles, and that this is sufficient to prove them innate, their way of arguing will stand thus, viz. that

whatever truths reason can certainly discover to us, and make us firmly assent to, those are all naturally imprinted on the mind; since that universal assent, which is made the mark of them, amounts to no more but this,—that by the use of reason we are capable to come to a certain knowledge of and assent to them; and, by this means, there will be no difference between the maxims of the mathematicians and theorems they deduce from them: all must be equally allowed innate, they being all discoveries made by the use of reason, and truths that a rational creature may certainly come to know, if he apply his thoughts rightly that way.

9. *It is false that Reason discovers them.* But how can these men think the use of reason necessary to discover principles that are supposed innate, when reason (if we may believe them) is nothing else but the faculty of deducing unknown truths from principles or propositions that are already known? That certainly can never be thought innate which we have need of reason to discover, unless, as I have said, we will have all the certain truths that reason ever teaches us to be innate. We may as well think the use of reason necessary to make our eyes discover visible objects, as that there should be need of reason, or the exercise thereof, to make the understanding see what is originally engraven in it, and cannot be in the understanding before it be perceived by it. So that to make reason discover those truths thus imprinted, is to say that the use of reason discovers to a man what he knew before; and if men have those innate impressed truths originally, and before the use of reason, and yet are always ignorant of them till they come to the use of reason, it is in effect to say, that men know and know them not at the same time.

10. It will here perhaps be said that mathematical demonstrations, and other truths that are not innate, are not assented to as soon as proposed, wherein they are distinguished from these maxims and other innate truths. I shall have occasion to speak of assent upon the first proposing more particularly by and by.[1] I shall here only, and that very readily, allow that these maxims and mathematical demonstrations are in this different: that the one has need of reason, using of proofs, to make them out and to gain our assent; but the other, as soon as understood, are, without any the least reasoning, embraced and assented to.

11. Those who will take the pains to reflect with a little attention on the operations of the understanding will find that this ready assent of the mind to some truths depends not either on native inscription or the use of reason, but on a faculty of the mind quite distinct from both of them, as we shall see hereafter.[2] Reason, therefore, having nothing to do in procuring our assent to these maxims, if by saying that "men know and assent to them, when they come to the use of reason" be meant that the use of reason assists us in the knowledge of these maxims, it is utterly false; and, were it true, would prove them not to be innate.

12. *The coming to the Use of Reason not the time we come to know these Maxims.* If by knowing and assenting to them "when we come to the use of reason" be meant that this is the time when they come to be taken notice of by the mind; and that, as soon as children come to the use of reason, they come also to know and assent to these maxims; this also is false and frivolous. First, it is false, because it is evident these maxims are not in the mind so early as the use of reason; and therefore the coming to the use of reason is falsely assigned as the time of their discovery. How many instances of the use of reason may we observe in children, a long time before they have any knowledge of this maxim, "That it is impossible for the same thing to be and not to be"? And a great part of illiterate people and savages pass many years, even of their rational age, without ever thinking on this and the like general propositions. I grant, men come not to the knowledge of these general and more abstract truths, which are thought innate, till they come to the use of reason; and I

add, nor then neither. Which is so, because, till after they come to the use of reason, those general abstract ideas are not framed in the mind, about which those general maxims are, which are mistaken for innate principles, but are indeed discoveries made and verities introduced and brought into the mind by the same way, and discovered by the same steps, as several other propositions, which nobody was ever so extravagant as to suppose innate.

14. *If coming to the Use of Reason were the time of their discovery, it would not prove them innate.* But, secondly, were it true that the precise time of their being known and assented to were when men come to the use of reason, neither would that prove them innate. This way of arguing is so frivolous as the supposition of itself is false. For, by what kind of logic will it appear that any notion is originally by nature imprinted in the mind in its first constitution, because it comes first to be observed and assented to when a faculty of the mind, which has quite a distinct province, begins to exert itself?

15. *The Steps by which the Mind attains several Truths.* The senses at first let in *particular* ideas, and furnish the yet empty cabinet, and, the mind by degrees growing familiar with some of them, they are lodged in the memory, and names got to them. Afterwards, the mind proceeding further abstracts them, and by degrees learns the use of general names. In this manner the mind comes to be furnished with ideas and language, the materials about which to exercise its discursive faculty. And the use of reason becomes daily more visible, as these materials that give it employment increase. But, though the having of general ideas and the use of general words and reason usually grow together, yet I see not how this any way proves them innate. The knowledge of some truths, I confess, is very early in the mind; but in a way that shows them not to be innate. For, if we will observe, we shall find it still to be about ideas, not innate, but acquired; it being about those first which are imprinted by external things, with which infants have earliest to do, which make the most frequent impressions on their senses. In ideas thus got the mind discovers that some agree and others differ, probably as soon as it has any use of memory, as soon as it is able to retain and receive distinct ideas. But whether it be then or no, this is certain, it does so long before it has the use of words, or comes to that which we commonly call "the use of reason". For a child knows as certainly before it can speak the difference between the ideas of sweet and bitter (i.e. that sweet is not bitter), as it knows afterwards (when it comes to speak) that wormwood and sugarplums are not the same thing.

16. A child knows not that three and four are equal to seven, till he comes to be able to count to seven, and has got the name and idea of equality; and then, upon explaining those words, he presently assents to, or rather perceives the truth of, that proposition. But neither does he then readily assent because it is an innate truth, nor was his assent wanting till then because he wanted the use of reason; but the truth of it appears to him as soon as he has settled in his mind the clear and distinct ideas that these names stand for. And then he knows the truth of that proposition upon the same grounds and by the same means, that he knew before that a rod and cherry are not the same thing; and upon the same grounds also that he may come to know afterwards "That it is impossible for the same thing to be and not to be". So that the later it is before anyone comes to have those general ideas about which those maxims are, or to know the signification of those general terms that stand for them, or to put together in his mind the ideas they stand for, the later also will it be before he comes to assent to those maxims;—whose terms, with the ideas they stand for, being no more innate than those of a cat or a weasel, he must stay till time and observation have acquainted him with them; and then he will be in a capacity to know the truth of these maxims, upon the first occasion that shall make him put together those ideas in his mind, and observe

whether they agree or disagree, according as is expressed in those propositions.

17. *Assenting as soon as proposed and understood, proves them not innate.* This evasion therefore of general assent when men come to the use of reason, failing as it does, and leaving no difference between those supposed innate and other truths that are afterwards acquired and learnt, men have endeavoured to secure an universal assent to those they call maxims, by saying they are generally assented to as soon as proposed, and the terms they are proposed in understood; seeing all men, even children, as soon as they hear and understand the terms, assent to these propositions, they think it is sufficient to prove them innate.

18. *If such an Assent be a mark of innate, then "that One and Two are equal to three, that Sweetness is not Bitterness" and a thousand the like, must be innate.* In answer to this I demand whether ready assent given to a proposition, upon first hearing and understanding the terms, be a certain mark of an innate principle? If it be not, such a general assent is in vain urged as a proof of them; if it be said that it is a mark of innate, they must then allow all such propositions to be innate which are generally assented to as soon as heard, whereby they will find themselves plentifully stored with innate principles. For upon the same ground, viz. of assent at first hearing and understanding the terms, that men would have those maxims pass for innate, they must also admit several propositions about numbers to be innate. Even natural philosophy, and all the other sciences, afford propositions which are sure to meet with assent as soon as they are understood. That "two bodies cannot be in the same place" is a truth that nobody any more sticks at than at this maxim, that "it is impossible for the same thing to be and not to be," that "white is not black," that "a square is not a circle," that "yellowness is not sweetness". But, since no proposition can be innate unless the *ideas* about which it is be innate, this will be to suppose all our ideas of colours, sounds, tastes, figure, &c., innate, than which there cannot be anything more opposite to reason and experience. Universal and ready assent upon hearing and understanding the terms is, I grant, a mark of self-evidence; but self-evidence, depending not on innate impressions but on something else, belongs to several propositions which nobody was yet so extravagant as to pretend to be innate.

19. *Such less general Propositions known before these universal Maxims.* Nor let it be said that those more particular self-evident propositions, which are assented to at first hearing, as that "one and two are equal to three," that "green is not red," &c., are received as the consequences of those more universal propositions which are looked on as innate principles, since anyone, who will but take the pains to observe what passes in the understanding, will certainly find that these, and the like less general propositions, are certainly known and firmly assented to by those who are utterly ignorant of those more general maxims; and so, being earlier in the mind than those (as they are called) first principles, cannot owe to them the assent wherewith they are received at first hearing.

21. *These Maxims not being known sometimes till proposed, proves them not innate.* Men grow first acquainted with many of these self-evident truths upon their being proposed; but it is clear that whosoever does so finds in himself that he then begins to know a proposition, which he knew not before, and which from thenceforth he never questions, not because it was innate, but because the consideration of the nature of the things contained in those words would not suffer him to think otherwise, how, or whensoever he is brought to reflect on them.

22. *Implicitly known before proposing, signifies that the Mind is capable of understanding them, or else signifies nothing.* If it be said the understanding hath an *implicit* knowledge of these principles, but not an *explicit,* before this first hearing (as they must who will say that they are in the understanding before they are known),

it will be hard to conceive what is meant by a principle imprinted on the understanding implicitly, unless it be this,—that the mind is capable of understanding and assenting firmly to such propositions. And thus all mathematical demonstrations, as well as first principles, must be received as native impressions on the mind.

23. *The Argument of assenting on first hearing, is upon a false supposition of no precedent teaching.* There is, I fear, this further weakness in the foregoing argument, that men are supposed not to be taught nor to learn anything *de novo,* when, in truth, they are taught, and do learn something they were ignorant of before. For, first, it is evident that they have learned the terms, and their signification, neither of which was born with them. But this is not all the acquired knowledge in the case: the ideas themselves, about which the proposition is, are not born with them, no more than their names, but got afterwards. For, though a child quickly assent to this proposition, "that an apple is not fire," when by familiar acquaintance he has got the ideas of those two different things distinctly imprinted on his mind, and has learnt that the names 'apple' and 'fire' stand for them, yet it will be some years after, perhaps, before the same child will assent to this proposition, "that it is impossible for the same thing to be and not to be"; because that, though perhaps the words are as easy to be learnt, yet the signification of them being more large, comprehensive, and abstract than of the names annexed to those sensible things the child hath to do with, it is longer before he learns their precise meaning, and it requires more time plainly to form in his mind those general ideas they stand for.

25. *These Maxims not the first known.* But that I may not be accused to argue from the thoughts of infants, which are unknown to us, and to conclude from what passes in their understandings before they express it, I say next that these two general propositions are not the truths that first possess the minds of children, nor are antecedent to all acquired and adventitious notions; which, if they were innate, they must needs be. Whether we can determine it or no, it matters not, there is certainly a time when children begin to think, and their words and actions do assure us that they do so. When therefore they are capable of thought, of knowledge, of assent, can it rationally be supposed they can be ignorant of those notions that nature has imprinted, were there any such? The child certainly knows that the nurse that feeds it is neither the cat it plays with, nor the blackamoor it is afraid of, that the wormseed or mustard it refuses is not the apple or sugar it cries for; this it is certainly and undoubtedly assured of; but will anyone say, it is by virtue of this principle, "That it is impossible for the same thing to be and not to be," that it so firmly assents to these and other parts of its knowledge?

26. *And so not innate.* Though therefore there be several general propositions that meet with constant and ready assent, as soon as proposed to men grown up, who have attained the use of more general and abstract ideas, and names standing for them, yet, they not being to be found in those of tender years, who nevertheless know other things, they cannot pretend to universal assent of intelligent persons, and so by no means can be supposed innate; it being impossible that any truth which is innate (if there were any such) should be unknown, at least to anyone who knows anything else. Since, if they are innate truths, they must be innate thoughts, there being nothing a truth in the mind that it has never thought on. Whereby it is evident, if there be any innate truths, they must necessarily be the first of any thought on, the first that appear there.

OF KNOWLEDGE IN GENERAL

1. *Our Knowledge conversant about our Ideas.* Since the mind in all its thoughts and reasonings hath no other immediate object but its own ideas, which it alone does or can contemplate, it

is evident that our knowledge is only conversant about them.

2. *Knowledge is the Perception of the Agreement or Disagreement of two Ideas. Knowledge* then seems to me to be nothing but *the perception of the connexion and agreement, or disagreement and repugnancy, of any of our ideas.* In this alone it consists. Where this perception is, there is knowledge, and where it is not, there, though we may fancy, guess, or believe, yet we always come short of knowledge. For when we know that white is not black, what do we else but perceive that these two ideas do not agree? When we possess ourselves with the utmost security of the demonstration that the three angles of a triangle are equal to two right ones, what do we more but perceive that equality to two right ones does necessarily agree to, and is inseparable from, the three angles of a triangle?

3. *This Agreement fourfold.* But to understand a little more distinctly wherein this agreement or disagreement consists, I think we may reduce it all to these four sorts:

1. *Identity,* or *diversity.*
2. *Relation.*
3. *Co-existence,* or *necessary connexion.*
4. *Real existence.*

4. *First, of Identity, or Diversity. First,* as to the first sort of agreement or disagreement, viz. *identity* or *diversity.* It is the first act of the mind, when it has any sentiments or ideas at all, to perceive its ideas; and so far as it perceives them, to know each what it is, and thereby also to perceive their difference, and that one is not another. This is so absolutely necessary that without it there could be no knowledge, no reasoning, no imagination, no distinct thoughts at all. By this the mind clearly and infallibly perceives each idea to agree with itself, and to be what it is, and all distinct ideas to disagree, i.e. the one not to be the other; and this it does without pains, labour, or deduction, but at first view, by its natural power of perception and distinction. And though men of art have reduced this into those general rules, *What is, is,* and *It is impossible for the same thing to be and not to be,* for ready application in all cases, wherein there may be occasion to reflect on it, yet it is certain that the first exercise of this faculty is about particular ideas. A man infallibly knows, as soon as ever he has them in his mind, that the ideas he calls *white* and *round* are the very ideas they are, and that they are not other ideas which he calls *red* or *square.* Nor can any maxim or proposition in the world make him know it clearer or surer than he did before, and without any such general rule. This then is the first agreement or disagreement which the mind perceives in its ideas, which it always perceives at first sight; and if there ever happen any doubt about it, it will always be found to be about the names, and not the ideas themselves, whose identity and diversity will always be perceived, as soon and as clearly as the ideas themselves are; nor can it possibly be otherwise.

5. *Secondly, Relative. Secondly,* the next sort of agreement or disagreement the mind perceives in any of its ideas may, I think, be called *relative,* and is nothing but the perception of the *relation* between any two ideas, of what kind soever, whether substances, modes, or any other. For, since all distinct ideas must eternally be known not to be the same, and so be universally and constantly denied one of another, there could be no room for any positive knowledge at all, if we could not perceive any relation between our ideas, and find out the agreement or disagreement they have one with another, in several ways the mind takes of comparing them.

6. *Thirdly, of Co-existence. Thirdly,* the third sort of agreement or disagreement to be found in our ideas, which the perception of the mind is employed about, is *co-existence* or *non-co-existence* in the *same subject;* and this belongs particularly to substances. Thus when we pronounce concerning gold that it is fixed, our knowledge of this truth amounts to no more but this, that fixedness, or a power to remain in the

fire unconsumed, is an idea that always accompanies and is joined with that particular sort of yellowness, weight, fusibility, malleableness, and solubility in *aqua regia,* which make our complex idea signified by the word 'gold'.

7. *Fourthly, of real Existence. Fourthly,* the fourth and last sort is that of *actual real existence* agreeing to any idea. Within these four sorts of agreement or disagreement is, I suppose, contained all the knowledge we have, or are capable of. For all the inquiries that we can make concerning any of our ideas, all that we know or can affirm concerning any of them, is that it is, or is not, the same with some other; that it does or does not always co-exist with some other idea in the same subject; that it has this or that relation to some other idea; or that it has a real existence without the mind. Thus, "Blue is not yellow" is of identity. "Two triangles upon equal bases between two parallels are equal" is of relation. "Iron is susceptible of magnetical impressions" is of co-existence. "God is" is of real existence. Though identity and co-existence are truly nothing but relations, yet they are so peculiar ways of agreement or disagreement of our ideas that they deserve well to be considered as distinct heads, and not under relation in general; since they are so different grounds of affirmation and negation, as will easily appear to anyone, who will but reflect on what is said in several places of this *Essay*. I should now proceed to examine the several degrees of our knowledge, but that it is necessary first to consider the different acceptations of the word 'knowledge'.

8. *Knowledge, actual or habitual.* There are several ways wherein the mind is possessed of truth; each of which is called knowledge.

1. There is *actual knowledge,* which is the present view the mind has of the agreement or disagreement of any of its ideas, or of the relation they have one to another.

2. A man is said to know any proposition, which having been once laid before his thoughts, he evidently perceived the agreement or disagreement of the ideas whereof it consists; and so lodged it in his memory that, whenever that proposition comes again to be reflected on, he, without doubt or hesitation, embraces the right side, assents to, and is certain of the truth of it. This, I think, one may call *habitual knowledge*. And thus a man may be said to know all those truths which are lodged in his memory, by a foregoing clear and full perception, whereof the mind is assured past doubt as often as it has occasion to reflect on them. For our finite understandings being able to think clearly and distinctly but on one thing at once, if men had no knowledge of any more than what they actually thought on, they would all be very ignorant; and he that knew most would know but one truth, that being all he was able to think on at one time.

9. *Habitual Knowledge twofold.* Of habitual knowledge there are, also, vulgarly speaking, two degrees:

First, the one is of such truths laid up in the memory as, whenever they occur to the mind, it *actually perceives the relation* is between those ideas. And this is in all those truths whereof we have an intuitive knowledge; where the ideas themselves, by an immediate view, discover their agreement or disagreement one with another.

Secondly, the other is of such truths whereof the mind having been convinced, it *retains the memory of the conviction, without the proofs*. Thus, a man that remembers certainly that he once perceived the demonstration that the three angles of a triangle are equal to two right ones, is certain that he knows it, because he cannot doubt of the truth of it. In his adherence to a truth, where the demonstration by which it was at first known is forgot, though a man may be thought rather to believe his memory than really to know, and this way of entertaining a truth seemed formerly to me like something between opinion and knowledge, a sort of assurance which exceeds bare belief, for that relies on the testimony of another, yet upon a due examination I find it comes not short of perfect certainty, and is in effect true knowledge. That which is apt to mislead our first thoughts into a mistake in this matter is that the agreement or disagreement of the ideas in this case is not perceived, as it was at first, by an actual view of all the intermediate ideas whereby the agreement or disagreement of those in the proposition was at first perceived, but by other intermediate ideas, that show the agreement or disagreement of the ideas contained in the proposition whose certainty we remember. For example: in this proposition, that the three angles of a triangle are equal to two right ones, one who has seen and clearly perceived the demonstration of this truth knows it to be true, when that demonstration is gone out of his mind; so that at present it is not actually in view, and possibly cannot be recollected: but he knows it in a different way from what he did before. The agreement of the two ideas joined in that proposition is perceived, but it is by the intervention of other ideas than those which at first produced that perception. He remembers, i.e. he knows (for remembrance is but the reviving of some past knowledge) that he was once certain of the truth of this proposition, that the three angles of a triangle are equal to two right ones. The immutability of the same relations between the same immutable things is now the idea that shows him that, if the three angles of a triangle were once equal to two right ones, they will always be equal to two right ones. And hence he comes to be certain that what was once true in the case is always true; what ideas once agreed will always agree; and consequently what he once knew to be true he will always know to be true, as long as he can remember that he once knew it. Upon this ground it is that particular demonstrations in mathematics afford general knowledge. If then the perception that the same ideas will *eternally* have the same habitudes and relations be not a sufficient ground of knowledge, there could be no knowledge of general propositions in mathematics; for no mathematical demonstration would be any other than particular, and, when a man had demonstrated any proposition concerning one triangle or circle, his knowledge would not reach beyond that particular diagram. If he would extend it further, he must renew his demonstration in another instance, before he could know it to be true in another like triangle, and so on; by which means one could never come to the knowledge of any general propositions. But because the memory is not always so clear as actual perception, and does in all men more or less decay in length of time, this, amongst other differences, is one which shows that *demonstrative* knowledge is much more imperfect than *intuitive,* as we shall see in the following chapter.

NOTES

1. §§ 17–21.
2. IV ii 1; vii 19; xvii 14.

2

On What is Independent of Sense and of Matter

(Letter to Queen Sophia Charlotte of Prussia, 1702)

GOTTFRIED WILHELM LEIBNIZ

I found the letter truly ingenious and beautiful which was sent some time ago from Paris to Osnabrück, and which I recently read by your order at Hanover. Since it deals with two important questions on which I admit I do not entirely share the opinion of its author—whether there is something in our thoughts which does not come from sense and whether there is something in nature which is not material—I wish I were able to explain myself with the same charm as his, in order to obey Your Majesty's orders and satisfy Your Majesty's curiosity.

To use the analogy of an ancient writer, we use the external senses as a blind man uses his stick, and they help us to know their particular objects, which are colors, sounds, odors, tastes, and tactual qualities. But they do not help us to know what these sensible qualities are or in what they consist. For example, if red is the whirling of certain small globes which, it is claimed, make light; if heat is an eddy of very fine dust; if sound is made in the air as are circles in the water when a stone is thrown in, as some philosophers hold, we at least do not see this, and we cannot even understand how this whirling, these eddies and circles, if they are real, should bring about just the particular perceptions which we have of red, of heat, and of noise. So it can be said that *sensible qualities* are in fact *occult qualities* and that there must be others *more manifest* which could render them understandable. Far from understanding sensible things only, it is just these which we understand the least. And even though we are familiar with them, we do not understand them the better for that, just as a pilot does not understand the nature of the magnetic needle, which turns to the north, better than other men, although he has it constantly before his eyes in the compass, and as a result scarcely even has any more curiosity about it.

Source: Leibniz, Gottfried Wilhelm, "On What Is Independent of Sense and Matter," *Philosophical Papers and Letters,* trans. L. Loemker. Dordrecht: D. Reidel Publishing Co., 1975, pp. 547–553 with kind permission from Kluwer Academic Publishers.

I do not deny that many discoveries have been made about the nature of these occult qualities. So, for example, we know what kind of refraction produces blue and yellow and how these two colors mixed produce green. But we still cannot understand as a result how the perception we have of these three colors follows from these causes. Also, we do not have even nominal definitions of such qualities, in order to explain the terms. The purpose of nominal definitions is to give marks sufficient to aid in recognizing things. For example, assayers have marks by which they distinguish gold from all other metals, and even if a man has never even seen gold, these marks could be taught him so that he could recognize it unmistakably should he some day encounter it. But this is not the case with these sensible qualities; no mark for recognizing blue, for example, can be given to one who has never seen it. Thus blue is itself its own mark, and in order that a man may know what blue is, one must of necessity show it to him.

For this reason it is usually said that the *concepts* of these qualities are *clear,* since they serve us in recognizing them, but that these same concepts are not *distinct,* because we cannot distinguish or develop the content included in them. It is an 'I know not what' which we perceive but for which we cannot account. On the other hand, we can make someone else understand what a thing is if we have some kind of description or nominal definition, even though we do not have the thing at hand to show him. We must do justice to the senses, however, by recognizing that besides these occult qualities, they enable us to know other qualities which are more manifest and furnish more distinct concepts. It is these which are ascribed to the *common sense,* because there is no external sense to which they are particularly attached and belong.[1] It is of these that definitions of the terms or words we use can be given. Such is the idea of *numbers,* which is found alike in sounds, colors, and the qualities of touch. It is thus, too, that we perceive the *figures* which are common to colors and to qualities of touch but which we do not observe in sounds. But it is true that in order to conceive numbers and even shapes distinctly and to build sciences from them, we must reach something which sense cannot furnish but which the understanding adds to it.[2]

Since therefore our soul compares the numbers and the shapes of colors, for example, with the numbers and shapes discovered by touch, there must be an *internal sense* where the perceptions of these different external senses are found united. This is called the *imagination,* which comprises at once the *concepts of particular senses,* which are *clear* but *confused,* and the *concepts of the common sense,* which are clear and distinct.[3] And these clear and distinct ideas which are subject to the imagination are the objects of the *mathematical sciences,* namely, arithmetic and geometry, which are the *pure* mathematical sciences, and their applications to nature, which make up *mixed* mathematics. It is seen also that particular sense qualities are capable of explanation and rationalization only insofar as they have a content common to the objects of several external senses and belong to the internal sense. For whenever one tries to explain sensible qualities distinctly, one always turns back to mathematical ideas, and these ideas always include *magnitude,* or multitude of parts. It is true that the mathematical sciences would not be demonstrative but would consist of a simple induction or observation which could never assure us of the perfect generality of the truths found in it, if something higher, which only the intellect can provide, did not come to the aid of *imagination* and *sense*.

There are thus also objects of another nature, which are not at all included in what we have observed in the objects of either the particular senses or the common sense, and which consequently are also not to be considered objects of the imagination. Besides what is *sensible* and *imaginable,* therefore, there is that which is only *intelligible,* since it is the object of the understanding alone. And such is the object of my thought when I think of myself.

This thought of *myself,* who perceive sensible objects, and of my own action which results from it, adds something to the objects of sense. To think of some color and to consider that I think of it—these two thoughts are very different, just as much as color itself differs from the ego who thinks of it. And since I conceive that there are other beings who also have the right to say 'I', or for whom this can be said, it is by this that I conceive what is called *substance* in general. It is the consideration of myself, also, which provides me with other concepts in *metaphysics,* such as those of cause, effect, action, similarity, etc., and even with those of *logic* and *ethics.* Thus it may be said that there is nothing in the understanding which has not come from the senses, except the understanding itself, or the one who understands.

There are thus three levels of concepts: those which are *sensible* only, which are the objects produced by each sense in particular; those which are at once *sensible and intelligible,* which appertain to the common sense; and those which are *intelligible only,* which belong to the understanding. The first and second together are imaginable, but the third lie beyond the imagination. The second and third are intelligible and distinct, but the first are confused, although they may be clear and recognizable.[4]

Being itself and *truth* are not understood completely through the senses. For it would not at all be impossible for a created being to have long and orderly dreams which resemble our lives, such that everything that it thought it perceived through the senses would be nothing but mere appearances. Something is thus needed beyond the senses, by which to distinguish the true from the apparent. But the truth of the demonstrative sciences is free[5] of such doubts and must even serve to judge the truth of sensible things. For as able ancient and modern philosophers have already well said, even if all that I think I see were only a dream, it would always be true that I who am thinking in my dream would be something and that I should in fact think in many ways for which there must always be a reason.

What the ancient Platonists have said is thus quite true and quite worthy of consideration—that the existence of intelligible things, particularly of the I who think and am called a mind or soul, is incomparably more certain than the existence of sensible things and that it would thus not be impossible, speaking with metaphysical rigor, that there should exist at bottom only intelligible substances, of which sensible things would be only the appearances. Instead, our lack of attention causes us to take sensible things for the only true ones. It is also well to observe that if I should discover some demonstrative truth, mathematical or other, in a dream (and this can in fact be done), it would be just as certain as if I were awake. This shows us that intelligible truth is independent of the truth or existence of sensible and material things outside of us.

This conception of *being* and of *truth* is thus found in the ego and in the understanding rather than in the external senses and the perception of exterior objects.

In the understanding we discover also what it means to affirm, deny, doubt, will, and act. But above all, we find there the *force of the conclusions* in reasoning, which are a part of what is called the *natural light.* For example, by reversing the terms, one can draw from the premise that no wise man is vicious the conclusion that no vicious man is wise. On the other hand, from the premise that every wise man is praiseworthy, one cannot conclude by reversing terms that every praiseworthy man is wise, but only that some praiseworthy men are wise. Although one can always convert particular affirmative propositions, this is impossible with particular negatives. For example, if some wise men are rich, it is necessary also that some rich men are wise. Yet one can say that there are charitable beings who are not just, for this happens when charity is not regular enough, but one cannot infer from this that there are just beings who are not charitable, for charity and the rule of reason are at once included in justice.

It is by this *natural light* that one may recognize also the *axioms* of mathematics; for example, that if the same quantity is taken away from two equals the remainders are equal and likewise that if both sides of a balance are equal neither will sink, a fact which we can foresee without ever having tried it. It is upon such foundations that arithmetic, geometry, mechanics, and the other demonstrative sciences are established, in which it is true that the senses are necessary to have definite ideas of sensible things, and experience is necessary to establish certain facts and even useful in verifying the reasoning involved, by a kind of check, as it were. But the force of the demonstrations depends upon intelligible concepts and truths, for it is these alone which enable us to draw conclusions which are necessary; they even make it possible for us, in the conjectural sciences, to determine demonstratively the degree of probability in certain given assumptions, so that we may choose reasonably, among conflicting appearances, that one whose probability is the greater. But this part of the art of reasoning has not yet been cultivated as much as it ought to be.

To return to *necessary truths,* however, it is universally true that we know them only by this natural light and not at all by sense experiences. For the senses can indeed help us after a fashion to know what is, but they cannot help us to know what *must* be or what cannot be otherwise.

For example, although we have countless times tested the fact that every heavy body falls toward the center of the earth, and is not sustained freely in the air, we are not sure that this is necessary until we have grasped the reason for it. Thus we cannot be sure that the same thing would happen in an altitude a hundred leagues or more higher than we are. There are philosophers who represent the earth as a magnet whose attractive force does not, they think, extend very far, any more than the ordinary magnet attracts a needle some distance away from it. I am not saying that they are right but only that we cannot proceed with much certainty beyond the experiences which we have had, unless we are aided by reason.

It is for this reason that the geometricians have always held that what has only been proved by *induction* or by examples, in geometry or arithmetic, has never been perfectly proved. For example, experience teaches us that the odd numbers when added together continuously in their order produce the square numbers in order, that is, the numbers produced by multiplying a number by itself. Thus 1 and 3 make 4, that is, 2^2; and 1 and 3 and 5 make 9, that is, 3^2; and 1 and 3 and 5 and 7 make 16, or 4^2 and 1 and 3 and 5 and 7 and 9 make 25, or 5^2; and so forth.

However, if one had tried this a hundred thousand times, extending the calculation very far, one might well judge it reasonable that this will always be true, but one could never be absolutely certain of it as long as he does not grasp the demonstrative reason for it which mathematicians long ago discovered. It is on the basis of this uncertainty of induction, pushed a little too far, that an Englishman has recently tried to argue that we can avoid death. For, says he, the following conclusion is not sound: my father, my grandfather, my great-grandfather have died, and so have all the rest whom we know to have lived before us; therefore we too will die. For their death has no influence upon us. The trouble with this argument is that we resemble them a little too much, in that the causes of their death subsist in us as well. For the similarity between us would itself not be sufficient to draw conclusions of complete certainty, without considering the same reasons.

There are in fact *experiments* which succeed countless times in ordinary circumstances, yet instances are found in some extraordinary cases in which the experiment does not succeed. For example, if we have shown a hundred thousand times that iron sinks to the bottom when placed in water, we are still not sure that this must always happen. Without appealing to the miracle of the prophet Elisha, who made iron float, we know that an iron pot can be made so hollow that it floats and can even carry a considerable load besides, as do boats made of copper and of tinplate. Even the abstract sciences like geometry provide cases in which what ordinarily happens does not happen. Ordinarily, for example, we find that two lines which approach each other continuously finally meet, and many people would be quick to swear that it could never happen otherwise. Yet geometry does furnish exceptional lines called *asymptotes* for this reason, that when extended to infinity they approach each other continuously, yet never meet.

This consideration also shows that there is a *light which is born with us*. For since the senses and induction can never teach us truths that are fully universal or absolutely necessary, but only what is and what is found in particular examples, and since we nonetheless know the universal and necessary truths of the sciences—in this we are privileged above the beasts—it follows that we have drawn these truths in part from what is within us. Thus one can lead a child to them by simple questions in the Socratic manner, without telling him anything, and without having him experiment at all about the truth of that which is asked him. This could most easily be carried out in numbers and similar matters.

I agree, however, that in our present state the external senses are necessary for our thinking and that if we had none, we would not think. But what is necessary for something need not therefore make up its essence. The air is necessary for our life, but our life is different from air. The senses furnish us with the matter for reasoning, and we never have thoughts so abstract that something is not mixed with them from sense. But reasoning demands something more than what is sensible.

As for the *second question, whether there are immaterial substances,* one must first explain it in order to answer it. Heretofore matter has been understood to mean that which includes only purely passive and indifferent concepts, such as extension and impenetrability, which need to be given determinate form or activity by something else. Thus when it is said that there are immaterial substances, one means by this that there are substances which include other concepts, namely, perception and the principle of action or of change, which cannot be explained either by extension or by impenetrability. When these beings have feeling, they are called *souls,* and when they are capable of reason, they are called *spirits*. Hence if anyone says that force and perception are essential to matter, he is taking matter for the complete corporeal substance which includes form and matter, or the soul along with the organs. This is the same as if he had said that there are souls everywhere. This could be true, yet not at all contrary to the doctrine of immaterial substances. For this does not require these souls to be free from matter but only to be something more than matter and not produced or destroyed by the change which matter undergoes or subject to dissolution, since they are not composed of parts.

It must also be admitted, however, that there is some *substance separate from matter*. To make this clear, we need only to consider that there is an infinity of possible orders which the totality of matter might have received in place of this particular sequence of changes which it has actually taken on. For it is clear, for example, that the stars could have moved quite differently, since space and time are indifferent to every kind of motion and figure. Hence the reason, or the universal determining cause which makes things be, and makes them be as they are rather than otherwise, must of necessity be free of matter. Even the existence of matter depends upon it, since one does not find anything in the concept of matter which carries a reason for its existence with it.

Now this ultimate reason for things which is common to all and universal because of the connection between all the parts of nature is what we call *God,* who must of necessity be an infinite and absolutely perfect substance. I am inclined to believe that all finite immaterial substances—in the opinion of the ancient Church Fathers, even the genii or angels—are joined to organs and accompany matter and even that souls or active forms are found everywhere. And to constitute a complete substance matter cannot dispense with them, since force and action are found everywhere in it. And the laws of force depend upon certain marvelous principles of metaphysics or upon intelligible concepts and cannot be explained by material or mathematical concepts alone or by those which fall within the jurisdiction of the imagination.

Perception, too, cannot be explained by any mechanism, whatever it may be. We can conclude then that there is also something immaterial everywhere in created beings, and particularly in us, where this force is accompanied by a fairly distinct perception, and even by that light of which I have spoken above, which makes us resemble God in miniature not only through our knowledge of order but also through the order which we can ourselves impart to the things within our grasp, in imitation of that which God imparts to the universe. It is in this, also, that our *virtue* and perfection consist, as our *felicity* consists in the pleasure which we take in it.

Now whenever we penetrate to the basis of anything, we find there the most beautiful order we can desire, surpassing anything we had expected, as anyone knows who has understood the sciences. We can therefore conclude that it is the same in all the rest and that not only do immaterial substances subsist always but their lives, progress, and changes are controlled to lead to a definite end or better, to approach it more and more, as do the asymptotes. Even though we may sometimes slip back, like curves which descend, the progression must finally prevail and win.

The natural light of reason is insufficient for us to recognize the details, and our experiences are still too limited to discover the laws of this order. Meanwhile the revealed light guides us when we heed it through faith. But there remains room to think that in the future we may know still more by experience itself and that there are spirits who already know more in this way than we.

Meanwhile philosophers and poets, lacking this knowledge, have had recourse to the fictions of metempsychosis or of the Elysian fields in order to provide some ideas which might be popularly appealing. But a consideration of the perfection of things, or what amounts to the same thing, of the sovereign power, wisdom, and goodness of God, who does everything for the best, that is, for the greatest order, is enough to make all reasonable people content and to convince us that our contentment should be the greater in the measure in which we are inclined to follow order and reason.

REFERENCES

1. For Leibniz's interpretation of Aristotle's doctrine of the common sense as the "mind itself" in reply to Locke see p. 294, note 2.
2. The selection of number and figures as examples is significant, since Leibniz used them from the beginning as fundamental categories, subforms of quantity and quality, upon which to base and to extend mathematics, particularly geometry and the art of combinations (see Nos. 1, 27, and 70).
3. Leibniz's distinction between imagination and sensation itself marks a point of deviation from Locke, since he emphasizes the dependence of the former upon the common sense and therefore its close relation to reflection and understanding.
4. At about this time Leibniz was developing his theory of apperception (probably suggested by the reflexive form *s'appercevoir,* which Coste used to translate Locke's *perceive*). Apperception or reflection is the basis of understanding, for without it there would be no perception of the content of perceptions and therefore no ground upon which to discover the universal principles of reason operative in the mind. While memory is the precondition of consciousness for Leibniz, apperception is the essential relation involved in the continuity of consciousness.
5. Reading *exempte* for *exemple* (G.).

 3 

Sceptical Solution of These Doubts

DAVID HUME

PART I

The passion for philosophy, like that for religion, seems liable to this inconvenience, that, though it aims at the correction of our manners, and extirpation of our vices, it may only serve, by imprudent management, to foster a predominant inclination, and push the mind, with more determined resolution, towards that side which already *draws* too much, by the bias and propensity of the natural temper. It is certain that, while we aspire to the magnanimous firmness of the philosophic sage, and endeavour to confine our pleasures altogether within our own minds, we may, at last, render our philosophy like that of Epictetus, and other *Stoics,* only a more refined system of selfishness, and reason ourselves out of all virtue as well as social enjoyment. While we study with attention the vanity of human life, and turn all our thoughts towards the empty and transitory nature of riches and honours, we are, perhaps, all the while flattering our natural indolence, which, hating the bustle of the world, and drudgery of business, seeks a pretence of reason to give itself a full and uncontrolled indulgence. There is, however, one species of philosophy which seems little liable to this inconvenience, and that because it strikes in with no disorderly passion of the human mind, nor can mingle itself with any natural affection or propensity; and that is the Academic or Sceptical philosophy. The academics always talk of doubt and suspense of judgement, of danger in hasty determinations, of confining to very narrow bounds the enquiries of the understanding, and of renouncing all speculations which lie not within the limits of common life and practice. Nothing, therefore, can be more contrary than such a philosophy to the supine indolence of the mind, its rash arrogance, its lofty pretensions, and its superstitious credulity. Every passion is mortified by it, except the love of truth; and that passion never is,

---

Source: David Hume, *An Enquiry Concerning Human Understanding,* originally published 1748.

nor can be, carried to too high a degree. It is surprising, therefore, that this philosophy, which, in almost every instance, must be harmless and innocent, should be the subject of so much groundless reproach and obloquy. But, perhaps, the very circumstance which renders it so innocent is what chiefly exposes it to the public hatred and resentment. By flattering no irregular passion, it gains few partizans: By opposing so many vices and follies, it raises to itself abundance of enemies, who stigmatize it as libertine, profane, and irreligious.

Nor need we fear that this philosophy, while it endeavours to limit our enquiries to common life, should ever undermine the reasonings of common life, and carry its doubts so far as to destroy all action, as well as speculation. Nature will always maintain her rights, and prevail in the end over any abstract reasoning whatsoever. Though we should conclude, for instance, as in the foregoing section, that, in all reasonings from experience, there is a step taken by the mind which is not supported by any argument or process of the understanding; there is no danger that these reasonings, on which almost all knowledge depends, will ever be affected by such a discovery. If the mind be not engaged by argument to make this step, it must be induced by some other principle of equal weight and authority; and that principle will preserve its influence as long as human nature remains the same. What that principle is may well be worth the pains of enquiry.

Suppose a person, though endowed with the strongest faculties of reason and reflection, to be brought on a sudden into this world; he would, indeed, immediately observe a continual succession of objects, and one event following another; but he would not be able to discover anything farther. He would not, at first, by any reasoning, be able to reach the idea of cause and effect; since the particular powers, by which all natural operations are performed, never appear to the senses; nor is it reasonable to conclude, merely because one event, in one instance, precedes another, that therefore the one is the cause, the other the effect. Their conjunction may be arbitrary and casual. There may be no reason to infer the existence of one from the appearance of the other. And in a word, such a person, without more experience, could never employ his conjecture or reasoning concerning any matter of fact, or be assured of anything beyond what was immediately present to his memory and senses.

Suppose, again, that he has acquired more experience, and has lived so long in the world as to have observed similar objects or events to be constantly conjoined together; what is the consequence of this experience? He immediately infers the existence of one object from the appearance of the other. Yet he has not, by all his experience, acquired any idea or knowledge of the secret power by which the one object produces the other; nor is it, by any process of reasoning, he is engaged to draw this inference. But still he finds himself determined to draw it: And though he should be convinced that his understanding has no part in the operation, he would nevertheless continue in the same course of thinking. There is some other principle which determines him to form such a conclusion.

This principle is Custom or Habit. For wherever the repetition of any particular act or operation produces a propensity to renew the same act or operation, without being impelled by any reasoning or process of the understanding, we always say, that this propensity is the effect of *Custom*. By employing that word, we pretend not to have given the ultimate reason of such a propensity. We only point out a principle of human nature, which is universally acknowledged, and which is well known by its effects. Perhaps we can push our enquiries no farther, or pretend to give the cause of this cause; but must rest contented with it as the ultimate principle, which we can assign, of all our conclusions from experience. It is sufficient satisfaction, that we can go so far, without repining at the narrowness of our faculties because they will carry us no farther. And it is certain we here advance a very intelligible proposition at least, if not a true one, when we assert that, after the constant conjunction of two objects—heat and flame, for instance, weight and solidity—we are determined by custom alone to expect the one from the appearance of the other. This hypothesis seems even the only one which explains the difficulty, why we draw from a thousand instances, an inference which we are not able to draw from one instance, that is, in no respect, different from them. Reason is incapable of any such variation. The conclusions which it draws from considering one circle are the same which it would form upon surveying all the circles in the universe. But no man, having seen only one body move after being impelled by another, could infer that every other body will move after a like impulse. All inferences from experience, therefore, are effects of custom, not of reasoning.[1]

Custom, then, is the great guide of human life. It is that principle alone which renders our experience useful to us, and makes us expect, for the future, a similar train of events with those which have appeared in the past. Without the influence of custom, we should be entirely ignorant of every matter of fact beyond what is immediately present to the memory and senses. We should never know how to adjust means to ends, or to employ our natural powers in the production of any effect. There would be an end at once of all action, as well as of the chief part of speculation.

But here it may be proper to remark, that though our conclusions from experience carry us beyond our memory and senses, and assure us of matters of fact which happened in the most distant places and most remote ages, yet some fact must always be present to the senses or memory, from which we may first proceed in drawing these conclusions. A man, who should find in a desert country the remains of pompous buildings, would conclude that the country had, in ancient times, been cultivated by civilized inhabitants; but did nothing of this nature occur to him, he could never form such an inference. We learn the events of former ages from history; but then we must peruse the volumes in which this instruction is contained, and thence carry up our inferences from one testimony to another, till we arrive at the eyewitnesses and spectators of these distant events. In a word, if we proceed not upon some fact, present to the memory or senses, our reasonings would be merely hypothetical; and however the particular links might be connected with each other, the whole chain of inferences would have nothing to support it, nor could we ever, by its means, arrive at the knowledge of any real existence. If I ask why you believe any particular matter of fact, which you relate, you must tell me some reason; and this reason will be some other fact, connected with it. But as you cannot proceed after this manner, *in infinitum,* you must at last terminate in some fact, which is present to your memory or senses; or must allow that your belief is entirely without foundation.

What, then, is the conclusion of the whole matter? A simple one; though, it must be confessed, pretty remote from the common theories of philosophy. All belief of matter of fact or real existence is derived merely from some object, present to the memory or senses, and a customary conjunction between that and some other object. Or in other words; having found, in many instances, that any two kinds of objects—flame and heat, snow and cold—have always been conjoined together; if flame or snow be presented anew to the senses, the mind is carried by custom to expect heat or cold, and to *believe* that such a quality does exist, and will discover itself upon a nearer approach. This belief is the necessary result of placing the mind in such circumstances. It is an operation of the soul, when we are so situated, as unavoidable as to feel the passion of love, when we receive benefits; or hatred, when we meet with injuries. All these operations are a species of natural instincts, which no reasoning or process of the thought and understanding is able either to produce or to prevent.

At this point, it would be very allowable for us to stop our philosophical researches. In most questions we can never make a single step farther; and in all questions we must terminate here at last, after our most restless and curious enquiries. But still our curiosity will be pardonable, perhaps commendable, if it carry us on to still farther researches, and make us examine more accurately the nature of this *belief,* and of the *customary conjunction,* whence it is derived. By this means we may meet with some explications and analogies that will give satisfaction; at least to such as love the abstract sciences, and can be entertained with speculations, which, however accurate, may still retain a degree of doubt and uncertainty. As to readers of a different taste; the remaining part of this section is not calculated for them, and the following enquiries may well be understood, though it be neglected.

NOTES

1. Nothing is more usual than for writers, even, on *moral, political,* or *physical* subjects, to distinguish between *reason* and *experience,* and to suppose, that these species of argumentation are entirely different from each other. The former are taken for the mere result of our intellectual faculties, which, by considering *à priori* the nature of things, and examining the effects, that must follow from their operation, establish particular principles of science and philosophy. The latter are supposed to be derived entirely from sense and observation, by which we learn what has actually resulted from the operation of particular objects, and are thence able to infer, what will, for the future, result from them. Thus, for instance, the limitations and restraints of civil government, and a legal constitution, may be defended, either from *reason,* which reflecting on the great frailty and corruption of human nature, teaches, that no man can safely be trusted with unlimited authority; or from *experience* and history, which inform us of the enormous abuses, that ambition, in every age and country, has been found to make of so imprudent a confidence.

   The same distinction between reason and experience is maintained in all our deliberations concerning the conduct of life; while the experienced statesman, general, physician, or merchant is trusted and followed; and the unpractised novice, with whatever natural talents endowed, neglected and despised. Though it be allowed, that reason may form very plausible conjectures with regard to the consequences of such a particular conduct in such particular circumstances; it is still supposed imperfect, without the assistance of experience, which is alone able to give stability and certainty to the maxims, derived from study and reflection.

   But notwithstanding that this distinction be thus universally received, both in the active and speculative scenes of life, I shall not scruple to pronounce, that it is, at bottom, erroneous, at least, superficial.

   If we examine those arguments, which, in any of the sciences above mentioned, are supposed to be the mere effects of reasoning and reflection, they will be found to terminate, at last, in some general principle or conclusion, for which we can assign no reason but observation and experience. The only difference between them and those maxims, which are vulgarly esteemed the result of pure experience, is, that the former cannot be established without some process of thought, and some reflection on what we have observed, in order to distinguish its circumstances, and trace its consequences: Whereas in the latter, the experienced event is exactly and fully similar to that which we infer as the result of any particular situation. The history of a TIBERIUS or a NERO makes us dread a like tyranny, were our monarchs freed from the restraints of laws and senates: But the observation of any fraud or cruelty in private life is sufficient, with the aid of a little thought, to give us the same apprehension; while it serves as an instance of the general corruption of human nature, and shows us the danger which we must incur by reposing an entire confidence in mankind. In both cases, it is experience which is ultimately the foundation of our inference and conclusion.

There is no man so young and unexperienced, as not to have formed, from observation, many general and just maxims concerning human affairs and the conduct of life; but it must be confessed, that, when a man comes to put these in practice, he will be extremely liable to error, till time and farther experience both enlarge these maxims, and teach him their proper use and application. In every situation or incident, there are many particular and seemingly minute circumstances, which the man of greatest talents is, at first, apt to overlook, though on them the justness of his conclusions, and consequently the prudence of his conduct, entirely depend. Not to mention, that, to a young beginner, the general observations and maxims occur not always on the proper occasions, nor can be immediately applied with due calmness and distinction. The truth is, an unexperienced reasoner could be no reasoner at all, were he absolutely unexperienced; and when we assign that character to any one, we mean it only in a comparative sense, and suppose him possessed of experience, in a smaller and more imperfect degree.

 4 

Introduction

IMMANUEL KANT

I. THE DISTINCTION BETWEEN PURE AND EMPIRICAL KNOWLEDGE

There can be no doubt that all our knowledge begins with experience. For how should our faculty of knowledge be awakened into action did not objects affecting our senses partly of themselves produce representations, partly arouse the activity of our understanding to compare these representations, and, by combining or separating them, work up the raw material of the sensible impressions into that knowledge of objects which is entitled experience? In the order of time, therefore, we have no knowledge antecedent to experience, and with experience all our knowledge begins.

But though all our knowledge begins with experience, it does not follow that it all arises out of experience. For it may well be that even our empirical knowledge is made up of what we receive through impressions and of what our own faculty of knowledge (sensible impressions serving merely as the occasion) supplies from itself. If our faculty of knowledge makes any such addition, it may be that we are not in a position to distinguish it from the raw material, until with long practice of attention we have become skilled in separating it.

This, then, is a question which at least calls for closer examination, and does not allow of any off-hand answer:—whether there is any knowledge that is thus independent of experience and even of all impressions of the senses. Such knowledge is entitled *a priori,* and distinguished from the *empirical,* which has its sources *a posteriori,* that is, in experience.

The expression '*a priori*' does not, however, indicate with sufficient precision the full meaning of our question. For it has been customary to say, even of much knowledge that is derived from empirical sources, that we have it or are

---

Source: Immanuel Kant, *The Critique of Pure Reason,* translated by Norman Kemp Smith. The second edition of this work published in 1787, known as the B version, is reprinted here.

capable of having it *a priori,* meaning thereby that we do not derive it immediately from experience, but from a universal rule—a rule which is itself, however, borrowed by us from experience. Thus we would say of a man who undermined the foundations of his house, that he might have known *a priori* that it would fall, that is, that he need not have waited for the experience of its actual falling. But still he could not know this completely *a priori*. For he had first to learn through experience that bodies are heavy, and therefore fall when their supports are withdrawn.

In what follows, therefore, we shall understand by *a priori* knowledge, not knowledge independent of this or that experience, but knowledge absolutely independent of all experience. Opposed to it is empirical knowledge, which is knowledge possible only *a posteriori,* that is, through experience. *A priori* modes of knowledge are entitled pure when there is no admixture of anything empirical. Thus, for instance, the proposition, 'every alteration has its cause', while an *a priori* proposition, is not a pure proposition, because alteration is a concept which can be derived only from experience.

II. WE ARE IN POSSESSION OF CERTAIN MODES OF *A PRIORI* KNOWLEDGE, AND EVEN THE COMMON UNDERSTANDING IS NEVER WITHOUT THEM

What we here require is a criterion by which to distinguish with certainty between pure and empirical knowledge. Experience teaches us that a thing is so and so, but not that it cannot be otherwise. First, then, if we have a proposition which in being thought is thought as *necessary,* it is an *a priori* judgement; and if, besides, it is not derived from any proposition except one which also has the validity of a necessary judgement, it is an absolutely *a priori* judgement. Secondly, experience never confers on its judgements true or strict, but only assumed and comparative *universality,* through induction. We can properly only say, therefore, that, so far as we have hitherto observed, there is no exception to this or that rule. If, then, a judgement is thought with strict universality, that is, in such manner that no exception is allowed as possible, it is not derived from experience, but is valid absolutely *a priori*. Empirical universality is only an arbitrary extension of a validity holding in most cases to one which holds in all, for instance, in the proposition, 'all bodies are heavy'. When, on the other hand, strict universality is essential to a judgement, this indicates a special source of knowledge, namely, a faculty of *a priori* knowledge. Necessity and strict universality are thus sure criteria of *a priori* knowledge, and are inseparable from one another. But since in the employment of these criteria the contingency of judgements is sometimes more easily shown than their empirical limitation, or, as sometimes also happens, their unlimited universality can be more convincingly proved than their necessity, it is advisable to use the two criteria separately, each by itself being infallible.

Now it is easy to show that there actually are in human knowledge judgements which are necessary and in the strictest sense universal, and which are therefore pure *a priori* judgements. If an example from the sciences be desired, we have only to look to any of the propositions of mathematics; if we seek an example from the understanding in its quite ordinary employment, the proposition, 'every alteration must have a cause', will serve our purpose. In the latter case, indeed, the very concept of a cause so manifestly contains the concept of a necessity of connection with an effect and of the strict universality of the rule, that the concept would be altogether lost if we attempted to derive it, as Hume has done, from a repeated association of that which happens with that which precedes, and from a custom of connecting representations, a custom originating in this repeated association, and constituting therefore a merely subjective necessity. Even without appealing to such examples, it is possible to show that pure *a priori* principles are indispensable for the possibility of experience, and so to prove their existence *a priori*. For whence could experience derive its certainty, if all the rules, according to which it proceeds, were always themselves empirical, and therefore contingent? Such rules could hardly be regarded as first principles. At present, however, we may be content to have established the fact that our faculty of knowledge does have a pure employment, and to have shown what are the criteria of such an employment.

Such *a priori* origin is manifest in certain concepts, no less than in judgements. If we remove from our empirical concept of a body, one by one, every feature in it which is [merely] empirical, the colour, the hardness or softness, the weight, even the impenetrability, there still remains the space which the body (now entirely vanished) occupied, and this cannot be removed. Again, if we remove from our empirical concept of any object, corporeal or incorporeal, all properties which experience has taught us, we yet cannot take away that property through which the object is thought as substance or as inhering in a substance (although this concept of substance is more determinate than that of an object in general). Owing, therefore, to the necessity with which this concept of substance forces itself upon us, we have no option save to admit that it has its seat in our faculty of *a priori* knowledge.

III. PHILOSOPHY STANDS IN NEED OF A SCIENCE WHICH SHALL DETERMINE THE POSSIBILITY, THE PRINCIPLES, AND THE EXTENT OF ALL *A PRIORI* KNOWLEDGE

But what is still more extraordinary than all the preceding is this, that certain modes of knowledge leave the field of all possible experiences and have the appearance of extending the scope of our judgements beyond all limits of experience, and this by means of concepts to which no corresponding object can ever be given in experience.

It is precisely by means of the latter modes of knowledge, in a realm beyond the world of the senses, where experience can yield neither guidance nor correction, that our reason carries on those enquiries which owing to their importance we consider to be far more excellent, and in their purpose far more lofty, than all that the understanding can learn in the field of appearances. Indeed we prefer to run every risk of error rather than desist from such urgent enquiries, on the ground of their dubious character, or from disdain and indifference. These unavoidable problems set by pure reason itself are *God, freedom,* and *immortality*. The science which, with all its preparations, is in its final intention directed solely to their solution is metaphysics; and its procedure is at first dogmatic, that is, it confidently sets itself to this task without any previous examination of the capacity or incapacity of reason for so great an undertaking.

Now it does indeed seem natural that, as soon as we have left the ground of experience, we should, through careful enquiries, assure ourselves as to the foundations of any building that we propose to erect, not making use of any knowledge that we possess without first determining whence it has come, and not trusting to principles without knowing their origin. It is natural, that is to say, that the question should first be considered, how the understanding can arrive at all this knowledge *a priori,* and what extent, validity, and worth it may have. Nothing, indeed, could be more natural, if by the term 'natural' we signify what fittingly and reasonably ought to happen. But if we mean by 'natural' what ordinarily happens, then on the contrary nothing is more natural and more intelligible than the fact that this enquiry has been so long neglected. For one part of this knowledge, the mathematical, has long been of established reliability, and so gives rise to a favourable presumption as regards the other part, which may yet be of quite different nature. Besides, once we are outside the circle of experience, we can be sure of not being *contradicted* by experience. The charm of extending our knowledge is so great that nothing short of encountering a direct contradiction can suffice to arrest us in our course; and this can be avoided, if we are careful in our fabrications—which none the less will still remain fabrications. Mathematics gives us a shining example of how far, independently of experience, we can progress in *a priori* knowledge. It does, indeed, occupy itself with objects and with knowledge solely in so far as they allow of being exhibited in intuition. But this circumstance is easily overlooked, since this intuition can itself be given *a priori,* and is therefore hardly to be distinguished from a bare and pure concept. Misled by such a proof of the power of reason, the demand for the extension of knowledge recognises no limits. The light dove, cleaving the air in her free flight, and feeling its resistance, might imagine that its flight would be still easier in empty space. It was thus that Plato left the world of the senses, as setting too narrow limits to the understanding, and ventured out beyond it on the wings of the ideas, in the empty space of the pure understanding. He did not observe that with all his efforts he made no advance—meeting no resistance that might, as it were, serve as a support upon which he could take a stand, to which he could apply his powers, and so set his understanding in motion. It is, indeed, the common fate of human reason to complete its speculative structures as speedily as may be, and only afterwards to enquire whether the foundations are reliable. All sorts of excuses will then be appealed to, in order to reassure us of their solidity, or rather indeed to enable us to dispense altogether with so late and so dangerous an enquiry. But what keeps us, during the actual building, free from all apprehension and suspicion, and flatters us with a seeming thoroughness, is this other circumstance, namely, that a great, perhaps the greatest, part of the business of our reason consists in analysis of the concepts which we already have of objects. This analysis supplies us with a considerable body of knowledge, which, while nothing but explanation or elucidation of what has already been thought in our concepts, though in a confused manner, is yet prized as being, at least as regards its form, new insight. But so far as the matter or content is concerned, there has been no extension of our previously possessed concepts, but only an analysis of them. Since this procedure yields real knowledge *a priori,* which progresses in an assured and useful fashion, reason is so far misled as surreptitiously to introduce, without itself being aware of so doing, assertions of an entirely different order, in which it attaches to given concepts others completely foreign to them, and moreover attaches them *a priori.* And yet it is not known how reason can be in position to do this. Such a question is never so much as thought of. I shall therefore at once proceed to deal with the difference between these two kinds of knowledge.

IV. THE DISTINCTION BETWEEN ANALYTIC AND SYNTHETIC JUDGEMENTS

In all judgements in which the relation of a subject to the predicate is thought (I take into consideration affirmative judgements only, the subsequent application to negative judgements being easily made), this relation is possible in two different ways. Either the predicate B belongs to the subject A, as something which is (covertly) contained in this concept A; or B lies outside the concept A, although it does indeed stand in connection with it. In the one case I entitle the judgement analytic, in the other synthetic. Analytic judgements (affirmative) are therefore those in which the connection of the predicate with the subject is thought through identity; those in which this connection is thought without identity should be entitled synthetic. The former, as adding nothing through the predicate to the concept of the subject, but merely breaking it up into those constituent concepts that have all along been thought in it, although confusedly, can also be entitled explicative. The latter, on the other hand, add to the concept of the subject a predicate which has not been in any wise thought in it, and which no analysis could possibly extract from it; and they may therefore be entitled ampliative. If I say, for instance, 'All bodies are extended', this is an analytic judgement. For I do not require to go beyond the concept which I connect with 'body' in order to find extension as bound up with it. To meet with this predicate, I have merely to analyse the concept, that is, to become conscious to myself of the manifold which I always think in that concept: The judgement is therefore analytic. But when I say, 'All bodies are heavy', the predicate is something quite different from anything that I think in the mere concept of body in general; and the addition of such a predicate therefore yields a synthetic judgement.

Judgements of experience, as such, are one and all synthetic. For it would be absurd to found an analytic judgement on experience. Since, in framing the judgement, I must not go outside my concept, there is no need to appeal to the testimony of experience in its support. That a body is extended is a proposition that holds *a priori* and is not empirical. For, before appealing to experience, I have already in the concept of body all the conditions required for my judgement. I have only to extract from it, in accordance with the principle of contradiction, the required predicate, and in so doing can at the same time become conscious of the necessity of the judgement—and that is what experience could never have taught me. On the other hand, though I do not include in the concept of a body in general the predicate 'weight', none the less this concept indicates an object of experience through one of its parts, and I can add to that part other parts of this same experience, as in this way belonging together with the concept. From the start I can apprehend the concept of body analytically through the characters of extension, impenetrability, figure, etc., all of which are thought in the concept. Now, however, looking back on the experience from which I have derived this concept of body, and finding weight to be invariably connected with the above characters, I attach it as a predicate to the concept; and in doing so I attach it synthetically, and am therefore extending my knowledge. The possibility of the synthesis of the predicate 'weight' with the concept of 'body' thus rests upon experience. While the one concept is not contained in the other, they yet belong to one another, though only contingently, as parts of a whole, namely, of an experience which is itself a synthetic combination of intuitions.

But in *a priori* synthetic judgements this help is entirely lacking: [I do not here have the advantage of looking around in the field of experience.] Upon what, then, am I to rely, when I seek to go beyond the concept A, and to know that another concept B is connected with it? Through what is the synthesis made possible? Let us take the proposition, 'Everything which happens has its cause' In the concept of 'something which happens', I do indeed think an existence which is preceded by a time, etc., and from this concept analytic judgements may be obtained. But the concept of a 'cause' lies entirely outside the other concept, and signifies something different from 'that which happens', and is not therefore in any way contained in this latter representation. How come I then to predicate of that which happens something quite different, and to apprehend that the concept of cause, though not contained in it, yet belongs, and indeed necessarily belongs, to it? What is here the unknown = X which gives support to the understanding when it believes that it can discover outside the concept A a predicate B foreign to this concept, which it yet at the same time considers to be connected with it? It cannot be experience, because the suggested principle has connected the second representation with the first, not only with greater universality, but also with the character of necessity, and therefore completely *a priori* and on the basis of mere concepts. Upon such synthetic, that is, ampliative principles, all our *a priori* speculative knowledge must ultimately rest; analytic judgements are very important, and indeed necessary, but only for obtaining that clearness in the concepts which is requisite for such a sure and wide synthesis as will lead to a genuinely new addition to all previous knowledge.

V. IN ALL THEORETICAL SCIENCES OF REASON SYNTHETIC *A PRIORI* JUDGEMENTS ARE CONTAINED AS PRINCIPLES

1. *All mathematical judgements, without exception, are synthetic.* This fact, though incontestably certain and in its consequences very important, has hitherto escaped the notice of those who are engaged in the analysis of human reason, and is, indeed, directly opposed to all their conjectures. For as it was found that all mathematical inferences proceed in accordance with the principle of contradiction (which the nature of all apodeictic certainty requires), it was supposed that the fundamental propositions of the science can themselves be known to be true through that principle. This is an erroneous view. For though a synthetic proposition can indeed be discerned in accordance with the principle of contradiction, this can only be if another synthetic proposition is presupposed, and if it can then be apprehended as following from this other proposition; it can never be so discerned in and by itself.

First of all, it has to be noted that mathematical propositions, strictly so called, are always judgements *a priori,* not empirical; because they carry with them necessity, which cannot be derived from experience. If this be demurred to, I am willing to limit my statement to *pure* mathematics, the very concept of which implies that it does not contain empirical, but only pure *a priori* knowledge.

We might, indeed, at first suppose that the proposition $7 + 5 = 12$ is a merely analytic proposition, and follows by the principle of contradiction from the concept of a sum of 7 and 5. But if we look more closely we find that the concept of the sum of 7 and 5 contains nothing save the union of the two numbers into one, and in this no thought is being taken as to what that single number may be which combines both. The concept of 12 is by no means already thought in merely thinking this union of 7 and 5; and I may analyse my concept of such a possible sum as long as I please, still I shall never find the 12 in it. We have to go outside these concepts, and call in the aid of the intuition which corresponds to one of them, our five fingers, for instance, or, as Segner does in his *Arithmetic,* five points, adding to the concept of 7, unit by unit, the five given in intuition. For starting with the number 7, and for the concept of 5 calling in the aid of the fingers of my hand as intuition, I now add one by one to the number 7 the units which I previously took together to form the number 5, and with the aid of that figure [the hand] see the number 12 come into being. That 5 should be added to 7, I have indeed already thought in the concept of a sum $= 7 + 5$, but not that this sum is equivalent to the number 12. Arithmetical propositions are therefore always synthetic. This is still more evident if we take larger numbers. For it is then obvious that, however we might turn and twist our concepts, we could never, by the mere analysis of them, and without the aid of intuition, discover what [the number is that] is the sum.

Just as little is any fundamental proposition of pure geometry analytic. That the straight line between two points is the shortest, is a synthetic proposition. For my concept of *straight* contains nothing of quantity, but only of quality. The concept of the shortest is wholly an addition, and cannot be derived, through any process of analysis, from the concept of the straight line.

Intuition, therefore, must here be called in; only by its aid is the synthesis possible. What here causes us commonly to believe that the predicate of such apodeictic judgements is already contained in our concept, and that the judgement is therefore analytic, is merely the ambiguous character of the terms used. We are required to join in thought a certain predicate to a given concept, and this necessity is inherent in the concepts themselves. But the question is not what we *ought* to join in thought to the given concept, but what we *actually* think in it, even if only obscurely; and it is then manifest that, while the predicate is indeed attached necessarily to the concept, it is so in virtue of an intuition which must be added to the concept, not as thought in the concept itself.

Some few fundamental propositions, presupposed by the geometrician, are, indeed, really analytic, and rest on the principle of contradiction. But, as identical propositions, they serve only as links in the chain of method and not as principles; for instance, $a = a$; the whole is equal to itself; or $(a + b) > a$, that is, the whole is greater than its part. And even these propositions, though they are valid according to pure concepts, are only admitted in mathematics because they can be exhibited in intuition.

2. *Natural science (physics) contains* a priori *synthetic judgements as principles.* I need cite only two such judgements: that in all changes of the material world the quantity of matter remains unchanged; and that in all communication of motion, action and reaction must always be equal. Both propositions, it is evident, are not only necessary, and therefore in their origin *a priori,* but also synthetic. For in the concept of matter I do not think its permanence, but only its presence in the space which it occupies. I go outside and beyond the concept of matter, joining to it *a priori* in thought something which I have not thought *in* it. The proposition is not, therefore, analytic, but synthetic, and yet is thought *a priori;* and so likewise are the other propositions of the pure part of natural science.

3. *Metaphysics,* even if we look upon it as having hitherto failed in all its endeavours, is yet, owing to the nature of human reason, a quite indispensable science, and *ought to contain a priori synthetic knowledge*. For its business is not merely to analyse concepts which we make for ourselves *a priori* of things, and thereby to clarify them analytically, but to extend our *a priori* knowledge. And for this purpose we must employ principles which add to the given concept something that was not contained in it, and through *a priori* synthetic judgements venture out so far that experience is quite unable to follow us, as, for instance, in the proposition, that the world must have a first beginning, and such like. Thus metaphysics consists, at least *in intention,* entirely of *a priori* synthetic propositions.

VI. THE GENERAL PROBLEM OF PURE REASON

Much is already gained if we can bring a number of investigations under the formula of a single problem. For we not only lighten our own task, by defining it accurately, but make it easier for others, who would test our results, to judge whether or not we have succeeded in what we set out to do. Now the proper problem of pure reason is contained in the question: How are *a priori* synthetic judgements possible?

That metaphysics has hitherto remained in so vacillating a state of uncertainty and contradiction, is entirely due to the fact that this problem, and perhaps even the distinction between analytic and synthetic judgements, has never previously been considered. Upon the solution of this problem, or upon a sufficient proof that the possibility which it desires to have explained does in fact not exist at all, depends the success or failure of metaphysics. Among philosophers, David Hume came nearest to envisaging this problem, but still was very far from conceiving it with sufficient definiteness and universality.

He occupied himself exclusively with the synthetic proposition regarding the connection of an effect with its cause (*principium causalitatis*), and he believed himself to have shown that such an *a priori* proposition is entirely impossible. If we accept his conclusions, then all that we call metaphysics is a mere delusion whereby we fancy ourselves to have rational insight into what, in actual fact, is borrowed solely from experience, and under the influence of custom has taken the illusory semblance of necessity. If he had envisaged our problem in all its universality, he would never have been guilty of this statement, so destructive of all pure philosophy. For he would then have recognised that, according to his own argument, pure mathematics, as certainly containing *a priori* synthetic propositions, would also not be possible; and from such an assertion his good sense would have saved him.

In the solution of the above problem, we are at the same time deciding as to the possibility of the employment of pure reason in establishing and developing all those sciences which contain a theoretical *a priori* knowledge of objects, and have therefore to answer the questions:

How is pure mathematics possible?
How is pure science of nature possible?

Since these sciences actually exist, it is quite proper to ask *how* they are possible; for that they must be possible is proved by the fact that they exist. But the poor progress which has hitherto been made in metaphysics, and the fact that no system yet propounded can, in view of the essential purpose of metaphysics, be said really to exist, leaves everyone sufficient ground for doubting as to its possibility.

Yet, in a certain sense, this *kind of knowledge* is to be looked upon as given; that is to say, metaphysics actually exists, if not as a science, yet still as natural disposition (*metaphysica naturalis*). For human reason, without being moved merely by the idle desire for extent and variety of knowledge, proceeds impetuously, driven on by an inward need, to questions such as cannot be answered by any empirical employment of reason, or by principles thence derived. Thus in all men, as soon as their reason has become ripe for speculation, there has always existed and will always continue to exist some kind of metaphysics. And so we have the question:

How is metaphysics, as natural disposition, possible?

that is, how from the nature of universal human reason do those questions arise which pure reason propounds to itself, and which it is impelled by its own need to answer as best it can?

But since all attempts which have hitherto been made to answer these natural questions—for instance, whether the world has a beginning or is from eternity—have always met with unavoidable contradictions, we cannot rest satisfied with the mere natural disposition to metaphysics, that is, with the pure faculty of reason itself, from which, indeed, some sort of metaphysics (be it what it may) always arises. It must be possible for reason to attain to certainty whether we know or do not know the objects of metaphysics, that is, to come to a decision either in regard to the objects of its enquiries or in regard to the capacity or incapacity of reason to pass any judgement upon them, so that we may either with confidence extend our pure reason or set to it sure and determinate limits. This last question, which arises out of the previous general problem, may, rightly stated, take the form:

How is metaphysics, as science, possible?

Thus the critique of reason, in the end, necessarily leads to scientific knowledge; while its dogmatic employment, on the other hand, lands us in dogmatic assertions to which other assertions, equally specious, can always be opposed—that is, in *scepticism*.

This science cannot be of any very formidable prolixity, since it has to deal not with the objects of reason, the variety of which is inexhaustible, but only with itself and the problems which arise entirely from within itself, and which are imposed upon it by its own nature, not by the nature of things which are distinct from it. When once reason has learnt completely to understand its own power in respect of objects which can be presented to it in experience, it should easily be able to determine, with completeness and certainty, the extent and the limits of its attempted employment beyond the bounds of all experience.

We may, then, and indeed we must, regard as abortive all attempts, hitherto made, to establish a metaphysic *dogmatically*. For the analytic part in any such attempted system, namely, the mere analysis of the concepts that inhere in our reason *a priori,* is by no means the aim of, but only a preparation for, metaphysics proper, that is, the extension of its *a priori* synthetic knowledge. For such a purpose, the analysis of concepts is useless, since it merely shows what is contained in these concepts, not how we arrive at them *a priori*. A solution of this latter problem is required, that we may be able to determine the valid employment of such concepts in regard to the objects of all knowledge in general. Nor is much self-denial needed to give up these claims, seeing that the undeniable, and in the dogmatic procedure of reason also unavoidable, contradictions of reason with itself have long since undermined the authority of every metaphysical system yet propounded. Greater firmness will be required if we are not to be deterred by inward difficulties and outward opposition from endeavouring, through application of a method entirely different from any hitherto employed, at last to bring to a prosperous and fruitful growth a science indispensable to human reason—a science whose every branch may be cut away but whose root cannot be destroyed.

VII. THE IDEA AND DIVISION OF A SPECIAL SCIENCE, UNDER THE TITLE "CRITIQUE OF PURE REASON"

In view of all these considerations, we arrive at the idea of a special science which can be entitled the Critique of Pure Reason. For reason is the faculty which supplies the principles of *a priori* knowledge. Pure reason is, therefore, that which contains the principles whereby we know anything absolutely *a priori*. An organon of pure reason would be the sum-total of those principles according to which all modes of pure *a priori* knowledge can be acquired and actually brought into being. The exhaustive application of such an organon would give rise to a system of pure reason. But as this would be asking rather much, and as it is still doubtful whether, and in what cases, any extension of our knowledge be here possible, we can regard a science of the mere examination of pure reason, of its sources and limits, as the *propaedeutic* to the system of pure reason. As such, it should be called a critique, not a doctrine, of pure reason. Its utility, in speculation, ought properly to be only negative, not to extend, but only to clarify our reason, and keep it free from errors—which is already a very great gain. I entitle *transcendental* all knowledge which is occupied not so much with objects as with the mode of our knowledge of objects in so far as this mode of knowledge is to be possible *a priori*. A system of such concepts might be entitled transcendental philosophy. But that is still, at this stage, too large an undertaking. For since such a science must contain, with completeness, both kinds of *a priori* knowledge, the analytic no less than the synthetic, it is, so far as our present purpose is concerned, much too comprehensive. We have to carry the analysis so far only as is indispensably necessary in order to comprehend, in their whole extent, the principles of *a priori* synthesis, with which alone we are called upon to deal. It is upon this enquiry, which should be entitled not a doctrine, but only a transcendental critique, that we are now engaged. Its purpose is not to extend knowledge, but only to correct it, and to supply a touchstone of the value, or lack of value, of all *a priori* knowledge. Such a critique is therefore a preparation, so far as may be possible, for an organon; and should this turn out not to be possible, then at least for a canon, according to which, in due course, the complete system of the philosophy of pure reason—be it in extension or merely in limitation of its knowledge—may be carried into execution, analytically as well as synthetically. That such a system is possible, and indeed that it may not be of such great extent as to cut us off from the hope of entirely completing it, may already be gathered from the fact that what here constitutes our subject-matter is not the nature of things, which is inexhaustible, but the understanding which passes judgement upon the nature of things; and this understanding, again, only in respect of its *a priori* knowledge. These *a priori* possessions of the understanding, since they have not to be sought for without, cannot remain hidden from us, and in all probability are sufficiently small in extent to allow of our apprehending them in their completeness, of judging as to their value or lack of value, and so of rightly appraising them. Still less may the reader here expect a critique of books and systems of pure reason; we are concerned only with the critique of the faculty of pure reason itself. Only in so far as we build upon this foundation do we have a reliable touchstone for estimating the philosophical value of old and new works in this field. Otherwise the unqualified historian or critic is passing judgements upon the groundless assertions of others by means of his own, which are equally groundless.

Transcendental philosophy is only the idea of a science, for which the critique of pure reason has to lay down the complete architectonic plan. That is to say, it has to guarantee, as following from principles, the completeness and certainty of the structure in all its parts. It is the system of all principles of pure reason. And if this critique is not itself to be entitled a transcendental philosophy, it is solely because, to be a complete system, it would also have to contain an exhaustive analysis of the whole of *a priori* human knowledge. Our critique must, indeed, supply a complete enumeration of all the fundamental concepts that go to constitute such pure knowledge. But it is not required to give an exhaustive analysis of these concepts, nor a complete review of those that can be derived from them. Such a demand would be unreasonable, partly because this analysis would not be appropriate to our main purpose, inasmuch as there is no such uncertainty in regard to analysis as we encounter in the case of synthesis, for the sake of which alone our whole critique is undertaken; and partly because it would be inconsistent with the unity of our plan to assume responsibility for the completeness of such an analysis and derivation, when in view of our purpose we can be excused from doing so. The analysis of these *a priori* concepts, which later we shall have to enumerate, and the derivation of other concepts from them, can easily, however, be made complete when once they have been established as exhausting the principles of synthesis, and if in this essential respect nothing be lacking in them.

The critique of pure reason therefore will contain all that is essential in transcendental philosophy. While it is the complete idea of transcendental philosophy, it is not equivalent to that latter science; for it carries the analysis only so far as is requisite for the complete examination of knowledge which is *a priori* and synthetic.

What has chiefly to be kept in view in the division of such a science, is that no concepts be allowed to enter which contain in themselves anything empirical, or, in other words, that it consist in knowledge wholly *a priori*. Accordingly, although the highest principles and fundamental concepts of morality are *a priori* knowledge, they have no place in transcendental philosophy, because, although they do not lay at the foundation of their precepts the concepts of pleasure and pain, of the desires and inclinations, etc., all of which are of empirical origin, yet in the construction of a system of pure morality these empirical concepts must necessarily be brought into the concept of duty, as representing either a hindrance, which we have to overcome, or an allurement, which must not be made into a motive. Transcendental philosophy is therefore a philosophy of pure and merely speculative reason. All that is practical, so far as it contains motives, relates to feelings, and these belong to the empirical sources of knowledge.

If we are to make a systematic division of the science which we are engaged in presenting, it must have first a *doctrine of the elements,* and secondly, a *doctrine of the method of pure reason.* Each of these chief divisions will have its subdivisions, but the grounds of these we are not yet in a position to explain. By way of introduction or anticipation we need only say that there are two stems of human knowledge, namely, *sensibility* and *understanding,* which perhaps spring from a common, but to us unknown, root. Through the former, objects are given to us; through the latter, they are thought. Now in so far as sensibility may be found to contain *a priori* representations constituting the condition under which objects are given to us, it will belong to transcendental philosophy. And since the conditions under which alone the objects of human knowledge are given must precede those under which they are thought, the transcendental doctrine of sensibility will constitute the first part of the science of the elements.

5

Two Dogmas of Empiricism[1]

W. V. O. QUINE

Modern empiricism has been conditioned in large part by two dogmas. One is a belief in some fundamental cleavage between truths which are *analytic,* or grounded in meanings independently of matters of fact, and truth which are *synthetic,* or grounded in fact. The other dogma is *reductionism:* the belief that each meaningful statement is equivalent to some logical construct upon terms which refer to immediate experience. Both dogmas, I shall argue, are ill founded. One effect of abandoning them is, as we shall see, a blurring of the supposed boundary between speculative metaphysics and natural science. Another effect is a shift toward pragmatism.

I. BACKGROUND FOR ANALYTICITY

Kant's cleavage between analytic and synthetic truths was foreshadowed in Hume's distinction between relations of ideas and matters of fact, and in Leibniz's distinction between truths of reason and truths of fact. Leibniz spoke of the truths of reason as true in all possible worlds. Picturesqueness aside, this is to say that the truths of reason are those which could not possibly be false. In the same vein we hear analytic statements defined as statements whose denials are self-contradictory. But this definition has small explanatory value; for the notion of self-contradictoriness, in the quite broad sense needed for this definition of analyticity, stands in exactly the same need of clarification as does the notion of analyticity itself.[2] The two notions are the two sides of a single dubious coin.

Kant conceived of an analytic statement as one that attributes to its subject no more than is already conceptually contained in the subject. This formulation has two shortcomings: it limits itself to statements of subject-predicate form, and it appeals to a notion of containment which is left at a metaphorical level. But Kant's intent, evident more from the use he makes of the notion

Source: W. V. O. Quine, "Two Dogmas of Empiricism," from *The Philosophical Review* (60) January 1951, pp. 20–43.

of analyticity than from his definition of it, can be restated thus: a statement is analytic when it is true by virtue of meanings and independently of fact. Pursuing this line, let us examine the concept of *meaning* which is presupposed.

We must observe to begin with that meaning is not to be identified with naming, or reference. Consider Frege's example of 'Evening Star' and 'Morning Star'. Understood not merely as a recurrent evening apparition but as a body, the Evening Star is the planet Venus, and the Morning Star is the same. The two singular terms *name* the same thing. But the meanings must be treated as distinct, since the identity 'Evening Star = Morning Star' is a statement of fact established by astronomical observation. If 'Evening Star' and 'Morning Star' were alike in meaning, the identity 'Evening Star = Morning Star' would be analytic.

Again there is Russell's example of 'Scott' and 'the author of *Waverley*'. Analysis of the meanings of words was by no means sufficient to reveal to George IV that the person named by these two singular terms was one and the same.

The distinction between meaning and naming is no less important at the level of abstract terms. The terms '9' and 'the number of planets' name one and the same abstract entity but presumably must be regarded as unlike in meaning; for astronomical observation was needed, and not mere reflection on meanings, to determine the sameness of the entity in question.

Thus far we have been considering singular terms. With general terms, or predicates, the situation is somewhat different but parallel. Whereas a singular term purports to name an entity, abstract or concrete, a general term does not; but a general term is *true of* an entity, or of each of many, or of none. The class of all entities of which a general term is true is called the *extension* of the term. Now paralleling the contrast between the meaning of a singular term and the entity named, we must distinguish equally between the meaning of a general term and its extension. The general terms 'creature with a heart' and 'creature with a kidney', e.g., are perhaps alike in extension but unlike in meaning.

Confusion of meaning with extension, in the case of general terms, is less common than confusion of meaning with naming in the case of singular terms. It is indeed a commonplace in philosophy to oppose intension (or meaning) to extension, or, in a variant vocabulary, connotation to denotation.

The Aristotelian notion of essence was the forerunner, no doubt, of the modern notion of intension or meaning. For Aristotle it was essential in men to be rational, accidental to be two-legged. But there is an important difference between this attitude and the doctrine of meaning. From the latter point of view it may indeed be conceded (if only for the sake of argument) that rationality is involved in the meaning of the word 'man' while two-leggedness is not; but two-leggedness may at the same time be viewed as involved in the meaning of 'biped' while rationality is not. Thus from the point of view of the doctrine of meaning it makes no sense to say of the actual individual, who is at once a man and a biped, that his rationality is essential and his two-leggedness accidental or vice versa. Things had essences, for Aristotle, but only linguistic forms have meanings. Meaning is what essence becomes when it is divorced from the object of reference and wedded to the word.

For the theory of meaning the most conspicuous question is as to the nature of its objects: what sort of things are meanings? They are evidently intended to be ideas, somehow—mental ideas for some semanticists, Platonic ideas for others. Objects of either sort are so elusive, not to say debatable, that there seems little hope of erecting a fruitful science about them. It is not even clear, granted meanings, when we have two and when we have one; it is not clear when linguistic forms should be regarded as *synonymous,* or alike in meaning, and when they should not. If a standard of synonymy should be arrived at, we may reasonably expect that the appeal to meanings as entities will not have played a very useful part in the enterprise.

A felt need for meant entities may derive from an earlier failure to appreciate that meaning and reference are distinct. Once the theory of meaning is sharply separated from the theory of reference, it is a short step to recognizing as the business of the theory of meaning simply the synonymy of linguistic forms and the analyticity of statements; meanings themselves, as obscure intermediary entities, may well be abandoned.

The description of analyticity as truth by virtue of meanings started us off in pursuit of a concept of meaning. But now we have abandoned the thought of any special realm of entities called meanings. So the problem of analyticity confronts us anew.

Statements which are analytic by general philosophical acclaim are not, indeed, far to seek. They fall into two classes. Those of the first class, which may be called *logically true,* are typified by:

(1) No unmarried man is married.

The relevant feature of this example is that it is not merely true as it stands, but remains true under any and all reinterpretations of 'man' and 'married'. If we suppose a prior inventory of *logical* particles, comprising 'no', 'un-', 'not', 'if', 'then', 'and', etc., then in general a logical truth is a statement which is true and remains true under all reinterpretations of its components other than the logical particles.

But there is also a second class of analytic statements, typified by:

(2) No bachelor is married.

The characteristic of such a statement is that it can be turned into a logical truth by putting synonyms for synonyms; thus (2) can be turned into (1) by putting 'unmarried man' for its synonym 'bachelor'. We still lack a proper characterization of this second class of analytic statements, and therewith of analyticity generally, inasmuch as we have had in the above description to lean on a notion of "synonymy" which is no less in need of clarification than analyticity itself.

In recent years Carnap has tended to explain analyticity by appeal to what he calls state-descriptions.[3] A state-description is any exhaustive assignment of truth values to the atomic, or noncompound, statements of the language. All other statements of the language are, Carnap assumes, built up of their component clauses by means of the familiar logical devices, in such a way that the truth value of any complex statement is fixed for each state-description by specifiable logical laws. A statement is then explained as analytic when it comes out true under every state-description. This account is an adaptation of Leibniz's "true in all possible worlds." But note that this version of analyticity serves its purpose only if the atomic statements of the language are, unlike 'John is a bachelor' and 'John is married', mutually independent. Otherwise there would be a state-description which assigned truth to 'John is a bachelor' and falsity to 'John is married', and consequently 'All bachelors are married' would turn out synthetic rather than analytic under the proposed criterion. Thus the criterion of analyticity in terms of state-descriptions serves only for languages devoid of extralogical synonym-pairs, such as 'bachelor' and 'unmarried man': synonym-pairs of the type which give rise to the "second class" of analytic statements. The criterion in terms of state-descriptions is a reconstruction at best of logical truth.

I do not mean to suggest that Carnap is under any illusions on this point. His simplified model language with its state-descriptions is aimed primarily not at the general problem of analyticity but at another purpose, the clarification of probability and induction. Our problem, however, is analyticity; and here the major difficulty lies not in the first class of analytic statements, the logical truths, but rather in the second class, which depends on the notion of synonymy.

II. DEFINITION

There are those who find it soothing to say that the analytic statements of the second class reduce to those of the first class, the logical truths, by *definition;* 'bachelor', e.g., is *defined* as 'unmarried man'. But how do we find that 'bachelor' is defined as 'unmarried man'? Who defined it thus, and when? Are we to appeal to the nearest dictionary, and accept the lexicographer's formulation as law? Clearly this would be to put the cart before the horse. The lexicographer is an empirical scientist, whose business is the recording of antecedent facts; and if he glosses 'bachelor' as 'unmarried man' it is because of his belief that there is a relation of synonymy between these forms, implicit in general or preferred usage prior to his own work. The notion of synonymy presupposed here has still to be clarified, presumably in terms relating to linguistic behavior. Certainly the "definition" which is the lexicographer's report of an observed synonymy cannot be taken as the ground of the synonymy.

Definition is not, indeed, an activity exclusively of philologists. Philosophers and scientists frequently have occasion to "define" a recondite term by paraphrasing it into terms of a more familiar vocabulary. But ordinarily such a definition, like the philologist's, is pure lexicography, affirming a relationship of synonymy antecedent to the exposition in hand.

Just what it means to affirm synonymy, just what the interconnections may be which are necessary and sufficient in order that two linguistic forms be properly describable as synonymous, is far from clear; but, whatever these interconnections may be, ordinarily they are grounded in usage. Definitions reporting selected instances of synonymy come then as reports upon usage.

There is also, however, a variant type of definitional activity which does not limit itself to the reporting of pre-existing synonymies. I have in mind what Carnap calls *explication*—an activity to which philosophers are given, and scientists also in their more philosophical moments. In explication the purpose is not merely to paraphrase the definiendum into an outright synonym, but actually to improve upon the definiendum by refining or supplementing its meaning. But even explication, though not merely reporting a pre-existing synonymy between definiendum and definiens, does rest nevertheless on *other* pre-existing synonymies. The matter may be viewed as follows. Any word worth explicating has some contexts which, as wholes, are clear and precise enough to be useful; and the purpose of explication is to preserve the usage of these favored contexts while sharpening the usage of other contexts. In order that a given definition be suitable for purposes of explication, therefore, what is required is not that the definiendum in its antecedent usage be synonymous with the definiens, but just that each of these favored contexts of the definiendum, taken as a whole in its antecedent usage, be synonymous with the corresponding context of the definiens.

Two alternative definientia may be equally appropriate for the purposes of a given task of explication and yet not be synonymous with each other; for they may serve interchangeably within the favored contexts but diverge elsewhere. By cleaving to one of these definientia rather than the other, a definition of explicative kind generates, by fiat, a relationship of synonymy between definiendum and definiens which did not hold before. But such a definition still owes its explicative function, as seen, to pre-existing synonymies.

There does, however, remain still an extreme sort of definition which does not hark back to prior synonymies at all; viz., the explicitly conventional introduction of novel notations for purposes of sheer abbreviation. Here the definiendum becomes synonymous with the definiens simply because it has been created expressly for the purpose of being synonymous with the definiens. Here we have a really transparent case of synonymy created by definition; would that all species of synonymy were as intelligible. For the rest, definition rests on synonymy rather than explaining it.

The word 'definition' has come to have a dangerously reassuring sound, due no doubt to its frequent occurrence in logical and mathematical writings. We shall do well to digress now into a brief appraisal of the role of definition in formal work.

In logical and mathematical systems either of two mutually antagonistic types of economy may be striven for, and each has its peculiar practical utility. On the one hand we may seek economy of practical expression: ease and brevity in the statement of multifarious relationships. This sort of economy calls usually for distinctive concise notations for a wealth of concepts. Second, however, and oppositely, we may seek economy in grammar and vocabulary; we may try to find a minimum of basic concepts such that, once a distinctive notation has been appropriated to each of them, it becomes possible to express any desired further concept by mere combination and iteration of our basic notations. This second sort of economy is impractical in one way, since a poverty in basic idioms tends to a necessary lengthening of discourse. But it is practical in another way: it greatly simplifies theoretical discourse *about* the language, through minimizing the terms and the forms of construction wherein the language consists.

Both sorts of economy, though prima facie incompatible, are valuable in their separate ways. The custom has consequently arisen of combining both sorts of economy by forging in effect two languages, the one a part of the other. The inclusive language, though redundant in grammar and vocabulary, is economical in message lengths, while the part, called *primitive notation,* is economical in grammar and vocabulary. Whole and part are correlated by rules of translation whereby each idiom not in primitive notation is equated to some complex built up of primitive notation. These rules of translation are the so-called *definitions* which appear in formalized systems. They are best viewed not as adjuncts to one language but as correlations between two languages, the one a part of the other.

But these correlations are not arbitrary. They are supposed to show how the primitive notations can accomplish all purposes, save brevity and convenience, of the redundant language. Hence the definiendum and its definiens may be expected, in each case, to be related in one or another of the three ways lately noted. The definiens may be a faithful paraphrase of the definiendum into the narrower notation, preserving a direct synonymy as of antecedent usage; or the definiens may, in the spirit of explication, improve upon the antecedent usage of the definiendum; or finally, the definiendum may be a newly created notation, newly endowed with meaning here and now.

In formal and informal work alike, thus, we find that definition—except in the extreme case of the explicitly conventional introduction of new notations—hinges on prior relationships of synonymy. Recognizing then that the notion of definition does not hold the key to synonymy and analyticity, let us look further into synonymy and say no more of definition.

III. INTERCHANGEABILITY

A natural suggestion, deserving close examination, is that the synonymy of two linguistic forms consists simply in their interchangeability in all contexts without change of truth value; interchangeability, in Leibniz's phrase, *salva veritate*. Note that synonyms so conceived need not even be free from vagueness, as long as the vaguenesses match.

But it is not quite true that the synonyms 'bachelor' and 'unmarried man' are everywhere interchangeable *salva veritate*. Truths which become false under substitution of 'unmarried man' for 'bachelor' are easily constructed with help of 'bachelor of arts' or 'bachelor's buttons'. Also with help of quotation, thus:

> 'Bachelor' has less than ten letters.

Such counterinstances can, however, perhaps be set aside by treating the phrases 'bachelor of arts' and 'bachelor's buttons' and the quotation "bachelor" each as a single indivisible word and then stipulating that the interchangeability *salva veritate* which is to be the touchstone of synonymy is not supposed to apply to fragmentary occurrences inside of a word. This account of synonymy, supposing it acceptable on other counts, has indeed the drawback of appealing to a prior conception of "word" which can be counted on to present difficulties of formulation in its turn. Nevertheless some progress might be claimed in having reduced the problem of synonymy to a problem of wordhood. Let us pursue this line a bit, taking "word" for granted.

The question remains whether interchangeability *salva veritate* (apart from occurrences within words) is a strong enough condition for synonymy, or whether, on the contrary, some nonsynonymous expressions might be thus interchangeable. Now let us be clear that we are not concerned here with synonymy in the sense of complete identity in psychological associations or poetic quality; indeed no two expressions are synonymous in such a sense. We are concerned only with what may be called *cognitive synonymy*. Just what this is cannot be said without successfully finishing the present study; but we know something about it from the need which arose for it in connection with analyticity in Section I. The sort of synonymy needed there was merely such that any analytic statement could be turned into a logical truth by putting synonyms for synonyms. Turning the tables and assuming analyticity, indeed, we could explain cognitive synonymy of terms as follows (keeping to the familiar example): to say that 'bachelor' and 'unmarried man' are cognitively synonymous is to say no more nor less than that the statement:

(3) All and only bachelors are unmarried men is analytic.[4]

What we need is an account of cognitive synonymy not presupposing analyticity—if we are to explain analyticity conversely with help of cognitive synonymy as undertaken in Section I. And indeed such an independent account of cognitive synonymy is at present up for consideration, viz., interchangeability *salva veritate* everywhere except within words. The question before us, to resume the thread at last, is whether such interchangeability is a sufficient condition for cognitive synonymy. We can quickly assure ourselves that it is, by examples of the following sort. The statement:

(4) Necessarily all and only bachelors are bachelors

is evidently true, even supposing 'necessarily' so narrowly construed as to be truly applicable only to analytic statements. Then, *if* 'bachelor' and 'unmarried man' are interchangeable *salva veritate,* the result

(5) Necessarily, all and only bachelors are unmarried men

of putting 'unmarried man' for an occurrence of 'bachelor' in (4) must, like (4), be true. But to say that (5) is true is to say that (3) is analytic, and hence that 'bachelor' and 'unmarried men' are cognitively synonymous.

Let us see what there is about the above argument that gives it its air of hocus-pocus. The condition of interchangeability *salva veritate* varies in its force with variations in the richness of the language at hand. The above argument supposes we are working with a language rich enough to contain the adverb 'necessarily', this adverb being so construed as to yield truth when and only when applied to an analytic statement. But can we condone a language which contains such an adverb? Does the adverb really make sense? To suppose that it does is to suppose that we have already made satisfactory sense of 'analytic'. Then what are we so hard at work on right now?

Our argument is not flatly circular, but something like it. It has the form, figuratively speaking, of a closed curve in space.

Interchangeability *salva veritate* is meaningless until relativized to a language whose extent is specified in relevant respects. Suppose now we consider a language containing just the following materials. There is an indefinitely large stock of one- and many-place predicates, mostly having to do with extralogical subject matter. The rest of the language is logical. The atomic sentences consist each of a predicate followed by one or more variables; and the complex sentences are built up of atomic ones by truth functions and quantification. In effect such a language enjoys the benefits also of descriptions and class names and indeed singular terms generally, these being contextually definable in known ways.[5] Such a language can be adequate to classical mathematics and indeed to scientific discourse generally, except in so far as the latter involves debatable devices such as modal adverbs and contrary-to-fact conditionals. Now a language of this type is *extensional,* in this sense: any two predicates which *agree extensionally* (i.e., are true of the same objects) are interchangeable *salva veritate*.

In an extensional language, therefore, interchangeability *salva veritate* is no assurance of cognitive synonymy of the desired type. That 'bachelor' and 'unmarried man' are interchangeable *salva veritate* in an extensional language assures us of no more than that (3) is true. There is no assurance here that the extensional agreement of 'bachelor' and 'unmarried man' rests on meaning rather than merely on accidental matters of fact, as does extensional agreement of 'creature with a heart' and 'creature with a kidney'.

For most purposes extensional agreement is the nearest approximation to synonymy we need care about. But the fact remains that extensional agreement falls far short of cognitive synonymy of the type required for explaining analyticity in the manner of Section I. The type of cognitive synonymy required there is such as to equate the synonymy of 'bachelor' and 'unmarried man' with the analyticity of (3), not merely with the truth of (3).

So we must recognize that interchangeability *salva veritate,* if construed in relation to an extensional language, is not a sufficient condition of cognitive synonymy in the sense needed for deriving analyticity in the manner of Section I. If a language contains an intensional adverb 'necessarily' in the sense lately noted, or other particles to the same effect, then interchangeability *salva veritate* in such a language does afford a sufficient condition of cognitive synonymy; but such a language is intelligible only if the notion of analyticity is already clearly understood in advance.

The effort to explain cognitive synonymy first, for the sake of deriving analyticity from it afterward as in Section I, is perhaps the wrong approach. Instead we might try explaining analyticity somehow without appeal to cognitive synonymy. Afterward we could doubtless derive cognitive synonymy from analyticity satisfactorily enough if desired. We have seen that cognitive synonymy of 'bachelor' and 'unmarried man' can be explained as analyticity of (3). The same explanation works for any pair of one-place predicates, of course, and it can be extended in obvious fashion to many-place predicates. Other syntactical categories can also be accommodated in fairly parallel fashion. Singular terms may be said to be cognitively synonymous when the statement of identity formed by putting '=' between them is analytic. Statements may be said simply to be cognitively synonymous when their biconditional (the result of joining them by 'if and only if') is analytic.[6] If we care to lump all categories into a single formulation, at the expense of assuming again the notion of "word" which was appealed to early in this section, we can describe any two linguistic forms as cognitively synonymous when the two forms are interchangeable (apart from occurrences within "words") *salva* (no longer *veritate* but) *analyticitate*. Certain technical questions arise, indeed, over cases of ambiguity or homonymy; let us not pause for them, however, for we are already digressing. Let us rather turn our backs on the problem of synonymy and address ourselves anew to that of analyticity.

IV. SEMANTICAL RULES

Analyticity at first seemed most naturally definable by appeal to a realm of meanings. On refinement, the appeal to meanings gave way to an appeal to synonymy or definition. But definition turned out to be a will-o'-the-wisp, and synonymy turned out to be best understood only by dint of a prior appeal to analyticity itself. So we are back at the problem of analyticity.

I do not know whether the statement 'Everything green is extended' is analytic. Now does my indecision over this example really betray an incomplete understanding, an incomplete grasp of the "meanings", of 'green' and 'extended'? I think not. The trouble is not with 'green' or 'extended', but with 'analytic'.

It is often hinted that the difficulty in separating analytic statements from synthetic ones in ordinary language is due to the vagueness of ordinary language and that the distinction is clear when we have a precise artificial language with explicit "semantical rules." This, however, as I shall now attempt to show, is a confusion.

The notion of analyticity about which we are worrying is a purported relation between statements and languages: a statement S is said to be *analytic for* a language L, and the problem is to make sense of this relation generally, i.e., for variable 'S' and 'L'. The point that I want to make is that the gravity of this problem is not perceptibly less for artificial languages than for natural ones. The problem of making sense of the idiom 'S is analytic for L', with variable 'S' and 'L', retains its stubbornness even if we limit the range of the variable 'L' to artificial languages. Let me now try to make this point evident.

For artificial languages and semantical rules we look naturally to the writings of Carnap. His semantical rules take various forms, and to make my point I shall have to distinguish certain of the forms. Let us suppose, to begin with, an artificial language L_0 whose semantical rules have the form explicitly of a specification, by recursion or otherwise, of all the analytic statements of L_0. The rules tell us that such and such statements, and only those, are the analytic statements of L_0. Now here the difficulty is simply that the rules contain the word 'analytic', which we do not understand! We understand what expressions the rules attribute analyticity to, but we do not understand what the rules attribute to those expressions. In short, before we can understand a rule which begins "A statement S is analytic for language L_0 if and only if . . . ," we must understand the general relative term 'analytic for'; we must understand 'S is analytic for L' where 'S' and 'L' are variables.

Alternatively we may, indeed, view the so-called rule as a conventional definition of a new simple symbol 'analytic-for-L_0', which might better be written untendentiously as 'K' so as not to seem to throw light on the interesting word 'analytic'. Obviously any number of classes K, M, N, etc. of statements of L_0 can be specified for various purposes or for no purpose; what does it mean to say that K, as against M, N, etc., is the class of the "analytic" statements of L_0?

By saying what statements are analytic for L_0 we explain 'analytic-for-L_0' but not 'analytic', not 'analytic for'. We do not begin to explain the idiom 'S is analytic for L' with variable 'S' and 'L', even though we be content to limit the range of 'L' to the realm of artificial languages.

Actually we do know enough about the intended significance of 'analytic' to know that analytic statements are supposed to be true. Let us then turn to a second form of semantical rule, which says not that such and such statements are analytic but simply that such and such statements are included among the truths. Such a rule is not subject to the criticism of containing the un-understood word 'analytic'; and we may grant for the sake of argument that there is no difficulty over the broader term 'true'. A semantical rule of this second type, a rule of truth, is not supposed to specify all the truths of the language; it merely stipulates, recursively or otherwise, a certain multitude of statements which, along with others unspecified, are to count as true. Such a rule may be conceded to be quite clear. Derivatively, afterward, analyticity can be demarcated thus: a statement is analytic if it is (not merely true but) true according to the semantical rule.

Still there is really no progress. Instead of appealing to an unexplained word 'analytic', we are now appealing to an unexplained phrase 'semantical rule'. Not every true statement which says that the statements of some class are true can count as a semantical rule—otherwise *all* truths would be "analytic" in the sense of being true according to semantical rules. Semantical rules are distinguishable, apparently, only by the fact of appearing on a page under the heading 'Semantical Rules', and this heading is itself then meaningless.

We can say indeed that a statement is *analytic-for-*L_0 if and only if it is true according to such and such specifically appended "semantical rules," but then we find ourselves back at essentially the same case which was originally discussed: "*S* is analytic-for-L_0 if and only if . . . ." Once we seek to explain '*S* is analytic for *L*' generally for variable '*L*' (even allowing limitation of '*L*' to artificial languages), the explanation 'true according to the semantical rules of *L*' is unavailing; for the relative term 'semantical rule of' is as much in need of clarification, at least, as 'analytic for'.

It might conceivably be protested that an artificial language *L* (unlike a natural one) is a language in the ordinary sense *plus* a set of explicit semantical rules—the whole constituting, let us say, an ordered pair; and that the semantical rules of *L* then are specifiable simply as the second component of the pair *L*. But, by the same token and more simply, we might construe an artificial language *L* outright as an ordered pair whose second component is the class of its analytic statements; and then the analytic statements of *L* become specifiable simply as the statements in the second component of *L*. Or better still, we might just stop tugging at our bootstraps altogether.

Not all the explanations of analyticity known to Carnap and his readers have been covered explicitly in the above considerations, but the extension to other forms is not hard to see. Just one additional factor should be mentioned which sometimes enters: sometimes the semantical rules are in effect rules of translation into ordinary language, in which case the analytic statements of the artificial language are in effect recognized as such from the analyticity of their specified translations in ordinary language. Here certainly there can be no thought of an illumination of the problem of analyticity from the side of the artificial language.

From the point of view of the problem of analyticity the notion of an artificial language with semantical rules is a *feu follet par excellence*. Semantical rules determining the analytic statements of an artificial language are of interest only in so far as we already understand the notion of analyticity; they are of no help in gaining this understanding.

Appeal to hypothetical languages of an artificially simple kind could conceivably be useful in clarifying analyticity, if the mental or behavioral or cultural factors relevant to analyticity—whatever they may be—were somehow sketched into the simplified model. But a model which takes analyticity merely as in irreducible character is unlikely to throw light on the problem of explicating analyticity.

It is obvious that truth in general depends on both language and extralinguistic fact. The statement 'Brutus killed Caesar' would be false if the world had been different in certain ways, but it would also be false if the word 'killed' happened rather to have the sense of 'begat'. Hence the temptation to suppose in general that the truth of a statement is somehow analyzable into a linguistic component and a factual component. Given this supposition, it next seems reasonable that in some statements the factual component should be null; and these are the analytic statements. But, for all its a priori reasonableness, a boundary between analytic and synthetic statements simply has not been drawn. That there is such a distinction to be drawn at all is an unempirical dogma of empiricists, a metaphysical article of faith.

V. THE VERIFICATION THEORY AND REDUCTIONISM

In the course of these somber reflections we have taken a dim view first of the notion of meaning, then of the notion of cognitive synonymy, and finally of the notion of analyticity. But what, it may be asked, of the verification theory of meaning? This phrase has established itself so firmly as a catchword of empiricism that we should be very unscientific indeed not to look beneath it for a possible key to the problem of meaning and the associated problems.

The verification theory of meaning, which has been conspicuous in the literature from Peirce onward, is that the meaning of a statement is the method of empirically confirming or infirming it. An analytic statement is that limiting case which is confirmed no matter what.

As urged in Section I, we can as well pass over the question of meanings as entities and move straight to sameness of meaning, or synonymy. Then what the verification theory says is that statements are synonymous if and only if they are alike in point of method of empirical confirmation or infirmation.

This is an account of cognitive synonymy not of linguistic forms generally, but of statements.[7] However, from the concept of synonymy of statements we could derive the concept of synonymy for other linguistic forms, by considerations somewhat similar to those at the end of Section III. Assuming the notion of "word," indeed, we could explain any two forms as synonymous when the putting of the one form for an occurrence of the other in any statement (apart from occurrences within "words") yields a synonymous statement. Finally, given the concept of synonymy thus for linguistic forms generally, we could define analyticity in terms of synonymy and logical truth as in Section I. For that matter, we could define analyticity more simply in terms of just synonymy of statements together with logical truth; it is not necessary to appeal to synonymy of linguistic forms other than statements. For a statement may be described as analytic simply when it is synonymous with a logically true statement.

So, if the verification theory can be accepted as an adequate account of statement synonymy, the notion of analyticity is saved after all. However, let us reflect. Statement synonymy is said to be likeness of method of empirical confirmation or infirmation. Just what are these methods which are to be compared for likeness? What, in other words, is the nature of the relationship between a statement and the experiences which contribute to or detract from its confirmation?

The most naive view of the relationship is that it is one of direct report. This is *radical reductionism*. Every meaningful statement is held to be translatable into a statement (true or false) about immediate experience. Radical reductionism, in one form or another, well ante dates the verification theory of meaning explicitly so-called. Thus Locke and Hume held that every idea must either originate directly in sense experience or else be compounded of ideas thus originating; and taking a hint from Tooke[8] we might rephrase this doctrine in semantical jargon by saying that a term, to be significant at all, must be either a name of a sense datum or a compound of such names or an abbreviation of such a compound. So stated, the doctrine remains ambiguous as between sense data as sensory events and sense data as sensory qualities; and it remains vague as to the admissible ways of compounding. Moreover, the doctrine is unnecessarily and intolerably restrictive in the term-by-term critique which it imposes. More reasonably, and without yet exceeding the limits of what I have called radical reductionism, we may take full statements as our significant units—thus demanding that our statements as wholes be translatable into sense-datum language, but not that they be translatable term by term.

This emendation would unquestionably have been welcome to Locke and Hume and Tooke, but historically it had to await two intermediate developments. One of these developments was the increasing emphasis on verification or confirmation, which came with the explicitly so-called verification theory of meaning. The objects of verification or confirmation being statements, this emphasis gave the statement an ascendency over the word or term as unit of significant discourse. The other development, consequent upon the first, was Russell's discovery of the concept of incomplete symbols defined in use.

Radical reductionism, conceived now with statements as units, sets itself the task of specifying a sense-datum language and showing how to translate the rest of significant discourse, statement by statement, into it. Carnap embarked on this project in the *Aufbau*.[9]

The language which Carnap adopted as his starting point was not a sense-datum language in the narrowest conceivable sense, for it included also the notations of logic, up through higher set theory. In effect it included the whole language of pure mathematics. The ontology implicit in it (i.e., the range of values of its variables) embraced not only sensory events but classes, classes of classes, and so on. Empiricists there are who would boggle at such prodigality. Carnap's starting point is very parsimonious, however, in its extralogical or sensory part. In a series of constructions in which he exploits the resources of modern logic with much ingenuity, he succeeds in defining a wide array of important additional sensory concepts which, but for his constructions, one would not have dreamed were definable on so slender a basis. Carnap was the first empiricist who, not content with asserting the reducibility of science to terms of immediate experience, took serious steps toward carrying out the reduction.

Even supposing Carnap's starting point satisfactory, his constructions were, as he himself stressed, only a fragment of the full program. The construction of even the simplest statements about the physical world was left in a sketchy state. Carnap's suggestions on this subject were, despite their sketchiness, very suggestive. He explained spatiotemporal point-instants as quadruples of real numbers and envisaged assignment of sense qualities to point-instants according to certain canons. Roughly summarized, the plan was that qualities should be assigned to point-instants in such a way as to achieve the laziest world compatible with our experience. The principle of least action was to be our guide in constructing a world from experience.

Carnap did not seem to recognize, however, that his treatment of physical objects fell short of reduction not merely through sketchiness, but in principle. Statements of the form 'Quality q is at point-instant x; y; z; t' were, according to his canons, to be apportioned truth values in such a way as to maximize and minimize certain over-all features, and with growth of experience the truth values were to be progressively revised in the same spirit. I think this is a good schematization (deliberately oversimplified, to be sure) of what science really does; but it provides no indication, not even the sketchiest, of how a statement of the form 'Quality q is at x; y; z; t' could ever be translated into Carnap's initial language of sense data and logic. The connective 'is at' remains an added undefined connective; the canons counsel us in its use but not in its elimination.

Carnap seems to have appreciated this point afterward; for in his later writings he abandoned all notion of the translatability of statements about the physical world into statements about immediate experience. Reductionism in its radical form has long since ceased to figure in Carnap's philosophy.

But the dogma of reductionism has, in a subtler and more tenuous form, continued to influence the thought of empiricists. The notion lingers that to each statement, or each synthetic statement, there is associated a unique range of possible sensory events such that the occurrence of any of them would add to the likelihood of truth of the statement, and that there is associated also another unique range of possible sensory events whose occurrence would detract from that likelihood. This notion is of course implicit in the verification theory of meaning.

The dogma of reductionism survives in the supposition that each statement, taken in isolation from its fellows, can admit of confirmation or infirmation at all. My countersuggestion, issuing essentially from Carnap's doctrine of the physical world in the *Aufbau,* is that our statements about the external world face the tribunal of sense experience not individually but only as a corporate body.

The dogma of reductionism, even in its attenuated form, is intimately connected with the other dogma: that there is a cleavage between the analytic and the synthetic. We have found ourselves led, indeed, from the latter problem to the former through the verification theory of meaning. More directly, the one dogma clearly supports the other in this way: as long as it is taken to be significant in general to speak of the confirmation and infirmation of a statement, it seems significant to speak also of a limiting kind of statement which is vacuously confirmed, *ipso facto,* come what may; and such a statement is analytic.

The two dogmas are, indeed, at root identical. We lately reflected that in general the truth of statements does obviously depend both upon language and upon extralinguistic fact; and we noted that this obvious circumstance carries in its train, not logically but all too naturally, a feeling that the truth of a statement is somehow analyzable into a linguistic component and a factual component. The factual component must, if we are empiricists, boil down to a range of confirmatory experiences. In the extreme case where the linguistic component is all that matters, a true statement is analytic. But I hope we are now impressed with how stubbornly the distinction between analytic and synthetic has resisted any straightforward drawing. I am impressed also, apart from prefabricated examples of black and white balls in an urn, with how baffling the problem has always been of arriving at any explicit theory of the empirical confirmation of a synthetic statement. My present suggestion is that it is nonsense, and the root of much nonsense, to speak of a linguistic component and a factual component in the truth of any individual statement. Taken collectively, science has its double dependence upon language and experience; but this duality is not significantly traceable into the statements of science taken one by one.

Russell's concept of definition in use was, as remarked, an advance over the impossible term-by-term empiricism of Locke and Hume. The statement, rather than the term, came with Russell to be recognized as the unit accountable to an empiricist critique. But what I am now urging is that even in taking the statement as unit we have drawn our grid too finely. The unit of empirical significance is the whole of science.

VI. EMPIRICISM WITHOUT THE DOGMAS

The totality of our so-called knowledge or beliefs, from the most casual matters of geography and history to the profoundest laws of atomic physics or even of pure mathematics and logic, is a man-made fabric which impinges on experience only along the edges. Or, to change the figure, total science is like a field of force whose boundary conditions are experience. A conflict with experience at the periphery occasions readjustments in the interior of the field. Truth values have to be redistributed over some of our statements. Re-evaluation of some statements entails re-evaluation of others, because of their logical interconnections—the logical laws being in turn simply certain further statements of the system, certain further elements of the field. Having re-evaluated one statement we must re-evaluate some others, whether they be statements logically connected with the first or whether they be the statements of logical connections themselves. But the total field is so undetermined by its boundary conditions, experience, that there is much latitude of choice as to what statements to re-evaluate in the light of any single contrary experience. No particular experiences are linked with any particular statements in the interior of the field, except indirectly through considerations of equilibrium affecting the field as a whole.

If this view is right, it is misleading to speak of the empirical content of an individual statement—especially if it be a statement at all remote from the experiential periphery of the field. Furthermore it becomes folly to seek a boundary between synthetic statements, which hold contingently on experience, and analytic statements which hold come what may. Any statement can be held true come what may, if we make drastic enough adjustments elsewhere in the system. Even a statement very close to the periphery can be held true in the face of recalcitrant experience by pleading hallucination or by amending certain statements of the kind called logical laws. Conversely, by the same token, no statement is immune to revision. Revision even of the logical law of the excluded middle has been proposed as a means of simplifying quantum mechanics; and what difference is there in principle between such a shift and the shift whereby Kepler superseded Ptolemy, or Einstein Newton, or Darwin Aristotle?

For vividness I have been speaking in terms of varying distances from a sensory periphery. Let me try now to clarify this notion without metaphor. Certain statements, though *about* physical objects and not sense experience, seem peculiarly germane to sense experience—and in a selective way: some statements to some experiences, others to others. Such statements, especially germane to particular experiences, I picture as near the periphery. But in this relation of "germaneness" I envisage nothing more than a loose association reflecting the relative likelihood, in practice, of our choosing one statement rather than another for revision in the event of recalcitrant experience. For example, we can imagine recalcitrant experiences to which we would surely be inclined to accommodate our system by re-evaluating just the statement that there are brick houses on Elm Street, together with related statements on the same topic. We can imagine other recalcitrant experiences to which we would be inclined to accommodate our system by re-evaluating just the statement that there are no centaurs, along with kindred statements. A recalcitrant experience can, I have already urged, be accommodated by any of various alternative re-evaluations in various alternative quarters of the total system; but, in the cases which we are now imagining, our natural tendency to disturb the total system as little as possible would lead us to focus our revisions upon these specific statements concerning brick houses or centaurs. These statements are felt, therefore, to have a sharper empirical reference than highly theoretical statements of physics or logic or ontology. The latter statements may be thought of as relatively centrally located within the total network, meaning merely that little preferential connection with any particular sense data obtrudes itself.

As an empiricist I continue to think of the conceptual scheme of science as a tool, ultimately, for predicting future experience in the light of past experience. Physical objects are conceptually imported into the situation as convenient intermediaries—not by definition in terms of experience, but simply as irreducible posits comparable, epistemologically, to the gods of Homer. Let me interject that for my part I do, qua lay physicist, believe in physical objects and not in Homer's gods; and I consider it a scientific error to believe otherwise. But in point of epistemological footing the physical objects and the gods differ only in degree and not in kind. Both sorts of entities enter our conception only as cultural posits. The myth of physical objects is epistemologically superior to most in that it has proved more efficacious than other myths as a device for working a manageable structure into the flux of experience.

Imagine, for the sake of analogy, that we are given the rational numbers. We develop an algebraic theory for reasoning about them, but we find it inconveniently complex, because certain functions such as square root lack values for some arguments. Then it is discovered that the rules of our algebra can be much simplified by conceptually augmenting our ontology with some mythical entities, to be called irrational numbers. All we continue to be really interested in, first and last, are rational numbers; but we find that we can commonly get from one law about rational numbers to another much more quickly and simply by pretending that the irrational numbers are there too.

I think this a fair account of the introduction of irrational numbers and other extensions of the number system. The fact that the mythical status of irrational numbers eventually gave way to the Dedekind-Russell version of them as certain infinite classes of ratios is irrelevant to my analogy. That version is impossible anyway as long as reality is limited to the rational numbers and not extended to classes of them.

Now I suggest that experience is analogous to the rational numbers and that the physical objects, in analogy to the irrational numbers, are posits which serve merely to simplify our treatment of experience. The physical objects are no more reducible to experience than the irrational numbers to rational numbers, but their incorporation into the theory enables us to get more easily from one statement about experience to another.

The salient differences between the positing of physical objects and the positing of irrational numbers are, I think, just two. First, the factor of simplification is more overwhelming in the case of physical objects than in the numerical case. Second, the positing of physical objects is far more archaic, being indeed coeval, I expect, with language itself. For language is social and so depends for its development upon intersubjective reference.

Positing does not stop with macroscopic physical objects. Objects at the atomic level and beyond are posited to make the laws of macroscopic objects, and ultimately the laws of experience, simpler and more manageable; and we need not expect or demand full definition of atomic and subatomic entities in terms of macroscopic ones, any more than definition of macroscopic things in terms of sense data. Science is a continuation of common sense, and it continues the common-sense expedient of swelling ontology to simplify theory.

Physical objects, small and large, are not the only posits. Forces are another example; and indeed we are told nowadays that the boundary between energy and matter is obsolete. Moreover, the abstract entities which are the substance of mathematics—ultimately classes and classes of classes and so on up—are another posit in the same spirit. Epistemologically these are myths on the same footing with physical objects and gods, neither better nor worse except for differences in the degree to which they expedite our dealings with sense experiences.

The over-all algebra of rational and irrational numbers is underdetermined by the algebra of rational numbers, but is smoother and more convenient; and it includes the algebra of rational numbers as a jagged or gerrymandered part. Total science, mathematical and natural and human, is similarly but more extremely underdetermined by experience. The edge of the system must be kept squared with experience; the rest, with all its elaborate myths or fictions, has as its objective the simplicity of laws.

Ontological questions, under this view, are on a par with questions of natural science. Consider the question whether to countenance classes as entities. This, as I have argued elsewhere,[10] is the question whether to quantify with respect to variables which take classes as values. Now Carnap has maintained[11] that this is a question not of matters of fact but of choosing a convenient language form, a convenient conceptual scheme or framework for science. With this I agree, but only on the proviso that the same be conceded regarding scientific hypotheses generally. Carnap has recognized[12] that he is able to preserve a double standard for ontological questions and scientific hypotheses only by assuming an absolute distinction between the analytic and the synthetic; and I need not say again that this is a distinction which I reject.

Some issues do, I grant, seem more a question of convenient conceptual scheme and others more a question of brute fact. The issue over there being classes seems more a question of convenient conceptual scheme; the issue over there being centaurs, or brick houses on Elm Street, seems more a question of fact. But I have been urging that this difference is only one of degree, and that it turns upon our vaguely pragmatic inclination to adjust one strand of the fabric of science rather than another in accommodating some particular recalcitrant experience. Conservatism figures in such choices, and so does the quest for simplicity.

Carnap, Lewis, and others take a pragmatic stand on the question of choosing between language forms, scientific frameworks; but their pragmatism leaves off at the imagined boundary between the analytic and the synthetic. In repudiating such a boundary I espouse a more thorough pragmatism. Each man is given a scientific heritage plus a continuing barrage of sensory stimulation; and the considerations which guide him in warping his scientific heritage to fit his continuing sensory promptings are, where rational, pragmatic.

NOTES

1. Much of this paper is devoted to a critique of analyticity which I have been urging orally and in correspondence for years past. My debt to the other participants in those discussions, notably Carnap, Church, Goodman, Tarski, and White, is large and indeterminate. White's excellent essay "The Analytic and the Synthetic: An Untenable Dualism," in *John Dewey: Philosopher of Science and Freedom* (New York, 1950), says much of what needed to be said on the topic; but in the present paper I touch on some further aspects of the problem. I am grateful to Dr. Donald L. Davidson for valuable criticism of the first draft.
2. See White, *op. cit.*, p. 324.
3. R. Carnap, *Meaning and Necessity* (Chicago, 1947), pp. 9ff.; *Logical Foundations of Probability* (Chicago, 1950), pp. 70ff.
4. This is cognitive synonymy in a primary, broad sense. Carnap. (*Meaning and Necessity,* pp. 56ff.) and Lewis (*Analysis of Knowledge and Valuation* [La Salle, Ill., 1946], pp. 83ff.) have suggested how, once this notion is at hand, a narrower sense of cognitive synonymy which is preferable for some purposes can in turn be derived. But this special ramification of concept-building lies aside from the

present purposes and must not be confused with the broad sort of cognitive synonymy here concerned.

5. See, e.g., my *Mathematical Logic* (New York, 1940; Cambridge, Mass., 1947), sec. 24, 26, 27; or *Methods of Logic* (New York, 1950), sec. 37ff.
6. The 'if and only if' itself is intended in the truth functional sense. See Carnap, *Meaning and Necessity,* p. 14.
7. The doctrine can indeed be formulated with terms rather than statements as the units. Thus C. I. Lewis describes the meaning of a term as "*a criterion in mind,* by reference to which one is able to apply or refuse to apply the expression in question in the case of presented, or imagined, things or situations" (*op. cit.,* p. 133).
8. John Horne Tooke, *The Diversions of Purley* (London, 1776; Boston, 1806), I, ch. ii.
9. R. Carnap, *Der logische Aufbau der Welt* (Berlin, 1928).
10. E.g., in "Notes on Existence and Necessity," *Journal of Philosophy,* XL (1943), 113–127.
11. Carnap, "Empiricism, Semantics, and Ontology," *Revue internationale de philosophie,* IV (1950), 20–40.
12. *Op. cit.,* p. 32, footnote.

 6 

Lecture I: January 20, 1970[1]

SAUL KRIPKE

I hope that some people see some connection between the two topics in the title. If not, anyway, such connections will be developed in the course of these talks. Furthermore, because of the use of tools involving reference and necessity in analytic philosophy today, our views on these topics really have wide-ranging implications for other problems in philosophy that traditionally might be thought far-removed, like arguments over the mind-body problem or the so-called 'identity thesis'. Materialism, in this form, often now gets involved in very intricate ways in questions about what is necessary or contingent in identity of properties—questions like that. . . .

The first topic in the pair of topics is naming. By a name here I will mean a proper name, i.e., the name of a person, a city, a country, etc. It is well known that modern logicians also are very interested in definite descriptions: phrases of the form 'the x such that φx', such as 'the man who corrupted Hadleyburg'. Now, if one and only one man ever corrupted Hadleyburg, then that man is the referent, in the logician's sense, of that description. We will use the term 'name' so that it does *not* include definite descriptions of that sort, but only those things which in ordinary language would be called 'proper names'. If we want a common term to cover names and descriptions, we may use the term 'designator'.

It is a point, made by Donnellan,[2] that under certain circumstances a particular speaker may use a definite description to refer, not to the proper referent, in the sense that I've just defined it, of that description, but to something else which he wants to single out and which he thinks is the proper referent of the description, but which in fact isn't. So you may say, 'The man over there with the champagne in his glass is happy', though he actually only has water in his

Source: Reprinted by permission of the publisher from NAMING AND NECESSITY by Saul Kripke, pp. 22–26, 34–44. Cambridge, MA: Harvard University Press, Copyright © 1972, 1980 by Saul Kripke.

glass. Now, even though there is no champagne in his glass, and there may be another man in the room who does have champagne in his glass, the speaker *intended* to refer, or maybe, in some sense of 'refer', *did* refer, to the man he thought had the champagne in his glass. Nevertheless, I'm just going to use the term 'referent of the description' to mean the object uniquely satisfying the conditions in the definite description. This is the sense in which it's been used in the logical tradition. So, if you have a description of the form 'the x such that φx', and there is exactly one x such that φx, that is the referent of the description.

. . . I want to talk about another distinction which will be important in the methodology of these talks. Philosophers have talked (and, of course, there has been considerable controversy in recent years over the meaningfulness of these notions) [about] various categories of truth, which are called '*a priori*', 'analytic', 'necessary'—and sometimes even 'certain' is thrown into this batch. The terms are often used as if *whether* there are things answering to these concepts is an interesting question, but we might as well regard them all as meaning the same thing. Now, everyone remembers Kant (a bit) as making a distinction between '*a priori*' and 'analytic'. So maybe this distinction is still made. In contemporary discussion very few people, if any, distinguish between the concepts of statements being *a priori* and their being necessary. At any rate I shall *not* use the terms '*a priori*' and 'necessary' interchangeably here.

Consider what the traditional characterizations of such terms as '*a priori*' and 'necessary' are. First the notion of a prioricity is a concept of epistemology. I guess the traditional characterization from Kant goes something like: *a priori* truths are those which can be known independently of any experience. This introduces another problem before we get off the ground, because there's another modality in the characterization of '*a priori*', namely, it is supposed to be something which *can* be known independently of any experience. That means that in some sense it's *possible* (whether we do or do not in fact know it independently of any experience) to know this independently of any experience. And possible for whom? For God? For the Martians? Or just for people with minds like ours? To make this all clear might [involve] a host of problems all of its own about what sort of possibility is in question here. It might be best therefore, instead of using the phrase '*a priori* truth', to the extent that one uses it at all, to stick to the question of whether a particular person or knower knows something *a priori* or believes it true on the basis of *a priori* evidence.

I won't go further too much into the problems that might arise with the notion of a prioricity here. I will say that some philosophers somehow change the modality in this characterization from *can* to *must*. They think that if something belongs to the realm of *a priori* knowledge, it couldn't possibly be known empirically. This is just a mistake. Something may belong in the realm of such statements that *can* be known *a priori* but still may be known by particular people on the basis of experience. To give a really common sense example: anyone who has worked with a computing machine knows that the computing machine may give an answer to whether such and such a number is prime. No one has calculated or proved that the number is prime; but the machine has given the answer: this number is prime. We, then, if we believe that the number is prime, believe it on the basis of our knowledge of the laws of physics, the construction of the machine, and so on. We therefore do not believe this on the basis of purely *a priori* evidence. We believe it (if anything is *a posteriori* at all) on the basis of *a posteriori* evidence. Nevertheless, maybe this could be known *a priori* by someone who made the requisite calculations. So '*can* be known *a priori*' doesn't mean '*must* be known *a priori*'.

The second concept which is in question is that of necessity. Sometimes this is used in an epistemological way and might then just mean *a priori*. And of course, sometimes it is used in a physical way when people distinguish between physical and logical necessity. But what I am concerned with here is a notion which is not a notion of epistemology but of metaphysics, in some (I hope) nonpejorative sense. We ask whether something might have been true, or might have been false. Well, if something is false, it's obviously not necessarily true. If it is true, might it have been otherwise? Is it possible that, in this respect, the world should have been different from the way it is? If the answer is 'no', then this fact about the world is a necessary one. If the answer is 'yes', then this fact about the world is a contingent one. This in and of itself has nothing to do with anyone's knowledge of anything. It's certainly a philosophical thesis, and not a matter of obvious definitional equivalence, either that everything *a priori* is necessary or that everything necessary is *a priori*. Both concepts may be vague. That may be another problem. But at any rate they are dealing with two different domains, two different areas, the epistemological and the metaphysical. Consider, say, Fermat's last theorem—or the Goldbach conjecture. The Goldbach conjecture says that an even number greater than 2 must be the sum of two prime numbers. If this is true, it is presumably necessary, and, if it is false, presumably necessarily false. We are taking the classical view of mathematics here and assume that in mathematical reality it is either true or false.

If the Goldbach conjecture is false, then there is an even number, n, greater than 2, such that for no primes p_1 and p_2, both $<n$, does $n = p_1 + p_2$. This fact about n, if true, is verifiable by direct computation, and thus is necessary if the results of arithmetical computations are necessary. On the other hand, if the conjecture is true, then every even number exceeding 2 is the sum of two primes. Could it then be the case that, although in fact every such even number is the sum of two primes, there might have been such an even number which was not the sum of two primes? What would that mean? Such a number would have to be one of 4, 6, 8, 10, . . . ; and, by hypothesis, since we are assuming Goldbach's conjecture to be true, each of these can be shown, again by direct computation, to be the sum of two primes. Goldbach's conjecture, then, cannot be contingently true or false; whatever truth-value it has belongs to it by necessity.

But what we can say, of course, is that right now, as far as we know, the question can come out either way. So, in the absence of a mathematical proof deciding this question, none of us has any *a priori* knowledge about this question in either direction. We don't know whether Goldbach's conjecture is true or false. So right now we certainly don't know anything *a priori* about it.

Perhaps it will be alleged that we *can* in principle know *a priori* whether it is true. Well, maybe we can. Of course an infinite mind which can search through all the numbers can or could. But I don't know whether a finite mind can or could. Maybe there just is no mathematical proof whatsoever which decides the conjecture. At any rate this might or might not be the case. Maybe there is a mathematical proof deciding this question; maybe every mathematical question is decidable by an intuitive proof or disproof. Hilbert thought so; others have thought not; still others have thought the question unintelligible unless the notion of intuitive proof is replaced by that of formal proof in a single system. Certainly no one formal system decides all mathematical questions, as we know from Gödel. At any rate, and this is the important thing, the question is not trivial; even though someone said that it's necessary, if true at all, that every even number is the sum of two primes, it doesn't follow that anyone knows anything *a priori* about it. It doesn't even seem to me to follow without some further philosophical argument (it is an interesting philosophical question) that anyone *could* know anything *a priori* about it. The 'could', as I said, involves some other modality. We mean that even if no one, perhaps even in the future, knows or will know *a priori* whether Goldbach's conjecture is right, in principle there is a way, which *could* have been used, of answering the question *a priori*. This assertion is not trivial.

The terms 'necessary' and '*a priori*', then, as applied to statements, are *not* obvious synonyms. There may be a philosophical argument connecting them, perhaps even identifying them; but an argument is required, not simply the observation that the two terms are clearly interchangeable. (I will argue below that in fact they are not even coextensive—that necessary *a posteriori* truths, and probably contingent *a priori* truths, both exist.)

I think people have thought that these two things must mean the same for these reasons:

First, if something not only happens to be true in the actual world but is also true in all possible worlds, then, of course, just by running through all the possible worlds in our heads, we ought to be able with enough effort to see, if a statement is necessary, that it is necessary, and thus know it *a priori*. But really this is not so obviously feasible at all.

Second, I guess it's thought that, conversely, if something is known *a priori* it must be necessary, because it was known without looking at the world. If it depended on some contingent feature of the actual world, how could you know it without looking? Maybe the actual world is one of the possible worlds in which it would have been false. This depends on the thesis that there can't be a way of knowing about the actual world without looking that wouldn't be a way of knowing the same thing about every possible world. This involves problems of epistemology and the nature of knowledge; and of course it is very vague as stated. But it is not really *trivial* either. More important than any particular example of something which is alleged to be necessary and not *a priori* or *a priori* and not necessary, is to see that the notions are different, that it's not trivial to argue on the basis of something's being something which maybe we can only know *a posteriori,* that it's not a necessary truth. It's not trivial, just because something is known in some sense *a priori,* that what is known is a necessary truth.

Another term used in philosophy is 'analytic'. Here it won't be too important to get any clearer about this in this talk. The common examples of analytic statements, nowadays, are like 'bachelors are unmarried'. Kant, (someone just pointed out to me) gives as an example 'gold is a yellow metal', which seems to me an extraordinary one, because it's something I think that can turn out to be false. At any rate, let's just make it a matter of stipulation that an analytic statement is, in some sense, true by virtue of its meaning and true in all possible worlds by virtue of its meaning. Then something which is analytically true will be both necessary and *a priori.* (That's sort of stipulative.)

Another category I mentioned was that of certainty. Whatever certainty is, it's clearly not obviously the case that everything which is necessary is certain. Certainty is another epistemological notion. Something can be known, or at least rationally believed, *a priori,* without being quite certain. You've read a proof in the math book; and, though you think it's correct, maybe you've made a mistake. You often do make mistakes of this kind. You've made a computation, perhaps with an error.

There is one more question I want to go into in a preliminary way. Some philosophers have distinguished between essentialism, the belief in modality *de re,* and a mere advocacy of necessity, the belief in modality *de dicto*. Now, some people say: Let's *give* you the concept of necessity.[3] A much worse thing, something creating great additional problems, is whether we can say of any particular that it has necessary or contingent properties, even make the distinction between necessary and contingent properties. Look, it's only a *statement* or a *state of affairs* that can be either necessary or contingent! Whether a *particular* necessarily or contingently has a certain property depends on the way it's described. This is perhaps closely related to the view that the way we refer to particular things is by a description. What is Quine's famous example? If we consider the number 9, does it have the property of necessary oddness? Has that number got to be odd in all possible worlds? Certainly it's true in all possible worlds, let's say, it couldn't have been otherwise, that *nine* is odd. Of course, 9 could also be equally well picked out as *the number of planets*. It is *not* necessary, not true in all possible worlds, that the number of planets is odd. For example if there had been eight planets, the number of planets would not have been odd. And so it's thought: Was it necessary or contingent that Nixon won the election? (It might seem contingent, unless one has some view of some inexorable processes. . . .) But this is a contingent property of Nixon only relative to our referring to him as 'Nixon' (assuming 'Nixon' doesn't mean 'the man who won the election at such and such a time'). But if we designate Nixon as 'the man who won the election in 1968', then it will be a necessary truth, of course, that the man who won the election in 1968, won the election in 1968. Similarly, whether an object has the same property in all possible worlds depends not just on the object itself, but on how it is described. So it's argued.

It is even suggested in the literature, that though a notion of necessity may have some sort of intuition behind it (we do think some things could have been otherwise; other things we don't think could have been otherwise), this notion [of a distinction between necessary and contingent properties] is just a doctrine made up by some bad philosopher, who (I guess) didn't realize that there are several ways of referring to the same thing. I don't know if some philosophers have not realized this; but at any rate it is very far from being true that this idea [that a property can meaningfully be held to be essential or accidental to an object independently of its description] is a notion which has no intuitive content, which means nothing to the ordinary man. Suppose that someone said, pointing to Nixon, 'That's the guy who might have lost'. Someone else says 'Oh no, if you describe him as "Nixon", then he might have lost; but, of course, describing him as the winner, then it is not true that he might have lost'. Now which one is being the philosopher, here, the unintuitive man? It seems to me obviously to be the second. The second man has a philosophical theory. The first man would say, and with great conviction, 'Well, of course, the winner of the election *might have been someone else*. The actual winner, had the course of the campaign been different, might have been the loser, and someone else the winner; or there might have been no election at all. So, such terms as "the winner" and "the loser" don't designate the same objects in all possible worlds. On the other hand, the term "Nixon" is just a *name* of *this man'*. When you ask whether it is necessary or contingent that *Nixon* won the election, you are asking the intuitive question whether in some counterfactual situation, *this man* would in fact have lost the election. If someone thinks that the notion of a necessary or contingent property (forget whether there *are* any non-trivial necessary properties [and consider] just the *meaningfulness* of the notion[4]) is a philosopher's notion with no intuitive content, he is wrong. Of course, some philosophers think that something's having intuitive content is very inconclusive evidence in favor of it. I think it is very heavy evidence in favor of anything, myself. I really don't know, in a way, what more conclusive evidence one can have about anything, ultimately speaking. But, in any event, people who think the notion of accidental property unintuitive have intuition reversed, I think.

Why have they thought this? While there are many motivations for people thinking this, one is this: The question of essential properties so-called is supposed to be equivalent (and it is equivalent) to the question of 'identity across possible worlds'. Suppose we have someone, Nixon, and there's another possible world where there is no one with all the properties Nixon has in the actual world. Which one of these other people, if any, is Nixon? Surely you must give some criterion of identity here! If you have a criterion of identity, then you just look in the other possible worlds at the man who is Nixon; and the question whether, in that other possible world, Nixon has certain properties, is well defined. It is also supposed to be well defined, in terms of such notions, whether it's true in all possible worlds, or there are some possible worlds in which Nixon didn't win the election. But, it's said, the problems of giving such criteria of identity are very difficult. Sometimes in the case of numbers it might seem easier (but even here it's argued that it's quite arbitrary). For example, one might say, and this is surely the truth, that if position in the series of numbers is what makes the number 9 what it is, then if (in another world) the number of planets had been 8, the number of planets would be a different number from the one it actually is. You wouldn't say that that number then is to be identified with our number 9 in this world. In the case of other types of objects, say people, material objects, things like that, has anyone given a set of necessary and sufficient conditions for identity across possible worlds?

Really, adequate necessary and sufficient conditions for identity which do not beg the question are very rare in any case. Mathematics is the only case I really know of where they are given even *within* a possible world, to tell the truth. I don't know of such conditions for identity of material objects over time, or for people. Everyone knows what a problem this is. But, let's forget about that. What seems to be more objectionable is that this depends on the wrong way of looking at what a possible world is. One thinks, in this picture, of a possible world as if it were like a foreign country. One looks upon it as an observer. Maybe Nixon has moved to the other country and maybe he hasn't, but one is given only qualities. One can observe all his qualities, but, of course, one doesn't observe that someone is Nixon. One observes that something has red hair (or green or yellow) but not whether something is Nixon. So we had better have a way of telling in terms of properties when we run into the same thing as we saw before; we had better have a way of telling, when we come across one of these other possible worlds, who was Nixon.

Some logicians in their formal treatment of modal logic may encourage this picture. A prominent example, perhaps, is myself. Nevertheless, intuitively speaking, it seems to me not to be the right way of thinking about the possible worlds. A possible world isn't a distant country that we are coming across, or viewing through a telescope. Generally speaking, another possible world is too far away. Even if we travel faster than light, we won't get to it. A possible world is *given by the descriptive conditions we associate with it*. What do we mean when we say 'In some other possible world I would not have given this lecture today?' We just imagine the situation where I didn't decide to give this lecture or decided to give it on some other day. Of course, we don't imagine everything that is true or false, but only those things relevant to my giving the lecture; but, in theory, everything needs to be decided to make a total description of the world. We can't really imagine that except in part; that, then, is a 'possible world'. Why can't it be part of the *description* of a possible world that it contains *Nixon* and that in that world *Nixon* didn't win the election? It might be a question, of course, whether such a world *is* possible. (Here it would seem, *prima facie*, to be clearly possible.) But, once we see that such a situation is possible, then we are given that the man who might have lost the election or did lose the election in this possible world is Nixon, because that's part of the description of the world. 'Possible worlds' are *stipulated,* not *discovered* by powerful telescopes. There is no reason why we cannot *stipulate* that, in talking about what would have happened to Nixon in a certain counterfactual situation, we are talking about what would have happened to *him*. . . .

It might be said 'Let's suppose that this is true. It comes down to the same thing, because whether Nixon could have had certain properties, different from the ones he actually has, is equivalent to the question whether the criteria of identity across possible worlds include that Nixon does not have these properties'. But it doesn't really come to the same thing, because the usual notion of a criterion of transworld identity demands that we give purely qualitative necessary and sufficient conditions for someone being Nixon. If we can't imagine a possible world in which Nixon doesn't have a certain property, then it's a necessary condition of someone being Nixon. Or a necessary property of Nixon that he [has] that property. For example, supposing Nixon is in fact a human being, it would seem that we cannot think of a possible counterfactual situation in which he was, say, an inanimate object; perhaps it is not even possible for him not to have been a human being. Then it will be a necessary fact about Nixon that in all possible worlds where he exists at all, he is human or anyway he is not an inanimate object. This has nothing to do with any requirement that there be purely qualitative *sufficient* conditions for Nixonhood which we can spell out. And should there be? Maybe there is some argument that there should be, but we can consider these questions about *necessary* conditions without going into any question about *sufficient* conditions. Further, even if there were a purely qualitative set of necessary and sufficient conditions for being Nixon, the view I advocate would not demand that we find these conditions *before* we can ask whether Nixon might have won the election, nor does it demand that we restate the question in terms of such conditions. We can simply consider *Nixon* and ask what might have happened to *him* had various circumstances been different. So the two views, the two ways of looking at things, do seem to me to make a difference.

Notice this question, whether Nixon could not have been a human being, is a clear case where the question asked is not epistemological. Suppose Nixon actually turned out to be an automaton. That might happen. We might need evidence whether Nixon is a human being or an automaton. But that is a question about our knowledge. The question of whether Nixon might have not been a human being, given that he is one, is not a question about knowledge, *a posteriori* or *a priori*. It's a question about, even though such and such things are the case, what might have been the case otherwise.

This table is composed of molecules. Might it not have been composed of molecules? Certainly it was a scientific discovery of great moment that it was composed of molecules (or atoms). But could anything be this very object and not be composed of molecules? Certainly there is some feeling that the answer to that must be 'no'. At any rate, it's hard to imagine under what circumstances you would have this very object and find that it is not composed of molecules. A quite different question is whether it is in fact composed of molecules in the actual world and how we know this. (I will go into more detail about these questions about essence later on.)

I wish at this point to introduce something which I need in the methodology of discussing the theory of names that I'm talking about. We need the notion of 'identity across possible worlds' as it's usually and, as I think, somewhat misleadingly called,[5] to explicate one distinction that I want to make now. What's the difference between asking whether it's necessary that 9 is greater than 7 or whether it's necessary that the number of planets is greater than 7? Why does one show anything more about essence than the other? The answer to this might be intuitively 'Well, look, the number of planets might have been different from what it in fact is.

It doesn't make any sense, though, to say that nine might have been different from what it in fact is'. Let's use some terms quasi-technically. Let's call something a *rigid designator* if in every possible world it designates the same object, a *nonrigid* or *accidental designator* if that is not the case. Of course we don't require that the objects exist in all possible worlds. Certainly Nixon might not have existed if his parents had not gotten married, in the normal course of things. When we think of a property as essential to an object we usually mean that it is true of that object in any case where it would have existed. A rigid designator of a necessary existent can be called *strongly rigid.*

One of the intuitive theses I will maintain in these talks is that *names* are rigid designators. Certainly they seem to satisfy the intuitive test mentioned above: although someone other than the U.S. President in 1970 might have been the U.S. President in 1970 (e.g., Humphrey might have), no one other than Nixon might have been Nixon. In the same way, a designator rigidly designates a certain object if it designates that object wherever the object exists; if, in addition, the object is a necessary existent, the designator can be called *strongly rigid.* For example, 'the President of the U.S. in 1970' designates a certain man, Nixon; but someone else (e.g., Humphrey) might have been the President in 1970, and Nixon might not have; so this designator is not rigid.

In these lectures, I will argue, intuitively, that proper names are rigid designators, for although the man (Nixon) might not have been the President, it is not the case that he might not have been Nixon (though he might not have been *called* 'Nixon'). Those who have argued that to make sense of the notion of rigid designator, we must antecedently make sense of 'criteria of transworld identity' have precisely reversed the cart and the horse; it is *because* we can refer (rigidly) to Nixon, and stipulate that we are speaking of what might have happened to *him* (under certain circumstances), that 'transworld identifications' are unproblematic in such cases.[6]

The tendency to demand purely qualitative descriptions of counterfactual situations has many sources. One, perhaps, is the confusion of the epistemological and the metaphysical, between a prioricity and necessity. If someone identifies necessity with a prioricity, and thinks that objects are named by means of uniquely identifying properties, he may think that it is the properties used to identify the object which, being known about it *a priori,* must be used to identify it in all possible worlds, to find out which object is Nixon. As against this, I repeat: (1) Generally, things aren't 'found out' about a counterfactual situation, they are stipulated; (2) possible worlds need not be given purely qualitatively, as if we were looking at them through a telescope. . . .

NOTES

1. In January of 1970, I gave three talks at Princeton University transcribed here. As the style of the transcript makes clear, I gave the talks without a written text, and, in fact, without notes. The present text is lightly edited from the *verbatim* transcript; an occasional passage has been added to expand the thought, an occasional sentence has been rewritten, but no attempt has been made to change the informal style of the original. Many of the footnotes have been added to the original, but a few were originally spoken asides in the talks themselves.

   I hope the reader will bear these facts in mind as he reads the text. Imagining it spoken, with proper pauses and emphases, may occasionally facilitate comprehension. I have agreed to publish the talks in this form with some reservations. The time allotted, and the informal style, necessitated a certain amount of compression of the argument, inability to treat certain objections, and the like. Especially in the concluding sections on scientific identities and the mind-body problem thoroughness had to be sacrificed. Some topics essential to a full presentation of the viewpoint argued here, especially that of existence statements and empty names, had to be omitted altogether. Further, the informality of the presentation may well have engendered a sacrifice of clarity at certain points. All these defects were accepted in the interest of early publication. I hope that perhaps I will have the chance to do a more thorough job later. To repeat, I hope the reader will bear in mind that he is largely reading informal lectures, not only when he encounters repetitions or infelicities, but also when he encounters irreverence or corn.

2. Keith Donnellan, 'Reference and Definite Descriptions', *Philosophical Review* 75 (1966), pp. 281–304. See also Leonard Linsky, 'Reference and Referents', in *Philosophy and Ordinary Language* (ed. Caton), University of Illinois Press, Urbana, 1963. Donnellan's distinction seems applicable to names as well as to descriptions. Two men glimpse someone at a distance and think they recognize him as Jones. 'What is Jones doing?' 'Raking the leaves'. If the distant leaf-raker is actually Smith, then in some sense they are *referring* to Smith, even though they both use 'Jones' *as a name of* Jones. In the text, I speak of the 'referent' of a name to mean the thing named by the name—e.g., Jones, not Smith—even though a speaker may sometimes properly be said to use the name to refer to someone else. Perhaps it would have been less misleading to use a technical term, such as 'denote' rather than 'refer'. My use of 'refer' is such as to satisfy the schema, 'The referent of "*X*" is *X*', where '*X*' is replaceable by any name or description. I am tentatively inclined to believe, in opposition to Donnellan, that his remarks about reference have little to do with semantics or truth-conditions, though they may be relevant to a theory of speech-acts. Space limitations do not permit me to explain what I mean by this, much less defend the view, except for a brief remark: Call the referent of a name or description in my sense the 'semantic referent'; for a name, this is the thing named, for a description, the thing uniquely satisfying the description.

   Then the speaker may *refer* so something other than the semantic referent if he has appropriate false beliefs. I think this is what happens in the naming (Smith-Jones) cases and also in the Donnellan 'champagne' case; the one requires no theory that names are ambiguous, and the other requires no modification of Russell's theory of descriptions.

3. By the way, it's a common attitude in philosophy to think that one shouldn't introduce a notion until it's been rigorously defined (according to some popular notion of rigor). Here I am just dealing with an intuitive notion and will keep on the level of an intuitive notion. That is, we think that some things, though they are in fact the case, might have been otherwise. I might not have given these lectures today. If that's right, then it is *possible* that I wouldn't have given these lectures today. Quite a different question is the epistemological question, how any particular person knows that I gave these lectures today. I suppose in that case he does know this is *a posteriori*. But, if someone were born with an innate belief that I was going to give these lectures today, who knows? Right now, anyway, let's suppose that people know this *a posteriori*. At any rate, the two questions being asked are different.

4. The example I gave asserts a certain property—electoral victory—to be *accidental* to Nixon, independently of how he is described. Of course, if the notion of accidental property is meaningful, the notion of essential property must be meaningful also. This is not to say that there *are* any essential properties—though, in fact, I think there are. The usual argument questions the *meaningfulness* of essentialism, and says that whether a property is accidental or essential to an object depends on how it is described. It is thus *not* the view that all properties are accidental. Of course, it is also not the view, held by some idealists, that all properties are essential, all relations internal.

5. Misleadingly, because the phrase suggests that there is a special problem of 'transworld identification', that we cannot trivially stipulate whom or what we are talking about when we imagine another possible world. The term

'possible world' may also mislead; perhaps it suggests the 'foreign country' picture. I have sometimes used 'counterfactual situation' in the text; Michael Slote has suggested that 'possible state (or history) of the world' might be less misleading than 'possible world'. It is better still, to avoid confusion, not to say, 'In some possible world, Humphrey would have won' but rather, simply, 'Humphrey might have won'. The apparatus of possible words has (I hope) been very useful as far as the set-theoretic model-theory of quantified modal logic is concerned, but has encouraged philosophical pseudo-problems and misleading pictures.

6. Of course I don't imply that language contains a name for every object. Demonstratives can be used as rigid designators, and free variables can be used as rigid designators of unspecified objects. Of course when we specify a counterfactual situation, we do not describe the whole possible world, but only the portion which interests us.

A Priori Knowledge

PHILIP KITCHER

I

"A priori" has been a popular term with philosophers at least since Kant distinguished between a priori and a posteriori knowledge. Yet, despite the frequency with which it has been used in twentieth century philosophy, there has been little discussion of the concept of apriority.[1] Some writers seem to take it for granted that there are propositions, such as the truths of logic and mathematics, which are a priori; others deny that there are any a priori propositions. In the absence of a clear characterization of the a priori/ a posteriori distinction, it is by no means obvious what is being asserted or what is being denied.

"A priori" is an epistemological predicate. What is *primarily* a priori is an item of knowledge.[2] Of course, we can introduce a derivative use of "a priori" as a predicate of propositions:[3] a priori propositions are those which we could know a priori. Somebody might protest that current practice is to define the notion of an a priori proposition outright, by taking the class of a priori propositions to consist of the truths of logic and mathematics (for example). But when philosophers allege that truths of logic and mathematics are a priori, they do not intend merely to recapitulate the definition of a priori propositions. Their aim is to advance a thesis about the epistemological status of logic and mathematics.

To understand the nature of such epistemological claims, we should return to Kant, who provided the most explicit characterization of a priori knowledge: "we shall understand by a priori knowledge, not knowledge which is independent of this or that experience, but knowledge absolutely independent of all experience."[4] While acknowledging that Kant's formulation sums up the classical notion of apriority, several recent writers who have discussed the topic have despaired of making sense of it.[5] I shall try to show that Kant's definition can be clarified,

Source: From *Philosophical Review* 89 (1980).

and that the concept of a priori knowledge can be embedded in a naturalistic epistemology.

II

Two questions naturally arise. What are we to understand by "experience"? And what is to be made of the idea of independence from experience? Apparently, there are easy answers. Count as a person's experience the stream of her sensory encounters with the world, where this includes both "outer experience," that is, sensory states caused by stimuli external to the body, and "inner experience," that is, those sensory states brought about by internal stimuli. Now we might propose that someone's knowledge is independent of her experience just in case she could have had that knowledge whatever experience she had had. To this obvious suggestion there is an equally obvious objection. The apriorist is not ipso facto a believer in innate knowledge: indeed, Kant emphasized the difference between the two types of knowledge. So we cannot accept an analysis which implies that a priori knowledge could have been obtained given minimal experiences.[6]

Many philosophers (Kant included) contend both that analytic truths can be known a priori and that some analytic truths involve concepts which could only be acquired if we were to have particular kinds of experience. If we are to defend their doctrines from immediate rejection, we must allow a minimal role to experience, even in a priori knowledge. Experience may be needed to provide some concepts. So we might modify our proposal: knowledge is independent of experience if any experience which would enable us to acquire the concepts involved would enable us to have the knowledge.

It is worth noting explicitly that we are concerned here with the *total* experience of the knower. Suppose that you acquire some knowledge empirically. Later you deduce some consequences of this empirical knowledge. We should reject the suggestion that your knowledge of those consequences is independent of experience because, at the time you perform the deduction, you are engaging in a process of reasoning which is independent of the sensations you are then having.[7] As Kant recognized,[8] your knowledge, in cases like this, is dependent on your total experience: different total sequences of sensations would not have given you the premises for your deductions.

Let us put together the points which have been made so far. A person's experience at a particular time will be identified with his sensory state at the time. (Such states are best regarded physicalistically in terms of stimulation of sensory receptors, but we should recognize that there are both "outer" and "inner" receptors.) The total sequence of experiences X has had up to time t is *X's life at t*. A life will be said to be *sufficient for X for p* just in case X could have had that life and gained sufficient understanding to believe that p. (I postpone, for the moment, questions about the nature of the modality involved here.) Our discussion above suggests the use of these notions in the analysis of a priori knowledge: X knows a priori that p if and only if X knows that p and, given any life sufficient for X for p, X could have had that life and still have known that p. Making temporal references explicit: at time t X knows a priori that p just in case, at time t, X knows that p and, given any life sufficient for X for p, X could have had that life at t and still have known, at t, that p. In subsequent discussions I shall usually leave the temporal references implicit.

Unfortunately, the proposed analysis will not do. A clearheaded apriorist should admit that people can have empirical knowledge of propositions which can be known a priori. However, on the account I have given, if somebody knows that p and if it is possible for her to know a priori that p, then, apparently, given any sufficiently rich life she could know that p, so that she would meet the conditions for a priori knowledge that p. (This presupposes that modalities "collapse," but I don't think the problem can be solved simply by denying the presupposition.) Hence it seems that my account will not allow for empirical knowledge of propositions that can be known a priori.

We need to amend the analysis. We must differentiate situations in which a person knows something empirically which could have been known a priori from situations of actual a priori knowledge. The remedy is obvious. What sets apart corresponding situations of the two types is a difference in the ways in which what is known is known. An analysis of a priori knowledge must probe the notion of knowledge more deeply than we have done so far.

III

We do not need a general analysis of knowledge, but we do need the *form* of such an analysis. I shall adopt an approach which extracts what is common to much recent work on knowledge, an approach which may appropriately be called "the psychologistic account of knowledge."[9] The root idea is that the question of whether a person's true belief counts as knowledge depends on whether the presence of that true belief can be explained in an appropriate fashion. The difference between an item of knowledge and mere true belief turns on the factors which produced the belief; thus the issue revolves around the way in which a particular mental state was generated. It is important to emphasize that, at different times, a person may have states of belief with the same content, and these states may be produced by different processes. The claim that a process produces a belief is to be understood as the assertion that the presence of the current state of belief is to be explained through a description of that process. Hence the account is not committed to supposing that the original formation of a belief is relevant to the epistemological status of later states of belief in the same proposition.[10]

The question of what conditions must be met if a belief is to be explained in an appropriate fashion is central to epistemology, but it need not concern us here. My thesis is that the distinction between knowledge and true belief depends on the characteristics of the process which generates the belief, and this thesis is independent of specific proposals about what characteristics are crucial. Introducing a useful term, let us say that some processes *warrant* the beliefs they produce, and that these processes are *warrants* for such beliefs. The general view of knowledge I have adopted can be recast as the thesis that X knows that p just in case X correctly believes that p and X's belief was produced by a process which is a warrant for it. Leaving the task of specifying the conditions on warrants to general epistemology, my aim is to distinguish a priori knowledge from a posteriori knowledge. We discovered above that the distinction requires us to consider the ways in which what is known is known. Hence I propose to reformulate the problem: let us say that X knows a priori that p just in case X has a true belief that p and that belief was produced by a process which is an *a priori warrant* for it. Now the crucial notion is that of an a priori warrant, and our task becomes that of specifying the conditions which distinguish a priori warrants from other warrants.

At this stage, some examples may help us to see how to draw the distinction. Perception is an obvious type of process which philosophers have supposed *not* to engender a priori knowledge. Putative a priori warrants are more controversial. I shall use Kant's notion of pure intuition as an example. This is not to endorse the claim that processes of pure intuition are a priori warrants, but only to see what features of such processes have prompted Kant (and others) to differentiate them from perceptual processes.

On Kant's theory, processes of pure intuition are supposed to yield a priori mathematical knowledge. Let us focus on a simple geometrical example. We are supposed to gain a priori knowledge of the elementary properties of triangles by using our grasp on the concept of triangle to construct a mental picture of a triangle and by inspecting this picture with the mind's eye.[11] What are the characteristics of this kind of process which make Kant want to say that it produces knowledge which is independent of experience? I believe that Kant's account implies that three conditions should be met. The same type of process must be *available* independently of experience. It must produce *warranted* belief independently of experience. And it must produce *true* belief independently of experience. Let us consider these conditions in turn.

According to the Kantian story, if our life were to enable us to acquire the appropriate concepts (the concept of a triangle and the other geometrical concepts involved) then the appropriate kind of pure intuition would be available to us. We could represent a triangle to ourselves, inspect it, and so reach the same beliefs. But, if the process is to generate *knowledge* independently of experience, Kant must require more of it. Given any sufficiently rich life, if we were to undergo the same type of process and gain the same beliefs, then those beliefs would be warranted by the process. Let us dramatize the point by imagining that experience is unkind. Suppose that we are presented with experiments which are cunningly contrived so as to make it appear that some of our basic geometrical beliefs are false. Kant's theory of geometrical knowledge presupposes that if, in the circumstances envisaged, a process of pure intuition were to produce geometrical belief then it would produce warranted belief, despite the background of misleading experience.

So far I have considered how a Kantian process of pure intuition might produce warranted belief independently of experience. But to generate *knowledge* independently of experience, a priori warrants must produce warranted *true* belief in counterfactual situations where experiences are different. This point does not emerge clearly in the Kantian case because the propositions which are alleged to be known a priori are taken to be necessary, so that the question of whether it would be possible to have an a priori warrant for a false belief does not arise. Plainly, we could ensure that a priori warrants produce warranted *true* belief independently of experience by declaring that a priori warrants only warrant necessary truths. But this proposal is unnecessarily strong. Our goal is to construe a priori knowledge as knowledge which is independent of experience, and this can be achieved, without closing the case against the contingent a priori, by supposing that, in a counterfactual situation in which an a priori warrant produces belief that p then p. On this account, a priori warrants are ultra-reliable; they never lead us astray.[12]

Summarizing the conditions that have been uncovered, I propose the following analysis of a priori knowledge.

1. X knows a priori that p if and only if X knows that p and X's belief that p was produced by a process which is an a priori warrant for it.
2. α is an a priori warrant for X's belief that p if and only if α is a process such that, given any life e, sufficient for X for p, then
   a. some process of the same type could produce in X a belief that p
   b. if a process of the same type were to produce in X a belief that p then it would warrant X in believing that p
   c. if a process of the same type were to produce in X a belief that p then p.

It should be clear that this analysis yields the desired result that, if a person knows a priori that p then she could know that p whatever (sufficiently rich) experience she had had. But it goes beyond the proposal of §II in spelling out the idea that the knowledge be obtainable in the same way. Hence we can distinguish cases of empirical knowledge of propositions which could be known a priori from cases of actual a priori knowledge.

IV

In this section, I want to be more explicit about the notion of "types of processes" which I have employed, and about the modal and conditional notions which figure in my analysis. To specify a process which produces a belief is to pick out some terminal segment of the causal ancestry of the belief. I think that, without loss of generality, we can restrict our attention to those segments which consist solely of states and events internal to the believer.[13] Tracing the causal ancestry of a belief beyond the believer would identify processes which would not be available independently of experience, so that they would violate our conditions on a priori warrants.

Given that we need only consider psychological processes, the next question which arises is how we divide processes into types. It may seem that the problem can be sidestepped: can't we simply propose that to defend the apriority of an item of knowledge is to claim that that knowledge was produced by a psychological process and that *that very process* would be available and would produce warranted true belief in counterfactual situations where experience is different? I think it is easy to see how to use this proposal to rewrite (2) in a way which avoids reference to "types of processes." I have not adopted this approach because I think that it shortcuts important questions about what makes a process the same in different counterfactual situations.

Our talk of processes which produce belief was originally introduced to articulate the idea that some items of knowledge are obtained in the same way while others are obtained in different ways. To return to our example, knowing a theorem on the basis of hearing a lecture and knowing the same theorem by following a proof count, intuitively, as different ways of knowing the theorem. Our intuitions about this example, and others, involve a number of different principles of classification, with different principles appearing in different cases. We seem to divide belief-forming processes into types by considering content of beliefs, inferential connections, causal connections, use of perceptual mechanisms and so forth. I suggest that these principles of classification probably do not give rise to one definite taxonomy, but that, by using them singly, or in combination, we obtain a number of different taxonomies which we can and do employ. Moreover, within each taxonomy, we can specify types of processes more or less narrowly.[14] Faced with such variety, what characterization should we pick?

There is probably no privileged way of dividing processes into types. This is not to say that our standard principles of classification will allow *anything* to count as a type. Somebody who proposed that the process of listening to a lecture (or the terminal segment of it which consists of psychological states and events) belongs to a type which consists of itself and instances of following a proof, would flout *all* our principles for dividing processes into types. Hence, while we may have many admissible notions of types of belief-forming processes, corresponding to different principles of classification, some collections of processes contravene all such principles, and these cannot be admitted as genuine types.[15]

My analysis can be read as issuing a challenge to the apriorist. If someone wishes to claim that a particular belief is an item of a priori knowledge then he must specify a segment of the causal ancestry of the belief, consisting of states and events internal to the believer, and type-identity conditions which conform to some principle (or set of principles) of classification which are standardly employed in our divisions of belief-forming processes (of which the principles I have indicated above furnish the most obvious examples). If he succeeds in doing this so that the requirements in (2) are met, his claim is sustained; if he cannot, then his claim is defeated.

The final issue which requires discussion in this section is that of explaining the modal and conditional notions I have used. There are all kinds of possibility, and claims about what is possible bear an implicit relativization to a set of facts which are held constant.[16] When we say, in (2), that, given any sufficiently rich life, X could have had a belief which was the product of a particular type of process, should we conceive of this as merely logical possibility or are there some features of the actual world which are tacitly regarded as fixed? I suggest that we are not just envisaging any logically possible world. We imagine a world in which X has similar mental powers to those he has in the actual world. By hypothesis, X's experience is different. Yet the capacities for thinking, reasoning, and acquiring knowledge which X possesses as a member of *homo sapiens* are to remain unaffected: we want to say that X, *with the kinds of cognitive capacities distinctive of humans,* could have undergone processes of the appropriate type, even if his experiences had been different.[17]

Humans might have had more faculties for acquiring knowledge than they actually have. For example, we might have had some strange ability to "see" what happens on the other side of the Earth. When we consider the status of a particular type of process as an a priori warrant, the existence of worlds in which such extra faculties come into play is entirely irrelevant. Our investigation focusses on the question of whether a particular type of process would be available to a person with the kinds of faculties people actually have, not on whether such processes would be available to creatures whose capacities for acquiring knowledge are augmented or diminished. Conditions (2(b)) and (2(c)) are to be read in similar fashion. Rewriting (2(b)) to make the form of the conditional explicit, we obtain: for any life e sufficient for X for p and for any world in which X has e, in which he believes that p, in which his belief is the product of a process of the appropriate kind, and *in which X has the cognitive capacities distinctive of humans,* X is warranted in believing that p. Similarly, (2(c)) becomes: for any life e sufficient for X for p and for any world in which X has e, in which he believes that p, in which his belief is the product of a process of the appropriate kind, *and in which X has the cognitive capacities distinctive of humans,* p. Finally, the notion of a life's being sufficient for X for p also bears an implicit reference to X's native powers. To say that a particular life enables X to form certain concepts is to maintain that, given the genetic programming with which X is endowed, that life allows for the formation of the concepts.

The account I have offered can be presented more graphically in the following way. Consider a human as a cognitive device, endowed initially with a particular kind of structure. Sensory experience is fed into the device and, as a result, the device forms certain concepts. For any proposition p, the class of experiences which are sufficiently rich for p consists of those experiences which would enable the device, with the kind of structure it actually has, to acquire the concepts to believe that p. To decide whether or not a particular item of knowledge that p is an item of a priori knowledge we consider whether the type of process which produced the belief that p is a process which would have been available to the device, with the kind of structure it actually has, if different sufficiently rich experiences had been fed into it, whether, under such circumstances, processes of the type would warrant belief that p, and would produce true belief that p.

Seen in this way, claims about apriority are implicitly indexical, in that they inherit the indexical features of "actual."[18] If this is not recognized, use of "a priori" in modal contexts can engender confusion. The truth value of "Possibly, X knows a priori that p" can be determined in one of two ways: we may consider the proposition expressed by the sentence at our world, and inquire whether there is a world at which that proposition is true; or we may ask whether there is a world at which the sentence expresses a true proposition. Because of the covert indexicality of "a priori," these lines of investigation may yield different answers. I suspect that failure to appreciate this point has caused trouble in assessing theses about the limits of the a priori. However, I shall not pursue the point here.[19]

V

At this point, I want to address worries that my analysis is too liberal, because it allows some of our knowledge of ourselves and our states to count as a priori. Given its Kantian psychologistic underpinnings, the theory appears to favor claims that some of our self-knowledge is a priori. However, two points should be kept in mind. Firstly, the analysis I have proposed can only be applied to cases in which we know enough about the ways in which our beliefs are warranted to decide whether or not the conditions of (2) are met. In some cases, our lack of a detailed account of how our beliefs are generated may mean that no firm decision about the apriority of an item of knowledge can be reached. Secondly, there may be cases, including cases of self-knowledge, in which we have no clear pre-analytic intuitions about whether a piece of knowledge is a priori.

Nevertheless, there are some clear cases. Obviously, any theory which implied that I can know a priori that I am seeing red (when, in fact, I am) would be suspect. But, when we apply my analysis, the unwanted conclusion does not follow. For, if the process which leads me to believe that I am seeing red (when I am) can be triggered in the absence of red, then (2(c)) would be violated. If the process cannot be triggered in the absence of red, then, given some sufficiently rich experiences, the process will not be available, so that (2(a)) will be violated. In general, knowledge of any involuntary mental state—such as pains, itches or hallucinations—will work in the same way. Either the process which leads from the occurrence of pain to the belief that I am in pain can be triggered in the absence of pain, or not: if it can, (2(c)) would be violated, if it cannot, then (2(a)) would be violated.

This line of argument can be sidestepped when we turn to cases in which we have the power, independently of experience, to put ourselves into the appropriate states. For, in such cases, one can propose that the processes which give us knowledge of the states cannot be triggered in the absence of the states themselves *and* that the processes are always available because we can always put ourselves into the states.[20] On this basis, we might try to conclude that we have a priori knowledge that we are imagining red (when we are) or thinking of Ann Arbor (when we are). However, the fact that such cases do not fall victim to the argument of the last paragraph does not mean that we are compelled to view them as cases of a priori knowledge. In the first place, the thesis that the processes through which we come to know our imaginative feats and our voluntary thoughts cannot be triggered in the absence of the states themselves requires evaluation—and, lacking detailed knowledge of those processes, we cannot arrive at a firm judgement here. Secondly, the processes in question will be required to meet (2(b)) if they are to be certified as a priori warrants. This means that, whatever experience hurls at us, beliefs produced by such processes will be warranted. We can cast doubt on this idea by imagining that our experience consists of a lengthy, and apparently reliable, training in neurophysiology, concluding with a presentation to ourselves of our own neurophysiological organization which appears to show that our detection of our imaginative states (say) is slightly defective, that we always make mistakes about the contents of our imaginings. If this type of story can be developed, then (2(b)) will be violated, and the knowledge in question will not count as a priori. But, even if it cannot be coherently extended, and even if my analysis does judge our knowledge of states of imagination (and other "voluntary" states) to be a priori, it is not clear to me that this consequence is counterintuitive.

In fact, I think that one can make a powerful case for supposing that *some* self-knowledge is a priori. At most, if not all, of our waking moments, each of us knows of herself that she exists.[21] Although traditional ideas to the effect that self-knowledge is produced by some "non-optical inner look" are clearly inadequate, I think it is plausible to maintain that there are processes which do warrant us in believing that we exist—processes of reflective thought, for example—and which belong to a general type whose members would be available to us independently of experience.[22] Trivially, when any such process produces in a person a belief that she exists that belief is true. All that remains, therefore, is to ask if the processes of the type in question inevitably warrant belief in our own existence, or whether they would fail to do so, given a suitably exotic background experience. It is difficult to settle this issue conclusively without a thorough survey of the ways in which reflective belief in one's existence can be challenged by experience, but perhaps there are Cartesian grounds for holding that, so long as the belief is the product of reflective thought, the believer is warranted, no matter how wild his experience may have been. If this is correct, then at least some of our self-knowledge will be a priori. However, in cases like this, attributions of apriority seem even less vulnerable to the criticism that they are obviously incorrect.

At this point we must consider a doctrinaire objection. If the conclusion of the last paragraph is upheld then we can know some contingent propositions a priori.[23] Frequently, however, it is maintained that only necessary truths can be known a priori. Behind this contention stands a popular argument.[24] Assume that a person knows a priori that p. His knowledge is independent of his experience. Hence he can know that p without any information about the kind of world he inhabits. So, necessarily p.

This hazy line of reasoning rests on an intuition which is captured in the analysis given above. The intuition is that a priori warrants must be ultra-reliable: if a person is entitled to ignore empirical information about the type of world she inhabits then that must be because she has at her disposal a method of arriving at belief which guarantees *true* belief. (This intuition can be defended by pointing out that if a method which could produce false belief were allowed to override experience, then we might be blocked from obtaining knowledge which we might otherwise have gained.) In my analysis, the intuition appears as (2(c)).[25]

However, when we try to clarify the popular argument we see that it contains an invalid step. Presenting it as a *reductio,* we obtain the following line of reasoning. Assume that a person knows a priori that p but that it is not necessary that p. Because p is contingent there are worlds at which p is false. Suppose that the person had inhabited such a world and behaved as she does at the actual world. Then she would have had an a priori warrant for a false belief. This is debarred by (2(c)). So we must conclude that the initial supposition is erroneous: if someone really does know a priori that p then p is necessary.

Spelled out in this way, the argument fails. We are not entitled to conclude from the premise that there are worlds at which p is false the thesis that there are worlds at which p is false *and* at which the person behaves as she does at the actual world. There are a number of propositions which, although they could be false, could not both be false and also believed by us. More generally, there are propositions which could not both be false and also believed by us in particular, definite ways. Obvious examples are propositions about ourselves and their logical consequences: such propositions as those expressed by tokens of the sentences "I exist," "I have some beliefs," "There are thoughts," and so forth. Hence the attempted *reductio* breaks down and allows for the possibility of a priori knowledge of some contingent propositions.

I conclude that my analysis is innocent of the charge of being too liberal in ascribing to us a priori knowledge of propositions about ourselves. Although it is plausible to hold that my account construes some of our self-knowledge as a priori, none of the self-knowledge it takes to be a priori is clearly empirical. Moreover, it shows how a popular argument against the contingent a priori is flawed, and how certain types of contingent propositions most notably propositions about ourselves—escape that argument. Thus I suggest that the analysis illuminates an area of traditional dispute.

VI

I now want to consider two different objections to my analysis. My replies to these objections will show how the approach I have developed can be further refined and extended.

The first objection, like those considered above, charges that the analysis is too liberal. My account apparently allows for the possibility that a priori knowledge could be gained through perception. We can imagine that some propositions are true at any world of which we can have experience, and that, given sufficient experience to entertain those propositions, we could always come to know them on the basis of perception. Promising examples are the proposition that there are objects, the proposition that some objects have shapes, and other, similar propositions. In these cases, one can argue that we cannot experience worlds at which they are false and that any (sufficiently rich) experience would provide perceptual warrant for belief in the propositions, regardless of the specific content of our perceptions. If these points are correct (and I shall concede them both, for the sake of argument), then perceptual processes would qualify as a priori warrants. Given any sufficiently rich experience, some perceptual process would be available to us, would produce warranted belief and, *ex hypothesi,* would produce warranted *true* belief.

Let us call cases of the type envisaged cases of *universally empirical* knowledge. The objection to my account is that it incorrectly classifies universally empirical knowledge as a priori knowledge. My response is that the classical notion of apriority is too vague to decide such cases: rather, this type of knowledge only becomes apparent when the classical notion is articulated. One could defend the classification of universally empirical knowledge as a priori by pointing out that such knowledge requires no particular type of experience (beyond that needed to obtain the concepts, of course). One could oppose that classification by pointing out that, even though the content of the experience is immaterial, the knowledge is still gained by perceiving, so that it should count as a posteriori.

If the second response should seem attractive, it can easily be accommodated by recognizing a stronger and a weaker notion of apriority. The weaker notion is captured in (1) and (2). The stronger adds an extra requirement: no process which involves the operation of a perceptual mechanism is to count as an a priori warrant.

At this point, it is natural to protest that the new condition makes the prior analysis irrelevant. Why not define a priori knowledge outright as knowledge which is produced by processes which do not involve perceptual mechanisms? The answer is that the prior conditions are not redundant: knowledge which is produced by a process which does not involve perceptual mechanisms need not be independent of experience. For the process may fail to generate warranted belief against a backdrop of misleading experience. (Nor may it generate true belief in all relevant counterfactual situations.) So, for example, certain kinds of thought-experiments may generate items of knowledge given a particular type of experience, but may not be able to sustain that knowledge against misleading experiences. Hence, if we choose to exclude universally empirical knowledge from the realm of the a priori in the way suggested, we are building on the analysis given in (1) and (2), rather than replacing it.

A different kind of criticism of my analysis is to accuse it of revealing the emptiness of the classical notion of apriority. Someone may suggest that, in exposing the constraints on a priori knowledge, I have shown that there could be very little a priori knowledge. Although I believe that this suggestion is incorrect, it is worth pointing out that, even if it is granted, my approach allows for the development of weaker notions which may prove epistemologically useful.

Let me first note that we can introduce approximations to a priori knowledge. Suppose that A is any type of process all of whose instances culminate in belief that p. Define the *supporting class* of A to be that class of lives, c, such that, (a) given c, some process in A could occur (and so produce belief that p), (b) given c, any process in A which occurred would produce warranted true belief that p. (Intuitively, the supporting class consists of those lives which enable processes of the type in question to produce knowledge.) The *defeating class* of A is the complement of the supporting class of A within the class of lives which are sufficient for p. A priori warrants are those processes which belong to a type whose defeating class is null. But we can be more liberal, and allow approximations to a priori knowledge by considering the size and/or nature of the defeating class. We might, for example, permit the defeating class to contain those radically disruptive experiences beloved of sceptics. Or we can define a notion of *contextual* apriority by allowing the defeating class to include experiences which undermine "framework principles."[26] Or we may employ a concept of *comparative* apriority by ordering defeating classes according to inclusion relations. Each of these notions can serve a useful function in delineating the structure of our knowledge.

VII

Finally, I want to address a systematic objection to my analysis. The approach I have taken is blatantly psychologistic. Some philosophers may regard these psychological complications as objectionable intrusions into epistemology. So I shall consider the possibility of rival apsychologistic approaches.

Is there an acceptable view of a priori knowledge which rivals the Kantian conception? The logical positivists hoped to understand a priori knowledge without dabbling in psychology. The simplest of their proposals was the suggestion that X knows a priori that p if and only if X believes that p and p is analytically true.[27]

Gilbert Harman has argued cogently that, in cases of factual belief, the nature of the reasons for which a person believes is relevant to the question of whether he has knowledge.[28] Similar considerations arise with respect to propositions which the positivists took to be a priori. Analytic propositions like synthetic propositions, can be believed for bad reasons, or for no reasons at all, and, when this occurs, we should deny that the believer knows the propositions in question. Assume, as the positivists did, that mathematics is analytic, and imagine a mathematician who comes to believe that some unobvious theorem is true. This belief is exhibited in her continued efforts to prove the theorem. Finally, she succeeds. We naturally describe her progress by saying that she has come to know something she only believed before. The positivistic proposal forces us to attribute knowledge from the beginning. Worse still, we can imagine that the mathematician has many colleagues who believe the theorem because of dreams, trances, fits of Pythagorean ecstasy, and so forth. Not only does the positivistic approach fail to separate the mathematician after she has found the proof from her younger self, but it also gives her the same status as her colleagues.

A natural modification suggests itself: distinguish among the class of analytic truths those which are elementary (basic laws of logic, immediate consequences of definitions, and, perhaps, a few others), and propose that elementary analytic truths can be known merely by being believed, while the rest are known, when they are known a priori, by inference from such truths. Even this restricted version of the original claim is vulnerable. If you believe the basic laws of logic because you have learned them from an eminent mathematician who has deluded himself into believing that the system of *Grundgesetze* is consistent and true, then you do not have a priori knowledge of those laws. Your belief in the laws of logic is undermined by evidence which you do not currently possess, namely the evidence which would expose your teacher as a misguided fanatic. The moral is obvious: apsychologistic approaches to a priori knowledge fail because, for a priori knowledge as for factual knowledge, the reasons for which a person believes are relevant to the question of whether he knows.

Although horror of psychologizing prevented the positivists from offering a defensible account of a priori knowledge, I think that my analysis can be used to articulate most of the doctrines that they wished to defend. Indeed, I believe that many classical theses, arguments and debates can be illuminated by applying the analysis presented here. My aim has been to prepare the way for investigations of traditional claims and disputes by developing in some detail Kant's conception of a priori knowledge. "A priori" has too often been a label which philosophers could attach to propositions they favored, without any clear criterion for doing so. I hope to have shown how a more systematic practice is possible.

NOTES

1. There are some exceptions. Passing attention to the problem of defining apriority is given in John Pollock. *Knowledge and Justification* (Princeton, 1974) Chapter 10; R. G. Swinburne "Analyticity. Necessity and Apriority." (*Mind,* LXXXIV, 1975, pp. 225–243), especially pp. 238–241; Edward Erwin "Are the Notions 'A Priori Truth' and 'Necessary Truth' Extensionally Equivalent?" (*Canadian Journal of Philosophy,* III, 1974, pp. 591–602), especially pp. 593–597. The inadequacy of much traditional thinking about apriority is forcefully presented in Saul Kripke's papers "Identity and Necessity" (in Milton K. Munitz (ed.), *Identity and Individuation,* New York, 1971, pp. 135–164), especially pp. 149–151, and "Naming and Necessity" (in D. Davidson and G. Harman (eds.), *Semantics of Natural Language,* D. Reidel, 1972, pp. 253–355, 763–769), especially pp. 260–264.
2. See Kripke, loc. cit.
3. For ease of reference, I take propositions to be the objects of belief and knowledge, and to be what declarative sentences express. I trust that my conclusions would survive any successful elimination of propositions in favor of some alternative approach to the objects of belief and knowledge.
4. *Critique of Pure Reason* (B2–3).
5. See Pollock, loc. cit., Swinburne, loc. cit., Erwin, loc. cit.
6. Someone might be tempted to propose, conversely, that all innate knowledge is a priori (cf. Swinburne op. cit. p. 239). In "The Nativist's Dilemma," (*Philosophical Quarterly,* 28, 1978, pp. 1–16). I have argued that there may well be no innate knowledge and that, if there were any such knowledge, it would not have to be a priori.
7. Pollock (op. cit. p. 301) claims that we can only resist the suggestion that this knowledge is independent of experience by complicating the notion of experience. For the reason given in the text, such desperate measures seem to me to be unnecessary.
8. See the example of the man who undermines the foundations of his house. (*Critique of Pure Reason,* B3).
9. Prominent exponents of this approach are Alvin Goldman, Gilbert Harman and David Armstrong. See: Alvin Goldman, "A Causal

Theory of Knowing" (*Journal of Philosophy,* LXIV, 1967, pp. 357–372), "Innate Knowledge" (in Stephen P. Stich (ed.) *Innate Ideas* [Berkeley, 1975] pp. 111–120), "Discrimination and Perceptual Knowledge" (*Journal of Philosophy,* LXXII, 1976, pp. 771–791), "What is Justified Belief?" (in George S. Pappas (ed.) *Justification and Knowledge,* [D. Reidel, forthcoming]); Gilbert Harman, *Thought* (Princeton, 1973); David Armstrong, *Belief, Truth and Knowledge* (Cambridge, 1973).

10. Psychologistic epistemologies are often accused of confusing the context of discovery with the context of justification. For a recent formulation of this type of objection, see Keith Lehrer, *Knowledge* (Oxford, 1974), pp. 123ff. I have tried to show that psychologistic epistemology is not committed to mistakes with which it is frequently associated in "Frege's Epistemology," (*Philosophical Review,* 88, 1979, pp. 235–62). I shall consider the possibility of an apsychologistic approach to apriority in §VII below.
11. More details about Kant's theory of pure intuition can be found in my paper "Kant and the Foundations of Mathematics" (*Philosophical Review,* 84, 1975, pp. 23–50), especially pp. 28–33.
12. For further discussion of this requirement and the possibility of the contingent a priori, see §V below.
13. For different reasons, Goldman proposes that an analysis of the general notion of warrant (or, in his terms, justification) can focus on psychological processes. See section 2 of "What is Justified Belief?"
14. Consider, for example, a Kantian process of pure intuition which begins with the construction of a triangle. Should we say that a process of the same type must begin with the construction of a triangle of the same size and shape, a triangle of the same shape, any triangle, or something even more general? Obviously there are many natural classifications here, and I think the best strategy is to suppose that an apriorist is entitled to pick any of them.
15. Strictly, the sets which do not constitute types are those which violate correct taxonomies. In making present decisions about types, we assume that our current principles of classification are correct. If it should turn out that those principles require revision then our judgements about types will have to be revised accordingly.
16. For a lucid and entertaining presentation of the point, see David Lewis, "The Paradoxes of Time Travel," (*American Philosophical Quarterly,* 13, 1976, pp. 145–152), pp. 149–151.
17. Of course, X might have been more intelligent, that is, he might have had better versions of the faculties he has. We allow for this type of change. But we are not interested in worlds where X has extra faculties.
18. The idea that "actual" is indexical is defended by David Lewis in "Anselm and Actuality," (*Noûs,* IV, 1970, pp. 175–188). In "The Only Necessity is Verbal Necessity," (*Journal of Philosophy,* LXXIV, 1977, pp. 71–85), Bas van Fraassen puts Lewis' ideas about "actual" in a general context. The machinery which van Fraassen presents in that paper can be used to elaborate the ideas of the present paragraph.
19. Jaegwon Kim has pointed out to me that, besides the "species-relative" notion of apriority presented in the text, there might be an absolute notion. Perhaps there is a class of propositions which would be knowable a priori by any being whom we would count as a rational being. Absolute a priori knowledge would thus be that a priori knowledge which is available to all possible knowers.
20. In characterizing pain as an involuntary state one paragraph back I may seem to have underestimated our powers of self-torture. But even a masochist could be defeated by unkind experience: as he goes to pinch himself his skin is anesthetized.
21. I shall ignore the tricky issue of trying to say exactly what is known when we know this and kindred things. For interesting explorations of this area, see Hector-Neri Castañeda, "Indicators and Quasi-indicators" (*American Philosophical Quarterly,* 4, 1967, pp. 85–100), "On the Logic of Attributions of Self-Knowledge to Others," (*Journal of Philosophy,* LXV, 1968, pp. 439–56); John Perry, "Frege on

Demonstratives," (*Philosophical Review,* 86, 1977, pp. 474–97), "The Problem of the Essential Indexical," (*Noûs,* 13, 1979, pp. 3–21). The issue of how to represent the content of items of self-knowledge may force revision of the position taken in footnote 3 above: it may not be possible to identify objects of belief with meanings of sentences. Although such revision would complicate my analysis, I don't think it would necessitate any fundamental modifications.

22. This presupposes that our knowledge of our existence does not result from some special kind of "inner sensation." For, if it did, different lives would deprive us of the warrant.
23. Kripke (loc. cit.) has attempted to construct examples of contingent propositions which can be known a priori. I have not tried to decide here whether his examples are successful, since full treatment of this question would lead into issues about the analysis of the propositions in question which are well beyond the scope of the present paper. For a discussion of some of the difficulties involved in Kripke's examples, see Keith Donnellan "The Contingent A Priori and Rigid Designators" (*Mid-West Studies in Philosophy,* Volume 2, 1977, pp. 12–27).
24. Kripke seems to take this to be the main argument against the contingent a priori. See "Naming and Necessity," p. 263.
25. As the discussion of this paragraph suggests, there is an intimate relation between my requirements (2(b)) and (2(c)). Indeed, one might argue that (2(b)) would not be met unless (2(c)) were also satisfied—on the grounds that one cannot allow a process to override experience unless it guarantees truth. The subsequent discussion will show that this type of reasoning is more complicated than appears. Hence, although I believe that the idea that a priori warrants function independently of experience does have implications for the reliability of these processes, I have chosen to add (2(c)) as a separate condition.
26. This notion of contextual apriority has been used by Hilary Putnam. See, for example, his paper "It Ain't Necessarily So," (Chapter 15 of H. Putnam, *Mathematics, Matter and Method,* Philosophical Papers, Volume I, Cambridge, 1975) and "There is At Least One A Priori Truth" (*Erkenntnis,* 13, 1978, pp. 153–70), especially p. 154.
27. See A. J. Ayer, *Language, Truth and Logic,* (London 1936), Chapter IV, and M. Schlick, "The Foundation of Knowledge" (in A. J. Ayer (ed.) *Logical Positivism* (New York, 1959) pp. 209–227) especially p. 224.
28. *Thought* Chapter 2; see also Goldman "What is Justified Belief?" Section 1.

 8 

Analyticity Reconsidered

PAUL ARTIN BOGHOSSIAN

I

This is what many philosophers believe today about the analytic/synthetic distinction: In his classic early writings on analyticity—in particular, in "Truth by Convention," "Two Dogmas of Empiricism," and "Carnap and Logical Truth"—Quine showed that there can be no distinction between sentences that are true purely by virtue of their meaning and those that are not. In so doing, Quine devastated the philosophical programs that depend upon a notion of analyticity—specifically, the linguistic theory of necessary truth, and the analytic theory of a priori knowledge.

Quine himself, so the story continues, went on to espouse far more radical views about meaning, including such theses as meaning-indeterminacy and meaning-skepticism. However, it is not necessary, and certainly not appealing, to follow him on this trajectory. As realists about meaning, we may treat Quine's self-contained discussion in the early papers as the basis for a profound *insight* into the nature of meaning facts, rather than any sort of rejection of them. We may discard the notions of the analytic and the a priori without thereby buying in on any sort of unpalatable skepticism about meaning.

Now, I don't know precisely how many philosophers believe all of the above, but I think it would be fair to say that it is the prevailing view. Philosophers with radically differing commitments—including radically differing commitments about the nature of meaning itself—subscribe to it: whatever precisely the correct construal of meaning, so they seem to think, Quine has shown that it will not sustain a distinction between the analytic and the

Source: Paul Boghossian, "Analyticity Reconsidered," *Nous,* Vol. 30 (1996), pp. 360–391. Reprinted with permission of the publisher.

synthetic. Listen, for example, to Bill Lycan:

> It has been nearly forty years since the publication of "Two Dogmas of Empiricism." Despite some vigorous rebuttals during that period, Quine's rejection of analyticity still prevails—in that philosophers en masse have either joined Quine in repudiating the "analytic/synthetic" distinction or remained (however mutinously) silent and made no claims of analyticity.
>
> This comprehensive capitulation is somewhat surprising, in light of the radical nature of Quine's views on linguistic meaning generally. In particular, I doubt that many philosophers accept his doctrine of the indeterminacy of translation. . . [1]

Lycan goes on to promise that in his paper, he is going to

> make a Quinean case against analyticity, without relying on the indeterminacy doctrine. For I join the majority in denying both analyticity and indeterminacy. . . .[2]

Now, my disagreement with the prevailing view is not total. There is *a* notion of 'truth by virtue of meaning'—what I shall call the metaphysical notion—that *is* undermined by a set of indeterminacy-independent considerations. Since this notion is presupposed by the linguistic theory of necessity, that project fails and must be abandoned.

However, I disagree with the prevailing view's assumption that those very same considerations also undermine the analytic explanation of the a priori. For it seems to me that an entirely distinct notion of analyticity underlies that explanation, a notion that is epistemic in character. And in contrast with the metaphysical notion, the epistemic notion can be defended, I think, provided that even a minimal realism about meaning is true. I'm inclined to hold, therefore, that there can be no effective Quinean critique of the a priori that does not ultimately depend on Quine's radical thesis of the indeterminacy of meaning, a thesis that, as I've stressed, many philosophers continue to reject.

All of this is what I propose to argue in this paper. I should emphasize right at the outset, however, that I am not a historian and my interest here is not historical. Think of me rather as asking, on behalf of all those who continue to reject Quine's later skepticism about meaning: Can something like the analytic explanation of the a priori be salvaged from the wreckage of the linguistic theory of necessity?

Belief, Apriority and Indeterminacy

We need to begin with some understanding—however brief and informal—of what it is to believe something and of what it is for a belief to count as a priori knowledge.

Let's work with a picture of belief that is as hospitable as possible to Quine's basic outlook. According to this 'linguistic' picture, the objects of belief are not propositions, but rather interpreted sentences: for a person **T** to believe that **p** is for **T** to hold true a sentence **S** which means that **p** in **T**'s idiolect.[3]

Against this rough and ready background, we may say that for **T** to know that **p** is for **T** to justifiably hold **S** true, with a strength sufficient for knowledge, and for **S** to be true. And to say that **T** knows **p** a priori is to say that **T**'s warrant for holding **S** true is independent of outer, sensory experience.[4] The interesting question in the analysis of the concept of apriority concerns this notion of warrant: what is it for a belief to be justified independently of outer sensory experience?

On a minimalist reading, to say that the warrant for a given belief is a priori is just to say that it is justified, with a strength sufficient for knowledge, without appeal to empirical evidence.[5] On a stronger reading, it is to say that *and* that the justification in question is not defeasible by any future empirical evidence.[6] Which of these two notions is at issue in the present debate?

My own view is that the minimal notion forms the core of the idea of apriority and, hence, that it would be achievement enough to demonstrate its possibility. However, in this paper I will aim to provide the materials with which to substantiate the claim that, under the appropriate circumstances, the notion of analyticty can help explain how we might have a priori knowledge even in the strong sense. A defense of the strong notion is particularly relevant in the present context, for Quine seems to have been most skeptical of the idea of empirical indefeasibility.

Before proceeding, we should also touch briefly on the notion of meaning-indeterminacy. In Chapter Two of *Word and Object,* Quine argued that, for any language, it is possible to find two incompatible translation manuals that nevertheless perfectly conform to the totality of the evidence that constrains translation. This is the famous doctrine of the indeterminacy of translation. Since Quine was furthermore prepared to assume that there could not be facts about meaning that are not captured in the constraints on best translation, he concluded that meaning facts themselves are indeterminate—that there is, strictly speaking, no determinate fact of the matter as to what a given expression in a language means. This is the doctrine that I have called the thesis of the indeterminacy of meaning.

An *acceptance* of meaning-indeterminacy can lead to a variety of *other* views about meaning. For instance, it might lead to an outright eliminativism about meaning. Or it might be taken as a reason to base the theory of meaning on the notion of likeness of meaning, rather than on that of sameness of meaning.[7] In this paper, I am not concerned with the question what moral should be drawn from the indeterminacy thesis, on the assumption that it is true; nor am I concerned with whether the indeterminacy thesis is true. I am only concerned to show that a skepticism about epistemic analyticity cannot stop short of the indeterminacy thesis, a thesis that, as I have stressed, most philosophers agree in rejecting.

Analyticity: Metaphysical or Epistemological?

Traditionally, three classes of statement have been thought to be the objects of a priori knowledge: logical statements, mathematical statements and such 'conceptual truths' as, for example, that all squares are four-sided. The problem has always been to explain what could justify us in holding such statements true on a priori grounds.

The history of philosophy has known a number of answers to this problem, among which the following has had considerable influence: We are equipped with a special evidence-gathering faculty of *intuition,* distinct from the standard five senses; by exercising this faculty, we are able to know a priori such truths as those of mathematics and logic.

The central impetus behind the *analytic* explanation of the a priori is a desire to explain the possibility of a priori knowledge without having to postulate such a special faculty, one that has never been described in satisfactory terms. The question is: How could a factual statement **S** be known a priori by **T**, without the help of a special evidence-gathering faculty?

Here, it would seem, is one way: *If mere grasp of* ***S****'s meaning by* ***T*** *sufficed for* ***T****'s being justified in holding* ***S*** *true*. If **S** were analytic in this sense, then, clearly, its apriority would be explainable without appeal to a special faculty of intuition: mere grasp of its meaning by **T** would suffice for explaining **T**'s justification for holding **S** true. On this understanding, then, 'analyticity' is an overtly *epistemological* notion: a statement is 'true' by virtue of its meaning' provided that grasp of its meaning alone suffices for justified belief in its truth.

Another, far more *metaphysical* reading of the phrase 'true by virtue of meaning' is also available, however, according to which a statement is analytic provided that, in some appropriate sense, it *owes its truth value completely to its meaning,* and not at all to 'the facts.'

Which of these two possible notions has been at stake in the dispute over analyticity? There has been a serious unclarity on the matter. Quine himself tends to label the doctrine of analyticity an epistemological doctrine, as for example in the following passage from "Carnap and Logical Truth":

> the linguistic doctrine of logical truth, which is an epistemological doctrine, goes on to say that logical truths are true purely by virtue of the intended meanings, or intended usage, of the logical words.[8]

However, his most biting criticisms seem often to be directed at what I have called the metaphysical notion. Consider, for example, the object of disapproval in the following famous passage, a passage that concludes the official discussion of analyticity in "Two Dogmas":

> It is obvious that truth in general depends on both language and extralinguistic fact. The statement 'Brutus killed Caesar' would be false if the world had been different in certain ways, but it would also be false if the word 'killed' happened rather to have the sense of 'begat'. Thus one is tempted to suppose in general that the truth of a statement is somehow analyzable into a linguistic component and a factual component. Given this supposition it next seems reasonable that in some statements the factual component should be null; and these are the analytic statements. But for all its a priori reasonableness, a boundary between analytic and synthetic statements simply has not been drawn. That there is such a distinction to be drawn at all is an unempirical dogma of empiricists, a metaphysical article of faith.[9]

Now, I think that there is no doubt that many of the proponents of the analytic theory of the a priori, among them especially its positivist proponents, intended the notion of analyticity to be understood in this metaphysical sense; very shortly I shall look at why.

Before doing that, however, I want to register my wholehearted agreement with Quine that the metaphysical notion is of dubious explanatory value and possibly also of dubious coherence. Fortunately for the analytic theory of the a priori, it can be shown that it need have nothing to do with this discredited idea.

The Metaphysical Concept

What could it possibly mean to say that the truth of a statement is fixed exclusively by its meaning and not by the facts? Isn't it in general true—indeed, isn't it in general a truism—that for any statement **S**,

S is true iff for some **p**, **S** means that **p** and **p**?

How could the *mere* fact that **S** means that **p** make it the case that **S** is true? Doesn't it also have to be the case that **p**? As Harman has usefully put it (he is discussing the sentence 'Copper is copper'):

> what is to prevent us from saying that the truth expressed by "Copper is copper" depends in part on a general feature of the way the world is, namely that everything is self-identical.[10]

The proponent of the metaphysical notion does have a comeback, one that has perhaps not been sufficiently addressed. If he is wise, he won't want to deny the meaning-truth truism. What he will want to say instead is that, in some appropriate sense, our meaning **p** by **S** *makes it the case that* ***p***.

But this line is itself fraught with difficulty. For how can we make sense of the idea that something is made true by our meaning something by a sentence?

Consider a sentence of the form 'Either **p** or not **p**'. It is easy, of course, to understand how the fact that we mean what we do by the ingredient terms fixes what is expressed by the sentence as a whole; and it is easy to understand, in consequence, how the fact that we mean what we do by the sentence determines whether the sentence expresses something true or false. But as Quine points out, that is just the normal dependence of truth on meaning. What is far more mysterious is the claim that the *truth of what the sentence expresses* depends on the fact that it is expressed by that sentence, so that we can say that what is expressed wouldn't have been true at all had it not been for the fact that it is expressed by that sentence. Are we really to suppose that, prior to our stipulating a meaning for the sentence

Either snow is white or it isn't

it wasn't the case that either snow was white or it wasn't? Isn't it overwhelmingly obvious that this claim was true *before* such an act of meaning, and that it would have been true even if no one had thought about it, or chosen it to be expressed by one of our sentences?

Why, if this idea is as problematic as I have claimed it to be, did it figure so prominently in positivist thinking about analyticity?

Much of the answer derives from the fact that the positivists didn't merely want to provide a theory of a priori knowledge; they also wanted to provide a reductive theory of necessity. The motivation was not purely epistemological, but metaphysical as well. Guided by the fear that objective, language-independent necessary connections would be both metaphysically and epistemologically odd, they attempted to show that all necessities could be understood to consist in linguistic necessities, in the shadows cast by conventional decisions concerning the meanings of words. Conventional linguistic meaning, by itself, was supposed to generate necessary truth; a fortiori, conventional linguistic meaning, by itself, was supposed to generate truth. Hence the play with the metaphysical concept of analyticity.

But this is, I believe, a futile project. In general, I have no idea what would constitute a better answer to the question: What is responsible for generating the truth of a given class of statements? than something bland like 'the world' or 'the facts'; and, for reasons that I have just been outlining, I cannot see how a good answer might be framed in terms of meaning, or convention, in particular.

So I have no sympathy with the linguistic theory of necessity or with its attendant Conventionalism. Unfortunately, the impression appears to be widespread that there is no way to disentangle that view from the analytic theory of the a priori; or, at a minimum, that there is no way to embrace the epistemic concept of analyticity without also embracing its metaphysical counterpart. I don't know whether Gil Harman believes something of the sort; he certainly gives the impression of doing so in his frequent suggestions that anyone deploying the notion of analyticity would have to be deploying both of its available readings simultaneously:

> It turned out that someone could be taught to make the analytic-synthetic distinction only by being taught a rather substantial theory, a theory including such principles as that meaning can make something true and that knowledge of meaning can give knowledge of truth.[11]

One of the main points of the present paper is that these two notions of analyticity are distinct and that the analytic theory of the a priori needs only the epistemological notion and has no use whatsoever for the metaphysical one. We can have an analytic theory of the a priori without in any way subscribing to a Conventionalism about anything. It is with the extended defense of this claim that much of the present essay is concerned.

The Epistemological Concept

Turning, then, to the epistemic notion of analyticity, we immediately confront a serious puzzle: How could any sentence be analytic in this sense? How could mere grasp of a sentence's meaning justify someone in holding it true?

Clearly, the answer to this question has to be *semantical:* something about the sentence's meaning, or about the way that meaning is fixed, must explain how its truth is knowable in this special way. What could this explanation be?

In the history of the subject, two different sorts of explanation have been especially important. Although these, too, have often been conflated, it is crucial to distinguish between them.

One idea was first formulated in full generality by Gottlob Frege. According to Frege, a statement's analyticity (in my epistemological sense) is to be explained by the fact that it is *transformable into a logical truth by the substitution of synonyms for synonyms*. When a statement satisfies this semantical condition, I shall say that it is 'Frege-analytic'.[12]

Now, it should be obvious that Frege-analyticity is at best an *incomplete* explanation of a statement's epistemic analyticity and, hence, of its apriority. For suppose that a given sentence **S** is Frege-analytic. How might this fact explain its analyticity? Clearly, two further assumptions are needed. First, that facts about synonymy are knowable a priori; and second, that the truths of logic are. Under the terms of these further assumptions, a satisfying explanation goes through. Given its Frege-analyticity, **S** is transformable into a logical truth by the substitution of synonyms for synonyms. Facts about synonymy are a priori, so it's a priori that **S** is so transformable. Furthermore, the sentence into which it is transformable is one whose truth is itself knowable a priori. Hence, **S**'s truth is knowable a priori.

Frege tended not to worry about these further assumptions, for two reasons. First, Frege thought it obviously constitutive of the idea of meaning, that meaning is transparent—that any competent user of two words would have to be able to know a priori whether or not they meant the same. Second, Frege also thought it obvious that there could be no substantive epistemology for logic—a fortiori, not one that could explain its apriority. As a consequence, he was happy to take logic's apriority for granted. For both of these reasons, he didn't worry about the fact that an explanation of apriority in terms of Frege-analyticity simply leaned on these further assumptions without explaining them.

I think the jury is still out on whether Frege was right to take these further assumptions for granted. There is certainly a very strong case to be made for the transparency of meaning.[13] And there are well-known difficulties providing a substantive epistemology for something as basic as logic, difficulties we shall have occasion to further review below. Nevertheless, because we cannot simply assume that Frege was right, we have to ask how a complete theory of the a priori would go about filling in the gaps left by the concept of Frege-analyticity.

I shall have very little to say about the first gap. The question whether facts about the sameness and difference of meaning are a priori cannot be discussed independently of the question what meaning is, and that is not an issue that I want to prejudge in the present context. On some views of meaning—for example, on certain conceptual role views—the apriority of synonymy is simply a by-product of the very nature of meaning facts, so that no substantive epistemology for synonymy is necessary or, indeed, possible. On other views—for example, on most externalist views of meaning—synonymy is not a priori, so there is no question of a sentence's Frege-analyticity fully explaining its epistemic analyticity.

Since this issue about the apriority of synonymy turns on questions that are currently unresolved, I propose to leave it for now. As we shall see, none of the analyticity-skeptical considerations we shall consider exploit it in any way. (Quine never argues that the trouble with Frege-analyticity is that synonymies are a posteriori.)

Putting aside, then, skepticism about the apriority of synonymy, and, for the moment anyway, skepticism about the very existence of Frege-analytic sentences, let us ask quite generally: What class of a priori statement would an account based on the notion of Frege-analyticity *fail* to explain?

Two classes come to mind. On the one hand, a priori statements that are not transformable into logical truths by the substitution of synonyms for synonyms; and, on the other hand, a priori statements that are trivially so transformable.

Taking the first class first, there do appear to be a significant number of a priori statements that are not Frege-analytic. For example:

Whatever is red all over is not blue.
Whatever is colored is extended.
If x is warmer than y, then y is not warmer than x.

These statements appear not to be transformable into logical truths by the appropriate substitutions: the ingredient descriptive terms seem not to be decomposable in the appropriate way.

The second class of recalcitrant statements consists precisely of the truths of logic. The truths of logic satisfy, of course, the conditions on Frege-analyticity. But they satisfy them trivially. And it seems obvious that we can't hope to explain our warrant for belief in the truths of logic by appealing to their analyticity in this sense: knowledge of Frege-analyticity presupposes knowledge of logical truth and so can't explain it.

How, then, is the epistemic analyticity of these recalcitrant truths to be explained? As we shall see below, the solution proposed by Carnap and the middle Wittgenstein turns on the suggestion that they are to be viewed as *implicit definitions* of their ingredient terms. When a statement satisfies this semantical condition, I shall sometimes say that it is 'Carnap-analytic'. However, before proceeding to a discussion of Carnap-analyticity, I want to re-examine Quine's famous rejection of the much weaker concept of Frege-analyticity.[14]

II

"Two Dogmas" and the Rejection of Frege-analyticity

For all its apparent limitations, the concept of Frege-analyticity is not without interest. Even though Quine made it fashionable to claim otherwise, the sentence "All bachelors are male," *does* seem to be transformable into a logical truth by the substitution of synonyms for synonyms and that fact *does* seem to have something important to do with its apriority. If, then, appearances are not misleading here, and a significant range of a priori statements are Frege-analytic, then the problem of their apriority is *reduced* to that of the apriority of logic and synonymy and, in this way, a significant economy in explanatory burden is achieved.

It was, therefore, an important threat to the analytic theory of the a priori to find Quine arguing, in one of the most celebrated articles of this century, that the apriority of no sentence could be explained by appeal to its Frege-analyticity, because no sentence of a natural language could *be* Frege-analytic.

It has not been sufficiently appreciated, it seems to me, that "Two Dogmas," is exclusively concerned with this weaker notion of Frege-analyticity, and not at all with the more demanding project of explaining the apriority of logic. But this is made very clear by Quine:

> Statements which are analytic by general philosophical acclaim are not, indeed, far to seek. They fall into two classes. Those of the first class, which may be called *logically true*, are typified by:
>
> (1) No unmarried man is married.

> The relevant feature of this example is that it is not merely true as it stands, but remains true under any and all reinterpretations of 'man' and 'married'. If we suppose a prior inventory of *logical* particles . . . then in general a logical truth is a statement that remains true under all reinterpretations of its components other than the logical particles.
>
> But there is also a second class of analytic statements, typified by:
>
> (2) No bachelor is married.
>
> The characteristic of such a statement is that it can be turned into a logical truth by putting synonyms for synonyms. (pp. 22–23)

Quine goes on to say very clearly:

> Our problem . . . is analyticity; and here the major difficulty lies not in the first class of analytic statements, the logical truths, but rather in the second class, which depends on the notion of synonymy. (p. 24)

Most of the rest of TD is devoted to arguing that no good sense can be made of such analyticities of the 'second class'.

None of this would make any sense unless Quine were intending in "Two Dogmas" to be restricting himself solely to the notion of Frege-analyticity. Of course, it is the point of two other important papers of his—"Truth by Convention" and "Carnap and Logical Truth"—to argue that there is no non-trivial sense in which *logic* is analytic. We will turn to that issue in due course. Relative to the Fregean notion, however, the logical truths are trivially analytic; and so, given his apparent desire to restrict his attention to that notion in TD, he simply concedes their 'analyticity' in the only sense he takes to be under discussion. What he wishes to resist in TD, he insists, is merely the claim that there are any *nontrivial instances of Frege-analyticity*.[15]

Skeptical Theses about Analyticity

What form does Quine's resistance take? We may agree that the result being advertised isn't anything modest, of the form: There are fewer analyticities than we had previously thought. Or, there are some analytic truths, but they are not important for the purposes of science. Or anything else of a similar ilk. Rather, as a very large number of Quine's remarks make clear, the sought-after result is something ambitious to the effect that the notion of Frege-analyticity is, somehow or other, not cogent. TD's many admirers have divided on whether to read this as the claim that the notion of Frege-analyticity does not have a well-defined, determinate factual content, or whether to read it merely as claiming that, although it has an intelligible content, it is necessarily uninstantiated. I'll call the first claim a *Non-factualism* about analyticity:

(NF) No coherent, determinate property is expressed by the predicate 'is analytic' (or, since these are correlative terms, the predicate 'is synthetic'); consequently, no coherent factual claim is expressed by sentences of the form 'S is analytic' and 'S is synthetic.'

And the second an *Error Thesis* about analyticity:

(ET) There is a coherent, determinate property expressed by 'is analytic', but it is necessarily uninstantiated; consequently, all sentences of the form 'S is analytic' are necessarily false.[16]

Regardless, however, of how TD's skepticism about Frege-analyticity is understood, I don't see how either thesis can plausibly stop short of a radical indeterminacy about meaning.

Non-Factualism about Frege-Analyticity

Let's begin with the non-factualist version. To say that there is no such property as the property of Frege-analyticity is essentially to say that, for *any* sentence, there is no fact of the matter as to whether it is transformable into a logical truth by the substitution of synonyms for synonyms. Presumably, this itself is possible only if, either there is no fact of the matter as to what counts as a logical truth, or no fact of the matter as to when two expressions are synonymous. Since the factuality of logic is not in dispute, the only option is a non-factualism about synonymy.

But, now, how can there fail to be facts about whether any two expressions mean the same—even where these are drawn from within a *single* speaker's idiolect, so that no questions of *inter*linguistic synonymy arise? Wouldn't this have to entail that there are no facts about what each expression means individually? Putting the question the other way: Could there be a fact of the matter about what each expression means, but no fact of the matter about whether they mean the same?[17]

Let's consider this question first against the background of an unQuinean relational construal of meaning, according to which an expression's meaning something is a relation **M** between it and its meaning, the meaning **C**. Someone who held that a non-factualism about synonymy could co-exist with a determinacy about meaning would have to hold that, although it might be true that some specific word—say, "cow"—bears some specific relation **M** to some specific meaning **C**, there is no fact of the matter about whether some *other* word—some other orthographically identified particular—bears precisely the same relation to precisely the same meaning.

But how could this be? How could it conceivably turn out that it is intelligible and true to say that "cow" bears **M** to **C**, and not merely false but *nonfactual* to say that some other word—"vache" as it may be—also does? What could be so special about the letters "c", "o", "w"?

The answer, of course, is that there is nothing special about them. If it is factual that one word bears **M** to **C**, it is surely factual that some other word does. Especially on a relational construal of meaning, it makes no sense to suppose that a determinacy about meaning could coexist with a non-factualism about synonymy.

The question naturally arises whether this result is forthcoming *only* against the background of a relational construal of meaning. I think it's quite clear that the answer is 'No'. To see why, suppose that instead of construing meaning facts as involving relations to meanings we construe them thus: "cow" means *cow* just in case "cow" has the monadic property **R**—a history of use, a disposition, or whatever your favorite candidate may be. Precisely the same arguments go through: it remains equally difficult to see how, given that "cow" has property **R**, it could fail to be factual whether some other word does.

The Error Thesis about Frege-Analyticity

I think, then, that if a plausible skepticism about Frege-analyticity is to be sustained, it cannot take the form of a non-factualism. Does an Error thesis fare any better? According to this view, although there are determinate facts about which sentences are transformable into logical truths by the appropriate manipulations of synonymy, this property is necessarily uninstantiated: it is nomically impossible for there to be any Frege-analytic sentences. Our question is: Does at least this form of skepticism about Frege-analyticity avoid collapse into the indeterminacy doctrine?

Well, I suppose that if we are being very strict about it, we may have to admit that it is barely *logically possible* to combine a denial of indeterminacy with an error thesis about synonymy, so that we can say that although there are determinate facts about what means what, it is impossible for any two things to mean the same thing. But is such a view plausible? Do we have any reason for believing it? I think not.

Let's begin with the fact that even Quine has to admit that it is possible for two *tokens of the same orthographic type* to be synonymous, for that much is presupposed by his own account of logical truth.[18]

What about two tokens of different types? Here again, our own argument can proceed from Quine's own admissions. For even Quine concedes that two expressions can mean the same thing, provided that they are explicitly stipulated to mean the same thing.[19] So his skepticism about synonymy has to boil down to the following somewhat peculiar claim: Although there is such a thing as the property of synonymy; and although it can be instantiated by pairs of tokens of the same orthographic type; and although it can be instantiated by pairs of tokens of distinct orthographic types, provided that they are related to each other by way of an explicit stipulation; it is, nevertheless, in principle impossible to generate instances of this property in some other way, via some other mechanism. For example, it is impossible that two expressions that were introduced independently of each other into the language, should have been introduced with exactly the same meanings.

But what conceivable rationale could there be for such a claim? As far as I am able to tell, there is precisely one argument in the literature that is supposed to provide support for it. It may be represented as follows:

Premise: Meaning is radically holistic in the sense that: "What our words mean depends on *everything* we believe, on *all* the assumptions we are making."[20]

Therefore,

Conclusion: It is very unlikely that, in any given language, there will be two words of distinct types that mean exactly the same thing.

I am inclined to agree that this argument (properly spelled out) is valid, and so, that if a radical holism about meaning were true, then synonymies between expressions of different types would be rare.

However, I note that "rare" does not mean the same as "impossible," which is the result we were promised. And, much more importantly, I am completely inclined to disagree that TD provides any sort of cogent argument for meaning holism in the first place.

It's easy to see why, if such a radical meaning holism were true, synonymies might be hard to come by. For although it is not unimaginable, it is unlikely that two words of distinct types will participate in *all* of the same beliefs and inferences. Presumably there will always be some beliefs that will discriminate between them—beliefs about their respective shapes, for example.

But what reason do we have for believing that *all* of a word's uses are constitutive of its meaning?

Many Quineans seem to hold that the crucial argument for this intuitively implausible view is to be found in the concluding sections of TD. In those concluding sections, Quine argues powerfully for the epistemological claim that has come to be known as the Quine-Duhem thesis: confirmation is holisitic in that the warrant for any given sentence depends on the warrant for every other sentence. In those concluding sections, Quine also assumes a Verificationist theory of meaning, according to which the meaning of a sentence is fixed by its method of confirmation. Putting these two theses together, one can speedily arrive at the view that a word's meaning depends on *all* of its inferential links to other words, and hence at the thesis of meaning-holism.[21]

This, however, is not a very convincing train of thought. First, and not all that importantly, this couldn't have been the argument that *Quine* intended against Frege-analyticity, for this argument for meaning holism is to be found in the very last pages of TD, well after the rejection of Frege-analyticity is taken to have been established.

Second, and more importantly, the argument is not very compelling because it depends crucially on a verificationism about meaning, a view that we have every good reason to reject, and which has in fact been rejected by most contemporary philosophers.

Finally, and perhaps most importantly, any such holism-based argument against the possibility of synonymy would need to be supported by something that no one has ever provided—a reason for believing that yielding such an intuitively implausible result about synonymy isn't itself simply a *reductio* of meaning holism.[22]

III

The Analyticity of Logic

If the preceding considerations are correct, then there is no principled objection to the existence of Frege-analyticities, and, hence, no principled objection to the existence of statements that are knowable a priori if logical truth is.[23]

But what about logical truth? Is it knowable a priori? And, if so, how?[24]

In the case of some logical truths, the explanation for how we have come to know them will be clear: we will have deduced them from others. So our question concerns only the most elementary laws of sentential or first-order logic. How do we know a priori, for example, that all the instances of the law of non-contradiction are true, or that all the instances of modus ponens are valid?

As I noted above, Frege thought it obvious that there could be no substantive answer to such questions; he was inclined, therefore, to take appearances at face value and to simply *assume* the apriority of logic.

What Frege probably has in mind is the following worry. 'Explaining our knowledge of logic' presumably involves finding some *other* thing that we know, on the basis of which our knowledge of logic is to be explained. However, regardless of what that other thing is taken to be, it's hard to see how the use of logic is to be avoided in moving from knowledge of that thing to knowledge of the relevant logical truth. And so it can come to seem as if any account of how we know logic will have to end up being vacuous, presupposing that we have the very capacity that's to be explained.

Michael Dummett has disputed the existence of a real problem here. As he has pointed out, the sort of circularity that's at issue isn't the gross circularity of an argument that consists of including the conclusion that's to be reached among the premisses. Rather, we have an argument that purports to prove the validity of a given logical law, at least one of whose inferential steps must be taken in accordance with that law. Dummett calls this a "pragmatic" circularity. He goes on to claim that a pragmatic circularity of this sort will be damaging only to a justificatory argument that

> is addressed to someone who genuinely doubts whether the law is valid, and is intended to persuade him that it is. . . . If, on the other hand, it is intended to satisfy the philosopher's perplexity about our entitlement to reason in accordance with such a law, it may well do so.[25]

The question whether Dummett's distinction fully allays Frege's worry is a large one, and I can't possibly hope to settle it here. If something along these general lines can't be made to work, then *any* explanation of logic's apriority—or aposteriority, for that matter—is bound to be futile, and the Fregean attitude will have been vindicated.

However, the question that particularly interests me in the present essay is this: Assuming that the very enterprise of explaining our knowledge of logic isn't shown to be hopeless by Frege's straightforward argument, is there any *special* reason for doubting an explanation based on the notion of analyticity? Quine's enormously influential claim was that there is. I shall try to argue that there isn't—that, in an important sense to be specified later on, our grasp of the meaning of logical claims can explain our a priori warrant for holding them true (provided that the Fregean worry doesn't defeat all such explanations in the first place).

The Classical View and Implicit Definition

It's important to understand, it seems to me, that the analytic theory of the apriority of logic arose indirectly, as a by-product of the attempt to explain in what a grasp of the meaning of the logical constants consists. Alberto Coffa lays this story out very nicely in his recent book.[26]

What account are we to give of our grasp of the logical constants, given that they are not to explicitly definable in terms of *other* concepts? Had they been explicitly definable, of course, we would have been able to say—however plausibly—that we grasp them by grasping their definitions. But as practically anybody who has thought about the matter has recognized, the logical constants are not explicitly definable in terms of other concepts, and so we are barred from giving that account. The question is, what account are we to give?

Historically, many philosophers were content to suggest that the state of grasping these constants was somehow primitive, not subject to further explanation. In particular, such a grasp of the meaning of, say, 'not', was to be thought of as prior to, and independent of, a decision on our part as to which of the various sentences involving 'not' to count as true. We may call this view, following Wittgenstein's lead, the doctrine of

Flash-Grasping: We grasp the meaning of, say, 'not' "in a flash"—prior to, and independently of, deciding which of the sentences involving 'not' are true.

On this historically influential picture, Flash-Grasping was combined with the doctrine of Intuition to generate an epistemology for logic:

Intuition: This grasp of the concept of, say, negation, along with our intuition of its logical properties, explains and justifies our logical beliefs involving negation—e.g., that 'If not not p, then p' is true.

As Coffa shows, this picture began to come under severe strain with the development of alternative geometries. Naturally enough, an analogous set of views had been used to explain the apriority of geometry. In particular, a flash-grasp of the indefinables of geometry, along with intuitions concerning their necessary properties, was said to explain and justify belief in the axioms of Euclidean geometry.

However, with the development of alternative geometries, such a view faced an unpleasant dilemma. Occupying one horn was the option of saying that Euclidean and non-Euclidean geometries are talking about the *same* geometrical properties, but disagreeing about what is true of them. But this option threatens the thesis of Intuition: If in fact we learn geometrical truths by intuition, how could this faculty have misled us for so long?

Occupying the other horn was the option of saying that Euclidean and non-Euclidean geometries are talking about *different* geometrical properties—attaching different meanings to, say, 'distance'—and so not disagreeing after all. But this option threatens the doctrine of Flash-Grasping. Suppose we grant that a Euclidean and a non-Euclidean geometer attach different meanings to 'distance'. In what does the difference in the respective psychological states consist? Officially, of course, the view is that one primitive state constitutes grasp of Euclidean distance, and another that of non-Euclidean distance. But absent some further detail about how to tell such states apart and the criteria that govern their attribution, this would appear to be a hopelessly ad hoc and non-explanatory maneuver.

The important upshot of these considerations was to make plausible the idea that grasp of the indefinables of geometry consists precisely in the adoption of one set of truths involving them, as opposed to another. Applied to the case of logic, it generates the semantical thesis that I shall call

Implicit definition: It is by arbitrarily stipulating that certain sentences of logic are to be true, or that certain inferences are to be valid, that we attach a meaning to the logical constants. More specifically, a particular constant means that logical object, if any, which makes valid a specified set of sentences and/or inferences involving it.

Now, the transition from this sort of implicit definition account of grasp, to the analytic theory of the apriority of logic, can seem pretty immediate. For it would seem that the following sort of argument is now in place:

1. If logical constant **C** is to mean what it does, then argument-form **A** has to be valid, for **C** means whatever logical object in fact makes **A** valid.
2. **C** means what it does.

Therefore,

3. **A** is valid.

I will return to various questions regarding this form of justification below.[27] For now I want to worry about the fact that neither Carnap nor Wittgenstein was content merely to replace Flash Grasping with Implicit Definition. Typically, both writers went on to embrace some form of anti-realism about logic. Intuitively, the statements of logic appear to be fully factual statements, expressing objective truths about the world, even if necessary ones, and even if (on occasion) highly obvious ones. Both Carnap and Wittgenstein, however, seemed inclined to deny such an intuitive realism about logic, affirming in its place either the thesis of logical Non-Factualism or the thesis of logical Conventionalism, or, on occasion, both theses at once.

By *logical* Non-Factualism[28], I mean the view that the sentences of logic that implicitly define the logical primitives do not express factual claims and, hence, are not capable of genuine truth or falsity. How, on such a view, are we to think of their semantic function? On the most popular version, we are to think of it as prescriptive, as a way of expressing a rule concerning the correct use of logical expressions. By contrast, logical Conventionalism is the view that, although the sentences of logic are factual—although they can express truths—their truth values are not objective, but are rather determined by our conventions.

Despite this important difference between them, there is an interesting sense in which the upshot of both views is the same, a fact that probably explains why they were often used interchangeably and why they often turn up simultaneously in the analytic theory of logic. For what both views imply is that, as between two different sets of decisions regarding which sentences of logic to hold true, there can be no epistemic fact of the matter. In short, both views imply an epistemic relativism about logic. Conventionalism implies this because it says that the truth in logic is up to us, so no substantive disagreement is possible; and Non-Factualism implies this because it says that there are no truths in logic, hence nothing to disagree about.

Nevertheless, for all this affinity of upshot, it should be quite plain that the two views are very different from each other—indeed, incompatible with each other. Conventionalism is a factualist view: it presupposes that the sentences of logic have truth values. It differs from a realist view of logic in its conception of the *source* of those truth values, not on their existence. Therefore, although it is possible, as I have noted, to find texts in which a rule-prescriptivism about logic is combined with Conventionalism, that can only be a confusion.

The important question is: Why did the proponents of Implicit Definition feel the need to go beyond it all the way to the far more radical doctrines of Non-Factualism and/or Conventionalism? Whatever problems it may eventually be discovered to harbor, Implicit Definition seems like a plausible candidate for explaining our grasp of the logical constants, especially in view of the difficulties encountered by its classical rival. But there would appear to be little that prima facie recommends either Nonfactualism or Conventionalism. So why combine these dubious doctrines with what looks to be a plausible theory of meaning?

Apparently, both Carnap and Wittgenstein seem to have thought that the issue was forced, that Implicit Definition entailed one or the other anti-realist thesis. It seems quite clear that Carnap, for example, believed that Implicit Definition brought Conventionalism immediately in its wake; and Quine seems to have agreed. What separated them was their attitude towards Conventionalism. Carnap embraced it; Quine, by contrast, seems to have been prepared to reject any premise that led to it; hence his assault on the doctrine of Implicit Definition.

But if this is in fact the correct account of Quine's motivations, then they are based, I believe, on a false assumption, for neither form of anti-realism about logic follows from the thesis of Implicit Definition.

I will proceed as follows. First, I will argue that Implicit Definition, properly understood, is completely independent of any form of anti-realism about logic. Second, I will defend the thesis of Implicit Definition against Quine's criticisms. Finally, I will examine the sort of account of the apriority of logic that this doctrine is able to provide.

Implicit Definition and Non-Factualism

Does Implicit Definition entail Non-Factualism? It is certainly very common to come across the claim that it does. Coffa, for instance, writes that from the new perspective afforded by the doctrine of Implicit Definition, the basic claims of logic are

> our access to certain meanings, definitions in disguise, devices that allow us to implement an explicit or tacit decision to constitute certain concepts. . . . From this standpoint, necessary claims do not tell us anything that is the case both in the world and in many others, as Leibniz thought, or anything that is the case for *formal* reasons, whatever that might mean, or anything that one is forced to believe due to features of our mind. They do not tell us anything that is the case; so they had better not be called claims or propositions. Since their role is to constitute meanings and since (apparently) we are free to endorse them or not, it is better to abandon the old terminology (a priori "principles", "laws," etc.) that misleadingly suggests a propositional status and to refer to them as "rules." (pp. 265–266)

I have no desire to engage the exegetical issues here; as far as I can tell, the middle Wittgenstein seems very much to have been a non-factualist about the implicit definers of logic, just as Coffa says. What I dispute is that it *follows* from the fact that a given sentence **Q** is being used to implicitly define one of its ingredient terms, that **Q** is not a factual sentence, not a sentence that "tells us anything that is the case." These two claims seem to me to be entirely independent of each other.

To help us think about this, consider Kripke's example of the introduction of the term 'meter'. As Kripke imagines it, someone introduces the term into his vocabulary by stipulating that the following sentence is to be true:

[1] Stick **S** is a meter long at **t**.

Suppose that stick **S** exists and is a certain length at **t**. Then it follows that 'meter' names that length and hence that [1] says that stick S is that length at t, and since it is that length at t, [1] is true.

Knowing all this may not be much of an epistemic achievement, but that isn't the point. The point is that there appears to be no inconsistency whatsoever between claiming that a given sentence serves to implicitly define an ingredient term and claiming that that very sentence expresses something factual.

Similarly, I don't see that there is any inconsistency between supposing that a given logical principle—for instance, the law of excluded middle—serves to implicitly define an ingredient logical constant, and supposing that that very sentence expresses a factual statement capable of genuine truth and falsity.[29]

Implicit Definition and Conventionalism

So far I have argued that it is consistent with a sentence's serving as an implicit definer that that very sentence come to express a fully factual claim, capable of genuine truth and falsity. Perhaps, however, when implicit definition is at issue, the truth of the claim that is thereby fixed has to be thought of as conventionally determined? Does at least Conventionalism follow from Implicit Definition?[30]

It is easy to see, I suppose, why these two ideas might have been run together. For according to Implicit Definition, 'if, then', for example, comes to mean the conditional precisely by my assigning the truth value True to certain basic sentences involving it, for example, to

If, if **p** then **q**, and **p**, then **q**.

And in an important sense, my assigning this sentence the value True is arbitrary. Prior to my assigning it that truth value, it didn't have a complete meaning, for one of its ingredient terms didn't have a meaning at all. The process of assigning it the value True is simply part of what fixes its meaning. Had I assigned it the value False, the sentence would then have had a *different* meaning. So, prior to the assignment there couldn't have been a substantive question regarding its truth value. And after the assignment there couldn't be a substantive question as to whether that assignment was correct. In this sense, then, the sentence's truth value is arbitrary and conventional. Doesn't it follow, then, that Implicit Definition entails Conventionalism?

Not at all. All that is involved in the thesis of Implicit Definition is the claim that the conventional assignment of truth to a sentence determines what claim that sentence expresses (if any); such a view is entirely silent about what (if anything) determines the truth of the claim that is thereby expressed—a fortiori, it is silent about whether our conventions determine it.

Think here again of Kripke's meter stick. If the stick exists and has such-and-so length at **t**, then it is conventional that 'meter' names that length and, therefore, conventional that [1] expresses the proposition stick ***S*** *has such-and-so length at* ***t***. However, that stick **S** has that length at **t** is hardly a fact generated by convention; it presumably had that length prior to the convention, and may continue to have it well after the convention has lapsed.[31]

I anticipate the complaint that the entailment between Implicit Definition and Conventionalism is blocked only through the tacit use of a distinction between a sentence and the proposition it expresses, a distinction that neither Carnap nor Quine would have approved.

Such a complaint would be mistaken, however. The argument I gave relies not so much on a distinction between a sentence and a proposition in the technical sense disapproved of by Quine, as on a distinction between a sentence and *what it expresses*. And it is hard to see how any adequate philosophy of language is to get by without some such distinction.[32] Even on a deflationary view of truth, there is presumably a distinction between the *sentence* 'Snow is white' and that which makes the sentence true, namely, snow's being white. And the essential point for my purposes is that it is one thing to say that 'Snow is white' comes to express the claim that snow is white as a result of being conventionally assigned the truth value True; and quite another to say that snow comes to be white as a result of our conventions. The first claim is Implicit Definition (however implausibly applied in this case); and the other is Conventionalism. Neither one seems to me to entail the other.

Quine against Implicit Definition: Regress

As I noted above, I am inclined to believe that erroneous opinion on this score has played an enormous role in the history of this subject. I conjecture that had Quine felt more confident that Implicit Definition could be sharply distinguished from Conventionalism, he might not have felt so strongly against it.

In any event, though, whatever the correct explanation of Quine's animus, we are indebted to him for a series of powerful critiques of the thesis of Implicit Definition, critiques that have persuaded many that that thesis, and with it any explanation of the apriority of logic that it might be able to ground, are fundamentally flawed. We must now confront Quine's arguments.

According to Implicit Definition, the logical constants come to have a particular meaning in our vocabulary by our conventionally stipulating that certain sentences (or inferences) involving them are to be true. For instance, let us assume that the meaning for 'and' is fixed by our stipulating that the following inferences involving it are to be valid:

$$[2] \qquad \frac{\text{A and B}}{\text{A}} \qquad \frac{\text{A and B}}{\text{B}} \qquad \frac{\text{A, B}}{\text{A and B}}$$

Now, Quine's first important criticism of this idea occurs in his early paper 'Truth by Convention'.[33] As Quine there pointed out, there are an infinite number of instances of schema [2]. Consequently, the inferences of this infinitary collection could not have been conventionally stipulated to be valid singly, one by one. Rather, Quine argued, if there is anything at all to this idea, it must be something along the following lines: We adopt certain general conventions from which it follows that all the sentences of the infinitary collection are assigned the value Valid. Such a general convention would presumably look like this:

> Let all results of putting a statement for 'p' and a statement for 'q' in 'p and q implies p' be valid.

However, the trouble is that in order to state such a general convention we have had, unavoidably, to use all sorts of logical terms—'every', 'and', and so on. So the claim, essential to the proposal under consideration, that all our logical constants acquire their meaning via the adoption of such explicitly formulated conventional assignments of validity must fail. Logical constants whose meaning is not fixed in this way are presupposed by the model itself.[34]

This argument of Quine's has been very influential; and I think that there is no doubt that it works against its target as specified. However, it is arguable that its target as specified isn't the view that needs defeating.

For, surely, it isn't compulsory to think of someone's following a rule **R** with respect to an expression **e** as consisting in his *explicitly stating* that rule in so many words in the way that Quine's argument presupposes. On the contrary, it seems far more plausible to construe **x**'s following rule **R** with respect to **e** as consisting in some sort of fact about **x**'s *behavior* with **e**.

In what would such a fact consist? Here there are at least a couple of options. According to a currently popular idea, following rule **R** with respect to **e** may consist in our being disposed to conform to rule **R** in our employment of **e**, under certain circumstances. On this version, the notion of rule-following would have been *reduced* to a certain sort of dispositional fact. Alternatively, one might wish to appeal to the notion of following a given rule, while resisting the claim that it can be reduced to a set of naturalistically acceptable dispositional facts. On such a non-reductionist version, there would be facts about what rule one is following, even if these are not cashable into facts about one's behavioral dispositions, however optimal.

For myself, I am inclined to think that the reductionist version won't work, that we will have to employ the notion of following a rule unreduced.[35] But because it is more familiar, and because nothing substantive hangs on it in the present context, I will work with the reductionist version of rule-following. Applied to the case we are considering, it issues in what is widely known in the literature as a "conceptual role semantics."

According to this view, then, the logical constants mean what they do by virtue of figuring in certain inferences and/or sentences involving them and not in others. If some expressions mean what they do by virtue of figuring in certain inferences and sentences, then some inferences and sentences are *constitutive* of an expression's meaning what it does, and others aren't. And any CRS must find a systematic way of saying which are which, of answering the question: What properties must an inference or sentence involving a constant **C** have, if that inference or sentence is to be constitutive of **C**'s meaning?

Quine against Implicit Definition: Constitutive Truth

Now, Quine's second objection to Implicit Definition can be put by saying that there will be no way of doing what I said any CRS must do—namely, systematically specify the meaning-constituting inferences. Quine formulated this point in a number of places. Here is a version that appears in 'Carnap and Logical Truth':

> if we try to warp the linguistic doctrine of logical truth into something like an experimental thesis, perhaps a first approximation will run thus: *Deductively irresoluble disagreement as to a logical truth is evidence of deviation in usage (or meanings) of words.* . . . [However] the obviousness or potential obviousness of elementary logic can be seen to present an insuperable obstacle to our assigning any experimental meaning to the linguistic doctrine of elementary logical truth. . . . For, that theory now seems to imply nothing that is not already implied by the fact that elementary logic is obvious or can be resolved into obvious steps.[36]

Elsewhere, Quine explained his use of the word "obvious" in this connection thus:

> In "Carnap and Logical Truth" I claimed that Carnap's arguments for the linguistic doctrine of logical truth boiled down to saying no more than that they were obvious, or potentially obvious—that is, generable from obvieties by obvious steps. I had been at pains to select the word 'obvious' from the vernacular, intending it as I did in the vernacular sense. A sentence is obvious if (a) it is true and (b) any speaker of the language is prepared, for any reason or none, to assent to it without hesitation, unless put off by being asked so obvious a question.[37]

Quine's important point here is that there will be no substantive way of distinguishing between a highly obvious, non-defining sentence and a sentence that is an implicit definer. Both types of sentence—if in fact both types exist—will have the feature that any speaker of the language will be prepared to assent to instances of them, "for any reason or none." So in what does the alleged difference between them consist? How is distinctive content to be given to the doctrine of Implicit Definition?[38]

Now, there is no doubt that this is a very good question; and the impression that it has no good answer has contributed greatly to the rejection of the doctrine of Implicit Definition. Jerry Fodor and Ernie Lepore, for example, base the entirety of their recent argument against a conceptual role semantics on their assumption that Quine showed this question to be unanswerable.[39]

If Quine's challenge is allowed to remain unanswered, then the threat to the analytic theory of the a priori is fairly straightforward. For if there is no fact of the matter as to whether **S** is a sentence that I must hold true if **S** is to mean what it does, then there is no basis on which to argue that I am entitled to hold **S** true without evidence.

But that would seem to be the least of our troubles, if Quine's argument is allowed to stand. For what's threatened is not only the apriority of logical truths but, far more extremely, the *determinacy* of what they claim. For as I've already pointed out, and as many philosophers are anyway inclined to believe, a conceptual role semantics seems to be the *only* plausible view about how the meaning of the logical constants is fixed. It follows, therefore, that if there is no fact of the matter as to which of the various inferences involving a constant are meaning-constituting, then there is also no fact of the matter as to what the logical constants themselves mean. And that, again, is just the dreaded indeterminacy of meaning on which the critique of analyticity was supposed not to depend.

The simple point here is that if the only view available about how the logical constants acquire their meaning is in terms of the inferences and/or sentences that they participate in, then any indeterminacy in what those meaning-constituting sentences and inferences are will translate into an indeterminacy about the meanings of the expressions themselves. This realization should give pause to any philosopher who thinks he can buy in on Quine's critique of implicit definition without following him all the way to the far headier doctrine of meaning-indeterminacy.

There has been a curious tendency to miss this relatively simple point. Jerry Fodor seems a particularly puzzling case. For Fodor holds all three of the following views. (1) He rejects indeterminacy, arguing forcefully against it. (2) He follows Quine in rejecting the notion of a meaning-constituting inference. (3) He holds a conceptual role view of the meanings of the logical constants. As far as I am able to judge, however, this combination of views is not consistent.[40]

Part of the explanation for this curious blindness derives from a tendency to view Quine's argument as issuing not in an indeterminacy about meaning, but, rather, in a *holism* about it. In fact, according to Fodor and Lepore, the master argument for meaning holism in the literature runs as follows:

A. Some of an expression's inferential liaisons are relevant to fixing its meaning.
B. There is no principled distinction between those inferential liaisons that are constitutive and those that aren't. (The Quinean result.)

Therefore,

C. All of an expression's inferential liaisons are relevant to fixing its meaning. (Meaning Holism)

Fearing this argument's validity, and seeing no way to answer Quine's challenge, they spend their whole book trying to undermine the argument's first premise, namely, the very plausible claim that at least *some* of an expression's inferential liaisons are relevant to fixing its meaning.[41]

But they needn't have bothered, for I don't see how the master argument could be valid in the first place. The claim that *all* of an expression's inferential liaisons are constitutive of it cannot cogently follow from the claim that it is *indeterminate* what the constitutive inferences are. If it's *indeterminate* what the constitutive inferences are, then it's genuinely *unsettled* what they are. And that is inconsistent with saying that they are *all* constitutive, and inconsistent with saying that *none* are constitutive and inconsistent with saying that some specified subset are constitutive.

Fodor and Lepore are not alone in not seeing the problem here. Let me cite just one more example. In his comments on an earlier version of the present paper, Gil Harman says:

> Can one accept Quine's argument against analyticity without being committed to the indeterminacy of meaning? Yes and no. By the "indeterminacy of meaning" might be meant an indeterminacy as to which of the principles one accepts determine the meanings of one's terms and which simple reflect one's opinions about the facts. Clearly, Quine's argument against analyticity is committed to that sort of indeterminacy. [However] that by itself does not imply full indeterminacy in the sense of Chapter Two of *Word and Object*.[42]

As Harman correctly says, Quine has to deny that there is a fact of the matter as to which of **T**'s principles determine the meanings of his terms and which simply reflect **T**'s opinions about the facts—that, after all, is just what it is to deny that there are facts about constitutivity. However, Harman insists, this denial in no way leads to the indeterminacy thesis of Chapter Two of *Word and Object*.

But this is very puzzling. Against the background of a conceptual role semantics, according to which the meaning of **T**'s term **C** is determined precisely by a certain subset of the principles involving **C** that **T** accepts, an indeterminacy in what the meaning-determining principles are will automatically lead to an indeterminacy in what the meaning is—in the full sense of Chapter Two of *Word and Object*. If a subset (not necessarily proper) of accepted principles is supposed to determine meaning; and if there is no fact of the matter as to which subset that is; then there is, to that extent, no fact of the matter as to what meaning has been determined.

I think there is really no avoiding the severe conclusion that meaning is indeterminate, if the Quinean challenge to constitutivity is allowed to remain unanswered. I'm inclined to think, therefore, that anyone who rejects radical indeterminacy of meaning must believe that a distinction between the meaning-constituting and the non-meaning-constituting can be drawn. The only question is how.

Well, that is not the task of the present paper. Although there are some good ideas about this, I don't have a fully thought-through proposal to present just now.[43] My main aim here is not to *solve* the fundamental problem for a conceptual role semantics for the logical constants; rather, as I have stressed, it is to show that, against the background of a rejection of indeterminacy, its insolubility cannot be conceded.

Pending the discovery of other problems, then, it seems open to us to suppose that a plausible theory of meaning for the logical constants is given by something like the following:

A logical constant **C** expresses that logical object, if any, that makes valid its meaning-constituting inferences.

Implicit Definition, Justification and Entitlement

Now, how does any of this help vindicate the analytic theory of the apriority of logic, the idea that logic is epistemically analytic? Let us consider a particular inference form, **A**, in a particular thinker's (**T**) repertoire; and let's suppose that that inference form is constitutive of the meaning of one of its ingredient constants **C**. How, exactly, might these facts help explain the epistemic analyticity of **A** for **T**?

To say that A is epistemically analytic for **T** is to say that **T**'s knowledge of **A**'s meaning alone suffices for **T**'s justification for **A**, so that empirical support is not required. And it does seem that a conceptual role semantics can provide us with a model of how that might be so. For given the relevant facts, we would appear to be able to argue as follows:

1. If **C** is to mean what it does, then **A** has to be valid, for **C** means whatever logical object in fact makes **A** valid.
2. **C** means what it does.

Therefore,

3. **A** is valid.

Now, it is true that this is tantamount to a fairly broad use of the phrase "knowledge of the meaning of **A**," for this knowledge includes not merely knowledge of what **A** means, strictly so-called, but also knowledge of how that meaning is fixed. But this is, of course, both predictable and unavoidable: there was never any real prospect of explaining apriority merely on the basis of a knowledge of propositional content. Even Carnap realized that one needed to know that a given inference or sentence had the status of a 'meaning postulate'.

But isn't it required, if this account is to genuinely explain **T**'s a priori justification for the basic truths of logic, that **T** know the premisses a priori as well? Yet, it hasn't been shown that **T** can know the premisses a priori.

It is quite correct that I have not attempted to show that the relevant facts about meaning cited in the premisses are knowable a priori, although I believe that it is intuitively quite clear that they are. I have purposely avoided discussing all issues relating to knowledge of meaning facts. My brief here has been to defend epistemic analyticity; and this requires showing only that certain sentences are such that, *if* someone knows the relevant facts about their meaning, *then* that person will be in a position to form a justified belief about their truth. It does not require showing that the knowledge of those meaning facts is itself a priori (although, I repeat, it seems quite clear to me that it will be).[44]

Isn't it a problem for the aspirations of the present account that a thinker would have to use modus ponens to get from the premisses to the desired conclusion?

Not if Dummett's distinction between pragmatic and vicious circularity is credited with opening a space for an epistemology for logic, as discussed above.

Finally, how could such an account possibly hope to explain the man in the street's justification for believing in the truths of logic? For such a person, not only would the relevant meaning facts be quite opaque, he probably wouldn't even be capable of framing them. Yet such a person is obviously quite justified in believing the elementary truths of logic. Thus, so our objector might continue, this sort of account cannot explain our ordinary warrant for believing in logic; at best, it can explain the warrant that sophisticates have.

I think that, strictly speaking, this objection is correct, but only in a sense that strips it of real bite. Philosophers are often in the position of articulating a warrant for an ordinary belief that the man in the street would not understand. If we insist that a person counts as justified only if they are aware of the reason that warrants their belief, then we will simply have to find another term for the kind of warrant that ordinary folk often have and that philosophers seek to articulate. Tyler Burge has called it an "entitlement":

> The distinction between justification and entitlement is this. Although both have positive force in rationally supporting a propositional attitude or cognitive practice, and in constituting an epistemic right to it, entitlements are epistemic rights or warrants that need not be understood by or even be accessible to the subject. . . . The unsophisticated are entitled to rely on their perceptual beliefs. Philosophers may articulate these entitlements. But being entitled does not require being

> able to justify reliance on these resources, or even to conceive such a justification. Justifications, in the narrow sense, involve reasons that people have and have access to.[45]

When someone is entitled, all the facts relevant to the person's justification are already in place, so to say; what's missing is the reflection that would reveal them.

Just so in the case at hand. If a conceptual role semantics is true, and if **A** is indeed constitutive of **C**'s meaning what it does, then those facts by themselves constitute a warrant for **A**; empirical support is not necessary. **A** can only be false by meaning something other than what it means. But these facts need not be known by the ordinary person. They suffice for his entitlement, even if not for his full-blown justification. This full-blown justification can be had only by knowing the relevant facts about meaning.

Conclusion

Quine helped us see the vacuity of the metaphysical concept of analyticity and, with it, the futility of the project it was supposed to underwrite—the linguistic theory of necessity. But I don't see that those arguments affect the epistemic notion of analyticity that is needed for the purposes of the theory of a priori knowledge. Indeed, it seems to me that epistemic analyticity can be defended quite vigorously, especially against the background of a realism about meaning.

On the assumption that our warrant for believing in elementary logical truths cannot be explained, the outstanding problem is to explain our a priori knowledge of conceptual truths. For this purpose, the crucial semantical notion is that of Frege-analyticity. I have argued that this notion is bound to be in good standing for a meaning realist.

If the project of explaining logic is not ruled hopeless, then I have tried to show how the doctrine that appears to offer the most promising account of how we grasp the meanings of the logical constants—namely, Implicit Definition—can explain the epistemic analyticity of our logical beliefs and, hence, our a priori warrant for believing them. As long as we are not prepared to countenance radical indeterminacy, we should have every confidence that this form of explanation can be made to work.[46]

NOTES

1. This is a shorter, and somewhat modified, version of a paper entitled "Analyticity," which is to appear in Crispin Wright and Bob Hale (eds.): *A Companion to the Philosophy of Language* (Cambridge: Blackwell, 1996). I am grateful to Blackwell, and to the editors, for permission to use some of that material here.
2. "Definition in a Quinean World," in J. Fetzer, D. Shatz, and G. Schlesinger (eds.): *Definitions and Definability: Philosophical Perspectives* (Dordrecht: Kluwer, 1991), pp. 111–131.
3. As I say, I am going to work with this linguistic picture out of deference to my opponents. I would prefer to work with a propositionalist picture of belief, according to which the objects of belief are propositions in the technical sense—mind- and language-independent, abstract objects which have their truth conditions essentially. Most of the crucial notions developed in this paper, and much of the argument involving them, can be translated, with suitable modifications, into this propositionalist framework.
4. The inclusion of the word "outer" here is partly stipulative. I have always found it natural to regard a priori knowledge as encompassing both knowledge that is based on no experience as well as knowledge that is based purely on *inner* experience.
5. In the interests of brevity, I shall henceforth take it as understood that "justification" means "justification with a strength sufficient for knowledge."
6. Even this strong notion is not as demanding as many have supposed. For instance, it is consistent with a belief's being a priori in the

strong sense that we should have *pragmatic* reasons for dropping it from our best overall theory. For illuminating discussion of the modesty of the notion of the a priori see Crispin Wright: "Inventing Logical Necessity," in Butterfield (ed.) *Language, Mind and Logic* (Cambridge: Cambridge University Press, 1984) and Bob Hale: *Abstract Objects* (Oxford: Blackwell, 1986), ch. 6.

7. See Gilbert Harman, *Thought* (Princeton: Princeton University Press, 1973).
8. *The Ways of Paradox* (Cambridge: Harvard University Press, 1976), p. 103.
9. *From a Logical Point of View* (Cambridge: Harvard University Press, 1953), pp. 36–7.
10. "Quine on Meaning and Existence I," *Review of Metaphysics* 21: 124–151, p. 128. I am grateful to Paul Horwich for emphasizing the importance of this point.
11. "Doubts About Conceptual Analysis," MS, p. 5. See also his "Quine on Meaning and Existence I."
12. See G. Frege (Austin, trans.): *The Foundations of Arithmetic,* sec 3, Oxford: Blackwell, 1950). (Some may regard the attribution of precisely this notion to Frege controversial. What matters to me is not who came up with the idea, but rather the philosophical role it has played.)

    My use of the term 'analytic' in connection with Frege's *semantical* notion as well as with the preceding epistemic and metaphysical concepts may be thought ill-advised. But I do so deliberately, to highlight the fact that the term has been used in the literature in general, and in Quine in particular, to stand for all three different sorts of notion, often without any acknowledgement of that fact. This terminological promiscuity has undoubtedly contributed to the confusion surrounding discussions of this issue.
13. For some discussion see my "The Transparency of Mental Content," in *Philosophical Perspectives,* v.8, 1994, pp. 33–50.
14. What follows is a compressed discussion of Frege-analyticity. For a fuller treatment see "Anayticity," *op. cit.*
15. Exegetically, this does leave us with a few puzzles. First, TD does contain a brief discussion of the implicit definition idea, under the guise of the notion of a "semantical rule." Given that, why does Quine insist that he intends only to discuss the notion of Frege-analyticity? Second, the notion of a semantical rule is discussed only in connection with non-logical truths; since, however, the deployment of this idea would be exactly the same in the logical case, why is the analyticity of logic expressly excluded? Third, given that the analyticity of logic is expressly excluded, on what basis does Quine allow himself to draw morals about logic's revisability towards the end of TD? I think there is no avoiding the conclusion that, on this and other related issues (see below), TD is confused. It would, in fact, have been surprising if these rather tricky problems had all been in clear focus in Quine's pioneering papers.
16. In this context, nothing fancy is meant by the use of such expressions as 'property' and 'proposition'. For present purposes they may be understood in a thoroughly deflationary manner.

    I have sometimes been asked why I consider just this particular weakening of a non-factualist thesis, one that involves, problematically from Quine's official point of view, a modal notion? Why not rather attribute to him the following *Very Weak Thesis:*

    > (VWT) There is a coherent, determinate property expressed by 'is analytic', but *as a matter of fact,* it has never been instantiated; consequently, all tokens of the sentence 'S is analytic' have been false up to now.

    There are two reasons. First, the VWT is not a philosophically interesting thesis and, second, it could not have been argued for on the basis of a *philosophy* paper—i.e., on the sorts of a priori grounds that Quine offers. So although Quine may not be entitled to precisely the ET, I am going to ignore that and not hold it against him.
17. This question was first asked by Grice and Strawson in their "In Defense of a Dogma," reprinted in Grice: *Studies in the Way of Words* (Cambridge: Harvard University Press, 1989). Grice and Strawson didn't sufficiently

stress, however, that Quine was committed to a skepticism even about *intra*linguistic synonymy, and not just about *inter*linguistic synonymy, for the theory of apriority doesn't care about the interlinguistic case.

18. See Peter Strawson, *Logico-Linguistic Papers,* (London: Methuen, 1971), p. 117.
19. See the discussion of stipulative definitions in TD. For further discussion see "Analyticity."
20. Harman: *Thought,* op. cit., p. 14, emphasis in the original.
21. Recent formulations of this argument may be found in Fodor: *Psychosemantics,* (Cambridge, MA: MIT Press, 1987), pp 62ff; Fodor and Lepore: *Holism: A Shopper's Guide* (Oxford: Blackwell, 1991), pp. 37ff; Devitt: *Coming to Our Senses,* (New York: Cambridge University Press, 1995), p. 17. None of the authors mentioned approve of the argument.
22. A further TD-based argument for meaning holism, this time invalid, will be considered further below, in connection with the discussion of the thesis of Implicit Definition.
23. As before, subject to the proviso about the apriority of synonymy.
24. I am ignoring for now the class of a priori truths that are neither logical nor Frege-analytic. As we shall see, the very same strategy—implicit definition—that can be applied to explain our knowledge of logic can be applied to them as well.
25. *The Logical Basis of Metaphysics* (Cambridge: Harvard University Press, 1991), p. 202.
26. Coffa, A.: *The Semantic Tradition*, (Cambridge: Cambridge University Press, 1991), ch. 14. In the next three paragraphs, I follow the general contours of the account that Coffa puts forward. However, the formulations are mine and they differ in important respects from Coffa's, as we shall see further on.
27. Readers who are acquainted with a paper of mine of mine entitled "Inferential Role Semantics and the Analytic/Synthetic Distinction," *Philosophical Studies,* Spring 1994, pp. 109–122, will be aware that I used to worry that Implicit Definition could not generate a priori knowledge because of the falsity of something I called "The Principle." The Principle is the thesis that it follows from a sentence's being an implicit definer that that sentence is true. This is a tangled issue that I cannot fully discuss here. I will have to settle for a few brief remarks. I stand by the letter of what I said in the earlier paper. However, *part* of the problem there highlighted for the theory of the a priori is taken care of here by a reformulation of the thesis of Implicit Defintion; another part is taken care of by a reformulation of the relation between Implicit Defintion and the a priori; and, finally, a residual problem, not discussed in this paper, is met by the section entitled "A Pragmatic Solution" in "Analyticity," op. cit.. Readers for whom this footnote reads darkly may ignore it in its entirety.
28. Not to be confused with the non-factualism about Frege-analyticity discussed earlier in the paper.
29. Someone may object that the two cases are not relevantly analogous. For the meter case is supposed to be a case of the *fixation of reference,* but the logical case an instance of the fixation of meaning. Doesn't this difference between them block the argument I gave?

    I don't see that it does. First, the two cases really are disanalogous only if there is an important difference between meaning and reference; yet, as is well-known, there are many philosophers of language who are inclined to think that there isn't an important such difference. Second, it seems to me that even if we allowed for a robust distinction between meaning and reference, the point would remain entirely unaffected. Whether we think of an implicit definer as fixing a term's reference directly, or we think of it as first fixing its meaning, which then in turn fixes its reference, seems to me entirely irrelevant to the claim that Implicit Definition does not entail Non-Factualism. As long as both processes are consistent with the fixation of a factual claim for the sentence at issue—as they very much seem to be—the important point stands.
30. Certainly many philosophers seem to have thought so. Richard Creath, for example,

sympathetically expounds Carnap's view that the basic axioms of logic implicitly define the ingredient logical terms by saying that on this view "the postulates (together with the other conventions) create the truths that they, the postulates express." See his "Carnap's Conventionalism," *Synthese* 93: 141–165, p. 147.

31. This point is also forcefully made by Nathan Salmon in "Analyticity and Apriority," *Philosophical Perspectives,* 1994, and by Stephen Yablo in his review of Sidelle, *Philosophical Review* 1988.
32. Notice that conventionalists themselves need to make crucial use of such a distinction when they describe their own position, as in the passage cited above from Creath:

> the postulates (together with the other conventions) create the truths that they, the postulates, express.

As Hilary Putnam pointed out some time ago, it's hard to see how distinctive content is to be given to Conventionalism without the use of some such distinction. For a conventionalism merely about linguistic expressions is trivial. A real issue is joined only when the view is formulated as a claim about the truths expressed. See Putnam, "The Refutation of Conventionalism," in his *Mind, Language and Reality: Philosophical Papers v.2* (NY: Cambridge University Press, 1975)

33. Quine's argument here is officially directed against a Conventionalism about logical truth, that is, against the idea that logical truth is determined by our conventions. This idea we have already rejected in our discussion of the metaphysical concept of analyticity. However, Quine attacks Conventionalism *by* attacking the semantical thesis of Implicit Definition. Hence, the need for the present discussion.
34. Quine claims that this argument may also be put as follows: The claim that the sentences of logic lack assignment of truth value until they are conventionally assigned such values must fail. For logic is needed in order to infer from a formulated general convention that the infinitely many instances of a given schema are true. Hence, sentences of logic whose truth value is not fixed as the model requires, are presupposed by the model itself.

It's unclear to me that this is a formulation of precisely the same argument. However, to the extent that it is distinct, it is also addressed by the proposal I put forth below.

35. For discussion see my "The Rule-Following Considerations," *Mind,* 1989, pp. 507–549.
36. p. 105, *op. cit.*
37. "Reply to Hellman," in Schilpp (ed.): "The Philosophy of WVO Quine," (La Salle: Open Court, 1975), p. 206.
38. For all its influence, it is still possible to find the force of the Quinean point being underestimated by the friends of Implicit Definition. Christopher Peacocke, for example, in a recent, subtle defense of an inferential role semantics claims that what makes the inferences involving the logical constants constitutive is that a thinker finds those inferences "primitively compelling" and does so because they are of those forms. He goes on to explain:

> To say that a thinker finds such instances primitively compelling is to say this: (1) he finds them compelling; (2) he does not find them compelling because he has inferred them from other premises and/or principles; and (3) for possession of the concept in question . . . he does not need to take the correctness of the transitions as answerable to anything else.

A Study of Concepts (Cambridge: MIT Press, 1992), p. 6. I think it is plain, however, that these conditions are insufficient for answering the Quinean challenge: a non-constitutive, though highly obvious, form of inference may also be found compelling because of its form, and not on the basis of inference from anything else. So these conditions cannot be what distinguish between a constitutive and a non-constitutive inference.

39. "Why Meaning (Probably) Isn't Conceptual Role," *op. cit.*
40. For Fodor's views on the mentioned issues, see his *Psychosemantics* (Cambridge: MIT Press, 1989) and *The Elm and the Expert* (Cambridge: MIT Press, 1994).

41. See Fodor and Lepore: *Holism: A Shopper's Guide* (Oxford: Blackwell, 1993).
42. Harman, "Comments on Boghossian," APA Symposium on Analytic Truth, Boston, MA, December 1994.
43. For a good start, see Peacocke: *A Study of Concepts, op. cit.*
44. For a discussion of why the second premiss is a priori see "Analyticity," *op. cit.*
45. Burge, "Content Preservation," *The Philosophical Review,* October 1993.
46. I am grateful to a number of audiences—at MIT, CUNY Graduate Center, Michigan State, the University of Chicago, the SOFIA Conference on Tenerife, the Chapel Hill Colloquium, Dartmouth College, London University and Oxford University. An earlier version of this paper was presented at the NEH Institute on the "Nature of Meaning," held at Rutgers University in the summer of 1992. It was there that I first became aware that Christopher Peacocke has been thinking along somewhat similar lines about the a priori—see his "How are A Priori Truths Possible?" presented at the Rutgers conference. Although there are a number of differences between our approaches, and although Peacocke's focus is not on the notion of analyticity, I have benefited from discussing these matters with him. I also benefited from presenting a version of this paper as part of a symposium on Analytic Truth, involving Gil Harman, Burton Dreben and WVO Quine, at the 1994 Eastern Division meetings of the APA. I am especially grateful to Gil Harman, Elizabeth Fricker, Hartry Field, Gary Gates, Bill Lycan, Stephen Schiffer and Barry Loewer for their detailed comments on previous versions of this paper. Special thanks are due to Bob Hale and Crispin Wright for their patience and for their very helpful reactions to several different drafts. For other helpful discussion and commentary, I want to thank Jennifer Church, Jerry Fodor, Albert Casullo, Norma Yunez, Neil Tennant, Peter Unger, Tom Nagel, Paul Horwich, Ned Block, Richard Creath, Allan Gibbard, Stephen Yablo and David Velleman.

REALITY

CHAPTER FIVE

IDENTITY, CHANGE, AND CAUSATION

We live in a world of constant change. From one moment to the next things move around, grow, shrink, cool, warm up, pass into being, perish, decay, and so on. Consider your own body. Many people would scoff at the notion that they have undergone a total body replacement over the years between childhood and adulthood. But clearly, if every cell that composed one's body as a child has died off and been replaced over the course of, let's say, twenty or so years, in what sense can a thirty-year-old man say he has the same body that he had at age five? It would seem ridiculous to insist that he did. But this is just a dramatic example of a phenomenon that has puzzled thinkers since the dawn of philosophy. Changing as things do from one moment to the next, in what sense can we say that they retain their identity while undergoing such change?

On the face of it, the fact of change seems contradictory. When we say that this sample of water is the same sample of water that was frozen a moment ago, we seem to be suggesting that the same thing (the water) is both frozen and not frozen. But this would be a straightforward contradiction. It does not help to simply assert that the *same* sample of water *was* solid and is *now* liquid, for our original question was how such a thing could be possible. If it is really the *same* sample of water, it cannot be both solid and liquid. And this puzzle generalizes to cover the full range of experience: the world seems like a river that cannot be stepped into twice because new waters are always rushing in upon us. Is there any way to reconcile the apparently persistent identity of things with the flux of experience?

We begin the chapter that follows with a collection of fragments from the pre-Socratic philosopher Heraclitus, to whom the metaphor of the ever-changing river is attributed. Heraclitus is puzzled by the flux of the world and attempts to make sense of it.

We then turn to Parmenides who argues that change, being contradictory, is simply unreal. Things seem to change. Furthermore, the world seems to present us with a multiplicity of beings. But, strictly speaking, the world is an immutable unity according to Parmenides. To think otherwise is to embrace a contradictory view of reality.

Zeno, a student of Parmenides, argues that motion, which is a form of change, is illogical. We have included accounts of his paradoxes of Motion, Achilles, The Arrow, Plurality, Place and Sound. Zeno challenges the advocate of motion to resolve several paradoxes based on seemingly incontestable and innocent premises. Consider moving from the top of a hill to the bottom of that hill. In order to do this, one must traverse the midpoint between the top of the hill and one's destination. But in order to get to the midpoint of the distance between the top and the bottom of the hill, one must get to the midpoint of *that distance* (the half-way point between the starting point and the midpoint of the top and bottom of the hill). But because this distance consists in an infinity of midpoints, and because it would be impossible to traverse an infinity of points in a finite stretch of time, Zeno concludes that motion is impossible.

A selection from Plato brings into harmony elements of both the Heraclitean and Parmenidean views. According to the myth of the cave, reality can be divided into two realms, one of which is unchanging, perfect, and purely intelligible. This is the world of the intellect, represented by the character of Socrates as the world outside the cave. Within the cave, there exist the ephemeral beings of the world of sense experience. But the world inside the cave is not really real.

Aristotle, Plato's student, wrestled with these problems as well. But he was not happy with his teacher's solution: the world of sense experience must be accounted for, not merely downplayed as an imitation of reality. We have here selections from his *Categories,* which contains his account of primary and secondary substances, *Physics,* which deals with beings in change, and his *Metaphysics,* which deals with things insofar as they are changeless. It may be helpful to note that Aristotle frequently divides his subject matter by considering the same thing(s) from different perspectives. So we can consider reality insofar as it is changing, but also insofar as it exists in a changeless way. In so doing, we have not necessarily moved from a realm of beings that are perfect and purely intelligible to a play of shadows on the cave wall, as a Platonist might argue. Rather we have simply changed theoretical standpoints.

In his classic paper, "Identity, Ostension, and Hypostasis," W. V. O. Quine wrestles with the problem of identity and change, arguing that even if we cannot step into the same stage of a river twice, since new waters are always rushing in upon us, we can step into the same river twice. The key to Quine's analysis here is that rivers, as well as all other perceivable objects, can be thought of as collections of temporal stages. No two temporal stages of any river are identical, yet the river, as a collection of river-stages, can be considered an enduring entity. The function of identity for Quine is not to pinpoint some otherworldly form or essence, but to allow us to specify borders around the sets of spatio temporally scattered stages that are presented to us in sense experience.

The remainder of the chapter deals with the related questions of causation and inductive reasoning. In changing, things seem to be involved in various causal transactions. Heat *causes* water to boil. But just what does this mean? Does this mean that sufficiently heated water *must, always,* and *everywhere* boil? Can we know what future samples of water will be like of the basis of past experience?

David Hume argues that causes do not necessitate effects. Properly speaking, our sense impressions of causes are merely "constantly conjoined" with our sense impressions of effects. We never experience anything like a causal power connecting causes and effects; nor is there a logical connection between them. Considered independently of experience, anything can cause anything, without any logical contradiction, according to Hume.

Nevertheless, causal reasoning is one of our main guides through experience. Hume then turns to the question of whether the beliefs that we form about the world on the basis of causal reasoning are logically warranted. Inductive reasoning in general, of which causal reasoning is a species, is the main target here. Can past experience provide any guide to the future? If so, how? It does not seem to logically guarantee anything, since it is always conceivable that the future might not resemble the past in certain ways. But if we say that past experience only renders probable some of our beliefs about the future, we have to ask on what basis the past may be used as a guide to assessing future probabilities.

We close the chapter with a piece by Nelson Goodman that builds on this puzzle. Goodman argues that what counts as inductive regularities is a matter relative to the predicates entrenched in our language. Consider for example the predicate *grue*. Updating Goodman's example just a bit, let's say that things are grue just in case they are green if observed before January 1, 2003 and blue if observed after that date. If this is true, then whatever inductive evidence supports the hypothesis that all emeralds are green also confirms the hypothesis that all emeralds are grue. But emeralds that are blue after January 1, 2003 would not count as supporting an inductive regularity for a linguistic community such as ours, which does not use a perverse predicate like "grue." However, for one that does, such findings would support a bona fide regularity.

Fragments

HÊRACLEITUS OF EPHESUS

Hêracleitus of Ephesus was in his prime about 500 B.C.

He wrote one book, covering all knowledge, metaphysical, scientific and political, in an oracular style.

1. The Law[1] (*of the universe*) is as here explained; but men are always incapable of understanding it, both before they hear it, and when they have heard it for the first time. For though all things come into being in accordance with this Law, men seem as if they had never met with it, when they meet with words (*theories*) and actions (*processes*) such as I expound, separating each thing according to its nature and explaining how it is made. As for the rest of mankind, they are unaware of what they are doing after they wake, just as they forget what they did while asleep.
2. Therefore one must follow (the universal Law, namely) that which is common (*to all*). But although the Law is universal, the majority live as if they had understanding peculiar to themselves.
3. (*On the size of the sun*): the breadth of a man's foot.
4. If happiness lay in bodily pleasures, we would call oxen happy when they find vetch to eat.
5. They purify themselves by staining themselves with other blood, as if one were to step into mud in order to wash off mud. But a man would be thought mad[2] if any of his fellow-men should perceive him acting thus. Moreover, they talk to these statues (*of theirs*) as if one were to hold conversation with houses, in his ignorance of the nature of both gods and heroes.
6. The sun is new each day.

Source: Kathleen Freeman, *Ancilla to the Pre-Socratic Philosophers,* Cambridge: Harvard University Press, 1983. Reprinted with permission.

7. If all existing things turned to smoke, the nose would be the discriminating organ.
8. That which is in opposition is in concert, and from things that differ comes the most beautiful harmony.
9. Donkeys prefer chaff to gold.
10. Joints: whole and not whole, connected-separate, consonant-dissonant.
11. Every creature is driven to pasture with a blow.
12. Anhalation (*vaporisation*). Those who step into the same river have different waters flowing ever upon them. (Souls also are vaporised from what is wet).
13. Do not revel in mud. (*Swine enjoy mud rather than pure water*).
14. Night-ramblers, magicians, Bacchants, Maenads, Mystics: the rites accepted by mankind in the Mysteries are an unholy performance.
15. If it were not in honour of Dionysus that they conducted the procession and sang the hymn to the male organ (*the phallic hymn*), their activity would be completely shameless. But Hades is the same as Dionysus, in whose honour they rave and perform the Bacchic revels.
16. How could anyone hide from that which never sets?
17. For many men—those who encounter such things—do not understand them, and do not grasp them after they have learnt; but to themselves they seem (*to understand*).
18. If one does not hope, one will not find the unhoped-for, since there is no trail leading to it and no path.
19. Men who do not know how to listen or how to speak.
20. When they are born, they are willing to live and accept their fate (*death*); and they leave behind children to become victims of fate.
21. All that we see when we have wakened is death; all that we see while slumbering is sleep.
22. Those who seek gold dig much earth and find little.
23. They would not know the name of Right, if these things (*i.e. the opposite*) did not exist.
24. Gods and men honour those slain in war.
25. The greater the fate (*death*), the greater the reward.
26. In the night, a man kindles[3] a light because his sight is quenched; while living, he approximates to[4] a dead man during sleep; while awake, he approximates to one who sleeps.
27. There await men after they are dead things which they do not expect or imagine.
28. The most wise-seeming man knows, (*that is*), preserves, only what seems; furthermore, retribution will seize the fabricators of lies and the (*false*) witnesses.
29. The best men choose one thing rather than all else: everlasting fame among mortal men.[4] The majority are satisfied, like well-fed cattle.
30. This ordered universe (*cosmos*), which is the same for all, was not created by any one of the gods or of mankind, but it was ever and is and shall be ever-living Fire, kindled in measure and quenched in measure.
31. The changes of fire: first, sea; and of sea, half is earth and half fiery water-spout . . . Earth[5] is liquified into sea, and retains its measure according to the same Law as existed before it became earth.
32. That which alone is wise is one; it is willing and unwilling to be called by the name of Zeus.
33. To obey the will of one man is also Law (*political law, Nomos*).
34. Not understanding, although they have heard, they are like the deaf. The proverb bears witness to them: 'Present yet absent.'
35. Men who love wisdom must be inquirers into very many things indeed.
36. To souls, it is death to become water; to water, it is death to become earth. From earth comes water, and from water, soul.

37. Pigs wash themselves in mud, birds in dust or ashes.
38. (*Thales was the first to study astronomy*).
39. In Priênê was born Bias son of Teutamos, whose fame (*or,* 'worth') is greater than that of the rest.
40. Much learning does not teach one to have intelligence; for it would have taught Hesiod and Pythagoras, and again, Xenophanes and Hecataeus.
41. That which is wise is one: to understand the purpose which steers all things through all things.
42. Homer deserves to be flung out of the contests and given a beating; and also Archilochus.
43. One should quench arrogance rather than a conflagration.
44. The people should fight for the Law (*Nomos*) as if for their city-wall.
45. You could not in your going find the ends of the soul, though you travelled the whole way: so deep is its Law (*Logos*).
46. Conceit: the sacred disease (*i.e. epilepsy*).
47. Let us not conjecture at random about the greatest things.
48. The bow is called Life,[6] but its work is death.
49. One man to me is (*worth*) ten thousand, if he is the best.

49a. In the same river, we both step and do not step, we are and we are not.

50. When you have listened, not to me but to the Law (*Logos*), it is wise to agree that all things are one.
51. They do not understand how that which differs with itself is in agreement: harmony consists of opposing tension, like that of the bow and the lyre.
52. Time is a child playing a game of draughts; the kingship is in the hands of a child.
53. War is both king of all and father of all, and it has revealed some as gods, others as men; some it has made slaves, others free.
54. The hidden harmony is stronger (*or,* 'better') than the visible.
55. Those things of which there is sight, hearing, knowledge: these are what I honour most.
56. Men are deceived over the recognition of visible things, in the same way as Homer, who was the wisest of all the Hellenes; for he too was deceived by boys killing lice, who said: 'What we saw and grasped, that we leave behind; but what we did not see and did not grasp, that we bring.'
57. Hesiod is the teacher of very many, he who did not understand day and night: for they are one.
58. For instance, physicians, who cut and burn, demand payment of a fee, though undeserving, since they produce the same (*pains as the disease*).
59. For the fuller's screw, the way, straight and crooked, is one and the same.
60. The way up and down is one and the same.
61. Sea water is the purest and most polluted: for fish, it is drinkable and life-giving; for men, not drinkable and destructive.
62. Immortals are mortal, mortals are immortal: (*each*) lives the death of the other, and dies their life.
63. When he (*God?*) is there, they (*the souls in Hades*) arise and become watchful guardians of the living and the dead.
64. The thunder-bolt (*i.e. Fire*) steers the universe.
65. Need and satiety.
66. Fire, having come upon them, will judge and seize upon (condemn) all things.
67. God is day-night, winter-summer, war-peace, satiety-famine. But he changes like (fire) which when it mingles with the smoke of incense, is named according to each man's pleasure.
68. (*Heracleitus called the shameful rites of the Mysteries*) Remedies.
69. (*There are two sorts of sacrifice: one kind offered by men entirely purified, as sometimes occurs, though rarely, in an individual, or a few easy to number; the other kind material*).[7]
70. Children's toys (*i.e. men's conjectures*).

71. (*One must remember also*) the man who forgets which way the road leads.
72. The Law (*Logos*): though men associate with it most closely, yet they are separated from it, and those things which they encounter daily seem to them strange.
73. We must not act and speak like men asleep.
74. (*We must not act like*) children of our parents.)
75. Those who sleep are workers and share in the activities going on in the universe.
76. Fire lives the death of earth, and air lives the death of fire; water lives the death of air, earth that of water.
77. It is delight, or rather death, to souls to become wet . . . We live their (*the souls'*) death, and they (*the souls*) live our death.
78. Human nature has no power of understanding; but the divine nature has it.
79. Man is called childish compared with divinity, just as a boy compared with a man.
80. One should know that war is general (*universal*) and jurisdiction is strife, and everything comes about by way of strife and necessity.
81. (*On Pythagoras*). Original chief of wranglers.
82. (*The most handsome ape is ugly compared with the human race*).[8]
83. (*The wisest man will appear an ape in relation to God, both in wisdom and beauty and everything else*).[8]

84a. It rests from change . . . (*Elemental Fire in the human body*).

84b. It is a weariness to the same (*elements forming the human body*) to toil and to obey.

85. It is hard to fight against impulse; whatever it wishes, it buys at the expense of the soul.
86. (*Most of what is divine*) escapes recognition through unbelief.
87. A foolish man is apt to be in a flutter at every word (*or, 'theory': Logos*).
88. And what is in us is the same thing: living and dead, awake and sleeping, as well as young and old; for the latter (*of each pair of opposites*) having changed becomes the former, and this again having changed becomes the latter.
89. To those who are awake, there is one ordered universe common (*to all*), whereas in sleep each man turns away (*from this world*) to one of his own.
90. There is an exchange: all things for Fire and Fire for all things, like goods for gold and gold for goods.
91. It is not possible to step twice into the same river. (*It is impossible to touch the same mortal substance twice, but through the rapidity of change*) they scatter and again combine (*or rather, not even 'again' or 'later', but the combination and separation are simultaneous*) and approach and separate.[9]
92. The Sibyl with raving mouth uttering her unlaughing, unadorned, unincensed words reaches out over a thousand years with her voice, through the (*inspiration of the*) god.
93. The lord whose oracle is that at Delphi neither speaks nor conceals, but indicates.
94. The sun will not transgress his measures, otherwise the Furies, ministers of Justice, will find him out.
95. It is better to hide ignorance (*though this is hard in relaxation and over wine*).
96. Corpses are more worthy to be thrown out than dung.
97. Dogs bark at those whom they do not recognise.
98. Souls have the sense of smell in Hades.
99. If there were no sun, so far as depended on the other stars it would be night.
100. (*The sun is in charge of the seasonal changes, and*) the Hours (Seasons) that bring all things.
101. I searched into myself.

101a. The eyes are more exact witnesses than the ears.

102. To God, all things are beautiful, good and just; but men have assumed some things to be unjust, others just.

103. Beginning and end are general in the circumference of the circle.
104. What intelligence or understanding have they? They believe the people's bards, and use as their teacher the populace, not knowing that 'the majority are bad, and the good are few'.[10]
105. Homer was an astrologer.
106. (*Heracleitus reproached Hesiod for regarding some days as bad and others as good*). Hesiod was unaware that the nature of every day is one.
107. The eyes and ears are bad witnesses for men if they have barbarian souls.
108. Of all those whose discourse I have heard, none arrives at the realisation that that which is wise is set apart from all things.
109. *See* 95.
110. It is not better for men to obtain all that they wish.
111. Disease makes health pleasant and good, hunger satisfaction, weariness rest.
112. Moderation is the greatest virtue, and wisdom is to speak the truth and to act according to nature, paying heed (*thereto*).
113. The thinking faculty is common to all.
114. If we speak with intelligence, we must base our strength on that which is common to all,[11] as the city on the Law (*Nomos*), and even more strongly. For all human laws are nourished by one, which is divine. For it governs as far as it will, and is sufficient for all, and more than enough.
115. The soul has its own Law (*Logos*), which increases itself (*i.e. grows according to its needs*).
116. All men have the capacity of knowing themselves and acting with moderation.
117. A man, when he gets drunk, is led stumbling along by an immature boy, not knowing where he is going, having his soul wet.
118. A dry (desiccated) soul is the wisest and best.
119. Character for man is destiny.
120. The limits of morning and evening are the Bear and, opposite the Bear, the boundary-mark of Zeus god of the clear sky.
121. The Ephesians would do well to hang themselves, every adult man, and bequeath their City-State to adolescents, since they have expelled Hermodôrus, the most valuable man among them, saying: 'Let us not have even one valuable man; but if we do, let him go elsewhere and live among others.'
122. (*Word for*) Approximation.
123. Nature likes to hide.
124. The fairest universe is but a dust-heap piled up at random.
125. The 'mixed drink' (*Kykeôn: mixture of wine, grated cheese and barley-meal*) also separates if it is not stirred.

125a. May wealth not fail you, men of Ephesus, so that you may be convicted of your wickedness.

126. Cold things grow hot, hot things grow cold, the wet dries, the parched is moistened.

NOTES

1. Logos, the intelligible Law of the universe, and its reasoned statement by Heracleitus. See *Companion*, pp. 115 *sqq*.
2. Pun on μιαινομενοι and μαινεσθαι, which cannot be reproduced in English.
3. Pun on απτεται, 'kindles', and 'touches upon' (approximates to).
4. Or: 'rather than things mortal'.
5. γη supplied by Kranz; otherwise, 'the sea is distributed'.
6. Pun on βίοσ, Life, and βιόσ, bow.
7. Paraphrase in Iamblichus.
8. Paraphrases in Plato, *Hippias Maior*.
9. Phrases of Heracleitus quoted in Aristotle, *Metaphysics*.
10. Saying attributed to Bias of Priênê. Diels, *Vors.*, ch. 10, 3, s. I.
11. Pun on ξεν νῶ and ξυνῶ.

Fragments

PARMENIDES OF ELEA

Parmenides of Elea was in his prime about 475 B.C.

He wrote a poem in hexameter verse, addressed to his pupil Zeno; it was divided into three parts: the Prologue, the Way of Truth, the Way of Opinion.

1. The mares which carry me conveyed me as far as my desire reached, when the goddesses who were driving had set me on the famous highway which bears a man who has knowledge through all the cities. Along this way I was carried; for by this way the exceedingly intelligent mares bore me, drawing the chariot, and the maidens directed the way. The axle in the naves gave forth a pipe-like sound as it glowed (for it was driven round by the two whirling circles (*wheels*) at each end) whenever the maidens, daughters of the Sun, having left the Palace of Night, hastened their driving towards the light, having pushed back their veils from their heads with their hands.

There (*in the Palace of Night*) are the gates of the paths of Night and Day, and they are enclosed with a lintel above and a stone threshold below. The gates themselves are filled with great folding doors; and of these Justice, mighty to punish, has the interchangeable keys. The maidens, skilfully cajoling her with soft words, persuaded her to push back the bolted bar without delay from the gates; and these, flung open, revealed a wide gaping space, having swung their jambs, richly-wrought in bronze, reciprocally in their sockets. This way, then, straight through them went the maidens, driving chariot and mares along the carriage-road.

And the goddess received me kindly, and took my right hand in hers, and thus she spoke and addressed me:

'Young man, companion of immortal charioteers, who comest by the help of the steeds which bring thee to our dwelling: welcome!—since no evil fate has despatched thee on thy

---

Source: Kathleen Freeman, *Ancilla to the Pres-Socratic Philosophers,* Cambridge: Harvard University Press, 1983. Reprinted with permission.

journey by this road (for truly it is far from the path trodden by mankind); no, it is divine command and Right. Thou shalt inquire into everything: both the motionless heart of well-rounded Truth, and also the opinions of mortals, in which there is no true reliability. But nevertheless thou shalt learn these things (*opinions*) also—how one should go through all the things-that-seem, without exception, and test them.[1]

2. Come, I will tell you—and you must accept my word when you have heard it—the ways of inquiry which alone are to be thought: the one that IT IS, and it is not possible for IT NOT TO BE, is the way of credibility, for it follows Truth; the other, that IT IS NOT, and that IT is bound NOT TO BE: this I tell you is a path that cannot be explored; for you could neither recognise that which IS NOT, nor express it.

3. For it is the same thing to think and to be.[2]

4. Observe nevertheless how things absent are securely present to the mind; for it will not sever Being from its connection with Being, whether it is scattered everywhere utterly throughout the universe, or whether it is collected together.

5. It is all the same to me from what point I begin, for I shall return again to this same point.

6. One should both say and think that Being Is; for To Be is possible, and Nothingness is not possible. This I command you to consider; for from the latter way of search first of all I debar you. But next I debar you from that way along which wander mortals knowing nothing, two-headed,[3] for perplexity in their bosoms steers their intelligence astray, and they are carried along as deaf as they are blind, amazed, uncritical hordes, by whom To Be and Not To Be are regarded as the same and not the same, and (*for whom*) in everything there is a way of opposing stress.[4]

7, 8. For this (*view*) can never predominate, that That Which Is Not exists. You must debar your thought from this way of search, nor let ordinary experience in its variety force you along this way, (*namely, that of allowing*) the eye, sightless as it is, and the ear, full of sound, and the tongue, to rule; but (*you must*) judge by means of the Reason (*Logos*) the much-contested proof which is expounded by me.

There is only one other description of the way remaining, (*namely*), that (*What Is*) Is. To this way there are very many sign-posts: that Being has no coming-into-being and no destruction, for it is whole of limb, without motion, and without end. And it never Was, nor Will Be, because it Is now, a Whole all together, One, continuous; for what creation of it will you look for? How, whence (*could it have*) sprung? Nor shall I allow you to speak or think of it as springing from Not-Being; for it is neither expressible nor thinkable that What-Is-Not Is. Also, what necessity impelled it, if it did spring from Nothing, to be produced later or earlier? Thus it must Be absolutely, or not at all. Nor will the force of credibility ever admit that anything should come into being, beside Being itself, out of Not-Being. So far as that is concerned, Justice has never released (*Being*) in its fetters and set it free either to come into being or to perish, but holds it fast. The decision on these matters depends on the following: IT IS, or IT IS NOT. It is therefore decided—as is inevitable—(*that one must*) ignore the one way as unthinkable and inexpressible (for it is no true way) and take the other as the way of Being and Reality. How could Being perish? How could it come into being? If it came into being, it Is Not; and so too if it is about-to-be at some future time. Thus Coming-into-Being is quenched, and Destruction also into the unseen.[5]

Nor is Being divisible, since it is all alike. Nor is there anything (*here or*) there which could prevent it from holding together, nor any lesser thing, but all is full of Being. Therefore it is altogether continuous; for Being is close to Being.

But it is motionless in the limits of mighty bonds, without beginning, without cease, since Becoming and Destruction have been driven very far away, and true conviction has rejected them. And remaining the same in the same place, it rests by itself and thus remains there fixed; for powerful Necessity holds it in the bonds of a Limit, which constrains it round about, because it is decreed by divine law that Being shall not be without boundary. For it is not lacking; but if it were (*spatially infinite*), it would be lacking everything.[6]

To think is the same as the thought that It Is; for you will not find thinking without Being, in (*regard to*) which there is an expression. For nothing else either is or shall be except Being, since Fate has tied it down to be a whole and motionless; therefore all things that mortals have established, believing in their truth, are just a name: Becoming and Perishing, Being and Not-Being, and Change of position, and alteration of bright colour.

But since there is a (*spatial*) Limit, it is complete on every side, like the mass of a well-rounded sphere, equally balanced from its centre in every direction; for it is not bound to be at all either greater or less in this direction or that; nor is there Not-Being which could check it from reaching to the same point, nor is it possible for Being to be more in this direction, less in that, than Being, because it is an inviolate whole. For, in all directions equal to itself, it reaches its limits uniformly.

At this point I cease my reliable theory (*Logos*) and thought, concerning Truth; from here onwards you must learn the opinions of mortals, listening to the deceptive order of my words.

They have established (*the custom of*) naming two forms, one of which ought not to be (*mentioned*): that is where they have gone astray. They have distinguished them as opposite in form, and have marked them off from another by giving them different signs: on one side the flaming fire in the heavens, mild, very light (*in weight*), the same as itself in every direction, and not the same as the other. This (*other*) also is by itself and opposite: dark Night, a dense and heavy body. This world-order I describe to you throughout as it appears with all its phenomena, in order that no intellect of mortal men may outstrip you.[7]

9. But since all things are named Light and Night, and names have been given to each class of things according to the power of one or the other (*Light or Night*), everything is full equally of Light and invisible Night, as both are equal, because to neither of them belongs any share (of the other). [8]

10. You shall know the nature of the heavens, and all the signs in the heavens, and the destructive works of the pure bright torch of the sun, and whence they came into being. And you shall learn of the wandering works of the round-faced moon, and its nature; and you shall know also the surrounding heaven, whence it sprang and how Necessity brought and constrained it to hold the limits of the stars.

11. (*I will describe*) how earth and sun and moon, and the aether common to all, and the Milky Way in the heavens, and outermost Olympus, and the hot power of the stars, hastened to come into being.

12. For the narrower rings were filled with unmixed Fire, and those next to them with Night, but between (*these*) rushes the portion of Flame. And in the centre of these is the goddess who guides everything; for throughout she rules over cruel Birth and Mating, sending the female to mate with the male, and conversely again the male with the female.

13. First of all the gods she devised Love.

14. (*The moon*): Shining by night with a light not her own, wandering round the earth.

15. (*The moon*): Always gazing towards the rays of the sun.

15a. (*Earth*): Rooted in water.

16. For according to the mixture of much-wandering limbs which each man has, so is the mind which is associated with mankind: for it is the same thing which thinks, namely the constitution of the limbs in men, all and individually; for it is excess which makes Thought.

17. On the right, boys, on the left, girls . . . (*in the womb*).

18. When a woman and a man mix the seeds of Love together, the power (*of the seeds*) which shapes (*the embryo*) in the veins out of different blood can mould well-constituted bodies only if it preserves proportion. For if the powers war (*with each other*) when the seed is mixed, and do not make a unity in the body formed by the mixture, they will terribly harass the growing (*embryo*) through the twofold seed of the (*two*) sexes.

19. Thus, therefore, according to opinion, were these things created, and are now, and shall hereafter from henceforth grow and then come to an end. And for these things men have established a name as a distinguishing mark for each.

NOTES

1. Reading δοκιμῶσ' (= δοκιμῶσαι) with Diels, *Vors.*, Edn. 4, and not with Kranz (Wilamowitz) δοκιμῶς (*Vors.*, 5). Wilamowitz took περῶντα with τα δοκουντα, and translated: ('Still, you shall learn these things too), how phenomena had to be on a plausible footing, because these extend throughout everything.' This interpretation is favoured by those who accept the view that Parmenides left the door open for 'Opinion' in some form; it was rejected by Diels, *Vors.*, 4, Nachträge, p. xxviii, as contrary to Parmenidean metaphysic. See *Companion,* pp. 141 *sqq.*
2. Or, reading εστιν: 'that which it is possible to think is identical with that which can Be'. (Zeller and Burnet, probably rightly).
3. *i.e.,* 'in two minds'.
4. Cp. Heracleitus, Frg. 8.
5. απυστος, 'beyond perception'; also απαυστος 'never-ending'.
6. Reading and meaning doubtful. Diels-Kranz: 'if it lacked Limit, it would fall short of being a Whole', but without any certainty.
7. Or, reading γνωμη (Stein): 'in order that no mortal may outstrip you in intelligence'.
8. Kranz takes επει with the previous line, and translates: 'For nothing is possible which does not come under either of the two' (*i.e.,* everything belongs to one or other of the two categories Light and Night).

 3

Paradoxes

ZENO

PARADOXES OF MOTION

These paradoxes are the most famous and have perhaps received more careful attention than the others. There are four paradoxes of motion: the Dichotomy, the Achilles, the Arrow, and the Stadium. The first and third deny motion altogether, the second and fourth assume motion and show the assumption leads to absurdities.

THE DICHOTOMY. The argument is that motion is impossible because for anything to move from one place to another it must first go halfway, but before going halfway it must go a quarter way, but before going a quarter way it must go an eighth way, and so on *ad infinitum*. Since one cannot exhaust an infinity in a finite time, motion cannot occur.

Source: Drew Hyland, *The Origins of Philosophy*. Atlantic Highlands, NJ: Humanities Press, 1973.

To understand the paradox more clearly let us consider the following diagram:

A G F E D C

. . . $(1/2)^4$ $(1/2)^3$ $(1/2)^2$ $(1/2)$

Interpretation A. Suppose the difficulty is how it is possible to do an infinite number of things in a finite time. Each of the tasks takes a finite amount of time and thus (it apparently seemed) that all of them would take an infinite time. However, we now know this need not be the case. If it takes 1 hour to go from A to B, 1/2 hour to go from A to C, 1/4 $(=(1/2)^2)$ hour to go from A to D, etc., then the amount of time is not infinite. In particular,

$$1/2 + (1/2)^2 + (1/2)^3 + \cdots = 1.$$

as can now be proven by many a schoolboy. However, the ancient Greeks had great difficulty in dealing with limits—in part due to a clumsy notation. (Our notation derives from the Indians and Arabs. To get some idea of the difficulty facing the Greeks, try dealing with infinite series in Roman numerals.) Even geometry—the first developed science in ancient Greece—was in a rapid state of flux in Zeno's time. Hence, it can hardly be expected that he would have understood even simple infinite series or that his hearers wouldn't be puzzled by them . . . .

THE ACHILLES. This paradox is Zeno's most famous and goes as follows: Achilles, born of a goddess and the fastest of human runners, cannot even catch a tortoise, the slowest of moving creatures. For suppose we have a race in which the tortoise is given a lead. However fast Achilles runs to reach the point where the tortoise was, he must take some time to do it. In that time the tortoise will move forward some (smaller) distance. This argument may now be repeated *ad infinitum*. Hence Achilles may get closer and closer to the tortoise, but he cannot catch the tortoise.

Again a diagram might be helpful. Let T_0 be the time of the start of the race and let's assume that Achilles is running twice as fast as the tortoise.

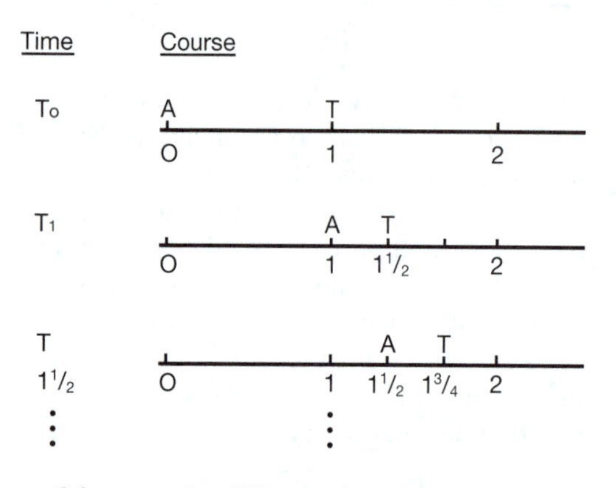

Of course the difficulty in the Achilles argument might be susceptible to the kinds of resolutions proposed in Interpretations A and B of the Dichotomy. But there are other possibilities.

. . . *Interpretation B.* Suppose the difficulty is in the comparison of infinite sets, and in particular with the assumption that the whole is greater than the part. To see this, consider that for each point on the line that Achilles is at, the tortoise is also at a point and yet the distance Achilles travels is greater than the distance the tortoise travels. The problem and its solution may be made clearer by considering the following diagram.

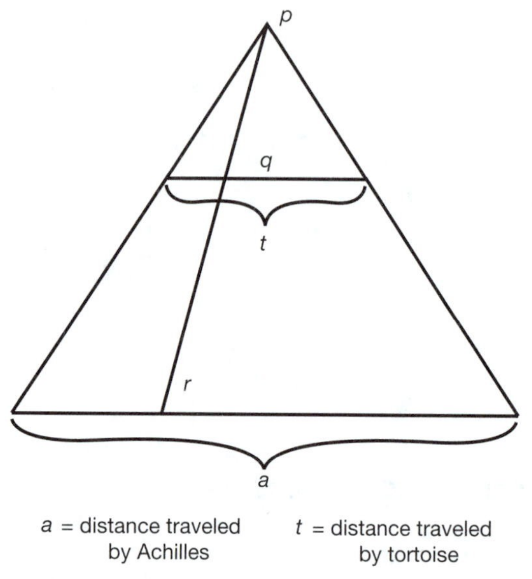

Now it is clear that to each point on a there corresponds a unique point on t, and vice versa. This can be easily seen by drawing straight lines through p which cross both t and a. Any point on line t (say, q) corresponds to a unique point (say, r) or line a, and vice versa. Hence if motion exists, the whole is not greater than the part. This difficulty may be resolved by denying that the whole is greater than the part for infinite sets. Such a possibility is now well known owing to the creation of set theory by Georg Cantor. For example, we can easily see that there are as many even positive integers as there are positive integers:

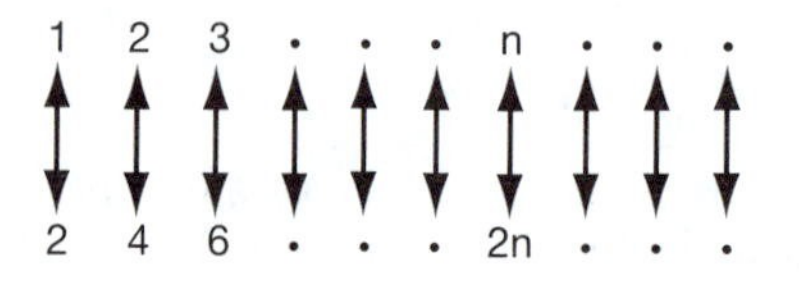

THE ARROW. The argument of the Arrow is as follows: at every instant a flying arrow occupies a space equal to itself, but if this is true, the arrow is at rest at every instant and therefore during the whole flight.

Interpretation A. Suppose the difficulty is in the inference that because at each and every instance the arrow is not in motion then it is not in motion during the whole time composed of instances. We may resolve the paradox by understanding this inference as an example of the fallacy of composition. Someone commits the fallacy of composition when he argues that a set of things has a certain property because each and every element has that property. For example, just because each and every page of a telephone book can be easily torn in half, it does not follow that the telephone book can be easily torn in half. Similarly, just because at each and every instant the arrow is not moving, it doesn't follow that the arrow doesn't move over the whole time interval. . . .

PARADOXES OF PLURALITY

Zeno composed a large number of arguments against plurality of which only three or four survive. We will consider two.

FIRST ARGUMENT. If there is a plurality of things, then things will be both infinitely small and infinitely large. On one hand, they must be infinitely small since if we have a plurality of units each unit must be indivisible (otherwise it would not be a unit since it has parts). But anything which is indivisible may not have size, and having no size (= no magnitude or thickness or mass) cannot exist at all. On the other hand, things must be infinitely big since each thing will have a certain size and hence parts, and those parts also parts, *ad infinitum*. If we add an infinite number of parts together, we naturally get something infinite in size.

Interpretation A. Suppose the difficulty is how something can be a unit and still have parts, that is, how something can be both one and many. One way around this difficulty is to consider something whose parts are not of like character with the whole. Thus a molecule of water is the unit of water. Yet it has parts but they are not water but the gases hydrogen and oxygen. Hence a molecule of water is both one (unit of water) and many (parts of hydrogen and oxygen).

Interpretation B. Suppose the difficulty consists in the necessity of getting an infinite-sized object from the addition of an infinite number of finite-sized objects. But this is not necessary as we have already seen in Interpretation A of the Dichotomy.

SECOND ARGUMENT. If there are a plurality of things then there are exactly as many as there are—neither more nor less. But then there will be a finite number of them. There will also be an infinite number since between any two things there must be another thing. And so the plurality of things is both finite and infinite.

Interpretation A. Suppose the difficulty consists in the question of whether or not infinite sets exist. Then we may get around Zeno's argument by pointing out some clear examples of infinite sets, as for instance the set of all positive integers. By Cantór's set theory we know there are different sizes of infinite sets which can be compared. Hence it doesn't follow that if in a plurality of things there are exactly as many things as there are then there must be a finite number of them.

Interpretation B. Suppose the difficulty is in the assumption that between any two existing things there must be another existing thing. Interpreting Zeno to be talking about the continuum, we may agree with the conclusion and deny that there is anything paradoxical about it. After all, between any two real numbers there is another real number but this fact, although perhaps an occasion for wonder, is not paradoxical.

PARADOX OF PLACE

This paradox concerns the following problem: If everything that exists, exists in a place, then the place itself has to have a place and so on *ad infinitum.*

Interpretation A. Suppose the difficulty concerns the infinite regress. We may then deny that a place has to be in another place. Instead we could allow a place to be in itself.

Interpretation B. Suppose the difficulty concerns the assumption that everything that exists, exists in a place. We can easily deny it. For example, numbers exist without existing in a place.

PARADOX OF SOUND: THE MILLET SEED

Since a single millet seed makes no sound when it is falling, the bushel of millet makes no sound when it falls; or contrarywise, since the bushel of millet makes a sound when it falls, so does the single millet seed.

Interpretation A. Suppose the difficulty consists in the question of why we do not hear the sound of a single falling millet seed. We may easily escape the paradoxical consequences by asserting that sound has a threshold and the "sound" of a single falling millet seed is below that threshold.

Interpretation B. Suppose the difficulty of the paradox depends on the fallacy of composition. Perhaps our hearing has no threshold and the individual millets make no sound. It does not follow that all of them together would make no sound. Conversely, if a bushel of millet makes a sound when falling, it doesn't follow that the individual grains do (fallacy of division). . . .

 4 

The Republic

PLATO

"THE DIVIDED LINE"

[509d]

You have to imagine, then, that there are two ruling powers, and that one of them is set over the intellectual world, the other over the visible. I do not say heaven, lest you should fancy that I am playing upon the name (ourhanoz, orhatoz). May I suppose that you have this distinction of the visible and intelligible fixed in your mind?

I have.

Now take a line which has been cut into two unequal parts, and divide each of them again in the same proportion, and suppose the two main divisions to answer, one to the visible and the other to the intelligible, and then compare the subdivisions in respect of their clearness and want of clearness, and you will find that the first section [509e] in the sphere of the visible consists of images. And by images I mean, [510a] in the first place, shadows, and in the second place, reflections in water and in solid, smooth and polished bodies and the like: Do you understand?

Yes, I understand.

Imagine, now, the other section, of which this is only the resemblance, to include the animals which we see, and everything that grows or is made.

Very good.

Would you not admit that both the sections of this division have different degrees of truth, and that the copy is to the original as [510b] the sphere of opinion is to the sphere of knowledge?

Most undoubtedly.

Next proceed to consider the manner in which the sphere of the intellectual is to be divided.

In what manner?

Thus:—There are two subdivisions, in the lower or which the soul uses the figures given by the former division as images; the enquiry can only be hypothetical, and instead of going

---

Source: Plato, *The Republic,* from *The Dialogues of Plato,* translated by Benjamin Jowett, 2nd edition, Oxford: Clarendon Press, 1875.

upwards to a principle descends to the other end; in the higher of the two, the soul passes out of hypotheses, and goes up to a principle which is above hypotheses, making no use of images as in the former case, but proceeding only in and through the ideas themselves.

I do not quite understand your meaning, he said.

Then I will try again; [510c] you will understand me better when I have made some preliminary remarks. You are aware that students of geometry, arithmetic, and the kindred sciences assume the odd and the even and the figures and three kinds of angles and the like in their several branches of science; these are their hypotheses, which they and everybody are supposed to know, and therefore they do not deign to give any account of them either to themselves or others; but they begin [510d] with them, and go on until they arrive at last, and in a consistent manner, at their conclusion?

Yes, he said, I know.

And do you not know also that although they make use of the visible forms and reason about them, they are thinking not of these, but of the ideals which they resemble; not of the figures which they draw, but of the absolute square and the absolute diameter, [510e] and so on—the forms which they draw or make, and which have shadows and reflections in water of their own, are converted by them into images, but they are really seeking to behold the things themselves, which can only be seen [511a] with the eye of the mind?

That is true.

And of this kind I spoke as the intelligible, although in the search after it the soul is compelled to use hypotheses; not ascending to a first principle, because she is unable to rise above the region of hypothesis, but employing the objects of which the shadows below are resemblances in their turn as images, they having in relation to the shadows and reflections of them a greater distinctness, and therefore a higher value.

I understand, [511b] he said, that you are speaking of the province of geometry and the sister arts.

And when I speak of the other division of the intelligible, you will understand me to speak of that other sort of knowledge which reason herself attains by the power of dialectic, using the hypotheses not as first principles, but only as hypotheses—that is to say, as steps and points of departure into a world which is above hypotheses, in order that she may soar beyond them to the first principle of the whole; and clinging to this and then to that which depends on this, by successive steps she descends again [511c] without the aid of any sensible object, from ideas, through ideas, and in ideas she ends.

I understand you, he replied; not perfectly, for you seem to me to be describing a task which is really tremendous; but, at any rate, I understand you to say that knowledge and being, which the science of dialectic contemplates, are clearer than the notions of the arts, as they are termed, which proceed from hypotheses only: these are also contemplated by the understanding, and not [511d] by the senses: yet, because they start from hypotheses and do not ascend to a principle, those who contemplate them appear to you not to exercise the higher reason upon them, although when a first principle is added to them they are cognizable by the higher reason. And the habit which is concerned with geometry and the cognate sciences I suppose that you would term understanding and not reason, as being intermediate between opinion and reason.

You have quite conceived my meaning, I said; and now, corresponding to these four divisions, let there be four faculties in the soul—reason answering to the highest, [511e] understanding to the second, faith (or conviction) to the third, and perception of shadows to the last—and let there be a scale of them, and let us suppose that the several faculties have clearness in the same degree that their objects have truth.

I understand, he replied, and give my assent, and accept your arrangement.

"THE ALLEGORY OF THE CAVE"

[514a]

And now, I said, let me show in a figure how far our nature is enlightened or unenlightened:—Behold! human beings living in a underground den, which has a mouth open towards the light and reaching all along the den; here they have been from their childhood, and have their legs and necks chained so that they cannot move, [514b] and can only see before them, being prevented by the chains from turning round their heads. Above and behind them a fire is blazing at a distance, and between the fire and the prisoners there is a raised way; and you will see, if you look, a low wall built along the way, like the screen which marionette players have in front of them, over which they show the puppets.

I see.

And do you see, I said, men passing along the wall carrying [514c] all sorts of vessels, and statues and figures of animals made of wood and stone and various materials, [515a] which appear over the wall? Some of them are talking, others silent.

You have shown me a strange image, and they are strange prisoners.

Like ourselves, I replied; and they see only their own shadows, or the shadows of one another, which the fire throws on the opposite wall of the cave?

True, he said; how could they see anything but the shadows if they were never allowed [515b] to move their heads?

And of the objects which are being carried in like manner they would only see the shadows?

Yes, he said.

And if they were able to converse with one another, would they not suppose that they were naming what was actually before them?

Very true.

And suppose further that the prison had an echo which came from the other side, would they not be sure to fancy when one of the passers-by spoke that the voice which they heard came from the passing shadow?

No question, he replied.

[515c]

To them, I said, the truth would be literally nothing but the shadows of the images.

That is certain.

And now look again, and see what will naturally follow if the prisoners are released and disabused of their error. At first, when any of them is liberated and compelled suddenly to stand up and turn his neck round and walk and look towards the light, he will suffer sharp pains; the glare will distress him, and he will be unable to see the realities of which in his former state he had seen the shadows; [515d] and then conceive some one saying to him, that what he saw before was an illusion, but that now, when he is approaching nearer to being and his eye is turned towards more real existence, he has a clearer vision,—what will be his reply? And you may further imagine that his instructor is pointing to the objects as they pass and requiring him to name them,—will he not be perplexed? Will he not fancy that the shadows which he formerly saw are truer than the objects which are now shown to him?

Far truer.

And if he is compelled to look straight at the light, [515e] will he not have a pain in his eyes which will make him turn away to take and take in the objects of vision which he can see, and which he will conceive to be in reality clearer than the things which are now being shown to him?

True, he said.

And suppose once more, that he is reluctantly dragged up a steep and rugged ascent, and held fast until he's forced into the presence of the sun himself, is he not likely to be pained and irritated? [516a] When he approaches the light his eyes will be dazzled, and he will not be able to see anything at all of what are now called realities.

Not all in a moment, he said.

He will require to grow accustomed to the sight of the upper world. And first he will see the shadows best, next the reflections of men and other objects in the water, and then the objects themselves; then he will gaze upon the light of the moon and the stars and the spangled heaven; and he will see the sky and the stars [516b] by night better than the sun or the light of the sun by day?

Certainly.

Last of he will be able to see the sun, and not mere reflections of him in the water, but he will see him in his own proper place, and not in another; and he will contemplate him as he is.

Certainly.

He will then proceed to argue that this is he who gives the season and the years, and is the guardian of all that is in the visible world, [516c] and in a certain way the cause of all things which he and his fellows have been accustomed to behold?

Clearly, he said, he would first see the sun and then reason about him.

And when he remembered his old habitation, and the wisdom of the den and his fellow-prisoners, do you not suppose that he would felicitate himself on the change, and pity them?

Certainly, he would.

And if they were in the habit of conferring honours among themselves on those who were quickest to observe the passing shadows and to remark which of them went before, [516d] and which followed after, and which were together; and who were therefore best able to draw conclusions as to the future, do you think that he would care for such honours and glories, or envy the possessors of them? Would he not say with *Homer,*

> "Better to be the poor servant of a poor master,"

and to endure anything, rather than think as they do [516e] and live after their manner?

Yes, he said, I think that he would rather suffer anything than entertain these false notions and live in this miserable manner.

Imagine once more, I said, such an one coming suddenly out of the sun to be replaced in his old situation; would he not be certain to have his eyes full of darkness?

To be sure, he said.

And if there were a contest, and he had to compete [517a] in measuring the shadows with the prisoners who had never moved out of the den, while his sight was still weak, and before his eyes had become steady (and the time which would be needed to acquire this new habit of sight might be very considerable) would he not be ridiculous? Men would say of him that up he went and down he came without his eyes; and that it was better not even to think of ascending; and if any one tried to loose another and lead him up to the light, let them only catch the offender, and they would put him to death.

No question, he said.

This entire allegory, I said, you may now append, dear *Glaucon,* to the previous argument; [517b] the prison-house is the world of sight, the light of the fire is the sun, and you will not misapprehend me if you interpret the journey upwards to be the ascent of the soul into the intellectual world according to my poor belief, which, at your desire, I have expressed—whether rightly or wrongly God knows. But, whether true or false, my opinion is that in the world of knowledge the idea of good appears last of all, and is seen only with an effort; [517c] and, when seen, is also inferred to be the universal author of all things beautiful and right, parent of light and of the lord of light in this visible world, and the immediate source of reason and truth in the intellectual; and that this is the power upon which he who would act rationally, either in public or private life must have his eye fixed.

I agree, he said, as far as I am able to understand you.

Moreover, I said, you must not wonder that those who attain to this beatific vision are unwilling to descend to human affairs; for their souls are ever hastening into the upper world [517d] where they desire to dwell; which desire of theirs is very natural, if our allegory may be trusted.

Yes, very natural.

And is there anything surprising in one who passes from divine contemplations to the evil state of man, misbehaving himself in a ridiculous manner; if, while his eyes are blinking and before he has become accustomed to the surrounding darkness, he is compelled to fight in courts of law, or in other places, about the images or the shadows of images of justice, and is endeavouring to meet [517e] the conceptions of those who have never yet seen absolute justice?

Anything but surprising, he replied.

Any one who has common sense [518a] will remember that the bewilderments of the eyes are of two kinds, and arise from two causes, either from coming out of the light or from going into the light, which is true of the mind's eye, quite as much as of the bodily eye; and he who remembers this when he sees any one whose vision is perplexed and weak, will not be too ready to laugh; he will first ask whether that soul of man has come out of the brighter light, and is unable to see because unaccustomed to the dark, [518b] or having turned from darkness to the day is dazzled by excess of light. And he will count the one happy in his condition and state of being, and he will pity the other; or, if he have a mind to laugh at the soul which comes from below into the light, there will be more reason in this than in the laugh which greets him who returns from above out of the light into the den.

That, he said, is a very just distinction.

But then, if I am right, certain professors of education must be wrong [518c] when they say that they can put a knowledge into the soul which was not there before, like sight into blind eyes.

They undoubtedly say this, he replied.

Whereas, our argument shows that the power and capacity of learning exists in the soul already; and that just as the eye was unable to turn from darkness to light without the whole body, so too the instrument of knowledge can only by the movement of the whole soul be turned from the world of becoming into that of being, and learn by degrees to endure the sight of being, and of the brightest and best of being, [518d] or in other words, of the good.

Very true.

 5

Categories

ARISTOTLE

PART 1

Things are said to be named 'equivocally' when, though they have a common name, the definition corresponding with the name differs for each. Thus, a real man and a figure in a picture can both lay claim to the name 'animal'; yet these are equivocally so named, for, though they have a common name, the definition corresponding with the name differs for each. For should any one define in what sense each is an animal, his definition in the one case will be appropriate to that case only.

On the other hand, things are said to be named 'univocally' which have both the name and the definition answering to the name in common. A man and an ox are both 'animal', and these are univocally so named, inasmuch as not only the name, but also the definition, is the same in both cases: for if a man should state in what sense each is an animal, the statement in the one case would be identical with that in the other.

Things are said to be named 'derivatively', which derive their name from some other name, but differ from it in termination. Thus the grammarian derives his name from the word 'grammar', and the courageous man from the word 'courage'.

PART 2

Forms of speech are either simple or composite. Examples of the latter are such expressions as 'the man runs', 'the man wins'; of the former 'man', 'ox', 'runs', 'wins'.

Of things themselves some are predicable of a subject, and are never present in a subject. Thus 'man' is predicable of the individual man, and is never present in a subject.

By being 'present in a subject' I do not mean present as parts are present in a whole, but being incapable of existence apart from the said subject.

Source: Aristotle, *Categories,* (347–323 B.C.E.), translated by E. M. Egdhill.

Some things, again, are present in a subject, but are never predicable of a subject. For instance, a certain point of grammatical knowledge is present in the mind, but is not predicable of any subject; or again, a certain whiteness may be present in the body (for colour requires a material basis), yet it is never predicable of anything.

Other things, again, are both predicable of a subject and present in a subject. Thus while knowledge is present in the human mind, it is predicable of grammar.

There is, lastly, a class of things which are neither present in a subject nor predicable of a subject, such as the individual man or the individual horse. But, to speak more generally, that which is individual and has the character of a unit is never predicable of a subject. Yet in some cases there is nothing to prevent such being present in a subject. Thus a certain point of grammatical knowledge is present in a subject.

PART 3

When one thing is predicated of another, all that which is predicable of the predicate will be predicable also of the subject. Thus, 'man' is predicated of the individual man; but 'animal' is predicated of 'man'; it will, therefore, be predicable of the individual man also: for the individual man is both 'man' and 'animal'.

If genera are different and co-ordinate, their differentiae are themselves different in kind. Take as an instance the genus 'animal' and the genus 'knowledge'. 'With feet', 'two-footed', 'winged', 'aquatic', are differentiae of 'animal'; the species of knowledge are not distinguished by the same differentiae. One species of knowledge does not differ from another in being 'two-footed'.

But where one genus is subordinate to another, there is nothing to prevent their having the same differentiae: for the greater class is predicated of the lesser, so that all the differentiae of the predicate will be differentiae also of the subject.

PART 4

Expressions which are in no way composite signify substance, quantity, quality, relation, place, time, position, state, action, or affection. To sketch my meaning roughly, examples of substance are 'man' or 'the horse', of quantity, such terms as 'two cubits long' or 'three cubits long', of quality, such attributes as 'white', 'grammatical'. 'Double', 'half', 'greater', fall under the category of relation; 'in a the market place', 'in the Lyceum', under that of place; 'yesterday', 'last year', under that of time. 'Lying', 'sitting', are terms indicating position, 'shod', 'armed', state; 'to lance', 'to cauterize', action; 'to be lanced', 'to be cauterized', affection.

No one of these terms, in and by itself, involves an affirmation; it is by the combination of such terms that positive or negative statements arise. For every assertion must, as is admitted, be either true or false, whereas expressions which are not in any way composite such as 'man', 'white', 'runs', 'wins', cannot be either true or false.

PART 5

Substance, in the truest and primary and most definite sense of the word, is that which is neither predicable of a subject nor present in a subject; for instance, the individual man or horse. But in a secondary sense those things are called substances within which, as species, the primary substances are included; also those which, as genera, include the species. For instance, the individual man is included in the species 'man', and the genus to which the species belongs is 'animal'; these, therefore—that is to say, the species 'man' and the genus 'animal,—are termed secondary substances.

It is plain from what has been said that both the name and the definition of the predicate must be predicable of the subject. For instance, 'man' is predicted of the individual man. Now in this case the name of the species 'man' is applied to the individual, for we use the term 'man' in describing the individual; and the definition of 'man' will also be predicated of the individual man, for the individual man is both man and animal. Thus, both the name and the definition of the species are predicable of the individual.

With regard, on the other hand, to those things which are present in a subject, it is generally the case that neither their name nor their definition is predicable of that in which they are present. Though, however, the definition is never predicable, there is nothing in certain cases to prevent the name being used. For instance, 'white' being present in a body is predicated of that in which it is present, for a body is called white: the definition, however, of the colour 'white' is never predicable of the body.

Everything except primary substances is either predicable of a primary substance or present in a primary substance. This becomes evident by reference to particular instances which occur. 'Animal' is predicated of the species 'man', therefore of the individual man, for if there were no individual man of whom it could be predicated, it could not be predicated of the species 'man' at all. Again, colour is present in body, therefore in individual bodies, for if there were no individual body in which it was present, it could not be present in body at all. Thus everything except primary substances is either predicated of primary substances, or is present in them, and if these last did not exist, it would be impossible for anything else to exist.

Of secondary substances, the species is more truly substance than the genus, being more nearly related to primary substance. For if any one should render an account of what a primary substance is, he would render a more instructive account, and one more proper to the subject, by stating the species than by stating the genus. Thus, he would give a more instructive account of an individual man by stating that he was man than by stating that he was animal, for the former description is peculiar to the individual in a greater degree, while the latter is too general. Again, the man who gives an account of the nature of an individual tree will give a more instructive account by mentioning the species 'tree' than by mentioning the genus 'plant'.

Moreover, primary substances are most properly called substances in virtue of the fact that they are the entities which underlie everything else, and that everything else is either predicated of them or present in them. Now the same relation which subsists between primary substance and everything else subsists also between the species and the genus: for the species is to the genus as subject is to predicate, since the genus is predicated of the species, whereas the species cannot be predicated of the genus. Thus we have a second ground for asserting that the species is more truly substance than the genus.

Of species themselves, except in the case of such as are genera, no one is more truly substance than another. We should not give a more appropriate account of the individual man by stating the species to which he belonged, than we should of an individual horse by adopting the same method of definition. In the same way, of primary substances, no one is more truly substance than another; an individual man is not more truly substance than an individual ox.

It is, then, with good reason that of all that remains, when we exclude primary substances, we concede to species and genera alone the name 'secondary substance', for these alone of all the predicates convey a knowledge of primary substance. For it is by stating the species or the genus that we appropriately define any individual man; and we shall make our definition more exact by stating the former than by stating the latter. All other things that we state, such as that he is white, that he runs, and so on, are irrelevant to the definition. Thus it is just that these alone, apart from primary substances, should be called substances.

Further, primary substances are most properly so called, because they underlie and are the subjects of everything else. Now the same relation that subsists between primary substance and everything else subsists also between the species and the genus to which the primary substance belongs, on the one hand, and every attribute which is not included within these, on the other. For these are the subjects of all such. If we call an individual man 'skilled in grammar', the predicate is applicable also to the species and to the genus to which he belongs. This law holds good in all cases.

It is a common characteristic of all substance that it is never present in a subject. For primary substance is neither present in a subject nor predicated of a subject; while, with regard to secondary substances, it is clear from the following arguments (apart from others) that they are not present in a subject. For 'man' is predicated of the individual man, but is not present in any subject: for manhood is not present in the individual man. In the same way, 'animal' is also predicated of the individual man, but is not present in him. Again, when a thing is present in a subject, though the name may quite well be applied to that in which it is present, the definition cannot be applied. Yet of secondary substances, not only the name, but also the definition, applies to the subject: we should use both the definition of the species and that of the genus with reference to the individual man. Thus substance cannot be present in a subject.

Yet this is not peculiar to substance, for it is also the case that differentiae cannot be present in subjects. The characteristics 'terrestrial' and 'two-footed' are predicated of the species 'man', but not present in it. For they are not in man. Moreover, the definition of the differentia may be predicated of that of which the differentia itself is predicated. For instance, if the characteristic 'terrestrial' is predicated of the species 'man', the definition also of that characteristic may be used to form the predicate of the species 'man': for 'man' is terrestrial.

The fact that the parts of substances appear to be present in the whole, as in a subject, should not make us apprehensive lest we should have to admit that such parts are not substances: for in explaining the phrase 'being present in a subject', we stated' that we meant 'otherwise than as parts in a whole'.

It is the mark of substances and of differentiae that, in all propositions of which they form the predicate, they are predicated univocally. For all such propositions have for their subject either the individual or the species. It is true that, inasmuch as primary substance is not predicable of anything, it can never form the predicate of any proposition. But of secondary substances, the species is predicated of the individual, the genus both of the species and of the individual. Similarly the differentiae are predicated of the species and of the individuals. Moreover, the definition of the species and that of the genus are applicable to the primary substance, and that of the genus to the species. For all that is predicated of the predicate will be predicated also of the subject. Similarly, the definition of the differentiae will be applicable to the species and to the individuals. But it was stated above that the word 'univocal' was applied to those things which had both name and definition in common. It is, therefore, established that in every proposition, of which either substance or a differentia forms the predicate, these are predicated univocally.

All substance appears to signify that which is individual. In the case of primary substance this is indisputably true, for the thing is a unit. In the case of secondary substances, when we speak, for instance, of 'man' or 'animal', our form of speech gives the impression that we are here also indicating that which is individual, but the impression is not strictly true; for a secondary substance is not an individual, but a class with a certain qualification; for it is not one and single as a primary substance is; the words 'man', 'animal', are predicable of more than one subject.

Yet species and genus do not merely indicate quality, like the term 'white'; 'white' indicates quality and nothing further, but species and genus determine the quality with reference to a substance: they signify substance qualitatively differentiated. The determinate qualification covers a larger field in the case of the genus that in that of the species: he who uses the word 'animal' is herein using a word of wider extension than he who uses the word 'man'.

Another mark of substance is that it has no contrary. What could be the contrary of any primary substance, such as the individual man or animal? It has none. Nor can the species or the genus have a contrary. Yet this characteristic is not peculiar to substance, but is true of many other things, such as quantity. There is nothing that forms the contrary of 'two cubits long' or of 'three cubits long', or of 'ten', or of any such term. A man may contend that 'much' is the contrary of 'little', or 'great' of 'small', but of definite quantitative terms no contrary exists.

Substance, again, does not appear to admit of variation of degree. I do not mean by this that one substance cannot be more or less truly substance than another, for it has already been stated that this is the case; but that no single substance admits of varying degrees within itself. For instance, one particular substance, 'man', cannot be more or less man either than himself at some other time or than some other man. One man cannot be more man than another, as that which is white may be more or less white than some other white object, or as that which is beautiful may be more or less beautiful than some other beautiful object. The same quality, moreover, is said to subsist in a thing in varying degrees at different times. A body, being white, is said to be whiter at one time than it was before, or, being warm, is said to be warmer or less warm than at some other time. But substance is not said to be more or less that which it is: a man is not more truly a man at one time than he was before, nor is anything, if it is substance, more or less what it is. Substance, then, does not admit of variation of degree.

The most distinctive mark of substance appears to be that, while remaining numerically one and the same, it is capable of admitting contrary qualities. From among things other than substance, we should find ourselves unable to bring forward any which possessed this mark. Thus, one and the same colour cannot be white and black. Nor can the same one action be good and bad: this law holds good with everything that is not substance. But one and the selfsame substance, while retaining its identity, is yet capable of admitting contrary qualities. The same individual person is at one time white, at another black, at one time warm, at another cold, at one time good, at another bad. This capacity is found nowhere else, though it might be maintained that a statement or opinion was an exception to the rule. The same statement, it is agreed, can be both true and false. For if the statement 'he is sitting' is true, yet, when the person in question has risen, the same statement will be false. The same applies to opinions. For if any one thinks truly that a person is sitting, yet, when that person has risen, this same opinion, if still held, will be false. Yet although this exception may be allowed, there is, nevertheless, a difference in the manner in which the thing takes place. It is by themselves changing that substances admit contrary qualities. It is thus that that which was hot becomes cold, for it has entered into a different state. Similarly that which was white becomes black, and that which was bad good, by a process of change; and in the same way in all other cases it is by changing that substances are capable of admitting contrary qualities. But statements and opinions themselves remain unaltered in all respects: it is by the alteration in the facts of the case that the contrary quality comes to be theirs. The statement 'he is sitting' remains unaltered, but it is at one time true, at another false, according to circumstances. What has been said of statements applies also to opinions. Thus, in respect of the manner in which the thing takes place, it is the peculiar mark of substance that it should be capable of admitting contrary qualities; for it is by itself changing that it does so.

If, then, a man should make this exception and contend that statements and opinions are capable of admitting contrary qualities, his contention is unsound. For statements and opinions are said to have this capacity, not because they themselves undergo modification, but because this modification occurs in the case of something else. The truth or falsity of a statement depends on facts, and not on any power on the part of the statement itself of admitting contrary qualities. In short, there is nothing which can alter the nature of statements and opinions. As, then, no change takes place in themselves, these cannot be said to be capable of admitting contrary qualities.

But it is by reason of the modification which takes place within the substance itself that a substance is said to be capable of admitting contrary qualities; for a substance admits within itself either disease or health, whiteness or blackness. It is in this sense that it is said to be capable of admitting contrary qualities.

To sum up, it is a distinctive mark of substance, that, while remaining numerically one and the same, it is capable of admitting contrary qualities, the modification taking place through a change in the substance itself.

Let these remarks suffice on the subject of substance.

 6

Physics

ARISTOTLE

I

Of things that exist, some exist by nature, some from other causes.

'By nature' the animals and their parts exist, and the plants and the simple bodies (earth, fire, air, water)—for we say that these and the like exist 'by nature'.

All the things mentioned present a feature in which they differ from things which are not constituted by nature. Each of them has within itself a principle of motion and of stationariness (in respect of place, or of growth and decrease, or by way of alteration). On the other hand, a bed and a coat and anything else of that sort, qua receiving these designations i.e. in so far as they are products of art—have no innate impulse to change. But in so far as they happen to be composed of stone or of earth or of a mixture of the two, they do have such an impulse, and just to that extent which seems to indicate that nature is a source or cause of being moved and of being at rest in that to which it belongs primarily, in virtue of itself and not in virtue of a concomitant attribute.

I say 'not in virtue of a concomitant attribute', because (for instance) a man who is a doctor might cure himself. Nevertheless it is not in so far as he is a patient that he possesses the art of medicine: it merely has happened that the same man is doctor and patient-and that is why these attributes are not always found together. So it is with all other artificial products. None of them has in itself the source of its own production. But while in some cases (for instance houses and the other products of manual labour) that principle is in something else external to the thing, in others those which may cause a change in themselves in virtue of a concomitant attribute—it lies in the things themselves (but not in virtue of what they are).

'Nature' then is what has been stated. Things 'have a nature' which have a principle of this

---

Source: Aristotle, *Physics,* (347–323 B.C.E.), translated by R. P. Hardie and R. K. Gaye.

kind. Each of them is a substance; for it is a subject, and nature always implies a subject in which it inheres.

The term 'according to nature' is applied to all these things and also to the attributes which belong to them in virtue of what they are, for instance the property of fire to be carried upwards—which is not a 'nature' nor 'has a nature' but is 'by nature' or 'according to nature'.

What nature is, then, and the meaning of the terms 'by nature' and 'according to nature', has been stated. That nature exists, it would be absurd to try to prove; for it is obvious that there are many things of this kind, and to prove what is obvious by what is not is the mark of a man who is unable to distinguish what is self-evident from what is not. (This state of mind is clearly possible. A man blind from birth might reason about colours. Presumably therefore such persons must be talking about words without any thought to correspond.)

Some identify the nature or substance of a natural object with that immediate constituent of it which taken by itself is without arrangement, e.g. the wood is the 'nature' of the bed, and the bronze the 'nature' of the statue.

As an indication of this Antiphon points out that if you planted a bed and the rotting wood acquired the power of sending up a shoot, it would not be a bed that would come up, but wood—which shows that the arrangement in accordance with the rules of the art is merely an incidental attribute, whereas the real nature is the other, which, further, persists continuously through the process of making.

But if the material of each of these objects has itself the same relation to something else, say bronze (or gold) to water, bones (or wood) to earth and so on, that (they say) would be their nature and essence. Consequently some assert earth, others fire or air or water or some or all of these, to be the nature of the things that are. For whatever any one of them supposed to have this character—whether one thing or more than one thing—this or these he declared to be the whole of substance, all else being its affections, states, or dispositions. Every such thing they held to be eternal (for it could not pass into anything else), but other things to come into being and cease to be times without number.

This then is one account of 'nature', namely that it is the immediate material substratum of things which have in themselves a principle of motion or change.

Another account is that 'nature' is the shape or form which is specified in the definition of the thing.

For the word 'nature' is applied to what is according to nature and the natural in the same way as 'art' is applied to what is artistic or a work of art. We should not say in the latter case that there is anything artistic about a thing, if it is a bed only potentially, not yet having the form of a bed; nor should we call it a work of art. The same is true of natural compounds. What is potentially flesh or bone has not yet its own 'nature', and does not exist until it receives the form specified in the definition, which we name in defining what flesh or bone is. Thus in the second sense of 'nature' it would be the shape or form (not separable except in statement) of things which have in themselves a source of motion. (The combination of the two, e.g. man, is not 'nature' but 'by nature' or 'natural'.)

The form indeed is 'nature' rather than the matter; for a thing is more properly said to be what it is when it has attained to fulfillment than when it exists potentially. Again man is born from man, but not bed from bed. That is why people say that the figure is not the nature of a bed, but the wood is—if the bed sprouted not a bed but wood would come up. But even if the figure is art, then on the same principle the shape of man is his nature. For man is born from man.

We also speak of a thing's nature as being exhibited in the process of growth by which its nature is attained. The 'nature' in this sense is not like 'doctoring', which leads not to the art of doctoring but to health. Doctoring must start from the art, not lead to it. But it is not in this way that nature (in the one sense) is related to nature (in the other). What grows qua growing grows from something into something. Into what then does it grow? Not into that from which it arose but into that to which it tends. The shape then is nature.

'Shape' and 'nature', it should be added, are in two senses. For the privation too is in a way form. But whether in unqualified coming to be there is privation, i.e. a contrary to what comes to be, we must consider later.

II

We have distinguished, then, the different ways in which the term 'nature' is used.

The next point to consider is how the mathematician differs from the physicist. Obviously physical bodies contain surfaces and volumes, lines and points, and these are the subject-matter of mathematics.

Further, is astronomy different from physics or a department of it? It seems absurd that the physicist should be supposed to know the nature of sun or moon, but not to know any of their essential attributes, particularly as the writers on physics obviously do discuss their shape also and whether the earth and the world are spherical or not.

Now the mathematician, though he too treats of these things, nevertheless does not treat of them as the limits of a physical body; nor does he consider the attributes indicated as the attributes of such bodies. That is why he separates them; for in thought they are separable from motion, and it makes no difference, nor does any falsity result, if they are separated. The holders of the theory of Forms do the same, though they are not aware of it; for they separate the objects of physics, which are less separable than those of mathematics. This becomes plain if one tries to state in each of the two cases the definitions of the things and of their attributes. 'Odd' and 'even', 'straight' and 'curved', and likewise 'number', 'line', and 'figure', do not involve motion; not so 'flesh' and 'bone' and 'man'—these are defined like 'snub nose', not like 'curved'.

Similar evidence is supplied by the more physical of the branches of mathematics, such as optics, harmonics, and astronomy. These are in a way the converse of geometry. While geometry investigates physical lines but not qua physical, optics investigates mathematical lines, but qua physical, not qua mathematical.

Since 'nature' has two senses, the form and the matter, we must investigate its objects as we would the essence of snubness. That is, such things are neither independent of matter nor can be defined in terms of matter only. Here too indeed one might raise a difficulty. Since there are two natures, with which is the physicist concerned? Or should he investigate the combination of the two? But if the combination of the two, then also each severally. Does it belong then to the same or to different sciences to know each severally?

If we look at the ancients, physics would to be concerned with the matter. (It was only very slightly that Empedocles and Democritus touched on the forms and the essence.)

But if on the other hand art imitates nature, and it is the part of the same discipline to know the form and the matter up to a point (e.g. the doctor has a knowledge of health and also of bile and phlegm, in which health is realized, and the builder both of the form of the house and of the matter, namely that it is bricks and beams, and so forth): if this is so, it would be the part of physics also to know nature in both its senses.

Again, 'that for the sake of which', or the end, belongs to the same department of knowledge as the means. But the nature is the end or 'that for the sake of which'. For if a thing undergoes a continuous change and there is a stage which is last, this stage is the end or 'that for the sake of which'. (That is why the poet was carried away into making an absurd statement when he said 'he has the end for the sake of which he was born'. For not every stage that is last claims to be an end, but only that which is best.)

For the arts make their material (some simply 'make' it, others make it serviceable), and we use everything as if it was there for our sake. (We also are in a sense an end. 'That for the sake of which' has two senses: the distinction is made in our work On Philosophy.) The arts, therefore, which govern the matter and have knowledge are two, namely the art which uses the product and the art which directs the production of it. That is why the using art also is in a sense directive; but it differs in that it knows the form, whereas the art which is directive as being concerned with production knows the matter. For the helmsman knows and prescribes what sort of form a helm should have, the other from what wood it should be made and by means of what operations. In the products of art, however, we make the material with a view to the function, whereas in the products of nature the matter is there all along.

Again, matter is a relative term: to each form there corresponds a special matter. How far then must the physicist know the form or essence? Up to a point, perhaps, as the doctor must know sinew or the smith bronze (i.e. until he understands the purpose of each): and the physicist is concerned only with things whose forms are separable indeed, but do not exist apart from matter. Man is begotten by man and by the sun as well. The mode of existence and essence of the separable it is the business of the primary type of philosophy to define.

III

Now that we have established these distinctions, we must proceed to consider causes, their character and number. Knowledge is the object of our inquiry, and men do not think they know a thing till they have grasped the 'why' of (which is to grasp its primary cause). So clearly we too must do this as regards both coming to be and passing away and every kind of physical change, in order that, knowing their principles, we may try to refer to these principles each of our problems.

In one sense, then, (1) that out of which a thing comes to be and which persists, is called 'cause', e.g. the bronze of the statue, the silver of the bowl, and the genera of which the bronze and the silver are species.

In another sense (2) the form or the archetype, i.e. the statement of the essence, and its genera, are called 'causes' (e.g. of the octave the relation of 2:1, and generally number), and the parts in the definition.

Again (3) the primary source of the change or coming to rest; e.g. the man who gave advice is a cause, the father is cause of the child, and generally what makes of what is made and what causes change of what is changed.

Again (4) in the sense of end or 'that for the sake of which' a thing is done, e.g. health is the cause of walking about. ('Why is he walking about?' we say. 'To be healthy', and, having said that, we think we have assigned the cause.) The same is true also of all the intermediate steps which are brought about through the action of something else as means towards the end, e.g. reduction of flesh, purging, drugs, or surgical instruments are means towards health. All these things are 'for the sake of' the end, though they differ from one another in that some are activities, others instruments.

This then perhaps exhausts the number of ways in which the term 'cause' is used.

As the word has several senses, it follows that there are several causes of the same thing not merely in virtue of a concomitant attribute, e.g. both the art of the sculptor and the bronze are causes of the statue. These are causes of the statue qua statue, not in virtue of anything else that it may be—only not in the same way, the one being the material cause, the other the cause whence the motion comes. Some things cause each other reciprocally, e.g. hard work causes fitness and vice versa, but again not in the same way, but the one as end, the other as the origin of change. Further the same thing is the cause of contrary results. For that which by its presence brings about one result is sometimes blamed for bringing about the contrary by its absence. Thus we ascribe the wreck of a ship to the absence of the pilot whose presence was the cause of its safety.

All the causes now mentioned fall into four familiar divisions. The letters are the causes of syllables, the material of artificial products, fire, &c., of bodies, the parts of the whole, and the premises of the conclusion, in the sense of 'that from which'. Of these pairs the one set are causes in the sense of substratum, e.g. the parts, the other set in the sense of essence—the whole and the combination and the form. But the seed and the doctor and the adviser, and generally the maker, are all sources whence the change or stationariness originates, while the others are causes in the sense of the end or the good of the rest; for 'that for the sake of which' means what is best and the end of the things that lead up to it. (Whether we say the 'good itself or the 'apparent good' makes no difference.)

Such then is the number and nature of the kinds of cause.

Now the modes of causation are many, though when brought under heads they too can be reduced in number. For 'cause' is used in many senses and even within the same kind one may be prior to another (e.g. the doctor and the expert are causes of health, the relation 2:1 and number of the octave), and always what is inclusive to what is particular. Another mode of causation is the incidental and its genera, e.g. in one way 'Polyclitus', in another 'sculptor' is the cause of a statue, because 'being Polyclitus' and 'sculptor' are incidentally conjoined. Also the classes in which the incidental attribute is included; thus 'a man' could be said to be the cause of a statue or, generally, 'a living creature'. An incidental attribute too may be more or less remote, e.g. suppose that 'a pale man' or 'a musical man' were said to be the cause of the statue.

All causes, both proper and incidental, may be spoken of either as potential or as actual; e.g. the cause of a house being built is either 'house-builder' or 'house-builder building'.

Similar distinctions can be made in the things of which the causes are causes, e.g. of 'this statue' or of 'statue' or of 'image' generally, of 'this bronze' or of 'bronze' or of 'material' generally. So too with the incidental attributes. Again we may use a complex expression for either and say, e.g. neither 'Polyclitus' nor 'sculptor' but 'Polyclitus, sculptor'.

All these various uses, however, come to six in number, under each of which again the usage is twofold. Cause means either what is particular or a genus, or an incidental attribute or a genus of that, and these either as a complex or each by itself; and all six either as actual or as potential. The difference is this much, that causes which are actually at work and particular exist and cease to exist simultaneously with their effect, e.g. this healing person with this being-healed person and that house-building man with that being-built house; but this is not always true of potential causes—the house and the house-builder do not pass away simultaneously.

In investigating the cause of each thing it is always necessary to seek what is most precise (as also in other things): thus man builds because he is a builder, and a builder builds in virtue of his art of building. This last cause then is prior: and so generally.

Further, generic effects should be assigned to generic causes, particular effects to particular causes, e.g. statue to sculptor, this statue to this sculptor; and powers are relative to possible effects, actually operating causes to things which are actually being effected.

This must suffice for our account of the number of causes and the modes of causation.

VII

It is clear then that there are causes, and that the number of them is what we have stated. The number is the same as that of the things comprehended under the question 'why'. The 'why' is referred ultimately either (1), in things which do not involve motion, e.g. in mathematics, to the 'what' (to the definition of 'straight line' or 'commensurable', &c.), or (2) to what initiated a motion, e.g. 'why did they go to war?-because there had been a raid'; or (3) we are inquiring 'for the sake of what?'-'that they may rule'; or (4), in the case of things that come into being, we are looking for the matter. The causes, therefore, are these and so many in number.

Now, the causes being four, it is the business of the physicist to know about them all, and if he refers his problems back to all of them, he will assign the 'why' in the way proper to his science-the matter, the form, the mover, 'that for the sake of which'. The last three often coincide; for the 'what' and 'that for the sake of which' are one, while the primary source of motion is the same in species as these (for man generates man), and so too, in general, are all things which cause movement by being themselves moved; and such as are not of this kind are no longer inside the province of physics, for they cause motion not by possessing motion or a source of motion in themselves, but being themselves incapable of motion. Hence there are three branches of study, one of things which are incapable of motion, the second of things in motion, but indestructible, the third of destructible things.

The question 'why', then, is answered by reference to the matter, to the form, and to the primary moving cause. For in respect of coming to be it is mostly in this last way that causes are investigated-'what comes to be after what? what was the primary agent or patient?' and so at each step of the series.

Now the principles which cause motion in a physical way are two, of which one is not physical, as it has no principle of motion in itself. Of this kind is whatever causes movement, not being itself moved, such as (1) that which is completely unchangeable, the primary reality, and (2) the essence of that which is coming to be, i.e. the form; for this is the end or 'that for the sake of which'. Hence since nature is for the sake of something, we must know this cause also. We must explain the 'why' in all the senses of the term, namely, (1) that from this that will necessarily result ('from this' either without qualification or in most cases); (2) that 'this must be so if that is to be so' (as the conclusion presupposes the premises); (3) that this was the essence of the thing; and (4) because it is better thus (not without qualification, but with reference to the essential nature in each case). . . .

VIII

We must explain then (1) that Nature belongs to the class of causes which act for the sake of something; (2) about the necessary and its place in physical problems, for all writers ascribe things to this cause, arguing that since the hot and the cold, &c., are of such and such a kind, therefore certain things necessarily are and come to be—and if they mention any other cause (one his 'friendship and strife', another his 'mind'), it is only to touch on it, and then good-bye to it.

A difficulty presents itself: why should not nature work, not for the sake of something, nor because it is better so, but just as the sky rains, not in order to make the corn grow, but of necessity? What is drawn up must cool, and what has been cooled must become water and descend, the result of this being that the corn grows. Similarly if a man's crop is spoiled on the threshing-floor, the rain did not fall for the sake of this—in order that the crop might be spoiled—but that result just followed. Why then should it not be the same with the parts in nature, e.g. that our teeth should come up of necessity—the front teeth sharp, fitted for tearing, the molars broad and useful for grinding down the food—since they did not arise for this end, but it was merely a coincident result; and so with all other parts in which we suppose that there is purpose? Wherever then all the parts came about just what they would have been if they had come to be for an end, such things survived, being organized spontaneously in a fitting way; whereas those which grew otherwise perished and continue to perish, as Empedocles says his 'man-faced ox-progeny' did.

Such are the arguments (and others of the kind) which may cause difficulty on this point. Yet it is impossible that this should be the true view. For teeth and all other natural things either invariably or normally come about in a given way; but of not one of the results of chance or spontaneity is this true. We do not ascribe to chance or mere coincidence the frequency of rain in winter, but frequent rain in summer we do; nor heat in the dog-days, but only if we have it in winter. If then, it is agreed that things are either the result of coincidence or for an end, and these cannot be the result of coincidence or spontaneity, it follows that they must be for an end; and that such things are all due to nature even the champions of the theory which is before us would agree. Therefore action for an end is present in things which come to be and are by nature.

Further, where a series has a completion, all the preceding steps are for the sake of that. Now surely as in intelligent action, so in nature; and as in nature, so it is in each action, if nothing interferes. Now intelligent action is for the sake of an end; therefore the nature of things also is so. Thus if a house, e.g. had been a thing made by nature, it would have been made in the same way as it is now by art; and if things made by nature were made also by art, they would come to be in the same way as by nature. Each step then in the series is for the sake of the next; and generally art partly completes what nature cannot bring to a finish, and partly imitates her. If, therefore, artificial products are for the sake of an end, so clearly also are natural products. The relation of the later to the earlier terms of the series is the same in both. This is most obvious in the animals other than man: they make things neither by art nor after inquiry or deliberation. Wherefore people discuss whether it is by intelligence or by some other faculty that these creatures work, spiders, ants, and the like. By gradual advance in this direction we come to see clearly that in plants too that is produced which is conducive to the end—leaves, e.g. grow to provide shade for the fruit. If then it is both by nature and for an end that the swallow makes its nest and the spider its web, and plants grow leaves for the sake of the fruit and send their roots down (not up) for the sake of nourishment, it is plain that this kind of cause is operative in things which come to be and are by nature. And since 'nature' means two things, the matter and the form, of which the latter is the end, and since all the rest is for the sake of the end, the form must be the cause in the sense of 'that for the sake of which'.

Now mistakes come to pass even in the operations of art: the grammarian makes a mistake in writing and the doctor pours out the wrong dose. Hence clearly mistakes are possible in the operations of nature also. If then in art there are cases in which what is rightly produced serves a purpose, and if where mistakes occur there was a purpose in what was attempted, only it was not attained, so must it be also in natural products, and monstrosities will be failures in the purposive effort. Thus in the original combinations the 'ox-progeny' if they failed to reach a determinate end must have arisen through the corruption of some principle corresponding to what is now the seed.

Further, seed must have come into being first, and not straightway the animals: the words 'whole-natured first . . .' must have meant seed.

Again, in plants too we find the relation of means to end, though the degree of organization is less. Were there then in plants also 'olive-headed vine-progeny', like the 'man-headed ox-progeny', or not? An absurd suggestion; yet there must have been, if there were such things among animals.

Moreover, among the seeds anything must have come to be at random. But the person who asserts this entirely does away with 'nature' and what exists 'by nature'. For those things are natural which, by a continuous movement originated from an internal principle, arrive at some completion: the same completion is not reached from every principle; nor any chance completion, but always the tendency in each is towards the same end, if there is no impediment.

The end and the means towards it may come about by chance. We say, for instance, that a stranger has come by chance, paid the ransom, and gone away, when he does so as if he had come for that purpose, though it was not for that that he came. This is incidental, for chance is an incidental cause, as I remarked before. But when an event takes place always or for the most part, it is not incidental or by chance. In natural products the sequence is invariable, if there is no impediment.

It is absurd to suppose that purpose is not present because we do not observe the agent deliberating. Art does not deliberate. If the ship-building art were in the wood, it would produce the same results by nature. If, therefore, purpose is present in art, it is present also in nature. The best illustration is a doctor doctoring himself: nature is like that.

It is plain then that nature is a cause, a cause that operates for a purpose.

IX

As regards what is 'of necessity', we must ask whether the necessity is 'hypothetical', or 'simple' as well. The current view places what is of necessity in the process of production, just as if one were to suppose that the wall of a house necessarily comes to be because what is heavy is naturally carried downwards and what is light to the top, wherefore the stones and foundations take the lowest place, with earth above because it is lighter, and wood at the top of all as being the lightest. Whereas, though the wall does not come to be without these, it is not due to these, except as its material cause: it comes to be for the sake of sheltering and guarding certain things. Similarly in all other things which involve production for an end; the product cannot come to be without things which have a necessary nature, but it is not due to these (except as its material); it comes to be for an end. For instance, why is a saw such as it is? To effect so-and-so and for the sake of so-and-so. This end, however, cannot be realized unless the saw is made of iron. It is, therefore, necessary for it to be of iron, if we are to have a saw and perform the operation of sawing. What is necessary then, is necessary on a hypothesis; it is not a result necessarily determined by antecedents. Necessity is in the matter, while 'that for the sake of which' is in the definition.

Necessity in mathematics is in a way similar to necessity in things which come to be through the operation of nature. Since a straight line is what it is, it is necessary that the angles of a triangle should equal two right angles. But not conversely; though if the angles are not equal to two right angles, then the straight line is not what it is either. But in things which come to be for an end, the reverse is true. If the end is to exist or does exist, that also which precedes it will exist or does exist; otherwise just as there, if the conclusion is not true, the premise will not be true, so here the end or 'that for the sake of which' will not exist. For this too is itself a starting-point, but of the reasoning, not of the action; while in mathematics the starting-point is the starting-point of the reasoning only, as there is no action. If then there is to be a house, such-and-such things must be made or be there already or exist, or generally the matter relative to the end, bricks and stones if it is a house. But the end is not due to these except as the matter, nor will it come to exist because of them. Yet if they do not exist at all, neither will the house, or the saw—the former in the absence of stones, the latter in the absence of iron—just as in the other case the premises will not be true, if the angles of the triangle are not equal to two right angles.

The necessary in nature, then, is plainly what we call by the name of matter, and the changes in it. Both causes must be stated by the physicist, but especially the end; for that is the cause of the matter, not vice versa; and the end is 'that for the sake of which', and the beginning starts from the definition or essence; as in artificial products, since a house is of such-and-such a kind, certain things must necessarily come to be or be there already, or since health is this, these things must necessarily come to be or be there already. Similarly if man is this, then these; if these, then those. Perhaps the necessary is present also in the definition. For if one defines the operation of sawing as being a certain kind of dividing, then this cannot come about unless the saw has teeth of a certain kind; and these cannot be unless it is of iron. For in the definition too there are some parts that are, as it were, its matter.

 7 

Metaphysics

ARISTOTLE

I

All men by nature desire to know. An indication of this is the delight we take in our senses; for even apart from their usefulness they are loved for themselves; and above all others the sense of sight. For not only with a view to action, but even when we are not going to do anything, we prefer seeing (one might say) to everything else. The reason is that this, most of all the senses, makes us know and brings to light many differences between things.

By nature animals are born with the faculty of sensation, and from sensation memory is produced in some of them, though not in others. And therefore the former are more intelligent and apt at learning than those which cannot remember; those which are incapable of hearing sounds are intelligent though they cannot be taught, e.g. the bee, and any other race of animals that may be like it; and those which besides memory have this sense of hearing can be taught.

The animals other than man live by appearances and memories, and have but little of connected experience; but the human race lives also by art and reasonings. Now from memory experience is produced in men; for the several memories of the same thing produce finally the capacity for a single experience. And experience seems pretty much like science and art, but really science and art come to men through experience; for 'experience made art', as Polus says, 'but inexperience luck'. Now art arises when from many notions gained by experience one universal judgement about a class of objects is produced. For to have a judgement that when Callias was ill of this disease this did him good, and similarly in the case of Socrates and in many individual cases, is a matter of experience; but to judge that it has done good to all persons of a certain constitution, marked off in one class, when they were ill of this disease,

Source: Aristotle, *Metaphysics* (347–323 B.C.E.), translated by W. D. Ross.

e.g. to phlegmatic or bilious people when burning with fevers—this is a matter of art.

With a view to action experience seems in no respect inferior to art, and men of experience succeed even better than those who have theory without experience. (The reason is that experience is knowledge of individuals, art of universals, and actions and productions are all concerned with the individual; for the physician does not cure man, except in an incidental way, but Callias or Socrates or some other called by some such individual name, who happens to be a man. If, then, a man has the theory without the experience, and recognizes the universal but does not know the individual included in this, he will often fail to cure; for it is the individual that is to be cured.) But yet we think that knowledge and understanding belong to art rather than to experience, and we suppose artists to be wiser than men of experience (which implies that Wisdom depends in all cases rather on knowledge); and this because the former know the cause, but the latter do not. For men of experience know that the thing is so, but do not know why, while the others know the 'why' and the cause. Hence we think also that the masterworkers in each craft are more honourable and know in a truer sense and are wiser than the manual workers, because they know the causes of the things that are done (we think the manual workers are like certain lifeless things which act indeed, but act without knowing what they do, as fire burns, but while the lifeless things perform each of their functions by a natural tendency, the labourers perform them through habit); thus we view them as being wiser not in virtue of being able to act, but of having the theory for themselves and knowing the causes. And in general it is a sign of the man who knows and of the man who does not know, that the former can teach, and therefore we think art more truly knowledge than experience is; for artists can teach, and men of mere experience cannot.

Again, we do not regard any of the senses as Wisdom; yet surely these give the most authoritative knowledge of particulars. But they do not tell us the 'why' of anything—e.g. why fire is hot; they only say that it is hot.

At first he who invented any art whatever that went beyond the common perceptions of man was naturally admired by men, not only because there was something useful in the inventions, but because he was thought wise and superior to the rest. But as more arts were invented, and some were directed to the necessities of life, others to recreation, the inventors of the latter were naturally always regarded as wiser than the inventors of the former, because their branches of knowledge did not aim at utility. Hence when all such inventions were already established, the sciences which do not aim at giving pleasure or at the necessities of life were discovered, and first in the places where men first began to have leisure. This is why the mathematical arts were founded in Egypt; for there the priestly caste was allowed to be at leisure.

We have said in the Ethics what the difference is between art and science and the other kindred faculties; but the point of our present discussion is this, that all men suppose what is called Wisdom to deal with the first causes and the principles of things; so that, as has been said before, the man of experience is thought to be wiser than the possessors of any sense-perception whatever, the artist wiser than the men of experience, the masterworker than the mechanic, and the theoretical kinds of knowledge to be more of the nature of Wisdom than the productive. Clearly then Wisdom is knowledge about certain principles and causes.

II

Since we are seeking this knowledge, we must inquire of what kind are the causes and the principles, the knowledge of which is Wisdom. If one were to take the notions we have about the wise man, this might perhaps make the answer more evident. We suppose first, then, that the wise man knows all things, as far as possible, although he has not knowledge of each of them in detail; secondly, that he who can learn things that are difficult, and not easy for man to know, is wise (sense-perception is common to all, and therefore easy and no mark of Wisdom); again, that he who is more exact and more capable of teaching the causes is wiser, in every branch of knowledge; and that of the sciences, also, that which is desirable on its own account and for the sake of knowing it is more of the nature of Wisdom than that which is desirable on account of its results, and the superior science is more of the nature of Wisdom than the ancillary; for the wise man must not be ordered but must order, and he must not obey another, but the less wise must obey him.

Such and so many are the notions, then, which we have about Wisdom and the wise. Now of these characteristics that of knowing all things must belong to him who has in the highest degree universal knowledge; for he knows in a sense all the instances that fall under the universal. And these things, the most universal, are on the whole the hardest for men to know; for they are farthest from the senses. And the most exact of the sciences are those which deal most with first principles; for those which involve fewer principles are more exact than those which involve additional principles, e.g. arithmetic than geometry. But the science which investigates causes is also instructive, in a higher degree, for the people who instruct us are those who tell the causes of each thing. And understanding and knowledge pursued for their own sake are found most in the knowledge of that which is most knowable (for he who chooses to know for the sake of knowing will choose most readily that which is most truly knowledge, and such is the knowledge of that which is most knowable); and the first principles and the causes are most knowable; for by reason of these, and from these, all other things come to be known, and not these by means of the things subordinate to them. And the science which knows to what end each thing must be done is the most authoritative of the sciences, and more authoritative than any ancillary science; and this end is the good of that thing, and in general the supreme good in the whole of nature. Judged by all the tests we have mentioned, then, the name in question falls to the same science; this must be a science that investigates the first principles and causes; for the good, i.e. the end, is one of the causes.

That it is not a science of production is clear even from the history of the earliest philosophers. For it is owing to their wonder that men both now begin and at first began to philosophize; they wondered originally at the obvious difficulties, then advanced little by little and stated difficulties about the greater matters, e.g. about the phenomena of the moon and those of the sun and of the stars, and about the genesis of the universe. And a man who is puzzled and wonders thinks himself ignorant (whence even the lover of myth is in a sense a lover of Wisdom, for the myth is composed of wonders); therefore since they philosophized order to escape from ignorance, evidently they were pursuing science in order to know, and not for any utilitarian end. And this is confirmed by the facts; for it was when almost all the necessities of life and the things that make for comfort and recreation had been secured, that such knowledge began to be sought. Evidently then we do not seek it for the sake of any other advantage; but as the man is free, we say, who exists for his own sake and not for another's, so we pursue this as the only free science, for it alone exists for its own sake.

Hence also the possession of it might be justly regarded as beyond human power; for in many ways human nature is in bondage, so that according to Simonides 'God alone can have this privilege', and it is unfitting that man should not be content to seek the knowledge that is suited to him. If, then, there is something in what the poets say, and jealousy is natural to the divine power, it would probably occur in this case above all, and all who excelled in this knowledge would be unfortunate. But the divine power cannot be jealous (nay, according to the proverb, 'bards tell a lie'), nor should any other science be thought more honourable than one of this sort. For the most divine science is also most honourable; and this science alone must be, in two ways, most divine. For the science which it would be most meet for God to have is a divine science, and so is any science that deals with divine objects; and this science alone has both these qualities; for (1) God is thought to be among the causes of all things and to be a first principle, and (2) such a science either God alone can have, or God above all others. All the sciences, indeed, are more necessary than this, but none is better.

Yet the acquisition of it must in a sense end in something which is the opposite of our original inquiries. For all men begin, as we said, by wondering that things are as they are, as they do about self-moving marionettes, or about the solstices or the incommensurability of the diagonal of a square with the side; for it seems wonderful to all who have not yet seen the reason, that there is a thing which cannot be measured even by the smallest unit. But we must end in the contrary and, according to the proverb, the better state, as is the case in these instances too when men learn the cause; for there is nothing which would surprise a geometer so much as if the diagonal turned out to be commensurable.

We have stated, then, what is the nature of the science we are searching for, and what is the mark which our search and our whole investigation must reach.

8

Identity, Ostension, and Hypostasis, excerpt

W. V. O. QUINE

I

Identity is a popular source of philosophical perplexity. Undergoing change as I do, how can I be said to continue to be myself? Considering that a complete replacement of my material substance takes place every few years, how can I be said to continue to be I for more than such a period at best?

It would be agreeable to be driven, by these or other considerations, to belief in a changeless and therefore immortal soul as the vehicle of my persisting self-identity. But we should be less eager to embrace a parallel solution of Heracleitus's parallel problem regarding a river: "You cannot bathe in the same river twice, for new waters are ever flowing in upon you."

The solution of Heracleitus's problem, though familiar, will afford a convenient approach to some less familiar matters. The truth is that you *can* bathe in the same *river* twice, but not in the same river stage. You can bathe in two river stages which are stages of the same river, and this is what constitutes bathing in the same river twice. A river is a process through time, and the river stages are its momentary parts. Identification of the river bathed in once with the river bathed in again is just what determines our subject matter to be a river process as opposed to a river stage.

Let me speak of any multiplicity of water molecules as a *water*. Now a river stage is at the same time a water stage, but two stages of the same river are not in general stages of the same water. River stages are water stages, but rivers are not waters. You may bathe in the same river twice without bathing in the same water twice,

---

and you may, in these days of fast transportation, bathe in the same water twice while bathing in two different rivers.

We begin, let us imagine, with momentary things and their interrelations. One of these momentary things, called *a*, is a momentary stage of the river Caÿster, in Lydia, around 400 B.C. Another, called *b*, is a momentary stage of the Caÿster two days later. A third, *c*, is a momentary stage, at this same latter date, of the same multiplicity of water molecules which were in the river at the time of *a*. Half of *c* is in the lower Caÿster valley, and the other half is to be found at diffuse points in the Aegean Sea. Thus *a*, *b*, and *c* are three objects, variously related. We may say that *a* and *b* stand in the relation of river kinship, and that *a* and *c* stand in the relation of water kinship.

Now the introduction of rivers as single entities, namely, processes or time-consuming objects, consists substantially in reading identity in place of river kinship. It would be wrong, indeed, to say that *a* and *b* are identical; they are merely river-kindred. But if we were to point to *a*, and then wait the required two days and point to *b*, and affirm identity of the objects pointed to, we should thereby show that our pointing was intended not as a pointing to two kindred river stages but as a pointing to a single river which included them both. The imputation of identity is essential, here, to fixing the reference of the ostension.

These reflections are reminiscent of Hume's account of our idea of external objects. Hume's theory was that the idea of external objects arises from an error of identification. Various similar impressions separated in time are mistakenly treated as identical; and then, as a means of resolving this contradiction of identifying momentary events which are separated in time, we invent a new nonmomentary object to serve as subject matter of our statement of identity. Hume's charge of erroneous identification here is interesting as a psychological conjecture on origins, but there is no need for us to share that conjecture. The important point to observe is merely the direct connection between identity and the positing of processes, or time-extended objects. To impute identity rather than river kinship is to talk of the river Caÿster rather than of *a* and *b*.

Pointing is of itself ambiguous as to the temporal spread of the indicated object. Even given that the indicated object is to be a process with considerable temporal spread, and hence a summation of momentary objects, still pointing does not tell us *which* summation of momentary objects is intended, beyond the fact that the momentary object at hand is to be in the desired summation. Pointing to *a*, if construed as referring to a time-extended process and not merely to the momentary object *a*, could be interpreted either as referring to the river Caÿster of which *a* and *b* are stages, or as referring to the water of which *a* and *c* are stages, or as referring to any one of an unlimited number of further less natural summations to which *a* also belongs.

Such ambiguity is commonly resolved by accompanying the pointing with such words as 'this river', thus appealing to a prior concept of a river as one distinctive type of time-consuming process, one distinctive form of summation of momentary objects. Pointing to *a* and saying 'this river'—or ὅδε ὁ ποταμός, since we are in 400 B.C.—leaves no ambiguity as to the object of reference if the word 'river' itself is already intelligible. 'This river' means 'the riverish summation of momentary objects which contains this momentary object'.

But here we have moved beyond pure ostension and have assumed conceptualization. Now suppose instead that the general term 'river' is not yet understood, so that we cannot specify the Caÿster by pointing and saying 'This river is the Caÿster'. Suppose also that we are deprived of other descriptive devices. What we may do then is point to *a* and two days later to *b* and say each time, 'This is the Caÿster'. The word 'this' so used must have referred not to *a* nor to *b*, but beyond to something more inclusive, identical in the two cases. Our specification of the Caÿster is not yet unique, however, for we might still mean any of a vast variety of other collections of momentary objects, related in other modes than that of river kinship; all we know is that *a* and *b* are among its constituents. By pointing to more and more stages additional to *a* and *b*, however, we eliminate more and more alternatives, until our listener, aided by his own tendency to favor the most natural groupings, has grasped the idea of the Caÿster. His learning of this idea is an induction: from our grouping the sample momentary objects *a*, *b*, *d*, *g*, and others under the head of Caÿster, he projects a correct general hypothesis as to what further momentary objects we would also be content to include.

Actually there is in the case of the Caÿster the question of its extent in space as well as in time. Our sample pointings need to be made not only on a variety of dates, but at various points up and down stream, if our listener is to have a representative basis for his inductive generalization as to the intended spatio-temporal spread of the four-dimensional object Caÿster.

In ostension, spatial spread is not wholly separable from temporal spread, for the successive ostensions which provide samples over the spatial spread are bound to consume time. The inseparability of space and time characteristic of relativity theory is foreshadowed, if only superficially, in this simple situation of ostension.

The concept of identity, then, is seen to perform a central function in the specifying of spatio-temporally broad objects by ostension. Without identity, *n* acts of ostension merely specify up to *n* objects, each of indeterminate spatio-temporal spread. But when we affirm identity of object from ostension to ostension, we cause our *n* ostensions to refer to the same large object, and so afford our listener an inductive ground from which to guess the intended reach of that object. Pure ostension plus identification conveys, with the help of some induction, spatio-temporal spread. . . .

9

Of the Idea of a Necessary Connection

DAVID HUME

There are no ideas, which occur in metaphysics, more obscure and uncertain, than those of *power, force, energy* or *necessary connexion,* of which it is every moment necessary for us to treat in all our disquisitions. We shall, therefore, endeavour, in this section, to fix, if possible, the precise meaning of these terms, and thereby remove some part of that obscurity, which is so much complained of in this species of philosophy.

It seems a proposition, which will not admit of much dispute, that all our ideas are nothing but copies of our impressions, or, in other words, that it is impossible for us to *think* of any thing, which we have not antecedently *felt,* either by our external or internal senses. I have endeavoured[1] to explain and prove this proposition, and have expressed my hopes, that, by a proper application of it, men may reach a greater clearness and precision in philosophical reasonings, than what they have hitherto been able to attain. Complex ideas may, perhaps, be well known by definition, which is nothing but an enumeration of those parts or simple ideas, that compose them. But when we have pushed up definitions to the most simple ideas, and find still some ambiguity and obscurity; what resource are we then possessed of? By what invention can we throw light upon these ideas, and render them altogether precise and determinate to our intellectual view? Produce the impressions or original sentiments, from which the ideas are copied. These impressions are all strong and sensible. They admit not of ambiguity. They are not only placed in a full light themselves, but may throw light on their correspondent ideas, which lie in obscurity. And by this means, we may, perhaps, attain a new microscope or species of optics, by which, in the moral sciences, the most minute, and most simple ideas may be so enlarged as to fall readily under our apprehension, and be equally known with the grossest and most sensible ideas, that can be the object of our enquiry.

Source: David Hume, *An Enquiry Concerning Human Understanding,* originally published 1748.

To be fully acquainted, therefore, with the idea of power or necessary connexion, let us examine its impression; and in order to find the impression with greater certainty, let us search for it in all the sources, from which it may possibly be derived.

When we look about us towards external objects, and consider the operation of causes, we are never able, in a single instance, to discover any power or necessary connexion; any quality, which binds the effect to the cause, and renders the one an infallible consequence of the other. We only find, that the one does actually, in fact, follow the other. The impulse of one billiard-ball is attended with motion in the second. This is the whole that appears to the *outward* senses. The mind feels no sentiment or *inward* impression from this succession of objects: Consequently, there is not, in any single, particular instance of cause and effect, any thing which can suggest the idea of power or necessary connexion.

From the first appearance of an object, we never can conjecture what effect will result from it. But were the power or energy of any cause discoverable by the mind, we could foresee the effect, even without experience; and might, at first, pronounce with certainty concerning it, by the mere dint of thought and reasoning.

In reality, there is no part of matter, that does ever, by its sensible qualities, discover any power or energy, or give us ground to imagine, that it could produce any thing, or be followed by any other object, which we could denominate its effect. Solidity, extension, motion; these qualities are all complete in themselves, and never point out any other event which may result from them. The scenes of the universe are continually shifting, and one object follows another in an uninterrupted succession; but the power or force, which actuates the whole machine, is entirely concealed from us, and never discovers itself in any of the sensible qualities of body. We know, that, in fact, heat is a constant attendant of flame; but what is the connexion between them, we have no room so much as to conjecture or imagine. It is impossible, therefore, that the idea of power can be derived from the contemplation of bodies, in single instances of their operation; because no bodies ever discover any power, which can be the original of this idea.[2] . . .

PART II

But to hasten to a conclusion of this argument, which is already drawn out to too great a length: We have sought in vain for an idea of power or necessary connexion in all the sources from which we could suppose it to be derived. It appears that, in single instances of the operation of bodies, we never can, by our utmost scrutiny, discover any thing but one event following another; without being able to comprehend any force or power by which the cause operates, or any connexion between it and its supposed effect. The same difficulty occurs in contemplating the operations of mind on body—where we observe the motion of the latter to follow upon the volition of the former, but are not able to observe or conceive the tie which binds together the motion and volition, or the energy by which the mind produces this effect. The authority of the will over its own faculties and ideas is not a whit more comprehensible: So that, upon the whole, there appears not, throughout all nature, any one instance of connexion which is conceivable by us. All events seem entirely loose and separate. One event follows another; but we never can observe any tie between them. They seem *conjoined,* but never *connected.* And as we can have no idea of any thing which never appeared to our outward sense or inward sentiment, the necessary conclusion *seems* to be that we have no idea of connexion or power at all, and that these words are absolutely without any meaning, when employed either in philosophical reasonings or common life.

But there still remains one method of avoiding this conclusion, and one source which we have not yet examined. When any natural object or event is presented, it is impossible for us, by any sagacity or penetration, to discover, or even conjecture, without experience, what event will result from it, or to carry our foresight beyond that object which is immediately present to the memory and senses. Even after one instance or experiment, where we have observed a particular event to follow upon another, we are not entitled to form a general rule, or foretell what will happen in like cases; it being justly esteemed an unpardonable temerity to judge of the whole course of nature from one single experiment, however accurate or certain. But when one particular species of event has always, in all instances, been conjoined with another, we make no longer any scruple of foretelling one upon the appearance of the other, and of employing that reasoning, which can alone assure us of any matter of fact or existence. We then call the one object, *Cause;* the other, *Effect*. We suppose that there is some connexion between them; some power in the one, by which it infallibly produces the other, and operates with the greatest certainty and strongest necessity.

It appears, then, that this idea of a necessary connexion among events arises from a number of similar instances which occur of the constant conjunction of these events; nor can that idea ever be suggested by any one of these instances, surveyed in all possible lights and positions. But there is nothing in a number of instances, different from every single instance, which is supposed to be exactly similar; except only, that after a repetition of similar instances, the mind is carried by habit, upon the appearance of one event, to expect its usual attendant, and to believe that it will exist. This connexion, therefore, which we *feel* in the mind, this customary transition of the imagination from one object to its usual attendant, is the sentiment or impression from which we form the idea of power or necessary connexion. Nothing farther is in the case. Contemplate the subject on all sides; you will never find any other origin of that idea. This is the sole difference between one instance, from which we can never receive the idea of connexion, and a number of similar instances, by which it is suggested. The first time a man saw the communication of motion by impulse, as by the shock of two billiard balls, he could not pronounce that the one event was *connected:* but only that it was *conjoined* with the other. After he has observed several instances of this nature, he then pronounces them to be *connected*. What alteration has happened to give rise to this new idea of *connexion?* Nothing but that he now *feels* these events to be *connected* in his imagination, and can readily foretell the existence of one from the appearance of the other. When we say, therefore, that one object is connected with another, we mean only that they have acquired a connexion in our thought, and give rise to this inference, by which they become proofs of each other's existence: A conclusion which is somewhat extraordinary, but which seems founded on sufficient evidence. Nor will its evidence be weakened by any general diffidence of the understanding, or sceptical suspicion concerning every conclusion which is new and extraordinary. No conclusions can be more agreeable to scepticism than such as make discoveries concerning the weakness and narrow limits of human reason and capacity.

And what stronger instance can be produced of the surprising ignorance and weakness of the understanding than the present? For surely, if there be any relation among objects which it imports to us to know perfectly, it is that of cause and effect. On this are founded all our reasonings concerning matter of fact or existence. By means of it alone we attain any assurance concerning objects which are removed from the present testimony of our memory and senses. The only immediate utility of all sciences, is to teach us, how to control and regulate future events by their causes. Our thoughts and enquiries are, therefore, every moment, employed about this relation: Yet so imperfect are the ideas which we form concerning it, that it is impossible to give any just definition of cause, except what is drawn from something extraneous and foreign to it. Similar objects are always conjoined with similar. Of this we have experience. Suitably to this experience, therefore, we may define a cause to be *an object, followed by another, and where all the objects similar to the first are followed by objects similar to the second.* Or in other words *where, if the first object had not been, the second never had existed.* The appearance of a cause always conveys the mind, by a customary transition, to the idea of the effect. Of this also we have experience. We may, therefore, suitably to this experience, form another definition of cause, and call it, *an object followed by another, and whose appearance always conveys the thought to that other.* But though both these definitions be drawn from circumstances foreign to the cause, we cannot remedy this inconvenience, or attain any more perfect definition, which may point out that circumstance in the cause, which gives it a connexion with its effect. We have no idea of this connexion, nor even any distinct notion what it is we desire to know, when we endeavour at a conception of it. We say, for instance, that the vibration of this string is the cause of this particular sound. But what do we mean by that affirmation? We either mean *that this vibration is followed by this sound, and that all similar vibrations have been followed by similar sounds:* Or, *that this vibration is followed by this sound, and that upon the appearance of one the mind anticipates the senses, and forms immediately an idea of the other.* We may consider the relation of cause and effect in either of these two lights; but beyond these, we have no idea of it.[3]

To recapitulate, therefore, the reasonings of this section: Every idea is copied from some preceding impression or sentiment; and where we cannot find any impression, we may be certain that there is no idea. In all single instances of the operation of bodies or minds, there is nothing that produces any impression, nor consequently can suggest any idea, of power or necessary connexion. But when many uniform instances appear, and the same object is always followed by the same event; we then begin to entertain the notion of cause and connexion. We then *feel* a new sentiment or impression, to wit, a customary connexion in the thought or imagination between one object and its usual attendant; and this sentiment is the original of that idea which we seek for. For as this idea arises from a number of similar instances, and not from any single instance, it must arise from that circumstance, in which the number of instances differ from every individual instance. But this customary connexion or transition of the imagination is the only circumstance in which they differ. In every other particular they are alike. The first instance which we saw of motion communicated by the shock of two billiard balls (to return to this obvious illustration) is exactly similar to any instance that may, at present, occur to us; except only, that we could not, at first, *infer* one event from the other; which we are enabled to do at present, after so long a course of uniform experience. I know not whether the reader will readily apprehend this reasoning. I am afraid that, should I multiply words about it, or throw it into a greater variety of lights, it would only become more obscure and intricate. In all abstract reasonings there is one point of view which, if we can happily hit, we shall go farther towards illustrating the subject than by all the eloquence and copious expression in the world. This point of view we should endeavour to reach, and reserve the flowers of rhetoric for subjects which are more adapted to them.

NOTES

1. Section II.
2. Mr. Locke, in his chapter of power, says that, finding from experience, that there are several new productions in matter, and concluding that there must somewhere be a power capable of

producing them, we arrive at last by this reasoning at the idea of power. But no reasoning can ever give us a new, original, simple idea; as this philosopher himself confesses. This, therefore, can never be the origin of that idea.

3. According to these explications and definitions, the idea of *power* is relative as much as that of *cause;* and both have a reference to an effect, or some other event constantly conjoined with the former. When we consider the *unknown* circumstance of an object, by which the degree or quantity of its effect is fixed and determined, we call that its power: And accordingly, it is allowed by all philosophers, that the effect is the measure of the power. But if they had any idea of power, as it is in itself, why could not they measure it in itself? The dispute whether the force of a body in motion be as its velocity, or the square of its velocity; this dispute, I say, needed not be decided by comparing its effects in equal or unequal times; but by a direct mensuration and comparison.

As to the frequent use of the words, Force, Power, Energy, &c., which every where occur in common conversation, as well as in philosophy; that is no proof, that we are acquainted, in any instance, with the connecting principle between cause and effect, or can account ultimately for the production of one thing by another. These words, as commonly used, have very loose meanings annexed to them; and their ideas are very uncertain and confused. No animal can put external bodies in motion without the sentiment of a *nisus* or endeavour; and every animal has a sentiment or feeling from the stroke or blow of an external object, that is in motion. These sensations, which are merely animal, and from which we can *à priori* draw no inference, we are apt to transfer to inanimate objects, and to suppose, that they have some such feelings, whenever they transfer or receive motion. With regard to energies, which are exerted, without our annexing to them any idea of communicated motion, we consider only the constant experienced conjunction of the events; and as we *feel* a customary connexion between the ideas, we transfer that feeling to the objects; as nothing is more usual than to apply to external bodies every internal sensation, which they occasion.

The New Riddle of Induction

NELSON GOODMAN

Confirmation of a hypothesis by an instance depends rather heavily upon features of the hypothesis other than its syntactical form. That a given piece of copper conducts electricity increases the credibility of statements asserting that other pieces of copper conduct electricity, and thus confirms the hypothesis that all copper conducts electricity. But the fact that a given man now in this room is a third son does not increase the credibility of statements asserting that other men now in this room are third sons, and so does not confirm the hypothesis that all men now in this room are third sons. Yet in both cases our hypothesis is a generalization of the evidence statement. The difference is that in the former case the hypothesis is a *lawlike* statement; while in the latter case, the hypothesis is a merely contingent or accidental generality. Only a statement that is *lawlike*—regardless of its truth or falsity or its scientific importance—is capable of receiving confirmation from an instance of it; accidental statements are not. Plainly, then, we must look for a way of distinguishing lawlike from accidental statements.

So long as what seems to be needed is merely a way of excluding a few odd and unwanted cases that are inadvertently admitted by our definition of confirmation, the problem may not seem very hard or very pressing. We fully expect that minor defects will be found in our definition and that the necessary refinements will have to be worked out patiently one after another. But some further examples will show that our present difficulty is of a much graver kind.

Suppose that all emeralds examined before a certain time t are green. At time t, then, our observations support the hypothesis that all emeralds are green; and this is in accord with our definition of confirmation. Our evidence

Source: Reprinted by permission of the publisher from FACT, FICTION, AND FORCAST by Nelson Goodman, pp. 72–81, Cambridge, MA: Harvard University Press,

statements assert that emerald *a* is green, that emerald *b* is green, and so on; and each confirms the general hypothesis that all emeralds are green. So far, so good.

Now let me introduce another predicate less familiar than "green". It is the predicate "grue" and it applies to all things examined before *t* just in case they are green but to other things just in case they are blue. Then at time *t* we have, for each evidence statement asserting that a given emerald is green, a parallel evidence statement asserting that that emerald is grue. And the statements that emerald *a* is grue, that emerald *b* is grue, and so on, will each confirm the general hypothesis that all emeralds are grue. Thus according to our definition, the prediction that all emeralds subsequently examined will be green and the prediction that all will be grue are alike confirmed by evidence statements describing the same observations. But if an emerald subsequently examined is grue, it is blue and hence not green. Thus although we are well aware which of the two incompatible predictions is genuinely confirmed, they are equally well confirmed according to our present definition. Moreover, it is clear that if we simply choose an appropriate predicate, then on the basis of these same observations we shall have equal confirmation, by our definition, for any prediction whatever about other emeralds—or indeed about anything else.[1] As in our earlier example, only the predictions subsumed under lawlike hypotheses are genuinely confirmed; but we have no criterion as yet for determining lawlikeness. And now we see that without some such criterion, our definition not merely includes a few unwanted cases, but is so completely ineffectual that it virtually excludes nothing. We are left once again with the intolerable result that anything confirms anything. This difficulty cannot be set aside as an annoying detail to be taken care of in due course. It has to be met before our definition will work at all.

Nevertheless, the difficulty is often slighted because on the surface there seem to be easy ways of dealing with it. Sometimes, for example, the problem is thought to be much like the paradox of the ravens. We are here again, it is pointed out, making tacit and illegitimate use of information outside the stated evidence: the information, for example, that different samples of one material are usually alike in conductivity, and the information that different men in a lecture audience are usually not alike in the number of their older brothers. But while it is true that such information is being smuggled in, this does not by itself settle the matter as it settles the matter of the ravens. There the point was that when the smuggled information is forthrightly declared, its effect upon the confirmation of the hypothesis in question is immediately and properly registered by the definition we are using. On the other hand, if to our initial evidence we add statements concerning the conductivity of pieces of other materials or concerning the number of older brothers of members of other lecture audiences, this will not in the least affect the confirmation, according to our definition, of the hypothesis concerning copper or of that concerning this lecture audience. Since our definition is insensitive to the bearing upon hypotheses of evidence so related to them, even when the evidence is fully declared, the difficulty about accidental hypotheses cannot be explained away on the ground that such evidence is being surreptitiously taken into account.

A more promising suggestion is to explain the matter in terms of the effect of this other evidence not directly upon the hypothesis in question but *in*directly through other hypotheses that *are* confirmed, according to our definition, by such evidence. Our information about other materials does by our definition confirm such hypotheses as that all pieces of iron conduct electricity, that no pieces of rubber do, and so on; and these hypotheses, the explanation runs, impart to the hypothesis that all pieces of copper conduct electricity (and also to the hypothesis that none do) the character of lawlikeness—that is, amenability to confirmation by direct positive instances when found. On the other hand, our information about other lecture audiences *dis*confirms many hypotheses to the effect that all the men in one audience are third sons, or that none are; and this strips any character of lawlikeness from the hypothesis that all (or the hypothesis that none) of the men in *this* audience are third sons. But clearly if this course is to be followed, the circumstances under which hypotheses are thus related to one another will have to be precisely articulated.

The problem, then, is to define the relevant way in which such hypotheses must be alike. Evidence for the hypothesis that all iron conducts electricity enhances the lawlikeness of the hypothesis that all zirconium conducts electricity, but does not similarly affect the hypothesis that all the objects on my desk conduct electricity. Wherein lies the difference? The first two hypotheses fall under the broader hypothesis—call it "*H*"—that every class of things of the same material is uniform in conductivity; the first and third fall only under some such hypothesis as—call it "*K*"—that every class of things that are either all of the same material or all on a desk is uniform in conductivity. Clearly the important difference here is that evidence for a statement affirming that one of the classes covered by *H* has the property in question increases the credibility of any statement affirming that another such class has this property; while nothing of the sort holds true with respect to *K*. But this is only to say that *H* is lawlike and *K* is not. We are faced anew with the very problem we are trying to solve: the problem of distinguishing between lawlike and accidental hypotheses.

The most popular way of attacking the problem takes its cue from the fact that accidental hypotheses seem typically to involve some spatial or temporal restriction, or reference to some particular individual. They seem to concern the people in some particular room, or the objects on some particular person's desk; while lawlike hypotheses characteristically concern all ravens or all pieces of copper whatsoever. Complete generality is thus very often supposed to be a sufficient condition of lawlikeness; but to define this complete generality is by no means easy. Merely to require that the hypothesis contain no term naming, describing, or indicating a particular thing or location will obviously not be enough. The troublesome hypothesis that all emeralds are grue contains no such term; and where such a term does occur, as in hypotheses about men in *this room,* it can be suppressed in favor of some predicate (short or long, new or old) that contains no such term but applies only to exactly the same things. One might think, then, of excluding not only hypotheses that actually contain terms for specific individuals but also all hypotheses that are equivalent to others that do contain such terms. But, as we have just seen, to exclude only hypotheses of which *all* equivalents contain such terms is to exclude nothing. On the other hand, to exclude all hypotheses that have *some* equivalent containing such a term is to exclude everything; for even the hypothesis

All grass is green
has as an equivalent
All grass in London or elsewhere is green.

The next step, therefore, has been to consider ruling out predicates of certain kinds. A syntactically universal hypothesis is lawlike, the proposal runs, if its predicates are 'purely qualitative' or 'non-positional'.[2] This will obviously accomplish nothing if a purely qualitative predicate is then conceived either as one that is equivalent to some expression free of terms for specific individuals, or as one that is equivalent to no expression that contains such a term; for this only raises again the difficulties just pointed out. The claim appears to be rather that at least in the case of a simple enough predicate we can readily determine by direct inspection of its meaning whether or not it is purely qualitative. But even aside from obscurities in the notion of 'the meaning' of a predicate, this claim seems to me wrong. I simply do not know how to tell whether a predicate is qualitative or positional, except perhaps by completely begging the question at issue and asking whether the predicate is 'well-behaved'—that is, whether simple syntactically universal hypotheses applying it are lawlike.

This statement will not go unprotested. "Consider", it will be argued, "the predicates 'blue' and 'green' and the predicate 'grue' introduced earlier, and also the predicate 'bleen' that applies to emeralds examined before time *t* just in case they are blue and to other emeralds just in case they are green. Surely it is clear", the argument runs, "that the first two are purely qualitative and the second two are not; for the meaning of each of the latter two plainly involves reference to a specific temporal position." To this I reply that indeed I do recognize the first two as well-behaved predicates admissible in lawlike hypotheses, and the second two as ill-behaved predicates. But the argument that the former but not the latter are purely qualitative seems to me quite unsound. True enough, if we start with "blue" and "green", then "grue" and "bleen" will be explained in terms of "blue" and "green" and a temporal term. But equally truly, if we start with "grue" and "bleen", then "blue" and "green" will be explained in terms of "grue" and "bleen" and a temporal term; "green", for example, applies to emeralds examined before time *t* just in case they are grue, and to other emeralds just in case they are bleen. Thus qualitativeness is an entirely relative matter and does not by itself establish any dichotomy of predicates. This relativity seems to be completely overlooked by those who contend that the qualitative character of a predicate is a criterion for its good behavior.

Of course, one may ask why we need worry about such unfamiliar predicates as "grue" or about accidental hypotheses in general, since we are unlikely to use them in making predictions. If our definition works for such hypotheses as are normally employed, isn't that all we need? In a sense, yes; but only in the sense that we need no definition, no theory of induction, and no philosophy of knowledge at all. We get along well enough without them in daily life and in scientific research. But if we seek a theory at all, we cannot excuse gross anomalies resulting from a proposed theory by pleading that we can avoid them in practice. The odd cases we have been considering are clinically pure cases that, though seldom encountered in practice, nevertheless display to best advantage the symptoms of a widespread and destructive malady.

We have so far neither any answer nor any promising clue to an answer to the question what distinguishes lawlike or confirmable hypotheses from accidental or nonconfirmable ones; and what may at first have seemed a minor technical difficulty has taken on the stature of a major obstacle to the development of a satisfactory theory of confirmation. It is this problem that I call the new riddle of induction. . . .

NOTES

1. For instance, we shall have equal confirmation, by our present definition, for the prediction that roses subsequently examined will be blue. Let "emerose" apply just to emeralds examined before time *t*, and to roses examined later. Then all emeroses so far examined are grue, and this confirms the hypothesis that all emeroses are grue and hence the prediction that roses subsequently examined will be blue. The problem raised by such antecedents has been little noticed, but is no easier to meet than that raised by similarly perverse consequents. . . .
2. Carnap took this course in his paper 'On the Application of Inductive Logic', *Philosophy and Phenomenological Research,* vol. 8 (1947), pp. 133–47. . . . The discussion was continued in my note 'On Infirmities of Confirmation Theory', *Philosophy and Phenomenological Research,* vol. 8 (1947), pp. 149–51; and in Carnap's 'Reply to Nelson Goodman', same journal, same volume, pp. 461–2.

CHAPTER SIX
UNIVERSALS AND PARTICULARS

Over two thousand years ago, the Greek philosopher Plato put forward a theory of reality according to which the world of appearances is but a pale reflection of the world of forms or "ideas." These forms or ideas were thought to be timeless and perfect exemplars of the imperfect, transient, shadows that make up the world of experience. Somehow, I am able to grasp how things as different from one another as a song, a sunset, a face, or a sculpture can all be beautiful. If I can do so, it must be because they share something in common—namely that they all are beautiful. Plato would explain this by saying that these things all partake of the "form of beauty." From a more common sense point of view, we might describe it by saying that they all share the property of being beautiful. This property, or form, would be something that, in itself, is not physical and cannot be directly perceived. I can destroy all these beautiful things in the world and still beauty, as a property, would exist. The fact that I can think about it, that I can understand what it is for something to be beautiful, would, for a Platonist, serve to underscore this point. After all, if I can think about beauty, mustn't it, in some sense, exist? The form of beauty exists in the world of thought while beautiful things exist in the world of the senses.

Although one might find it odd to claim that beauty is not itself perceivable, we can perhaps see Plato's point by considering the fact that different beautiful things may not resemble each other in any perceivable way. They may be of completely different sizes, shapes, colors, etc. And when we talk about things in general, we invariably invoke properties. Although we may be able to perceive the redness of a sweater and compare it to the visible redness of a sunset, still we have to reckon with the fact that it is the *same* property that is being referred to in both instances. Even if this sunset and this sweater pass out of existence, redness does not cease to exist. Redness then, as an entity that can be instantiated in many instances at the same time may be thought to be a universal. Whenever we speak about things having various properties or relations, we seem to invoke universals. When we say that the Bronx is north of Manhattan and that Milan is north of Rome, for example, we seem to be talking about the same relation—being north of—in both cases. If this is so, mustn't we say that the relation, being north of, is a universal, and that it exists?

In what follows we have included readings that address these and related questions. We start off the section with a selection from Plato's *Parmenides* in which the great Greek philosopher subjects his own theory of forms to merciless philosophical criticism. We then turn to his student Aristotle's critique. Next we move to a classic formulation of nominalism—the claim by William of Ockham that only particulars exist. The section is rounded off with contemporary treatment of the issues by Frank Jackson, and a debate between Michael Devitt and David Armstrong. We close the section with a piece by Keith Campbell in which he introduces a position on the question of universals commonly referred to as trope theory. Traditionally this position has not received very much attention, but in recent philosophy it has been gaining in popularity. Attempting to reconcile features of both nominalism and universalism, this theory allows for the existence of properties, but denies the existence of universals.

1

Parmenides, excerpts

PLATO

. . . While Socrates was speaking, Pythodorus thought that Parmenides and Zeno were not altogether pleased at the successive steps of the argument; but still they gave the closest attention, and often looked at one another, and smiled as if in admiration of him. When he had finished, Parmenides expressed their feelings in the following words:—

Socrates, he said, I admire the bent of your mind towards philosophy; tell me now, was this your own distinction between ideas in themselves and the things which partake of them? and do you think that there is an idea of likeness apart from the likeness which we possess, and of the one and many, and of the other things which Zeno mentioned?

I think that there are such ideas, said Socrates.

Source: Plato, *Parmenides,* from *The Dialogues of Plato,* translated by Benjamin Jowett, 2nd ed. Oxford: Clarendon Press, 1875.

Parmenides proceeded: And would you also make absolute ideas of the just and the beautiful and the good, and of all that class?

Yes, he said, I should.

And would you make an idea of man apart from us and from all other human creatures, or of fire and water?

I am often undecided, Parmenides, as to whether I ought to include them or not.

And would you feel equally undecided, Socrates, about things of which the mention may provoke a smile?—I mean such things as hair, mud, dirt, or anything else which is vile and paltry; is it hard to decide whether each of these has an idea distinct from the actual objects with which we come into contact, or not?

Certainly not, said Socrates; visible things like these are such as they appear to us, and I am afraid that there would be an absurdity in assuming any idea of them, although I sometimes get disturbed, and begin to think that there is nothing without an idea; but then again, when I have taken up this position, I run away, because I am afraid that I may fall into a bottomless pit of nonsense, and perish; and so I return to the ideas of which I was just now speaking, and occupy myself with them.

Yes, Socrates, said Parmenides; that is because you are still young; the time will come, if I am not mistaken, when philosophy will have a firmer grasp of you, and then you will not despise even the meanest things; at your age, you are too much disposed to regard the opinions of men. But I should like to know whether you mean that there are certain ideas of which all other things partake, and from which they derive their names; that similars, for example, become similar, because they partake of similarity; and great things become great, because they partake of greatness; and that just and beautiful things become just and beautiful, because they partake of justice and beauty?

Yes, certainly, said Socrates, that is my meaning.

Then each individual partakes either of the whole of the idea or else of a part of the idea? Can there be any other mode of participation?

There cannot be, he said.

Then do you think that the whole idea is one, and yet, being one, is in each one of the many?

What objection is there, Parmenides? said Socrates.

The result will be that one and the same thing will exist as a whole at the same time in many separate individuals, and will therefore be in a state of separation from itself.

Nay, but the idea may be like the day which is one and the same in many places at once, and yet continuous with itself; in this way each idea may be one and the same in all at the same time.

I like your way, Socrates, of making one in many places at once. You mean to say, that if I were to spread out a sail and cover a number of men, there would be one whole including many—is not that your meaning?

I think so.

And would you say that the whole sail includes each man, or a part of it only, and different parts different men?

The latter.

Then, Socrates, the ideas themselves will be divisible, and things which participate in them will have a part of them only and not the whole idea existing in each of them?

That seems to follow.

Then would you like to say, Socrates, that the one idea is really divisible and yet remains one?

Certainly not, he said.

Suppose that you divide absolute greatness, and that of the many great things each one is great in virtue of a portion of greatness less than absolute greatness—is that conceivable?

No.

Or will each equal thing, if possessing some small portion of equality less than absolute equality, be equal to some other thing by virtue of that portion only?

Impossible.

Or suppose one of us to have a portion of smallness; this is but a part of the small, and therefore the absolutely small will be greater; while that to which the abstracted part of the small is added will be smaller and not greater than before.

That, indeed, can scarcely be.

Then in what way, Socrates, will all things participate in the ideas, if they are unable to participate in them either as parts or wholes?

Indeed, he said, you have asked a question which is not easily answered.

Well, said Parmenides, and what do you say of another question?

What question?

I imagine that your reason for assuming one idea of each kind is as follows:—Whenever a number of objects appear to you to be great there doubtless seems to you to be one and the same idea (or nature) visible in them all; hence you conceive of greatness as one.

Very true, said Socrates.

But now, if you allow your mind in like manner to embrace in one view this real greatness and those other great things, will not one more greatness arise, being required to account for the semblance of greatness in all these?

It would seem so.

Then another idea of greatness now comes into view over and above absolute greatness and the individuals which partake of it; and then another, over and above all these, by virtue of which they will all be great, and so you will be left not with a single idea in every case, but with an infinite number.

But may not the ideas, asked Socrates, be thoughts only, and have no proper existence except in our minds, Parmenides? For in that case each idea may still be one, and not experience this infinite multiplication.

Tell me, then: can each thought have its own definite nature, and yet be a thought of nothing?

Impossible, he said.

The thought must be of something?

Yes.

Of something which is or which is not?

Of something which is.

Must it not be of a single something, which the thought recognizes as attaching to all, being a single form or nature?

Yes.

And will not the something, which is apprehended as one and the same in all, be an idea?

From that, again, there is no escape.

Then, said Parmenides, if you say that everything else must participate in the ideas, must you not say either that everything is made up of thoughts, and that all things think; or that they are thoughts but have no thought?

So this view, Parmenides, is no more rational than the previous one. In my opinion the ideas are, as it were, patterns fixed in nature, and other things are like them and resemblances of them—what is meant by the participation of other things in the ideas, is really assimilation to them.

But if, said he, the individual is like the idea, is it possible that the idea should not be like the copy, in so far as this has been fashioned in resemblance of the idea? That which is like, cannot be conceived of as other than the like of like.

Impossible.

And when two things are alike, must they not partake of the same idea?

They must.

And will not that, by partaking in which like things are alike, be the idea itself?

Certainly.

Then the idea cannot be like the individual, or the individual like the idea; for if they are alike, some further idea of likeness will always be coming to light, and if that be like anything else, another; and new ideas will be always arising, if the idea resembles that which partakes of it?

Quite true.

The theory, then, that other things participate in the ideas by resemblance, has to be given up, and some other mode of participation devised?

It would seem so.

Do you see then, Socrates, how great is the difficulty of making this distinction of ideas (or classes) existing by themselves?

Yes, indeed.

And, further, let me say that as yet you only understand a small part of the difficulty which is involved if you make of each thing a single idea, parting it off from other things.

What difficulty? he said.

There are many, but the greatest of all is this:—If an opponent argues that these ideas, being such as we say they ought to be, must remain unknown, no one can prove to him that he is wrong, unless he who denies their existence be a man of great natural ability and experience, and is willing to follow a long and laborious demonstration; he will remain unconvinced, and still insist that they cannot be known.

What do you mean, Parmenides? said Socrates.

In the first place, I think, Socrates, that you, or anyone who maintains the existence of absolute essences, will admit that they cannot exist in us.

No, said Socrates; for then they would be no longer absolute.

True, he said; and therefore when ideas are what they are in relation to one another, their essence is determined by a relation among themselves, and has nothing to do with the resemblances, or whatever they are to be termed, which are in our sphere, and from which we receive this or that name when we partake of them. And the things which are within our sphere and have the same names with them, are likewise only relative to one another, and not to the ideas which have the same names with them, but belong to themselves and not to them.

What do you mean? said Socrates.

I may illustrate my meaning in this way, said Parmenides. Suppose a man to be a master or a slave—he is obviously not a slave of the abstract idea of a master, or a master of the abstract idea of a slave; the relation is one of man to man. The idea of mastership in the abstract must be defined by relation to the idea of slavery in the abstract, and vice versa. But the things familiar to us are not empowered to act on those ideas, nor the ideas to act upon familiar things; but, as I have said, the ideas belong to and stand in relation to each other, as also do the things in our familiar world. Do you see my meaning?

Yes, said Socrates, I quite see your meaning.

And will not knowledge—I mean absolute knowledge—answer to absolute truth?

Certainly.

And each kind of absolute knowledge will answer to each kind of absolute being?

Yes.

But the knowledge which we have, will answer to the truth which we have; and again, each kind of knowledge which we have, will be a knowledge of each kind of being which we have?

Certainly.

But the ideas themselves, as you admit, we have not, and cannot have?

No, we cannot.

And the absolute natures or kinds are known severally by the absolute idea of knowledge?

Yes.

And we have not got the idea of knowledge?

No.

Then none of the ideas are known, at least by us, because we have no share in absolute knowledge?

I suppose not.

Then the nature of the beautiful in itself, and of the good in itself, and all other ideas which we suppose to exist absolutely, are unknown to us?

It would seem so.

Observe that there is a stranger consequence still.

What is it?

Would you, or would you not, say that absolute knowledge, if there is such a thing, must be a far more exact knowledge than our knowledge; and the same of beauty and of the rest?

Yes.

And no one is more likely than God to have this most exact knowledge, if other things can share in it at all?

Certainly.

But then, will God, having the true knowledge, also be capable of knowledge of human things?

Why not?

Because, Socrates, said Parmenides, we have admitted that the ideas are not valid in relation to human things; nor human things in relation to them; the relations of either are limited to their respective spheres.

Yes, that has been admitted.

And if God has this perfect authority and perfect knowledge, his authority cannot rule us, nor his knowledge know us or any human thing; just as our authority does not extend to the gods, nor our knowledge know anything which is divine, so by parity of reason they, being gods, are not our masters, neither do they know the things of men.

Yet, surely, said Socrates, to deprive God of knowledge is monstrous.

These, Socrates, said Parmenides, are a few and only a few of the difficulties in which we are involved if ideas really are and we determine each one of them to be an absolute unity. He who hears what may be said against them will deny the very existence of them—and even if they do exist, he will say that they must of necessity be unknown to man; and he will seem to have reason on his side, and as we were remarking just now, will be very difficult to convince; a man must be gifted with very considerable ability before he can learn that everything has a class and an absolute essence; and still more remarkable will he be who discovers all these things for himself, and having thoroughly investigated them is able to teach them to others.

I agree with you, Parmenides, said Socrates; and what you say is very much to my mind.

And yet, Socrates, said Parmenides, if a man, fixing his attention on these and the like difficulties, does away with ideas of things and will not admit that every individual thing has its own determinate idea which is always one and the same, he will have nothing on which his mind can rest; and so he will utterly destroy the power of reasoning, as you seem to me to have particularly noted.

Very true, he said.

But, then, what is to become of philosophy? Whither shall we turn, if the ideas are unknown?

I certainly do not see my way at present. . . .

2

Criticisms of the Theory of the Forms, excerpts

ARISTOTLE

VI

After the systems we have named came the philosophy of Plato, which in most respects followed these thinkers, but had peculiarities that distinguished it from the philosophy of the Italians. For, having in his youth first become familiar with Cratylus and with the Heraclitean doctrines (that all sensible things are ever in a state of flux and there is no knowledge about them), these views he held even in later years. Socrates, however, was busying himself about ethical matters and neglecting the world of nature as a whole but seeking the universal in these ethical matters, and fixed thought for the first time on definitions; Plato accepted his teaching, but held that the problem applied not to sensible things but to entities of another kind—for this reason, that the common definition could not be a definition of any sensible thing, as they were always changing. Things of this other sort, then, he called Ideas, and sensible things, he said, were all named after these, and in virtue of a relation to these; for the many existed by participation in the Ideas that have the same name as they. Only the name 'participation' was new; for the Pythagoreans say that things exist by 'imitation' of numbers, and Plato says they exist by participation, changing the name. But what the participation or the imitation of the Forms could be they left an open question.

Further, besides sensible things and Forms he says there are the objects of mathematics, which occupy an intermediate position, differing from sensible things in being eternal and unchangeable, from Forms in that there are many alike, while the Form itself is in each case unique.

Since the Forms were the causes of all other things, he thought their elements were the elements of all things. As matter, the great and the small were principles; as essential reality, the

---

Source: Aristotle, *Criticisms of the Theory of Forms* (347–323 B.C.E.), translated by W. D. Ross.

One; for from the great and the small, by participation in the One, come the Numbers.

But he agreed with the Pythagoreans in saying that the One is substance and not a predicate of something else; and in saying that the Numbers are the causes of the reality of other things he agreed with them; but positing a dyad and constructing the infinite out of great and small, instead of treating the infinite as one, is peculiar to him; and so is his view that the Numbers exist apart from sensible things, while they say that the things themselves are Numbers, and do not place the objects of mathematics between Forms and sensible things. His divergence from the Pythagoreans in making the One and the Numbers separate from things, and his introduction of the Forms, were due to his inquiries in the region of definitions (for the earlier thinkers had no tincture of dialectic), and his making the other entity besides the One a dyad was due to the belief that the numbers, except those which were prime, could be neatly produced out of the dyad as out of some plastic material. Yet what happens is the contrary; the theory is not a reasonable one. For they make many things out of the matter, and the form generates only once, but what we observe is that one table is made from one matter, while the man who applies the form, though he is one, makes many tables. And the relation of the male to the female is similar; for the latter is impregnated by one copulation, but the male impregnates many females; yet these are analogues of those first principles.

Plato, then, declared himself thus on the points in question; it is evident from what has been said that he has used only two causes, that of the essence and the material cause (for the Forms are the causes of the essence of all other things, and the One is the cause of the essence of the Forms); and it is evident what the underlying matter is, of which the Forms are predicated in the case of sensible things, and the One in the case of Forms, viz. that this is a dyad, the great and the small. Further, he has assigned the cause of good and that of evil to the elements, one to each of the two, as we say some of his predecessors sought to do, e.g. Empedocles and Anaxagoras.

VII

Our review of those who have spoken about first principles and reality and of the way in which they have spoken, has been concise and summary; but yet we have learnt this much from them, that of those who speak about 'principle' and 'cause' no one has mentioned any principle except those which have been distinguished in our work on nature, but all evidently have some inkling of them, though only vaguely. For some speak of the first principle as matter, whether they suppose one or more first principles, and whether they suppose this to be a body or to be incorporeal; e.g. Plato spoke of the great and the small, the Italians of the infinite, Empedocles of fire, earth, water, and air, Anaxagoras of the infinity of things composed of similar parts. These, then, have all had a notion of this kind of cause, and so have all who speak of air or fire or water, or something denser than fire and rarer than air; for some have said the prime element is of this kind.

These thinkers grasped this cause only; but certain others have mentioned the source of movement, e.g. those who make friendship and strife, or reason, or love, a principle.

The essence, i.e. the substantial reality, no one has expressed distinctly. It is hinted at chiefly by those who believe in the Forms; for they do not suppose either that the Forms are the matter of sensible things, and the One the matter of the Forms, or that they are the source of movement (for they say these are causes rather of immobility and of being at rest), but they furnish the Forms as the essence of every other thing, and the One as the essence of the Forms.

That for whose sake actions and changes and movements take place, they assert to be a cause in a way, but not in this way, i.e. not in the way in which it is its nature to be a cause. For those who speak of reason or friendship class these causes as goods; they do not speak, however, as if anything that exists either existed or came into being for the sake of these, but as if movements started from these. In the same way those who say the One or the existent is the good, say that it is the cause of substance, but not that substance either is or comes to be for the sake of this. Therefore it turns out that in a sense they both say and do not say the good is a cause; for they do not call it a cause qua good but only incidentally.

All these thinkers then, as they cannot pitch on another cause, seem to testify that we have determined rightly both how many and of what sort the causes are. Besides this it is plain that when the causes are being looked for, either all four must be sought thus or they must be sought in one of these four ways. Let us next discuss the possible difficulties with regard to the way in which each of these thinkers has spoken, and with regard to his situation relatively to the first principles.

VIII

Those, then, who say the universe is one and posit one kind of thing as matter, and as corporeal matter which has spatial magnitude, evidently go astray in many ways. For they posit the elements of bodies only, not of incorporeal things, though there are also incorporeal things. And in trying to state the causes of generation and destruction, and in giving a physical account of all things, they do away with the cause of movement. Further, they err in not positing the substance, i.e. the essence, as the cause of anything, and besides this in lightly calling any of the simple bodies except earth the first principle, without inquiring how they are produced out of one another—I mean fire, water, earth, and air. For some things are produced out of each other by combination, others by separation, and this makes the greatest difference to their priority and posteriority. For (1) in a way the property of being most elementary of all would seem to belong to the first thing from which they are produced by combination, and this property would belong to the most fine-grained and subtle of bodies. For this reason those who make fire the principle would be most in agreement with this argument. But each of the other thinkers agrees that the element of corporeal things is of this sort. At least none of those who named one element claimed that earth was the element, evidently because of the coarseness of its grain. (Of the other three elements each has found some judge on its side; for some maintain that fire, others that water, others that air is the element. Yet why, after all, do they not name earth also, as most men do? For people say all things are earth Hesiod says earth was produced first of corporeal things; so primitive and popular has the opinion been.) According to this argument, then, no one would be right who either says the first principle is any of the elements other than fire, or supposes it to be denser than air but rarer than water. But (2) if that which is later in generation is prior in nature, and that which is concocted and compounded is later in generation, the contrary of what we have been saying must be true,—water must be prior to air, and earth to water. . . .

So much, then, for those who posit one cause such as we mentioned; but the same is true if one supposes more of these, as Empedocles says matter of things is four bodies. For he too is confronted by consequences some of which are the same as have been mentioned, while others are peculiar to him. For we see these bodies produced from one another, which implies that the same body does not always remain fire or earth (we have spoken about this in our works on nature); and regarding the cause of movement and the question whether we must posit one or two, he must be thought to have spoken neither correctly nor altogether plausibly. And in general, change of quality is necessarily done away with for those who speak thus, for on their view cold will not come from hot nor hot from cold. For if it did there would be something that accepted the contraries themselves, and there would be some one entity that became fire and water, which Empedocles denies.

As regards Anaxagoras, if one were to suppose that he said there were two elements, the supposition would accord thoroughly with an argument which Anaxagoras himself did not state articulately, but which he must have accepted if any one had led him on to it. True, to say that in the beginning all things were mixed is absurd both on other grounds and because it follows that they must have existed before in an unmixed form, and because nature does not allow any chance thing to be mixed with any chance thing, and also because on this view modifications and accidents could be separated from substances (for the same things which are mixed can be separated); yet if one were to follow him up, piecing together what he means, he would perhaps be seen to be somewhat modern in his views. For when nothing was separated out, evidently nothing could be truly asserted of the substance that then existed. I mean, e.g. that it was neither white nor black, nor grey nor any other colour, but of necessity colourless; for if it had been coloured, it would have had one of these colours. And similarly, by this same argument, it was flavourless, nor had it any similar attribute; for it could not be either of any quality or of any size, nor could it be any definite kind of thing. For if it were, one of the particular forms would have belonged to it, and this is impossible, since all were mixed together; for the particular form would necessarily have been already separated out, but he all were mixed except reason, and this alone was unmixed and pure. From this it follows, then, that he must say the principles are the One (for this is simple and unmixed) and the Other, which is of such a nature as we suppose the indefinite to be before it is defined and partakes of some form. Therefore, while expressing himself neither rightly nor clearly, he means something like what the later thinkers say and what is now more clearly seen to be the case.

But these thinkers are, after all, at home only in arguments about generation and destruction and movement; for it is practically only of this sort of substance that they seek the principles and the causes. But those who extend their vision to all things that exist, and of existing things suppose some to be perceptible and others not perceptible, evidently study both classes, which is all the more reason why one should devote some time to seeing what is good in their views and what bad from the standpoint of the inquiry we have now before us.

The 'Pythagoreans' treat of principles and elements stranger than those of the physical philosophers (the reason is that they got the principles from non-sensible things, for the objects of mathematics, except those of astronomy, are of the class of things without movement); yet their discussions and investigations are all about nature; for they generate the heavens, and with regard to their parts and attributes and functions they observe the phenomena, and use up the principles and the causes in explaining these, which implies that they agree with the others, the physical philosophers, that the real is just all that which is perceptible and contained by the so-called 'heavens'. But the causes and the principles which they mention are, as we said, sufficient to act as steps even up to the higher realms of reality, and are more suited to these than to theories about nature. They do not tell us at all, however, how there can be movement if limit and unlimited and odd and even are the only things assumed, or how without movement and change there can be generation and destruction, or the bodies that move through the heavens can do what they do.

Further, if one either granted them that spatial magnitude consists of these elements, or this were proved, still how would some bodies be light and others have weight? To judge from what they assume and maintain they are speaking no more of mathematical bodies than of perceptible; hence they have said nothing whatever about fire or earth or the other bodies of this sort, I suppose because they have nothing to say which applies peculiarly to perceptible things.

Further, how are we to combine the beliefs that the attributes of number, and number itself, are causes of what exists and happens in the heavens both from the beginning and now, and that there is no other number than this number out of which the world is composed? When in one particular region they place opinion and opportunity, and, a little above or below, injustice and decision or mixture, and allege, as proof, that each of these is a number, and that there happens to be already in this place a plurality of the extended bodies composed of numbers, because these attributes of number attach to the various places,—this being so, is this number, which we must suppose each of these abstractions to be, the same number which is exhibited in the material universe, or is it another than this? Plato says it is different; yet even he thinks that both these bodies and their causes are numbers, but that the intelligible numbers are causes, while the others are sensible.

IX

Let us leave the Pythagoreans for the present; for it is enough to have touched on them as much as we have done. But as for those who posit the Ideas as causes, firstly, in seeking to grasp the causes of the things around us, they introduced others equal in number to these, as if a man who wanted to count things thought he would not be able to do it while they were few, but tried to count them when he had added to their number. For the Forms are practically equal to—or not fewer than—the things, in trying to explain which these thinkers proceeded from them to the Forms. For to each thing there answers an entity which has the same name and exists apart from the substances, and so also in the case of all other groups there is a one over many, whether the many are in this world or are eternal.

Further, of the ways in which we prove that the Forms exist, none is convincing; for from some no inference necessarily follows, and from some arise Forms even of things of which we think there are no Forms. For according to the arguments from the existence of the sciences there will be Forms of all things of which there are sciences and according to the 'one over many' argument there will be Forms even of negations, and according to the argument that there is an object for thought even when the thing has perished, there will be Forms of perishable things; for we have an image of these. Further, of the more accurate arguments, some lead to Ideas of relations, of which we say there is no independent class, and others introduce the 'third man'.

And in general the arguments for the Forms destroy the things for whose existence we are more zealous than for the existence of the Ideas; for it follows that not the dyad but number is first, i.e. that the relative is prior to the absolute,—besides all the other points on which certain people by following out the opinions held about the Ideas have come into conflict with the principles of the theory.

Further, according to the assumption on which our belief in the Ideas rests, there will be Forms not only of substances but also of many other things (for the concept is single not only in the case of substances but also in the other cases, and there are sciences not only of substance but also of other things, and a thousand other such difficulties confront them). But according to the necessities of the case and the opinions held about the Forms, if Forms can be shared in there must be Ideas of substances only. For they are not shared in incidentally, but a thing must share in its Form as in something not predicated of a subject (by 'being shared in incidentally' I mean that e.g. if a thing shares in 'double itself', it shares also in 'eternal', but incidentally; for 'eternal' happens to be predicable of the 'double'). Therefore the Forms will be substance; but the same terms indicate substance in this and in the ideal world (or what will be the meaning of saying that there is something apart from the particulars—the one over many?). And if the Ideas and the particulars that share in them have the same form, there will be something common to these; for why should '2' be one and the same in the perishable 2's or in those which are many but eternal, and not the same in the '2' itself' as in the particular 2? But if they have not the same form, they must have only the name in common, and it is as if one were to call both Callias and a wooden image a 'man', without observing any community between them.

Above all one might discuss the question what on earth the Forms contribute to sensible things, either to those that are eternal or to those that come into being and cease to be. For they cause neither movement nor any change in them. But again they help in no wise either towards the knowledge of the other things (for they are not even the substance of these, else they would have been in them), or towards their being, if they are not in the particulars which share in them; though if they were, they might be thought to be causes, as white causes whiteness in a white object by entering into its composition. But this argument, which first Anaxagoras and later Eudoxus and certain others used, is very easily upset; for it is not difficult to collect many insuperable objections to such a view.

But, further, all other things cannot come from the Forms in any of the usual senses of 'form'. And to say that they are patterns and the other things share in them is to use empty words and poetical metaphors. For what is it that works, looking to the Ideas? And anything can either be, or become, like another without being copied from it, so that whether Socrates or not a man Socrates like might come to be; and evidently this might be so even if Socrates were eternal. And there will be several patterns of the same thing, and therefore several Forms; e.g. 'animal' and 'two-footed' and also 'man himself' will be Forms of man. Again, the Forms are patterns not only sensible things, but of Forms themselves also; i.e. the genus, as genus of various species, will be so; therefore the same thing will be pattern and copy.

Again, it would seem impossible that the substance and that of which it is the substance should exist apart; how, therefore, could the Ideas, being the substances of things, exist apart? In the 'Phaedo' the case is stated in this way—that the Forms are causes both of being and of becoming; yet when the Forms exist, still the things that share in them do not come into being, unless there is something to originate movement; and many other things come into being (e.g. a house or a ring) of which we say there are no Forms. Clearly, therefore, even the other things can both be and come into being owing to such causes as produce the things just mentioned.

Again, if the Forms are numbers, how can they be causes? Is it because existing things are other numbers, e.g. one number is man, another is Socrates, another Callias? Why then are the one set of numbers causes of the other set? It will not make any difference even if the former are eternal and the latter are not. But if it is because things in this sensible world (e.g. harmony) are ratios of numbers, evidently the things between which they are ratios are some one class of things. If, then, this—the matter—is some definite thing, evidently the numbers themselves too will be ratios of something to something else. E.g. if Callias is a numerical ratio between fire and earth and water and air, his Idea also will be a number of certain other underlying things; and man himself, whether it is a number in a sense or not, will still be a numerical ratio of certain things and not a number proper, nor will it be of a number merely because it is a numerical ratio.

Again, from many numbers one number is produced, but how can one Form come from many Forms? And if the number comes not from the many numbers themselves but from the units in them, e.g. in 10,000, how is it with the units? If they are specifically alike, numerous absurdities will follow, and also if they are not alike (neither the units in one number being themselves like one another nor those in other numbers being all like to all); for in what will they differ, as they are without quality? This is not a plausible view, nor is it consistent with our thought on the matter.

Further, they must set up a second kind of number (with which arithmetic deals), and all the objects which are called 'intermediate' by some thinkers; and how do these exist or from what principles do they proceed? Or why must they be intermediate between the things in this sensible world and the things-themselves?

Further, the units in must each come from a prior but this is impossible.

Further, why is a number, when taken all together, one?

Again, besides what has been said, if the units are diverse the Platonists should have spoken like those who say there are four, or two, elements; for each of these thinkers gives the name of element not to that which is common, e.g. to body, but to fire and earth, whether there is something common to them, viz. body, or not. But in fact the Platonists speak as if the One were homogeneous like fire or water; and if this is so, the numbers will not be substances. Evidently, if there is a One itself and this is a first principle, 'one' is being used in more than one sense; for otherwise the theory is impossible.

When we wish to reduce substances to their principles, we state that lines come from the short and long (i.e. from a kind of small and great), and the plane from the broad and narrow, and body from the deep and shallow. Yet how then can either the plane contain a line, or the solid a line or a plane? For the broad and narrow is a different class from the deep and shallow. Therefore, just as number is not present in these, because the many and few are different from these, evidently no other of the higher classes will be present in the lower. But again the broad is not a genus which includes the deep, for then the solid would have been a species of plane. Further, from what principle will the presence of the points in the line be derived? Plato even used to object to this class of things as being a geometrical fiction. He gave the name of principle of the line—and this he often posited—to the indivisible lines. Yet these must have a limit; therefore the argument from which the existence of the line follows proves also the existence of the point.

In general, though philosophy seeks the cause of perceptible things, we have given this up (for we say nothing of the cause from which change takes its start), but while we fancy we are stating the substance of perceptible things, we assert the existence of a second class of substances, while our account of the way in which they are the substances of perceptible things is empty talk; for 'sharing', as we said before, means nothing.

Nor have the Forms any connection with what we see to be the cause in the case of the arts, that for whose sake both all mind and the whole of nature are operative,—with this cause which we assert to be one of the first principles; but mathematics has come to be identical with philosophy for modern thinkers, though they say that it should be studied for the sake of other things. Further, one might suppose that the substance which according to them underlies as matter is too mathematical, and is a predicate and differentia of the substance, i.e., of the matter, rather than matter itself; i.e. the great and the small are like the rare and the dense which the physical philosophers speak of, calling these the primary differentiae of the substratum; for these are a kind of excess and defect. And regarding movement, if the great and the small are to be movement, evidently the Forms will be moved; but if they are not to be movement, whence did movement come? The whole study of nature has been annihilated.

And what is thought to be easy—to show that all things are one—is not done; for what is proved by the method of setting out instances is not that all things are one but that there is a One itself,—if we grant all the assumptions. And not even this follows, if we do not grant that the universal is a genus; and this in some cases it cannot be.

Nor can it be explained either how the lines and planes and solids that come after the numbers exist or can exist, or what significance they have; for these can neither be Forms (for they are not numbers), nor the intermediates (for those are the objects of mathematics), nor the perishable things. This is evidently a distinct fourth class.

In general, if we search for the elements of existing things without distinguishing the many senses in which things are said to exist, we cannot find them, especially if the search for the elements of which things are made is conducted in this manner. For it is surely impossible to discover what 'acting' or 'being acted on', or 'the straight', is made of, but if elements can be discovered at all, it is only the elements of substances; therefore either to seek the elements of all existing things or to think one has them is incorrect.

And how could we learn the elements of all things? Evidently we cannot start by knowing anything before. For as he who is learning geometry, though he may know other things before, knows none of the things with which the science deals and about which he is to learn, so is it in all other cases. Therefore if there is a science of all things, such as some assert to exist, he who is learning this will know nothing before. Yet all learning is by means of premises which are (either all or some of them) known before,—whether the learning be by demonstration or by definitions; for the elements of the definition must be known before and be familiar; and learning by induction proceeds similarly. But again, if the science were actually innate, it were strange that we are unaware of our possession of the greatest of sciences.

Again, how is one to come to know what all things are made of, and how is this to be made evident? This also affords a difficulty; for there might be a conflict of opinion, as there is about certain syllables; some say za is made out of s and d and a, while others say it is a distinct sound and none of those that are familiar.

Further, how could we know the objects of sense without having the sense in question? Yet we ought to, if the elements of which all things consist, as complex sounds consist of the elements proper to sound, are the same.

3 

Universals

WILLIAM OF OCKHAM

. . . ON THE UNIVERSAL

It is not enough for the logician to have a merely general knowledge of terms; he needs a deep understanding of the concept of a term. Therefore, after discussing some general divisions among terms we should examine in detail the various headings under these divisions.

First, we should deal with terms of second intention and afterwards with terms of first intention. I have said that 'universal', 'genus', and 'species' are examples of terms of second intention. We must discuss those terms of second intention which are called the five universals, but first we should consider the common term 'universal'. It is predicated of every universal and is opposed to the notion of a particular.

First, it should be noted that the term 'particular' has two senses. In the first sense a particular is that which is one and not many. Those who hold that a universal is a certain quality residing in the mind which is predicable of many (not suppositing for itself, of course, but for the many of which it is predicated) must grant that, in this sense of the word, every universal is a particular. Just as a word, even if convention makes it common, is a particular, the intention of the soul signifying many is numerically one thing a particular; for although it signifies many things it is nonetheless one thing and not many.

In another sense of the word we use 'particular' to mean that which is one and not many and which cannot function as a sign of many. Taking 'particular' in this sense no universal is a particular, since every universal is capable of signifying many and of being predicated of many. Thus, if we take the term 'universal' to mean that which is not one in number, as many do, then, I want to say that nothing is a universal.

Source: William of Ockham, *Ockham's Theory of Terms: Part I of the Summa Logicae,* trans. M. Loux, Notre Dame, IN: University of Notre Dame Press, 1974. Reprinted with permission.

One could, of course, abuse the expression and say that a population constitutes a single universal because it is not one but many. But that would be puerile.

Therefore, it ought to be said that every universal is one particular thing and that it is not a universal except in its signification, in its signifying many things. This is what Avicenna means to say in his commentary on the fifth book of the *Metaphysics*. He says, "One form in the intellect is related to many things, and in this respect it is a universal; for it is an intention of the intellect which has an invariant relationship to anything you choose." He then continues, "Although this form is a universal in its relationship to individuals, it is a particular in its relationship to the particular soul in which it resides; for it is just one form among many in the intellect."[1] He means to say that a universal is an intention of a particular soul. Insofar as it can be predicated of many things not for itself but for these many, it is said to be a universal; but insofar as it is a particular form actually existing in the intellect, it is said to be a particular. Thus 'particular' is predicated of a universal in the first sense but not in the second. In the same way we say that the sun is a universal cause and, nevertheless, that it is really and truly a particular or individual cause. For the sun is said to be a universal cause because it is the cause of many things (i.e., every object that is generable and corruptible), but it is said to be a particular cause because it is one cause and not many. In the same way the intention of the soul is said to be a universal because it is a sign predicable of many things, but it is said to be a particular because it is one thing and not many.

But it should be noted that there are two kinds of universals. Some things are universal by nature; that is, by nature they are signs predicable of many in the same way that the smoke is by nature a sign of fire; weeping, a sign of grief; and laughter, a sign of internal joy. The intention of the soul, of course, is a universal by nature. Thus, no substance outside the soul, nor any accident outside the soul is a universal of this sort. It is of this kind of universal that I shall speak in the following chapters.

Other things are universals by convention. Thus, a spoken word, which is numerically one quality, is a universal; it is a sign conventionally appointed for the signification of many things. Thus, since the word is said to be common, it can be called a universal. But notice it is not by nature, but only by convention, that this label applies.

. . . THAT THE UNIVERSAL IS NOT A THING OUTSIDE THE MIND

But it is not enough just to state one's position; one must defend it by philosophical arguments. Therefore, I shall set forth some arguments for my view, and then corroborate it by an appeal to the authorities.

That no universal is a substance existing outside the mind can be proved in a number of ways:

No universal is a particular substance, numerically one; for if this were the case, then it would follow that Socrates is a universal; for there is no good reason why one substance should be a universal rather than another. Therefore no particular substance is a universal; every substance is numerically one and a particular. For every substance is either one thing and not many or it is many things. Now, if a substance is one thing and not many, then it is numerically one; for that is what we mean by 'numerically one'. But if, on the other hand, some substance is several things, it is either several particular things or several universal things. If the first alternative is chosen, then it follows that some substance would be several particular substances; and consequently that some substance would be several men. But although the universal would be distinguished from a single particular, it would not be distinguished from several particulars. If, however, some substance were to be several universal entities, I take one of those universal entities and ask, "Is it many things or is it one and not many?" If the second is the case then it follows that the thing is particular. If the first is the case then I ask, "Is it several particular things or several universal things?" Thus, either an infinite regress will follow or it will be granted that no substance is a universal in a way that would be incompatible with its also being a particular. From this it follows that no substance is a universal.

Again, if some universal were to be one substance existing in particular substances, yet distinct from them, it would follow that it could exist without them; for everything that is naturally prior to something else can, by God's power, exist without that thing; but the consequence is absurd.

Again, if the view in question were true, no individual would be able to be created. Something of the individual would pre-exist it, for the whole individual would not take its existence from nothing if the universal which is in it were already in something else. For the same reason it would follow that God could not annihilate an individual substance without destroying the other individuals of the same kind. If He were to annihilate some individual, he would destroy the whole which is essentially that individual and, consequently, He would destroy the universal which is in that thing and in others of the same essence. Consequently, other things of the same essence would not remain, for they could not continue to exist without the universal which constitutes a part of them.

Again, such a universal could not be construed as something completely extrinsic to the essence of an individual; therefore, it would belong to the essence of the individual; and, consequently, an individual would be composed of universals, so that the individual would not be any more a particular than a universal.

Again, it follows that something of the essence of Christ would be miserable and damned, since that common nature really existing in Christ would be damned in the damned individual; for surely that essence is also in Judas. But this is absurd.

Many other arguments could be brought forth, but in the interests of brevity, I shall dispense with them. Instead, I shall corroborate my account by an appeal to authorities.

First, in the seventh book of the *Metaphysics,* Aristotle is treating the question of whether a universal is a substance. He shows that no universal is a substance. Thus, he says, "it is impossible that substance be something that can be predicated universally."[2]

Again, in the tenth book of the *Metaphysics,* he says, "Thus, if, as we argued in the discussions on substance and being, no universal can be a substance, it is not possible that a universal be a substance in the sense of a one over and against the many."[3]

From these remarks it is clear that, in Aristotle's view, although universals can supposit for substances, no universal is a substance.

Again, the Commentator in his forty-fourth comment on the seventh book of the *Metaphysics* says, "In the individual, the only substance is the particular form and matter out of which the individual is composed."[4]

Again, in the forty-fifth comment, he says, "Let us say, therefore, that it is impossible that one of those things we call universals be the substance of anything, although they do express the substances of things."[5]

And, again, in the forty-seventh comment, "It is impossible that they (universals) be parts of substances existing of and by themselves."[6]

Again, in the second comment on the eighth book of the *Metaphysics,* he says, "No universal is either a substance or a genus."[7]

Again, in the sixth comment on the tenth book, he says, "Since universals are not substances, it is clear that the common notion of being is not a substance existing outside the mind."[8]

Using these and many other authorities, the general point emerges: no universal is a substance regardless of the viewpoint from which we consider the matter. Thus, the viewpoint from which we consider the matter is irrelevant to the question of whether something is a substance. Nevertheless, the meaning of a term is relevant to the question of whether the expression 'substance' can be predicated of the term. Thus, if the term 'dog' in the proposition 'The dog is an animal' is used to stand for the barking animal, the proposition is true; but if it is used for the celestial body which goes by that name, the proposition is false. But it is impossible that one and the same thing should be a substance from one viewpoint and not a substance from another.

Therefore, it ought to be granted that no universal is a substance regardless of how it is considered. On the contrary, every universal is an intention of the mind which, on the most probable account, is identical with the act of understanding. Thus, it is said that the act of understanding by which I grasp men is a natural sign of men in the same way that weeping is a natural sign of grief. It is a natural sign such that it can stand for men in mental propositions in the same way that a spoken word can stand for things in spoken propositions.

That the universal is an intention of the soul is clearly expressed by Avicenna in the fifth book of the *Metaphysics,* in which he comments, "I say, therefore, that there are three senses of 'universal'. For we say that something is a universal if (like 'man') it is actually predicated of many things; and we also call an intention a universal if it could be predicated of many." Then follows the remark, "An intention is also called a universal if there is nothing inconceivable in its being predicated of many."[9]

From these remarks it is clear that the universal is an intention of the soul capable of being predicated of many. The claim can be corroborated by argument. For every one agrees that a universal is something predicable of many, but only an intention of the soul or a conventional sign is predicated. No substance is ever predicated of anything. Therefore, only an intention of the soul or a conventional sign is a universal; but I am not here using the term 'universal' for conventional signs, but only for signs that are universals by nature. That substance is not capable of functioning as predicate is clear; for if it were, it would follow that a proposition would be composed of particular substances; and, consequently, the subject would be in Rome and the predicate in England which is absurd.

Furthermore, propositions occur only in the mind, in speech, or in writing; therefore, their parts can exist only in the mind, in speech, and in writing. Particular substances, however, cannot themselves exist in the mind, in speech, or in writing. Thus, no proposition can be composed of particular substances. Propositions are, however, composed of universals; therefore, universals cannot conceivably be substances.

NOTES

1. *Avicennae Metaphysica,* Tract. V, chapter 1–E, 140–141.
2. 1038^b 8–9.
3. 1053^b 17–19.
4. *Aristotelis Opera Cum Averrois Commentariis* (Frankfurt: Minerva, 1962 (a photostat of the 1562–1574 edition)), vol. 8, 197, recto, B.
5. *Ibid.,* 198, verso, B.
6. *Ibid.,* 198, recto, B.
7. *Ibid.,* 210, recto, B.
8. *Ibid.,* 256, verso, A-B.
9. *Avicennae Metaphysica,* Tract. V, chapter 1–E, 140.

4

Empiricism, Semantics, and Ontology[1]

RUDOLF CARNAP

1. THE PROBLEM OF ABSTRACT ENTITIES

Empiricists are in general rather suspicious with respect to any kind of abstract entities like properties, classes, relations, numbers, propositions, etc. They usually feel much more in sympathy with nominalists than with realists (in the medieval sense). As far as possible they try to avoid any reference to abstract entities and to restrict themselves to what is sometimes called a nominalistic language, i.e., one not containing such references. However, within certain scientific contexts it seems hardly possible to avoid them. In the case of mathematics, some empiricists try to find a way out by treating the whole of mathematics as a mere calculus, a formal system for which no interpretation is given or can be given. Accordingly, the mathematician is said to speak not about numbers, functions, and infinite classes, but merely about meaningless symbols and formulas manipulated according to given formal rules. In physics it is more difficult to shun the suspected entities, because the language of physics serves for the communication of reports and predictions and hence cannot be taken as a mere calculus. A physicist who is suspicious of abstract entities may perhaps try to declare a certain part of the language of physics as uninterpreted and uninterpretable, that part which refers to real numbers as space-time coordinates or as values of physical magnitudes, to functions, limits, etc. More probably he will just speak about all these things like anybody else but with an uneasy conscience, like a man who in his everyday life does with qualms many things which are not in accord with the high moral principles he professes on Sundays. Recently the problem of abstract entities has arisen again in connection with semantics, the theory of meaning and truth. Some semanticists

Source: Excerpt from Rudolf Carnap, MEANING AND NECESSITY, Chicago: University of Chicago Press, pp. 205–211.

say that certain expressions designate certain entities, and among these designated entities they include not only concrete material things but also abstract entities, e.g., properties as designated by predicates and propositions as designated by sentences.[2] Others object strongly to this procedure as violating the basic principles of empiricism and leading back to a metaphysical ontology of the Platonic kind.

It is the purpose of this article to clarify this controversial issue. The nature and implications of the acceptance of a language referring to abstract entities will first be discussed in general; it will be shown that using such a language does not imply embracing a Platonic ontology but is perfectly compatible with empiricism and strictly scientific thinking. Then the special question of the role of abstract entities in semantics will be discussed. It is hoped that the clarification of the issue will be useful to those who would like to accept abstract entities in their work in mathematics, physics, semantics, or any other field; it may help them to overcome nominalistic scruples.

2. LINGUISTIC FRAMEWORKS

Are there properties, classes, numbers, propositions? In order to understand more clearly the nature of these and related problems, it is above all necessary to recognize a fundamental distinction between two kinds of questions concerning the existence or reality of entities. If someone wishes to speak in his language about a new kind of entities, he has to introduce a system of new ways of speaking, subject to new rules; we shall call this procedure the construction of a linguistic *framework* for the new entities in question. And now we must distinguish two kinds of questions of existence: first, questions of the existence of certain entities of the new kind *within the framework;* we call them *internal questions;* and second, questions concerning the existence or reality *of the system of entities as a whole,* called *external questions*. Internal questions and possible answers to them are formulated with the help of the new forms of expressions. The answers may be found either by purely logical methods or by empirical methods, depending upon whether the framework is a logical or a factual one. An external question is of a problematic character which is in need of closer examination.

The world of things. Let us consider as an example the simplest kind of entities dealt with in the everyday language: the spatio-temporally ordered system of observable things and events. Once we have accepted the thing language with its framework for things, we can raise and answer internal questions, e.g., "Is there a white piece of paper on my desk?", "Did King Arthur actually live?", "Are unicorns and centaurs real or merely imaginary?", and the like. These questions are to be answered by empirical investigations. Results of observations are evaluated according to certain rules as confirming or disconfirming evidence for possible answers. (This evaluation is usually carried out, of course, as a matter of habit rather than a deliberate, rational procedure. But it is possible, in a rational reconstruction, to lay down explicit rules for the evaluation. This is one of the main tasks of a pure, as distinguished from a psychological epistemology.) The concept of reality occurring in these internal questions is an empirical, scientific, non-metaphysical concept. To recognize something as a real thing or event means to succeed in incorporating it into the system of things at a particular space-time position so that it fits together with the other things recognized as real, according to the rules of the framework.

From these questions we must distinguish the external question of the reality of the thing world itself. In contrast to the former questions, this question is raised neither by the man in the street nor by scientists, but only by philosophers. Realists give an affirmative answer, subjective idealists a negative one, and the controversy goes on for centuries without ever being solved.

And it cannot be solved because it is framed in a wrong way. To be real in the scientific sense means to be an element of the system; hence this concept cannot be meaningfully applied to the system itself. Those who raise the question of the reality of the thing world itself have perhaps in mind not a theoretical question as their formulation seems to suggest, but rather a practical question, a matter of a practical decision concerning the structure of our language. We have to make the choice whether or not to accept and use the forms of expression in the framework in question.

In the case of this particular example, there is usually no deliberate choice because we all have accepted the thing language early in our lives as a matter of course. Nevertheless, we may regard it as a matter of decision in this sense: we are free to choose to continue using the thing language or not; in the latter case we could restrict ourselves to a language of sense-data and other "phenomenal" entities, or construct an alternative to the customary thing language with another structure, or, finally, we could refrain from speaking. If someone decides to accept the thing language, there is no objection against saying that he has accepted the world of things. But this must not be interpreted as if it meant his acceptance of a *belief* in the reality of the thing world; there is no such belief or assertion or assumption, because it is not a theoretical question. To accept the thing world means nothing more than to accept a certain form of language, in other words, to accept rules for forming statements and for testing, accepting, or rejecting them. The acceptance of the thing language leads, on the basis of observations made, also to the acceptance, belief, and assertion of certain statements. But the thesis of the reality of the thing world cannot be among these statements, because it cannot be formulated in the thing language or, it seems, in any other theoretical language.

The decision of accepting the thing language, although itself not of a cognitive nature, will nevertheless usually be influenced by theoretical knowledge, just like any other deliberate decision concerning the acceptance of linguistic or other rules. The purposes for which the language is intended to be used, for instance, the purpose of communicating factual knowledge, will determine which factors are relevant for the decision. The efficiency, fruitfulness, and simplicity of the use of the thing language may be among the decisive factors. And the questions concerning these qualities are indeed of a theoretical nature. But these questions cannot be identified with the question of realism. They are not yes-no questions but questions of degree. The thing language in the customary form works indeed with a high degree of efficiency for most purposes of everyday life. This is a matter of fact, based upon the content of our experiences. However, it would be wrong to describe this situation by saying: "The fact of the efficiency of the thing language is confirming evidence for the reality of the thing world"; we should rather say instead: "This fact makes it advisable to accept the thing language."

The system of numbers. As an example of a system which is of a logical rather than a factual nature let us take the system of natural numbers. The framework for this system is constructed by introducing into the language new expressions with suitable rules: (1) numerals like "five" and sentence forms like "there are five books on the table"; (2) the general term "number" for the new entities, and sentence forms like "five is a number"; (3) expressions for properties of numbers (e.g., "odd", "prime"), relations (e.g., "greater than"), and functions (e.g., "plus"), and sentence forms like "two plus three is five"; (4) numerical variables ("*m*", "*n*", etc.) and quantifiers for universal sentences ("for every *n*, . . . ") and existential sentences ("there is an *n* such that . . . ") with the customary deductive rules.

Here again there are internal questions, e.g., "Is there a prime number greater than a hundred?" Here, however, the answers are found, not by empirical investigation based on observations, but by logical analysis based on the rules for the new expressions. Therefore the answers are here analytic, i.e., logically true.

What is now the nature of the philosophical question concerning the existence or reality of numbers? To begin with, there is the internal question which, together with the affirmative answer, can be formulated in the new terms, say, by "There are numbers" or, more explicitly, "There is an *n* such that *n* is a number". This statement follows from the analytic statement "five is a number" and is therefore itself analytic. Moreover, it is rather trivial (in contradistinction to a statement like "There is a prime number greater than a million", which is likewise analytic but far from trivial), because it does not say more than that the new system is not empty; but this is immediately seen from the rule which states that words like "five" are substitutable for the new variables. Therefore nobody who meant the question "Are there numbers?" in the internal sense would either assert or even seriously consider a negative answer. This makes it plausible to assume that those philosophers who treat the question of the existence of numbers as a serious philosophical problem and offer lengthy arguments on either side, do not have in mind the internal question. And, indeed, if we were to ask them: "Do you mean the question as to whether the framework of numbers, *if* we were to accept it, would be found to be empty or not?", they would probably reply: "Not at all; we mean a question *prior* to the acceptance of the new framework". They might try to explain what they mean by saying that it is a question of the ontological status of numbers; the question whether or not numbers have a certain metaphysical characteristic called reality (but a kind of ideal reality, different from the material reality of the thing world) or subsistence or status of "independent entities". Unfortunately, these philosophers have so far not given a formulation of their question in terms of the common scientific language. Therefore our judgement must be that they have not succeeded in giving to the external question and to the possible answers any cognitive content. Unless and until they supply a clear cognitive interpretation, we are justified in our suspicion that their question is a pseudo-question, that is, one disguised in the form of a theoretical question while in fact it is non-theoretical; in the present case it is the practical problem whether or not to incorporate into the language the new linguistic forms which constitute the framework of numbers.

The system of propositions. New variables, "*p*", "*q*", etc., are introduced with a rule to the effect that any (declarative) sentence may be substituted for a variable of this kind; this includes, in addition to the sentences of the original thing language, also all general sentences with variables of any kind which may have been introduced into the language. Further, the general term "proposition" is introduced. "*p* is a proposition" may be defined by "*p* or not *p*" (or by any other sentence form yielding only analytic sentences). Therefore, every sentence of the form ". . . is a proposition" (where any sentence may stand in the place of the dots) is analytic. This holds, for example, for the sentence:

(*a*) "Chicago is large is a proposition."

(We disregard here the fact that the rules of English grammar require not a sentence but a that-clause as the subject of another sentence; accordingly, instead of (*a*) we should have to say "That Chicago is large is a proposition".) Predicates may be admitted whose argument expressions are sentences; these predicates may be either extensional (e.g., the customary truth-functional connectives) or not (e.g., modal predicates like "possible", "necessary", etc.). With the help of the new variables, general sentences may be formed, e.g.,

(*b*) "For every *p*, either *p* or not-*p*."

(*c*) "There is a *p* such that *p* is not necessary and not-*p* is not necessary."

(*d*) "There is a *p* such that *p* is a proposition."

(*c*) and (*d*) are internal assertions of existence. The statement "There are propositions" may be meant in the sense of (*d*); in this case it is analytic (since it follows from (*a*)) and even trivial. If, however, the statement is meant in an external sense, then it is non-cognitive.

It is important to notice that the system of rules for the linguistic expressions of the propositional framework (of which only a few rules have here been briefly indicated) is sufficient for the introduction of the framework. Any further explanations as to the nature of the propositions (i.e., the elements of the system indicated, the values of the variables "*p*", "*q*", etc.) are theoretically unnecessary because, if correct, they follow from the rules. For example, are propositions mental events (as in Russell's theory)? A look at the rules shows us that they are not, because otherwise existential statements would be of the form: "If the mental state of the person in question fulfils such and such conditions, then there is a *p* such that . . .". The fact that no references to mental conditions occur in existential statements (like (*c*), (*d*), etc.) shows that propositions are not mental entities. Further, a statement of the existence of linguistic entities (e.g., expressions, classes of expressions, etc.) must contain a reference to a language. The fact that no such reference occurs in the existential statements here, shows that propositions are not linguistic entities. The fact that in these statements no reference to a subject (an observer or knower) occurs (nothing like: "There is a *p* which is necessary for Mr. *X*"), shows that the propositions (and their properties, like necessity, etc.) are not subjective. Although characterizations of these or similar kinds are, strictly speaking, unnecessary, they may nevertheless be practically useful. If they are given, they should be understood, not as ingredient parts of the system, but merely as marginal notes with the purpose of supplying to the reader helpful hints or convenient pictorial associations which may make his learning of the use of the expressions easier than the bare system of the rules would do. Such a characterization is analogous to an extra-systematic explanation which a physicist sometimes gives to the beginner. He might, for example, tell him to imagine the atoms of a gas as small balls rushing around with great speed, or the electromagnetic field and its oscillations as quasi-elastic tensions and vibrations in an ether. In fact, however, all that can accurately be said about atoms or the field is implicitly contained in the physical laws of the theories in question.[3]

The system of thing properties. The thing language contains words like "red", "hard", "stone", "house", etc., which are used for describing what things are like. Now we may introduce new variables, say "*f*", "*g*", etc., for which those words are substitutable and furthermore the general term "property". New rules are laid down which admit sentences like "Red is a property", "Red is a color", "These two pieces of paper have at least one color in common" (i.e., "There is an *f* such that *f* is a color, and . . ."). The last sentence is an internal assertion. It is of an empirical, factual nature. However, the external statement, the philosophical statement of the reality of properties—a special case of the thesis of the reality of universals—is devoid of cognitive content.

The systems of integers and rational numbers. Into a language containing the framework of natural numbers we may introduce first the (positive and negative) integers as relations among natural numbers and then the rational numbers as relations among integers. This involves introducing new types of variables, expressions substitutable for them, and the general terms "integer" and "rational number."

The system of real numbers. On the basis of the rational numbers, the real numbers may be introduced as classes of a special kind (segments) of rational numbers (according to the method developed by Dedekind and Frege). Here again a new type of variables is introduced, expressions substitutable for them (e.g., "$\sqrt{2}$"), and the general term "real number."

The spatio-temporal coordinate system for physics. The new entities are the space-time points. Each is an ordered quadruple of four real numbers, called its coordinates, consisting of three spatial and one temporal coordinates. The physical state of a spatio-temporal point or region is described either with the help of qualitative predicates (e.g., "hot") or by ascribing numbers as values of a physical magnitude (e.g., mass, temperature, and the like). The step from the system of things (which does not contain space-time points but only extended objects with spatial and temporal relations between them) to the physical coordinate system is again a matter of decision. Our choice of certain features, although itself not theoretical, is suggested by theoretical knowledge, either logical or factual. For example, the choice of real numbers rather than rational numbers or integers as coordinates is not much influenced by the facts of experience but mainly due to considerations of mathematical simplicity. The restriction to rational coordinates would not be in conflict with any experimental knowledge we have, because the result of any measurement is a rational number. However, it would prevent the use of ordinary geometry (which says, e.g., that the diagonal of a square with the side 1 has the irrational value $\sqrt{2}$) and thus lead to great complications. On the other hand, the decision to use three rather than two or four spatial coordinates is strongly suggested, but still not forced upon us, by the result of common observations. If certain events allegedly observed in spiritualistic séances, e.g., a ball moving out of a sealed box, were confirmed beyond any reasonable doubt, it might seem advisable to use four spatial coordinates. Internal questions are here, in general, empirical questions to be answered by empirical investigations. On the other hand, the external questions of the reality of physical space and physical time are pseudo-questions. A question like "Are there (really) space-time points?" is ambiguous. It may be meant as an internal question; then the affirmative answer is, of course, analytic and trivial. Or it may be meant in the external sense: "Shall we introduce such and such forms into our language?"; in this case it is not a theoretical but a practical question, a matter of decision rather than assertion, and hence the proposed formulation would be misleading. Or finally, it may be meant in the following sense: "Are our experiences such that the use of the linguistic forms in question will be expedient and fruitful?" This is a theoretical question of a factual, empirical nature. But it concerns a matter of degree; therefore a formulation in the form "real or not?" would be inadequate.

3. WHAT DOES ACCEPTANCE OF A KIND OF ENTITIES MEAN?

Let us now summarize the essential characteristics of situations involving the introduction of a new kind of entities, characteristics which are common to the various examples outlined above.

The acceptance of a new kind of entities is represented in the language by the introduction of a framework of new forms of expressions to be used according to a new set of rules. There may be new names for particular entities of the kind in question; but some such names may already occur in the language before the introduction of the new framework. (Thus, for example, the thing language contains certainly words of the type of "blue" and "house" before the framework of properties is introduced; and it may contain words like "ten" in sentences of the form "I have ten fingers" before the framework of numbers is introduced.) The latter fact shows that the occurrence of constants of the type in question—regarded as names of entities of the new kind after the new framework is introduced—is not a sure sign of the acceptance of the new kind of entities. Therefore the introduction of such constants is not to be regarded as an essential step in the introduction of the framework. The two essential steps are rather the following. First, the introduction of a general term, a predicate of higher level, for the new kind of entities, permitting us to say of any particular entity that it belongs to this kind (e.g., "Red is a *property*," "Five is a *number*"). Second, the introduction of variables of the new type. The new entities are values of these variables; the constants (and the closed compound expressions, if any) are substitutable for the variables.[4] With the help of the variables, general sentences concerning the new entities can be formulated.

After the new forms are introduced into the language, it is possible to formulate with their help internal questions and possible answers to them. A question of this kind may be either empirical or logical; accordingly a true answer is either factually true or analytic.

From the internal questions we must clearly distinguish external questions, i.e., philosophical questions concerning the existence or reality of the total system of the new entities. Many philosophers regard a question of this kind as an ontological question which must be raised and answered *before* the introduction of the new language forms. The latter introduction, they believe, is legitimate only if it can be justified by an ontological insight supplying an affirmative answer to the question of reality. In contrast to this view, we take the position that the introduction of the new ways of speaking does not need any theoretical justification because it does not imply any assertion of reality. We may still speak (and have done so) of "the acceptance of the new entities" since this form of speech is customary; but one must keep in mind that this phrase does not mean for us anything more than acceptance of the new framework, i.e., of the new linguistic forms. Above all, it must not be interpreted as referring to an assumption, belief, or assertion of "the reality of the entities". There is no such assertion. An alleged statement of the reality of the system of entities is a pseudo-statement without cognitive content. To be sure, we have to face at this point an important question; but it is a practical, not a theoretical question; it is the question of whether or not to accept the new linguistic forms. The acceptance cannot be judged as being either true or false because it is not an assertion. It can only be judged as being more or less expedient, fruitful, conducive to the aim for which the language is intended. Judgements of this kind supply the motivation for the decision of accepting or rejecting the kind of entities.[5]

Thus it is clear that the acceptance of a linguistic framework must not be regarded as implying a metaphysical doctrine concerning the reality of the entities in question. It seems to me due to a neglect of this important distinction that some contemporary nominalists label the admission of variables of abstract types as "Platonism".[6] This is, to say the least, an extremely misleading terminology. It leads to the absurd consequence, that the position of everybody who accepts the language of physics with its real number variables (as a language of communication, not merely as a calculus) would be called Platonistic, even if he is a strict empiricist who rejects Platonic metaphysics.

A brief historical remark may here be inserted. The non-cognitive character of the questions which we have called here external questions was recognized and emphasized already by the Vienna Circle under the leadership of Moritz Schlick, the group from which the movement of logical empiricism originated. Influenced by ideas of Ludwig Wittgenstein, the Circle rejected both the thesis of the reality of the external world and the thesis of its irreality as pseudo-statements;[7] the same was the case for both the thesis of the reality of universals (abstract entities, in our present terminology) and the nominalistic thesis that they are not real and that their alleged names are not names of anything but merely *flatus vocis*. (It is obvious that the apparent negation of a pseudo-statement must also be a pseudo-statement.) It is therefore not correct to classify the members of the Vienna Circle as nominalists, as is sometimes done. However, if we look at the basic anti-metaphysical and pro-scientific attitude of most nominalists (and the same holds for many materialists and realists in the modern sense), disregarding their occasional pseudo-theoretical formulations, then it is, of course, true to say that the Vienna Circle was much closer to those philosophers than to their opponents.

4. ABSTRACT ENTITIES IN SEMANTICS

The problem of the legitimacy and the status of abstract entities has recently again led to controversial discussions in connection with semantics. In a semantical meaning analysis certain expressions in a language are often said to designate (or name or denote or signify or refer to) certain extra-linguistic entities.[8] As long as physical things or events (e.g., Chicago or Caesar's death) are taken as designata (entities designated), no serious doubts arise. But strong objections have been raised, especially by some empiricists, against abstract entities as designata, e.g., against semantical statements of the following kind:

1. "The word 'red' designates a property of things";
2. "The word 'color' designates a property of properties of things";
3. "The word 'five' designates a number";
4. "The word 'odd' designates a property of numbers";
5. "The sentence 'Chicago is large' designates a proposition."

Those who criticize these statements do not, of course, reject the use of the expressions in question, like "red" or "five"; nor would they deny that these expressions are meaningful. But to be meaningful, they would say, is not the same as having a meaning in the sense of an entity designated. They reject the belief, which they regard as implicitly presupposed by those semantical statements, that to each expression of the types in question (adjectives like "red," numerals like "five," etc.) there is a particular real entity to which the expression stands in the relation of designation. This belief is rejected as incompatible with the basic principles of empiricism or of scientific thinking. Derogatory labels like "Platonic realism," "hypostatization," or " 'Fido'-Fido principle" are attached to it. The latter is the name given by Gilbert Ryle [Meaning] to the criticized belief, which, in his view, arises by a naïve inference of analogy: just as there is an entity well known to me, viz. my dog Fido, which is designated by the name "Fido," thus there must be for every meaningful expression a particular entity to which it stands in the relation of designation or naming, i.e., the relation exemplified by "Fido"-Fido. The belief criticized is thus a case of hypostatization, i.e., of treating as names expressions which are not names. While "Fido" is a name, expressions like "red," "five," etc., are said not to be names, not to designate anything.

Our previous discussion concerning the acceptance of frameworks enables us now to clarify the situation with respect to abstract entities as designata. Let us take as an example the statement:

(*a*) " 'Five' designates a number."

The formulation of this statement presupposes that our language L contains the forms of expressions which we have called the framework of numbers, in particular, numerical variables and the general term "number." If L contains these forms, the following is an analytic statement in L:

(*b*) "Five is a number."

Further, to make the statement (*a*) possible, L must contain an expression like "designates" or "is a name of" for the semantical relation of designation. If suitable rules for this term are laid down, the following is likewise analytic:

(*c*) " 'Five' designates five."

(Generally speaking, any expression of the form " ' . . . ' designates . . . " is an analytic statement provided the term " . . . " is a constant in an accepted framework. If the latter condition is not fulfilled, the expression is not a statement.) Since (*a*) follows from (*c*) and (*b*), (*a*) is likewise analytic.

Thus it is clear that *if* someone accepts the framework of numbers, then he must acknowledge (*c*) and (*b*) and hence (*a*) as true statements. Generally speaking, if someone accepts a framework for a certain kind of entities, then he is bound to admit the entities as possible designata. Thus the question of the admissibility of entities of a certain type or of abstract entities in general as designata is reduced to the question of the acceptability of the linguistic framework for those entities. Both the nominalistic critics, who refuse the status of designators or names to expressions like "red," "five," etc., because they deny the existence of abstract entities, and the skeptics, who express doubts concerning the existence and demand evidence for it, treat the question of existence as a theoretical question. They do, of course, not mean the internal question; the affirmative answer to *this* question is analytic and trivial and too obvious for doubt or denial, as we have seen. Their doubts refer rather to the system of entities itself; hence they mean the external question. They believe that only after making sure that there really is a system of entities of the kind in question are we justified in accepting the framework by incorporating the linguistic forms into our language. However, we have seen that the external question is not a theoretical question but rather the practical question whether or not to accept those linguistic forms. This acceptance is not in need of a theoretical justification (except with respect to expediency and fruitfulness), because it does not imply a belief or assertion. Ryle says that the "Fido"-Fido principle is "a grotesque theory." Grotesque or not, Ryle is wrong in calling it a theory. It is rather the practical decision to accept certain frameworks. Maybe Ryle is historically right with respect to those whom he mentions as previous representatives of the principle, viz. John Stuart Mill, Frege, and Russell. If these philosophers regarded the acceptance of a system of entities as a theory, an assertion, they were victims of the same old, metaphysical confusion. But it is certainly wrong to regard *my* semantical method as involving a belief in the reality of abstract entities, since I reject a thesis of this kind as a metaphysical pseudo-statement.

The critics of the use of abstract entities in semantics overlook the fundamental difference between the acceptance of a system of entities and an internal assertion, e.g., an assertion that there are elephants or electrons or prime numbers greater than a million. Whoever makes an internal assertion is certainly obliged to justify it by providing evidence, empirical evidence in the case of electrons, logical proof in the case of the prime numbers. The demand for a theoretical justification, correct in the case of internal assertions, is sometimes wrongly applied to the acceptance of a system of entities. Thus, for example, Ernest Nagel in [Review C.] asks for "evidence relevant for affirming with warrant that there are such entities as infinitesimals or propositions". He characterizes the evidence required in these cases—in distinction to the empirical evidence in the case of electrons—as "in the broad sense logical and dialectical". Beyond this no hint is given as to what might be regarded as relevant evidence. Some nominalists regard the acceptance of abstract entities as a kind of superstition or myth populating the world with fictitious or at least dubious entities, analogous to the belief in centaurs or demons. This shows again the confusion mentioned, because a superstition or myth is a false (or dubious) internal statement.

Let us take as example the natural numbers as cardinal numbers, i.e., in contexts like "Here are three books." The linguistic forms of the framework of numbers, including variables and the general term "number," are generally used in our common language of communication; and it is easy to formulate explicit rules for their use. Thus the logical characteristics of this framework are sufficiently clear (while many internal questions, i.e., arithmetical questions, are, of course, still open). In spite of this, the controversy concerning the external question of the ontological reality of the system of numbers continues. Suppose that one philosopher says: "I believe that there are numbers as real entities. This gives me the right to use the linguistic forms of the numerical framework and to make semantical statements about numbers as designata of numerals." His nominalistic opponent replies: "You are wrong; there are no numbers. The numerals may still be used as meaningful expressions. But they are not names, there are no entities designated by them. Therefore the word "number" and numerical variables must not be used (unless a way were found to introduce them as merely abbreviating devices, a way of translating them into the nominalistic thing language)." I cannot think of any possible evidence that would be regarded as relevant by both philosophers, and therefore, if actually found, would decide the controversy or at least make one of the opposite theses more probable than the other. (To construe the numbers as classes or properties of the second level, according to the Frege-Russell method, does, of course, not solve the controversy, because the first philosopher would affirm and the second deny the existence of the system of classes or properties of the second level.) Therefore I feel compelled to regard the external question as a pseudo-question, until both parties to the controversy offer a common interpretation of the question as a cognitive question; this would involve an indication of possible evidence regarded as relevant by both sides.

There is a particular kind of misinterpretation of the acceptance of abstract entities in various fields of science and in semantics, that needs to be cleared up. Certain early British empiricists (e.g., Berkeley and Hume) denied the existence of abstract entities on the ground that immediate experience presents us only with particulars, not with universals, e.g., with this red patch, but not with Redness or Color-in-General; with this scalene triangle, but not with Scalene Triangularity or Triangularity-in-General. Only entities belonging to a type of which examples were to be found within immediate experience could be accepted as ultimate constituents of reality. Thus, according to this way of thinking, the existence of abstract entities could be asserted only if one could show either that some abstract entities fall within the given, or that abstract entities can be defined in terms of the types of entity which are given. Since these empiricists found no abstract entities within the realm of sense-data, they either denied their existence, or else made a futile attempt to define universals in terms of particulars. Some contemporary philosophers, especially English philosophers following Bertrand Russell, think in basically similar terms. They emphasize a distinction between the data (that which is immediately given in consciousness, e.g., sense-data, immediately past experiences, etc.) and the constructs based on the data. Existence or reality is ascribed only to the data; the constructs are not real entities; the corresponding linguistic expressions are merely ways of speech not actually designating anything (reminiscent of the nominalists' *flatus vocis*). We shall not criticize here this general conception. (As far as it is a principle of accepting certain entities and not accepting others, leaving aside any ontological, phenomenalistic and nominalistic pseudo-statements, there cannot be any theoretical objection to it.) But if this conception leads to the view that other philosophers or scientists who accept abstract entities thereby assert or imply their occurrence as immediate data, then such a view must be rejected as a misinterpretation. References to space-time points, the electromagnetic field, or electrons in physics, to real or complex numbers and their functions in mathematics, to the excitatory potential or unconscious complexes in psychology, to an inflationary trend in economics, and the like, do not imply the assertion that entities of these kinds occur as immediate data. And the same holds for references to abstract entities as designata in semantics. Some of the criticisms by English philosophers against such references give the impression that, probably due to the misinterpretation just indicated, they accuse the semanticist not so much of bad metaphysics (as some nominalists would do) but of bad psychology. The fact that they regard a semantical method involving abstract entities not merely as doubtful and perhaps wrong, but as manifestly absurd, preposterous and grotesque, and that they show a deep horror and indignation against this method, is perhaps to be explained by a misinterpretation of the kind described. In fact, of course, the semanticist does not in the least assert or imply that the abstract entities to which he refers can be experienced as immediately given either by sensation or by a kind of rational intuition. An assertion of this kind would indeed be very dubious psychology. The psychological question as to which kinds of entities do and which do not occur as immediate data is entirely irrelevant for semantics, just as it is for physics, mathematics, economics, etc., with respect to the examples mentioned above.[9]

5. CONCLUSION

For those who want to develop or use semantical methods, the decisive question is not the alleged ontological question of the existence of abstract entities but rather the question whether the use of abstract linguistic forms or, in technical terms, the use of variables beyond those for things (or phenomenal data), is expedient and fruitful for the purposes for which semantical analyses are made, viz. the analysis, interpretation, clarification, or construction of languages of communication, especially languages of science. This question is here neither decided nor even discussed. It is not a question simply of yes or no, but a matter of degree. Among those philosophers who have carried out semantical analyses and thought about suitable tools for this work, beginning with Plato and Aristotle and, in a more technical way on the basis of modern logic, with C. S. Peirce and Frege, a great majority accepted abstract entities. This does, of course, not prove the case. After all, semantics in the technical sense is still in the initial phases of its development, and we must be prepared for possible fundamental changes in methods. Let us therefore admit that the nominalistic critics may possibly be right. But if so, they will have to offer better arguments than they have so far. Appeal to ontological insight will not carry much weight. The critics will have to show that it is possible to construct a semantical method which avoids all references to abstract entities and achieves by simpler means essentially the same results as the other methods.

The acceptance or rejection of abstract linguistic forms, just as the acceptance or rejection of any other linguistic forms in any branch of science, will finally be decided by their efficiency as instruments, the ratio of the results achieved to the amount and complexity of the efforts required. To decree dogmatic prohibitions of certain linguistic forms instead of testing them by their success or failure in practical use, is worse than futile; it is positively harmful because it may obstruct scientific progress. The history of science shows examples of such prohibitions based on prejudices deriving from religious, mythological, metaphysical, or other irrational sources, which slowed up the developments for shorter or longer periods of time. Let us learn from the lessons of history. Let us grant to those who work in any special field of investigation the freedom to use any form of expression which seems useful to them; the work in the field will sooner or later lead to the elimination of those forms which have no useful function. *Let us be cautious in making assertions and critical in examining them, but tolerant in permitting linguistic forms.*

NOTES

1. I have made here some minor changes in the formulations to the effect that the term "framework" is now used only for the system of linguistic expressions, and not for the system of the entities in question.
2. The terms "sentence" and "statement" are here used synonymously for declarative (indicative, propositional) sentences.
3. In my book *Meaning and Necessity* (Chicago, 1947) I have developed a semantical method which takes propositions as entities designated by sentences (more specifically, as intensions of sentences). In order to facilitate the understanding of the systematic development, I added some informal, extra-systematic explanations concerning the nature of propositions. I said that the term "proposition" "is used neither for a linguistic expression nor for a subjective, mental occurrence, but rather for something objective that may or may not be exemplified in nature. . . . We apply the term 'proposition' to any entities of a certain logical type, namely, those that may be expressed by (declarative) sentences in a language" (p. 27). After some more detailed discussions concerning the relation between propositions and facts, and the nature of false propositions, I added: "It has been the purpose of the preceding remarks to facilitate the understanding of our conception of propositions. If, however, a reader should find these explanations more puzzling than clarifying, or even unacceptable, he may disregard them" (p. 31) (that is, disregard these extra-systematic explanations, not the whole theory of the propositions as intensions of sentences, as one reviewer understood). In spite of this warning, it seems that some of those readers who were puzzled by the explanations, did not disregard them but thought that by raising objections against them they could refute the theory. This is analogous to the procedure of some laymen who by (correctly) criticizing the ether picture or other visualizations of physical theories, thought they had refuted those theories. Perhaps the discussions in the present paper will help in clarifying the role of the system of linguistic rules for the introduction of a framework for entities on the one hand, and that of extra-systematic explanations concerning the nature of the entities on the other.
4. W. V. Quine was the first to recognize the importance of the introduction of variables as indicating the acceptance of entities. "The ontology to which one's use of language commits him comprises simply the objects that he treats as falling . . . within the range of values of his variables" ([Notes], p. 118; compare also his [Designation] and [Universals]).
5. For a closely related point of view on these questions see the detailed discussions in Herbert Feigl, "Existential Hypotheses," *Philosophy of Science,* 17 (1950), 35–62.
6. Paul Bernays, "Sur le platonisme dans les mathématiques" (*L'Enseignement math.,* 34 (1935), 52–69). W. V. Quine, see previous footnote and a recent paper [What]. Quine does not acknowledge the distinction which I emphasize above, because according to his general conception there are no sharp boundary lines between logical and factual truth, between questions of meaning and questions of fact, between the acceptance of a language structure and the acceptance of an assertion formulated in the language. This conception, which seems to deviate considerably from customary ways of thinking, will be explained in his article [Semantics]. When Quine in the article [What] classifies my logicistic conception of mathematics (derived from Frege and Russell) as "platonic realism" (p. 33), this is meant (according to a personal communication from him) not as ascribing to me agreement with Plato's metaphysical doctrine of universals, but merely as referring to the fact that I accept a language of mathematics containing variables

of higher levels. With respect to the basic attitude to take in choosing a language form (an "ontology" in Quine's terminology, which seems to me misleading), there appears now to be agreement between us: "the obvious counsel is tolerance and an experimental spirit" ([What], p. 38).

7. See Carnap, *Scheinprobleme in der Philosophie; das Fremdpsychische und der Realismusstreit,* Berlin, 1928. Moritz Schlick, *Positivismus und Realismus,* reprinted in *Gesammelte Aufsätze,* Wien, 1938.
8. See [I]; *Meaning and Necessity* (Chicago, 1947). The distinction I have drawn in the latter book between the method of the name-relation and the method of intension and extension is not essential for our present discussion. The term "designation" is used in the present article in a neutral way; it may be understood as referring to the name-relation or to the intension-relation or to the extension-relation or to any similar relations used in other semantical methods.
9. Wilfrid Sellars ("Acquaintance and Description Again", in *Journal of Philos.,* 46 (1949), 496–504; see pp. 502 f.) analyzes clearly the roots of the mistake "of taking the designation relation of semantic theory to be a reconstruction of *being present to an experience.*"

5

Statements About Universals

FRANK JACKSON

A feature of many versions of Nominalism is the claim that all statements putatively about universals can be translated as statements about particulars. This is certainly possible in some cases, for instance, 'Wisdom was a characteristic of Plato' is equivalent to 'Plato was wise'. I will argue that it is not, however, always possible; in particular, that it is not possible for 'Red is a colour' and 'Red resembles pink more than blue'.

The usual nominalist suggestion is that 'Red is a colour' is equivalent to something like 'Everything red is coloured'. There is a standard objection to this translation (see, e.g., A. N. Prior, 'Existence', *Encyclopedia of Philosophy,* New York, 1967, vol. 3, p. 146). Consider the scattered location, L, of all the red things. Everything L-located is coloured, but evidently L-location is not a colour. Likewise, everything red might have been triangular and vice-versa, so that everything triangular was coloured; but triangularity still would not have been a colour.

The nominalist particularist can, however, side-step this objection by offering 'Necessarily, everything red is coloured' as his translation of 'Red is a colour'. For it is, at best, only contingently true that everything L-located or triangular is coloured. This reply gives a hostage to fortune, namely, the ontic commitments of such assertions of necessity. But it is arguable that these do not include a commitment to universals.

It is, thus, important that the following, apparently decisive, objection is available to the realist about universals. Everything red is both shaped and extended, but red is neither a shape nor an extension. And, further, it is necessarily true that everything red is shaped and extended. This is not to deny that 'Red is a colour' entails that necessarily everything red is coloured. But the former says more than the latter. If red's being a colour were nothing more than a matter

Source: Frank Jackson, "Statements About Universals", *MIND,* Vol. 86 (343), pp. 427–429, by permission of Oxford University Press.

of every red thing necessarily being coloured, then red's being a shape and an extension would be nothing more than the fact that necessarily every red thing is shaped and extended. And red is not a shape and not an extension. It seems that 'Red is a colour' says, as realists maintain, something about red not reducible to something about red things.

The nominalist might have recourse at this point to the distinction between *analytic* truth in the Fregean sense of reducibility to a logical truth by synonomy substitution and necessity in the wide sense. He might, that is, suggest 'It is analytic that everything red is coloured' as his translation. However, there are difficulties in the way of reducing 'Everything red is coloured' to a logical truth. For instance, one cannot replace 'is coloured' by 'is yellow or red or . . .'. Because one cannot complete the disjunction, there being no finite list of all the possible colours; and further, the nominalist cannot explicate the dots by saying 'and so on for all the colours' for this ontically commits him to all the colours (as well as being circular).

In general, appeal to relations (of synonomy or whatever) between linguistic entities is beside the point when seeking an analysis of red being a colour. Red did not become a colour the day we first commented on the fact in our languages, and its being a colour is in no way dependent on the existence of English or French or whatever language the linguistic entities may belong to.

Similar difficulties face nominalist attempts to give a particularist translation of:

(1) Red resembles pink more than blue.

Following Arthur Pap ('Nominalism, Empiricism and Universals: I', *Philosophical Quarterly,* 9 (1959)), (1) is not equivalent to 'Anything red resembles anything pink more than anything blue'. For some red things resemble some blue things more than some pink things because of factors other than colour. For example, a red ball resembles a blue ball more than a pink elephant. The nominalist must offer instead:

(2) Anything red colour-resembles anything pink more than anything blue.

The standard realist objection to (2) (again from Pap, ibid.) is that 'x colour-resembles y' is analysable as 'x resembles y in colour', where the latter is obtained from 'x resembles y in z' by substitution for 'z'. Hence (2) is ontically committed to universals, albeit in disguise, for it contains a three-place relation with a place for designations of universals. Notoriously, the trouble with this objection is that it is hard to *prove* the realist's analysis of colour-resemblance without begging the question of the existence of universals. There is, however, a further objection to (2) which avoids this difficulty.

Consider the possible world in which 'red' and 'triangular' are co-extensive, 'pink' and 'sweet' are co-extensive, and 'blue' and 'square' are co-extensive. In this world, anything triangular colour-resembles anything sweet more than anything square. But no-one will want to say that in this world triangularity resembles sweetness more than squareness. Hence, arguing along the same lines as before, there is more to red's resembling pink more than blue than the fact that red things colour-resemble pink things more than blue things. For triangular things might colour-resemble sweet things more than square things without triangularity resembling sweetness more than squareness.

It may be suggested that I am here misconstruing the nominalist's suggestion. It is not that 'Anything F ϕ-resembles anything G more than anything H' is invariably equivalent to 'F resembles G more than H', it is only equivalent to the latter when F, G, H are all ϕ. Now I have no doubt this is true, but it is not something a nominalist can say. It re-introduces universals, for it is *they* which are required all to be ϕ.

The obvious response for the nominalist is to point out that (2) is true in all worlds, and so to advocate 'Necessarily, anything red colour-resembles anything pink more than anything blue' as his translation of (1). (This also has the advantage of avoiding difficulties arising from the possibility of there being no red, pink, or blue things making (2) trivially true in some worlds.)

This response has, however, a crucial shortcoming. It cannot handle 'The colour of ripe tomatoes resembles the colour associated with girl babies more than the colour associated with boy babies'. For this statement is true, while 'Necessarily, anything with the colour of ripe tomatoes colour-resembles anything with the colour associated with girl babies more than anything with the colour associated with boy babies' is *false*. The statement governed by 'necessarily' is true, but only contingently so—tomatoes and baby lore might have been such that it was false. (Of course, the nominalist will want to write, for example, 'anything same-coloured as ripe tomatoes' rather than 'anything with the colour of ripe tomatoes', but this is not germane to the present point.)

Finally, the line of argument just outlined can be modified to apply to our first statement, 'Red is a colour'. Red is, let us suppose, the most conspicuous property of ripe tomatoes; then the most conspicuous property of ripe tomatoes is a colour. This cannot be nominalistically translated as 'Everything with the most conspicuous property of ripe tomatoes is coloured'. (I leave aside the question of what further translation the nominalist might attempt to eliminate 'the most conspicuous property . . .'). Because the most conspicuous property of ripe tomatoes might have been their smell while it remained true that all tomatoes were coloured (though not so conspicuously); then 'Everything with the most conspicuous property of ripe tomatoes is coloured' would be true together with the falsity of 'The most conspicuous property of ripe tomatoes is a colour'. And, of course, it would be wrong to offer 'Necessarily, everything with the most conspicuous property of ripe tomatoes is coloured' as the translation of 'The most conspicuous property of ripe tomatoes is a colour'. The former is false, there is no *necessity* about it: the most conspicuous property of ripe tomatoes might have been, as we have just noted, their smell, and some things with that smell might have been transparent, so that some things with the most conspicuous property of ripe tomatoes might not have been coloured. On the other hand 'The most conspicuous property of ripe tomatoes is a colour' is true.

It seems then that—though some criticisms in the literature of particularist translations of 'Red is a colour' and 'Red resembles pink more than blue' and the like may not be decisive—there are decisive criticisms of these translations available to the realist.

6

"Ostrich Nominalism" or "Mirage Realism"?

MICHAEL DEVITT

David Armstrong's approach to 'the problem of universals' has a contemporary gloss: he leaves it to 'total science ... to determine what universals there are'. Nevertheless his conception of the problem shows him to be a devotee of the 'old-time' metaphysics. The problem is the traditional one allegedly posed by the premise of Plato's One over Many argument: 'Many different particulars can all have what appears to be the same nature' (p. xiii).[1] It is a pity that Armstrong takes no serious account of the 'new' metaphysics of W. V. Quine and others, according to which there is no such problem as Armstrong seeks to solve.[2] In my view this Quinean position is a much stronger rival to Armstrong's Realism about universals than the many others he carefully demolishes.

Source: Michael Devitt, "'Ostrich Nominalism' or 'Mirage Realism'?" *Pacific Philosophical Quarterly*, Vol. 61 (1980), pp. 433–439. Reprinted by permission of the publisher.

The universals we are concerned with here are properties (what Quine calls 'attributes') and relations. 'Realists' believe in them, 'Nominalists' don't. After outlining five versions of Nominalism, Armstrong mentions the Quinean position as a possible sixth under the title 'Ostrich or Cloak-and-dagger Nominalism'.

> I have in mind those philosophers who refuse to countenance universals but who at the same time see no need for any reductive analyses of the sorts just outlined. There are no universals but the proposition that *a* is *F* is perfectly all right as it is. Quine's refusal to take predicates with any ontological seriousness seems to make him a Nominalist of this kind (p. 16).

Worse, these philosophers are guilty of trying to have it both ways: denying universals whilst, *prima facie,* unashamedly making use of them. They commit the sin of failing to answer 'a compulsory question in the examination paper' (p. 17). In Quinean language, they fail to face up to their ontological commitments.

Ostriches are reputed to ignore problems by putting their heads in the sand. Mirages are another feature of desert life: people see things that aren't there. An 'Ostrich Nominalist' is a person who maintains Nominalism whilst ignoring a problem. A 'Mirage Realist' is a person who adopts Realism because he sees a problem that isn't there. My major thesis is as follows:

1. To maintain Nominalism whilst ignoring the One over Many argument is not to be an Ostrich Nominalist; rather to adopt Realism because of that argument is to be a Mirage Realist.

Establishing this thesis would not, of course, show Realism to be unjustified (let alone false): there might be problems independent of the One over Many argument for which Realism is a possible solution. Armstrong thinks there are. I agree. To the extent that he is responding to those problems he is not a Mirage Realist. My thesis about him is as follows:

2. Armstrong is largely though not entirely a Mirage Realist.

Correspondingly, a Nominalist could be an Ostrich by putting his head in the sand as *real* problems loom. However correct his stand on the One over Many argument he could *otherwise* commit the sin that Armstrong complains of. I don't know whether there are any Ostrich Nominalists, but the only philosopher Armstrong alleges (tentatively) to be one, Quine, is not:

3. Quine is not an Ostrich Nominalist.

ARGUMENT FOR THESIS 1

According to Armstrong, the problem posed by the One over Many argument is that of explaining 'how numerically different particulars can nevertheless be identical in nature, all be of the same "type"' (p. 41). What phenomena are supposed to need explaining here? I take it that what Armstrong is alluding to is the common habit of expressing, assenting to, and believing, statements of the following form:

(1) *a* and *b* have the same property (are of the same type), *F*-ness.

To settle ontological questions we need a criterion of ontological commitment. Perhaps Quine's criterion has difficulties, but something along that line is mandatory. The key idea is that a person is committed to the existence of those things that must exist for the sentences he accepts to be true. What must exist for a given sentence to be true is a semantic question to which our best theory may give no answer in which we have confidence. Furthermore the sentence may, by its use of quantifiers or singular terms, suggest an answer which the person would want to resist. Hence, in my view, the importance of Quine's mention of paraphrase in this context. Suppose the given sentence *seems* to require for its truth the existence of *G*s yet the person can offer another sentence, which serves his purposes well enough, and which is known not to have that requirement. This is known because our semantic theory can be applied to this other sentence, in a way that it cannot to the given sentence, to show that the sentence can be true even though *G*s do not exist. We can then say that the person's apparent commitment to *G*s in the given sentence arises from 'a mere manner of speaking'; he is not really committed to them.

Now in the ordinary course of conversation a Quinean is prepared to express or assent to the likes of (1). (1) seems to require the existence of an *F*-ness for it to be true. So he appears committed to that existence. To this extent the One over Many argument does pose a problem to the Quinean Nominalist, but it is a negligible extent. He has a suitable paraphrase readily to hand:

(2) *a* and *b* are both *F*.

When the ontological chips are down, he can drop (1). There is no problem about identities in nature beyond a trivial one of paraphrase.

Armstrong will not be satisfied by this, of course: 'You have simply shifted the problem. In virtue of what are *a* and *b* both *F*?' The Quinean sees only a trivial problem here too. It is in virtue of the following:

(3) *a* is *F*;
(4) *b* is *F*.

Armstrong will still be dissatisfied: 'In virtue of what is *a* (or *b*) *F*?' If the One over Many argument poses a problem it is this. That was historically the case and, though Armstrong always *states* the problem in terms of identities in nature, it is the case for him too.[3] If there is no problem for the Nominalist in (3) and (4) *as they stand* then he has an easy explanation of identities in nature.

The Realist who accepts the One over Many problem attempts to solve it here by claiming the existence of a universal, *F*-ness, which both *a* and *b* have. The Nominalist who accepts the problem attempts to solve it without that claim. The Quinean rejects the problem.

The Quinean sees no problem for Nominalism in the likes of (3) because there is a well-known semantic theory which shows that (3) can be true without there being any universals:

(3) is true if and only if there exists an *x* such that '*a*' designates *x* and '*F*' applies to *x*.

So (3) can be true without the existence of *F*-ness. There is no refusal here 'to take predicates with any ontological seriousness'. The Quinean thinks that there *really must exist something* (said as firmly as you like) that the predicate '*F*' applies to. However that thing is not a universal but simply an object. Further, in denying that this object need have properties, the Quinean is not denying that it *really is F* (or *G*, or whatever). He is not claiming that it is 'a bare particular'. He sees no need to play that game.

The Realist may reply that this is a mistaken statement of the truth conditions of (3) and that the correct one *does* require the existence of *F*-ness for (3)'s truth. Until a good argument for this reply is produced the Quinean is entitled to go on thinking he has no problem.

All of this is not to say that there is nothing further about (3), or about *a* being *F*, that might need explanation. I can think of four possible problems here. None of them pose any special difficulty for the Nominalist: they are irrelevant to 'the problem of universals'.

(i) We might need to explain what *caused a* to be *F*. (ii) We might need to explain what was *the purpose* of *a* being *F*. Nobody interested in 'the problem of universals' is likely to confuse their problem with (i) or (ii) and so I shall set them aside immediately.

It is not so easy to keep the next two problems distinct from 'the problem of universals'. (iii) If '*F*' is not a fundamental predicate then as reductivists we might need to explain what *constitutes a* being *F*: perhaps we will want to be told that it is in virtue of being *G*, where '*G*' is some physical predicate (*a* is a gene in virtue of being a DNA molecule). (iv) We might need to explain the *semantics* of '*F*': we might want to know what makes it the case that '*F*' applies to *a*.

The traditional 'problem of universals' has often appeared in a misleading semantic guise: how can '*F*' 'be applied to an indefinite multiplicity of particulars' (p. xiii; Armstrong does not approve of this way of putting the problem)? The strictly semantic problem of multiplicity does not have anything to do with universals. We need to explain the link between '*F*' and all *F* things in virtue of which the former applies to the latter. This is not different *in principle* from explaining the link between '*a*' and one object, *a*, in virtue of which the former designates the latter. The explanation of '*F*''s application depends on a theory of one semantic relation, application, the explanation of '*a*''s designation depends on a theory of another, designation. A feature of the explanations will be that it is *F* things that are linked to '*F*', and *a* that is linked to '*a*'. The *F*-ness of *F* things and the *a*-ness of *a* need not go unexplained in the semantics. Thus I think it is part of a good explanation of the link between 'tiger' and the many objects that it applies to that those objects are genetically of a certain sort. So the semantic problem may require *some* answer to the question: in virtue of what is *a F*? But the answer required is of type (iii), a reductivist answer.

In denying that there is any problem for the Nominalist about (3) it is important to see that we are not denying the reductivist problem (iii), nor the semanticist problem (iv), nor some combination of (iii) and (iv). What we are denying can be brought out vividly by taking '*F*' to be a fundamental predicate, say a physical predicate. Then there is no problem (iii): we have nothing to say about what makes *a F*, it just *is F*; that is a basic and inexplicable fact[4] about the universe. Problem (iv) remains: it is the problem of explaining the link between the predicate '*F*' and that basic fact. Nothing else remains to be explained.

Why be dissatisfied with this? Explanation must stop somewhere. What better place than with a fundamental physical fact of our world?

Armstrong feels that we need to go further. How can we tell who is right? There is one sure sign that explanation has not gone far enough: an explanation that goes further. Thus if Armstrong's Realist response to the One over Many argument is a genuine explanation then there must be a genuine problem here to be explained. My final remarks in support of thesis 1 will consider Armstrong's response.

One Realist response, but not Armstrong's, to the One over Many argument runs as follows: *a* is *F* in virtue of having the property *F*-ness. We explain (3) by

(5) *a* has *F*-ness.

An obvious question arises: how is (5) to be explained? The Realist feels that the one-place predication (3) left something unexplained, yet all he has done to explain it is offer a two-place predication (a relational statement). If there is a problem about *a being F* then there is at least an equal problem about *a having F*-ness. Furthermore, the point of this manoeuvre for the Realist is to commit us to universals. In ontology, the less the better. Therefore this sort of Realist makes us ontologically worse off without explanatory gain. Any attempt by him to achieve explanatory power by explaining (5) seems doomed before it starts: it will simply raise the same problem as (5); he is in a vicious regress. If there is a problem about (3) this sort of Realist *cannot* solve it.

Armstrong calls the doctrine we have just considered 'relational Immanent Realism', and rejects it for reasons not unconnected to mine (pp. 104–7). In its place he offers us 'non-relational Immanent Realism'. This doctrine is obscure. Armstrong offers us (5), or the similar, '*F*-ness is *in a*,' and simply *declares* it to be non-relational and inexplicable: particulars are not *related* to universals but bonded to them in a metaphysical unity (pp. 108–11). We have just seen that (5), taken at face value, cannot explain any problem about (3): it is a relational statement and so any problem for (3) is a problem for it. Armstrong avoids this grievous difficulty for Realism by fiat: (5) is not to be taken at face value. How then is it to be taken? Do we have even the remotest idea of what the words 'in' and 'have' mean here if they are not construed as relational predicates? Armstrong's Realism replaces the explanatory failings of relational Realism with a complete mystery. I suspect that Armstrong views sentences like (5) as attempts to speak the unspeakable: to talk about 'the link' between particulars and universals without saying they are related. (Note the scare-quotes around 'in' on p. 108 and the use of a special hyphenating device on p. 111.)

Talk of 'particulars' and 'universals' clutters the landscape without adding to our understanding. We should rest with the basic fact that *a* is *F*. Even the alleged unity of particular and universal can be captured without mystery:

a predication must involve both a singular term and a predicate; drop either partner and you say nothing. For the Nominalist the unity of predication is an unexciting linguistic fact. The move to relational Realism loses the unity. Armstrong's non-relational Realism attempts to bring it back with metaphysical glue. These are 'degenerating problem shifts' (Lakatos).

Armstrong sees the One over Many argument as posing a problem for Nominalism and offers a Realist solution. If his solution were real then the problem would be real. The solution is not real. So it throws no doubt on my earlier argument that the problem is not real.

Indeed the Quinean can gain much comfort from Armstrong's book: it is a powerful argument for thesis 1. We have just demonstrated the failings of Armstrong's response to the One over Many argument. Armstrong himself carefully, and convincingly, demolishes every other known response to it. This chronicle of two thousand years of failure makes the task seem hopeless. The alternative view that there is no problem to solve becomes very attractive.

I take my major thesis to be established:

1. To maintain Nominalism whilst ignoring the One over Many argument is not to be an Ostrich Nominalist; rather to adopt Realism because of that argument is to be a Mirage Realist.

Even if there *are* universals they cannot form part of a solution to the One over Many problem, because that problem is a mirage.

ARGUMENT FOR THESIS 2

The arguments for theses 2 and 3 will be brief. It follows from thesis 1 that in so far as Armstrong adopts Realism because of the One over Many argument, he is a Mirage Realist. At the beginning of his book he indicates that he sees that argument as the main one for universals (p. xiii). When he talks of 'the problem of universals' it is the problem allegedly posed by that argument that he is referring to (e.g. p. 41). Almost the whole book is taken up with the consideration of responses to that argument. Armstrong is largely a Mirage Realist.

In one chapter, drawing on the ideas of Arthur Pap and Frank Jackson, Armstrong offers quite independent reasons for Realism (pp. 58–63).[5] We all assent to, express, believe, statements like the following:

(6) Red resembles orange more than it resembles blue;
(7) Red is a colour;
(8) He has the same virtues as his father;
(9) The dresses were of the same colour.

Unlike (3) these seem to require the existence of properties for them to be true. Whether or not they are sufficient for Realism depends on whether or not we can find acceptable paraphrases without that commitment. There is nothing illusory about this problem for a Nominalist. Armstrong is not entirely a Mirage Realist. So,

(2) Armstrong is largely though not entirely a Mirage Realist.

ARGUMENT FOR THESIS 3

For Quine to be an Ostrich Nominalist would be for him to ignore the ontological problem posed by his acceptance of statements like (6) to (9). *A priori* it is unlikely that this would be so. Quine, more than any other philosopher, has pointed out what constitutes an ontological commitment and has preached against ignoring such. Philosophers, like others, can fail to practise what they preach, but I suggest that it is unlikely that Quine would fail here, about as unlikely as that he would confuse use and mention.

A quick glance through *Word and Object*[6] shows that he does not fail. In a section on abstract terms he considers, e.g., the sentence,

(10) Humanity is a virtue,

a sentence that raises much the same problem as Armstrong's (8), and sees it as committing him to the existence of 'an abstract object' (p. 119), in fact to 'an attribute', what Armstrong would call 'a property'. He goes on to 'deplore the facile line of thought' that allows us to ignore this (pp. 119–20). He considers ways to paraphrase away this apparent commitment to attributes and admits the difficulties (pp. 121–3). The issues are postponed until chapter VII. He does not there discuss sentences like (6) to (10) directly, so far as I can see, but his strategy for them is clear enough: all talk of attributes is to be dispensed with in favour of talk of eternal open sentences or talk of classes (p. 209). Whatever the merits of this approach it is not the behaviour of an Ostrich. So,

(3) Quine is not an Ostrich Nominalist.

NOTES

1. Such references are to *Nominalism and Realism: Universals and Scientific Realism, Volume 1* (Cambridge: Cambridge University Press, 1978).
2. See particularly Quine's discussion in 'On What There Is' [chapter V in this volume]. Quine's discussion is largely aimed at a position like Armstrong's ('For "McX" read "McArmstrong" ': Elizabeth Prior).
3. See, e.g., his remarks on Ostrich Nominalism (quoted above) and his discussion of the varieties of Nominalism, pp. 12–16.
4. Lest an uncharitable reader should take this talk as committing me to the existence of facts, let me hasten to add that such talk is a mere manner of speaking, eliminable at the cost of style and emphasis.
5. Given the importance Armstrong attaches to the One over Many argument for Realism, this chapter's title, 'Arguments for Realism', is misleading.
6. W. V. Quine, *Word and Object* (Cambridge, Mass.: M.I.T., 1960).

7

Against "Ostrich" Nominalism: A Reply to Michael Devitt

D. M. ARMSTRONG

I am dissatisfied with my treatment, in Volume 1 of *Universals and Scientific Realism,*[1] of what I there called 'Ostrich' Nominalism. Michael Devitt's vigorous defence of Quine, whom I accused of being such a Nominalist, gives me a second opportunity. (I should like to thank Devitt for comments on earlier drafts, and for the pleasant spirit in which this controversy has been conducted.)

1. QUINE AND THE 'ONE OVER MANY'

I think that the main argument for the existence of universals is Plato's 'One over Many'. I do not think that it proves straight off that there are universals. But I think that it shows that there is a strong preliminary case for accepting universals. There are various sorts of Nominalists (I spoke of Predicate, Concept, Class, Mereological, and Resemblance Nominalists) who seem to perceive the strength of the 'One over Many' but who maintain their Nominalism nevertheless. There are, however, Nominalists who deny that the argument has any force. These I christened, tendentiously enough, Ostrich Nominalists. Quine is certainly one who denies the force of the 'One over Many'.

In chapter 1 of *From a Logical Point of View* (1953), that is, the well-known paper 'On What There Is' [chapter V in this volume], Quine makes a philosopher whom he calls 'McX'[2] advance the 'One over Many':

> Speaking of attributes, he [McX] says: 'There are red houses, red roses, and red sunsets; this much is prephilosophical common sense in which we must all agree. These houses, roses and sunsets, then, have something in common: and this which they have in common is all I mean by the attribute of redness.' For McX, thus, there being attributes

Source: David M. Armstrong, "Against 'Ostrich' Nominalism: A Reply to Michael Devitt," *Pacific Philosophical Quarterly,* Vol. 61 (1980), pp. 440–449. Reprinted by permission of the publisher.

> is even more obvious and trivial than the obvious and trivial fact of there being red houses, roses, and sunsets (p. 81).

In my view, Quine has here made McX considerably overplay his hand. I would wish to start in a much more cautious way by saying, as I say on p. xiii, that:

> many different particulars can all have what appears to be the same nature.

and draw the conclusion that, as a result, there is a *prima facie* case for postulating universals.

Quine, I think, admits or half-admits the truth of this premiss, though in a back-handed way, when he says, in the course of his assault on McX:

> One may admit that there are red houses, roses and sunsets, but deny, except as a popular and misleading manner of speaking, that they have anything in common (p. 81).

Quine here allows that there is a popular manner of speaking in which different red things are said to have something in common. But he does not seem to realize just how ubiquitous such manners of speaking are. We (that is, everybody) are continually talking about the *sameness* of things. And most of the time when we talk about the sameness of things we are talking about the sameness of *different* things. We are continually talking about different things having the same property or quality, being of the same sort or kind, having the same nature, and so on.

Philosophers have formalized the matter a little. They draw the enormously useful Peircean distinction between sameness of token and sameness of type. But they are only formalizing, making explicit, a distinction which ordinary language (and so, ordinary thought) perfectly recognizes.

G. E. Moore thought, correctly I believe, that there are many facts which even philosophers should not deny, whatever philosophical account or analysis they gave of these facts. He gave as an example the existence of his hands. We can argue about the philosophical account which ought to be given of material objects, such as Moore's hands. But we should not deny that there are such things. (He was not arguing that their existence was a logically necessary or logically indubitable truth.) I suggest that the fact of sameness of type is a Moorean fact.

Any comprehensive philosophy must try to give some account of Moorean facts. They constitute the compulsory questions in the philosophical examination paper. If sameness of type is a Moorean fact, then, because Quine sees no need to give an account of it, he is refusing to answer a compulsory question.

Here is one answer to the question. When we speak of sameness of token, the sameness of the Morning and the Evening star to coin an example, we are speaking of *identity*. But when we speak of sameness of type, of two dresses being the same shade of colour for instance, sameness is merely a matter of *resemblance* (on one view between the dresses, on another between two property-instances). Resemblance is not to be analysed in terms of identity. Hence *sameness* with respect to token is not the same as (is not identical with) sameness with respect to type. The word 'same' is fundamentally ambiguous.

This is not a view which I accept. But it is an attempt to grapple with the problem.

Again, it may be held that sameness of token and sameness of type is sameness in exactly the same sense, *viz.* identity. This Realist view seems to be nearer the truth of the matter. I think it is a bit crude as it stands, because it appears to require recognition of a universal wherever we recognize sameness of type, a universal corresponding to each general word. However, the rightness or wrongness of the answer is not what is in debate here. The point is that the philosophical problem of the nature of sameness of type is faced, not evaded.

By comparison, what does Quine offer us? He simply says:

> That the houses and roses and sunsets are all of them red may be taken as ultimate and irreducible, . . . (p. 81).

What does he mean by this? This remark might be made by a Realist, or at any rate by a Realist who believes that *redness* is a property. But, of course, Quine is engaged in rejecting Realism, personified by the unfortunate McX.

It is natural to interpret him instead as saying that, although these tokens are all of the same type, yet we have no need to consider what sameness of type is. (And, *a fortiori,* sameness of type is not a matter of identity of property.)

If this is the way to interpret Quine, then is he not an ostrich about types? Like an Oxford philosopher of yore, he keeps on saying that he does not deny that many different objects are all of them red, but what this ostensible sameness is he refuses to explain (except to say it is ultimate and irreducible). Instead, he thrusts his head back into his desert landscape.

But perhaps there is a still deeper level of scepticism in Quine. Perhaps he would object to this foisting upon him of talk about types. Suppose *a* is red and *b* is red, then, Quine might say, we can by a convenient abbreviation say that *a* and *b* are *both* red. If *a* is red and *b* is red and *c* is red, we can by a convenient abbreviation say that *a*, *b* and *c* are *all of them* red. But nothing here justifies talking of sameness of type, unless this too is mere abbreviation.

Such scepticism cannot be maintained. It is true that '*a* and *b* are both red' is an abbreviation of '*a* is red and *b* is red.' But the abbreviation does not hold just for these particular sentences (much less for the above sentence-tokens), but is a rule-governed, projectible, transformation which we are capable of applying to an indefinite multiplicity of sentences. And what is the rule? It goes something like this. Suppose that we are given a sentence of the form '*a* is—and *b* is—.' If but only if the two blanks are filled by the *same* predicate, it is permitted to rewrite the sentence as '*a* and *b* are both—,' with that same predicate in the new blank. But 'same predicate' here is a type-notion. It is not meant that the very same predicate-token be plugged successively into three gaps!

It appears, then, that just to understand phrases like 'are both red' requires that we understand at least what a *predicate*-type is. And if this notion is understood, and at least at a Moorean level accepted, then there can be no bar to understanding, and at least at the Moorean level accepting, type-notions generally. Some account must then be given, reductive or otherwise, of what sameness of type is.

But perhaps Quine failed to appreciate this point when he wrote 'On What There Is'. The insight on which the argument of the penultimate paragraph is based was not available to contemporary philosophers until the work of Donald Davidson. For this, see Davidson, who criticises Quine for a similar failure to appreciate the projectible semantic structure of sentences attributing beliefs in *Word and Object*.[3]

It may be, then, that Quine did not perceive at least the full urgency of the need to give an account of types. But however it was with Quine (or is with Devitt), the distinction between tokens and types cannot be ignored. Hence a philosophical account of a general sort is required of what it is for different tokens to be of the same type. To refuse to give such an account is to be a metaphysical ostrich.

2. QUINE'S CRITERION OF ONTOLOGICAL COMMITMENT

But there is, of course, something else which insulates Quine from the full impact of the problem of types, from the problem of the One over Many. The insulating material is his extraordinary doctrine that predicates involve no ontological commitment. In a statement of the form '*Fa*', he holds, the predicate '*F*' need not be taken with ontological seriousness. Quine gives the predicate what has been said to be the privilege of the harlot: power without responsibility. The predicate is informative, it makes a vital contribution to telling us what is the case, the world is different if it is different, yet ontologically it is supposed not to commit us. Nice work: if you can get it.

It is at this very point, however, that Quine may protest, as Devitt does on his behalf, that his Nominalism is at least not an *Ostrich* Nominalism. For although Quine is perfectly cavalier about predicates, he is deadly serious about referring expressions. Suppose that a statement meets three conditions. (1) It makes ostensible *reference* to universals. (2) We account it true. (3) It is impossible to find a satisfactory paraphrase of the statement in which this reference to universals is eliminated. Under these conditions, Quine allows, indeed insists, we ought to admit universals into our ontology. Perhaps the three conditions cannot be met, but if they can be met, why then Quine will turn Realist.

I grant freely that to put forward such a set of conditions is not the behaviour of a philosophical ostrich. On the other hand, I do think that Quine is an ostrich *with respect to the One over Many argument*. Furthermore I think that Quine (and his followers) have been distinctly perfunctory in considering the many statements which answer to conditions (1) and (2) and which *appear* to answer to condition (3).

In chapter 6 of my book[4] I consider the statements:

(1) Red resembles orange more than it resembles blue
(2) Red is a colour
(3) He has the same virtues as his father.

Basing myself upon work by Pap and Jackson, I argue that these statements cannot be analyzed in a way which removes their ostensible reference to universals, or at least to property-instances.[5] (I try to show the incoherence of the doctrine of property-instances, that is, particularized properties, in chapter 8.)

It would in fact have been desirable also to have made reference to Hilary Putnam's 'On Properties'[6] which considers the statement:

(4) There are undiscovered fundamental physical properties.

To this might be added an example suggested by David Stove:

(5) Acquired characteristics are never inherited,

and many others.

Now we might expect reasonably extended discussions of examples of this sort in Quine. Our expectation, however, is disappointed. In 'On What There Is' he does mention:

(6) Some zoological species are cross-fertile

and says that, unless we can paraphrase it in some way, it commits us to 'abstract'[7] objects, *viz.* species. But he does not say what account he would give of (6).

As Devitt points out, in §25 of *Word and Object,* Quine does give brief consideration to:

(7) Humility is a virtue

along with:

(8) Redness is a sign of ripeness.

For (8) he suggests

(8′) Red fruits are ripe

which perhaps may be allowed to pass. But (7), which resembles (2), cannot be rendered, as he seems to suggest, by:

(7′) Humble persons are virtuous.

First, the truth of (7) is compatible with there being humble persons who are not virtuous.

Indeed, it is compatible with *no* humble persons being virtuous. For it may be that every humble person is so full of glaring faults that, although they have the virtue of humility, they are not virtuous persons.

Second, and more seriously, the truth of (7′) is compatible with humility not being a virtue. Consider an example suggested by Graham Nerlich. Suppose it was true, and well known to be true, that tall people are always virtuous.

(7″) Tall persons are virtuous

is exactly parallel to:

(7′) Humble persons are virtuous.

But nobody would wish to suggest that it would then be a truth that:

(7‴) Tallness is a virtue.[8]

So not only does (7) fail to entail (7′) which was the first objection, but (7′) fails to entail (7).

As Devitt says, Quine then postpones general discussion of the problems of 'abstract objects' until chapter VII. In that chapter, Quine, without discussing examples, suggests that all apparent reference to attributes and relations should be dispensed with in favour of talk of 'eternal' open sentences (or general terms) and/or talk of classes.

Here, I agree, he has moved beyond his original position to some form of Predicate and/or Class Nominalism. But he does not discuss the rather well-known difficulties for these varieties of Nominalism. (Devitt, it may be noticed, appears to think that the difficulties are insoluble.)

It seems, then, that Quine is in trouble, even under his own rules. But the more important question, I think, is why we should grant him his rules. Devitt can only say that:

> . . . we need a criterion of ontological commitment. Perhaps Quine's criterion has difficulties, but something along that line is mandatory (pp. 94–5).

After this less than full-blooded defence, one can only ask 'Why not a criterion which allows predicates a role in ontological commitment?'

At this point, appeal may be made to semantics. Devitt makes such an appeal. He says that one can give the truth conditions of '*Fa*' by saying that it is true if and only if '*a*' denotes some particular which '*F*' applies to. He says that this shows that '*Fa*' can be true even though the '*F*' carries no ontological commitment. But two points may be made in reply. First, there may be alternative, and perhaps more satisfying, ways of giving the semantics for '*Fa*'. Devitt offers no argument against this possibility. Second, and more important, the semantics of 'applies' has been left totally obscure. The Realist may well argue, correctly I believe, that a convincing account of the semantics of 'applies' cannot be given without appeal to the properties and/or relations of the object *a*. (I owe this point to John Bishop.)

3. PROBLEMS FOR REALISM

Besides supporting Quine in his rejection of the One over Many argument, Devitt also argues directly against Realism. He confines himself to the problem, familiar to all Realists, of how particulars stand to universals. I agree with Devitt that this is the central difficulty in the Realist position. So I will finish what I have to say by making some remarks about it. But Devitt's own remarks are brief, and I think it best to expound the problem anew.

The problem is a sub-problem of the problem about the nature of particulars. For one who denies the existence of properties *in re* (whether these properties be universals or particulars), particulars are a sort of structureless blob. They can have parts. Predicates can be hung on them, concepts applied to them, they can be herded into classes, they may even have resemblances to other particulars if a Resemblance Nominalism is adopted, but they lack real internal structure. For those who accept properties *in re,* however, particulars are sort of layer-cake. The *one* particular somehow unites within itself *many* different properties (another One over Many). The question is: how is this possible?

The problem divides at this point because a defender of properties *in re* may develop the theory of particulars in different ways. According to one view, a particular is nothing but its properties. It is not, of course, a mere class of properties, but is a certain *bundling* of properties. A certain relation holds between all and only the properties of a particular, and the holding of this relation is what makes it a particular. This 'Bundle' view in turn divides into two, because the properties in the bundle may be conceived either as universals or as property-instances. Russell held the Bundle view in its first form, Donald Williams in its second.

However, the more orthodox view among those who accept properties *in re* is that, besides their properties, particulars involve a factor of particularity, an individuating component. This view in turn divides into two in the same way as before. There are those who make the properties into particulars. Locke is a probable example. However, the more orthodox version of this more orthodox view takes the properties to be universals.

Since our special concern here is with the problems of *Realism,* we may ignore the views which give an account of particulars by appealing to property-instances. The view that a particular is nothing but a bundle of universals is exposed to many grave difficulties (some of which I try to spell out in chapter 9 of my book), but I do not think that the difficulty raised by Devitt is among them. The problem proposed by Devitt only arises, I think, if one holds (as I do hold) that a particular involves a factor of particularity (*haeccitas,* thisness) together with properties which are universals. The question is then this: how are the two components of a particular to be put together?

There are, broadly, two sorts of answer to the question which Realists have given. According to the first, the factor of particularity stands in a certain *relation* to the properties. It really is correct to speak of the *related components* of a full-blooded particular. For this line of thought it is quite natural to reify the factor of particularity and to think of it as a 'bare particular'. This line of thought, it seems further, ought to be reasonably sympathetic to the idea that bare particulars might exist without any properties, and properties might exist which are not properties of any particular. For why should not the relation fail to hold? A synthetic necessity could be postulated to ensure that the factors only exist in relation, but it is hard to see the necessity for this necessity.

But whether or not bare particulars can exist apart from properties, or properties from bare particulars, difficulties arise for this conception of a particular. Let the relation be I, a bare particular be B, and wholly distinct properties of the particular be P', P''. . . . An ordinary particular containing B will then be constituted by a conjunction of states of affairs $I(B, P)$, $I(B, P')$ . . . etc. The difficulty then is that I is a *relation* and so, on this view, is a universal. As a result, a *new* relation of instantiation will be required to hold between I, on the one hand, and the elements which it relates, on the other. The new relation will then be involved in the same difficulty. The difficulty has been appreciated at least since the work of F. H. Bradley.

Various shifts may be attempted in the face of this regress, for instance, it may be suggested that the regress exists, but is not vicious. Without arguing the matter here, I will just say that I do not think that this way out, or any other, succeeds.

In common with many other Realists, I therefore favour the view that, while we can *distinguish* the particularity of a particular from its properties, nevertheless the two 'factors' are too intimately together to speak of a *relation* between them. The thisness and the nature are incapable of existing apart from each other. Bare particulars and uninstantiated universals are vicious abstractions (in the non-Quinean sense of 'abstraction', of course!) from what may be called states of affairs: this-of-a-certain-nature. The thisness and the nature are therefore not related.

Frege says of his concepts that they are 'unsaturated'. Fregean concepts are not something mental. They are close to being the Realist's properties and relations. His idea, I think, was that the concepts have, as it were, a gap in their being, a gap which must be filled by particulars. If we think of the particularity of particulars as *also* 'unsaturated', then I think Frege's metaphor is helpful.

All this is profoundly puzzling. As a result, Devitt is able to claim, not implausibly, that all I have done is to substitute inexplicable mystery for the relational view. Realism requires a relation between particularity and universality. Yet to postulate such a relation appears to lead to insoluble problems. So, he says, I simply 'unite' the two factors in an incomprehensible manner.

I accept some of the force of this. But I have three things to say which I think ought to make Devitt look upon this 'Non-Relational Immanent Realism' with a little more sympathy.

First, as was made clear already, the problem arises not simply where a particular has a property, but where two or more particulars are related. Suppose *a* has *R* to *b*. If *R* is a universal, and *a* and *b* are particulars, and if we think that a relation is needed to link a universal to its particulars, then we shall require a further relation or relations to link *R* to *a* and *b*. This seems intolerable. It seems much better, therefore, to say that, while we can distinguish the relation from the particulars, yet the three 'entities' are together in a way which does not require any further relation to *get* them together. Now, if we think this way about the polyadic case, it seems to me that when we go back to the monadic case we ought in consistency to take the same line, and deny that the particularity of a particular is related to the properties of the particular. Contrariwise, if we admit a relation in the monadic case, should we not admit an extra relation in the polyadic case?

I hope that this generalization of the problem will at least show Devitt how strong an intellectual pressure there is for a Realist to adopt a non-relational view. It may be crooked, but it looks to be the best (Realist) game in town.

Second, I appeal to what Devitt says himself. He says:

> Talk of 'particulars' and 'universals' clutters the landscape without adding to our understanding. We should rest with the basic fact that *a* is *F* (p. 98).

Now, of course, I accept the *second* sentence just as much as Devitt. (There is, as it were, *f.a.* in my philosophy as much as there is in Devitt's.) Let us consider the sentence. Devitt will surely admit that '*a*' is a token-word, picking out just this thing *a*, while '*F*' is a type-word, applicable, potentially at least, to many things. Now why should we need two words of just this semantic sort to record the basic fact? Does not some explanation seem called for? Is it so very extreme an hypothesis that, while '*a*' names a particular, '*F*' captures something repeatable, something universal, about the situation?

I might add that I think that the dispute between Devitt and myself here is an instance of a very deep dispute indeed. There are those who, apparently like Devitt, think of reality as made up of *things*. There are others who, like me, think of it as made up of *facts* or *states of affairs*. We cannot expect any easy resolution of such an argument. (All the more reason to try to argue it of course.)

Third, I offer a second *ad hominem* criticism of Devitt's position. Devitt rejects the 'One over Many'. But he agrees that the problems posed for Quine by the arguments of Arthur Pap and Frank Jackson, retailed by me in the chapter 'Arguments for Realism', are hard to solve. He makes no attempt to improve upon the unsatisfactory paraphrases suggested by Quine of statements ostensibly referring to universals. So it seems that he thinks that it may be necessary to postulate universals. If he does have to postulate them, how will *he* solve the problem of how universals stand to their particulars? I think he will end up saying something similar to what I (and indefinitely many other Realists) have had to say.

NOTES

1. [D. M. Armstrong, *Nominalism and Realism* (Cambridge: Cambridge University Press, 1978).]
2. Devitt, following E. Prior, suggests that for the variable 'X' be substituted the name 'Armstrong'. However, Devitt and Prior overlook the fact that 'McArmstrong' is ill-formed. 'Armstrong' is a *Lowland* Scottish name.
3. Donald Davidson (1965), 'Theories of Meaning and Learnable Languages', in his *Inquiries into Truth and Interpretation* (Oxford: Clarendon Press, 1984), 3–36; W. V. O. Quine, *Word and Object* (Cambridge, Mass.: M.I.T. Press, 1960).
4. Devitt correctly noted that it was misleading to call the chapter 'Arguments for Realism' in spite of the fact that what I take to be the main argument for Realism, the One over Many, is deployed in earlier chapters and is not deployed in chapter 6. As Frank Jackson has pointed out, the title should really be 'Arguments for Realism that work even if Quine is right about ontological commitment'.
5. Arthur Pap, 'Nominalism, Empiricism and Universals: I', *Philosophical Quarterly,* 9 (1959), 330–40; Frank Jackson, 'Statements About Universals [chapter VI of this volume].
6. [*Essays in Honor of Carl G. Hempel,* edited by Nicholas Rescher (Dordrecht: Reidel, 1970), 235–54).]
7. Quine appears to mean by an 'abstract' entity one that is outside space and time. This is a misuse of the term, on a par with using 'disinterested' to mean the same as 'uninterested'. An abstract object is one which can be *considered* apart from something else, but cannot *exist* apart from that thing. Being outside space and time has no special connection with abstraction. He holds that both classes, if they exist, and universals, if they exist, are abstract in his sense. He also says that classes *are* universals (pp. 115–23), probably because he takes 'universal' to be a convenient synonym for 'abstract'. In fact classes are particulars, even if, as Quine claims, non-spatio-temporal particulars. This is because unlike universals, they are not ones which may run through many. There can be many instances of redness, but not many instances of the class of men or the class of colours. A 'Nominalist', for Quine, is simply one who does not recognize abstract objects in his sense, a 'Platonist' is one who does recognize them. So when he reluctantly admitted classes Quine became a 'Platonist'. The misuse of all these terms has contributed to muddling a whole philosophical generation about the Problem of Universals.
8. Equally, supposing it to be true that:

   (7'''') Humble persons are amphibious

   it does not follow that:

   (7''''') Humility is an amphibian.

The Metaphysic of Abstract Particulars

KEITH CAMPBELL

1. THE CONCEPTION OF PROPERTIES AS PARTICULAR

A classic tradition in first philosophy, descending from Plato and Aristotle, and recently reaffirmed by D. M. Armstrong,[1] proposes two equally essential, yet mutually exclusive, categories of reality: Substances (or Particulars), which are particular and concrete, and Properties (and Relations), which are universal and abstract. Material bodies are the most familiar examples of Concrete Particulars, and their characteristics, conceived of as repeatable entities common to many different objects, are paradigms of Abstract Universals.

Particular being's distinguishing mark is that it is exhausted in the one embodiment, or occasion, or example. For the realm of space, this restricts particulars to a single location at any one time. Particulars thus seem to enjoy a relatively unproblematic mode of being.

Universals, by contrast, are unrestricted in the plurality of different locations in space-time at which they may be wholly present. Altering the number of instances of a universal (*being a bee,* for example), increasing or decreasing it by millions, in no way either augments or diminishes the universal itself. In my opinion, the difficulty in comprehending how any item could enjoy this sort of reality has been the scandal which has motivated much implausible Nominalism in which, with varying degrees of candor, the existence of properties and relations is denied.

The scandal would disappear if properties were not really universal after all. In modern times, it was G. F. Stout who first explicitly made the proposal that properties and relations are as particular as the substances that they

---

Source: Keith Campbell, "The Metaphysic of Abstract Particulars," in Peter French, Howard Wettstein, and Theodore Uehling, eds., *Midwest Studies in Philosophy V: Studies in Epistemology* (University of Minnesota Press, 1980), pp. 477–488. Reprinted with permission of the publisher and author.

qualify.[2] Others have given the notion some countenance,[3] but its most wholehearted advocate, perhaps, has been D. C. Williams.[4] What are its merits?

In the first place, that a property should, in some sense, enjoy particular being, is not a contradiction in terms. The opposite of *Particular* is *Universal,* whereas the opposite of *Concrete* is *Abstract*. In this context, an item is abstract if it is got before the mind by an act of abstraction, that is, by concentrating attention on some, but not all, of what is presented. A complete material body, a shoe, ship, or lump of sealing wax, is concrete; all of what is where the shoe is belongs to the shoe—its color, texture, chemical composition, temperature, elasticity, and so on are all aspects or elements included in the being of the shoe. But these features or characteristics considered individually, e.g., the shoe's color or texture, are by comparison abstract.

The distinction between abstract and concrete is different from that between universal and particular, and logically independent of it. That some particulars as well as universals should be abstract, and that, specifically, cases or instances of properties should be particulars, is at least a formal possibility.

In the second place, it is plain that one way or another, properties must take on or meet particularity in their instances. Consider two pieces of red cloth. There are two pieces of cloth, *ex hypothesi*. Each is red. So there are two occurrences of redness. Let them be two occurrences of the very same shade of redness, so that difference in quality between them does not cloud the issue. We can show that there really are two pieces of cloth (and not, for example, that one is just a reflection of the other) by selective destruction—burn one, leaving the other unaffected. We can show that there really are two cases of redness in the same sort of way; dye one blue, leaving the other unaffected. In this case there remain two pieces of cloth. But there do *not* remain two cases of redness. So the cases of redness here are not to be identified with the pieces of cloth. They are a pair of somethings, distinct from the pair of pieces of cloth. A pair of what? The fact that there are two of them, each with its bounded location, shows that they are particulars. The fact that they are a pair of *rednesses* shows them to be qualitative in nature. The simplest thesis about them is that they are not the compound or intersection of two distinct categories, but are as they seem to reflection to be, items both abstract and particular. Williams dubs abstract particulars *tropes*.

The argument above is to the effect that tropes are required in any proper understanding of the nature of concrete particulars (in this case specimen material bodies, pieces of cloth) and that this becomes evident in the analysis of local qualitative change.

A third ground for admitting tropes in our ontology is to be found in the problem of universals itself. The problem of universals is the problem of determining the minimum ontological schedule adequate to account for the similarities between different things, or the recurrence of like qualities in different objects. Take a certain shade of red as an example. Many different items are the same color, this certain shade of red. There is a multiple occurrence involved. But what, exactly, is multiple? The *universal* quality, the shade of red, is common to all the cases but is not plural. On the other hand, the red *objects* are plural enough, but they are heterogeneous. Some are pieces of cloth, others bits of the skin of berries, others exotic leaves, dollops of paint, bits of the backs of dangerous spiders, and so on. There is no common recurrent substance.

What does recur, the only element that does recur, is the color. But it must be the color as a particular that is involved in the recurrence, for only particulars can be many in the way required for recurrence.

It is the existence of resembling tropes which poses the problem of universals. The accurate expression of that problem is: What, if anything, is common to a set of resembling tropes?

2. TROPES AS INDEPENDENT EXISTENCES

Williams claims more for tropes than just a place in our ontology; he claims a fundamental place. Tropes constitute, for him, "the very alphabet of being," the independent, primitive elements which in combination constitute the variegated and somewhat intelligible world in which we find ourselves.

To take this line, we must overcome a long-standing and deeply ingrained prejudice to the effect that *concrete* particulars, atoms or molecules or larger swarms, are the minimal beings logically capable of independent existence.

We are used to the idea that the redness of our piece of cloth, or Julius Caesar's baldness, if they are beings at all, are essentially dependent ones. Without Julius Caesar to support it, so the familiar idea runs, his baldness would be utterly forlorn. Without the cloth, no redness of the cloth. On this view, concrete particulars are the basic particulars. Tropes are at best parasitic.

Being used to an idea, of course, is not a sufficient recommendation for it. When it is conceded that, as a matter of fact, tropes tend to come in clusters and that a substantial collection of them, clinging together in a clump, is the normal minimum which we do in fact encounter, we have conceded all that this traditional point of view has a right to claim. The question at issue, however, is not what is in fact the ordinary minimum in what is "apt for being," but what that minimum is of metaphysical necessity. The least which could exist on its own may well be less than a whole man or a whole piece of cloth. It may be just a single trope or even a minimal part of a single trope.

And some aspects of experience encourage the view that abstract particulars are capable of independent existence. Consider the sky; it is, to appearance at least, an instance of color quite lacking the complexity of a concrete particular. The color bands in a rainbow seem to be tropes dissociated from any concrete particular.

All Williams requires here, of course, is that dissociated tropes be possible (capable of independent existence), not that they be actual. So the possibility of a Cheshire Cat face, as areas of color, or a massless inert, impenetrable zone as a solidity trope, or free-floating sounds and smells, are sufficient to carry the point.

The way concrete particularity dissolves in the subatomic world, and in the case of black holes, suggests that dissociated tropes are not just possibilities but are actually to be encountered in this world.

On the view that tropes are the basic particulars, concrete particulars, the whole man and the whole piece of cloth, count as dependent realities. They are collections of co-located tropes, depending on these tropes as a fleet does upon its component ships.

3. THE ANALYSIS OF CAUSATION

D. Davidson has provided powerful reasons why some singular causal statements, like

The short circuit caused the fire,

are best interpreted as making reference to events.[5] Davidson's example is a specimen of an *event-event* singular causal claim.

But by no means all singular causal statements are of this type. Many involve *conditions* as terms in causal connections. For example:

Condition-event:	The weakness of the cable caused the collapse of the bridge.
Event-condition:	The firing of the auxiliary rocket produced the eccentricity in the satellite's orbit.
Condition-condition:	The high temperature of the frying pan arises from its contact with the stove.

Now the conditions referred to in these examples, the cable's weakness, the orbit's eccentricity, the frying pan's temperature, are properties, but the particular cases of properties involved in particular causal transactions. It is the weakness of this particular cable, not weakness in general or the weakness of anything else, which is involved in the collapse of this bridge on this occasion. And it is not the cable's steeliness, rustiness, mass, magnetism, or temperature which is at all involved. To hold that the whole cable, as concrete particular, is the cause of the collapse is to introduce a mass of irrelevant characteristics.

The cause of the collapse is the weakness of this cable (and not any other), the whole weakness, and nothing but the weakness. It is a particular, a specific condition at a place and time: so it is an abstract particular. It is, in short, a trope.

Events, the other protagonists in singular causal transactions, are widely acknowledged to be particulars. They are plainly not ordinary concrete particulars.[6] They are, in my opinion, best viewed as trope-sequences, in which one condition gives way to others. Events, on this view, are changes in which tropes replace one another. This is a promising schema for many sorts of change.

Attempts to avert reference to tropes by use of *qua*-clauses do not succeed. If we affirm that

The cable *qua* weak caused the collapse

yet deny that

The cable *qua* steely caused the collapse,

then we are committed to the view that

The cable *qua* weak $\neq$ the cable *qua* steely.

So at least one of these terms refers to something other than the cable. What could it be referring to?—only the weakness (or steeliness) of the cable, that is, only to the trope.

The philosophy of cause calls for tropes. That on its own is virtually sufficient recommendation for a place in the ontological sun.

4. PERCEPTION AND EVALUATION

The introduction of tropes into our ontology gives us an extremely serviceable machinery for analyzing any situation in which specific *respects* of concrete particulars are involved.

In the philosophy of perception, tropes appear not only as terms of the causal relations involved but also, epistemically, as the immediate objects of perception. The difficulties involved in Direct Realism with material objects disappear. Notoriously, we do not see an entire cat, all there is to a cat, for a cat has a back not now perceived and an interior never perceived. The immediate object of vision cannot even be part of the front surface of the cat, for that front surface has a texture and temperature which are not visible, and a microscopic structure not perceptible by any means. So that when you look at a cat what you most directly see is neither a cat nor part of its front surface. This conclusion has, to say the least, encouraged Idealist claims that the immediate object of perception is of a mental nature, a percept or representation standing in some special relation to the cat.

In the trope philosophy, a Direct Realist theory of perception would hold that not cats, but tropes of cats, are what is seen, touched, and so on. The cat's shape and color, but not its temperature or the number of molecules it contains, are objects of vision. Some of the tropes belonging to the cat are perceptible, some not. On any one occasion, some of the perceptible ones are perceived, others are hidden. That is the way in which the senses are selectively sensitive; that is why there is no need for embarrassment in admitting that the senses can give us knowledge only of certain aspects of concrete particulars.

Evaluation is another field in which the admission of tropes does away with awkwardness. Concrete particulars can be simultaneously subject to conflicting evaluations—in different respects, of course. A wine's flavor can be admirable and its clarity execrable, a pole vaulter's strength be splendid and his manners ill. On a trope analysis, the immediate object of evaluation is the trope, so that strictly speaking, different objects are being evaluated when we consider the flavor and the clarity of the wine, and thus the incompatible evaluations give rise to no problem at all.

5. THE PROBLEM OF CONCRETE INDIVIDUALS

The problem of concrete individuals is the problem of how it is possible for many different qualities to belong to one and the same thing. To answer it is to give the constitution of a single individual. For convenience's sake, we tend to discuss the issue in terms of items of medium scale, such as books, chairs, or tables, although we know such objects are not really single units but assemblies of parts which are themselves also individuals. The question of the constitution of a single individual is, of course, quite distinct from the relationship between complex wholes and their simpler parts. To avoid confusion we might do better to use as an example some more plausible specimen of a single concrete individual, such as one corpuscle in classical Atomism. Our question is: what is it, in the reality of one corpuscle, in virtue of which it is one, single, complete, distinct individual?

In an ontology that recognizes properties and relations only as *universals,* no satisfactory solution to this question can be found. There are two ways of tackling it:

(i) A complete individual is the union of universal properties with some additional, particularizing reality. For Aristotelians, this will be the Prime Matter that qualities inform, for Lockeans the substratum in which qualities inhere. The common ground of objection to solutions of this type lies in their introduction of a somewhat which, because it lies beyond qualities, lies by its very nature beyond our explorations, describings, and imaginings, all of which are of necessity restricted to the qualities things have. We do well to postpone as long as possible the admission into our ontology of elements essentially elusive and opaque to the understanding.

To avoid such elements, we must deny that in the ontic structure of an individual is to be found any non-qualitative element. Which is precisely the course followed in the other main tradition:

(ii) A complete individual is no more than a Bundle of qualities, viz., all and only the qualities that, as we would ordinarily say, the thing has. In banishing "meta-physical" particularizers, such views are appealing to Empiricists, for as long as they can forget their Nominalism, which is, of course, incompatible with any Bundle theory.

Where the bundle is a bundle of universals, the very same repeatable item crops up in many different bundles (the same property occurs in many different instances). And herein lies the theory's downfall. For it is a necessary truth that each individual is distinct from each other individual. So each bundle must be different from every other bundle. Since the bundles contain nothing but qualities, there must be at least one qualitative difference between any two bundles. In short, this theory requires that the Identity of Indiscernibles be a necessary truth.

Unfortunately, the Identity of Indiscernibles is not a necessary truth. There are possible worlds in which it fails, ranging from very simple worlds with two uniform spheres in a non-absolute space to very complex ones, without temporal beginning or end, in which the same sequence of events is cyclically repeated, with non-identical indiscernibles occurring in the different cycles.

Bundle theories with elements that are universal qualities thus come to grief over the status of the Identity of Indiscernibles. But where the elements in the bundle are not repeatable universals but particular cases of qualities, not smoothness-in-general but the particular smoothness here, in this place, qualifying this particular tile, the situation is quite different. Now the elements in the bundles are tropes, and no matter how similar they are to one another, the smoothness trope in one tile is quite distinct from the smoothness trope in every other tile. So the bundles can never have any common elements, let alone coincide completely. The question of the Identity of Indiscernibles becomes the question whether all the elements in one bundle match perfectly with all the elements in any other, which is, as it should be, an *a posteriori* question of contingent fact.

Tropes of different sorts can be *compresent* (present at the same place). In being compresent they, in common speech, "belong to the same thing." Taken together, the maximal sum of compresent tropes constitutes a complete being, a fully concrete particular. Each fully concrete individual is, of necessity, distinct from every other.

There is no need for any non-qualitative particularizer, nor any problem over the Identity of Indiscernibles. In the trope philosophy, the Problem of Individuals has an elegant solution.

A. Quinton recently proposed that an individual is the union of a group of qualities and a position, and D. M. Armstrong has endorsed a similar view.[7] If we take this as a version of the Lockean *substratum* strategy, it invites the criticism that it involves an *a priori* commitment to absolute space or space-time, anterior to the placing of qualities. To avoid such objectionable *a priori* cosmology, we must hold not that place and the quality present at that place are distinct beings, one the particularizer and the other a universal, but that quality-at-a-place is itself a single, particular, reality. And this second view is just the trope doctrine re-expressed.

6. THE PROBLEM OF UNIVERSALS

Tropes can be compresent; this makes possible a solution to the problem of individuals. Tropes can also resemble one another, more or less closely. Williams holds that this facilitates a solution to the problem of universals. I regret to report that I cannot fully share his optimism.

The Problem of Universals is the problem of how the same property can occur in any number of different instances. "The Problem of Universals" is not really a good name, since the principal issue is whether there *are* any universals; the problem is: what ontological structure, what array of real entities, is necessary and sufficient to account for the likenesses among different objects which ground the use on different occasions of the same general term, 'round', 'square', 'blue', 'black', or whatever. "The Problem of Resemblance" would thus be a better name; proposed solutions consist in theories of the nature of properties.

As with the problem of individuals, philosophical tradition exhibits an ominous unstable oscillation between unsatisfactory alternatives. Realism claims the existence of a new category of entities, not particular, not having any restricted location, literally completely present, the very same item, in each and every different circular object, or square one, or blue one, or whatever. Nominalism holds that roundness and squareness are no more than shadows cast by the human activity of classifying together, and applying the same description to, sundry distinct particular objects. The classic objection to Realism is Locke's *dictum* that all things that exist are only particulars. This amounts to the difficulty of believing in universal beings. The objection to Nominalism is its consequence that if there were no human race (or other living things), nothing would be like anything else.

Can a philosophy of abstract particulars be of any assistance? Williams claims that a property, such as smoothness, is a set of resembling tropes. Members of this set are instances of the property. Tile A's smoothness, tile B's smoothness, tile C's smoothness, insofar as they resemble one another, all belong to a set S. There are no *a priori* limits on how many members S should have, or how they should be distributed through space and time. So in this respect S behaves as a universal must. Moreover, since the members of S are particular smoothnesses, each of them is fully smooth, not merely partly smooth. This is again a condition which anything proposed as a universal must meet.

The closeness of resemblance between the tropes in a set can vary. These variations correspond to the different degrees to which different properties are specific. According to this view, Resemblance is taken as an unanalyzable primitive, and there are no non-particular realities beyond the sets of resembling tropes. So this view holds that there is *no* entity literally common to the resembling tropes; it is a version of Particularism.

Can we take Resemblance as a primitive? Resemblance between tropes, rather than between concrete particulars, avoids two classic objections to this line.

Objection 1. The Companionship Difficulty[8]

Attempts to construct a property as a Resemblance-Class of the items that "have the property" face this objection: there could be two *different* properties (say, *having a heart* and *having a kidney*) which, as a matter of fact, happen to be present in the very same objects. But if each property is no more than the Resemblance-Class containing all and only those objects, since these two different properties determine the same Resemblance-Class it will turn out that the 'two' properties are not different after all. The theory falsely identifies *having a heart* with *having a kidney,* and indeed any pair of co-extensive properties.

This problem cannot arise where the members of the Resemblance-Class are *tropes* rather than whole concrete particulars. Although the *animals* that have hearts coincide with the animals with kidneys, the instances of having a heart, as abstract particulars, are quite different items from the instances of having a kidney. The Resemblance-Classes for the two properties have no members in common, and there is no basis for the objectionable identification.

Objection 2. The Difficulty of Imperfect Community[9]

In constructing a Resemblance-Class, we cannot just select some object O and take all the objects that resemble O in some way or other. That would yield an utterly heterogeneous collection, with 'nothing in common', as we would intuitively put it.

To avoid saying that the members of the Resemblance-Class must all resemble O in the same respect, which introduces *respects* as Realistically conceived universals, we have to require that all the members of the Resemblance-Class must not only resemble O but must also resemble one another.

But although necessary, this restriction is not sufficient. For consider the case where

O_1 has features P Q R
O_2 has features Q R S
O_3 has features R S T
O_4 has features S T P

Each of these objects does resemble all the others. But they share no common property. This is the phenomenon of *imperfect community*. Family resemblance classes are examples. Not all resemblance classes pick out a genuine universal property. More precisely, this is the case where the members of the resemblance classes are objects with many different features.

The problem of imperfect community cannot arise where our resemblance sets are sets of tropes. For tropes, by their very nature and mode of differentiation, *can* only resemble in one respect. An instance of solidity, unlike a complete material object, does not resemble a host of different objects in a host of heterogeneous ways. The difficulty of imperfect community springs from the complexity of concrete particulars. The simplicity of tropes puts a stop to it.

Although the prospects for a resolution of the problem of universals through appeal to resemblances between tropes are better than those for resemblance between concrete particulars, it is by no means plain that this line succeeds.

The difficulty is that we have an answer to the question: What do two smooth tiles have in common, in virtue of which they are both smooth? They both contain a trope of smoothness; *matching* tropes occur in their makeup. But then we at once invite the question: What do two smooth tropes have in common, in virtue of which they match? And now we have no answer, or only answers that restate the situation: These tropes resemble, or are alike, in virtue of their nature, in virtue of what they are. This leaves us with no answer to the question: Why isn't the way a rough trope is, a ground for matching a smooth trope? We cannot say it is the wrong *sort* of thing. We must just say: because it isn't.

Now explanations must stop somewhere. But is this a satisfactory place to stop?

7. THE ROLE OF SPACE IN A FIRST PHILOSOPHY

The metaphysic of abstract particulars gives a central place to Space, or Space-Time, as the frame of the world. It is through *location* that tropes get their particularity. Further, they are identified, and distinguished from one another, by location. Further yet, the continuing identity over time of the tropes that can move is connected with a continuous track in space-time.

Still further, space (and time) are involved in *co-location,* or compresence, which is essential to the theory's account of concrete particulars. So the theory seems to be committed to the thesis that every reality is a spatio-temporal one. This would make a clean sweep of transcendent gods, Thomist angels, Cartesian minds, Kantian noumena, and Berkeley's entire ontology. But that is too swift, too dismissive.

There is, in fact, a less drastic possibility open. That is, that to the extent that there can be non-spatial particulars, to that extent there must be some analogue of the locational order of space.[10] And in that case, there will be an analogue of location to serve as the principle of individuation for non-spatial abstract particulars.

To concede that there can be non-spatial particulars to the extent that they belong in an array analogous to space is generous enough toward such dubious items.

We are, however, not yet at the end of the special status of space. The geometric features of things, their form and volume, have a special role. Form and volume are not tropes like any others. Their presence in any particular sum of tropes is not an optional, contingent, matter. For the color, taste, solidity, salinity, and so on, which any thing has are essentially spread out. They exist, if they exist at all, *all over* a specific area or volume. They cannot be present except by being present in a formed volume. Tropes are, of their essence, regional. And this carries with it the essential presence of shape and size in any trope occurrence. The often-noticed fact that shape and size, like Siamese twins, are never found except together, is part of this special status of the geometrical features.

Color, solidity, strength are never found except as the-color-of-this-region, the-solidity-of-this-region, and so on. So wherever a trope is, there is formed volume. Conversely, shape and size are not genuinely found except in company with other characteristics. A mere region, a region whose boundaries mark no material distinction whatever, is only artificially a single and distinct being.

So the geometric features are doubly special; they are essential to ordinary tropes and in themselves insufficient to count as proper beings. Form and volume are therefore best considered not as tropes in their own right at all. Real tropes are qualities-of-a-formed-volume. The distinctions we can make between color, shape, and size are distinctions in thought to which correspond no distinctions in reality. A change in the size or shape of an occurrence of redness is not the association of the same red trope with different size and shape tropes, but the occurrence of an (at least partly) different trope of redness.

There is no straightforward correlation between distinct *descriptions* and distinct tropes. That predicates may not go hand-in-hand with tropes is important, for therein lies the possibility of reduction, exhibiting one trope as consisting in tropes which before the discovery of the reduction would have been considered "other" tropes. Reduction is the life and soul of any scientific cosmology. Reductions involving elements in familiar human-scale material bodies provide the best of explanations why tropes ordinarily occur in compresent bundles which cannot be dissociated and whose members resist independent manipulation.

8. THE PHILOSOPHY OF CHANGE AND MODERN COSMOLOGY

The admission of abstract particulars as the basic ontological category gives us a way into the philosophy of change. We all feel in our bones that there is a quite radical distinction to be made between the sorts of changes involved in becoming bald and the sorts involved in becoming a grandfather. The first sort are closer to home. They are intrinsic, whereas the others are in some way derivative, dependent, or secondary. If we content ourselves with an analysis of change in terms of the applicability of descriptions, however, the two sorts of change seem to be on a par.

We can do justice to the feeling in our bones by distinguishing changes in which different descriptions apply to O in virtue of a new trope situation at O itself, from changes in which the new descriptions apply as a consequence of a new trope situation elsewhere. Trope changes become the metaphysical base from which other sorts of change derive.

We can recognize three basic types of change into which tropes enter:

1. *Motions,* the shifting about of tropes which retain their identity. When a cricket ball moves from the bat to the boundary, it retains its identity, and the tropes that constitute it retain their identity also. Many *instances of relations,* of being so far, in such direction, from such and such, are involved. For all that has been said so far, these are tropes too. Many such enjoy a brief occurrence during any motion. Because there cannot be relations without terms, in a metaphysic that makes first-order tropes the terms of all relations, relational tropes must belong to a second, derivative order.

2. *Substitutions,* in which one, or more, trope passes away and others take its place. Burning is a classic case. The object consumed does not retain its identity. Its constituent tropes are no more. In their place are others which formerly had no existence.

3. *Variations.* An object gets harder or softer, warmer or cooler. With such qualities which admit of degree, I think we should allow that the same trope, determinable in character though determinate at any given point in time, is involved. Call an abstract element in a situation, extending over time, a *thread.* Variations are homogeneous threads; processes, such as burning, are heterogeneous ones.

The concept of a thread is very useful in ordering categories. Stability is represented by the most homogeneous threads of all. Variations in a quantity, as we have seen, involve no deep discontinuity; different parts of the thread are plainly instances of the same type of property. *Events* are of various sorts: a rise in temperature is a quantitative alteration along a homogeneous thread: an explosion terminates many threads and initiates many different ones. Events, processes, stabilities, and continuities are all explicable as variations in the pattern of presence of tropes. All these are categories constructable from the same basis in abstract particulars.

Attempts to relate these three kinds of change are of course a perfectly proper part of cosmology. Classical Atomism, for example, the very apotheosis of concrete particularism, involves the thesis that all three types of change resolve, on finer analysis, into motions, in particular the motions of corpuscles.

But Classical Atomism is false, and any type of atomism looks unpromising at the present time. The cosmology of General Relativity takes a holistic view of space-time. And it seems positively to call for a trope metaphysic and a break with concrete particularism. The distinction between "matter" and "space" is no longer absolute. All regions have, to some degree, those quantities which in sufficient measure constitute the matter of the objects among which we live and move and have our being.

The world is resolved into six quantities, whose values at each point specify the tensor for curved space-time at that point. Material bodies are zones of relatively high curvature.

The familiar concept of a complex, distinct, concrete individual dissolves. In its place we get the concept of quantities with values in regions. Such quantities, at particular locations, are dissociated abstract particulars, or tropes. Considered in their occurrence and variation across all space and all time, they are pandemic homogeneous threads.

The metaphysic of abstract particulars thus finds a vindication in providing the most suitable materials for the expression of contemporary cosmology.

NOTES

1. D. M. Armstrong, *Universals and Scientific Realism* (Cambridge, 1978).
2. G. F. Stout, *The Nature of Universals and Propositions* (Oxford [British Academy Lecture], 1921).
3. G. E. L. Owen, "Inherence," *Phronesis* 10 (1965): 97–108; N. Wolterstorff, "Qualities," *Philosophical Review* 69 (1960): 183–200 and *On Universals* (Chicago, 1970). A. Quinton, "Objects and Events," *Mind* 87 (1979): 197–214. J. Levinson, "The Particularisation of Attributes," *Australian Journal of Philosophy* 58 (1980): 102–15. P. Butchvarov, *Being Qua Being* (Indiana, 1979), pp. 184–206, discusses but rejects the view.
4. D. C. Williams, "The Elements of Being," in *Principles of Empirical Realism* (Springfield, Ill., 1966).
5. D. Davidson, "Causal Relations," *The Journal of Philosophy* 64 (1967): 691–703; "The Logical Form of Action Statements," in *Logic of Decision and Action,* ed. N. Rescher (Pittsburgh, 1966).
6. If Quine is right, they are four-dimensional concrete particulars whose boundaries are determined not by material discontinuities but by discontinuities in other respects, which we pre-theoretically describe as discontinuities in *activity*.
7. A. Quinton, *The Nature of Things,* part 1 (London, 1973); D. M. Armstrong, *Universals,* chap. 11.
8. See N. Goodman, *The Structure of Appearance,* 2nd ed. (Indianapolis, 1966), chap. 5.
9. See *ibid.,* chaps. 5 and 6.
10. Cf. P. F. Strawson, *Individuals* (London, 1959), chap. 2.

CHAPTER SEVEN

SENSORY PERCEPTION AND THE EXTERNAL WORLD

What connection, if any, exists between the senses and the physical world? Do we, in perception, get to the world as it really is, independently of our minds? Or is there some distinction between the way things really are, out there, and the way they *seem* to us, on the basis of sense experience?

René Descartes famously argued that on the basis of experience it is very difficult to determine whether we are connected to an external world or are merely dreaming. On the basis of how things seem to us, Descartes would argue, we are in no position to distinguish between a genuine waking experience and a dream. We kick off this section with a selection from Descartes's *Meditations* in which he poses his infamous "dream argument."

Supposing, somehow, we are able to determine with certainty whether or not there exists an external world, and furthermore, *when* we perceive it. Do our senses get to the way the world is in itself? John Locke, an Empiricist, famously argued that the mind faithfully mirrors the world in some cases, but not in others. When it comes to "primary qualities," such as size, shape, temperature, motion, solidity, and others, we can, in principle, get at the way these properties exist independently of our minds. Whether something is solid or liquid, in motion or at rest, according to Locke, can be known on the basis of sense experience—but it is independent of that experience and the subject having the experience. By contrast, when we consider properties like being sweet, loud, bright, or hot to the touch, so called "secondary qualities," we are considering properties whose appearance does not faithfully mirror properties of the external world. The sweetness of a sugar cube, according to Locke, is dependent on a relation between the molecular properties the sugar cube and a perceiver. There is nothing quite like the sweetness I experience in the sugar cube, for Locke. By contrast, the sugar cube is solid, whether or not I can see it. If I can perceive the solidity of the cube, my perception matches reality.

Bishop George Berkeley carries Locke's Empiricist starting point to a radical extreme. He argues that all qualities, as perceived qualities, are secondary in nature. Size and shape, as well as taste and sound, are known through sense experience and are vulnerable to arguments based on the relativity of perception. The sizes and shapes of things, no less than the colors, tastes, and sounds, vary from one individual, and species, to the next. Indeed, even for the same individual, the size and shape of an object will appear dramatically different when viewed with the naked eye and then under a microscope. Berkeley concludes that all qualities are dependent on perceiving minds and that the notion of a mind independent of reality is incoherent. This is the view commonly referred to as "subjective idealism." Berkeley called it "immaterialism."

In "Idealism," Bertrand Russell argues that Berkeley's system rests on a conflation of two senses of "idea," according to which an idea is a mental entity *and* whatever is thought of in an idea is also a mental entity. Russell disputes the latter usage, claiming that it is simply false. When I say I am thinking about a tree, while my thinking is mental, and my idea of the tree is mental, it does not follow that the tree itself is also mental. Like Russell, J. L. Austin discusses the use of the term "real" in his chapter from *Sense and Sensibilia*. This chapter reminds us that the philosopher's choices in examples may mislead us into thinking that there are clear-cut criteria for applying the term "real," when, under closer scrutiny, we find that we can only distinguish what we mean by "real" in respect to particular cases; and that the criteria for particular applications are subject to change and revision.

William Poundstone presents the classic problem of the "Brain in the Vat," a problem that can also be found in Descartes's use of methodological skepticism in Meditation II. Poundstone presents the possibility that all of our experiences of what we believe to be the external world are fed to us through the machinations of an "evil scientist" (or evil genius, in Descartes's case). Skepticism about the existence of the external world depends on the way that such a possibility, however unlikely, cannot be eliminated. If this possibility cannot be eliminated, then perhaps everything we experience is only in our own minds. Solipsism is the result. We can only know our own minds, not the external world or other minds. In the selection ". . . How Are Hallucinations Possible?" Daniel Dennett contends that these sorts of thought experiments, although representing possibilities *in principle*, represent combinatorial impossibilities.

The chapter ends with Michael Devitt's "A Naturalistic Defense of Realism." In this paper, Devitt defends the view that metaphysics must be distinguished from questions of meaning or semantics. Our commonsense commitment to the "reality" of objects in the external world comes prior to other philosophical questions we can ask about the external world. Other inquiries, most importantly scientific inquiry, presuppose the commonsense realism Devitt defends.

Meditations on First Philosophy
In Which Are Demonstrated the Existence of God and the Distinction Between the Human Soul and the Body

RENÉ DESCARTES

FIRST MEDITATION
What Can Be Called into Doubt

Some years ago I was struck by the large number of falsehoods that I had accepted as true in my childhood, and by the highly doubtful nature of the whole edifice that I had subsequently based on them. I realized that it was necessary, once in the course of my life, to demolish everything completely and start again right from the foundations if I wanted to establish anything at all in the sciences that was stable and likely to last. But the task looked an enormous one, and I began to wait until I should reach a mature enough age to ensure that no subsequent time of life would be more suitable for tackling such inquiries. This led me to put the project off for so long that I would now be to blame if by pondering over it any further I wasted the time still left for carrying it out. So today I have expressly rid my mind of all worries and arranged for myself a clear stretch of free time. I am here quite alone, and at last I will devote myself sincerely and without reservation to the general demolition of my opinions.

But to accomplish this, it will not be necessary for me to show that all my opinions are false, which is something I could perhaps never manage. Reason now leads me to think that I should hold back my assent from opinions which are not completely certain and indubitable just as carefully as I do from those which are patently false. So, for the purpose of rejecting all my opinions, it will be enough if I find in each of them at least some reason for doubt. And to do this I will not need to run through them all individually, which would be an endless task. Once the foundations of a building are undermined, anything built on them collapses of

Source: René Descartes, *Meditations on First Philosophy,* revised ed. John Cottingham, Trans. New York: Cambridge University Press, pp. 12–23.

its own accord; so I will go straight for the basic principles on which all my former beliefs rested.

Whatever I have up till now accepted as most true I have acquired either from the senses or through the senses. But from time to time I have found that the senses deceive, and it is prudent never to trust completely those who have deceived us even once.

Yet although the senses occasionally deceive us with respect to objects which are very small or in the distance, there are many other beliefs about which doubt is quite impossible, even though they are derived from the senses—for example, that I am here, sitting by the fire, wearing a winter dressing-gown, holding this piece of paper in my hands, and so on. Again, how could it be denied that these hands or this whole body are mine? Unless perhaps I were to liken myself to madmen, whose brains are so damaged by the persistent vapours of melancholia that they firmly maintain they are kings when they are paupers, or say they are dressed in purple when they are naked, or that their heads are made or earthenware, or that they are pumpkins, or made of glass. But such people are insane, and I would be thought equally mad if I took anything from them as a model for myself.

A brilliant piece of reasoning! As if I were not a man who sleeps at night, and regularly has all the same experiences[1] while asleep as madmen do when awake—indeed sometimes even more improbable ones. How often, asleep at night, am I convinced of just such familiar events—that I am here in my dressing-gown, sitting by the fire—when in fact I am lying undressed in bed! Yet at the moment my eyes are certainly wide awake when I look at this piece of paper; I shake my head and it is not asleep; as I stretch out and feel my hand I do so deliberately, and I know what I am doing. All this would not happen with such distinctness to someone asleep. Indeed! As if I did not remember other occasions when I have been tricked by exactly similar thoughts while asleep! As I think about this more carefully, I see plainly that there are never any sure signs by means of which being awake can be distinguished from being asleep. The result is that I begin to feel dazed, and this very feeling only reinforces the notion that I may be asleep.

Suppose then that I am dreaming, and that these particulars—that my eyes are open, that I am moving my head and stretching out my hands—are not true. Perhaps, indeed, I do not even have such hands or such a body at all. Nonetheless, it must surely be admitted that the visions which come in sleep are like paintings, which must have been fashioned in the likeness of things that are real, and hence that at least these general kinds of things—eyes, head, hands and the body as a whole—are things which are not imaginary but are real and exist. For even when painters try to create sirens and satyrs with the most extraordinary bodies, they cannot give them natures which are new in all respects; they simply jumble up the limbs of different animals. Or if perhaps they manage to think up something so new that nothing remotely similar has ever been seen before—something which is therefore completely fictitious and unreal—at least the colours used in the composition must be real. By similar reasoning, although these general kinds of things—eyes, head, hands and so on—could be imaginary, it must at least be admitted that certain other even simpler and more universal things are real. These are as it were the real colours from which we form all the images of things, whether true or false, that occur in our thought.

This class appears to include corporeal nature in general, and its extension; the shape of extended things; the quantity, or size and number of these things; the place in which they may exist, the time through which they may endure,[2] and so on.

So a reasonable conclusion from this might be that physics, astronomy, medicine, and all other disciplines which depend on the study of composite things, are doubtful; while arithmetic, geometry and other subjects of this kind, which deal only with the simplest and most general things, regardless of whether they really exist in nature or not, contain something certain and indubitable. For whether I am awake or asleep, two and three added together are five, and a square has no more than four sides. It seems impossible that such transparent truths should incur any suspicion of being false.

And yet firmly rooted in my mind is the long-standing opinion that there is an omnipotent God who made me the kind of creature that I am. How do I know that he has not brought it about that there is no earth, no sky, no extended thing, no shape, no size, no place, while at the same time ensuring that all these things appear to me to exist just as they do now? What is more, since I sometimes believe that others go astray in cases where they think they have the most perfect knowledge, may I not similarly go wrong every time I add two and three or count the sides of a square, or in some even simpler matter, if that is imaginable? But perhaps God would not have allowed me to be deceived in this way, since he is said to be supremely good. But if it were inconsistent with his goodness to have created me such that I am deceived all the time, it would seem equally foreign to his goodness to allow me to be deceived even occasionally; yet this last assertion cannot be made.[3]

Perhaps there may be some who would prefer to deny the existence of so powerful a God rather than believe that everything else is uncertain. Let us not argue with them, but grant them that everything said about God is a fiction. According to their supposition, then, I have arrived at my present state by fate or chance or a continuous chain of events, or by some other means; yet since deception and error seem to be imperfections, the less powerful they make my original cause, the more likely it is that I am so imperfect as to be deceived all the time. I have no answer to these arguments, but am finally compelled to admit that there is not one of my former beliefs about which a doubt may not properly be raised; and this is not a flippant or ill-considered conclusion, but is based on powerful and well thought-out reasons. So in future I must withhold my assent from these former beliefs just as carefully as I would from obvious falsehoods, if I want to discover any certainty.[4]

But it is not enough merely to have noticed this; I must make an effort to remember it. My habitual opinions keep coming back, and, despite my wishes, they capture my belief, which is as it were bound over to them as a result of long occupation and the law of custom. I shall never get out of the habit of confidently assenting to these opinions, so long as I suppose them to be what in fact they are, namely highly probable opinions—opinions which, despite the fact that they are in a sense doubtful, as has just been shown, it is still much more reasonable to believe than to deny. In view of this, I think it will be a good plan to turn my will in completely the opposite direction and deceive myself, by pretending for a time that these former opinions are utterly false and imaginary. I shall do this until the weight of preconceived opinion is counter-balanced and the distorting influence of habit no longer prevents my judgement from perceiving things correctly. In the meantime, I know that no danger or error will result from my plan, and that I cannot possibly go too far in my distrustful attitude. This is because the task now in hand does not involve action but merely the acquisition of knowledge.

I will suppose therefore that not God, who is supremely good and the source of truth, but rather some malicious demon of the utmost power and cunning has employed all his energies in order to deceive me. I shall think that the sky, the air, the earth, colours, shapes, sounds and all external things are merely the delusions of dreams which he has devised to ensnare my judgement. I shall consider myself as not having hands or eyes, or flesh, or blood or senses, but as falsely believing that I have all these things. I shall stubbornly and firmly persist in this meditation; and, even if it is not in my power to know any truth, I shall at least do what is in my power,[5] that is, resolutely guard against assenting to any falsehoods, so that the deceiver, however powerful and cunning he may be, will be unable to impose on me in the slightest degree. But this is an arduous undertaking, and a kind of laziness brings me back to normal life. I am like a prisoner who is enjoying an imaginary freedom while asleep; as he begins to suspect that he is asleep, he dreads being woken up, and goes along with the pleasant illusion as long as he can. In the same way, I happily slide back into my old opinions and dread being shaken out of them, for fear that my peaceful sleep may be followed by hard labour when I wake, and that I shall have to toil not in the light, but amid the inextricable darkness of the problems I have now raised.

SECOND MEDITATION
The Nature of the Human Mind, and How It Is Better Known than the Body

So serious are the doubts into which I have been thrown as a result of yesterday's meditation that I can neither put them out of my mind nor see any way of resolving them. It feels as if I have fallen unexpectedly into a deep whirlpool which tumbles me around so that I can neither stand on the bottom nor swim up to the top. Nevertheless I will make an effort and once more attempt the same path which I started on yesterday. Anything which admits of the slightest doubt I will set aside just as if I had found it to be wholly false; and I will proceed in this way until I recognize something certain, or, if nothing else, until I at least recognize for certain that there is no certainty. Archimedes used to demand just one firm and immovable point in order to shift the entire earth; so I too can hope for great things if I manage to find just one thing, however slight, that is certain and unshakeable.

I will suppose then, that everything I see is spurious. I will believe that my memory tells me lies, and that none of the things that it reports ever happened. I have no senses. Body, shape, extension, movement and place are chimeras. So what remains true? Perhaps just the one fact that nothing is certain.

Yet apart from everything I have just listed, how do I know that there is not something else which does not allow even the slightest occasion for doubt? Is there not a *God,* or whatever I may call him, who puts into me[6] the thoughts I am now having? But why do I think this, since I myself may perhaps be the author of these thoughts? In that case am not I, at least, something? But I have just said that I have no senses and no body. This is the sticking point: what follows from this? Am I not so bound up with a body and with senses that I cannot exist without them? But I have convinced myself that there is absolutely nothing in the world, no sky, no earth, no minds, no bodies. Does it now follow that I too do not exist? No: if I convinced myself of something[7] then I certainly existed. But there is a deceiver of supreme power and cunning who is deliberately and constantly deceiving me. In that case I too undoubtedly exist, if he is deceiving me; and let him deceive me as much as he can, he will never bring it about that I am nothing so long as I think that I am something. So after considering everything very thoroughly, I must finally conclude that this proposition, *I am, I exist,* is necessarily true whenever it is put forward by me or conceived in my mind.

But I do not yet have a sufficient understanding of what this 'I' is, that now necessarily exists. So I must be on my guard against carelessly taking something else to be this 'I', and so making a mistake in the very item of knowledge that I maintain is the most certain and evident of all. I will therefore go back and meditate on what I originally believed myself to be, before I embarked on this present train of thought. I will then subtract anything capable of being weakened, even minimally, by the arguments now introduced, so that what is left at the end may be exactly and only what is certain and unshakeable.

What then did I formerly think I was? A man. But what is a man? Shall I say 'a rational animal'? No; for then I should have to inquire what an animal is, what rationality is, and in this way one question would lead me down the slope to other harder ones, and I do not now have the time to waste on subtleties of this kind. Instead I propose to concentrate on what came into my thoughts spontaneously and quite naturally whenever I used to consider what I was. Well, the first thought to come to mind was that I had a face, hands, arms and the whole mechanical structure of limbs which can be seen in a corpse, and which I called the body. The next thought was that I was nourished, that I moved about, and that I engaged in sense-perception and thinking; and these actions I attributed to the soul. But as to the nature of this soul, either I did not think about this or else I imagined it to be something tenuous, like a wind or fire or ether, which permeated my more solid parts. As to the body, however, I had no doubts about it, but thought I knew its nature distinctly. If I had tried to describe the mental conception I had of it, I would have expressed it as follows: by a body I understand whatever has a determinable shape and a definable location and can occupy a space in such a way as to exclude any other body; it can be perceived by touch, sight, hearing, taste or smell, and can be moved in various ways, not by itself but by whatever else comes into contact with it. For, according to my judgement, the power of self-movement, like the power of sensation or of thought, was quite foreign to the nature of a body; indeed, it was a source of wonder to me that certain bodies were found to contain faculties of this kind.

But what shall I now say that I am, when I am supposing that there is some supremely powerful and, if it is permissible to say so, malicious deceiver, who is deliberately trying to trick me in every way he can? Can I now assert that I possess even the most insignificant of all the attributes which I have just said belong to the nature of a body? I scrutinize them, think about them, go over them again, but nothing suggests itself; it is tiresome and pointless to go through the list once more. But what about the attributes I assigned to the soul? Nutrition or movement? Since now I do not have a body, these are mere fabrications. Sense-perception? This surely does not occur without a body, and besides, when asleep I have appeared to perceive through the senses many things which I afterwards realized I did not perceive through the senses at all. Thinking? At last I have discovered it—thought; this alone is inseparable from me. I am, I exist—that is certain. But for how long? For as long as I am thinking. For it could be that were I totally to cease from thinking, I should totally cease to exist. At present I am not admitting anything except what is necessarily true. I am, then, in the strict sense only a thing that thinks;[8] that is, I am a mind, or intelligence, or intellect, or reason—words whose meaning I have been ignorant of until now. But for all that I am a thing which is real and which truly exists. But what kind of a thing? As I have just said—a thinking thing.

What else am I? I will use my imagination.[9] I am not that structure of limbs which is called a human body. I am not even some thin vapour which permeates the limbs—a wind, fire, air, breath, or whatever I depict in my imagination; for these are things which I have supposed to be nothing. Let this supposition stand;[10] for all that I am still something. And yet may it not perhaps be the case that these very things which I am supposing to be nothing, because they are unknown to me, are in reality identical with the 'I' of which I am aware? I do not know, and for the moment I shall not argue the point, since I can make judgements only about things which are known to me. I know that I exist; the question is, what is this 'I' that I know? If the 'I' is understood strictly as we have been taking it, then it is quite certain that knowledge of it does not depend on things of whose existence I am as yet unaware; so it cannot depend on any of the things which I invent in my imagination. And this very word 'invent' shows me my mistake. It would indeed be a case of fictitious invention if I used my imagination to establish that I was something or other; for imagining is simply contemplating the shape or image of a corporeal thing. Yet now I know for certain both that I exist and at the same time that all such images and, in general, everything relating to the nature of body, could be mere dreams <and chimeras>. Once this point has been grasped, to say 'I will use my imagination to get to know more distinctly what I am' would seem to be as silly as saying 'I am now awake, and see some truth; but since my vision is not yet clear enough, I will deliberately fall asleep so that my dreams may provide a truer and clearer representation.' I thus realize that none of the things that the imagination enables me to grasp is at all relevant to this knowledge of myself which I possess, and that the mind must therefore be most carefully diverted from such things[11] if it is to perceive its own nature as distinctly as possible.

But what then am I? A thing that thinks. What is that? A thing that doubts, understands, affirms, denies, is willing, is unwilling, and also imagines and has sensory perceptions.

This is a considerable list, if everything on it belongs to me. But does it? Is it not one and the same 'I' who is now doubting almost everything, who nonetheless understands some things, who affirms that this one thing is true, denies everything else, desires to know more, is unwilling to be deceived, imagines many things even involuntarily, and is aware of many things which apparently come from the senses? Are not all these things just as true as the fact that I exist, even if I am asleep all the time, and even if he who created me is doing all he can to deceive me? Which of all these activities is distinct from my thinking? Which of them can be said to be separate from myself? The fact that it is I who am doubting and understanding and willing is so evident that I see no way of making it any clearer. But it is also the case that the 'I' who imagines is the same 'I'. For even if, as I have supposed, none of the objects of imagination are real, the power of imagination is something which really exists and is part of my thinking. Lastly, it is also the same 'I' who has sensory perceptions, or is aware of bodily things as it were through the senses. For example, I am now seeing light, hearing a noise, feeling heat. But I am asleep, so all this is false. Yet I certainly *seem* to see, to hear, and to be warmed. This cannot be false; what is called 'having a sensory perception' is strictly just this, and in this restricted sense of the term it is simply thinking.

From all this I am beginning to have a rather better understanding of what I am. But it still appears—and I cannot stop thinking this—that the corporeal things of which images are formed in my thought, and which the senses investigate, are known with much more distinctness than this puzzling 'I' which cannot be pictured in the imagination. And yet it is surely surprising that I should have a more distinct grasp of things which I realize are doubtful, unknown and foreign to me, than I have of that which is true and known—my own self. But I see what it is: my mind enjoys wandering off and will not yet submit to being restrained within the bounds of truth. Very well then; just this once let us give it a completely free rein, so that after a while, when it is time to tighten the reins, it may more readily submit to being curbed.

Let us consider the things which people commonly think they understand most distinctly of all; that is, the bodies which we touch and see. I do not mean bodies in general—for general perceptions are apt to be somewhat more confused—but one particular body. Let us take, for example, this piece of wax. It has just been taken from the honeycomb; it has not yet quite lost the taste of the honey; it retains some of the scent of the flowers from which it was gathered; its colour, shape and size are plain to see; it is hard, cold and can be handled without difficulty; if you rap it with your knuckle it makes a sound. In short, it has everything which appears necessary to enable a body to be known as distinctly as possible. But even as I speak, I put the wax by the fire, and look: the residual taste is eliminated, the smell goes away, the colour changes, the shape is lost, the size increases; it becomes liquid and hot; you can hardly touch it, and if you strike it, it no longer makes a sound. But does the same wax remain? It must be admitted that it does; no one denies it, no one thinks otherwise. So what was it in the wax that I understood with such distinctness? Evidently none of the features which I arrived at by means of the senses; for whatever came under taste, smell, sight, touch or hearing has now altered—yet the wax remains.

Perhaps the answer lies in the thought which now comes to my mind; namely, the wax was not after all the sweetness of the honey, or the fragrance of the flowers, or the whiteness, or the shape, or the sound, but was rather a body which presented itself to me in these various forms a little while ago, but which now exhibits different ones. But what exactly is it that I am now imagining? Let us concentrate, take away everything which does not belong to the wax, and see what is left: merely something extended, flexible and changeable. But what is meant here by 'flexible' and 'changeable'? Is it what I picture in my imagination: that this piece of wax is capable of changing from a round shape to a square shape, or from a square shape to a triangular shape? Not at all; for I can grasp that the wax is capable of countless changes of this kind, yet I am unable to run through this immeasurable number of changes in my imagination, from which it follows that it is not the faculty of imagination that gives me my grasp of the wax as flexible and changeable. And what is meant by 'extended'? Is the extension of the wax also unknown? For it increases if the wax melts, increases again if it boils, and is greater still if the heat is increased. I would not be making a correct judgement about the nature of wax unless I believed it capable of being extended in many more different ways than I will ever encompass in my imagination. I must therefore admit that the nature of this piece of wax is in no way revealed by my imagination, but is perceived by the mind alone. (I am speaking of this particular piece of wax; the point is even clearer with regard to wax in general.) But what is this wax which is perceived by the mind alone?[12] It is of course the same wax which I see, which I touch, which I picture in my imagination, in short the same wax which I thought it to be from the start. And yet, and here is the point, the perception I have of it[13] is a case not of vision or touch or imagination—nor has it ever been, despite previous appearances—but of purely mental scrutiny; and this can be imperfect and confused, as it was before, or clear and distinct as it is now, depending on how carefully I concentrate on what the wax consists in.

But as I reach this conclusion I am amazed at how <weak and> prone to error my mind is. For although I am thinking about these matters within myself, silently and without speaking, nonetheless the actual words bring me up short, and I am almost tricked by ordinary ways of talking. We say that we see the wax itself, if it is there before us, not that we judge it to be there from its colour or shape; and this might lead me to conclude without more ado that knowledge of the wax comes from what the eye sees, and not from the scrutiny of the mind alone. But then if I look out of the window and see men crossing the square, as I just happen to have done, I normally say that I see the men themselves, just as I say that I see the wax. Yet do I see any more than hats and coats which could conceal automatons? I *judge* that they are men. And so something which I thought I was seeing with my eyes is in fact grasped solely by the faculty of judgement which is in my mind.

However, one who wants to achieve knowledge above the ordinary level should feel ashamed at having taken ordinary ways of talking as a basis for doubt. So let us proceed, and consider on which occasion my perception of the nature of the wax was more perfect and evident. Was it when I first looked at it, and believed I knew it by my external senses, or at least by what they call the 'common' sense[14]—that is, the power of imagination? Or is my knowledge more perfect now, after a more careful investigation of the nature of the wax and of the means by which it is known? Any doubt on this issue would clearly be foolish; for what distinctness was there in my earlier perception? Was there anything in it which an animal could not possess? But when I distinguish the wax from its outward forms—take the clothes off, as it were, and consider it naked—then although my judgement may still contain errors, at least my perception now requires a human mind.

But what am I to say about this mind, or about myself? (So far, remember, I am not admitting that there is anything else in me except a mind.) What, I ask, is this 'I' which seems to perceive the wax so distinctly? Surely my awareness of my own self is not merely much truer and more certain than my awareness of the wax, but also much more distinct and evident. For if I judge that the wax exists from the fact that I see it, clearly this same fact entails much more evidently that I myself also exist. It is possible that what I see is not really the wax; it is possible that I do not even have eyes with which to see anything. But when I see, or think I see (I am not here distinguishing the two), it is simply not possible that I who am now thinking am not something. By the same token, if I judge that the wax exists from the fact that I touch it, the same result follows, namely that I exist. If I judge that it exists from the fact that I imagine it, or for any other reason, exactly the same thing follows. And the result that I have grasped in the case of the wax may be applied to everything else located outside me. Moreover, if my perception of the wax seemed more distinct[15] after it was established not just by sight or touch but by many other considerations, it must be admitted that I now know myself even more distinctly. This is because every consideration whatsoever which contributes to my perception of the wax, or of any other body, cannot but establish even more effectively the nature of my own mind. But besides this, there is so much else in the mind itself which can serve to make my knowledge of it more distinct, that it scarcely seems worth going through the contributions made by considering bodily things.

I see that without any effort I have now finally got back to where I wanted. I now know that even bodies are not strictly perceived by the senses or the faculty of imagination but by the intellect alone, and that this perception derives not from their being touched or seen but from their being understood; and in view of this I know plainly that I can achieve an easier and more evident perception of my own mind than of anything else. But since the habit of holding on to old opinions cannot be set aside so quickly, I should like to stop here and meditate for some time on this new knowledge I have gained, so as to fix it more deeply in my memory.

NOTES

1. '. . . and in my dreams regularly represent to myself the same things' (French version).
2. '. . . the place where they are, the time which measures their duration' (French version).
3. '. . . yet I cannot doubt that he does allow this' (French version).
4. '. . . in the sciences' (added in French version).
5. '. . . nevertheless it is in my power to suspend my judgement' (French version).
6. '. . . puts into my mind' (French version).
7. '. . . or thought anything at all' (French version).
8. The word 'only' is most naturally taken as going with 'a thing that thinks', and this interpretation is followed in the French version. When discussing this passage with Gassendi, however, Descartes suggests that he meant

the 'only' to govern 'in the strict sense'; see below p. 276.

9. '. . . to see if I am not something more' (added in French version).
10. Lat. *maneat* ('let it stand'), first edition. The second edition has the indicative *manet:* 'The proposition still stands, *viz.* that I am none-theless something.' The French version reads: 'without changing this supposition, I find that I am still certain that I am something'.
11. '. . . from this manner of conceiving things' (French version).
12. '. . . which can be conceived only by the un-derstanding or the mind' (French version).
13. '. . . or rather the act whereby it is perceived' (added in French version).
14. See note p. 59 below.
15. The French version has 'more clear and dis-tinct' and, at the end of this sentence, 'more evidently, distinctly and clearly'.

2

Of Power

JOHN LOCKE

1. The mind being every day informed, by the senses, of the alteration of those simple ideas it observes in things without; and taking notice how one comes to an end, and ceases to be, and another begins to exist which was not before; reflecting also on what passes within itself, and observing a constant change of its ideas, sometimes by the impression of outward objects on the senses, and sometimes by the determination of its own choice; and concluding from what it has so constantly observed to have been, that the like changes will for the future be made in the same things, by like agents, and by the like ways,—considers in one thing the possibility of having any of its simple ideas changed, and in another the possibility of making that change; and so comes by that idea which we call *power*. Thus we say, Fire has a power to melt gold, i.e. to destroy the consistency of its insensible parts, and consequently its hardness, and make it fluid; and gold has a power to be melted; that the sun has a power to blanch wax, and wax a power to be blanched by the sun, whereby the yellowness is destroyed, and whiteness made to exist in its room. In which, and the like cases, the power we consider is in reference to the change of perceivable ideas. For we cannot observe any alteration to be made in, or operation upon anything, but by the observable change of its sensible ideas; nor conceive any alteration to be made, but by conceiving a change of some of its ideas.

2. Power thus considered is two-fold, viz. as able to make, or able to receive any change. The one may be called *active,* and the other *passive* power. Whether matter be not wholly destitute of active power, as its author, God, is truly above all passive power; and whether the intermediate state of created spirits be not that alone which is capable of both active and passive power, may be worth consideration. I shall not now enter into that inquiry, my present business being not to search into the original of power, but how we come by the *idea* of it. But since active powers make so great a part of our

Source: John Locke, *An Essay Concerning Human Nature,* first published in 1690. Footnotes have been deleted from this excerpt.

complex ideas of natural substances, (as we shall see hereafter,) and I mention them as such, according to common apprehension; yet they being not, perhaps, so truly *active* powers as our hasty thoughts are apt to represent them, I judge it not amiss, by this intimation, to direct our minds to the consideration of God and spirits, for the clearest idea of *active* power.

3. I confess power includes in it some kind of *relation,* (a relation to action or change,) as indeed which of our ideas, of what kind soever, when attentively considered, does not? For, our ideas of extension, duration, and number, do they not all contain in them a secret relation of the parts? Figure and motion have something relative in them much more visibly. And sensible qualities, as colours and smells, &c., what are they but the powers of different bodies, in relation to our perception, &c.? And, if considered in the things themselves, do they not depend on the bulk, figure, texture, and motion of the parts? All which include some kind of relation in them. Our idea therefore of power, I think, may well have a place amongst other *simple ideas,* and be considered as one of them; being one of those that make a principal ingredient in our complex ideas of substances, as we shall hereafter have occasion to observe.

4. [We are abundantly furnished with the idea of *passive* power by almost all sorts of sensible things. In most of them we cannot avoid observing their sensible qualities, nay, their very substances, to be in a continual flux.] And therefore with reason we look on them as liable still to the same change. Nor have we of *active* power (which is the more proper signification of the word power) fewer instances. Since whatever change is observed, the mind must collect a power somewhere able to make that change, as well as a possibility in the thing itself to receive it. But yet, if we will consider it attentively, bodies, by our senses, do not afford us so clear and distinct an idea of active power, as we have from reflection on the operations of our minds. For all power relating to action, and there being but two sorts of action whereof we have an idea, viz. thinking and motion, let us consider whence we have the clearest ideas of the powers which produce these actions. (1) Of thinking, body affords us no idea at all; it is only from reflection that we have that. (2) Neither have we from body any idea of the beginning of motion. A body at rest affords us no idea of any active power to move; and when it is set in motion itself, that motion is rather a passion than an action in it. For, when the ball obeys the motion of a billiard-stick, it is not any action of the ball, but bare passion. Also when by impulse it sets another ball in motion that lay in its way, it only communicates the motion it had received from another, and loses in itself so much as the other received: which gives us but a very obscure idea of an *active* power of moving in body, whilst we observe it only to *transfer,* but not *produce* any motion. For it is but a very obscure idea of power which reaches not the production of the action, but the continuation of the passion. For so is motion in a body impelled by another; the continuation of the alteration made in it from rest to motion being little more an action, than the continuation of the alteration of its figure by the same blow is an action. The idea of the *beginning* of motion we have only from reflection on what passes in ourselves; where we find by experience, that, barely by willing it, barely by a thought of the mind, we can move the parts of our bodies, which were before at rest. So that it seems to me, we have, from the observation of the operation of bodies by our senses, but a very imperfect obscure idea of *active* power; since they afford us not any idea in themselves of the power to begin any action, either motion or thought. But if, from the impulse bodies are observed to make one upon another, any one thinks he has a clear idea of power, it serves as well to my purpose; sensation being one of those ways whereby the mind comes by its ideas: only I thought it worth while to consider here, by the way, whether the mind doth not receive its idea of active power clearer from reflection on its own operations, than it doth from any external sensation.

 3 

Dialogues I and II Between Hylas and Philonous

GEORGE BERKELEY

THE FIRST DIALOGUE

PHILONOUS. Good morrow, Hylas: I did not expect to find you abroad so early.

HYLAS. It is indeed something unusual; but my thoughts were so taken up with a subject I was discoursing of last night, that finding I could not sleep, I resolved to rise and take a turn in the garden.

PHILONOUS. It happened well, to let you see what innocent and agreeable pleasures you lose every morning. Can there be a pleasanter time of the day, or a more delightful season of the year? That purple sky, these wild but sweet notes of birds, the fragrant bloom upon the trees and flowers, the gentle influence of the rising sun, these and a thousand nameless beauties of nature inspire the soul with secret transports; its faculties too being at this time fresh and lively, are fit for those meditations, which the solitude of a garden and tranquillity of the morning naturally dispose us to. But I am afraid I interrupt your thoughts: for you seemed very intent on something.

HYLAS. It is true, I was, and shall be obliged to you if you will permit me to go on in the same vein; not that I would by any means deprive my self of your company, for my thoughts always flow more easily in conversation with a friend, than when I am alone: but my request is, that you would suffer me to impart my reflexions to you.

PHILONOUS. With all my heart, it is what I should have requested myself, if you had not prevented me.

HYLAS. I was considering the odd fate of those men who have in all ages, through an affectation of being distinguished from the vulgar, or some unaccountable turn of thought, pretended either to believe nothing at all, or to believe the most extravagant things in the world. This however might be borne, if their

---

Source: George Berkeley, *Three Dialogues between Hylas and Philonous,* first published in 1713.

paradoxes and scepticism did not draw after them some consequences of general disadvantage to mankind. But the mischief lieth here; that when men of less leisure see them who are supposed to have spent their whole time in the pursuits of knowledge, professing an entire ignorance of all things, or advancing such notions as are repugnant to plain and commonly received principles, they will be tempted to entertain suspicions concerning the most important truths, which they had hitherto held sacred and unquestionable.

PHILONOUS. I entirely agree with you, as to the ill tendency of the affected doubts of some philosophers, and fantastical conceits of others. I am even so far gone of late in this way of thinking, that I have quitted several of the sublime notions I had got in their schools for vulgar opinions. And I give it you on my word, since this revolt from metaphysical notions to the plain dictates of Nature and common sense, I find my understanding strangely enlightened, so that I can now easily comprehend a great many things which before were all mystery and riddle.

HYLAS. I am glad to find there was nothing in the accounts I heard of you.

PHILONOUS. Pray, what were those?

HYLAS. You were represented in last night's conversation, as one who maintained the most extravagant opinion that ever entered into the mind of man, to wit, that there is no such thing as *material substance* in the world.

PHILONOUS. That there is no such thing as what philosophers call *material substance,* I am seriously persuaded: but if I were made to see any thing absurd or sceptical in this, I should then have the same reason to renounce this, that I imagine I have now to reject the contrary opinion.

HYLAS. What! can any thing be more fantastical, more repugnant to common sense, or a more manifest piece of scepticism, than to believe there is no such thing as *matter?*

PHILONOUS. Softly, good Hylas. What if it should prove, that you, who hold there is, are by virtue of that opinion a greater *sceptic,* and maintain more paradoxes and repugnancies to common sense, than I who believe no such thing?

HYLAS. You may as soon persuade me, the part is greater than the whole, as that, in order to avoid absurdity and scepticism, I should ever be obliged to give up my opinion in this point.

PHILONOUS. Well then, are you content to admit that opinion for true, which upon examination shall appear most agreeable to common sense, and remote from scepticism?

HYLAS. With all my heart. Since you are raising disputes about the plainest things in Nature, I am content for once to hear what you have to say.

PHILONOUS. Pray, Hylas, what do you mean by a *sceptic?*

HYLAS. I mean what all men mean, one that doubts of every thing.

PHILONOUS. He then who entertains no doubt concerning some particular point, with regard to that point cannot be thought a *sceptic.*

HYLAS. I agree with you.

PHILONOUS. Whether doth doubting consist in embracing the affirmative or negative side of a question?

HYLAS. In neither; for whoever understands English, cannot but know that *doubting* signifies a suspense between both.

PHILONOUS. He then that denieth any point, can no more be said to doubt of it, than he who affirmeth it with the same degree of assurance.

HYLAS. True.

PHILONOUS. And consequently, for such his denial is no more to be esteemed a *sceptic* than the other.

HYLAS. I acknowledge it.

PHILONOUS. How cometh it to pass then, Hylas, that you pronounce me a *sceptic,* because I deny what you affirm, to wit, the existence of matter? Since, for ought you can tell, I am as peremptory in my denial, as you in your affirmation.

HYLAS. Hold, Philonous, I have been a little out in my definition; but every false step a man makes in discourse is not to be insisted on. I said indeed, that a *sceptic* was one who doubted of every thing; but I should have added, or who denies the reality and truth of things.

PHILONOUS. What things? Do you mean the principles and theorems of sciences? But these you know are universal intellectual notions, and consequently independent of matter; the denial therefore of this doth not imply the denying them.

HYLAS. I grant it. But are there no other things? What think you of distrusting the senses, of denying the real existence of sensible things, or pretending to know nothing of them. Is not this sufficient to denominate a man a *sceptic?*

PHILONOUS. Shall we therefore examine which of us it is that denies the reality of sensible things, or professes the greatest ignorance of them; since, if I take you rightly, he is to be esteemed the greatest *sceptic?*

HYLAS. That is what I desire.

PHILONOUS. What mean you by sensible things?

HYLAS. Those things which are perceived by the senses. Can you imagine that I mean any thing else?

PHILONOUS. Pardon me, Hylas, if I am desirous clearly to apprehend your notions, since this may much shorten our inquiry. Suffer me then to ask you this farther question. Are those things only perceived by the senses which are perceived immediately? Or may those things properly be said to be *sensible,* which are perceived mediately, or not without the intervention of others?

HYLAS. I do not sufficiently understand you.

PHILONOUS. In reading a book, what I immediately perceive are the letters, but mediately, or by means of these, are suggested to my mind the notions of God, virtue, truth, *&c.* Now, that the letters are truly sensible things, or perceived by sense, there is no doubt: but I would know whether you take the things suggested by them to be so too.

HYLAS. No certainly, it were absurd to think *God* or *Virtue* sensible things, though they may be signified and suggested to the mind by sensible marks, with which they have an arbitrary connexion.

PHILONOUS. It seems then, that by *sensible things* you mean those only which can be perceived immediately by sense.

HYLAS. Right.

PHILONOUS. Doth it not follow from this, that though I see one part of the sky red, and another blue, and that my reason doth thence evidently conclude there must be some cause of that diversity of colours, yet that cause cannot be said to be a sensible thing, or perceived by the sense of seeing?

HYLAS. It doth.

PHILONOUS. In like manner, though I hear variety of sounds, yet I cannot be said to hear the causes of those sounds.

HYLAS. You cannot.

PHILONOUS. And when by my touch I perceive a thing to be hot and heavy, I cannot say with any truth or propriety, that I feel the cause of its heat or weight.

HYLAS. To prevent any more questions of this kind, I tell you once for all, that by *sensible things* I mean those only which are perceived by sense, and that in truth the senses perceive nothing which they do not perceive immediately: for they make no inferences. The deducing therefore of causes or occasions from effects and appearances, which alone are perceived by sense, entirely relates to reason.

PHILONOUS. This point then is agreed between us, that *sensible things are those only which are immediately perceived by sense.* You will farther inform me, whether we immediately perceive by sight any thing beside light, and colours, and figures: or by hearing, any thing but sounds: by the palate, any thing beside tastes: by the smell, beside odours: or by the touch, more than tangible qualities.

HYLAS. We do not.

PHILONOUS. It seems therefore, that if you take away all sensible qualities, there remains nothing sensible.

HYLAS. I grant it.

PHILONOUS. Sensible things therefore are nothing else but so many sensible qualities, or combinations of sensible qualities.

HYLAS. Nothing else.

PHILONOUS. Heat then is a sensible thing.

HYLAS. Certainly.

PHILONOUS. Doth the reality of sensible things consist in being perceived? or, is it something distinct from their being perceived, and that bears no relation to the mind?

HYLAS. To *exist* is one thing, and to be *perceived* is another.

PHILONOUS. I speak with regard to sensible things only: and of these I ask, whether by their real existence you mean a subsistence exterior to the mind, and distinct from their being perceived.

HYLAS. I mean a real absolute being distinct from, and without any relation to their being perceived.

PHILONOUS. Heat therefore, if it be allowed a real being, must exist without the mind.

HYLAS. It must.

PHILONOUS. Tell me, Hylas, is this real existence equally compatible to all degrees of heat, which we perceive: or is there any reason why we should attribute it to some, and deny it others? And if there be, pray let me know that reason.

HYLAS. Whatever degree of heat we perceive by sense, we may be sure the same exists in the object that occasions it.

PHILONOUS. What, the greatest as well as the least?

HYLAS. I tell you, the reason is plainly the same in respect of both: they are both perceived by sense; nay, the greater degree of heat is more sensibly perceived; and consequently, if there is any difference, we are more certain of its real existence than we can be of the reality of a lesser degree.

PHILONOUS. But is not the most vehement and intense degree of heat a very great pain?

HYLAS. No one can deny it.

PHILONOUS. And is any unperceiving thing capable of pain or pleasure?

HYLAS. No certainly.

PHILONOUS. Is your material substance a senseless being, or a being endowed with sense and perception?

HYLAS. It is senseless, without doubt.

PHILONOUS. It cannot therefore be the subject of pain.

HYLAS. By no means.

PHILONOUS. Nor consequently of the greatest heat perceived by sense, since you acknowledge this to be no small pain.

HYLAS. I grant it.

PHILONOUS. What shall we say then of your external object; is it a material substance, or no?

HYLAS. It is a material substance with the sensible qualities inhering in it.

PHILONOUS. How then can a great heat exist in it, since you own it cannot in a material substance? I desire you would clear this point.

HYLAS. Hold, Philonous, I fear I was out in yielding intense heat to be a pain. It should seem rather, that pain is something distinct from heat, and the consequence or effect of it.

PHILONOUS. Upon putting your hand near the fire, do you perceive one simple uniform sensation, or two distinct sensations?

HYLAS. But one simple sensation.

PHILONOUS. Is not the heat immediately perceived?

HYLAS. It is.

PHILONOUS. And the pain?

HYLAS. True.

PHILONOUS. Seeing therefore they are both immediately perceived at the same time, and the fire affects you only with one simple, or uncompounded idea, it follows that this same simple idea is both the intense heat immediately perceived, and the pain; and consequently, that the intense heat immediately perceived, is nothing distinct from a particular sort of pain.

HYLAS. It seems so.

PHILONOUS. Again, try in your thoughts, Hylas, if you can conceive a vehement sensation to be without pain, or pleasure.

HYLAS. I cannot.

PHILONOUS. Or can you frame to yourself an idea of sensible pain or pleasure in general, abstracted from every particular idea of heat, cold, tastes, smells? *&c.*

HYLAS. I do not find that I can.

PHILONOUS. Doth it not therefore follow, that sensible pain is nothing distinct from those sensations or ideas, in an intense degree?

HYLAS. It is undeniable; and to speak the truth, I begin to suspect a very great heat cannot exist but in a mind perceiving it.

PHILONOUS. What! are you then in that *sceptical* state of suspense, between affirming and denying?

HYLAS. I think I may be positive in the point. A very violent and painful heat cannot exist without the mind.

PHILONOUS. It hath not therefore, according to you, any real being.

HYLAS. I own it.

PHILONOUS. Is it therefore certain, that there is no body in nature really hot?

HYLAS. I have not denied there is any real heat in bodies. I only say, there is no such thing as an intense real heat.

PHILONOUS. But did you not say before, that all degrees of heat were equally real: or if there was any difference, that the greater were more undoubtedly real than the lesser?

HYLAS. True: but it was, because I did not then consider the ground there is for distinguishing between them, which I now plainly see. And it is this: because intense heat is nothing else but a particular kind of painful sensation; and pain cannot exist but in a perceiving being; it follows that no intense heat can really exist in an unperceiving corporeal substance. But this is no reason why we should deny heat in an inferior degree to exist in such a substance.

PHILONOUS. But how shall we be able to discern those degrees of heat which exist only in the mind, from those which exist without it?

HYLAS. That is no difficult matter. You know, the least pain cannot exist unperceived; whatever therefore degree of heat is a pain, exists only in the mind. But as for all other degrees of heat, nothing obliges us to think the same of them.

PHILONOUS. I think you granted before, that no unperceiving being was capable of pleasure, any more than of pain.

HYLAS. I did.

PHILONOUS. And is not warmth, or a more gentle degree of heat than what causes uneasiness, as pleasure?

HYLAS. What then?

PHILONOUS. Consequently it cannot exist without the mind in any unperceiving substance, or body.

HYLAS. So it seems.

PHILONOUS. Since therefore, as well those degrees of heat that are not painful, as those that are, can exist only in a thinking substance; may we not conclude that external bodies are absolutely incapable of any degree of heat whatsoever?

HYLAS. On second thoughts, I do not think it so evident that warmth is a pleasure, as that a great degree of heat is a pain.

PHILONOUS. I do not pretend that warmth is as great a pleasure as heat is a pain. But if you grant it to be even a small pleasure, it serves to make good my conclusion.

HYLAS. I could rather call it an *indolence.* It seems to be nothing more than a privation of both pain and pleasure. And that such a quality or state as this may agree to an unthinking substance, I hope you will not deny.

Philonous. If you are resolved to maintain that warmth, or a gentle degree of heat, is no pleasure, I know not how to convince you otherwise, than by appealing to your own sense. But what think you of cold?

Hylas. The same that I do of heat. An intense degree of cold is a pain; for to feel a very great cold, is to perceive a great uneasiness: it cannot therefore exist without the mind; but a lesser degree of cold may, as well as a lesser degree of heat.

Philonous. Those bodies therefore, upon whose application to our own, we perceive a moderate degree of heat, must be concluded to have a moderate degree of heat or warmth in them: and those, upon whose application we feel a like degree of cold, must be thought to have cold in them.

Hylas. They must.

Philonous. Can any doctrine be true that necessarily leads a man into an absurdity?

Hylas. Without doubt it cannot.

Philonous. Is it not an absurdity to think that the same thing should be at the same time both cold and warm?

Hylas. It is.

Philonous. Suppose now one of your hands hot, and the other cold, and that they are both at once put into the same vessel of water, in an intermediate state; will not the water seem cold to one hand, and warm to the other?

Hylas. It will.

Philonous. Ought we not therefore by your principles to conclude, it is really both cold and warm at the same time, that is, according to your own concession, to believe an absurdity.

Hylas. I confess it seems so.

Philonous. Consequently, the principles themselves are false, since you have granted that no true principle leads to an absurdity.

Hylas. But after all, can any thing be more absurd than to say, *there is no heat in the fire?*

Philonous. To make the point still clearer; tell me, whether in two cases exactly alike, we ought not to make the same judgement?

Hylas. We ought.

Philonous. When a pin pricks your finger, doth is not rend and divide the fibres of your flesh?

Hylas. It doth.

Philonous. And when a coal burns your finger, doth it any more?

Hylas. It doth not.

Philonous. Since therefore you neither judge the sensation itself occasioned by the pin, nor any thing like it to be in the pin; you should not, conformably to what you have now granted, judge the sensation occasioned by the fire, or any thing like it, to be in the fire.

Hylas. Well, since it must be so, I am content to yield this point, and acknowledge, that heat and cold are only sensations existing in our minds: but there still remain qualities enough to secure the reality of external things.

Philonous. But what will you say, Hylas, if it shall appear that the case is the same with regard to all other sensible qualities, and that they can no more be supposed to exist without the mind, than heat and cold?

Hylas. Then indeed you will have done something to the purpose; but that is what I despair of seeing proved.

Philonous. Let us examine them in order. What think you of tastes, do they exist without the mind, or no?

Hylas. Can any man in his senses doubt whether sugar is sweet, or wormwood bitter?

Philonous. Inform me, Hylas. Is a sweet taste a particular kind of pleasure or pleasant sensation, or is it not?

Hylas. It is.

Philonous. And is not bitterness some kind of uneasiness or pain?

Hylas. I grant it.

Philonous. If therefore sugar and wormwood are unthinking corporeal substances existing without the mind, how can sweetness and bitterness, that is, pleasure and pain, agree to them?

Hylas. Hold, Philonous, I now see what it was deluded me all this time. You asked whether heat and cold, sweetness and bitterness, were not particular sorts of pleasure and pain; to which I answered simply, that they were. Whereas I should have thus distinguished: those qualities, as perceived by us, are pleasures or pains, but not as existing in the external objects. We must not therefore conclude absolutely, that there is no heat in the fire, or sweetness in the sugar, but only that heat or sweetness, as perceived by us, are not in the fire or sugar. What say you to this?

PHILONOUS. I say it is nothing to the purpose. Our discourse proceeded altogether concerning sensible things, which you defined to be the things we *immediately perceive by our senses*. Whatever other qualities therefore you speak of, as distinct from these, I know nothing of them, neither do they at all belong to the point in dispute. You may indeed pretend to have discovered certain qualities which you do not perceive, and assert those insensible qualities exist in fire and sugar. But what use can be made of this to your present purpose, I am at a loss to conceive. Tell me then once more, do you acknowledge that heat and cold, sweetness and bitterness (meaning those qualities which are perceived by the senses) do not exist without the mind?

HYLAS. I see it is to no purpose to hold out, so I give up the cause as to those mentioned qualities. Though I profess it sounds oddly, to say that sugar is not sweet.

PHILONOUS. But for your farther satisfaction, take this along with you: that which at other times seems sweet, shall to a distempered palate appear bitter. And nothing can be plainer, than that divers persons perceive different tastes in the same food, since that which one man delights in, another abhors. And how could this be, if the taste was something really inherent in the food?

HYLAS. I acknowledge I know not how.

PHILONOUS. In the next place, odours are to be considered. And with regard to these, I would fain know, whether what hath been said of tastes doth not exactly agree to them? Are they not so many pleasing or displeasing sensations?

HYLAS. They are.

PHILONOUS. Can you then conceive it possible that they should exist in an unperceiving thing?

HYLAS. I cannot.

PHILONOUS. Or can you imagine, that filth and ordure affect those brute animals that feed on them out of choice, with the same smells which we perceive in them?

HYLAS. By no means.

PHILONOUS. May we not therefore conclude of smells, as of the other forementioned qualities, that they cannot exist in any but a perceiving substance or mind?

HYLAS. I think so.

PHILONOUS. Then as to sounds, what must we think of them: are they accidents really inherent in external bodies, or not?

HYLAS. That they inhere not in the sonorous bodies, is plain from hence; because a bell struck in the exhausted receiver of an air-pump, sends forth no sound. The air therefore must be thought the subject of sound.

PHILONOUS. What reason is there for that, Hylas?

HYLAS. Because when any motion is raised in the air, we perceive a sound greater or lesser, in proportion to the air's motion; but without some motion in the air, we never hear any sound at all.

PHILONOUS. And granting that we never hear a sound but when some motion is produced in the air, yet I do not see how you can infer from thence, that the sound itself is in the air.

HYLAS. It is this very motion in the external air, that produces in the mind the sensation of *sound*. For, striking on the drum of the ear, it causeth a vibration, which by the auditory nerves being communicated to the brain, the soul is thereupon affected with the sensation called *sound*.

PHILONOUS. What! is sound then a sensation?

HYLAS. I tell you, as perceived by us, it is a particular sensation in the mind.

PHILONOUS. And can any sensation exist without the mind?

HYLAS. No certainly.

PHILONOUS. How then can sound, being a sensation exist in the air, if by the *air* you mean a senseless substance existing without the mind?

HYLAS. You must distinguish, Philonous, between sound as it is perceived by us, and as it is in itself; or (which is the same thing) between the sound we immediately perceive, and that which exists without us. The former indeed is a particular kind of sensation, but the latter is merely a vibrative or undulatory motion in the air.

PHILONOUS. I thought I had already obviated that distinction by the answer I gave when you were applying it in a like case before. But to say no more of that; are you sure then that sound is really nothing but motion?

HYLAS. I am.

PHILONOUS. Whatever therefore agrees to real sound, may with truth be attributed to motion.

HYLAS. It may.

PHILONOUS. It is then good sense to speak of *motion,* as of a thing that is *loud, sweet, acute,* or *grave*.

HYLAS. I see you are resolved not to understand me. Is it not evident, those accidents or modes belong only to sensible sound, or *sound* in the common acceptation of the word, but not to *sound* in the real and philosophic sense, which, as I just now told you, is nothing but a certain motion of the air?

PHILONOUS. It seems then there are two sorts of sound, the one vulgar, or that which is heard, the other philosophical and real.

HYLAS. Even so.

PHILONOUS. And the latter consists in motion.

HYLAS. I told you so before.

PHILONOUS. Tell me, Hylas, to which of the senses think you, the idea of motion belongs: to the hearing?

HYLAS. No certainly, but to the sight and touch.

PHILONOUS. It should follow then, that according to you, real sounds may possibly be *seen* or *felt,* but never *heard.*

HYLAS. Look you, Philonous, you may if you please make a jest of my opinion, but that will not alter the truth of things. I own indeed, the inferences you draw me into, sound something oddly; but common language, you know, is framed by, and for the use of the vulgar: we must not therefore wonder, if expressions adapted to exact philosophic notions, seem uncouth and out of the way.

PHILONOUS. Is it come to that? I assure you, I imagine myself to have gained no small point, since you make so light of departing from common phrases and opinions; it being a main part of our inquiry, to examine whose notions are widest of the common road, and most repugnant to the general sense of the world. But can you think it no more than a philosophical paradox, to say that *real sounds are never heard,* and that the idea of them is obtained by some other sense. And is there nothing in this contrary to nature and the truth of things?

HYLAS. To deal ingenuously, I do not like it. And after the concessions already made, I had as well grant that sounds too have no real being without the mind.

PHILONOUS. And I hope you will make no difficulty to acknowledge the same of colours.

HYLAS. Pardon me: the case of colours is very different. Can any thing be plainer, than that we see them on the objects?

PHILONOUS. The objects you speak of are, I suppose, corporeal substances existing without the mind.

HYLAS. They are.

PHILONOUS. And have true and real colours inhering in them?

HYLAS. Each visible object hath that colour which we see in it.

PHILONOUS. How! Is there any thing visible but what we perceive by sight?

HYLAS. There is not.

PHILONOUS. And do we perceive any thing by sense, which we do not perceive immediately?

HYLAS. How often must I be obliged to repeat the same thing? I tell you, we do not.

PHILONOUS. Have patience, good Hylas; and tell me once more, whether there is any thing immediately perceived by the senses, except sensible qualities. I know you asserted there was not: but I would now be informed, whether you still persist in the same opinion.

HYLAS. I do.

PHILONOUS. Pray, is your corporeal substance either a sensible quality, or made up of sensible qualities?

HYLAS. What a question that is! who ever thought it was?

PHILONOUS. My reason for asking was, because in saying, *each visible object hath that colour which we see in it,* you make visible objects to be corporeal substances; which implies either that corporeal substances are sensible qualities, or else that there is something beside sensible qualities perceived by sight: but as this point was formerly agreed between us, and is still maintained by you, it is a clear consequence, that your corporeal substance is nothing distinct from sensible qualities.

HYLAS. You may draw as many absurd consequences as you please, and endeavour to perplex and plainest things; but you shall never persuade me out of my senses. I clearly understand my own meaning.

PHILONOUS. I wish you would make me understand it too. But since you are unwilling to have your notion of corporeal substance examined, I shall urge that point no farther. Only be pleased to let me know, whether the same colours which we see, exist in external bodies, or some other.

HYLAS. The very same.

PHILONOUS. What! are then the beautiful red and purple we see on yonder clouds, really in them? Or do you imagine they have in themselves any other form, than that of a dark mist or vapour?

HYLAS. I must own, Philonous, those colours are not really in the clouds as they seem to be at this distance. They are only apparent colours.

PHILONOUS. *Apparent* call you them? how shall we distinguish these apparent colours from real?

HYLAS. Very easily. Those are to be thought apparent, which appearing only at a distance, vanish upon a nearer approach.

PHILONOUS. And those I suppose are to be thought real, which are discovered by the most near and exact survey.

HYLAS. Right.

PHILONOUS. Is the nearest and exactest survey made by the help of a microscope, or by the naked eye?

HYLAS. By a microscope, doubtless.

PHILONOUS. But a microscope often discovers colours in an object different from those perceived by the unassisted sight. And in case we had microscopes magnifying to any assigned degree; it is certain, that no object whatsoever viewed through them, would appear in the same colour which it exhibits to the naked eye.

HYLAS. And what will you conclude from all this? You cannot argue that there are really and naturally no colours on objects: because by artificial managements they may be altered, or made to vanish.

PHILONOUS. I think it may evidently be concluded from your own concessions, that all the colours we see with our naked eyes, are only apparent as those on the clouds, since they vanish upon a more close and accurate inspection, which is afforded us by a microscope. Then as to what you say by way of prevention: I ask you, whether the real and natural state of an object is better discovered by a very sharp and piercing sight, or by one which is less sharp?

HYLAS. By the former without doubt.

Philonous. Is it not plain from *dioptrics,* that microscopes make the sight more penetrating, and represent objects as they would appear to the eye, in case it were naturally endowed with a most exquisite sharpness?

Hylas. It is.

Philonous. Consequently the microscopical representation is to be thought that which best sets forth the real nature of the thing, or what it is in itself. The colours therefore by it perceived, are more genuine and real, than those perceived otherwise.

Hylas. I confess there is something in what you say.

Philonous. Besides, it is not only possible but manifest, that there actually are animals, whose eyes are by Nature framed to perceive those things, which by reason of their minuteness escape our sight. What think you of those inconceivably small animals perceived by glasses? Must we suppose they are all stark blind? Or, in case they see, can it be imagined their sight hath not the same use in preserving their bodies from injuries, which appears in that of all other animals? And if it hath, is it not evident, they must see particles less than their own bodies, which will present them with a far different view in each object, from that which strikes our senses? Even our own eyes do not always represent objects to us after the same manner. In the *jaundice,* every one knows that all things seem yellow. Is it not therefore highly probable, those animals in whose eyes we discern a very different texture from that of ours, and whose bodies abound with different humours, do not see the same colours in every object that we do? From all which, should it not seem to follow, that all colours are equally apparent, and that none of those which we perceive are really inherent in any outward object?

Hylas. It should.

Philonous. The point will be past all doubt, if you consider, that in case colours were real properties or affections inherent in external bodies, they could admit of no alteration, without some change wrought in the very bodies themselves: but is it not evident from what hath been said, that upon the use of microscopes, upon a change happening in the humours of the eye, or a variation of distance, without any manner of real alteration in the thing itself, the colours of any object are either changed, or totally disappear? Nay all other circumstances remaining the same, change but the situation of some objects, and they shall present different colours to the eye. The same thing happens upon viewing an object in various degrees of light. And what is more known, than that the same bodies appear differently coloured by candlelight, from what they do in the open day? Add to these the experiment of a prism, which separating the heterogeneous rays of light, alters the colour of any object; and will cause the whitest to appear of a deep blue or red to the naked eye. And now tell me, whether you are still of opinion, that every body hath its true real colour inhering in it; and if you think it hath, I would fain know farther from you, what certain distance and position of the object, what peculiar texture and formation of the eye, what degree or kind of light is necessary for ascertaining that true colour, and distinguishing it from apparent ones.

Hylas. I own myself entirely satisfied, that they are all equally apparent; and that there is no such thing as colour really inhering in external bodies, but that it is altogether in the light. And what confirms me in this opinion is, that in proportion to the light, colours are still more or less vivid; and if there be no light, then are there no colours perceived. Besides, allowing there are colours on external objects, yet how is it possible for us to perceive them? For no external body affects the mind, unless it act first on our organs of sense. But the only action of bodies is motion; and motion cannot be communicated otherwise than by impulse. A distant object therefore cannot act on the eye, nor consequently make itself or its properties perceivable to the soul. Whence it plainly follows, that it is immediately some contiguous substance, which operating on the eye occasions a perception of colours: and such is light.

PHILONOUS. How! is light then a substance?

HYLAS. I tell you, Philonous, external light is nothing but a thin fluid substance, whose minute particles being agitated with a brisk motion, and in various manners reflected from the different surfaces of outward objects to the eyes, communicate different motions to the optic nerves; which being propagated to the brain, cause therein various impressions: and these are attended with the sensations of red, blue, yellow, *&c.*

PHILONOUS. It seems then, the light doth no more than shake the optic nerves.

HYLAS. Nothing else.

PHILONOUS. And consequent to each particular motion of the nerves the mind is affected with a sensation, which is some particular colour.

HYLAS. Right.

PHILONOUS. And these sensations have no existence without the mind.

HYLAS. They have not.

PHILONOUS. How then do you affirm that colours are in the light, since by *light* you understand a corporeal substance external to the mind?

HYLAS. Light and colours, as immediately perceived by us, I grant cannot exist without the mind. But in themselves they are only the motions and configurations of certain insensible particles of matter.

PHILONOUS. Colours then in the vulgar sense, or taken for the immediate objects of sight, cannot agree to any but a perceiving substance.

HYLAS. That is what I say.

PHILONOUS. Well then, since you give up the point as to those sensible qualities, which are alone thought colours by all mankind beside, you may hold what you please with regard to those invisible ones of the philosophers. It is not my business to dispute about them; only I would advise you to bethink your self, whether considering the inquiry we are upon, it be prudent for you to affirm, *the red and blue which we see are not real colours, but certain unknown motions and figures which no man ever did or can see, are truly so.* Are not these shocking notions, and are not they subject to as many ridiculous inferences, as those you were obliged to renounce before in the case of sounds?

HYLAS. I frankly own, Philonous, that it is in vain to stand out any longer. Colours, sounds, tastes, in a word, all those termed *secondary qualities,* have certainly no existence without the mind. But by this acknowledgment I must not be supposed to derogate any thing from the reality of matter or external objects, seeing it is no more than several philosophers maintain, who nevertheless are the farthest imaginable from denying matter. For the clearer understanding of this, you must know sensible qualities are by philosophers divided into *primary* and *secondary.* The former are extension, figure, solidity, gravity, motion, and rest. And these they hold exist really in bodies. The latter are those above enumerated; or briefly, all sensible qualities beside the primary, which they assert are only so many sensations or ideas existing no where but in the mind. But all this, I doubt not, you are already apprised of. For my part, I have been a long time sensible there was such an opinion current among philosophers, but was never thoroughly convinced of its truth till now.

PHILONOUS. You are still then of opinion, that extension and figures are inherent in external unthinking substances.

HYLAS. I am.

PHILONOUS. But what if the same arguments which are brought against secondary qualities, will hold good against these also?

HYLAS. Why then I shall be obliged to think, they too exist only in the mind.

PHILONOUS. Is it your opinion, the very figure and extension which you perceive by sense, exist in the outward object or material substance?

HYLAS. It is.

PHILONOUS. Have all other animals as good grounds to think the same of the figure and extension which they see and feel?

HYLAS. Without doubt, if they have any thought at all.

PHILONOUS. Answer me, Hylas. Think you the senses were bestowed upon all animals for their preservation and well-being in life? or were they given to men alone for this end?

HYLAS. I make no question but they have the same use in all other animals.

PHILONOUS. If so, is it not necessary they should be enabled by them to perceive their own limbs, and those bodies which are capable of harming them?

HYLAS. Certainly.

PHILONOUS. A mite therefore must be supposed to see his own foot, and things equal or even less than it, as bodies of some considerable dimension; though at the same time they appear to you scarce discernible, or at best as so many visible points.

HYLAS. I cannot deny it.

PHILONOUS. And to creatures less than the mite they will seem yet larger.

HYLAS. They will.

PHILONOUS. Insomuch that what you can hardly discern, will to another extremely minute animal appear as some huge mountain.

HYLAS. All this I grant.

PHILONOUS. Can one and the same thing be at the same time in itself of different dimensions?

HYLAS. That were absurd to imagine.

PHILONOUS. But from what you have laid down it follows, that both the extension by you perceived, and that perceived by the mite itself, as likewise all those perceived by lesser animals, are each of them the true extension of the mite's foot, that is to say, by your own principles you are led into an absurdity.

HYLAS. There seems to be some difficulty in the point.

PHILONOUS. Again, have you not acknowledged that no real inherent property of any object can be changed, without some change in the thing itself?

HYLAS. I have.

PHILONOUS. But as we approach to or recede from an object, the visible extension varies, being at one distance ten or an hundred times greater than at another. Doth it not therefore follow from hence likewise, that it is not really inherent in the object?

HYLAS. I own I am at a loss what to think.

PHILONOUS. Your judgement will soon be determined, if you will venture to think as freely concerning this quality, as you have done concerning the rest. Was it not admitted as a good argument, that neither heat nor cold was in the water, because it seemed warm to one hand, and cold to the other?

HYLAS. It was.

PHILONOUS. Is it not the very same reasoning to conclude, there is no extension or figure in an object, because to one eye it shall seem little, smooth, and round, when at the same time it appears to the other, great, uneven, and angular?

HYLAS. The very same. But doth this latter fact ever happen?

PHILONOUS. You may at any time make the experiment, by looking with one eye bare, and with the other through a microscope.

HYLAS. I know not how to maintain it, and yet I am loth to give up *extension,* I see so many odd consequences following upon such a concession.

PHILONOUS. Odd, say you? After the concessions already made, I hope you will stick at nothing for its oddness. But on the other hand should it not seem very odd, if the general reasoning which includes all other sensible qualities did not also include extension? If it be allowed that no idea nor any thing like an idea can exist in an unperceiving substance, then surely it follows, that no figure or mode of extension, which we can either perceive or imagine, or have any idea of, can be really inherent in matter; not to mention the peculiar difficulty there must be, in conceiving a material substance, prior to and distinct from extension, to be the *substratum* of extension. Be the sensible quality what it will, figure, or sound, or colour; it seems alike impossible it should subsist in that which doth not perceive it.

HYLAS. I give up the point for the present, reserving still a right to retract my opinion, in case I shall hereafter discover any false step in my progress to it.

PHILONOUS. That is a right you cannot be denied. Figures and extension being dispatched, we proceed next to *motion*. Can a real motion in any external body be at the same time both very swift and very slow?

HYLAS. It cannot.

PHILONOUS. Is not the motion of a body swift in a reciprocal proportion to the time it takes up in describing any given space? Thus a body that describes a mile in an hour, moves three times faster than it would in case it described only a mile in three hours.

HYLAS. I agree with you.

PHILONOUS. And is not time measured by the succession of ideas in our minds?

HYLAS. It is.

PHILONOUS. And is it not possible ideas should succeed one another twice as fast in your mind, as they do in mine, or in that of some spirit of another kind.

HYLAS. I own it.

PHILONOUS. Consequently the same body may to another seem to perform its motion over any space in half the time that it doth to you. And the same reasoning will hold as to any other proportion: that is to say, according to your principles (since the motions perceived are both really in the object) it is possible one and the same body shall be really moved the same way at once, both very swift and very slow. How is this consistent either with common sense, or with what you just now granted?

HYLAS. I have nothing to say to it.

PHILONOUS. Then as for *solidity;* either you do not mean any sensible quality by that word, and so it is beside our inquiry: or if you do, it must be either hardness or resistance. But both the one and the other are plainly relative to our senses: it being evident, that what seems hard to one animal, may appear soft to another, who hath greater force and firmness of limbs. Nor is it less plain, that the resistance I feel is not in the body.

HYLAS. I own the very sensation of resistance, which is all you immediately perceive, is not in the *body,* but the cause of that sensation is.

PHILONOUS. But the causes of our sensations are not things immediately perceived, and therefore not sensible. This point I thought had been already determined.

HYLAS. I own it was; but you will pardon me if I seem a little embarrassed: I know not how to quit my old notions.

PHILONOUS. To help you out, do but consider, that if extension be once acknowledged to have no existence without the mind, the same must necessarily be granted of motion, solidity, and gravity, since they all evidently suppose extension. It is therefore superfluous to inquire particularly concerning each of them. In denying extension, you have denied them all to have any real existence.

HYLAS. I wonder, Philonous, if what you say be true, why those philosophers who deny the secondary qualities any real existence, should yet attribute it to the primary. If there is no difference between them, how can this be accounted for?

PHILONOUS. It is not my business to account for every opinion of the philosophers. But among other reasons which may be assigned for this, it seems probable, that pleasure and pain being rather annexed to the former than the latter, may be one. Heat and cold, tastes and smells, have something more vividly pleasing or disagreeable than the ideas of extension, figure, and motion, affect us with. And it being too visibly absurd to hold, that pain or pleasure can be in an unperceiving substance, men are more easily weaned from believing the external existence of the secondary, than the primary qualities. You will be satisfied there is something in this, if you recollect the difference you made between an intense and more moderate degree of heat, allowing the one a real existence, while you denied it to the other. But after all, there is no rational ground for that distinction; for surely an indifferent sensation is as truly *a sensation,* as one more pleasing or painful; and consequently should not any more than they be supposed to exist in an unthinking subject.

HYLAS. It is just come into my head, Philonous, that I have somewhere heard of a distinction between absolute and sensible extension. Now though it be acknowledged that *great* and *small,* consisting merely in the relation which other extended beings have to the parts of our own bodies, do not really inhere in the substances themselves; yet nothing obliges us to hold the same with regard to *absolute extension,* which is something abstracted from *great* and *small,* from this or that particular magnitude or figure. So likewise as to motion, *swift* and *slow* are altogether relative to the succession of ideas in our own minds. But it doth not follow, because those modifications of motion exist not without the mind, that therefore absolute motion abstracted from them doth not.

PHILONOUS. Pray what is it that distinguishes one motion, or one part of extension from another? Is it not something sensible, as some degree of swiftness or slowness, some certain magnitude or figure peculiar to each?

HYLAS. I think so.

PHILONOUS. These qualities therefore stripped of all sensible properties, are without all specific and numerical differences, as the Schools call them.

HYLAS. They are.

PHILONOUS. That is to say, they are extension in general, and motion in general.

HYLAS. Let it be so.

PHILONOUS. But it is an universally received maxim, that *every thing which exists, is particular.* How then can motion in general, or extension in general exist in any corporeal substance?

HYLAS. I will take time to solve your difficulty.

PHILONOUS. But I think the point may be speedily decided. Without doubt you can tell, whether you are able to frame this or that idea. Now I am content to put our dispute on this issue. If you can frame in your thoughts a distinct abstract idea of motion or extension, divested of all those sensible modes, as swift and slow, great and small, round and square, and the like, which are acknowledged to exist only in the mind, I will then yield the point you contend for. But if you cannot, it will be unreasonable on your side to insist any longer upon what you have no notion of.

HYLAS. To confess ingenuously, I cannot.

PHILONOUS. Can you even separate the ideas of extension and motion, from the ideas of all those qualities which they who make the distinction, term *secondary.*

HYLAS. What! is it not an easy matter, to consider extension and motion by themselves, abstracted from all other sensible qualities? Pray how do the mathematicians treat of them?

PHILONOUS. I acknowledge, Hylas, it is not difficult to form general propositions and reasonings about those qualities, without mentioning any other; and in this sense to consider or treat of them abstractedly. But how doth it follow that because I can pronounce the word *motion* by itself, I can form the idea of it in my mind exclusive of body?

Or because theorems may be made of extension and figures, without any mention of *great* or *small,* or any other sensible mode or quality; that therefore it is possible such an abstract idea of extension, without any particular size or figure, or sensible quality, should be distinctly formed, and apprehended by the mind? Mathematicians treat of quantity, without regarding what other sensible qualities it is attended with, as being altogether indifferent to their demonstrations. But when laying aside the words, they contemplate the bare ideas, I believe you will find, they are not the pure abstracted ideas of extension.

HYLAS. But what say you to *pure intellect?* May not abstracted ideas be framed by that faculty?

PHILONOUS. Since I cannot frame abstract ideas at all, it is plain, I cannot frame them by the help of *pure intellect,* whatsoever faculty you understand by those words. Besides, not to inquire into the nature of pure intellect and its spiritual objects, as *virtue, reason, God,* or the like; thus much seems manifest, that sensible things are only to be perceived by sense, or represented by the imagination. Figures therefore and extension being originally perceived by sense, do not belong to pure intellect. But for your farther satisfaction, try if you can frame the idea of any figure, abstracted from all particularities of size, or even from other sensible qualities.

HYLAS. Let me think a little—I do not find that I can.

PHILONOUS. And can you think it possible, that should really exist in Nature, which implies a repugnancy in its conception?

HYLAS. By no means.

PHILONOUS. Since therefore it is impossible even for the mind to disunite the ideas of extension and motion from all other sensible qualities, doth it not follow, that where the one exist, there necessarily the other exist likewise?

HYLAS. It should seem so.

PHILONOUS. Consequently the very same arguments which you admitted, as conclusive against the secondary qualities, are without any farther application of force against the primary too. Besides, if you will trust your senses, is it not plain all sensible qualities coexist, or to them, appear as being in the same place? Do they ever represent a motion, or figure, as being divested of all other visible and tangible qualities?

HYLAS. You need say no more on this head. I am free to own, if there be no secret error or oversight in our proceedings hitherto, that all sensible qualities are alike to be denied existence without the mind. But my fear is, that I have been too liberal in my former concessions, or overlooked some fallacy or other. In short, I did not take time to think.

PHILONOUS. For that matter, Hylas, you may take what time you please in reviewing the progress of our inquiry. You are at liberty to recover any slips you might have made, or offer whatever you have omitted, which makes for your first opinion.

HYLAS. One great oversight I take to be this: that I did not sufficiently distinguish the *object* from the *sensation.* Now though this latter may not exist without the mind, yet it will not thence follow that the former cannot.

PHILONOUS. What object do you mean? The object of the senses?

HYLAS. The same.

PHILONOUS. It is then immediately perceived.

HYLAS. Right.

PHILONOUS. Make me to understand the difference between what is immediately perceived, and a sensation.

HYLAS. The sensation I take to be an act of the mind perceiving; beside which, there is something perceived; and this I call the *object.* For example, there is red and yellow on that tulip. But then the act of perceiving those colours is in me only, and not in the tulip.

PHILONOUS. What tulip do you speak of? is it that which you see?

HYLAS. The same.

PHILONOUS. And what do you see beside colour, figure, and extension?

HYLAS. Nothing.

PHILONOUS. What you would say then is, that the red and yellow are coexistent with the extension; is it not?

HYLAS. That is not all; I would say, they have a real existence without the mind, in some unthinking substance.

PHILONOUS. That the colours are really in the tulip which I see, is manifest. Neither can it be denied, that this tulip may exist independent of your mind or mine, but that any immediate object of the senses, that is, any idea, or combination of ideas, should exist in an unthinking substance, or exterior to all minds, is in itself an evident contradiction. Nor can I imagine how this follows from what you said just now, to wit that the red and yellow were on the tulip *you saw,* since you do not pretend to *see* that unthinking substance.

HYLAS. You have an artful way, Philonous, of diverting our inquiry from the subject.

PHILONOUS. I see you have no mind to be pressed that way. To return then to your distinction between *sensation* and *object;* if I take you right, you distinguish in every perception two things, the one an action of the mind, the other not.

HYLAS. True.

PHILONOUS. And this action cannot exist in, or belong to any unthinking thing; but whatever beside is implied in a perception, may.

HYLAS. That is my meaning.

PHILONOUS. So that if there was a perception without any act of the mind, it were possible such a perception should exist in an unthinking substance.

HYLAS. I grant it. But it is impossible there should be such a perception.

PHILONOUS. When is the mind said to be active?

HYLAS. When it produces, puts an end to, or changes any thing.

PHILONOUS. Can the mind produce, discontinue, or change any thing but by an act of the will?

HYLAS. It cannot.

PHILONOUS. The mind therefore is to be accounted active in its perceptions, so far forth as volition is included in them.

HYLAS. It is.

PHILONOUS. In plucking this flower, I am active, because I do it by the motion of my hand, which was consequent upon my volition; so likewise in applying it to my nose. But is either of these smelling?

HYLAS. No.

PHILONOUS. I act too in drawing the air through my nose; because my breathing so rather than otherwise, is the effect of my volition. But neither can this be called *smelling:* for if it were, I should smell every time I breathed in that manner.

HYLAS. True.

PHILONOUS. Smelling then is somewhat consequent to all this.

HYLAS. It is.

PHILONOUS. But I do not find my will concerned any farther. Whatever more there is, as that I perceive such a particular smell or any smell at all, this is independent of my will, and therein I am altogether passive. Do you find it otherwise with you, Hylas?

HYLAS. No, the very same.

PHILONOUS. Then as to seeing, is it not in your power to open your eyes, or keep them shut; to turn them this or that way?

HYLAS. Without doubt.

PHILONOUS. But doth it in like manner depend on your will, that in looking on this flower, you perceive *white* rather than any other colour? Or directing your open eyes toward yonder part of the heaven, can you avoid seeing the sun? Or is light or darkness the effect of your volition?

HYLAS. No certainly.

PHILONOUS. You are then in these respects altogether passive.

HYLAS. I am.

PHILONOUS. Tell me now, whether *seeing* consists in perceiving light and colours, or in opening and turning the eyes?

HYLAS. Without doubt, in the former.

PHILONOUS. Since therefore you are in the very perception of light and colours altogether passive, what is become of that action you were speaking of, as an ingredient in every sensation? And doth it not follow from your own concessions, that the perception of light and colours, including no action in it, may exist in an unperceiving substance? And is not this a plain contradiction?

HYLAS. I know not what to think of it.

PHILONOUS. Besides, since you distinguish the *active* and *passive* in every perception, you must do it in that of pain. But how is it possible that pain, be it as little active as you please, should exist in an unperceiving substance? In short, do but consider the point, and then confess ingenuously, whether light and colours, tastes, sounds, *&c.* are not all equally passions or sensations in the soul. You may indeed call them *external objects,* and give them in words what subsistence you please. But examine your own thoughts, and then tell me whether it be not as I say?

HYLAS. I acknowledge, Philonous, that upon a fair observation of what passes in my mind, I can discover nothing else, but that I am a thinking being, affected with variety of sensations; neither is it possible to conceive how a sensation should exist in an unperceiving substance. But then on the other hand, when I look on sensible things in a different view, considering them as so many modes and qualities, I find it necessary to suppose a material *substratum,* without which they cannot be conceived to exist.

PHILONOUS. *Material substratum* call you it? Pray, by which of your senses came you acquainted with that being?

HYLAS. It is not itself sensible; its modes and qualities only being perceived by the senses.

PHILONOUS. I presume then, it was by reflexion and reason you obtained the idea of it.

HYLAS. I do not pretend to any proper positive idea of it. However I conclude it exists, because qualities cannot be conceived to exist without a support.

PHILONOUS. It seems then you have only a relative notion of it, or that you conceive it not otherwise than by conceiving the relation it bears to sensible qualities.

HYLAS. Right.

PHILONOUS. Be pleased therefore to let me know wherein that relation consists.

HYLAS. Is it not sufficiently expressed in the term *substratum,* or *substance?*

PHILONOUS. If so, the word *substratum* should import, that it is spread under the sensible qualities or accidents.

HYLAS. True.

PHILONOUS. And consequently under extension.

HYLAS. I own it.

PHILONOUS. It is therefore somewhat in its own nature entirely distinct from extension.

HYLAS. I tell you, extension is only a mode, and matter is something that supports modes. And is it not evident the thing supported is different from the thing supporting?

PHILONOUS. So that something distinct from, and exclusive of extension, is supposed to be the *substratum* of extension.

HYLAS. Just so.

PHILONOUS. Answer me, Hylas. Can a thing be spread without extension? or is not the idea of extension necessarily included in *spreading?*

HYLAS. It is.

PHILONOUS. Whatsoever therefore you suppose spread under any thing, must have in itself an extension distinct from the extension of that thing under which it is spread.

HYLAS. It must.

PHILONOUS. Consequently every corporeal substance being the *substratum* of extension, must have in itself another extension by which it is qualified to be a *substratum:* and so on to infinity. And I ask whether this be not absurd in itself, and repugnant to what you granted just now, to wit, that the *substratum* was something distinct from, and exclusive of extension.

HYLAS. Ay but, Philonous, you take me wrong. I do not mean that matter is *spread* in a gross literal sense under extension. The word *substratum* is used only to express in general the same thing with *substance*.

PHILONOUS. Well then, let us examine the relation implied in the term *substance*. Is it not that it stands under accidents?

HYLAS. The very same.

PHILONOUS. But that one thing may stand under or support another, must it not be extended?

HYLAS. It must.

PHILONOUS. Is not therefore this supposition liable to the same absurdity with the former?

HYLAS. You still take things in a strict literal sense: that is not fair, Philonous.

PHILONOUS. I am not for imposing any sense on your words: you are at liberty to explain them as you please. Only I beseech you, make me understand something by them. You tell me, matter supports or stands under accidents. How! is it as your legs support your body?

HYLAS. No; that is the literal sense.

PHILONOUS. Pray let me know any sense, literal or not literal, that you understand it in. ______ How long must I wait for an answer, Hylas?

HYLAS. I declare I know not what to say. I once thought I understood well enough what was meant by matter's supporting accidents. But now the more I think on it, the less can I comprehend it; in short, I find that I know nothing of it.

PHILONOUS. It seems then you have no idea at all, neither relative nor positive of matter; you know neither what it is in itself, nor what relation it bears to accidents.

HYLAS. I acknowledge it.

PHILONOUS. And yet you asserted, that you could not conceive how qualities or accidents should really exist, without conceiving at the same time a material support of them.

HYLAS. I did.

PHILONOUS. That is to say, when you conceive the real existence of qualities, you do withal conceive something which you cannot conceive.

HYLAS. It was wrong I own. But still I fear there is some fallacy or other. Pray what think you of this? It is just come into my head, that the ground of all our mistakes lies in your treating of each quality by itself. Now, I grant that each quality cannot singly subsist without the mind. Colour cannot without extension, neither can figure without some other sensible quality. But as the several qualities united or blended together form entire sensible things, nothing hinders why such things may not be supposed to exist without the mind.

PHILONOUS. Either, Hylas, you are jesting, or have a very bad memory. Though indeed we went through all the qualities by name one after another; yet my arguments, or rather your concessions no where tended to prove, that the secondary qualities did not subsist each alone by itself; but that they were not *at all* without the mind. Indeed in treating of figure and motion, we concluded they could not exist without the mind, because it was impossible even in thought to separate them from all secondary qualities, so as to conceive them existing by themselves. But then this was not the only argument made use of upon that occasion. But (to pass by all that hath been hitherto said, and reckon it for nothing, it you will have it so) I am content to put the whole upon this issue. If you can conceive it possible for any mixture or combination of qualities, or any sensible object whatever, to exist without the mind, then I will grant it actually to be so.

HYLAS. If it comes to that, the point will soon be decided. What more easy than to conceive a tree or house existing by itself, independent of, and unperceived by any mind whatsoever? I do at this present time conceive them existing after that manner.

PHILONOUS. How say you, Hylas, can you see a thing which is at the same time unseen?

HYLAS. No, that were a contradiction.

PHILONOUS. Is it not as great a contradiction to talk of *conceiving* a thing which is *unconceived?*

HYLAS. It is.

PHILONOUS. The tree or house therefore which you think of, is conceived by you.

HYLAS. How should it be otherwise?

PHILONOUS. And what is conceived, is surely in the mind.

HYLAS. Without question, that which is conceived is in the mind.

PHILONOUS. How then came you to say, you conceived a house or tree existing independent and out of all minds whatsoever?

HYLAS. That was I own an oversight; but stay, let me consider what led me into it.—It is a pleasant mistake enough. As I was thinking of a tree in a solitary place, where no one was present to see it, methought that was to conceive a tree as existing unperceived or unthought of, not considering that I myself conceived it all the while. But now I plainly see, that all I can do is to frame ideas in my own mind. I may indeed conceive in my own thoughts the idea of a tree, or a house, or a mountain, but that is all. And this is far from proving, that I can conceive them *existing out of the minds of all spirits.*

PHILONOUS. You acknowledge then that you cannot possibly conceive, how any one corporeal sensible thing should exist otherwise than in a mind.

HYLAS. I do.

PHILONOUS. And yet you will earnestly contend for the truth of that which you cannot so much as conceive.

HYLAS. I profess I know not what to think, but still there are some scruples remain with me. Is it not certain I see things at a distance? Do we not perceive the stars and moon, for example, to be a great way off? Is not this, I say, manifest to the senses?

PHILONOUS. Do you not in a dream too perceive those or the like objects?

HYLAS. I do.

PHILONOUS. And have they not then the same appearance of being distant?

HYLAS. They have.

PHILONOUS. But you do not thence conclude the apparitions in a dream to be without the mind?

HYLAS. By no means.

PHILONOUS. You ought not therefore to conclude that sensible objects are without the mind, from their appearance or manner wherein they are perceived.

HYLAS. I acknowledge it. But doth not my sense deceive me in those cases?

PHILONOUS. By no means. The idea or thing which you immediately perceive, neither sense nor reason inform you that it actually exists without the mind. By sense you only know that you are affected with such certain sensations of light and colours, *&c.* And these you will not say are without the mind.

HYLAS. True: but beside all that, do you not think the sight suggests something of *outness* or *distance?*

PHILONOUS. Upon approaching a distant object, do the visible size and figure change perpetually, or do they appear the same at all distances?

HYLAS. They are in a continual change.

PHILONOUS. Sight therefore doth not suggest or any way inform you, that the visible object you immediately perceive, exists at a distance, or will be perceived when you advance farther onward, there being a continued series of visible objects succeeding each other, during the whole time of your approach.

HYLAS. It doth not; but still I know, upon seeing an object, what object I shall perceive after having passed over a certain distance:

no matter whether it be exactly the same or no: there is still something of distance suggested in the case.

PHILONOUS. Good Hylas, do but reflect a little on the point, and then tell me whether there be any more in it than this. From the ideas you actually perceive by sight, you have by experience learned to collect what other ideas you will (according to the standing order of Nature) be affected with, after such a certain succession of time and motion.

HYLAS. Upon the whole, I take it to be nothing else.

PHILONOUS. Now is it not plain, that if we suppose a man born blind was on a sudden made to see, he could at first have no experience of what may be suggested by sight.

HYLAS. It is.

PHILONOUS. He would not then according to you have any notion of distance annexed to the things he saw; but would take them for a new set of sensations existing only in his mind.

HYLAS. It is undeniable.

PHILONOUS. But to make it still more plain: Is not *distance* a line turned endwise to the eye?

HYLAS. It is.

PHILONOUS. And can a line so situated be perceived by sight?

HYLAS. It cannot.

PHILONOUS. Doth it not therefore follow that distance is not properly and immediately perceived by sight?

HYLAS. It should seem so.

PHILONOUS. Again, is it your opinion that colours are at a distance?

HYLAS. It must be acknowledged, they are only in the mind.

PHILONOUS. But do not colours appear to the eye as coexisting in the same place with extension and figures?

HYLAS. They do.

PHILONOUS. How can you then conclude from sight, that figures exist without, when you acknowledge colours do not; the sensible appearance being the very same with regard to both?

HYLAS. I know not what to answer.

PHILONOUS. But allowing that distance was truly and immediately perceived by the mind, yet it would not thence follow it existed out of the mind. For whatever is immediately perceived is an idea: and can any *idea* exist out of the mind?

HYLAS. To suppose that, were absurd: but inform me, Philonous, can we perceive or know nothing beside our ideas?

PHILONOUS. As for the rational deducing of causes from effects, that is beside our inquiry. And by the senses you can best tell, whether you perceive any thing which is not immediately perceived. And I ask you, whether the things immediately perceived, are other than your own sensations or ideas? You have indeed more than once, in the course of this conversation, declared yourself on those points; but you seem by this last question to have departed from what you then thought.

HYLAS. To speak the truth, Philonous, I think there are two kinds of objects, the one perceived immediately, which are likewise called *ideas;* the other are real things or external objects perceived by the mediation of ideas, which are their images and representations. Now I own, ideas do not exist without the mind; but the latter sort of objects do. I am sorry I did not think of this distinction sooner; it would probably have cut short your discourse.

PHILONOUS. Are those external objects perceived by sense, or by some other faculty?

HYLAS. They are perceived by sense.

PHILONOUS. How! is there any thing perceived by sense, which is not immediately perceived?

HYLAS. Yes, Philonous, in some sort there is. For example, when I look on a picture or statue of Julius Cæsar, I may be said after a manner to perceive him (though not immediately) by my senses.

PHILONOUS. It seems then, you will have our ideas, which alone are immediately perceived, to be pictures of external things: and that these also are perceived by sense, inasmuch as they have a conformity or resemblance to our ideas.

HYLAS. That is my meaning.

PHILONOUS. And in the same way that Julius Cæsar, in himself invisible, is nevertheless perceived by sight; real things in themselves imperceptible, are perceived by sense.

HYLAS. In the very same.

PHILONOUS. Tell me, Hylas, when you behold the picture of Julius Cæsar, do you see with your eyes any more than some colours and figures with a certain symmetry and composition of the whole?

HYLAS. Nothing else.

PHILONOUS. And would not a man, who had never known any thing of Julius Cæsar, see as much?

HYLAS. He would.

PHILONOUS. Consequently he hath his sight, and the use of it, in as perfect a degree as you.

HYLAS. I agree with you.

PHILONOUS. Whence comes it then that your thoughts are directed to the Roman Emperor, and his are not? This cannot proceed from the sensations or ideas of sense by you then perceived; since you acknowledge you have no advantage over him in that respect. It should seem therefore to proceed from reason and memory: should it not?

HYLAS. It should.

PHILONOUS. Consequently it will not follow from that instance, that any thing is perceived by sense which is not immediately perceived. Though I grant we may in one acceptation be said to perceive sensible things mediately be sense: that is, when from a frequently perceived connexion, the immediate perception of ideas by one sense suggests to the mind others perhaps belonging to another sense, which are wont to be connected with them. For instance, when I hear a coach drive along the streets, immediately I perceive only the sound; but from the experience I have had that such a sound is connected with a coach, I am said to hear the coach. It is nevertheless evident, that in truth and strictness, nothing can be *heard* but *sound:* and the coach is not then properly perceived by sense, but suggested from experience. So likewise when we are said to see a red-hot bar of iron; the solidity and heat of the iron are not the objects of sight, but suggested to the imagination by the colour and figure, which are properly perceived by that sense. In short, those things alone are actually and strictly perceived by any sense, which would have been perceived, in case that same sense had then been first conferred on us. As for other things, it is plain they are only suggested to the mind by experience grounded on former perceptions. But to return to your comparison of Cæsar's picture, it is plain, if you keep to that, you must hold the real things or archetypes of our ideas are not perceived by sense, but by some internal faculty of the soul, as reason or memory. I would therefore fain know, what arguments you can draw from reason for the existence of what you call *real things* or *material objects*. Or whether you remember to have seen them formerly as they are in themselves? or if you have heard or read of any one that did.

HYLAS. I see, Philonous, you are disposed to raillery; but that will never convince me.

PHILONOUS. My aim is only to learn from you, the way to come at the knowledge of *material beings*. Whatever we perceive, is perceived either immediately or mediately: by sense, or by reason and reflexion. But as you have excluded sense, pray shew me what reason you have to believe their existence; or what *medium* you can possibly make use of, to prove it either to mine or your own understanding.

HYLAS. To deal ingenuously, Philonous, now I consider the point, I do not find I can give you any good reason for it. But thus much seems pretty plain, that it is at least possible such things may really exist. And as long as there is no absurdity in supposing them, I am resolved to believe as I did, till you bring good reasons to the contrary.

PHILONOUS. What! is it come to this, that you only believe the existence of material objects, and that your belief is founded barely on the possibility of its being true? Then you will have me bring reasons against it: though another would think it reasonable, the proof should lie on him who holds the affirmative. And after all, this very point which you are now resolved to maintain without any reason, is in effect what you have more than once during this discourse seen good reason to give up. But to pass over all this; if I understand you rightly, you say our ideas do not exist without the mind; but that they are copies, images, or representations of certain originals that do.

HYLAS. You take me right.

PHILONOUS. They are then like external things.

HYLAS. They are.

PHILONOUS. Have those things a stable and permanent nature independent of our senses; or are they in a perpetual change, upon our producing any motions in our bodies, suspending, exerting, or altering our faculties or organs of sense.

HYLAS. Real things, it is plain, have a fixed and real nature, which remains the same, notwithstanding any change in our senses, or in the posture and motion of our bodies; which indeed may affect the ideas in our minds, but it were absurd to think they had the same effect on things existing without the mind.

PHILONOUS. How then is it possible, that things perpetually fleeting and variable as our ideas, should be copies or images of any thing fixed and constant? Or in other words, since all sensible qualities, as size, figure, colour, *&c.* that is, our ideas are continually changing upon every alteration in the distance, medium, or instruments of sensation; how can any determinate material objects be properly represented or painted forth by several distinct things, each of which is so different from and unlike the rest? Or if you say it resembles some one only of our ideas, how shall we be able to distinguish the true copy from all the false ones?

HYLAS. I profess, Philonous, I am at a loss. I know not what to say to this.

PHILONOUS. But neither is this all. Which are material objects in themselves, perceptible or imperceptible?

HYLAS. Properly and immediately nothing can be perceived but ideas. All material things therefore are in themselves insensible, and to be perceived only by their ideas.

PHILONOUS. Ideas then are sensible, and their archetypes or originals insensible.

HYLAS. Right.

PHILONOUS. But how can that which is sensible be like that which is insensible? Can a real thing in itself *invisible* be like a *colour;* or a real thing which is not *audible,* be like a *sound?* In a word, can any thing be like a sensation or idea, but another sensation or idea?

HYLAS. I must own, I think not.

PHILONOUS. Is it possible there should be any doubt in the point? Do you not perfectly know your own ideas?

HYLAS. I know them perfectly; since what I do not perceive or know, can be no part of my idea.

PHILONOUS. Consider therefore, and examine them, and then tell me if there be any thing in them which can exist without the mind: or if you can conceive any thing like them existing without the mind.

HYLAS. Upon inquiry, I find it is impossible for me to conceive or understand how any thing but an idea can be like an idea. And it is most evident, that *no idea can exist without the mind.*

PHILONOUS. You are therefore by your principles forced to deny the reality of sensible things, since you made it to consist in an absolute existence exterior to the mind. That is to say, you are a downright *sceptic*. So I have gained my point, which was to shew your principles led to scepticism.

HYLAS. For the present I am, if not entirely convinced, at least silenced.

PHILONOUS. I would fain know what more you would require in order to a perfect conviction. Have you not had the liberty of explaining yourself all manner of ways? Were any little slips in discourse laid hold and insisted on? Or were you not allowed to retract or reinforce any thing you had offered, as best served your purpose? Hath not every thing you could say been heard and examined with all the fairness imaginable? In a word, have you not in every point been convinced out of your own mouth? And if you can at present discover any flaw in any of your former concessions, or think of any remaining subterfuge, any new distinction, colour, or comment whatsoever, why do you not produce it?

HYLAS. A little patience, Philonous. I am at present so amazed to see myself ensnared, and as it were imprisoned in the labyrinths you have drawn me into, that on the sudden it cannot be expected I should find my way out. You must give me time to look about me, and recollect myself.

PHILONOUS. Hark; is not this the college-bell?

HYLAS. It rings for prayers.

PHILONOUS. We will go in then if you please, and meet here again to-morrow morning. In the mean time you may employ your thoughts on this morning's discourse, and try if you can find any fallacy in it, or invent any new means to extricate yourself.

HYLAS. Agreed.

THE SECOND DIALOGUE

HYLAS. I beg your pardon, Philonous, for not meeting you sooner. All this morning my head was so filled with our late conversation, that I had not leisure to think of the time of the day, or indeed of any thing else.

PHILONOUS. I am glad you were so intent upon it, in hopes if there were any mistakes in your concessions, or fallacies in my reasonings from them, you will now discover them to me.

HYLAS. I assure you, I have done nothing ever since I saw you, but search after mistakes and fallacies, and with that view have minutely examined the whole series of yesterday's discourse: but all in vain, for the notions it led me into, upon review appear still more clear and evident; and the more I consider them, the more irresistibly do they force my assent.

PHILONOUS. And is not this, think you, a sign that they are genuine, that they proceed from Nature, and are conformable to right reason? Truth and beauty are in this alike, that the strictest survey sets them both off to advantage. While the false lustre of error and disguise cannot endure being reviewed, or too nearly inspected.

HYLAS. I own there is a great deal in what you say. Nor can any one be more entirely satisfied of the truth of those odd consequences, so long as I have in view the reasonings that lead to them. But when these are out of my thoughts, there seems on the other hand something so satisfactory, so natural and intelligible in the modern way of explaining things, that I profess I know not how to reject it.

PHILONOUS. I know not what way you mean.

HYLAS. I mean the way of accounting for our sensations or ideas.

PHILONOUS. How is that?

HYLAS. It is supposed the soul makes her residence in some part of the brain, from which the nerves take their rise, and are thence extended to all parts of the body: and that outward objects by the different impressions they make on the organs of sense, communicate certain vibrative motions to the nerves;

and these being filled with spirits, propagate them to the brain or seat of the soul, which according to the various impressions or traces thereby made in the brain, is various affected with ideas.

PHILONOUS. And call you this an explication of the manner whereby we are affected with ideas?

HYLAS. Why not, Philonous, have you any thing to object against it?

PHILONOUS. I would first know whether I rightly understand your hypothesis. You make certain traces in the brain to be the causes or occasions of our ideas. Pray tell me, whether by the *brain* you mean any sensible thing?

HYLAS. What else think you I could mean?

PHILONOUS. Sensible things are all immediately perceivable; and those things which are immediately perceivable, are ideas; and these exist only in the mind. Thus much you have, if I mistake not, long since agreed to.

HYLAS. I do not deny it.

PHILONOUS. The brain therefore you speak of, being a sensible thing, exists only in the mind. Now, I would fain know whether you think it reasonable to suppose, that one idea or thing existing in the mind, occasions all other ideas. And if you think so, pray how do you account for the origin of that primary idea or brain itself?

HYLAS. I do not explain the origin of our ideas by that brain which is perceivable to sense, this being itself only a combination of sensible ideas, but by another which I imagine.

PHILONOUS. But are not things imagined as truly in the mind as things perceived?

HYLAS. I must confess they are.

PHILONOUS. It comes therefore to the same thing; and you have been all this while accounting for ideas, by certain motions or impressions in the brain, that is, by some alterations in an idea, whether sensible or imaginable it matters not.

HYLAS. I begin to suspect my hypothesis.

PHILONOUS. Beside spirits, all that we know or conceive are our own ideas. When therefore you say, all ideas are occasioned by impressions in the brain, do you conceive this brain or no? If you do, then you talk of ideas imprinted in an idea, causing that same idea, which is absurd. If you do not conceive it, you talk unintelligibly, instead of forming a reasonable hypothesis.

HYLAS. I now clearly see it was a mere dream. There is nothing in it.

PHILONOUS. You need not be much concerned at it: for after all, this way of explaining things, as you called it, could never have satisfied any reasonable man. What connexion is there between a motion in the nerves, and the sensations of sound or colour in the mind? or how is it possible these should be the effect of that?

HYLAS. But I could never think it had so little in it, as now it seems to have.

PHILONOUS. Well then, are you at length satisfied that no sensible things have a real existence; and that you are in truth an arrant *sceptic?*

HYLAS. It is too plain to be denied.

PHILONOUS. Look! are not the fields covered with a delightful verdure? Is there not something in the woods and groves, in the rivers and clear springs that soothes, that delights, that transports the soul? At the prospect of the wide and deep ocean, or some huge mountain whose top is lost in the clouds, or of an old gloomy forest, are not our minds filled with a pleasing horror? Even in rocks and deserts, is there not an agreeable wildness? How sincere a pleasure is it to behold the natural beauties of the earth! To preserve and renew our relish for them, is not the veil of night alternately drawn over her face, and doth she not change her dress with the seasons? How aptly are the elements disposed? What variety and use in the meanest productions of Nature? What delicacy, what beauty, what contrivance in animal and vegetable bodies? How exquisitely are all things suited, as well to their particular ends, as to constitute apposite parts of the whole! And while they mutually aid and support, do they not also set off and illustrate each other? Raise now your thoughts from this ball of earth, to all those glorious luminaries that adorn the high arch of heaven. The motion and situation of the planets, are they not admirable for use and order? Were those (miscalled *erratic*) globes ever known to stray, in their repeated journeys through the pathless void? Do they not measure areas round the sun ever proportioned to the times? So fixed, so immutable are the laws by which the unseen Author of Nature actuates the universe. How vivid and radiant is the lustre of the fixed stars! How magnificent and rich that negligent profusion, with which they appear to be scattered throughout the whole azure vault! Yet if you take the telescope, it brings into your sight a new host of stars that escape the naked eye. Here they seem contiguous and minute, but to a nearer view immense orbs of light at various distances, far sunk in the abyss of space. Now you must call imagination to your aid. The feeble narrow sense cannot descry innumerable worlds revolving round the central fires; and in those worlds the energy of an all-perfect mind displayed in endless forms. But neither sense nor imagination are big enough to comprehend the boundless extent with all its glittering furniture. Though the labouring mind exert and strain each power to its utmost reach, there still stands out ungrasped a surplusage immeasurable. Yet all the vast bodies that compose this mighty frame, how distant and remote soever, are by some secret mechanism, some divine art and force linked in a mutual dependence and intercourse with each other, even with this earth, which was almost slipt from my thoughts, and lost in the crowd of worlds. Is not the whole system immense, beautiful, glorious beyond expression and beyond thought! What treatment then do those philosophers deserve, who would deprive these noble and delightful scenes of all reality? How should those principles be entertained, that lead us to think all the visible beauty of the creation a false imaginary glare? To be plain, can you expect this scepticism of yours will not be thought extravagantly absurd by all men of sense?

HYLAS. Other men may think as they please: but for your part you have nothing to reproach me with. My comfort is, you are as much a *sceptic* as I am.

PHILONOUS. There, Hylas, I must beg leave to differ from you.

HYLAS. What! have you all along agreed to the premises, and do you now deny the conclusion, and leave me to maintain those paradoxes by myself which you led me into? This surely is not fair.

PHILONOUS. I deny that I agreed with you in those notions that led to scepticism. You indeed said, the reality of sensible things consisted in an *absolute existence* out of the minds of spirits, or distinct from their being perceived. And pursuant to this notion of reality, you are obliged to deny sensible things any real existence: that is, according to your own definition, you profess yourself a *sceptic*. But I neither said nor thought the reality of sensible things was to be defined after that manner. To me it is evident, for the reasons you allow of, that sensible things cannot exist otherwise than in a mind or spirit. Whence I conclude, not that they have no real existence, but that seeing they depend not on my thought, and have an existence distinct from being perceived by me, *there must be some other mind wherein they exist*. As sure therefore as the sensible world really exists, so sure is there an infinite omnipresent spirit who contains and supports it.

HYLAS. What! this is no more than I and all Christians hold; nay, and all others too who believe there is a God, and that he knows and comprehends all things.

PHILONOUS. Ay, but here lies the difference. Men commonly believe that all things are known or perceived by God, because they believe the being of a God, whereas I on the other side, immediately and necessarily conclude the being of a God, because all sensible things must be perceived by him.

HYLAS. But so long as we all believe the same thing, what matter is it how we come by that belief?

PHILONOUS. But neither do we agree in the same opinion. For philosophers, though they acknowledge all corporeal beings to be perceived by God, yet they attribute to them an absolute subsistence distinct from their being perceived by any mind whatever, which I do not. Besides, is there no difference between saying, *there is a God, therefore he perceives all things:* and saying, *sensible things do really exist: and if they really exist, they are necessarily perceived by an infinite mind: therefore there is an infinite mind, or God.* This furnishes you with a direct and immediate demonstration, from a most evident principle, of the *being of a God.* Divines and philosophers had proved beyond all controversy, from the beauty and usefulness of the several parts of the creation, that it was the workmanship of God. But that setting aside all help of astronomy and natural philosophy, all contemplation of the contrivance, order, and adjustment of things, an infinite mind should be necessarily inferred from the bare existence of the sensible world, is an advantage peculiar to them only who have made this easy reflexion: that the sensible world is that which we perceive by our several senses; and that nothing is perceived by the senses beside ideas; and that no idea or archetype of an idea can exist otherwise than in a mind. You may now, without any laborious search into the sciences, without any subtlety of reason, or tedious length of discourse, oppose and baffle the most strenuous advocate for atheism. Those miserable refuges, whether in an eternal succession of unthinking causes and effects, or in a fortuitous concourse of atoms; those wild imaginations of Vanini, Hobbes, and Spinoza; in a word the whole system of atheism, is it not entirely overthrown by this single reflexion on the repugnancy included in supposing the whole, or any part, even the most rude and shapeless of the visible world, to exist without a mind? Let any one of those abettors of impiety but look into his own thoughts, and there try if he can conceive how so much as a rock, a desert, a chaos, or confused jumble of atoms; how any thing at all, either sensible or imaginable, can exist independent of a mind, and he need go no farther to be convinced of his folly. Can any thing be fairer than to put a dispute on such an issue, and leave it to a man himself to see if he can conceive, even in thought, what he holds to be true in fact, and from a notional to allow it a real existence?

HYLAS. It cannot be denied, there is something highly serviceable to religion in what you advance. But do you not think it looks very like a notion entertained by some eminent moderns, of *seeing all things in God?*

PHILONOUS. I would gladly know that opinion; pray explain it to me.

HYLAS. They conceive that the soul being immaterial, is incapable of being united with material things, so as to perceive them in themselves, but that she perceives them by her union with the substance of God, which being spiritual is therefore purely intelligible, or capable of being the immediate object of a spirit's thought. Besides, the divine essence contains in it perfections correspondent to each created being; and which are for that reason proper to exhibit or represent them to the mind.

PHILONOUS. I do not understand how our ideas, which are things altogether passive and inert, can be the essence, or any part (or like any part) of the essence or substance of God, who is an impassive, indivisible, purely active being. Many more difficulties and objections there are, which occur at first view against this hypothesis; but I shall only add that it is liable to all the absurdities of the common hypotheses, in making a created world exist otherwise than in the mind of a spirit. Beside all which is hath this peculiar to itself; that it makes that material world serve to no purpose. And if it pass for a good argument against other hypotheses in the sciences, that they suppose Nature or the divine wisdom to make something in vain, or do that by tedious round-about methods, which might have been performed in a much more easy and compendious way, what shall we think of that hypothesis which supposes the whole world made in vain?

HYLAS. But what say you, are not you too of opinion that we see all things in God? If I mistake not, what you advance comes near it.

PHILONOUS. Few men think, yet all will have opinions. Hence men's opinions are superficial and confused. It is nothing strange that tenets, which in themselves are ever so different, should nevertheless be confounded with each other by those who do not consider them attentively. I shall not therefore be surprised, if some men imagine that I run into the enthusiasm of Malbranche, though in truth I am very remote from it. He builds on the most abstract general ideas, which I entirely disclaim. He asserts an absolute external world, which I deny. He maintains that we are deceived by our senses, and know not the real natures or the true forms and figures of extended beings; of all which I hold the direct contrary. So that upon the whole there are no principles more fundamentally opposite than his and mine. It must be owned I entirely agree with what the holy Scripture faith, *that in God we live, and move, and have our being*. But that we see things in his essence after the manner above set forth, I am far from believing, Take here in brief my meaning. It is evident that the things I perceive are my own ideas, and that no idea can exist unless it be in a mind. Nor is it less plain that these ideas or things by me perceived, either themselves or their archetypes, exist independently of my mind, since I know myself not to be their author, it being out of my power to determine at pleasure, what particular ideas I shall be affected with upon opening my eyes or ears. They must therefore exist in some other mind, whose will it is they should be exhibited to me. The things, I say, immediately perceived, are ideas or sensations, call them which you will. But how can any idea or sensation exist in, or be produced by, any thing but a mind or spirit? This indeed is inconceivable; and to assert that which is inconceivable, is to talk nonsense: Is it not?

HYLAS. Without doubt.

PHILONOUS. But on the other hand, it is very conceivable that they should exist in, and be produced by, a spirit; since this is no more than I daily experience in myself, inasmuch as I perceive numberless ideas; and by an act of my Will can form a great variety of them, and raise them up in my imagination: though it must be confessed, these creatures of the fancy are not altogether so distinct, so strong, vivid, and permanent, as those perceived by my senses, which latter are called *real things*. From all which I conclude, *there is a mind which affects me every moment with all the sensible impressions I perceive*. And from the variety, order, and manner of these, I conclude the Author of them to be *wise, powerful, and good, beyond comprehension*. Mark it well; I do not say, I see things by perceiving that which represents them in the intelligible substance of God. This I do not understand; but I say, the things by me perceived are known by the understanding, and produced by the will, of an infinite spirit. And is not all this most plain and evident? Is there any more in it, than what a little observation of our own minds, and that which passes in them not only enableth us to conceive, but also obligeth us to acknowledge?

HYLAS. I think I understand you very clearly; and own the proof you give of a Deity seems no less evident, than it is surprising. But allowing that God is the Supreme and Universal Cause of all things, yet may not there be still a third nature besides spirits and ideas? May we not admit a subordinate and limited cause of our ideas? In a word, may there not for all that be *matter?*

PHILONOUS. How often must I inculcate the same thing? You allow the things immediately perceived by sense to exist no where without the mind: but there is nothing perceived by sense, which is not perceived immediately: therefore there is nothing sensible that exists without the mind. The matter therefore which you still insist on, is something intelligible, I suppose; something that may be discovered by reason, and not by sense.

HYLAS. You are in the right.

PHILONOUS. Pray let me know what reasoning your belief of matter is grounded on; and what this matter is in your present sense of it.

HYLAS. I find myself affected with various ideas, whereof I know I am not the cause; neither are they the cause of themselves, or of one another, or capable of subsisting by themselves, as being altogether inactive, fleeting, dependent beings. They have therefore some cause distinct from me and them: of which I pretend to know no more, than that it is *the cause of my ideas.* And this things, whatever it be, I call matter.

PHILONOUS. Tell me, Hylas, hath every one a liberty to change the current proper signification annexed to a common name in any language? For example, suppose a traveller should tell you, that in a certain country men might pass unhurt through the fire; and, upon explaining himself, you found he meant by the word *fire* that which others call *water:* or if he should assert there are trees which walk upon two legs, meaning men by the term *trees.* Would you think this reasonable?

HYLAS. No; I should think it very absurd. Common custom is the standard of propriety in language. And for any man to affect speaking improperly, is to pervert the use of speech, and can never serve to a better purpose, than to protract and multiply disputes where there is no difference in opinion.

PHILONOUS. And doth not *matter,* in the common current acceptation of the word, signify an extended, solid, moveable, unthinking, inactive substance?

HYLAS. It doth?

PHILONOUS. And hath it not been made evident, that no such substance can possibly exist? And though it should be allowed to exist, yet how can that which is *inactive* be a *cause;* or that which is *unthinking* be a *cause of thought?* You may indeed, if you please, annex to the word *matter* a contrary meaning to what is vulgarly received; and tell me you understand by it an unextended, thinking, active being, which is the cause of our ideas. But what else is this, than to play with words, and run into that very fault you just now condemned with so much reason? I do by no means find fault with your reasoning, in that you collect a cause from the phenomena: but I deny that the cause deducible by reason can properly be termed *matter.*

HYLAS. There is indeed something in what you say. But I am afraid you do not thoroughly comprehend my meaning. I would by no means be thought to deny that God or an Infinite Spirit is the supreme cause of all things. All I contend for, is, that subordinate to the supreme agent there is a cause of a limited and inferior nature, which concurs in the production of our ideas, not by any act of will or spiritual efficiency, but by that kind of action which belongs to matter, *viz. motion.*

PHILONOUS. I find, you are at every turn relapsing into your old exploded conceit, of a moveable and consequently an extended substance existing without the mind. What! Have you already forgot you were convinced, or are you willing I should repeat what has been said on that head? In truth this is not fair dealing in you, still to suppose the being of that which you have so often acknowledged to have no being. But not to insist farther on what has been so largely handled, I ask whether all your ideas are not perfectly passive and inert, including nothing of action in them?

HYLAS. They are.

PHILONOUS. And are sensible qualities any thing else but ideas?

HYLAS. How often have I acknowledged that they are not?

PHILONOUS. But is not motion a sensible quality?

HYLAS. It is.

PHILONOUS. Consequently it is no action.

HYLAS. I agree with you. And indeed it is very plain, that when I stir my finger, it remains passive; but my will which produced the motion, is active.

PHILONOUS. Now I desire to know in the first place, whether motion being allowed to be no action, you can conceive any action besides volition: and in the second place, whether to say something and conceive nothing be not to talk nonsense: and lastly, whether having considered the premises, you do not perceive that to suppose any efficient or active cause of our ideas, other than *spirit,* is highly absurd and unreasonable?

HYLAS. I give up the point entirely. But though matter may not be a cause, yet what hinders its being an *instrument* subservient to the supreme agent in the production of our ideas?

PHILONOUS. An instrument, say you; pray what may be the figure, springs, wheels, and motions of that instrument?

HYLAS. Those I pretend to determine nothing of, both the substance and its qualities being entirely unknown to me.

PHILONOUS. What? You are then of opinion, it is made up of unknown parts, that it hath unknown motions, and an unknown shape.

HYLAS. I do not believe it hath any figure or motion at all, being already convinced, that no sensible qualities can exist in an unperceiving substance.

PHILONOUS. But what notion is it possible to frame of an instrument void of all sensible qualities, even extension itself?

HYLAS. I do not pretend to have any notion of it.

PHILONOUS. And what reason have you to think, this unknown, this inconceivable somewhat doth exist? Is it that you imagine God cannot act as well without it, or that you find by experience the use of some such thing, when you form ideas in your own mind?

HYLAS. You are always teasing me for reasons of my belief. Pray, what reasons have you not to believe it?

PHILONOUS. It is to me a sufficient reason not to believe the existence of any thing, if I see no reason for believing it. But not to insist on reasons for believing, you will not so much as let me know what it is you would have me believe, since you say you have no manner of notion of it. After all, let me entreat you to consider whether it be like a philosopher, or even like a man of common sense, to pretend to believe you know not what, and you know not why.

HYLAS. Hold, Philonous. When I tell you matter is an *instrument,* I do not mean altogether nothing. It is true, I know not the particular kind of instrument; but however I have some notion of *instrument in general,* which I apply to it.

PHILONOUS. But what if it should prove that there is something, even in the most general notion of *instrument,* as taken in a distinct sense from *cause,* which makes the use of it inconsistent with the divine attributes?

HYLAS. Make that appear, and I shall give up the point.

PHILONOUS. What mean you by the general nature or notion of *instrument?*

HYLAS. That which is common to all particular instruments, composeth the general notion.

PHILONOUS. Is it not common to all instruments, that they are applied to the doing those things only, which cannot be performed by the mere act of our wills? Thus for instance, I never use an instrument to move my finger, because it is done by a volition. But I should use one, if I were to remove part of a rock, or tear up a tree by the roots. Are you of the same mind? Or can you shew any example where an instrument is made use of in producing an effect immediately depending on the will of the agent?

HYLAS. I own, I cannot.

PHILONOUS. How therefore can you suppose, that an all-perfect spirit, on whose will all things have an absolute and immediate dependence, should need an instrument in his operations, or not needing it make use of it? Thus it seems to me that you are obliged to own the use of a lifeless inactive instrument, to be incompatible with the infinite perfection of God; that is, by your own confession, to give up the point.

HYLAS. It doth not readily occur what I can answer you.

PHILONOUS. But methinks you should be ready to own the truth, when it hath been fairly proved to you. We indeed, who are beings of finite powers, are forced to make use of instruments. And the use of an instrument sheweth the agent to be limited by rules of another's prescription, and that he cannot obtain his end, but in such a way and by such conditions. Whence it seems a clear consequence, that the supreme unlimited agent useth no tool or instrument at all. The will of an omnipotent spirit is no sooner exerted than executed, without the application of means, which, if they are employed by inferior agents, it is not upon account of any real efficacy that is in them, or necessary aptitude to produce any effect, but merely in compliance with the laws of Nature, or those conditions prescribed to them by the first cause, who is himself above all limitation or prescription whatsoever.

HYLAS. I will no longer maintain that matter is an instrument. However, I would not be understood to give up its existence neither; since, notwithstanding what hath been said, it may still be an *occasion*.

PHILONOUS. How many shapes is your matter to take? Or how often must it be proved not to exist, before you are content to part with it? But to say no more of this (though by all the laws of disputation I may justly blame you for so frequently changing the signification of the principal term) I would fain know what you mean by affirming that matter is an occasion, having already denied it to be a cause. And when you have shewn in what sense you understand *occasion,* pray in the next place be pleased to shew me what reason induceth you to believe there is such an occasion of our ideas.

HYLAS. As to the first point: by *occasion* I mean an inactive unthinking being, at the presence whereof God excites ideas in our minds.

PHILONOUS. And what may be the nature of that inactive unthinking being?

HYLAS. I know nothing of its nature.

PHILONOUS. Proceed then to the second point, and assign some reason why we should allow an existence to this inactive, unthinking, unknown thing.

HYLAS. When we see ideas produced in our minds after an orderly and constant manner, it is natural to think they have some fixed and regular occasions, at the presence of which they are excited.

PHILONOUS. You acknowledge then God alone to be the cause of our ideas, and that he causes them at the presence of those occasions.

HYLAS. That is my opinion.

PHILONOUS. Those things which you say are present to God, without doubt He perceives.

HYLAS. Certainly; otherwise they could not be to Him an occasion of acting.

PHILONOUS. Not to insist now on your making sense of this hypothesis, or answering all the puzzling questions and difficulties it is liable to: I only ask whether the order and regularity observable in the series of our ideas, or the course of Nature, be not sufficiently accounted for by the wisdom and power of God; and whether it doth not derogate from those attributes, to suppose He is influenced, directed, or put in mind, when and what He is to act, by any unthinking substance. And lastly whether, in case I granted all you contend for, it would make any thing to your purpose, it not being easy to conceive how the external or absolute existence of an unthinking substance, distinct from its being perceived, can be inferred from my allowing that there are certain things perceived by the mind of God, which are to Him the occasion of producing ideas in us.

HYLAS. I am perfectly at a loss what to think, this notion of *occasion* seeming now altogether as groundless as the rest.

PHILONOUS. Do you not at length perceive, that in all these different acceptations of *matter,* you have been only supposing you know not what, for no manner of reason, and to no kind of use?

HYLAS. I freely own my self less fond of my notions, since they have been so accurately examined. But still, methinks I have some confused perception that there is such a thing as *matter*.

PHILONOUS. Either you perceive the being of matter immediately, or mediately. If immediately, pray inform me by which of the senses you perceive it. If mediately, let me know by what reasoning it is inferred from those things which you perceive immediately. So much for the perception. Then for the matter it self, I ask whether it is object, *substratum,* cause, instrument, or occasion? You have already pleaded for each of these, shifting your notions, and making matter to appear sometimes in one shape, then in another. And what you have offered hath been disapproved and rejected by your self. If you have anything new to advance, I would gladly hear it.

HYLAS. I think I have already offered all I had to say on those heads. I am at a loss what more to urge.

PHILONOUS. And yet you are loth to part with your old prejudice. But to make you quit it more easily, I desire that, beside what has been hitherto suggested, you will farther consider whether, upon supposition that matter exists, you can possibly conceive how you should be affected by it? Or supposing it did not exist, whether it be not evident you might for all that be affected with the same ideas you now are, and consequently have the very same reasons to believe its existence that you now can have?

HYLAS. I acknowledge it is possible we might perceive all things just as we do now, though there was no matter in the world; neither can I conceive, if there be matter, how it should produce any idea in our minds. And I do farther grant, you have entirely satisfied me, that it is impossible there should be such a thing as matter in any of the foregoing acceptations. But still I cannot help supposing that there is *matter* in some sense or other. What that is I do not indeed pretend to determine.

PHILONOUS. I do not expect you should define exactly the nature of that unknown being. Only be pleased to tell me, whether it is a substance: and if so, whether you can suppose a substance without accidents; or in case you suppose it to have accidents or qualities, I desire you will let me know what those qualities are, at least what is meant by matter's supporting them.

HYLAS. We have already argued on those points. I have no more to say to them. But to prevent any farther questions, let me tell you, I at present understand by *matter* neither substance nor accident, thinking nor extended being, neither cause, instrument, nor occasion, but something entirely unknown, distinct from all these.

PHILONOUS. It seems then you include in your present notion of matter, nothing but the general abstract idea of *entity*.

HYLAS. Nothing else, save only that I superadd to this general idea the negation of all those particular things, qualities, or ideas that I perceive, imagine, or in any wise apprehend.

PHILONOUS. Pray where do you suppose this unknown matter to exist?

HYLAS. Oh Philonous! now you think you have entangled me; for if I say it exists in place, then you will infer that it exists in the mind, since it is agreed, that place or extension exists only in the mind: but I am not ashamed to own my ignorance. I know not where it exists; only I am sure it exists not in place. There is a negative answer for you: and you must expect no other to all the questions you put for the future about matter.

PHILONOUS. Since you will not tell me where it exists, be pleased to inform me after what manner you suppose it to exist, or what you mean by its *existence.*

HYLAS. It neither thinks nor acts, neither perceives, nor is perceived.

PHILONOUS. But what is there positive in your abstracted notion of its existence?

HYLAS. Upon a nice observation, I do not find I have any positive notion or meaning at all. I tell you again I am not ashamed to own my ignorance. I know not what is meant by its *existence,* or how it exists.

PHILONOUS. Continue, good Hylas, to act the same ingenuous part, and tell me sincerely whether you can frame a distinct idea of entity in general, prescinded from and exclusive of all thinking and corporeal beings, all particular things whatsoever.

HYLAS. Hold, let me think a little—I profess, Philonous, I do not find that I can. At first glance methought I had some dilute and airy notion of pure entity in abstract; but upon closer attention it hath quite vanished out of sight. The more I think on it, the more am I confirmed in my prudent resolution of giving none but negative answers, and not pretending to the least degree of any positive knowledge or conception of matter, its *where,* its *how,* its *entity,* or any thing belonging to it.

PHILONOUS. When therefore you speak of the existence of matter, you have not any notion in your mind.

HYLAS. None at all.

PHILONOUS. Pray tell me if the case stands not thus: at first, from a belief of material substance you would have it that the immediate objects existed without the mind; then that their archetypes; then causes; next instruments; then occasions: lastly, *something in general,* which being interpreted proves *nothing.* So matter comes to nothing. What think you, Hylas, is not this a fair summary of your whole proceeding?

HYLAS. Be that as it will, yet I still insist upon it, that our not being able to conceive a thing, is no argument against its existence.

PHILONOUS. That from a cause, effect, operation, sign, or other circumstance, there may reasonably be inferred the existence of a thing not immediately perceived, and that it were absurd for any man to argue against the existence of that thing, from his having no direct and positive notion of it, I freely own. But where there is nothing of all this; where neither reason nor revelation induce us to believe the existence of a thing; where we have not even a relative notion of it; where an abstraction is made from perceiving and being perceived, from spirit and idea: lastly, where there is not so much as the most inadequate or faint idea pretended to: I will not indeed thence conclude against the reality of any notion or existence of any thing: but my inference shall be, that you mean nothing at all: that you employ words to no manner of purpose, without any design or signification whatsoever. And I leave it to you to consider how mere jargon should be treated.

HYLAS. To deal frankly with you, Philonous, your arguments seem in themselves unanswerable, but they have not so great an effect on me as to produce that entire conviction, that hearty acquiescence which attends demonstration. I find myself still relapsing into an obscure surmise of I know not what, *matter*.

PHILONOUS. But are you not sensible, Hylas, that two things must concur to take away all scruple, and work a plenary assent in the mind? Let a visible object be set in never so clear a light, yet if there is any imperfection in the sight, or if the eye is not directed towards it, it will not be distinctly seen. And though a demonstration be never so well grounded and fairly proposed, yet if there is withal a stain of prejudice, or a wrong bias on the understanding, can it be expected on a sudden to perceive clearly and adhere firmly to the truth? No, there is need of time and pains: the attention must be awakened and detained by a frequent repetition of the same thing placed oft in the same, oft in different lights. I have said it already, and find I must still repeat and inculcate, that it is an unaccountable licence you take in pretending to maintain you know not what, for you know not what reason, to you know not what purpose? Can this be paralleled in any art or science, any sect or profession of men? Or is there any thing so barefacedly groundless and unreasonable to be met with even in the lowest of common conversation? But perhaps you will still say, matter may exist, though at the same time you neither know what is meant by *matter,* or by its *existence.* This indeed is surprising, and the more so because it is altogether voluntary, you not being led to it by any one reason; for I challenge you to shew me that thing in Nature which needs matter to explain or account for it.

HYLAS. The reality of things cannot be maintained without supposing the existence of matter. And is not this, think you, a good reason why I should be earnest in its defence?

PHILONOUS. The reality of things! What things, sensible or intelligible?

HYLAS. Sensible things.

PHILONOUS. My glove, for example?

HYLAS. That or any other thing perceived by the senses.

PHILONOUS. But to fix on some particular thing; is it not a sufficient evidence to me of the existence of this *glove,* that I see it, and feel it, and wear it? Or if this will not do, how is it possible I should be assured of the reality of this thing, which I actually see in this place, by supposing that some unknown thing which I never did or can see, exists after an unknown manner, in an unknown place, or in no place at all? How can the supposed reality of that which is intangible, be a proof that any thing tangible really exists? or of that which is invisible, that any visible thing, or in general of any thing which is imperceptible, that a perceptible exists? Do but explain this, and I shall think nothing too hard for you.

HYLAS. Upon the whole, I am content to own the existence of matter is highly improbable; but the direct and absolute impossibility of it does not appear to me.

PHILONOUS. But granting matter to be possible, yet upon that account merely it can have no more claim to existence, than a golden mountain or a centaur.

HYLAS. I acknowledge it; but still you do not deny it is possible; and that which is possible, for aught you know, may actually exist.

PHILONOUS. I deny it to be possible; and have, if I mistake not, evidently proved from your own concessions that it is not. In the common sense of the word *matter,* is there any more implied, than an extended, solid, figured, moveable substance existing without the mind? And have not you acknowledged over and over, that you have seen evident reason for denying the possibility of such a substance?

HYLAS. True, but that is only one sense of the term *matter*.

PHILONOUS. But is it not the only proper genuine received sense? And if matter in such a sense be proved impossible, may it not be thought with good grounds absolutely impossible? Else how could any thing be proved impossible? Or indeed how could there be any proof at all one way or other, to a man who takes the liberty to unsettle and change the common signification of words?

HYLAS. I thought philosophers might be allowed to speak more accurately than the vulgar, and were not always confined to the common acceptation of a term.

PHILONOUS. But this now mentioned is the common received sense among philosophers themselves. But not to insist on that, have you not been allowed to take matter in what sense you pleased? And have you not used this privilege in the utmost extent, sometimes entirely changing, at others leaving out or putting into the definition of it whatever for the present best served your design, contrary to all the known rules of reason and logic? And hath not this shifting unfair method of yours spun out our dispute to an unnecessary length; matter having been particularly examined, and by your own confession refuted in each of those senses? And can any more be required to prove the absolute impossibility of a thing, than the proving it impossible in every particular sense, that either you or any one else understands it in?

HYLAS. But I am not so thoroughly satisfied that you have proved the impossibility of matter in the last most obscure abstracted and indefinite sense.

PHILONOUS. When is a thing shewn to be impossible?

HYLAS. When a repugnancy is demonstrated between the ideas comprehended in its definition.

PHILONOUS. But where there are no ideas, there no repugnancy can be demonstrated between ideas.

HYLAS. I agree with you.

PHILONOUS. Now in that which you call the obscure indefinite sense of the word *matter,* it is plain, by your own confession, there was included no idea at all, no sense except an unknown sense, which is the same thing as none. You are not therefore to expect I should prove a repugnancy between ideas where there are no ideas; or the impossibility of matter taken in an *unknown* sense, that is no sense at all. My business was only to shew, you meant *nothing;* and this you were brought to own. So that in all your various senses, you have been shewed either to mean nothing at all, or if any thing, an absurdity. And if this be not sufficient to prove the impossibility of a thing, I desire you will let me know what is.

HYLAS. I acknowledge you have proved that matter is impossible; nor do I see what more can be said in defence of it. But at the same time that I give up this, I suspect all my other notions. For surely none could be more seemingly evident than this once was: and yet it now seems as false and absurd as ever it did true before. But I think we have discussed the point sufficiently for the present. The remaining part of the day I would willingly spend, in running over in my thoughts the several heads of this morning's conversation, and to-morrow shall be glad to meet you here again about the same time.

PHILONOUS. I will not fail to attend you.

4

Idealism

BERTRAND RUSSELL

The word 'idealism' is used by different philosophers in somewhat different senses. We shall understand by it the doctrine that whatever exists, or at any rate whatever can be known to exist, must be in some sense mental. This doctrine, which is very widely held among philosophers, has several forms, and is advocated on several different grounds. The doctrine is so widely held, and so interesting in itself, that even the briefest survey of philosophy must give some account of it.

Those who are unaccustomed to philosophical speculation may be inclined to dismiss such a doctrine as obviously absurd. There is no doubt that common sense regards tables and chairs and the sun and moon and material objects generally as something radically different from minds and the contents of minds, and as having an existence which might continue if minds ceased. We think of matter as having existed long before there were any minds, and it is hard to think of it as a mere product of mental activity. But whether true or false, idealism is not to be dismissed as obviously absurd.

We have seen that, even if physical objects do have an independent existence, they must differ very widely from sense-data, and can only have a *correspondence* with sense-data, in the same sort of way in which a catalogue has a correspondence with the things catalogued. Hence common sense leaves us completely in the dark as to the true intrinsic nature of physical objects, and if there were good reason to regard them as mental, we could not legitimately reject this opinion merely because it strikes us as strange. The truth about physical objects *must* be strange. It *may* be unattainable, but if any philosopher believes that he has attained it, the fact that what he offers as the truth is strange ought not to be made a ground of objection to his opinion.

The grounds on which idealism is advocated are generally grounds derived from the theory

Source: Pp. 37–45 from *The Problems of Philosophy* by Bertrand Russell (1912). Reprinted by permission of Oxford University Press.

of knowledge, that is to say, from a discussion of the conditions which things must satisfy in order that we may be able to know them. The first serious attempt to establish idealism on such grounds was that of Bishop Berkeley. He proved first, by arguments which were largely valid, that our sense-data cannot be supposed to have an existence independent of us, but must be, in part at least, 'in' the mind, in the sense that their existence would not continue if there were no seeing or hearing or touching or smelling or tasting. So far, his contention was almost certainly valid, even if some of his arguments were not so. But he went on to argue that sense-data were the only things of whose existence our perceptions could assure us, and that to be known is to be 'in' a mind, and therefore to be mental. Hence he concluded that nothing can ever be known except what is in some mind, and that whatever is known without being in my mind must be in some other mind.

In order to understand his argument, it is necessary to understand his use of the word 'idea'. He gives the name 'idea' to anything which is *immediately* known, as, for example, sense-data are known. Thus a particular colour which we see is an idea; so is a voice which we hear, and so on. But the term is not wholly confined to sense-data. There will also be things remembered or imagined, for with such things also we have immediate acquaintance at the moment of remembering or imagining. All such immediate data he calls 'ideas'.

He then proceeds to consider common objects, such as a tree, for instance. He shows that all we know immediately when we 'perceive' the tree consists of ideas in his sense of the word, and he argues that there is not the slightest ground for supposing that there is anything real about the tree except what is perceived. Its being, he says, consists in being perceived: in the Latin of the schoolmen its '*esse*' is '*percipi*'. He fully admits that the tree must continue to exist even when we shut our eyes or when no human being is near it. But this continued existence, he says, is due to the fact that God continues to perceive it; the 'real' tree, which corresponds to what we called the physical object, consists of ideas in the mind of God, ideas more or less like those we have when we see the tree, but differing in the fact that they are permanent in God's mind so long as the tree continues to exist. All our perceptions, according to him, consist in a partial participation in God's perceptions, and it is because of this participation that different people see more or less the same tree. Thus apart from minds and their ideas there is nothing in the world, nor is it possible that anything else should ever be known, since whatever is known is necessarily an idea.

There are in this argument a good many fallacies which have been important in the history of philosophy, and which it will be as well to bring to light. In the first place, there is a confusion engendered by the use of the word 'idea'. We think of an idea as essentially something *in* somebody's mind, and thus when we are told that a tree consists entirely of ideas, it is natural to suppose that, if so, the tree must be entirely in minds. But the notion of being 'in' the mind is ambiguous. We speak of bearing a person in mind, not meaning that the person is in our minds, but that a thought of him is in our minds. When a man says that some business he had to arrange went clean out of his mind, he does not mean to imply that the business itself was ever in his mind, but only that a thought of the business was formerly in his mind, but afterwards ceased to be in his mind. And so when Berkeley says that the tree must be in our minds if we can know it, all that he really has a right to say is that a thought of the tree must be in our minds. To argue that the tree itself must be in our minds is like arguing that a person whom we bear in mind is himself in our minds. This confusion may seem too gross to have been really committed by any competent philosopher, but various attendant circumstances rendered it possible. In order to see how it was possible, we must go more deeply into the question as to the nature of ideas.

Before taking up the general question of the nature of ideas, we must disentangle two entirely separate questions which arise concerning sense-data and physical objects. We saw that, for various reasons of detail, Berkeley was right in treating the sense-data which constitute our perception of the tree as more or less subjective, in the sense that they depend upon us as much as upon the tree, and would not exist if the tree were not being perceived. But this is an entirely different point from the one by which Berkeley seeks to prove that whatever can be immediately known *must* be in a mind. For this purpose arguments of detail as to the dependence of sense-data upon us are useless. It is necessary to prove, generally, that by being known, things are shown to be mental. This is what Berkeley believes himself to have done. It is this question, and not our previous question as to the difference between sense-data and the physical object, that must now concern us.

Taking the word 'idea' in Berkeley's sense, there are two quite distinct things to be considered whenever an idea is before the mind. There is on the one hand the thing of which we are aware—say the colour of my table—and on the other hand the actual awareness itself, the mental act of apprehending the thing. The mental act is undoubtedly mental, but is there any reason to suppose that the thing apprehended is in any sense mental? Our previous arguments concerning the colour did not prove it to be mental; they only proved that its existence depends upon the relation of our sense organs to the physical object—in our case, the table. That is to say, they proved that a certain colour will exist, in a certain light, if a normal eye is placed at a certain point relatively to the table. They did not prove that the colour is in the mind of the percipient.

Berkeley's view, that obviously the colour *must* be in the mind, seems to depend for its plausibility upon confusing the thing apprehended with the act of apprehension. Either of these might be called an 'idea'; probably either would have been called an idea by Berkeley. The act is undoubtedly in the mind; hence, when we are thinking of the act, we readily assent to the view that ideas must be in the mind. Then, forgetting that this was only true when ideas were taken as acts of apprehension, we transfer the proposition that 'ideas are in the mind' to ideas in the other sense, i.e. to the things apprehended by our acts of apprehension. Thus, by an unconscious equivocation, we arrive at the conclusion that whatever we can apprehend must be in our minds. This seems to be the true analysis of Berkeley's argument, and the ultimate fallacy upon which it rests.

This question of the distinction between act and object in our apprehending of things is vitally important, since our whole power of acquiring knowledge is bound up with it. The faculty of being acquainted with things other than itself is the main characteristic of a mind. Acquaintance with objects essentially consists in a relation between the mind and something other than the mind; it is this that constitutes the mind's power of knowing things. If we say that the things known must be in the mind, we are either unduly limiting the mind's power of knowing, or we are uttering a mere tautology. We are uttering a mere tautology if we mean by '*in* the mind' the same as by '*before* the mind', i.e. if we mean merely being apprehended by the mind. But if we mean this, we shall have to admit that what, *in this sense,* is in the mind, may nevertheless be not mental. Thus when we realize the nature of knowledge, Berkeley's argument is seen to be wrong in substance as well as in form, and his grounds for supposing that 'ideas'—i.e. the objects apprehended—must be mental, are found to have no validity whatever. Hence his grounds in favour of idealism may be dismissed. It remains to see whether there are any other grounds.

It is often said, as though it were a self-evident truism, that we cannot know that anything exists which we do not know. It is inferred that whatever can in any way be relevant to our experience must be at least capable of being known by us; whence it follows that if matter were essentially something with which we could not become acquainted, matter would be something which we could not know to exist, and which could have for us no importance whatever. It is generally also implied, for reasons which remain obscure, that what can have no importance for us cannot be real, and that therefore matter, if it is not composed of minds or of mental ideas, is impossible and a mere chimaera.

To go into this argument fully at our present stage would be impossible, since it raises points requiring a considerable preliminary discussion; but certain reasons for rejecting the argument may be noticed at once. To begin at the end: there is no reason why what cannot have any *practical* importance for us should not be real. It is true that, if *theoretical* importance is included, everything real is of *some* importance to us, since, as persons desirous of knowing the truth about the universe, we have some interest in everything that the universe contains. But if this sort of interest is included, it is not the case that matter has no importance for us, provided it exists, even if we cannot know that it exists. We can, obviously, suspect that it may exist, and wonder whether it does; hence it is connected with our desire for knowledge, and has the importance of either satisfying or thwarting this desire.

Again, it is by no means a truism, and is in fact false, that we cannot know that anything exists which we do not know. The word 'know' is here used in two different senses. (1) In its first use it is applicable to the sort of knowledge which is opposed to error, the sense in which what we know is *true,* the sense which applies to our beliefs and convictions, i.e. to what are called *judgements*. In this sense of the word we know *that* something is the case. This sort of knowledge may be described as knowledge of *truths*. (2) In the second use of the word 'know' above, the word applies to our knowledge of *things,* which we may call *acquaintance*. This is the sense in which we know sense-data. (The distinction involved is roughly that between *savoir* and *connaître* in French, or between *wissen* and *kennen* in German.)

Thus the statement which seemed like a truism becomes, when re-stated, the following: 'We can never truly judge that something with which we are not acquainted exists.' This is by no means a truism, but on the contrary a palpable falsehood. I have not the honour to be acquainted with the Emperor of China, but I truly judge that he exists. It may be said, of course, that I judge this because of other people's acquaintance with him. This, however, would be an irrelevant retort, since, if the principle were true, I could not know that any one else is acquainted with him. But further: there is no reason why I should not know of the existence of something with which *nobody* is acquainted. This point is important, and demands elucidation.

If I am acquainted with a thing which exists, my acquaintance gives me the knowledge that it exists. But it is not true that, conversely, whenever I can know that a thing of a certain sort exists, I or some one else must be acquainted with the thing. What happens, in cases where I have true judgement without acquaintance, is that the thing is known to me by *description,* and that, in virtue of some general principle, the existence of a thing answering to this description can be inferred from the existence of something with which I am acquainted. In order to understand this point fully, it will be well first to deal with the difference between knowledge by acquaintance and knowledge by description, and then to consider what knowledge of general principles, if any, has the same kind of certainty as our knowledge of the existence of our own experiences. These subjects will be dealt with in the following chapters.

 5 

Sense and Sensibilia

J. L. AUSTIN

But now, provoked largely by the frequent and unexamined occurrences of 'real', 'really', 'real shape', &c., in the arguments we have just been considering, I want to take a closer look at this little word 'real'. I propose, if you like, to discuss the Nature of Reality—a genuinely important topic, though in general I don't much like making this claim.

There are two things, first of all, which it is immensely important to understand here.

1. 'Real' is an absolutely *normal* word, with nothing new-fangled or technical or highly specialized about it. It is, that is to say, already firmly established in, and very frequently used in, the ordinary language we all use every day. Thus *in this sense* it is a word which has a fixed meaning, and so can't, any more than can any other word which is firmly established, be fooled around with *ad lib.* Philosophers often seem to think that they can just 'assign' any meaning whatever to any word; and so no doubt, in an absolutely trivial sense, they can (like Humpty-Dumpty). There are some expressions, of course, 'material thing' for example, which only philosophers use, and in such cases they can, within reason, please themselves; but most words are *in fact* used in a particular way already, and this fact can't be just disregarded. (For example, some meanings that have been assigned to 'know' and 'certain' have made it seem outrageous that we should use these terms as we actually do; but what this shows is that the meanings assigned by some philosophers are *wrong*.) Certainly, when we have discovered how a word is in fact used, that may not be the end of the matter; there is certainly no reason why, in general, things should be left exactly as we find them; we may wish to tidy the situation up a bit, revise the map here and there, draw the boundaries and distinctions rather differently. But still, it is advisable always to bear in mind

Source: Pp. 62–77 from *Sense and Sensibilia* by J. L. Austin, edited by G. J. Warnock (1963). Reprinted by permission of Oxford University Press.

(*a*) that the distinctions embodied in our vast and, for the most part, relatively ancient stock of ordinary words are neither few nor always very obvious, and almost never just arbitrary; (*b*) that in any case, before indulging in any tampering on our own account, we need to find out what it is that we have to deal with; and (*c*) that tampering with words in what we take to be one little corner of the field is always *liable* to have unforeseen repercussions in the adjoining territory. Tampering, in fact, is not so easy as is often supposed, is not justified or needed so often as is often supposed, and is often thought to be necessary just because what we've got already has been misrepresented. And we must always be particularly wary of the philosophical habit of dismissing some (if not all) the ordinary uses of a word as 'unimportant', a habit which makes distortion practically unavoidable. For instance, if we are going to talk about 'real', we must not dismiss as beneath contempt such humble but familiar expressions as 'not real cream'; this may save us from saying, for example, or seeming to say that what is not real cream must be a fleeting product of our cerebral processes.

2. The other immensely important point to grasp is that 'real' is *not* a normal word at all, but highly exceptional; exceptional in this respect that, unlike 'yellow' or 'horse' or 'walk', it does not have one single, specifiable, always-the-same *meaning*. (Even Aristotle saw through this idea.) *Nor* does it have a large number of different meanings—it is not *ambiguous,* even 'systematically'. Now words of this sort have been responsible for a great deal of perplexity. Consider the expressions 'cricket ball', 'cricket bat', 'cricket pavilion', 'cricket weather'. If someone did not know about cricket and were obsessed with the use of such 'normal' words as 'yellow', he might gaze at the ball, the bat, the building, the weather, trying to detect the 'common quality' which (he assumes) is attributed to these things by the prefix 'cricket'. But no such quality meets his eye; and so perhaps he concludes that 'cricket' must designate a *non-natural* quality, a quality to be detected not in any ordinary way but by *intuition*. If this story strikes you as too absurd, remember what philosophers have said about the word 'good'; and reflect that many philosophers, failing to detect any ordinary quality common to real ducks, real cream, and real progress, have decided that Reality must be an *a priori* concept apprehended by reason alone.

Let us begin, then, with a preliminary, no doubt rather haphazard, survey of some of the complexities in the use of 'real'. Consider, for instance, a case which at first sight one might think was pretty straightforward—the case of 'real colour'. What is meant by the 'real' colour of a thing? Well, one may say with some confidence, that's easy enough: the *real* colour of the thing is the colour that it looks to a normal observer in conditions of normal or standard illumination; and to find out what a thing's real colour is, we just need to be normal and to observe it in those conditions.

But suppose (*a*) that I remark to you of a third party, 'That isn't the real colour of her hair.' Do I mean by this that, if you were to observe her in conditions of standard illumination, you would find that her hair did not look that colour? Plainly not—the conditions of illumination may be standard already. I mean, of course, that her hair has been *dyed,* and normal illumination just doesn't come into it at all. Or suppose that you are looking at a ball of wool in a shop, and I say, 'That's not its real colour.' Here I *may* mean that it won't look that colour in ordinary daylight; but I *may* mean that wool isn't that colour before it's dyed. As so often, you can't tell what I mean just from the words that I use; it makes a difference, for instance, whether the thing under discussion is or is not of a type which is *customarily* dyed.

Suppose (*b*) that there is a species of fish which looks vividly multi-coloured, slightly glowing perhaps, at a depth of a thousand feet. I ask you what its real colour is. So you catch a specimen and lay it out on deck, making sure the condition of the light is just about normal, and you find that it looks a muddy sort of greyish white. Well, is *that* its real colour? It's clear enough at any rate that we don't have to say so. In fact, is there any right answer in such a case?

Compare: 'What is the real taste of saccharine?' We dissolve a tablet in a cup of tea and we find that it makes the tea taste sweet; we then take a tablet neat, and we find that it tastes bitter. Is it *really* bitter, or *really* sweet?

(*c*) What is the real colour of the sky? Of the sun? Of the moon? Of a chameleon? We say that the sun in the evening sometimes looks red—well, what colour is it *really?* (What are the 'conditions of standard illumination' for the sun?)

(*d*) Consider a *pointilliste* painting of a meadow, say; if the general effect is of green, the painting may be composed of predominantly blue and yellow dots. What is the real colour of the painting?

(*e*) What is the real colour of an after-image? The trouble with this one is that we have no idea what an alternative to its 'real colour' might be. Its apparent colour, the colour that it looks, the colour that it appears to be?—but these phrases have no application here. (You might ask me, 'What colour is it really?' if you suspected that I had lied in telling you its colour. But 'What colour is it really?' is not quite the same as 'What is its real colour?')

Or consider 'real shape' for a moment. This notion cropped up, you may remember, seeming quite unproblematic, when we were considering the coin which was said to 'look elliptical' from some points of view; it had a real shape, we insisted, which remained unchanged. But coins in fact are rather special cases. For one thing their outlines are well defined and very highly stable, and for another they have a *known* and a *nameable* shape. But there are plenty of things of which this is not true. What is the real shape of a cloud? And if it be objected, as I dare say it could be, that a cloud is not a 'material thing' and so not the kind of thing which has to have a real shape, consider this case: what is the real shape of a cat? Does its real shape change whenever it moves? If not, in what posture *is* its real shape on display? Furthermore, is its real shape such as to be fairly smooth-outlined, or must it be finely enough serrated to take account of each hair? It is pretty obvious that there is *no* answer to these questions—no rules according to which, no procedure by which, answers are to be determined. Of course, there are plenty of shapes which the cat definitely is not—cylindrical, for instance. But only a desperate man would toy with the idea of ascertaining the cat's real shape 'by elimination'.

Contrast this with cases in which we *do* know how to proceed: 'Are those real diamonds?', 'Is that a real duck?' Items of jewellery that more or less closely resemble diamonds may not be real diamonds because they are paste or glass; that may not be a real duck because it is a decoy, or a toy duck, or a species of goose closely resembling a duck, or because I am having a hallucination. These are all of course quite different cases. And notice in particular (*a*) that, in most of them 'observation by a normal observer in standard conditions' is completely irrelevant; (*b*) that something which is not a real duck is not a *non-existent* duck, or indeed a non-existent anything; and (*c*) that something existent, e.g. a toy, may perfectly well not be real, e.g. not a real duck.[1]

Perhaps by now we have said enough to establish that there is more in the use of 'real' than meets the cursory eye; it has many and diverse uses in many diverse contexts. We must next, then, try to tidy things up a little; and I shall now mention under four headings what might be called the salient features of the use of 'real'—though not *all* these features are equally conspicuous in all its uses.

1. First, 'real' is a word that we may call *substantive-hungry*. Consider:

'These diamonds are real';
'These are real diamonds.'

This pair of sentences looks like, in an obvious grammatical respect, this other pair:

'These diamonds are pink';
'These are pink diamonds'.

But whereas we can *just* say of something 'This is pink', we can't *just* say of something 'This is real'. And it is not very difficult to see why. We can perfectly well say of something that it is pink without knowing, without any reference to, what it *is*. But not so with 'real'. For one and the same object may be both a real *x* and not a real *y*; an object looking rather like a duck may be a real decoy duck (not just a toy) but not a real duck. When it isn't a real duck but a hallucination, it may still be a real hallucination—as opposed, for instance, to a passing quirk of a vivid imagination. That is, we must have an answer to the question 'A real *what?*', if the question 'Real or not?' is to have a definite sense, to get any foothold. And perhaps we should also mention here another point—that the question 'Real or not?' does not always come up, can't always be raised. We *do* raise this question only when, to speak rather roughly, suspicion assails us—in some way or other things may be not what they seem; and we *can* raise this question only if there *is* a way, or ways, in which things may be not what they seem. What alternative is there to being a 'real' after-image?

'Real' is not, of course, the only word we have that is substantive-hungry. Other examples, perhaps better known ones, are 'the same' and 'one.' The same *team* may not be the same *collection of players;* a body of troops may be one *company* and also three *platoons*. Then what about 'good'? We have here a variety of gaps crying out for substantives—'A good *what?*', 'Good *at* what?'—a good book, perhaps, but not a good novel; good at pruning roses, but not good at mending cars.[2]

2. Next, 'real' is what we may call a *trouser-word*. It is usually thought, and I dare say usually rightly thought, that what one might call the affirmative use of a term is basic—that, to understand '*x*', we need to know what it is to be *x*, or to be an *x*, and that knowing this apprises us of what it is *not* to be *x*, not to be an *x*. But with 'real' (as we briefly noted earlier) it is the *negative* use that wears the trousers. That is, a definite sense attaches to the assertion that something is real, a real such-and-such, only in the light of a specific way in which it might be, or might have been, *not* real. 'A real duck' differs from the simple 'a duck' only in that it is used to exclude various ways of being not a real duck—but a dummy, a toy, a picture, a decoy, &c.; and moreover I don't know *just* how to take the assertion that it's a real duck unless I know *just* what, on that particular occasion, the speaker has it in mind to exclude. This, of course, is why the attempt to find a characteristic common to all things that are or could be called 'real' is doomed to failure; the function of 'real' is not to contribute positively to the characterization of anything, but to exclude possible ways of being *not* real—and these ways are both numerous for particular kinds of things, and liable to be quite different for things of different kinds. It is this identity of general function combined with immense diversity in specific applications which gives to the word 'real' the, at first sight, baffling feature of having neither one single 'meaning', nor yet ambiguity, a number of different meanings.

3. Thirdly, 'real' is (like 'good') a *dimension-word*. I mean by this that it is the most general and comprehensive term in a whole group of terms of the same kind, terms that fulfil the same function. Other members of this group, on the affirmative side, are, for example, 'proper', 'genuine', 'live', 'true', 'authentic', 'natural'; and on the negative side, 'artificial', 'fake', 'false', 'bogus', 'makeshift', 'dummy', 'synthetic', 'toy'—and such nouns as 'dream', 'illusion', 'mirage', 'hallucination' belong here as well.[3] It is worth noticing here that, naturally enough, the *less* general terms on the affirmative side have the merit, in many cases, of suggesting

more or less definitely what it is that is being excluded; they tend to pair off, that is, with particular terms on the negative side and thus, so to speak, to narrow the range of possibilities. If I say that I wish the university had a proper theatre, this suggests that it has at present a *makeshift* theatre; pictures are genuine as opposed to *fake,* silk is natural as opposed to *artificial,* ammunition is live as opposed to *dummy,* and so on. In practice, of course, we often get a clue to what it is that is in question from the substantive in the case, since we frequently have a well-founded antecedent idea in what respects the kind of thing mentioned could (and could not) be 'not real'. For instance, if you ask me 'Is this real silk?' I shall tend to supply 'as opposed to artificial', since I already know that silk is the kind of thing which can be very closely simulated by an artificial product. The notion of its being *toy* silk, for instance, will not occur to me.[4]

A large number of questions arises here—which I shall not go into—concerning both the composition of these families of 'reality'-words and 'unreality'-words, and also the distinctions to be drawn between their individual members. Why, for instance, is being a *proper* carving-knife one way of being a real carving-knife, whereas being *pure* cream seems not to be one way of being *real* cream? Or to put it differently: how does the distinction between real cream and synthetic cream differ from the distinction between pure cream and adulterated cream? Is it just that adulterated cream still is, after all, *cream?* And why are false teeth called 'false' rather than, say, 'artificial'? Why are artificial limbs so-called, in *preference* to 'false'? Is it that false teeth, besides doing much the same job as real teeth, look, and are meant to look, *deceptively* like real teeth? Whereas an artificial limb, perhaps, is meant to do the same job, but is neither intended, nor likely, to be *passed off* as a real limb.

Another philosophically notorious dimension-word, which has already been mentioned in another connexion as closely comparable with 'real', is 'good'. 'Good' is the most general of a very large and diverse list of more specific words, which share with it the general function of expressing commendation, but differ among themselves in their aptness to, and implications in, particular contexts. It is a curious point, of which Idealist philosophers used to make much at one time, that 'real' itself, in certain uses, may belong to this family. 'Now this is a *real* carving-knife!' may be one way of saying that this is a good carving-knife.[5] And it is sometimes said of a bad poem, for instance, that it isn't really a poem at all; a certain standard must be reached, as it were, even to *qualify.*

4. Lastly, 'real' also belongs to a large and important family of words that we may call *adjuster-words*—words, that is, by the use of which other words are adjusted to meet the innumerable and unforeseeable demands of the world upon language. The position, considerably oversimplified no doubt, is that at a given time our language contains words that enable us (more or less) to say what we want to say in most situations that (we think) are liable to turn up. But vocabularies are finite; and the variety of possible situations that may confront us is neither finite nor precisely foreseeable. So situations are practically bound to crop up sometimes with which our vocabulary is not already fitted to cope in any tidy, straightforward style. We have the word 'pig', for instance, and a pretty clear idea which animals, among those that we fairly commonly encounter, are and are not to be so called. But one day we come across a new kind of animal, which looks and behaves very much as pigs do, but not *quite* as pigs do; it is somehow different. Well, we might just keep silent, not knowing what to say; we don't want to say positively that it *is* a pig, or that it is *not.* Or we might, if for instance we expected to want to refer to these new creatures pretty often, invent a quite new word for them. But what we could do, and probably would do first of all, is to say, 'It's *like* a pig.' ('Like' is *the* great adjuster-word, or, alternatively put, the main

flexibility-device by whose aid, in spite of the limited scope of our vocabulary, we can always avoid being left completely speechless.) And then, having said of this animal that it's *like* a pig, we may proceed with the remark, 'But it isn't a *real* pig'—or more specifically, and using a term that naturalists favour, 'not a *true* pig'. If we think of words as being shot like arrows at the world, the function of these adjuster-words is to free us from the disability of being able to shoot only straight ahead; by their use on occasion, such words as 'pig' can be, so to speak, brought into connexion with targets lying slightly off the simple, straightforward line on which they are ordinarily aimed. And in this way we gain, besides flexibility, precision; for if I can say, 'Not a real pig, but like a pig', I don't have to tamper with the meaning of 'pig' itself.

But, one might ask, do we *have* to have 'like' to serve this purpose? We have, after all, other flexibility-devices. For instance, I might say that animals of this new species are 'piggish'; I might perhaps call them 'quasi-pigs', or describe them (in the style of vendors of peculiar wines) as 'pig-type' creatures. But these devices, excellent no doubt in their way, can't be regarded as substitutes for 'like', for this reason: they equip us simply with new expressions on the same level as, functioning in the same way as, the word 'pig' itself; and thus, though they may perhaps help us out of our immediate difficulty, they themselves may land us in exactly the same *kind* of difficulty at any time. We have this kind of wine, not real port, but a tolerably close approximation to port, and we call it 'port type'. But then someone produces a new kind of wine, not port exactly, but also not quite the same as what we now call 'port type'. So what are we to say? Is it port-type type? It would be tedious to have to say so, and besides there would clearly be no future in it. But as it is we can say that it is *like* port-type wine (and for that matter rather like port, too); and in saying this we don't saddle ourselves with a *new word,* whose application may itself prove problematic if the vintners spring yet another surprise on us. The word 'like' equips us *generally* to handle the unforeseen, in a way in which new words invented *ad hoc* don't, and can't.

(Why then do we need 'real' as an adjuster-word as well as 'like'? Why exactly do we want to say, sometimes 'It is like a pig', sometimes 'It is not a real pig'? To answer these questions properly would be to go a long way towards making really clear the use, the 'meaning', of 'real'.)[6]

It should be quite clear, then, that there are no criteria to be laid down *in general* for distinguishing the real from the not real. How this is to be done must depend on *what* it is with respect to which the problem arises in particular cases. Furthermore, even for particular kinds of things, there may be many different ways in which the distinction may be made (there is not just *one* way of being 'not a real pig')—this depends on the number and variety of the surprises and dilemmas nature and our fellow men may spring on us, and on the surprises and dilemmas we have been faced with hitherto. And of course, if there is *never* any dilemma or surprise, the question simply doesn't come up; if we had simply never had occasion to distinguish anything as being in any way like a pig but not a *real* pig, then the words 'real pig' themselves would have no application—as perhaps the words 'real after-image' have no application.

Again, the criteria we employ at a given time can't be taken as *final,* not liable to change. Suppose that one day a creature of the kind we now call a cat takes to talking. Well, we say to begin with, I suppose, 'This cat can talk.' But then other cats, not all, take to talking as well; we now have to say that some cats talk, we distinguish between talking and non-talking cats. But again we may, if talking becomes prevalent and the distinction between talking and not talking seems to us to be really important, come to insist that a *real* cat be a creature that can talk.

And this will give us a new case of being 'not a real cat', i.e. being a creature just like a cat except for not talking.

Of course—this may seem perhaps hardly worth saying, but in philosophy it seems it does need to be said—we make a distinction between 'a real *x*' and 'not a real *x*' only if there is a way of telling the difference between what is a real *x* and what is not. A distinction which we are not in fact able to draw is—to put it politely—not worth making.

NOTES

1. 'Exist', of course, is itself extremely tricky. The word is a verb, but it does not describe something that things do all the time, like breathing, only quieter—ticking over, as it were, in a metaphysical sort of way. It is only too easy to start wondering what, then, existing *is*. The Greeks were worse off than we are in this region of discourse—for our different expressions 'to be', 'to exist', and 'real' they made do with the single word εἶναι. We have not their excuse for getting confused on this admittedly confusing topic.
2. In Greek the case of σοφός is of some importance; Aristotle seems to get into difficulties by trying to use σοφία 'absolutely', so to speak, without specification of the field in which σοφία is exercised and shown. Compare on δεινότης too.
3. Of course, not all the uses of all these words are of the kind we are here considering—though it would be wise not to assume, either, that any of their uses are *completely* different, *completely* unconnected.
4. Why not? Because silk can't be 'toy'. Yes, but why not? Is it that a toy is, strictly speaking, something quite small, and specially made or designed to be manipulated in play? The water in toy beer-bottles is not toy beer, but *pretend* beer. Could a toy watch actually have clockwork inside and show the time correctly? Or would that be just a *miniature* watch?
5. Colloquially at least, the converse is also found: 'I gave him a good hiding'—'a real hiding'—'a proper hiding'.
6. Incidentally, nothing is gained at all by saying that 'real' is a *normative* word and leaving it at that, for 'normative' itself is much too general and vague. Just how, in what way, is 'real' normative? Not, presumably, in just the same way as 'good' is. And it's the differences that matter.

 6 

Brains in Vats

WILLIAM POUNDSTONE

Blue sky, sunshine, déjà vu glazed with dread. Something horrible is going to happen about now. It is a perfect summer day in a meadow of tall grass. J.V. is following her brothers, lagging lazily behind. A shadow falls on the ground; something rustles the grass. J.V. turns—she cannot help it, it is what happens next—and sees a strange man. He has no face, like a minor character in a dream. The man holds something writhing and indistinct. He asks, "How would you like to get into this bag with the snakes?"

J.V.'s encounter is an unlikely milestone of twentieth-century thought. J.V., a fourteen-year-old girl, was not in a summer field but on an operating table in the Montreal Neurological Institute. Her physician, Wilder Penfield, was attempting an experimental operation to relieve her violent epileptic seizures. The operating team had removed the side of J.V.'s skull to expose the temporal lobe of the brain. In order to locate the site of the attacks, Penfield probed the brain with an electrode connected to an EEG machine. The surgery was a collaboration between physician and patient. J.V. had to remain conscious throughout and help locate the site of the seizures. When Penfield touched the probe to a certain spot on J.V.'s temporal lobe, she again found herself in the field of grass. . . .

J.V.'s experience with the strange man had occurred seven years earlier, in Canada, in what we call the real world. She reported seeing herself as she was then, a seven-year-old girl. J.V. had been frightened but not physically harmed, and ran crying home to her mother. These few moments of terror were to haunt her over and over. The man with the bag of snakes entered her dreams, made them nightmares. The trauma became interwoven with her epileptic seizures.

Like a madeleine, a fleeting recollection would trigger the whole memory, then an attack.

Under the EEG probe, J.V. not merely recalled but *relived* the encounter. All the richness of detail, all the lucid horror of the original experience, came back. Penfield's probe caused the brain to replay past experiences like a movie. With bits of lettered or numbered paper, Penfield kept track of the sites on the cerebral cortex associated with the recollection. Touching nearby points produced different sensations. When the probe touched one point, J.V. recalled people scolding her for doing something wrong. Other sites produced only a phantasmagoria of colored stars.

BRAINS IN VATS

Penfield's classic brain experiments of the 1930s inspired a certain famous riddle, long since dubbed "brains in vats" by philosophy students. It goes like this: You think you're sitting there reading this book. Actually, you could be a disembodied brain in a laboratory somewhere, soaking in a vat of nutrients. Electrodes are attached to the brain, and a mad scientist is feeding it a stream of electrical impulses that exactly *simulates* the experience of reading this book.!

Let's expand a little on the anecdote to see the full force of this. At some indistinct past time, while you were sleeping, your brain was removed from your body. Every nerve was severed by skilled surgeons and attached to a microscopic electrode. Each of these millions of electrodes is hooked to a machine that produces tiny electrical pulses just as the original nerves did.

When you turn the page, it *feels* like a page because the electrodes send your brain exactly the same nerve impulses that would have come from real fingers grasping a real page. But the page and the fingers are illusion. Bringing the book closer to your face makes it look bigger; holding it at arm's length makes it look smaller . . . 3-D perspective is simulated by judiciously adjusting the voltages of the electrodes attached to the stump of the optic nerve. If, right this instant, you can smell spaghetti cooking and hear dulcimer music in the background, that is part of the illusion too. You can pinch yourself and receive the expected sensation, but it will prove nothing. In fact, *there's no way you can prove that this isn't so*. How, then, can you justify your belief that the external world exists?

DREAMS AND EVIL GENIUSES

To anyone with a skeptical turn of mind, the brains-in-vats-paradox is both appealing and infuriating. There is something fascinating about the demonstration that, just possibly, everything you know is wrong!

Despite the influence of Penfield and other brain researchers, doubts about the reality of the world are not a uniquely modern malaise. Brains-in-vats is simply a stronger version of older riddles asking "How do you know this isn't all a dream?" Best known of these is the Chinese tale of Chuang-tzu, dating from the fourth century B.C. Chuang-tzu was the man who dreamt he was a butterfly, then awoke to wonder if he was a butterfly dreaming he was a man.

Chuang-tzu's fable is unconvincing. It is true that we usually don't realize we're dreaming in our dreams. But a waking person always knows that he is not dreaming. Doesn't he?

Opinions differ. In his "First Meditation" (1641), French philosopher and mathematician René Descartes decided he could not be *absolutely* sure he wasn't dreaming. Most people would probably disagree with Descartes. You're not dreaming right now, and you know it because experiences in dreams are different from those in waking life.

Saying exactly *how* they're different is difficult. If waking life is absolutely, unmistakably different from a dream, there ought to be some surefire test you can perform to distinguish the two. For instance:

- There's the old gag about pinching yourself to see if you're dreaming. The rationale is apparently that you don't feel pain in dreams. But I *have* felt pain in dreams, and suspect that everyone must from time to time. Scratch that test.
- Since few dreams are in color, the red rose on your desk proves you're awake. Again, the dream sensation of color is not all that rare. Many people dream in color, and even if you never have, this could be the first time.
- Real life usually seems more detailed and coherent than dreams. If you can examine the wall before you and see every minute crack, that means you're awake. If you can add a column of figures, then check the result with a calculator, you're awake. These tests are more telling though still not foolproof. (Might not you dream about seeing tiny cracks in the wall after hearing that the cracks "prove" you are awake?)
- Some say that the very fact that you are wondering whether you are dreaming or awake proves you are awake. In waking life, you are aware of the dream state, but while dreaming you forget the distinction (and think you are awake). But if that were ture, you could never have a dream in which you realize you are dreaming, and such dreams are fairly common with many people.
- I propose this test, based on what might be called "coherent novelty." Keep a book of limericks by your bed. Don't read the book; just use it thus. Whenever you want to know if you are dreaming, go into your bedroom and open the book at random (it may of course be a dream bedroom and a dream book). Read a limerick, making sure it is one you have never read or heard before. Most likely you cannot compose a bona fide limerick on a moment's notice. You can't do it when awake, and certainly not when asleep either. Nonetheless, anyone can *recognize* a limerick when he sees it. It has a precise rhyme and metrical scheme, and it is funny (or more likely *not* funny, but in a certain way). If the limerick meets all these tests, it must be part of the external world and not a figment of your dreaming mind.[1]

There was a young girl at Bryn Mawr
Who committed a dreadful faux pas;
  She loosened a stay
  Of her décolleté
Exposing her je-ne-sais-quoi.

My real point is that you don't need to use any of these tests to establish that you're awake; you just *know*. The suggestion that Chuang Tzu's, or anyone's, "real" life is literally a nighttime dream lacks credibility.

It may however be a "dream" of a different sort. The most famous discussion along these lines is in Descartes's *Meditations*. There Descartes wonders if the external world, including his body, is an illusion created by an "evil genius" bent on deceiving him. "I will suppose that . . . some malicious demon of the utmost power and cunning has employed all his energies in order to deceive me. I shall think that the sky, the air, the earth, colours, shapes, sounds and all external things are merely the delusions of dreams which he has devised to ensnare my judgement. I shall consider myself as not having hands or eyes, or flesh, or blood or senses, but as falsely believing that I have all these things."

That the demon and Descartes's mind were the only two realities would be the very pinnacle of deception, Descartes reasoned. Were there even one other mind as "audience" for the deception, Descartes would at least be correct about the existence of minds such as his own.

Descartes's evil genius anticipates the brains-in-vats paradox in all meaningful particulars. The Penfield experiments merely showed how Descartes's metaphysical fantasy might be physically conceivable. The illusion in the Penfield experiments was more realistic than a dream or memory, though not complete. Penfield's patients described it as a double consciousness: Even while reliving the past experience in detail, they were also aware of being on the operating table.

One can readily envision the more complete neurological illusion supposed in the brains-in-vats riddle. The eyes do not send the brain pictures, nor the ears sound. The senses communicate with the brain via electrochemical impulses in the nerve cells. Each cell in the nervous system "sees" only the impulses of neighboring cells, not the external stimulus that caused them.

If we knew more about the original sensory nerve communication with the brain (as may be the case in a century or so), it might be possible to simulate any experience artificially. That contingency throws all experience into doubt. Even the current embryonic stage of neurology is no guarantee of the validity of our senses. It might be the twenty-fifth century right now, and the forces behind the brains-in-vats laboratory want you to think it's the twentieth, when such things don't happen!

The existence of one's brain is just as open to doubt as the external world. We talk of "brains in vats" because it is a convenient picture, wryly suggestive of bad science fiction. The brain is shorthand for "mind." We no more know, with unimpeachable certainty, that our consciousness is contained in a brain than that it is contained in a body. A yet more complete version of the fantasy would have your mind hallucinating the entire world, including Penfield, J.V., and the brains-in-vats riddle.

AMBIGUITY

"Brains in vats" is the quintessential illustration of what philosophers call the "problem of knowledge." The point is not the remote possibility that we are brains in vats but that we may be just as deluded in ways we cannot even imagine. Few persons reach their fifteenth birthday without having some thoughts along this line. How do we know *anything* for sure?

The whole of our experience is a stream of nerve impulses. The sheen of a baroque pearl, the sound of a dial tone, and the odor of apricots are suppositions from these nerve impulses. We have all *imagined* a world that might account for the unique set of nerve impulses we have received since (and several months before) birth. The conventional picture of a real, external world is not the only possible explanation for that neural experience. We are forced to admit that an evil genius or a brains-in-vats experiment could explain the neural experience just as well. Experience is forever equivocal.

Science places great faith in the evidence of the senses. Most people are skeptical about ghosts, the Loch Ness monster, and flying saucers, not because they are inherently stupid notions, but only because no one has produced unquestionable sensory evidence for them. Brains-in-vats turns this (apparently reasonable!) skepticism inside out. How can you know, by the evidence of your senses, that you are not a brain in a vat? You can't! The belief that you are *not* a brain in a vat can never be disproven empirically. In the jargon of philosophy, it is "evidence-transcendent."

This is a serious blow to the idea that "everything can be determined scientifically." At issue is not some bit of trivia such as the color of a tyrannosaurus. If we cannot even know whether the external world exists, then there are profound limitations on knowledge. Our conventional view of things might be outrageously wrong.

Ambiguity underlies a famous analogy proposed by Albert Einstein and Leopold Infeld. In 1938 they wrote:

> In our endeavour to understand reality we are somewhat like a man trying to understand the mechanism of a closed watch. He sees the face and the moving hands, even hears its ticking, but he has no way of opening the case. If he is ingenious he may form some picture of a mechanism which could be responsible for all the things he observes, but he may never be quite sure his picture is the only one which could explain his observations. He will never be able to compare his picture with the real mechanism and he cannot even imagine the possibility of the meaning of such a comparison.

NOTE

1. Samuel Taylor Coleridge composed his masterwork, "Kubla Khan," in a dream. Coleridge fell asleep reading a history of the emperor and dreamed, with startling lucidity, a poem of 300 verses. Upon awakening, Coleridge scrambled to write down the poem before it eluded him. He wrote about 50 verses—the "Kubla Khan" we know—then was interrupted by a visitor. Afterward, he could remember but a few scattered lines of the remaining 250 verses. Coleridge, however, was a poet in waking life. I recommend the limerick test only to people who can't easily compose a limerick. Also, Coleridge's dream was perhaps atypical, for he had taken laudanum to get to sleep.

7

. . . How Are Hallucinations Possible?

DANIEL DENNETT

1. THE BRAIN IN THE VAT

Suppose evil scientists removed your brain from your body while you slept, and set it up in a life-support system in a vat. Suppose they then set out to trick you into believing that you were not just a brain in a vat, but still up and about, engaging in a normally embodied round of activities in the real world. This old saw, the brain in the vat, is a favorite thought experiment in the toolkit of many philosophers. It is a modern-day version of Descartes's (1641) evil demon, an imagined illusionist bent on tricking Descartes about absolutely everything, including his own existence. But as Descartes observed, even an infinitely powerful evil demon couldn't trick him into thinking he himself existed if he didn't exist: *cogito ergo sum,* "I think, therefore I am." Philosophers today are less concerned with proving one's own existence as a thinking thing (perhaps because they have decided that Descartes settled that matter quite satisfactorily) and more concerned about what, in principle, we may conclude from our experience about our nature, and about the nature of the world in which we (apparently) live. Might you be nothing but a brain in a vat? Might you have *always* been just a brain in a vat? If so, could you even conceive of your predicament (let alone confirm it)?

The idea of the brain in the vat is a vivid way of exploring these questions, but I want to put the old saw to another use. I want to use it to uncover some curious facts about hallucinations, which in turn will lead us to the beginnings of a theory—an empirical, scientifically respectable theory—of human consciousness. In the standard thought experiment, it is obvious that the scientists would have their hands full providing the nerve stumps from all your senses with just the right stimulations to carry off the trickery, but philosophers have assumed for the sake of argument that however technically difficult the task might be, it is "possible in principle." One should be leery of these possibilities in principle. It is also possible in principle to build a stainless-steel ladder to the moon, and to write out, in alphabetical order, all intelligible English conversations consisting of less than a thousand words. But neither of these are remotely possible in fact and sometimes an *impossibility in fact* is theoretically more interesting than a *possibility in principle,* as we shall see.

Let's take a moment to consider, then, just how daunting the task facing the evil scientists would be. We can imagine them building up to the hard tasks from some easy beginnings. They begin with a conveniently comatose brain, kept alive but lacking all input from the optic nerves, the auditory nerves, the somatosensory nerves, and all the other afferent, or input, paths to the brain. It is sometimes assumed that such a "deafferented" brain would naturally stay in a comatose state forever, needing no morphine to keep it dormant, but there is some empirical evidence to suggest that spontaneous waking might still occur in these dire circumstances. I think we can suppose that were you to awake in such a state, you would find yourself in horrible straits: blind, deaf, completely numb, with no sense of your body's orientation.

Not wanting to horrify you, then, the scientists arrange to wake you up by piping stereo music (suitably encoded as nerve impulses) into your auditory nerves. They also arrange for the signals that would normally come from your vestibular system or inner ear to indicate that you are lying on your back, but otherwise paralyzed, numb, blind. This much should be within the limits of technical virtuosity in the near future—perhaps possible even today. They might then go on to stimulate the tracts that used to innervate your epidermis, providing it with the input that would normally have been produced by a gentle, even warmth over the ventral (belly) surface of your body, and (getting fancier) they might stimulate the dorsal (back) epidermal nerves in a way that simulated the tingly texture of grains of sand pressing into your back. "Great!" you say to yourself: "Here I am, lying on my back on the beach, paralyzed and blind, listening to rather nice music, but probably in danger of sunburn. How did I get here, and how can I call for help?"

But now suppose the scientists, having accomplished all this, tackle the more difficult problem of convincing you that you are not a mere beach potato, but an agent capable of engaging in some form of activity in the world. Starting with little steps, they decide to lift part of the "paralysis" of your phantom body and let you wiggle your right index finger in the sand. They permit the sensory experience of moving your finger to occur, which is accomplished by giving you the kinesthetic feedback associated with the relevant volitional or motor signals in the output or efferent part of your nervous system, but they must also arrange to remove the numbness from your phantom finger, and provide the stimulation for the feeling that the motion of the imaginary sand around your finger would provoke.

Suddenly, they are faced with a problem that will quickly get out of hand, for just how the sand will feel depends on just how you decide to move your finger. The problem of calculating the proper feedback, generating or composing it, and then presenting it to you in real time is going to be computationally intractable on even the fastest computer, and if the evil scientists decide to solve the real-time problem by pre-calculating and "canning" all the possible responses for playback, they will just trade one insoluble problem for another: there are too many possibilities to store. In short, our evil scientists will be swamped by *combinatorial explosion* as soon as they give you any genuine exploratory powers in this imaginary world.[1]

It is a familiar wall these scientists have hit; we see its shadow in the boring stereotypes in every video game. The alternatives open for action have to be strictly—and unrealistically—limited to keep the task of the world-representers within feasible bounds. If the scientists can do no better than convince you that you are doomed to a lifetime of playing Donkey Kong, they are evil scientists indeed.

There is a solution of sorts to this technical problem. It is the solution used, for instance, to ease the computational burden in highly realistic flight simulators: use *replicas* of the items in the simulated world. Use a real cockpit and push and pull it with hydraulic lifters, instead of trying to simulate all that input to the seat of the pants of the pilot in training. In short, there is only one way for you to store for ready access that much information about an imaginary world to be explored, and that is to use a *real* (if tiny or artificial or plaster-of-paris) world to store its own information! This is "cheating" if you're the evil demon claiming to have deceived Descartes about the existence of absolutely everything, but it's a way of actually getting the job done with less than infinite resources.

Descartes was wise to endow his imagined evil demon with *infinite* powers of trickery. Although the task is not, strictly speaking, infinite, the amount of information obtainable in short order by an inquisitive human being is staggeringly large. Engineers measure information flow in bits per second, or speak of the *bandwidth* of the channels through which the information flows. Television requires a greater bandwidth than radio, and high-definition television has a still greater bandwidth. High-definition smello-feelo television would have a still greater bandwidth, and *interactive* smello-feelo television would have an astronomical bandwidth, because it constantly branches into thousands of slightly different trajectories through the (imaginary) world. Throw a skeptic a dubious coin, and in a second or two of hefting, scratching, ringing, tasting, and just plain looking at how the sun glints on its surface, the skeptic will consume more bits of information than a Cray supercomputer can organize in a year. Making a *real* but counterfeit coin is child's play; making a *simulated* coin out of nothing but organized nerve stimulations is beyond human technology now and probably forever.[2]

One conclusion we can draw from this is that we are not brains in vats—in case you were worried. Another conclusion it seems that we can draw from this is that strong hallucinations are simply impossible! By a strong hallucination I mean a hallucination of an apparently concrete and persisting three-dimensional object in the real world—as contrasted to flashes, geometric distortions, auras, afterimages, fleeting phantom-limb experiences, and other anomalous sensations. A strong hallucination would be, say, a ghost that talked back, that permitted you to touch it, that resisted with a sense of solidity, that cast a shadow, that was visible from any angle so that you might walk around it and see what its back looked like.

Hallucinations can be roughly ranked in strength by the number of such features they have. Reports of *very* strong hallucinations are rare, and we can now see why it is no coincidence that the credibility of such reports seems, intuitively, to be inversely proportional to the strength of the hallucination reported. We are—and should be—particularly skeptical of reports of very strong hallucinations because we don't believe in ghosts, and we think that only a real ghost could produce a strong hallucination. (It was primarily the telltale strength of the hallucinations reported by Carlos Castañeda in *The Teachings of Don Juan: A Yaqui Way of Knowledge* [1968] that first suggested to scientists that the book, in spite of having been a successful Ph.D. thesis in anthropology at UCLA, was fiction, not fact.)

But if *really* strong hallucinations are not known to occur, there can be no doubt that convincing, multimodal hallucinations are frequently experienced. The hallucinations that are well attested in the literature of clinical psychology are often detailed fantasies far beyond the generative capacities of current technology. How on earth can a single brain do what teams of scientists and computer animators would find to be almost impossible? If such experiences are not genuine or veridical perceptions of some real thing "outside" the mind, they must be produced entirely inside the mind (or the brain), concocted out of whole cloth but lifelike enough to fool the very mind that concocts them.

2. PRANKSTERS IN THE BRAIN

The standard way of thinking of this is to suppose that hallucinations occur when there is some sort of freakish autostimulation of the brain, in particular, an entirely internally generated stimulation of some parts or levels of the brain's perceptual systems. Descartes, in the seventeenth century, saw this prospect quite clearly, in his discussion of phantom limb, the startling but quite normal hallucination in which amputees seem to feel not just the presence of the amputated part, but itches and tingles and pains in it. (It often happens that new amputees, after surgery, simply cannot believe that a leg or foot has been amputated until they *see* that it is gone, so vivid and realistic are their sensations of its continued presence.) Descartes's analogy was the bell-pull. Before there were electric bells, intercoms, and walkie-talkies, great houses were equipped with marvelous systems of wires and pulleys that permitted one to call for a servant from any room in the house. A sharp tug on the velvet sash dangling from a hole in the wall pulled a wire that ran over pulleys all the way to the pantry, where it jangled one of a number of labeled bells, informing the butler that service was required in the master bedroom or the parlor or the billiards room. The systems worked well, but were tailor-made for pranks. Tugging on the parlor wire anywhere along its length would send the butler scurrying to the parlor, under the heartfelt misapprehension that someone had called him from there—a modest little hallucination of sorts. Similarly, Descartes thought, since perceptions are caused by various complicated chains of events in the nervous system that lead eventually to the control center of the conscious mind, if one could intervene somewhere along the chain (anywhere on the optic nerve, for instance, between the eyeball and consciousness), tugging just right on the nerves would produce exactly the chain of events that would be caused by a normal, veridical perception of something, and this would produce, at the receiving end in the mind, exactly the effect of such a conscious perception.

The brain—or some part of it—inadvertently played a mechanical trick on the mind. That was Descartes's explanation of phantom-limb hallucinations. Phantom-limb hallucinations, while remarkably vivid, are—by our terminology—relatively weak; they consist of unorganized pains and itches, all in one sensory modality. Amputees don't see or hear or (so far as I know) smell their phantom feet. So something like Descartes's account *could* be the right way to explain phantom limbs, setting aside for the time being the notorious mysteries about how the physical brain could interact with the nonphysical conscious mind. But we can see that even the purely mechanical part of Descartes's story must be wrong as an account of relatively strong hallucinations; there is no way the brain as illusionist could store and manipulate enough false information to fool an inquiring mind. The brain can relax, and let the real world provide a surfeit of *true* information, but if it starts trying to short-circuit its own nerves (or pull its own wires, as Descartes would have said), the results will be only the weakest of fleeting hallucinations. (Similarly, the malfunctioning of your neighbor's electric hairdryer might cause "snow" or "static," or hums and buzzes, or odd flashes to appear on your television set, but if you see a bogus version of the evening news, you *know* it had an elaborately organized cause far beyond the talents of a hairdryer.)

It is tempting to suppose that perhaps we have been too gullible about hallucinations; perhaps only mild, fleeting, thin hallucinations ever occur—the strong ones don't occur because they can't occur! A cursory review of the literature on hallucinations certainly does suggest that there is something of an inverse relation between strength and frequency—as well as between strength and credibility. But that review also provides a clue leading to another theory of the mechanism of hallucination-production: one of the endemic features of hallucination reports is that the victim will comment on his or her rather unusual passivity in the face of the hallucination. Hallucinators usually just stand and marvel. Typically, they feel no desire to probe, challenge, or query, and take no steps to interact with the apparitions. It is likely, for the reasons we have just explored, that this passivity is not an inessential feature of hallucination but a necessary precondition for any moderately detailed and sustained hallucination to occur.

Passivity, however, is only a special case of a way in which relatively strong hallucinations could survive. The reason these hallucinations can survive is that the illusionist—meaning by that, whatever it is that produces the hallucination—can "count on" a particular line of exploration by the victim—in the case of total passivity, the *null* line of exploration. So long as the illusionist can predict in detail the line of exploration actually to be taken, it only has to prepare for the illusion to be sustained "in the directions that the victim will look." Cinema set designers insist on knowing the location of the camera in advance—or if it is not going to be stationary, its exact trajectory and angle—for then they have to prepare only enough material to cover the perspectives actually taken. (Not for nothing does *cinéma verité* make extensive use of the freely roaming hand-held camera.) In real life the same principle was used by Potemkin to economize on the show villages to be reviewed by Catherine the Great; her itinerary had to be ironclad.

So one solution to the problem of strong hallucination is to suppose that there is a link between the victim and illusionist that makes it possible for the illusionist to build the illusion *dependent on,* and hence capable of anticipating, the exploratory intentions and decisions of the victim. Where the illusionist is unable to "read the victim's mind" in order to obtain this information, it is still sometimes possible in real life for an illusionist (a stage magician, for instance) to *entrain* a particular line of inquiry through subtle but powerful "psychological forcing." Thus a card magician has many standard ways of giving the victim the illusion that he is exercising his free choice in what cards on the table he examines, when in fact there is only one card that may be turned over. To revert to our earlier thought experiment, if the evil scientists can *force* the brain in the vat to have a particular set of exploratory intentions, they can solve the combinatorial explosion problem by preparing only the anticipated material; the system will be only *apparently* interactive. Similarly, Descartes's evil demon can sustain the illusion with less than infinite power if he can sustain an illusion of free will in the victim, whose investigation of the imaginary world he minutely controls.[3]

But there is an even more economical (and realistic) way in which hallucinations could be produced in a brain, a way that harnesses the very freewheeling curiosity of the victim. We can understand how it works by analogy with a party game.

3. A PARTY GAME CALLED PSYCHOANALYSIS

In this game one person, the dupe, is told that while he is out of the room, one member of the assembled party will be called upon to relate a recent dream. This will give everybody else in the room the story line of that dream so that when the dupe returns to the room and begins questioning the assembled party, the dreamer's identity will be hidden in the crowd of responders. The dupe's job is to ask yes/no questions of the assembled group until he has figured out the dream narrative to a suitable degree of detail, at which point the dupe is to psychoanalyze the dreamer, and use the analysis to identify him or her.

Once the dupe is out of the room, the host explains to the rest of the party that no one is to relate a dream, that the party is to answer the dupe's questions according to the following simple rule: if the last letter of the last word of the question is in the first half of the alphabet, the questions is to be answered in the affirmative, and all other questions are to be answered in the negative, with one proviso: a non-contradiction override rule to the effect that later questions are not to be given answers that contradict earlier answers. For example:

Q: Is the dream about a girl?
A: Yes.

but if later our forgetful dupe asks

Q: Are there any female characters in it?
A: Yes [in spite of the final *t*, applying the non-contradiction override rule].[4]

When the dupe returns to the room and begins questioning, he gets a more or less random, or at any rate arbitrary, series of yeses and noes in response. The results are often entertaining. Sometimes the process terminates swiftly in absurdity, as one can see at a glance by supposing the initial question asked were "Is the story line of the dream word-for-word identical to the story line of *War and Peace?*" or, alternatively, "Are there any animate beings in it?" A more usual outcome is for a bizarre and often obscene story of ludicrous misadventure to unfold, to the amusement of all. When the dupe eventually decides that the dreamer—whoever he or she is—must be a very sick and troubled individual, the assembled party gleefully retorts that the dupe himself is the author of the "dream." This is not strictly true, of course. In one sense, the dupe is the author by virtue of the questions he was inspired to ask. (No one *else* proposed putting the three gorillas in the rowboat with the nun.) But in another sense, the dream simply has no author, and that is the whole point. Here we see a process of narrative production, of detail accumulation, with no authorial intentions or plans at all—an illusion with no illusionist.

The structure of this party game bears a striking resemblance to the structure of a family of well-regarded models of perceptual systems. It is widely held that human vision, for instance, cannot be explained as an *entirely* "data-driven" or "bottom-up" process, but needs, at the highest levels, to be supplemented by a few "expectation-driven" rounds of hypothesis testing (or something analogous to hypothesis testing). Another member of the family is the "analysis-by-synthesis" model of perception that also supposes that perceptions are built up in a process that weaves back and forth between centrally generated expectations, on the one hand, and confirmations (and disconfirmations) arising from the periphery on the other hand (e.g., Neisser, 1967). The general idea of these theories is that after a certain amount of "pre-processing" has occurred in the early or peripheral layers of the perceptual system, the tasks of perception are completed—objects are identified, recognized, categorized—by generate-and-test cycles. In such a cycle, one's current expectations and interests shape hypotheses for one's perceptual systems to confirm or disconfirm, and a rapid sequence of such hypothesis generations and confirmations produces the ultimate product, the ongoing, updated "model" of the world of the perceiver. Such accounts of perception are motivated by a variety of considerations, both biological and epistemological, and while I wouldn't say that any such model has been proven, experiments inspired by the approach have borne up well. Some theorists have been so bold as to claim that perception *must* have this fundamental structure.

Whatever the ultimate verdict turns out to be on generate-and-test theories of perception, we can see that they support a simple and powerful account of hallucination. All we need suppose must happen for an otherwise normal perceptual system to be thrown into a hallucinatory mode is for the hypothesis-generation side of the cycle (the expectation-driven side) to operate normally, while the data-driven side of the cycle (the confirmation side) goes into a disordered or random or arbitrary round of confirmation and disconfirmation, just as in the party game. In other words, if noise in the data channel is arbitrarily amplified into "confirmations" and "disconfirmations" (the arbitrary yes and no answers in the party game), the current expectations, concerns, obsessions, and worries of the victim will lead to framing questions or hypotheses whose content is guaranteed to reflect those interests, and so a "story" will unfold in the perceptual system without an author. We don't have to suppose the story is written in advance; we don't have to suppose that information is stored or composed in the illusionist part of the brain. All we suppose is that the illusionist goes into an arbitrary confirmation mode and the victim provides the content by asking the questions.

This provides in the most direct possible way a link between the emotional state of the hallucinator and the content of the hallucinations produced. Hallucinations are usually related in their content to the current concerns of the hallucinator, and this model of hallucination provides for that feature without the intervention of an implausibly knowledgeable internal storyteller who has a theory or model of the victim's psychology. Why, for instance, does the hunter on the last day of deer season see a deer, complete with antlers and white tail, while looking at a black cow or another hunter in an orange jacket? Because his internal questioner is obsessively asking: "Is it a deer?" and getting NO for an answer until finally a bit of noise in the system gets mistakenly amplified into a YES, with catastrophic results.

A number of findings fit nicely with this picture of hallucination. For instance, it is well known that hallucinations are the normal result of prolonged sensory deprivation (see, e.g., Vosberg, Fraser, and Guehl, 1960). A plausible explanation of this is that in sensory deprivation, the data-driven side of the hypothesis-generation-and-test system, lacking any data, lowers its threshold for noise, which then gets amplified into arbitrary patterns of confirmation and disconfirmation signals, producing, eventually, detailed hallucinations whose content is the product of nothing more than anxious expectation and chance confirmation. Moreover, in most reports, hallucinations are only gradually elaborated (under conditions of either sensory deprivation or drugs). They start out weak—e.g., geometric—and then become stronger ("objective" or "narrative"), and this is just what this model would predict (see, e.g., Siegel and West, 1975).

Finally, the mere fact that a drug, by diffusion in the nervous system, can produce such elaborate and contentful effects requires explanation—the drug *itself* surely can't "contain the story," even if some credulous people like to think so. It is implausible that a drug, by diffuse activity, could create or even turn on an elaborate illusionist system, while it is easy to see how a drug could act directly to raise or lower or disorder in some arbitrary way a confirmation threshold in a hypothesis-generation system.

The model of hallucination generation inspired by the party game could also explain the composition of dreams, of course. Ever since Freud there has been little doubt that the thematic content of dreams is tellingly symptomatic of the deepest drives, anxieties, and preoccupations of the dreamer, but the clues the dreams provide are notoriously well concealed under layers of symbolism and misdirection.

What kind of process could produce stories that speak so effectively and incessantly to a dreamer's deepest concerns, while clothing the whole business in layers of metaphor and displacement? The more or less standard answer of the Freudian has been the extravagant hypothesis of an internal dream playwright composing therapeutic dream-plays for the benefit of the ego and cunningly sneaking them past an internal censor by disguising their true meaning. (We might call the Freudian model the Hamlet model, for it is reminiscent of Hamlet's devious ploy of staging "The Mousetrap" just for Claudius; it takes a clever devil indeed to dream up such a subtle stratagem, but if Freud is to be believed, we all harbor such narrative virtuosi.) As we shall see later on, theories that posit such *homunculi* ("little men" in the brain) are not always to be shunned, but whenever homunculi are rung in to help, they had better be relatively stupid functionaries—not like the brilliant Freudian playwrights who are supposed to produce new dream-scenes every night for each of us! The model we are considering eliminates the playwright altogether, and counts on the "audience" (analogous to the one who is "it" in the party game) to provide the content. The audience is no dummy, of course, but at least it doesn't have to have a theory of its own anxieties; it just has to be driven by them to ask questions.

It is interesting to note, by the way, that one feature of the party game that would not be necessary for a process producing dreams or hallucinations is the noncontradiction override rule. Since one's perceptual systems are presumably always exploring an ongoing situation (rather than a *fait accompli,* a finished dream narrative already told) subsequent "contradictory" confirmations can be interpreted by the machinery as indicating a new change in the world, rather than a revision in the story known by the dream relaters. The ghost was blue when last I looked, but has now suddenly turned green; its hands have turned into claws, and so forth. The volatility of metamorphosis of objects in dreams and hallucinations is one of the most striking features of those narratives, and what is even more striking is how seldom these noticed metamorphoses "bother" us while we are dreaming. So the farmhouse in Vermont is now suddenly revealed to be a bank in Puerto Rico, and the horse I was riding is now a car, no a speedboat, and my companion began the ride as my grandmother but has become the Pope. These things happen.

This volatility is just what we would expect from an active but insufficiently skeptical question-asker confronted by a random sample of yeses and noes. At the same time, the persistence of some themes and objects in dreams, their refusal to metamorphose or disappear, can also be tidily explained by our model. Pretending, for the moment, that the brain uses the alphabet rule and conducts its processing in English, we can imagine how subterranean questioning goes to create an obsessive dream:

Q. Is it about father?
A. No.
Q. Is it about a telephone?
A. Yes.
Q. Okay. Is it about mother?
A. No.
Q. Is it about father?
A. No.
Q. Is it about father on the telephone?
A. Yes.
Q. I *knew* it was about father! Now, was he talking to me?
A. Yes. . . .

This little theory sketch could hardly be said to prove anything (yet) about hallucinations or dreams. It does show—metaphorically—how a mechanistic explanation of these phenomena *might* go, and that's an important prelude, since some people are tempted by the defeatist thesis that science couldn't "in principle" explain the various "mysteries" of the mind. The sketch so far, however, does not even address the problem of our *consciousness* of dreams and hallucinations. Moreover, although we have exercised one unlikely homunculus, the clever illusionist/playwright who plays pranks on the mind, we have left in his place not only the stupid question-answerers (who arguably can be "replaced by machines") but also the still quite clever and unexplained question-poser, the "audience." If we have eliminated a villain, we haven't even begun to give an account of the victim.

We have made some progress, however. We have seen how attention to the "engineering" requirements of a mental phenomenon can raise new, and more readily answerable, questions, such as: What models of hallucination can avoid combinatorial explosion? How might the content of experience be elaborated by (relatively) stupid, uncomprehending processes? What sort of links between processes or systems could explain the results of their interaction? If we are to compose a scientific theory of consciousness, we will have to address many questions of this sort.

. . . . The key element in our various explanations of how hallucinations and dreams are possible at all was the theme that the only work that the brain must do is whatever it takes to *assuage epistemic hunger*—to satisfy "curiosity" in all its forms. If the "victim" is passive or incurious about topic *x*, if the victim doesn't seek answers to any questions about topic *x*, then no material about topic *x* needs to be prepared. (Where it doesn't itch, don't scratch.) The world provides an inexhaustible deluge of information bombarding our senses, and when we concentrate on how much is coming in, or continuously available, we often succumb to the illusion that it all must be used, all the time. But our capacities to use information, and our epistemic appetites, are limited. If our brains can just satisfy all our particular epistemic hungers as they arise, we will never find grounds for complaint. We will never be able to tell, in fact, that our brains are provisioning us with less than everything that is available in the world.

So far, this thrifty principle has only been introduced, not established. . . . The brain doesn't always avail itself of this option in any case, but it's important not to overlook the possibility. The power of this principle to dissolve ancient conundrums has not been generally recognized.

NOTES

1. The term *combinatorial explosion* comes from computer science, but the phenomenon was recognized long before computers, for instance in the fable of the emperor who agrees to reward the peasant who saved his life one grain of rice on the first square of the checkerboard, two grains on the second, four on the third, and so forth, doubling the amount for each of the sixty-four squares. He ends up owing the wily peasant millions of billions of grains of rice ($2^{64} - 1$ to be exact). Closer to our example is the plight of the French "aleatoric" novelists who set out to write novels in which, after reading chapter 1, the reader flips a coin and then reads chapter 2a or 2b, depending on the outcome, and then reads chapter 3aa, 3ab, 3ba, or 3bb after that, and so on, flipping a coin at the end of every chapter. These novelists soon came to realize that they had better minimize the number of choice points if they wanted to avoid an explosion of fiction that would prevent anyone from carrying the whole "book" home from the bookstore.
2. The development of "Virtual Reality" systems for recreation and research is currently undergoing a boom. The state of the art is impressive: electronically rigged gloves that provide a convincing interface for "manipulating" virtual objects, and headmounted visual displays that permit you to explore virtual environments of considerable complexity. The limitations of these systems are apparent, however, and

they bear out my point: it is only by various combinations of physical replicas and schematization (a *relatively* coarse-grained representation) that robust illusions can be sustained. And even at their best, they are experiences of virtual surreality, not something that you might mistake for the real thing for more than a moment. If you really want to fool someone into thinking he is in a cage with a gorilla, enlisting the help of an actor in a gorilla suit is going to be your best bet for a long time.

3. For a more detailed discussion of the issues of free will, control, mindreading, and anticipation, see my *Elbow Room: The Varieties of Free Will Worth Wanting,* 1984, especially chapters 3 and 4.
4. Empirical testing suggests that the game is more likely to produce a good story if in fact you favor affirmative answers slightly, by making p/q the alphabetic dividing line between yes and no.

 8 

A Naturalistic Defense of Realism

MICHAEL DEVITT

Anti-realism about the physical world is an occupational hazard of philosophy. Most of the great philosophers have been anti-realists in one way or another. Many of the cleverest contemporary philosophers are also: Michael Dummett, Nelson Goodman, Hilary Putnam, and Bas van Fraassen. Yet anti-realism is enormously implausible on the face of it.

The defense of realism depends on distinguishing it from other doctrines and on choosing the right place to start the argument. And the defense of that choice depends on naturalism. In part I, I shall say what realism is, distinguishing it from semantic doctrines with which it is often confused. In part II, I shall consider the arguments for and against realism about observables. In part III, I shall consider the arguments for and against realism about unobservables, "scientific" realism. The discussion is based on my book, *Realism and Truth* (1997; unidentified references are to this work).

I. WHAT IS REALISM?

A striking aspect of the contemporary realism debate is that it contains almost as many doctrines under the name 'realism' as it contains participants.[1] However, some common features can be discerned in this chaos. First, nearly all the doctrines are, or seem to be, partly semantic. Consider, for example, Jarrett Leplin's editorial introduction to a collection of papers on scientific realism. He lists ten "characteristic realist claims" (1984b: 1–2). Nearly all of these are about the truth and reference of theories. Not one is straightforwardly metaphysical.[2] However, second, amongst all the semantic talk, it is usually possible to discern a metaphysical doctrine, a doctrine about what there is and what it

Source: Michael Devitt, "A Naturalistic Defense of Realism," in *Metaphysics: Contemporary Readings*, S. Hales, Ed. Belmont CA: Wadsworth Publishing Co., 1999, pp. 90–103. Permission granted by the author.

is like. Thus 'realism' is now usually taken to refer to some combination of a metaphysical doctrine with a doctrine about truth, particularly with a correspondence doctrine.[3]

The metaphysical doctrine has two dimensions, an existence dimension and an independence dimension (ch. 2 and sec. A.1). The existence dimension commits the realist to the existence of such common-sense entities as stones, trees and cats, and such scientific entities as electrons, muons and curved spacetime. Typically, idealists, the traditional opponent of realists, have not denied this dimension; or, at least, have not straightforwardly denied it. What they have denied is the independence dimension. According to some idealists, the entities identified by the first dimension are made up of mental items, "ideas" or "sense data," and so are not external to the mind. In recent times another sort of idealist has been much more common. According to these idealists, the entities are not, in a certain respect, "objective": they depend for their existence and nature on the cognitive activities and capacities of our minds. Realists reject all such mind dependencies. Relations between minds and those entities are limited to familiar causal interactions long noted by the folk: we throw stones, plant trees, kick cats, and so on.

Though the focus of the debate has mostly been on the independence dimension, the existence dimension is important. First, it identifies the entities that are the subject of the dispute over independence. In particular, it distinguishes a realism worth fighting for from what I call "Weak, or Fig-Leaf, Realism" (p. 23): a commitment merely to there being *something* independent of us. Second, in the discussion of unobservables—the debate about *scientific* realism—the main controversy has been over existence.

I capture the two dimensions in the following doctrine:

> *Realism:* Tokens of most common-sense, and scientific, physical types objectively exist independently of the mental.

This doctrine covers both the observable and the unobservable worlds. Some philosophers, like van Fraassen, have adopted a different attitude to these two worlds. So, for the purpose of argument, we can split the doctrine in two: *Common-Sense Realism* concerned with observables, and *Scientific Realism* concerned with unobservables.

In insisting on the objectivity of the world, Realists are not saying that it is unknowable. They are saying that it is not *constituted by* our knowledge, by our epistemic values, by our capacity to refer to it, by the synthesizing power of the mind, nor by our imposition of concepts, theories, or languages; it is not limited by what we can believe or discover. Many worlds lack this sort of objectivity and independence: Kant's "phenomenal" world; Dummett's verifiable world; the stars made by a Goodman "version"; the constructed world of Putnam's "internal realism"; Kuhn's world of theoretical ontologies[4], the many worlds created by the "discourses" of structuralists and post-structuralists.

Realism accepts both the ontology of science and common sense as well as the folk epistemological view that this ontology is objective and independent. Science and common sense are not, for the most part, to be "reinterpreted." It is not just that our experiences are *as if* there are cats, there are cats. It is not just that the observable world is *as if* there are atoms, there are atoms. As Putnam once put it, Realism takes science at "face value" (1978: 37).

Realism is the minimal realist doctrine worth fighting for, once it is established, the battle against anti-realism is won; all that remains are skirmishes. Furthermore, Realism provides the place to stand in order to solve the many other difficult problems that have become entangled with it.

Any semantic doctrine needs to be disentangled from Realism (ch. 4 and sec. A.2). In particular, the correspondence theory of truth needs to be disentangled: it is in no way constitutive of Realism nor of any similarly metaphysical doctrine.[5]

On the one hand, Realism does not entail any theory of truth or meaning at all, as is obvious from our definition. So it does not entail the correspondence theory. On the other hand, the correspondence theory does not entail Realism. The correspondence theory claims that a sentence (or thought) is true in virtue of its structure, its relations to reality, usually reference relations, and the nature of reality. *This is compatible with absolutely any metaphysics.* The theory is often taken to require the objective mind-independent existence of the reality which makes sentences true or false. This addition of Realism's independence dimension does, of course, bring us closer to Realism. However, the addition seems like a gratuitous intrusion of metaphysics into semantics. And even with the addition, the correspondence theory is still distant from Realism, because it is silent on the existence dimension. It tells us what it is for a sentence to be true or false, but it does not tell us which ones are true and so *could* not tell us which particular entities exist.

Realism is about the nature of reality in general, about what there is and what it is like; it is about the largely inanimate impersonal world. If correspondence truth has a place, it is in our theory of only a small part of that reality: it is in our theory of people and their language.[6]

Not only is Realism independent of any *doctrine* of truth, we do not even need to use 'true' and its cognates to *state* Realism, as our definition shows. This is not to say that there is anything "wrong" with using 'true' for this purpose. Any predicate worthy of the name "truth" has a "disquotational" property captured by the "equivalence thesis." The thesis is that appropriate instances of

s is true if and only if *p*

hold, where an appropriate instance is obtained by substituting for '*p*' a sentence which is the same as (or a translation of) the sentence referred to by the term substituted for '*s*.'[7] Because of this disquotational property, we can use 'true' to talk about *anything* by referring to sentences. Thus we can talk about the whiteness of snow by saying "'Snow is white' is true." And we can redefine the metaphysical doctrine Realism as follows:

Most common-sense, and scientific, physical existence statements are objectively and mind-independently true.

This redefinition does not make Realism semantic (else every doctrine could be made semantic); it does not change the subject matter at all. It does not involve commitment to the correspondence *theory* of truth, nor to any other theory. Indeed, it is compatible with a *deflationary* view of truth according to which, roughly, the equivalence thesis captures all there is to truth.[8] This inessential redefinition *exhausts* the involvement of truth in constituting Realism.[9]

My view that realism does not involve correspondence truth flies so much in the face of entrenched opinion, and has received so little support, that I shall labor the point. I shall do so by considering a fairly typical contemporary statement of "Scientific Realism":

Contemporary Realism: Most scientific statements about unobservables are (approximately) correspondence-true.

Why would people believe this? I suggest only because they believed something like the following two doctrines:

Strong Scientific Realism: Tokens of most unobservable scientific types objectively exist independently of the mental and (approximately) obey the laws of science.

Correspondence Truth: Sentences have correspondence-truth conditions.

These two doctrines, together with the equivalence thesis, imply Contemporary Realism. Yet the two doctrines have almost nothing to do with each other. *Contemporary Realism is an unfortunate hybrid.*

Strong Scientific Realism is stronger than my minimal doctrine, Scientific Realism, in requiring that science be mostly right not only about which unobservables exist but also about the properties of those unobservables. But the key point here is that both these doctrines are *metaphysical,* concerned with the underlying nature of the world in general. To accept Strong Scientific Realism, we have to be confident that science is discovering things about the unobservable world. Does the success of science show that we can be confident about this? Is inference to the best explanation appropriate here? Should we take skeptical worries seriously? These are just the sort of epistemological questions that have been, and still largely are, at the center of the realism debate. *Their home is with Strong Scientific Realism, not with Correspondence Truth.*

Correspondence Truth is a semantic doctrine about the pretensions of one small part of the world to represent the rest. The doctrine is the subject of lively debate in the philosophy of language, the philosophy of mind, and cognitive science. Do we need to ascribe truth conditions to sentences and thoughts to account for their roles in the explanation of behavior and as guides to reality? Do we need reference to explain truth conditions? Should we prefer a conceptual-role semantics? Or should we, perhaps, near enough eliminate meaning altogether? These are interesting and difficult questions (ch. 6 and secs. A.12–A.15), but they have no immediate bearing on scientific realism.

Semantic questions are not particularly concerned with the language of science. Even less are they particularly concerned with "theoretical" language "about unobservables." Insofar as the questions are concerned with that language, they have no direct relevance to the metaphysical *concerns of* Strong Scientific Realism. They bear directly on the sciences of language and mind and, via that, on the other human sciences. They do not bear directly on science in general. Many philosophers concerned with semantics and not in any way tainted by anti-realism are dubious of the need for a correspondence notion of truth.[10]

Are there atoms? Are there molecules? If there are, what are they like? How are they related to each other? Strong Scientific Realism says that we should take science's answers pretty much at face value. So there really are atoms and they really do make up molecules. That is one issue. Another issue altogether is about meaning. Do statements have correspondence truth conditions? Correspondence Truth says that they do. This applies as much to 'Cats make up atoms' as to 'Atoms make up molecules'; indeed it applies as much to 'The Moon is made of green cheese.' Put the first issue together with the second and we get a third: Is 'Atoms make up molecules' correspondence-true? My point is that this issue is completely derivative from the other two. It arises only if we are wondering about, first, the meanings of sentences ranging from the scientific to the silly; and about, second, the nature of the unobservable world.

Suppose that we had established that Correspondence Truth was right for the familiar everyday language. Suppose further that we believed that atoms do make up molecules, and the like. Then, *of course,* we would conclude that Correspondence Truth applies to 'Atoms make up molecules,' and the like, and so conclude that such sentences are correspondence-true. What possible motive could there be for not concluding this? Scientific theories raise special metaphysical questions not semantic ones.

Strong Scientific Realism and Correspondence Truth have very different subject matters and should be supported by very different evidence. Underlying Contemporary Realism is a conflation of these two doctrines that has been detrimental to both.

It follows from this discussion that a metaphysical doctrine like Realism cannot be attacked *simply* by arguing against certain semantic theories of truth or reference; for example, against Correspondence Truth. . . .[11]

. . . I have emphasized that Realism is a metaphysical doctrine and hence different from semantic doctrines like Correspondence Truth. However, Realism is a little bit semantic in requiring that the world be independent of our semantic capacities. Similarly, it is a little bit epistemic in requiring that the world be independent of our epistemic capacities. But these are only minor qualifications to the metaphysical nature of Realism.

Why has the metaphysical issue been conflated with semantic issues? This is a difficult question, but part of the answer is surely the "linguistic turn" in twentieth-century philosophy. At its most extreme, this turn treats all philosophical issues as about language (sec. 4.5).

I claim that no semantic doctrine is in any way *constitutive* of Realism (or any metaphysical doctrine of realism). This is not to claim that there is no *evidential* connection between the two sorts of doctrines. Indeed, I favor the Quinean view that, roughly, everything is evidentially connected to everything else. So distinguishing Realism from anything semantic is only the first step in saving it. We have to consider the extent to which contemporary semantic arguments, once conflations are removed, might be used as evidence against Realism: although their conclusions do not *amount to* anti-Realism, they may *count in favor of* anti-Realism. Traditionally, philosophers started with an epistemological view and typically used this as evidence against Realism. We should reconstrue contemporary philosophers so that they are doing something similar: starting with a semantic view and using it as evidence against Realism.

In part II, I shall assess these arguments against Realism, claiming that they start in the wrong place. I shall first consider traditional arguments from epistemology and then, reconstrued contemporary arguments from semantics. The concern here is with realism about observables, Common-Sense Realism. Having established the case for this, I shall argue for Scientific Realism in part III.

II. WHY BE A COMMON-SENSE REALIST?

Realism about the ordinary observable physical world is a compelling doctrine. It is almost universally held outside intellectual circles. From an early age we come to believe that such objects as stones, cats, and trees exist. Furthermore, we believe that these objects exist even when we are not perceiving them, and that they do not depend for their existence on our opinions nor on anything mental. These beliefs about ordinary objects are central to our whole way of viewing the world. Common-Sense Realism is aptly named because it is the core of common sense.

What, then, has persuaded so many philosophers out of it? A clear answer emerges from the tradition before the linguistic turn (ch. 5). If we have knowledge of the external world, it is obvious that we acquire it through our sensory experiences. Yet how can we rely on these, Descartes (1641) asks? First, the Realist must allow that our senses sometimes deceive us: there are the familiar examples of illusion and hallucination. How, then, can we ever be justified in relying on our senses? Second, how can we be sure that we are not dreaming? Though we think we are perceiving the external world, perhaps we are only dreaming that we are. Finally, perhaps there is a deceitful demon causing us to have sensory experiences *as if* of an external world, when in fact there is no such world. If we are not certain that this is not the case, how can we know that Realism is correct? How can it be rational to believe Realism?

One traditional way of responding to the challenge of this extreme Cartesian skepticism is to seek an area of knowledge which is not open to skeptical doubt and which can serve as a "foundation" for all or most claims to knowledge. Since even the most basic common-sense and scientific knowledge—including that of the existence of the external world—is open to doubt, this search is for a special philosophical realm of knowledge outside science. The foundationalist has always found this realm in the same place. "In the search for certainty, it is natural to begin with our present experiences" (Russell 1912: 1). This natural beginning led traditionally to the view that we could not be mistaken about mental entities called "ideas." More recently, it has led to the similar view that we could not be mistaken about entities called "sense data." These entities are the "given" of experience. I shall talk of "sense data."

From this perspective, the justification of Realism can seem hopeless. The perspective yields what is sometimes called, anachronistically, "the movie-show model" of the mind. Sense data are the immediate objects of perception. They are like images playing on a screen in the inner theater of a person's mind. The person (a homunculus really) sits watching this movie and asks herself: (1) Is there anything outside the mind *causing* the show? (2) If so, does it *resemble* the images on the screen? To answer these questions "Yes," as Locke (1690) does with a qualification or two, is to be a "representative realist." But Locke's justification for his answers is desperately thin, as Berkeley (1710) shows: there seems to be no basis for the inference from the inner show to the external world. Certainly, there is no reason why a Cartesian skeptic should accept the inference.

The problem for Realism is the "gap" between the object known and the knowing mind. According to the Realist, the object known is external to the person's mind and independent of it. Yet the person has immediate knowledge only of her own sense data. She can never leave the inner theater to compare those sense data with the external world. So how could she ever know about such a world?

To save our knowledge, it seemed to Berkeley and many others, we must give up Realism and adopt idealism: the world is constructed, in some sense, out of sense data. The gap is closed by bringing objects, one way or another, "into the mind." But the problem is that even this desperate metaphysics does not save our knowledge. Idealism too is open to skeptical doubt.

First, consider the foundations of idealism: our allegedly indubitable knowledge of our own sense data. Why should the skeptic accept that there are any such mental objects as sense data? Even if there are, why should the skeptic accept that the person has indubitable knowledge of them? Why is this any more plausible than the view that we have indubitable knowledge of external objects?

Even if the foundations are granted, and Realism is abandoned, the task of building our familiar knowledge to Cartesian skeptical standards on these foundations has proved impossible.

The simplest part of this knowledge is singular knowledge of physical objects; for example, the knowledge that Nana is a cat. How can we get this knowledge from knowledge of sense data? This task might seem easy if Nana were literally constructed out of sense data, if she were nothing but a bundle of them. But then how could we explain the fact that Nana can exist unobserved? The obvious answer that *sense data* can exist unobserved is quite gratuitous from the skeptical viewpoint.

So idealists favored a different sort of construction, the "logical construction" proposed by "phenomenalism." Each statement about a physical object was to be translated, in some loose sense, into statements about sense data. Since the latter statements are the sort that the foundationalist thinks we know, it was hoped in this way to save our knowledge, albeit in a new form. However, the total failure of all attempts to fulfill this translation program over many years of trying is so impressive as to make it "overwhelmingly likely" that the program *cannot* be fulfilled (Putnam 1975b: 20).

From a Realist perspective, it is easy to see the problem for phenomenalism: there is a loose link between a physical object and any set of experiences we might have of it. As a result, no finite set of sense-datum statements is either necessary or sufficient for a physical-object statement.

In sum, the foundationalist anti-Realist cannot save physical objects. He cannot save even our singular knowledge of the world. We have already noted the failure of foundationalist Realism. The Cartesian skeptical challenge leaves the foundationalist no place to stand and no way to move: he is left, very likely, only with the knowledge that he is now experiencing, with "instantaneous solipsism." The foundationalist program is hopeless.[12]

Kant is responsible for another traditional idealist response to the skeptical challenge. Kant's way of saving knowledge is very different from foundationalism's. He closes the gap between the knowing mind and the object known with his view that the object is partly constituted by the cognitive activities of the mind. He distinguished objects as we know them—stones, trees, cats, and so on—from objects as they are independent of our knowledge. Kant calls the former "appearances" and the latter "things-in-themselves." Appearances are obtained by our *imposition* of *a priori* concepts; for example, causality, time and the Euclidian principles of spatial relations. Only things-in-themselves, forever beyond our ken, have the objectivity and independence required by Realism. Appearances do not, as they are partly our construction. And, it must be emphasized, the familiar furniture of the world are appearances not things-in-themselves. Although an idealist, Kant is a Weak Realist (p. 23).

How does this view help with skepticism? We can know about appearances because, crudely, we make them. Indeed, Kant thinks that we could not know about them unless we made them: it is a condition on the possibility of knowledge that we make them.

Many contemporary anti-Realisms combine Kantianism with relativism to yield what is known as "constructivism." Kant was no relativist: the concepts imposed to constitute the known world were common to all mankind. Contemporary anti-Realisms tend to retain Kant's ideas of things-in-themselves and of imposition, but drop the universality of what is imposed. Instead, different languages, theories, and world views are imposed to create different known worlds. Goodman, Putnam, and Kuhn are among the constructivists.

Constructivism is so bizarre and mysterious—how could we, literally, make dinosaurs and stars?—that one is tempted to seek a charitable reinterpretation of constructivist talk. But, sadly, charity is out of place here (13.1–13.3).[13]

Something has gone seriously wrong. The Cartesian skeptical challenge that has persuaded so many to abandon Realism has led us to disaster: either to a lack of any worthwhile knowledge or to knowledge at the expense of a truly bizarre metaphysics. It is time to think again.

The disaster has come from epistemological speculations about what we can know and how we can know it. But why should we have any confidence in these speculations? In particular, why should we have such confidence in them that they can undermine Realism? Over a few years of living people come to the conclusion that there are stones, trees, cats, and the like, existing largely independent of us. This Realism is confirmed day by day in their experience. It seems much more firmly based than the epistemological speculations. Perhaps, then, we have started the argument in the wrong place: rather than using the epistemological speculations as evidence against Realism, perhaps we should use Realism as evidence against the speculations.

Indeed, what support are these troubling speculations thought to have? Not the empirical support of the claims of science, for that sort of support is itself being doubted. The support is thought to be a priori, as is the support for our knowledge of mathematics and logic. Reflecting from the comfort of armchairs, foundationalists and Kantians decide what knowledge *must* be like, and from this, infer what the world *must* be like:

a priori epistemology → a priori metaphysics.

The disaster alone casts doubt on this procedure and the philosophical method it exemplifies, the a priori method of "First Philosophy." This doubt is confirmed by the sorts of considerations adduced by Quine (1952: Introduction; 1953: 42–46). These considerations should lead us to reject a priori knowledge and embrace "naturalism," the view that there is only one way of knowing, the empirical way that is the basis of science.[14] From the naturalistic perspective, philosophy becomes continuous with science. And the troubling epistemological speculations have no special status: they are simply some among many empirical hypotheses about the world we live in. As such; they do not compare in evidential support with Realism. Experience has taught us a great deal about the world of stones, trees, and cats, but rather little about how we know about this world. So epistemology is just the wrong place to start the argument: the skeptical challenge should be rejected. Instead, we should start with an empirically based metaphysics and use that as evidence in an empirical study of what we can know and how we can know it: epistemology itself becomes part of science, "naturalized epistemology":

empirical metaphysics → empirical epistemology.

And when we approach our metaphysics empirically, Realism is irresistible.[15] Indeed, it faces no rival we should take seriously. Thus naturalism supports the order of procedure suggested tentatively in the last paragraph.

Quine is fond of a vivid image taken from Otto Neurath. He likens our knowledge—our "web of belief" to a boat that we continually rebuild while staying afloat on it. We can rebuild any part of the boat, but in so doing we must take a stand on the rest of the boat for the time being. So we cannot rebuild it all at once. Similarly, we can revise any part of our knowledge, but in so doing we must accept the rest for the time being. So we cannot revise it all at once. And just as we should start rebuilding the boat by standing on the firmest parts, so also should we start rebuilding our web.[16] Epistemology is one of the weakest parts to stand on. So also is semantics.

We noted in part I that semantics has been at the center of contemporary anti-Realist arguments. Setting aside the frequent conflation of semantics with metaphysics, I suggested that we reconstrue these arguments as simply offering evidence against Realism. So just as traditional philosophers argued for epistemological doctrines that show that we could not *know* the Realist world, we should see Dummett and Putnam as arguing for semantic doctrines that show that we could not *refer to* the Realist world. Since we obviously do know about and refer to the world, the arguments run, the world cannot be Realist. The objection to traditional arguments was that they started with a priori speculations on what knowledge *must* be like and inferred what the world *must* be like. The objection to contemporary arguments is that they start with *a priori* speculations on what meaning and reference *must* be like and infer what the world *must* be like:

a priori semantics → a priori metaphysics.

From the naturalistic perspective, this inference uses the wrong methodology and proceeds in the wrong direction. We should proceed:

empirical metaphysics → empirical semantics.

We should, as I like to say, "put metaphysics first.". . .

The mistaken methodology is reflected in a certain caricature of Realism that tends to accompany contemporary anti-Realist polemics (sec. 12.6). Thus, according to Putnam, Realism requires a "God's Eye View" (1981: 74); that we have "direct access to a ready made world" (p. 146) and so can compare theories with "unconceptualized reality" (1979: 611); that we can make "a transcendental match between our representation and the world in itself" (1981: 134).[17] According to Richard Rorty, the Realist believes that we can "step out of our skins" (1982: xix) to judge, without dependence on any concepts, whether theories are true of reality.[18] But, of course, no sane person believes any of this. What Realists believe is that we can judge whether theories are true of reality, *the nature of which* does not depend on any theories or concepts.

What lies behind these views of Realism? The answer is clear: the Cartesian picture that leads to the skeptical challenge. According to this picture we are theorizing *from scratch,* locked in our mental theaters, trying to bridge the gap between our sense data and the external world. But we are not starting from scratch in epistemology and semantics. We can use well-established theories in physics, biology, and so forth; we already have the entities and relations which those theories posit. And if we were starting from scratch, skeptical doubts would condemn us to instantaneous solipsism. The picture puts the epistemic and semantic carts before the metaphysical horse.

To put the carts back where they belong, we take a naturalistic approach to epistemology and semantics. Reflection on our best science has committed us to the many entities of the largely impersonal and inanimate world. It has not committed us to sense data and so there is no gap between sense data and the world to be bridged. We go on to seek empirical explanations of that small part of the world in which there are problems of knowledge and reference: people and language. From the naturalistic perspective, the relations between our minds and reality are not, in principle, any more inaccessible than any other relations. Without jumping out of our skins, we can have well-based theories about the relations between, say, Michael and Scottie. Similarly, we can have such theories about our epistemic and semantic relations to Michael and Scottie.

In sum, objections to Common-Sense Realism have come from speculations in epistemology and semantics. From the naturalistic perspective, there can be no question of these speculations being known a priori. Once they are seen as empirical, they are far too ill-based to justify any metaphysical conclusion. We should put metaphysics first, and then Realism is the only doctrine that can be taken seriously.

III. WHY BE A SCIENTIFIC REALIST?

The argument for Scientific Realism—Realism about the unobservables of science—starts by assuming Common-Sense Realism. And, setting aside some deep and difficult problems in quantum theory, the issue is over the existence dimension, over whether these unobservables exist. For the independence dimension mostly goes without saying once Common-Sense Realism has been accepted.

The basic argument for Scientific Realism is simple (sec. 7.1). By supposing the unobservables of science exist, we can give good explanations of the behavior and characteristics of observed entities, behavior and characteristics which would otherwise remain completely inexplicable. Furthermore, such a supposition leads to predictions about observables which are well confirmed; the supposition is successful.

This argument should not be confused with one version of the popular and much discussed argument that "realism explains success" (sec. 7.3).[19] This version is most naturally expressed talking of truth. First we define success: for a theory to be successful is for its observational predictions to be true. Why is a theory thus successful? The Realist argument claims: because the theory is true. However, given the conflation of Realism with Correspondence Truth criticized in part I, it is worth noting that this talk exploits only the disquotational property of "true" and so does not require any robust notion of truth. This can be seen by rewriting the explanation without any talk of truth at all. Suppose a theory says that *S*. The rewrite defines success: for this theory to be successful is for the world to be observationally as if *S*. Why is the theory thus successful? The rewrite claims: because *S*. For example, why is the world observationally as if there are atoms? Why are all the observations we make just the sort we would make if there were atoms? Answer: because there *are* atoms. This Realist explanation has a trivial air to it because it is only if we suppose that *there aren't x's* that we feel any need to explain why it is *as if there are x's*. Still, it is a good explanation. And the strength of Scientific Realism is that the anti-Realist has no explanation of this success: if Scientific Realism were not correct, Realists are fond of saying, it would be "a miracle" that the observable world is as if it is correct.

This popular argument is good but it is different from my simple one and not as basic—Where the popular argument uses Realism to explain the observational success of theories, my simple one uses Realism to explain the observed phenomena, the behavior and characteristics of observed entities. This is not to say that observational success is unimportant to the simple argument: the explanation of observed phenomena, like any explanation, is *tested* by its observational success. So according to the simple argument, Scientific Realism *is* successful; according to the popular one, it explains success. There is not even an air of triviality about the simple argument.

I shall conclude by briefly considering three arguments against Scientific Realism. (1) The first is an influential empiricist argument. Richard Boyd, who does not agree with its conclusion, has nicely expressed the argument as follows:

> Suppose that *T* is a proposed theory of unobservable phenomena. . . . A theory is said to be empirically equivalent to *T* just in case it makes the same predictions about observable phenomena that *T* does. Now, it is always possible, given *T*, to construct arbitrarily many alternative theories that are empirically equivalent to *T* but which offer contradictory accounts of the nature of unobservable phenomena. . . . *T* and each of the theories empirically equivalent to it will be equally well confirmed or disconfirmed by any possible observational evidence. . . . scientific evidence can never decide the question between theories of unobservable phenomena and, therefore, knowledge of unobservable phenomena is impossible. (1984: 42–44)

One way of putting this is: we should not believe *T* because it is *underdetermined by the possible evidence*. Commitment to the existence of the entities posited by *T*, rather than merely to the pragmatic advantages of the theory that talks of them, makes no evidential difference, and so is surely a piece of misguided metaphysics; it reflects super-empirical values, not hard facts.

Talk of "possible evidence" is vague (sec. 3.5). If it is construed in a restricted way, then theories may indeed be underdetermined by the possible evidence. Yet for underdetermination to threaten Scientific Realism, I argue (sec. 7.4), the talk of "possible evidence" must be construed in a very liberal way. And construed in this way, there is no reason to believe in underdetermination.

One sense of 'possible evidence' (see Quine 1970: 179; van Fraassen 1980: 12, 60, 64) is restricted in that it does not cover anything nonactual *except acts of observation:* it is restricted to all the points of *actual* space-time that we would have observed had we been around. Yet there are many things that we do not do, but could do, other than merely observing. If we had the time, talent, and money, perhaps we could invent the right instruments and conduct the right experiments to discriminate between T and its rival T'. There may be many differences between the theories which we would not have detected if we had *passively observed* each point of actual space-time but which we would have detected if we had *actively intervened* (Hacking 1983) to change what happened at points of space-time. In this liberal sense that allows for our capacity to *create* phenomena, the class of possible evidence seems totally open.

In the light of this consideration, given any T, what possible reason could there be for thinking *a priori* that *we could not* distinguish it empirically from any rival if we were ingenious enough in constructing experiments and auxiliary hypotheses? It is of course *possible* that we should be unable to distinguish two theories: we humans have finite capacities. The point is that we have no good reason for believing it in a particular case. Even less do we have a good reason for believing it in *all* cases; that is to say, for believing that *every* theory faces rivals that are not detectably different.

Behind these Realist doubts about underdetermination lies the following picture. T and T' describe different causal structures alleged to underlie the phenomena. We can manipulate the actual underlying structure to get observable effects. We have no reason to believe that we *could not* organize these manipulations so that, if the structure were as T says, the effects would be of one sort, whereas if the structure were as T' says, the effects would be of a different sort.

If the liberally interpreted underdetermination thesis were true, Realism might be in trouble. But why should the Realist be bothered by the restricted thesis? A consequence of that thesis is that we *do not,* as a matter of fact, ever conduct a crucial experiment for deciding between T and T'. This does not show that we *could not* conduct one. And the latter is what needs to be established for the empiricist argument against Realism (Boyd 1984: 50). The restricted empirical equivalence of T and T' does *not* show, *in any epistemologically interesting sense,* that they make "the same predictions about observable phenomena," nor that they "will be equally well confirmed or disconfirmed by any possible evidence." It does *not* show that "scientific evidence can never decide the question between theories of unobservable phenomena and [that], therefore, knowledge of unobservable phenomena is impossible." It does *not* show that commitment to T rather than T' is superempirical and hence a piece of misguided metaphysics.

(2) Van Fraassen (1980, 1985) has proposed a doctrine he calls "constructive empiricism." It is Common-Sense but not Scientific Realist. Suppose that a theory says that *S*. Van Fraassen holds that we may be justified in believing that the observable world is as if *S* but we are never justified in believing that *S*. So Scientific Realism is unjustified. From the Realist perspective, such a position amounts to an unprincipled selective skepticism against unobservables: it offends against unobservable rights.[20] An epistemology that justifies a belief in observables will also justify a belief in unobservables. An argument that undermines Scientific Realism, will also undermine Common-Sense Realism.

So the Realist has a simple strategy against such anti-Realism. First, she demands from the anti-Realist a justification of the knowledge that he claims to have about observables. Using this she attempts to show, positively, that the epistemology involved in this justification will also justify knowledge of unobservables. Second, she attempts to show, negatively, that the case for skepticism about unobservables produced by the anti-Realist is no better than the case for skepticism about observables. I claim that arguments along these lines work against van Fraassen (ch. 8).[21]

(3) Finally, perhaps the most influential recent argument against Scientific Realism arose from the revolution in the philosophy of science led by Kuhn (1962). It is the earlier-mentioned "meta-induction": past theories posited entities that, from the perspective of our current theories, we no longer think exist; so, probably, from the perspective of future theories we will come to think that the posits of our present theories do not exist. In part II I argued that the case offered for the premise of this meta-induction rests on two mistakes: first, the mistake of putting semantics before metaphysics; second, the mistake of taking a description theory of reference for granted. These arguments are enough to remove concern about the existence of past observables, but not of past unobservables. For, even without these mistakes there is plausibility to the idea that we no longer believe in the existence of past unobservables; phlogiston is a popular example. The meta-induction against Scientific Realism is a powerful argument. Still, I think that the Realist has a number of defenses against it which are jointly sufficient (sec. 9.4).

In conclusion, I have argued that the metaphysical issue of Realism about the external world is quite distinct from semantic issues about truth. Furthermore, we should not follow the tradition and argue the metaphysical issue from a perspective in epistemology, nor follow the recent linguistic turn and argue it from a perspective in semantics. Rather, we should adopt naturalism and argue the metaphysical issue first. When we do, the case for Common-Sense Realism is overwhelming and the case for Scientific Realism is very strong.

The realism dispute arises from the age-old metaphysical question, "What ultimately is there, and what is it like?" I am sympathetic to the complaint that Realism, as part of an answer to this question, is rather boring. Certainly it brings no mystical glow. Nevertheless, it needs to be kept firmly at the front of the mind to avoid mistakes in theorizing about other, more interesting, matters in semantics and epistemology where it makes a difference.[22]

NOTES

1. Susan Haack (1987) distinguishes *nine* "senses" of "realism"!
2. Some other examples: Hesse 1967: 407; Hooker 1974: 409; Papineau 1979: 126; Ellis 1979: 28; Boyd 1984: 41–42; Miller 1987; Fales 1988: 253–54; Jennings 1989: 240; Matheson 1989; Kitcher 1993; Brown 1994.
3. Two examples are Putnam's "metaphysical realism" (1978, 123–25), and the account of realism by Arthur Fine (1986a: 115–16, 136–37).
4. For fairly accessible accounts of these worlds see, respectively: Kant 1783; Dummett 1978: preface and chs. 10 and 14; Goodman 1978; Putnam 1981; Kuhn 1962.

   In characterizing the independence of the paradigm Realist objects, stones, trees, cats, and the like, we deny that they have *any* dependence on us except the occasional familiar causal one. Other physical objects that have a more interesting dependence on us—for example, hammers and money—pose more of a challenge to the characterization. But, with careful attention to the differences between this sort of dependence and the dependence that anti-realists allege, the challenge can be met (secs. 13.5–13.7).
5. Cf. Putnam 1985: 78; 1987: 15–16. Most philosophers who tie realism to correspondence truth do not argue for their position. Dummett is one exception, criticized in my ch. 14. Michael Williams (1993: 212n) is another, criticized in my sec. A.2.
6. Note that the point is not a verbal one about how the word 'realism' should be used. The point is to distinguish two doctrines, whatever they are called (p. 40).

7. More needs to be said to allow for the paradoxes, ambiguity, indexicals, and truth-value gaps.
8. The utility of 'true' that comes from its disquotational property is much greater than the examples in this paragraph show. On this, and the idea of deflationary truth, see my sec. 3.4 and the works it draws on.
9. Some will object that we cannot assess Realism until we have *interpreted* it and this requires a semantic theory that talks of truth. I argue against this objection in secs. 4.6–4.9, A.2–A.11.
10. See, e.g., Leeds 1978, Field 1978, Churchland 1979, Stich 1983.
11. Two other examples are: Rorty 1979, discussed in my ch. 11; Laudan 1981, discussed in my ch. 9.
12. Note that the program we are talking about attempts to answer the Cartesian skeptic by rebuilding our knowledge on the foundation of indubitable knowledge of sense data, mental entities that are the immediate objects of perception. Less demanding forms of foundationalism that do not make this attempt to answer the skeptic may well be promising; see note 18.
13. Because constructivism is so bizarre and mysterious, its popularity cries out for explanation. I have tried to offer some *rational* explanations (13.4–13.7). For some learned, and very entertaining, explanations of a different sort, see Stove 1991. Stove thinks that anti-Realism, like religion, stems from our need to have a *congenial* world. For some suggestions by Georges Rey along similar lines, see my p. 257, n. 11.
14. A particularly important consideration against the a priori, in my view (1996: 2.2), is that we lack anything close to a satisfactory *explanation* of a nonempirical way of knowing. We are told what this way of knowing is *not*—it is *not* the empirical way of deriving knowledge from experience–but we are not told what it *is*. Rey 1998 and Field 1998 have a more tolerant view of the a priori. My 1998 is a response.
15. Some people think that science itself undermines Realism. I think that this is a mistake (secs. 5.10, 7.9).
16. It is plausible to think that the firmest parts are our singular beliefs about the objects we observe. So we might hope for a new foundationalism built on these beliefs, one with no pretensions to answer the unanswerable Cartesian skeptic, and with no presumption that the beliefs are indubitable.
17. Putnam attributes this view to realist friends "in places like Princeton and Australia" (1979: 611). The Dummettians have more bad news for Australians (particularly black ones): "there is no sense to supposing that [Australia] either determinately did or did not exist [in 1682]" (Luntley 1988: 249–50).
18. See also 1979: 293; Fine 1986a: 131–12; 1986b: 151–52.
19. I identify eight versions of the argument by distinguishing different senses of 'realism,' and 'success' (sec. 6.6).
20. This, not the legitimacy of "abduction," is the primary issue in the defense of Scientific Realism; cf. Laudan 1981: 45; Fine 1986a: 114–15; 1986b: 162.
21. However, it should be noted that my discussion does not take account of van Fraassen's radical nonjustificationist epistemology (1989).
22. My thanks to Steven Hales and Georges Rey for comments on a draft of this paper.

REFERENCES

Berkeley, George. 1710. *Principles of Human Knowledge*.

Boyd, Richard N. 1984. "The Current Status of Scientific Realism." In Leplin 1984a: 41–82.

Brown, James Robert. 1994. *Smoke and Mirrors: How Science Reflects Reality*. New York: Routledge.

Churchland, Paul M. 1979. *Scientific Realism and the Plasticity of Mind*. Cambridge: Cambridge University Press.

Descartes, Rene. 1641. *Meditations on First Philosophy*.

Devitt, Michael. 1996. *Coming to Our Senses: A Naturalistic Defense of Semantic Localism*. New York: Cambridge University Press.

______. 1997. *Realism and Truth*. 2nd ed. with a new afterword (1st ed. 1984, 2nd ed. 1991). Princeton: Princeton University Press.

______. 1998. "Naturalism and the A Priori." *Philosophical Studies* 92: 45–65.

Dretske, Fred I. 1981. *Knowledge and the Flow of Information*. Cambridge, MA: MIT Press.

Dummett, Michael. 1978. *Truth and Other Enigmas*. Cambridge, MA: Harvard University Press.

Ellis, Brian. 1979. *Rational Belief Systems*. Oxford: Basil Blackwell.

Fales, Evan. 1988. "How to be a Metaphysical Realist." In *Midwest Studies in Philosophy*. Vol. 12: *Realism and Antirealism*, ed. Peter A. French, Theodore E. Uehling, Jr., and Howard K. Wettstein. Minneapolis: University of Minnesota Press: 253–74.

Field, Hartry. 1978. "Mental Representation." *Erkenntnis* 13: 9–61.

Field, Hartry. 1998. "Epistemological Nonfactualism and the A Priority of Logic." *Philosophical Studies* 92: 1–24.

Fine, Arthur. 1986a. *The Shaky Game: Einstein, Realism, and the Quantum Theory*. Chicago: University of Chicago Press.

Fine, Arthur. 1986b. "Unnatural Attitudes: Realist and Instrumentalist Attachments to Science." *Mind* 95: 149–77.

Goodman, Nelson. 1978. *Ways of Worldmaking*. Indianapolis: Hackett.

Haack, Susan. 1987. "'Realism.'" *Synthese* 73: 275–99.

Hacking, Ian. 1983. *Representing and Intervening: Introductory Topics in the Philosophy of Natural-Science*. Cambridge: Cambridge University Press.

Hesse, Mary. 1967: "Laws and Theories." In *The Encyclopedia of Philosophy,* ed. Paul Edwards. New York: Macmillan: vol. 4, pp. 404–10.

Hooker, Clifford A. 1974. "Systematic Realism." *Synthese,* 51, 409–97.

Jennings, Richard. 1989. "Scientific Quasi-Realism." *Mind,* 98, 223–45.

Kant, Immanuel. 1783. *Prolegomena to Any Future Metaphysics*.

Kitcher, Philip. 1993. *The Advancement of Science: Science without Legend, Objectivity without Illusions*. New York: Oxford University Press.

Kripke, Saul A. 1980. *Naming and Necessity*. Cambridge, MA: Harvard University Press.

Kuhn, Thomas S. 1962: *The Structure of Scientific Revolutions*. Chicago: Chicago University Press. 2nd ed. 1970.

Laudan, Larry. 1981. "A Confutation of Convergent Realism." *Philosophy of Science* 48: 19–49. Reprinted in Leplin 1984a.

Leeds, Stephen. 1978. "Theories of Reference and Truth." *Erkenntnis* 13: 111–29.

Leplin, Jarrett, ed. 1984a. *Scientific Realism*. Berkeley: University of California Press.

Leplin, Jarrett. 1984b. "Introduction." In Leplin 1984a: 1–7.

Locke, John. 1690. *An Essay Concerning Human Understanding*.

Luntley, Michael. 1988. *Language, Logic and Experience: The Case for Anti-Realism*. La Salle: Open court.

Matheson, Carl. 1989. "Is the Naturalist Really Naturally a Realist?" *Mind,* 98, 247–58.

Miller, Richard W. 1987. *Fact and Method: Explanation, Confirmation and Reality in the Natural and Social Sciences*. Princeton: Princeton University Press.

Millikan, Ruth. 1984. *Language, Thought, and Other Biological Categories: New Foundations for Realism*. Cambridge, MA: MIT Press.

Papineau, David. 1979. *Theory and Meaning*. Oxford: Clarendon Press.

Putnam, Hilary. 1975. *Mind, Language and Reality: Philosophical Papers,* vol. 2. Cambridge: Cambridge University Press.

______. 1978. *Meaning and the Moral Sciences*. London: Routledge & Kegan Paul.

______. 1979. "Reflections on Goodman's *Ways of World-Making*." *Journal of Philosophy* 76: 603–18.

______. 1981. *Reason, Truth and History*. Cambridge: Cambridge University Press.

______. 1983. *Realism and Reason: Philosophical Papers,* vol. 3. Cambridge: Cambridge University Press.

______. 1985. "A Comparison of Something with Something Else." *New Literary History* 17: 61–79.

______. 1987. *The Many Faces of Realism*. La Salle: Open Court.

Quine, W. V. 1952. *Methods of Logic*. London: Routledge & Kegan Paul.

______. 1953. *From a Logical Point of View*. Cambridge, MA: Harvard University Press, 2nd ed. rev., 1st ed. 1953.

______. 1970. *Philosophy of Logic*. Cambridge, MA: Harvard University Press.

Rey, Georges. 1998. "A Naturalistic A Priori." *Philosophical Studies* 92: 25–43.

Rorty, Richard. 1979. *Philosophy and the Mirror of Nature*. Princeton: Princeton University Press.

Rorty, Richard. 1982. *Consequences of Pragmaticism [Essays: 1972–1980]*. Minneapolis: University of Minnesota Press.

Russell, Bertrand. 1912. *The Problems of Philosophy*. London: Oxford Paperbacks, 1967. [Original publ. 1912.]

Stich, Stephen P. 1983. *From Folk Psychology to Cognitive Science: The Case Against Belief*. Cambridge, MA: MIT Press.

Stove, David. 1991: *The Plato Cult and Other Philosophical Follies*. Oxford: Basil Blackwell.

Van Fraassen, Bas C. 1980. *The Scientific Image*. Oxford: The Clarendon Press.

______. 1985. "Empiricism in the Philosophy of Science." In *Images of Science: Essays on Realism and Empiricism, with a Reply from Bas C. van Fraassen*, ed. Paul M. Churchland and Clifford A. Hooker. Chicago: University of Chicago Press: 245–308.

______. 1989. *Laws and Symmetry*. Oxford: Clarendon Press.

Williams, Michael. 1993. "Realism and Scepticism." In *Reality. Representation, and Projection*, ed. John Haldane and Crispin Wright. New York: Oxford University Press: 193–214.